THE SEVENTIES

The Seventies

PROBLEMS AND PROPOSALS

EDITED BY Irving Howe AND Michael Harrington

HARPER & ROW, PUBLISHERS

NEW YORK, EVANSTON, SAN FRANCISCO, LONDON

1817

The essays in this book originally appeared in *Dissent* magazine, and portions of "Corporate Takeover and Popular Challenge" appeared in slightly different form in Ben B. Seligman, *The Potentates: Business and Businessmen in American History* (New York: The Dial Press). Copyright © 1971 by the Estate of Ben B. Seligman. Reprinted by permission of The Dial Press.

"The Politics of Pollution" first appeared in *Commonweal*, Vol. 92, No. 5 (April 17, 1970). Reprinted by permission of the author and publisher.

"Nixon and Neo-Jeffersonianism" first appeared in the *New York Times*, January 30, 1971, under the title "Is It Jeffersonian? A Critical View of Local Vs. National Government." Reprinted by permission of the author.

THE SEVENTIES: PROBLEMS AND PROPOSALS. *Introduction, compilation copyright © 1972 by Irving Howe and Michael Harrington. All rights reserved. Printed in the United States of America. No part of this book may be used or reproduced in any manner whatsoever without written permission except in the case of brief quotations embodied in critical articles and reviews. For information address Harper & Row, Publishers, Inc., 10 East 53rd Street, New York, N.Y. 10022. Published simultaneously in Canada by Fitzhenry & Whiteside Limited, Toronto.*

FIRST EDITION

STANDARD BOOK NUMBER: 06-011973-X

LIBRARY OF CONGRESS CATALOG CARD NUMBER: 71-181628

Contents

Introduction

This book is based on a cluster of premises: that the United States in the 1970s is experiencing a major social and political crisis; that radical changes are required in our society if we are to cope with this crisis; and that these changes can be brought about only through loyalty to and reinvigoration of the democratic process. Each contributor to this book has, no doubt, some political differences with the others, yet all of them would surely agree with these crucial assumptions.

The general outlook, then, from which most of us write can be described as democratic socialist. Because we believe that the United States needs, immediately, a major extension of the reforms which in their sum we designate as the welfare state; because we desire, as soon as possible, a significant redistribution of income, wealth, and power; because we are convinced that if there is enough social will, imagination, and money put into the job we can all but eradicate racism and poverty in the near future—for reasons such as these, we wish to work with people of varying political views, with liberals, trade unionists, insurgent students, and aroused minority groups, toward creating a majority political coalition that will bring about the necessary changes. Because we believe that the creation of a good society requires that major components of the economy be collectively owned and democratically controlled, we are socialists. And because we believe that both of these sets of goals, short-range and long-range, can be achieved—and are meaningful—only under conditions of political liberty, we are democrats.

Any book, no matter how comprehensive its claims, requires editorial selection. We have chosen, in this volume, to emphasize the immediate and middle-range domestic problems facing American society during the next decade or so. Only one piece on foreign policy appears in these pages, though obviously the United States will be facing severe problems in this area. But we had to make a choice—and besides, there has already appeared a volume (*A Dissenter's Guide to Foreign Policy,* edited by Irving Howe) which provides a representation of our views. Similarly, this volume does not contain very much about our views on socialism. But again, choices had to be made—and again, there is available a volume (*Essential Works of Socialism,* edited by Irving Howe) which provides a comprehensive selection on that topic.

Since we feel that the future of this country will be decided in the arena of domestic politics and social policy within the next period, we have concentrated on such matters. Inevitably a problem arises: Have we been specific enough or too specific? Does our analysis provide a large enough framework for the understanding of American society today? The reader will no doubt make his own judgments, but we should say that it has been our intention to provide articles of both kinds, all written in the knowledge that what had to be omitted by one author would be taken up by another. And of course there are gaps— sometimes because of space limits, sometimes because we couldn't find the right author, sometimes because we didn't know the answers or even the questions.

This book represents another instance in the collaboration of a number of writers grouped around the magazine *Dissent,* which over the years has come to be recognized as an authoritative voice of democratic socialism in the United States. We offer this book in the hope that its readers—young and old, students and unionists, white and black, men and women—will be stirred by what follows to reflection, argument, disagreement, and amendment. And then, to the necessary task of setting things right.

I.H.
M.H.

THE SEVENTIES

Michael Harrington

American Society: Burdens, Problems, Solutions

Our technology has produced unprecedented wealth, rotted great cities, threatened the very air and water, and embittered races, generations, and social classes.

Our vision of society, even when most liberal, is too conservative to resolve these contradictions, for they are aspects of a system that has a deep, even principled commitment to the wrong priorities. And while significant reforms—often socialist in inspiration—have modified some of the extreme forms of capitalist injustice, the post-Keynesian welfare state still allows huge corporations to make decisions of fundamental social importance without consulting either those who are affected or those who work for them.

But isn't it an act of leftist nostalgia to indict American society in this way? Today, one is told, the United States is the richest country in the history of mankind, and its remaining problems can be taken care of by pragmatic technicians acting within the framework of the welfare state.

It is precisely this conventional assumption about our present and future that I propose to challenge. I will show that our affluence is so misshapen that it does not even meet the needs of the majority of the people. The most humane of technocrats cannot cope with the basic causes of these antisocial policies, if only because they are located in an entrenched and possessive system of power. Only a democratic mass movement could challenge this vested interest in our current crises.

1

There are three basic reasons why the reform of the welfare state will not solve our most urgent problems:

• the class structure of capitalist society vitiates, or subverts, almost every such effort toward social justice;

• private, corporate power cannot tolerate the comprehensive and democratic planning we desperately need;

• and even if these first two obstacles to providing every citizen with a decent house, income, and job were overcome, the system still has an inherent tendency to make affluence self-destructive.

The welfare state was an enormous advance over the cruelty and indifference to human suffering that characterized early capitalism. It was achieved through struggle and great sacrifice—sometimes of life itself—on the part of "ordinary" people who, even though they had usually been denied an adequate education, tutored the wealthy in some of the fundamentals of social decency. And to the extent that there is a mass "left wing" in the United States, it is composed largely of precisely those groups—trade unionists, minorities, middle-class idealists—which fought these great battles and are determined to preserve the gains they brought.

Far from being simply a matter of keeping the record straight, this point has profound political implications for the future. It is important that socialists demonstrate the inherent inability of the welfare state, based as it is upon a capitalist economy and social structure, to deal with problems that demand anticapitalist allocations of resources. But that does not mean, as some young leftists in recent times have thought, that the welfare state is to be dismissed as a "fraud" that prevents the people from coming to truly radical conclusions. In this context, the following analysis of the severe limits capitalism imposes upon the welfare state is designed not to prove that liberals are foolish and deluded but that their liberal values can be completely realized only on the basis of a socialist program.

The welfare state, for all its value, tends to provide benefits in inverse relationship to human need. And not—the point is crucial—because there is a conspiracy of the affluent, but as a "natural consequence of the division of society into unequal social classes."

Through vigorous and radical reforms it is possible to offset—

though not to remove—this inherent tendency within capitalist society to distribute public benefits according to the inequalities of private wealth. Any movement that attempts to carry out such reforms will be going against the grain of the system itself. This has not kept socialists from participating in every one of these struggles, nor will it in the future. But if the gains are to be permanent, if they are not to be reversed when a period of social innovation is followed by a swing back to capitalist normality, then there must be basic, structural changes. Instead of episodic victories within an antisocial environment, there must be a concerted effort to create a new human environment.

How Inequality Is Built into the System

The class divisions of welfare capitalism that are the root cause of this problem are not, it must be stressed, simply unfair in some abstract sense. Were that the case, a sophisticated conservative argument might be persuasive: since to some extent the growth of the economy benefits everyone, even those who are worst off, there is no point in endangering these gains on behalf of a vision of egalitarianism. What really concerns the poor, this argument continues, is not the rise or fall of their *relative* share of affluence but the steady increase in their absolute standard of living. In fact, however, inequality means not merely that there are sharply unequal proportions of goods distributed among the various social sectors of the population. It also signifies a socioeconomic process, at once dynamic and destructive, which determines that public and private resources shall be spent in an increasingly antisocial way, thereby threatening the well-being of the entire society.

Housing is a crucial case in point. Even under liberal administrations, the government has been much more solicitous about the comfort of the rich than the shelter of the poor. Not only is this policy morally outrageous; it has had disastrous social consequences. Yet it must be emphasized that in thus investing billions in the creation of public problems, Washington did not act maliciously but only followed—unconsciously, automatically, "naturally"—the priorities structured into our society's class divisions. Thus:

• in 1962 the value of a single tax deduction to the 20 percent of Americans with the highest incomes was worth twice as much as all the moneys spent on public housing for the one-fifth who were poorest,[1] and this figure does not even take into account the government support for below-market rates of interest to build suburbia;

• in 1969, the *Wall Street Journal* reported, the $2.5 billion for urban freeways was a far greater subsidy to car owners who daily fled the central city than was the $175 million subsidy to mass transit,[2] and Richard Nixon's 1970 budget continues this perverse allocation of resources by providing public transportation with only 6 percent of the funds assigned to highways;

• as the National Commission on Civil Disorders (the "Riot Commission" of 1968) computed the figures, during roughly the same thirty-year period the government helped to construct over 10 million housing units for home builders, that is, for the middle class and the rich, but provided only 650,000 units of low-cost housing for the poor.[3]

Skewed Priorities and Social Consequences

It would be a mistake to think Washington discriminated only against the poor. For, as the White House Conference told President Johnson in 1966, *the entire lower half of the American population is excluded from the market for new housing,* a market that could not exist without massive federal support.[4] This point needs special emphasis if only because many people, with the best of intentions, concluded from the rediscovery of poverty in America in the sixties that the bulk of the nation was affluent while only a minority was poor. The statistics, far from describing a simple division between the rich and the poverty-stricken, show that we have in this country a *majority*—composed of the poor, the near-poor, more than half the

1. Alvin Schorr, *Explorations in Social Policy* (New York: Basic Books, 1968), p. 275.
2. Alan Otten, in the *Wall Street Journal,* February 25, 1969.
3. National Commission on Civil Disorders, *Report, 1968* (Washington, D.C.: Government Printing Office [cited hereafter as GPO; years of publications are omitted unless they vary from dates given in titles]), p. 28.
4. White House Conference on Civil Rights, *Report and Recommendations of the Council, 1966* (Washington, D.C.: GPO), p. 67.

workers and lower-middle class—which does not even have a "moderate standard of living" as defined by the government.[5]

When Washington used its powers to improve conditions for a wealthy elite, the poor suffered most because they had the most urgent claim on the funds thus squandered on the upper class; but a majority of the people, including tens of millions who were not poor, were also deprived of benefits that should have rightfully been theirs. Worse, in carrying out these discriminatory policies, the federal programs did positive harm to those most in need. As an American presidential commission recently reported, "over the last decades, government action through urban renewal, highway programs, demolitions on public housing sites, code enforcement, and other programs has destroyed more housing for the poor than government at all levels has built for them."[6] But then this is a familiar injustice: "Fifty years ago," wrote Alvin Schorr in 1968, "a British Royal Commission for Inquiry into the Housing of the Working Classes observed, with dismay, that poor people rarely benefited when land was cleared and model housing erected."[7]

In the America of the seventies these fantastically skewed priorities will have momentous social consequences. For Washington has, in effect, been aggravating the very social problems to which it points with alarm. By financing the flight of the middle class from the metropolis and helping industry to locate in the suburbs, the federal government has allowed the central city to rot. As a result such related evils as violence, bitter old age, intensified racism, the decay of the traditional centers of culture, all grew worse. A study commissioned by the government and chaired by Milton Eisenhower gave the darkest view of these trends. The National Commission on the Causes and Prevention of Violence said that, "lacking effective public action," the centers of the great American cities would be safe only in the daytime when crowds gave the individual some security, and that they would be dangerous and empty at night. The big downtown apartment buildings would become "fortified cells for upper-

5. Rudolph Oswald, "The City Worker's Budget," *Federationist,* February 1969.
6. National Commission on Urban Problems, *Building the American City: Report, 1968* (Washington, D.C.: GPO), p. 67.
7. Schorr, *Explorations in Social Policy,* p. 275.

middle and high-income populations living at prime locations in the city." The ghettos would become "places of terror with widespread crime, perhaps entirely out of police control during nighttime hours." And the suburbs would be ringed by freeways patrolled by lightly armored cars.[8]

So the government's discriminatory social policies have done much more than exacerbate inequality; they have helped to promote a fantastic anti-design for living. How, then, can we explain why sincere and dedicated men—as those who presided over these disastrous programs often were—would lavish public funds to aggravate social problems? The answer is to be found in the class character of American society and in the commercial logic that both derives from it and pervades governmental decisions.

The 1969 Report of the Council of Economic Advisers provides candid documentation of this pattern. "Investing in new housing for low-income families—particularly in big cities—is usually a losing proposition," the Council said. "Indeed the *most profitable investment* is often one that demolishes homes of low-income families to make room for business and higher-income families [emphasis added]."[9] It is obvious that the criterion of profitability to which the Council refers is private since, as the gloomy projections of the Violence Commission demonstrate, the social cost of the present system is bankrupting the society. Yet precisely this private calculus is the one the government follows. As the Urban Problems Commission put it, "renewal was and is too often looked upon as a federally financed gimmick to provide relatively cheap land for a miscellany of profitable or prestigious enterprises."[10]

In a society based on class inequality and suffused with commercial values, it just doesn't "make sense" to waste resources on social uses or beauty—or anything that cannot be quantified in dollars and cents. Our legislators, drawn almost exclusively from the middle and upper classes, cannot bring themselves to forget those principles that are

8. National Commission on the Causes and Prevention of Violence, *To Establish Justice, To Insure Domestic Tranquility: Final Report, 1969* (Washington, D.C.: GPO), pp. 44–45.

9. *Economic Report of the President, 1969* (Washington, D.C.: GPO), p. 175.

10. National Commission on Urban Problems, *Building the American City: Report, 1968,* p. 153.

sacred to a private economy. To them it seems logical to invest the federal dollar in undertakings that run the lowest risk and will show the highest and most immediate return.

Housing is only one example of how the welfare state observes the priorities of maldistributed wealth even when it attempts to serve the common good. Other cases in point can be found in literally every department of government. The American welfare system in the sixties reached only a third of the poor and provided them, on a national average, with only half of what they needed.[11] Meanwhile, in 1969, the richest one-sixth among the farmers (individuals and corporations) received two-thirds of the agricultural subsidies, or about $2.5 billion.[12] Given the relation of social classes in this field, America's commitment to promote "agriculture" is also a commitment to help the rich at the expense of the poor. And if one considers the various deductions in the tax codes as an indirect form of government expense —by not collecting money from an individual, Washington increases his income as surely as if it had sent him a check—one will note that they total up to $50 billion, with the bulk of that sum going to oil men, home builders, stock-market speculators, and others from the top of the economic pyramid.

Education and Social Inequality

It is in education that the effect of systematic inequality is most damaging. America is becoming a "knowledge economy," in which higher and higher educational credentials are required, sometimes unnecessarily, in order to get a good job. This is one of the most important areas of socialized effort since, either through public schools or aid to private education, the state supplies the modern economy with "its decisive factor of production, which is trained manpower." Although public spending on education in the sixties increased at a rate faster than that of the Gross National Product,[13] those Americans in the most desperate straits were not reached.

11. National Commission on Civil Disorders, *Report, 1968,* pp. 150, 458.
12. Charles Schultze, "Budget Alternatives After Vietnam," in *Agenda for the Nation,* Kermit Gordon, ed. (Washington, D.C.: Brookings Institution), p. 44.
13. Christopher Jencks and David Riesman, *The Academic Revolution* (New York: Doubleday Anchor, 1969), p. 111.

So it is that in the sixties a rather optimistic study of social mobility in the United States found that there is an "oversupply" of youth at the bottom of the economic structure:[14] the *Manpower Report of the President, 1969,* reported that the unprecedented recent boom had clearly revealed "economic expansion alone was insufficient to employ many people who had been bypassed in the general advance because of inexperience, lack of skills, and cultural deprivation."[15] Now, it is bad enough that such a group should exist at all. What is truly intolerable is the extent to which the social class structure denies its effective access to tax-supported education and works and thereby makes it both self-perpetuating and hereditary.

For if, as Christopher Jencks and David Riesman document in *The Academic Revolution,* society is divided into blue- and white-collar groups, the high school seniors from the white-collar background are four times as likely to score in the top rather than in the bottom 10 percent, while the blue-collar students are twice as likely to be at the bottom rather than at the top.[16] One way of coping with such depressing statistics is to argue that they reflect the "middle-class bias" of the tests used to evaluate students. There have been demands to do away with IQ tests and standard grading, to assign each racial and ethnic group a quota of admissions in state-supported colleges (the top 10 percent of Negroes, Puerto Ricans, Mexican-Americans, and others would have places reserved for them, so there would be competition only within these communities but not among them or with the nonethnics).

To those who charge that the tests are "unfair to the poor," Riesman and Jencks cogently reply, "Life is unfair to the poor. Tests are merely the results. Urban middle-class life in general and professional work in particular seem to nourish potential academic skills and interests in parents, while lower-class life does the opposite."[17] The conclusion they come to is much more radical than that offered by people who simply denounce "educational racism"—or even pro-

14. Peter M. Blair and Otis Dudley Duncan, *The American Occupational Structure* (New York: John Wiley & Sons, 1967), p. 79.

15. *Manpower Report of the President, 1969* (Washington, D.C.: GPO), p. 26.

16. Jencks and Reisman, *Academic Revolution,* p. 175.

17. *Ibid.,* p. 125.

pose separate but inferior college faculties for the children of the poor and the minorities. Riesman and Jencks write:

So long as the distribution of power and privilege remains radically unequal, so long as some children are raised by adults at the bottom while others are raised by adults at the top, the children will more often than not turn out unequal. . . . We suspect that these differences account for more of the class variation in college changes than all other differences combined.[18]

Jencks and Riesman then raise a basic psychological point. Suppose by an act of political will the schools could be transformed so as to favor the minorities while the fundamental social inequalities were left intact. That, they hold, "could be a formula for misery. A mobile, fluid society in which men move up and down is simultaneously a competitive, insecure, and invidious society."[19] "What America needs," they conclude, "is not more mobility but more equality. So long as American life is premised on dramatic inequalities of wealth and power, *no* system for allocating social roles will be very satisfactory."[20] Exactly!

In education, housing, and agriculture, in welfare and every other area of social life, it is therefore necessary to attack the systematic concentration of economic power in order to achieve serious reform. The fulfillment of liberal values, in short, requires structural changes in our class relationships, changes transcending the capitalist limits of today's welfare state.

Planning Under Capitalism

The second major reason why American society cannot deal with its crises is that we need national economic and social planning on a scale that our present institutional arrangements tend to make impossible.

Now there is no question that the seventies will see planning in the United States. The really crucial questions are: What kind of planning? Planning for whom? The problems of welfare capitalist society are becoming so obvious and overwhelming that conservatives

18. *Ibid.,* p. 147.
19. *Ibid.,* p. 148.
20. *Ibid.,* p. 150.

and even reactionaries have understood the need for state intervention —if only to maintain as much of the old order as possible.

In 1969, Spiro Agnew wrote an enthusiastic introduction to the report of the National Committee on Urban Growth Policy, which concluded that the nation should spend public funds in building ten new cities for 2 million people each and ten new towns each for 100,000 citizens.[21] If it was surprising to find a conservative Republican endorsing such an idea, it was even more remarkable that Richard Nixon proceeded to criticize it from "the left." In his Population Message of July 1969, Mr. Nixon noted that by the year 2000 the number of Americans was going to increase to 300 million and that this growth would be predominantly urban. "Are our cities prepared for such an influx? The chaotic history of urban growth suggests they are not, and that many problems will be severely aggravated by a dramatic increase in numbers."

The "radical" proposal for new towns and cities that Agnew had approved was criticized by Nixon because

the total number of people who would be accommodated if even this bold plan were implemented is *only* 20 million—a *mere* one-fifth of the expected 30-year increase. If we were to accommodate the full 100 million persons in new communities we would have to build a new city of 250,000 persons each month from now to the end of the century. [Emphasis added.]

And then, in rephrasing what would once have been regarded as a classic Marxian critique of capitalism, the Republican President defined the fundamental problem: "Perhaps the most dangerous element in the present situation is that so few people are examining the questions from the viewpoint of the whole society."

Mr. Nixon is the representative of precisely those special interests, concentrated in the Republican party, which were able to enlist a good part of the welfare state in behalf of their private purposes. And, though he uses a patch or two of Marxist-sounding rhetoric, he could hardly afford to acknowledge the basis of Marx's insight: that an economy dominated by self-seeking units is, precisely because of that fact, incapable of seeking the common good of the "whole

21. National Committee on Urban Growth Policy, *The New City* (New York: Praeger, 1969), pp. 3 ff.

society." So, when Mr. Nixon talks in this manner, there is no real question of innovations that could threaten the power and privilege of his most important supporters. He and other conservatives are sophisticated enough to understand that the "chaotic" growth of modern society is no longer tolerable and that, in order to contain the future, a modicum of planning and discipline must be imposed on the corporations. This realization has penetrated to all advanced societies in the West, so much so that the British economist Andrew Shonfeld can write that planning is "the most characteristic expression of the new capitalism."[22] We must, then, define the limits of new capitalist planning and contrast them sharply with socialist proposals in the same area.

Two Systems and Their Values

The first distinction between capitalist and socialist planning has to do with money. For meeting the social problems that have just been described will require an investment of billions of public dollars. In 1967 Senator Ribicoff noted that the various existing programs don't even reach people with incomes of $8,000 a year.[23] And in December 1969, three years of inflation later, *Fortune* magazine reported that "the shortage of acceptable shelter that has been afflicting the poor and the black is reaching to the white middle class and even to quite affluent families."[24] To deal with a crisis of this magnitude will clearly require a shift of massive resources from the private to the public sector, since the market is not even reaching a majority of the people. But while Mr. Nixon criticizes the proposals for new towns and cities as inadequate, it is obvious that he and his conservative colleagues are not about to propose such a basic revision in the uses of the national wealth. They are, after all, principled pinchpennies with regard to federal spending—that is, they sincerely believe that the common good is maximized by keeping the allocation of resources as private as possible. Given this basic and capitalist limit

22. Andrew Shonfeld, *Modern Capitalism: The Changing Balance of Public and Private Power* (London: Oxford University Press, 1965), p. 115.
23. Senator Abraham Ribicoff, "The Competent City," Address, January 23, 1967, *Congressional Record,* 113, no. 8.
24. Lawrence A. Mayer, "The Housing Shortage Goes Critical," *Fortune,* December 1969.

to their thinking, any planning measures they urge are going to be inadequately funded. It is significant that in all the Nixon administration's talk about new cities and towns one of the key conclusions of the Urban Growth Policy report is ignored: *"The development of new communities by solely private means will occur in those rare circumstances where the dynamics of growth in particular areas will afford a timely and reasonable return on private investment* [emphasis added]."[25] The infrastructure for a metropolis of one million is, of course, extremely costly, and even though such undertakings have paid for themselves in Europe, the time period before there is any return is quite long. Yet in February 1970, when Nixon's Secretary of Commerce Maurice Stans made the most authoritative and detailed administration statement on the new-city proposal, all he advocated was some tax and other government subsidies to the private sector. If, as Stans and Nixon himself insisted, we will need a new city of 250,000 every month between 1970 and 2000, just to house the increase in population, their timid program is doomed to failure even before it begins.

A second basic distinction between capitalist and socialist planning concerns comprehensiveness.

When Dwight Eisenhower proposed in May 1968 that there be new, integrated communities with jobs, schools, parks, and high-speed transportation links to the old cities, he was unwittingly committing himself to radical innovation. Assembling an integrated population and providing its members with decent work, education, and transportation is not something to be accomplished by the "invisible hand" of Adam Smith. It requires long-range projections and a conscious coordination of government policies. It cannot be done, to take but one crucial example, if land is left to private speculation. For in order to assemble the huge areas needed for such extensive projects at a remotely reasonable cost, the public authority would have to use its power of eminent domain and bank land.

Conservatives may be forced to recognize the magnitude of the urban crisis, but they cannot solve it within their own economic calculus. In their advocacy of new cities Eisenhower, Nixon, and Stans really were talking about a version of the old schemes providing

25. National Committee on Urban Growth Policy, *The New City*, p. 171.

federal subsidies for private interests, which are then supposed to fulfill a social purpose. Supposing even that such a tactic could provide the billions of dollars needed (it cannot), the housing industry hardly has the resources, the overview, or the legal right to engage in national, regional, and metropolitan planning.

But, if it is easy enough to demonstrate that planning within a capitalist context is, at best, utterly and necessarily inadequate, that does not mean socialist planning is without problems. These problems have to be faced candidly.

The Nightmares of Affluence

The third major reason for the basic transformation of capitalist society is this:

Let us assume that the system proves to be much more ingenious than the preceding analysis suggests. Suppose it constructs a welfare state that really does respond to the needs of the poor and that it manages, without fundamental changes in structure, to accommodate itself to democratic planning. Even then—and I admit this possibility for the purpose of argument only—it would be necessary to go beyond capitalism and toward socialism. For, if this society somehow found a way to deal with poverty, racism, inequality, and unmet social needs, it would still be incapable of dealing with its own prosperity.

This problem is not a consequence of wrong-headed choices on the part of muddled executives; it is a trend within the system itself and cannot be corrected without sweeping change. The economic theory of "external economies" and "external diseconomies" helps to explain why.

An external economy occurs when an act of consumption creates a collective good, for example, when the decision of a high school student to remain in school raises his skill level and makes him a more productive worker rather than a candidate for welfare. External economies usually derive from public investments in schools, hospitals, and the like.[26] External diseconomies are a result of an opposite phenomenon: acts of consumption that create a collective evil—for

26. Robert Dorfman, in *Measuring the Benefits of Government Investment*, Robert Dorfman, ed. (Washington, D.C.: Brookings Institution, 1965), pp. 4–5.

example, the air pollution visited upon society by a private automobile. These are particularly associated with giant industries and, as one moderate economist put it, "seem to be far more prevalent than external economies."[27]

So the fundamental tendencies of late-capitalist economies toward bigness and concentration will produce goods whose social costs often exceed their social benefits. This, it must be emphasized, is an inherent pattern in a society where huge investments are made privately. To offset this trend, such decisions have to be made with major consideration of the social costs—a kind of calculus (as will be seen shortly) that is at odds with the very character of the capitalist economy. There follows an extraordinary paradox: the richer capitalism becomes, the more self-destructive it is.

So that as the seventies began—to cite one striking example—the President of the United States could tell the nation: "Based on present trends it is quite possible that by 1980 the increase in the sheer number of cars in densely populated areas will begin outrunning the technological limits of our capacity to reduce pollution from the internal combustion engine."[28] One would think that such an apocalyptic presentiment in Mr. Nixon's Message on the Environment would have been the prelude to decisive action. Yet, only one week before he thus warned that the society was destroying the very air it breathes, Nixon proposed a budget in which mass transportation (which would cut down "the sheer number of cars" as well as serve a number of other social purposes) received 6 percent of the money assigned to building highways, that is, making sure that the sheer number of cars would increase.

The automobile is only one case in point. As Jerome C. Pickard of the Urban Land Institute has commented,

the concentrated character of future urban regional development will place a great strain on regional resources: with water supply, air, and the land itself. The pollutants generated in such large-scale urban and industrial concentration may threaten a large segment of the environment inhabited by a majority of the United States population.[29]

27. Robert Dorfman, *The Price System* (Englewood Cliffs: Prentice-Hall, 1964), p. 140.
28. *New York Times,* February 11, 1970.
29. National Committee on Urban Growth Policy, *The New City,* p. 53.

By the seventies, the menacing consequences of uncontrolled and maldistributed affluence had become so obvious that even the thoughtful business press had begun to doubt whether the market on its own could maximize welfare. Thus one of Marx's fundamental theories was vindicated in a way he himself would never have imagined. The forces of production, Marx held, come into contradiction with the mode of capitalist production, that is, the revolutionary technology cannot be contained within the social and economic system. In Marx's view, evidence of this clash was to be found in the recurrence of depressions. Today, however, precisely because capitalism has moderated the tendency toward periodic crises, it throws up a new form of the Marxian contradiction—for private decision-making is no longer capable of regulating a technology whose social consequences become more and more destructive.

Lyndon Johnson stated the problem well enough in his 1967 message on "Protecting Our National Heritage" but, like his successor, he could not bring himself to urge the radical measures necessary to deal with it. "We must realize," Johnson said, "that in dealing with fuels for motor vehicles we are dealing with matters of enormous importance to every section of the nation and to many economic units. America's technology and natural resources development are intimately involved in any program that affects fuels and their uses." And then Mr. Johnson proceeded to express the wish that corporate polluters would realize that "out of personal interest, as out of public duty, industry has a stake in making the air fit to breathe."[30]

The day Mr. Johnson made that statement, the president of the Ford Motor Company attacked the dangers of government over-regulation, and the *Wall Street Journal* observed that business was mobilizing to fight Johnson's modest reforms. When he signed the Air Quality Act of 1967, President Johnson pretended that he had been given "new power to stop pollution before it chokes our children and strangles our elderly—before it drives us indoors or into the hospital." The *Wall Street Journal* was more realistic: "This was a major victory for such industrial groups as the coal producers, who vigorously opposed toughening federal standards."[31]

In his 1970 Message on the Environment, Richard Nixon confirmed

30. *New York Times,* January 30, 1967.
31. *Wall Street Journal,* May 1, 1967.

that the *Wall Street Journal* had been right and Johnson wrong. There were, he said, "insufficient federal enforcement powers" to fight air pollution. But Nixon could not, of course, hint at why this was so: that the corporations, which had become conscience-stricken about pollution at the precise moment there was a public outcry and the possibility of punitive legislation, had themselves subverted previous efforts to clean up the atmosphere. And, even though Mr. Nixon's antipollution proposals were much less bold than his generalities, the *Wall Street Journal* editorially cautioned him about too sweeping an attack on the internal combustion engine. That, it said, might lead to "severe disruption of many of the nation's largest industries."[32]

There, in the example of the automobile, is the essence of the problem: it is foolish to think that giant industries will voluntarily desist from the profitable spoliation of the environment; and it is impossible for a government committed to maximizing the autonomy of those corporations to take the drastic action we require.

Corporate Interests and the Social Good

In the not so distant past, such a conflict between corporate interest and common good was thought of as exceptional. As Gardner Ackley, a leading new economist of the sixties, put it concisely a few years ago, "If one were to examine all of the thousands of decisions made daily by the managers of the modern corporation, I think he would be struck by the relatively small number in which significant questions of conflict between public and private interests arise."[33] A year later Carl Kaysen, another distinguished liberal economist, challenged Ackley's faith in devastating fashion:

The interrelated set of questions involving urban renewal, urban planning and transportation planning raises questions that go right to the heart of the usual value assumptions of the economist. The whole field is dominated by the existence of externalities, i.e., it is clear that there is no simple meaningful sense in which the range of decisons can be left to market forces. It is further clear that our past methods for dealing with the major externalities are increasingly inadequate, if they ever were adequate. Zoning by a fragmented set of competing jurisdictions, highway

32. *Wall Street Journal*, February 16, 1970.
33. *Wall Street Journal*, May 1, 1967.

planning uncoordinated with land-use planning or without comprehensive urban-suburban transportation planning simply fails to meet the issues. What alternate decision-mechanisms are available?

The natural bias of economists is toward believing that consumers "ought" to get what they want in some ethical sense of the word. Economists accordingly tend to resist, as a matter of fundamental principle, changes in decision-making processes that substitute planners' choices for consumers' choices. Yet in the face of what consumers' choices are leading to, some such substitution appears inevitable. At the very least, planners will determine, much more narrowly than present processes do, the range of alternatives from which consumers may choose. The key question becomes, "By what political mechanism are planners' choices reviewed and controlled?"[34]

This is a remarkable admission. Yet, much as I agree with Kaysen's perspective on the future, I think he is too easy on the capitalist past. He contrasts the market choices, which supposedly pampered the consumer, with planners' choices, which are said to be more restrictive. Yet a good deal of the consumer's desires are in fact engineered, and even when that is not the case, his freedom is circumscribed by the possibilities open to him. Many people in the middle class "freely chose" single-unit suburban homes because decent, reasonably priced housing in the city was not available. The citizen faced with shoddy public transportation or the private automobile was hardly exercising an exhilarating discretion when he chose the latter. In other words, planning could and should broaden the range of choice for the majority.

Nor has this consciousness of the inadequacy of the classic capitalist model been confined to economists. In September 1969 the Yankelovich polling organization surveyed a representative sample of the chief executives of the five hundred largest corporations and fifty largest banks. It concluded that there was a "coming conflict in business discipline" because of the contradiction between social need and private investment. "We predict," the article in *Fortune* reporting on the survey said, "that nothing that has happened since the 1930s will inject more confusion, sow more dissension and conflict, and threaten

34. Carl Kaysen, "Model Makers and Decision Makers," in *Economic Means and Social Ends,* Robert Heilbroner, ed. (Englewood Cliffs: Prentice-Hall, 1969), p. 149.

more chaos than the effect of these pressures [for meeting social needs] as they mount in the early years of the 1970s."[35]

Not only, then, is contemporary capitalism heir to many of the traditional evils of the system, even if sometimes in ameliorated ways; it also cannot deal adequately, no matter how sophisticated it has become, with either poverty or affluence. Left to itself, the system creates a welfare state that provides some benefits for all yet favors the rich and discriminates against the deprived; it generates problems, like those of the urban environment, which demand comprehensive planning; and even when it functions to produce the highest living standard in the world, the social consequences of that achievement are so appalling as to vitiate much of it. There must be a radically new economic calculus, a radically new political and social structure.

The Face of Socialism

In Marx's view history was not predetermined; there was no "inevitable" upward curve of progress. The class struggle within capitalist society, he said, could lead to socialism—or to barbarism. The latter Marx saw as a stalemate, "the common ruin of the contending classes," which would keep the contradictions of society from being resolved on a new and higher plane.[36] In his comments on the "Asiatic mode of production," he even described a system in which state control of a decisive means of production (water in an economy based on irrigation) could provide the basis for a kind of bureaucratic class rule.[37] Yet Marx did not anticipate that a sort of antisocialist "socialism" could be the successor to capitalism in one-third of the world, or that capitalism itself could be planned and rationalized for an entire historical period.

But Marx did clearly assert a basic value judgment that makes it possible to distinguish socialism from other forms of collectivism.

35. *Fortune*, September 1969, p. 95.
36. Karl Marx, *The Communist Manifesto,* quoted here from Karl Marx and Friedrich Engels, *Werke* (Berlin: Dietz Verlag, 1960–   ) 4:462.
37. Karl Marx, *Pre-Capitalist Economic Formations,* Eric Hobsbawn, ed. (New York: International Publishers, 1966). See also Karl Wittfogel, *Oriental Despotism* (New Haven: Yale University Press, 1957).

Nationalization of industry, planning cooperative production—these, he insisted, were only means to an end. The crucial questions about such techniques and institutions are who employs them and according to what priorities? If the state owns the means of production, we must then ask, who owns the state? And there is only one way for the people to "own" the state which owns the means of production: through the exercise of their democratic right to determine its policies and personnel.

For capitalism, it is "natural" to assign resources where there will be the greatest commercial return, and without regard for social consequence. For socialism, by contrast, it is "natural" to allocate them on the basis of human need as democratically determined. As a group of independent French leftists have put it, "By socialism . . . one means a global conception of man and the world which seeks to substitute the principle of conscious solidarity for the traditional resort to domination and private interest in the organization and functioning of society."[38] If this solidarity does not suffuse the new institutions, then it is possible to nationalize all the means of production, to plan the economy meticulously, and yet to end up, not with democratic socialism, but with a new and oppressive form of class society.

The Port Authority in New York City is a useful example of such an antisocial collectivism. Originally it was given considerable autonomy in order to take it out of "politics." Even though it was designed to be high-minded and serve the public, and even though there are no private owners, it acts at least as irresponsibly as any private corporation. As Theodore Kheel has described the Port Authority:

It has preferred to grow huge—and hugely profitable—by catering to motorists. Without even the flimsy justification of acting in the interests of stockholders—it has none—the Port Authority pursues money, not service, with the arrogance, indifference and contempt for the public welfare characteristic of nineteenth-century robber barons.[39]

38. Claude Bruclain [pseudonym for a group of members of the Club Jean Moulin], *Le Socialisme et L'Europe* (Paris: Le Seuil, 1965), p. 56.
39. Theodore Kheel, "How the Port Authority Is Strangling New York," *New York Magazine*, November 17, 1969.

And then, in a perceptive statement of the kind of economic calculation that should rule in a publicly owned enterprise, Kheel writes:

Austin J. Tobin, executive director [of the Port Authority] for 27 years, once said, "Above all else, the people expect their officials to give them prudent and conservative management of public funds." That is disingenuous. Public servants are expected to manage public funds as conservatively as their essential purpose permits. A seemingly unprofitable venture, such as helping mass transportation, might be more genuinely productive than any seemingly self-supporting service the Port Authority has yet turned its hand to—and ultimately would cost us far less.

The Port Authority in New York, like many of the nationalized industries in Europe, shows that public ownership in and of itself, especially within the framework of an economy still basically capitalist, is no guarantee that a corporation will follow social priorities. It behaves exactly like the capitalist enterprises that surround it. This would not be the case under socialism—even though such a society would still have to take costs and alternate uses of resources into account. Karl Kautsky, who prided himself on his Marxian orthodoxy, argued that accounting, and even interest, would exist in socialist undertakings, and he opposed the notion that the omnipotent state would simply command the economy to produce this or that good.[40] Socialist planning would seek to get as precise a measure of costs as possible; yet an investment would not be made simply because it could bring a high return and in spite of its social cost, as is the case under capitalism; nor would totalitarian bureaucrats ruthlessly sacrifice the present needs of the masses in order to build up heavy industry and a war machine, as under Communism.

In the following attempt to make a rough outline of socialist institutions, the point will be to describe how the contradictions of capitalist society can be resolved so that the needs of the people, as they themselves democratically determine them, are met. But, in imagining this future, it is obviously not enough to invent "ideal" solutions. We begin with the specific problems that have just been identified, and within a context established by capitalism where

40. Karl Kautsky, *The Labour Revolution*, H. J. Stenning, transl. (London: Allen & Unwin, n.d. [1925]).

resources are limited and choices have to be made. Then, after having described the social classes and strata that need such innovations and can become politically conscious of this fact, we come to an ultimate vision of socialism. This ultimate vision assumes that the basic material desires of the people have been satisfied and productivity has grown to such an extent that man can free himself from the psychology and economics of scarcity. But, if it is indeed impossible to take a single, giant stride into utopia, one surely cannot arrive at a society of brotherhood by way of gradual terror and coercion, as under Communism.

For Socialization of Investment

First of all—and it is urgent practical politics within the present confines of capitalism as well as a step toward socialism—investment must be socialized.

There are, as has just been seen, huge and decisive areas of economic life in which private capital will not invest because there is no prospect of sufficient profitability (or, what amounts to the same thing, where antisocial allocations are more profitable than social ones). This is true of the fundamental determinants of the urban environment, such as housing and transportation. Therefore, the society must shift resources from the privately profitable sector of the economy to the socially necessary. This decision can be made only by government and must be made only as a result of a democratic process. It can be accomplished only on a national scale and within the framework of planning.

I do not mean to say that the housing design or the exact mix of public and private transport will be settled by a ukase from Washington. A qualitative increase in the rate of social spending can be channeled through the most diverse kinds of organizations: through departments of national, regional, and local government, public corporations, cooperatives, private nonprofit institutions, neighborhood associations, and so on. A progressive income tax, nationally administered, is the only source of funds for such a gigantic appropriation, and the various regional and local choices—where to build a new city, for instance—have to be integrated into a national plan.

In areas such as housing and transportation, this program obviously requires much more than simply the spending of money. For even conservatives have come to realize that government programs have to be coordinated: the Nixon administration talks of a national urban policy and has used five-year projections in its 1970 budget. The National Commission on Urban Problems (chaired by the liberal economist Paul Douglas) recommended that

the President and his Economic Advisers, the Federal Reserve Board, the Treasury Department, and other major agencies of government be required to state what effect any major change in economic policy [e.g., interest-rate changes, tax reductions or increases, balance of payments proposals] would have on the successful building of the number of housing units set by the President in his annual housing construction goal message.[41]

All these suggestions, the liberal as well as the conservative, assume the continuation of the present structure of the housing "industry"—if so modern a word can be used to describe so backward a sector. Yet the government will fail in its commitments unless it creates a new industry. New cities cannot be built by a myriad of private developers, each making his own decisions about a small parcel of real estate. The present procedure of clearing areas that are already urban and then turning them over to profit-seekers has indeed had the disastrous effect of subtracting from the housing supply, increasing the rent on existing, inadequate dwellings, and in general making life more miserable for the poor and minorities. There must consequently be a social land bank, a new technology, an industry created to modern scale and to national and regional plans. And that will take more ingenuity than just writing a federal check.

This one case could be duplicated in every other area of social need, and it points up the second socialist proposal for changing our institutional structure: that decisive investments must be democratically planned as well as financially socialized.

There should be an Office of the Future in the White House. Each year the President should make a Report on the Future—with projections ranging five, ten, or even twenty years ahead—which would be submitted to a Joint Congressional Committee, where it would be

41. National Commission on Urban Problems, *Building the American City: Report, 1970,* p. 182.

debated and amended, and then be presented to the entire Congress for decision. This process should establish the broad priorities of the society and annually monitor the result of past efforts. It would be, for instance, the proper forum where the broad concept of regional planning would be established; but it would not engage in the actual planning of individual projects.

At this point, a candid admission is in order. The changes outlined in the previous paragraph could be welcomed by social engineers determined to impose their values on the people. They might even be used by sophisticated corporate leaders to make the status quo more rational and stable. And they might create an entrenched bureaucracy with a self-interest of its own. The critics of socialism who cite such dangers ignore, or conceal, the fact that these are the consequence of the complexity of *all forms* of modern, technological society and that socialism is the only movement which seeks to offer a structural and democratic challenge to that trend. Even more important, it must be understood that there is no institutional reform which, in and of itself, can "guarantee" genuine popular participation. Only a vibrant movement of the people can do that. That is why socialists do not foresee an ultimate stage of human existence in which all conflicts are resolved. In the very best of societies both the democratic majority and the critical minority must be on the alert.

There is, however, one important area where planning is made more simple because of tendencies within the economy itself. The dominant trend of this century is to move economic activity away from primary pursuits, such as agriculture, and even away from industry, into areas like service and education. This is one of the reasons why college expenditures have increased faster than the GNP since 1950, and why schoolteaching has been one of the fastest-growing professions.[42]

A great many of the areas thereby expanded have been traditionally public or private nonprofit: schools, hospitals, social services, and the like. A 1970 analysis in *Fortune* has even suggested that it is impossible for the nation to achieve its health goals unless there is an even greater increase in the employment of paraprofessionals.[43] When there was a renewal of social consciousness in the sixties, the corporations

42. Jencks and Riesman, *Academic Revolution*, p. 111.
43. Dan Cordtz, "Change Begins in the Doctor's Office," *Fortune*, January 1970.

began to move into these new markets and designed various human-care programs according to the logic of profit. Yet education, health, and personal problems are obviously antagonistic to commercialism, for these are spheres in which one should not stint in order to cut costs and increase the return. The only humane criterion is that of need, and these growth "industries" are therefore natural candidates for social investment.

A Case for Social Ownership

But even if society would thus socialize more and more investment, consciously planning the allocation of resources for cities, transportation, and human care, that in itself would not change the prevailing order. For the control of the means of production and of wealth is not simply economic power; it is political power as well. If over a long period of time private ownership of huge corporations were to coexist with planned social investments, the corporate rich, be they managers or owners, would come to dominate the new, supposedly democratic institutions. Socialists cannot abandon their insistence on social ownership.

Paradoxically, the case for social ownership can be argued on the basis of the same economic trend—the separation of ownership and control under contemporary capitalism—which was cited by many socialists in the sixties as a reason for giving up the traditional position on the nationalization of industry. Moreover, I think there is a strategy for achieving social ownership that does not involve a sudden, apocalyptic leap (impossible under democratic conditions) but rather employs structural reforms. This is a response to present, so far limited problems that nevertheless point toward fundamental changes in the relations of wealth and power.

There is a trend toward the separation of ownership and control and its bearing on social ownership.

For the continental socialists who revised their basic programs in the late fifties and early sixties, this development made the classic case for nationalization seem irrelevant. Now that rational, plan-oriented managers have taken over from individualistic capitalists, they argued, it is no longer necessary to change the title to property. For the socialists in control of the government will follow full-employment policies that will yield a growing fund for social spending and, in any case, the corporate executives will see that it is to their interest to observe the broad priorities established by the state. I would argue that this very trend of separating ownership and control increasingly demonstrates the functionless character of the legal title to property and suggests a very practical, unapocalyptic method of doing away with it.

Marx, as I noted earlier, understood that the joint stock company —the first institutional expression of the separation of ownership from control—contained an anticapitalist premise insofar as it made economic functions independent of capital itself. That, he felt, was one more sign of the transition to socialism. In the 1920s John Maynard Keynes described the self-socializing tendencies of capitalism as the "euthanasia of the rentiers."[44] It was a distinguished conservative, however, who most clearly drew the socialist conclusions from this economic tendency. Frederick A. Hayek has said,

So long as the management is supposed to serve the interests of the stockholders it is reasonable to leave the control of its actions to the stockholders. But if the management is supposed to serve wider public interest, it becomes a logical consequence of this conception that the appointed representatives of the public interests should control the management.[45]

There are two reasons why I believe this straightforward proposal of socialization is to be preferred to the European social democratic notion of the state programming a market economy with social goals. First, the recent experience of the continental social democrats confirms the tendency of the corporations to try to dominate, rather than obey, the government that is supposed to control them. Second, it is now possible to have a relatively painless transition to social ownership if socialists will only learn how to give direction to the underlying trends of the corporate economy.

Harold Wilson's problems in England during the sixties provide an example of the first point. Whenever Wilson, who had received a democratic mandate, sought to raise pensions or to introduce other

44. Quoted in John Strachey, *Contemporary Capitalism* (New York: Random House, 1965), p. 56.
45. *Management and Corporations, 1985,* Melvin Anshen and George Bach, eds. (New York: McGraw-Hill, 1960), p. 107.

reforms, bankers in London and throughout the world took reprisals against the pound sterling. Industry was quite ready to maximize the advantages of production for the domestic market rather than to become the efficient exporter that the government urged it to be. And while Labour did manage to put through a qualitative expansion of social spending, the proportion of unearned income in Britain rose.[46] For in Britain, as in America, private economic power seeks to veto democratic majorities and to make the state an instrument of private purposes as far as is possible. That is one reason why an extension of social ownership is necessary.

"Euthanasia for Rentiers": A Modest Proposal

Social ownership now seems easier to achieve if socialists will encourage the "euthanasia of the rentiers." The Swedish socialists bring an ingenious contribution to this area. They propose to socialize the functions of property while leaving the title to it temporarily undisturbed. In this way socialization will be part of a historic process rather than a sudden and drastic leap to new forms of property.[47]

We tend to reify private property into something indivisible, so that one either owns or does not own. But, in the case of the means of production (and they, not personal property, are what is of concern to socialists), one can think of private property as conferring series of functional and divisible rights. In the class theory of *laissez faire,* ownership allowed a man to utilize existing fixed capital resources; to determine investment policy; to deploy the labor force; to set wage levels; to distribute profits; to retain profits; and so on. This model has, of course, already been modified: wage levels are fixed through collective-bargaining agreements overseen and encouraged by the state; tax policies can provide incentives for internal financing or for distributing profits; etc. Now a much more profound and conscious socialization is required of more of the functions of property. Taking property as, in A. A. Berle's phrase, a "packet of permissions,"[48]

46. John Hughes, "The Increase in Inequality," *New Statesman* (London), November 8, 1968.

47. Gunnar Adler-Karlson, *Functional Socialism: A Swedish Theory for Democratic Socialization* (Stockholm: Prismen, [in English] 1969).

48. A. A. Berle, *Power* (New York: Harcourt, Brace & World, 1969), p. 258.

what is proposed is not a sudden, wholesale takeover by the state but a process that progressively abolishes all these private permissions and that substitutes democratic decisions for them.

For example, private investment decisions must be socialized. The right to locate or relocate a plant in a given area can no longer be considered a private matter. For in order to engage in regional planning and to aid in the construction of new cities and towns, the geography of employment has to be publicly determined. A strict system of licensing the permission to build a factory could work toward this end. (The Attlee government initiated some measures of this type, and various Italian governments have tried to use such techniques to promote the development of the South.)

Technology also has to be monitored. The decision to build a supersonic transport has so many consequences (noise, air traffic congestion, airport construction) that even if it were not a government-subsidized project, the public interest would have to be asserted. There is a need, as a National Academy of Sciences panel pointed out, for "technological forecasting." One cannot trust these matters, as the *Wall Street Journal* put it in a telling anticapitalist phrase, to the "mindless market."[49]

The panel also made another important point about technological forecasting: that it must be carried out by an independent agency and not by an interested bureaucracy. For "the Bureau of Public Roads has hardly been noted for its devotion to the natural beauty of the countryside." More generally, as the example of the New York Port Authority suggests, it is quite possible for a publicly owned enterprise to behave in the same aggressive, self-interested way as a private corporation. Here again, the crucial issue is not so much the legal form of ownership as the kind of economic calculus it follows.

Profit is another function of property that must be subjected to social control. In 1967, the Council of Economic Advisers—hardly an anticapitalist agency—noted that government direction of the economy had smoothed out the cycle of boom and bust and therefore removed a great deal of the risk in the marketplace. Under such conditions, the council argued, business should be prepared to take a

49. Arlen J. Large, "Technology in the Mindless Market," *Wall Street Journal,* October 17, 1969.

lower rate of return.[50] But, in point of fact, American corporations chafed under the voluntary controls of the Kennedy and Johnson administrations even though their profits rose by 78.7 percent between 1960 and 1970, and their cash flow (profits plus depreciation) was up by 85 percent in the same period.[51] When Richard Nixon came into office, he abandoned all efforts to persuade industry and labor to obey guidelines in price and wage policy. Whereupon, the London *Economist* reported, the steel industry increased its prices in twelve months by 7 percent—as contrasted to a 6 percent rise in the previous ten years.[52]

Government, we must conclude, cannot leave profit policy to the "conscience" of the corporations. It can use an array of techniques to socialize this important area of economic life: price and wage controls in an inflationary period; a requirement that big companies open up their books and justify any increase in prices before an independent board; the use of vigorous tax policy (more on this shortly). However this be done, the fundamental purpose of the reform is clear enough. The society cannot afford to leave to private decision the pricing of basic goods—or how the huge annual increments in wealth are to be distributed.

There are other structural changes that could socialize some of the functions of property. The voting rights of all speculative, short-term shareholders could be abolished.[53] (This would make it clear that many of the transactions on the stock market are nothing but a socially approved form of gambling—and an enormous waste of resources and energy.) It has been proposed that the government give itself the right to act as if it were a majority stockholder in all major industries, but without taking legal title.[54] In this scheme, the corporation would be left to its own devices as long as it conformed to the national plan and did not irresponsibly impose social costs upon the country. When its private egotism led to antisocial behavior, the

50. *Economic Report of the President, 1967* (Washington, D.C.: GPO), p. 133.

51. "Corporate Profits and the Wage Gap," *Federationist*, July, 1968.

52. *Economist* (London), January 31, 1970.

53. Andrew Shonfeld, "Business in the Twenty-First Century," *Daedalus*, Winter 1969, p. 202.

54. *Ibid.,* p. 202. See also C. A. R. Crosland, *The Conservative Enemy* (New York: Schocken Books, 1962), p. 48.

government would intervene in the same way major shareholders confront poor management. The state would not assume permanent control but see to it that the direction of corporate policy was changed so as to observe the proper social priorities.

In France in 1970, the Radical party under the urging of Jean-Jacques Servan-Schreiber adopted a policy "to abolish the hereditary transmission of property in the means of production." In effect, Servan-Schreiber advocated a confiscatory tax on the stock holdings of very wealthy individuals. There have been debates on how effective such measures would be, yet the principle is both clear and excellent.[55] A quite similar idea was proposed by Douglas Jay of the British Labour party, which would make a government investment bank the recipient of the stock paid as death duty.[56]

Taken individually, none of these changes would basically transform the power relations within capitalist society. But, if they were part of a comprehensive policy which sought to limit progressively the rights of property in the means of production, they could encourage and direct the "euthanasia of the rentiers." The gradualism of this strategy is not derived from any abstract principle but from the actual experience of socialist governments over half a century—as well as from a sense of what may be acceptable to the American people.

Social Change and Human Psychology

Discussion of the practical limits of man's idealism has been confused because it has so often turned on the experience of Communism, and on what happens to human psychology in a regime of totalitarian scarcity and class privileges. Alienation—and greed and invidious striving—can only be overcome, as Marx observed, when the means of production are so developed that they provide the material basis for general abundance. When an impoverished economy is socialized, he said, "*want is made general, and with want the need to struggle for necessities must begin again and all of the old crap will be reproduced.*" (Emphasis added.)[57] And "the old crap" is precisely that

---

55. Gilbert Mathieu, "Revolution ou voeu pieux," *Le Monde*, February 7, 1970.

56. Douglas Jay, *Socialism in the New Society* (New York: St. Martin's Press, 1963), pp. 281–82.

57. Karl Marx, *Die Deutsche Ideologie*, 3:34–35.

pervasive venality that is to be found in any form of class society, capitalist or Communist.

Must an analysis then conclude, as Robert Heilbroner has suggested, with an acknowledgment that the socialist aspiration toward equality necessarily and always conflicts with the socialist determination to produce enough for all?[58] I think not. For, as soon as one examines the question of motivation within the context of affluent societies, there emerges the possibility of a productive egalitarianism—and trends in this direction can be seen despite the outrageous inequality still prevailing in these nations. The evidence is provided by the children of the rich and the mothers of the poor in contemporary America; the optimistic generalizations come from men as counterposed as Keynes and Trotsky.

Heilbroner speculates on how advanced capitalism may be changing economic psychology. It is possible, he writes, that in such a society "affluence will weaken the conditions of economic dependency on which the market system is tacitly based, opening up the prospect that normal differentials of income payment will no longer suffice to attract men to less desirable jobs, and thereby requiring that capitalism resort more and more to planning and coercion."[59] Yet, if Heilbroner's observations of this trend are accurate, his conclusions are overly pessimistic.

For it has been noted in New York that when welfare benefits to the mothers of dependent children became competitive with or superior to the pay for unskilled jobs in the labor market these people did not seek work. They were hardly enjoying affluence, yet they certainly exemplified a breakdown of the old market compulsions. There is, as Nathan Glazer commented on the phenomenon, "a massive change in values which makes various kinds of work which used to support families undesirable to a large number of potential workers today."[60] Now, one possible conclusion is to force welfare women to work. That was the response of the Nixon administration in 1969,

58. Robert Heilbroner, "Socialism and the Future," *Commentary,* December 1969.

59. *Ibid.*

60. Nathan Glazer, "Beyond Income Maintenance," *The Public Interest,* Summer 1969. p. 120.

when it made the benefits of its proposed minimum family income program conditional on the recipient's working or training for a job. It was, in effect, a vicious public policy forcing mothers into the labor market (by 1969 there were practically no able-bodied men on public assistance).

But there is another way of handling this situation, one that socialists propose here and now, even within the context of welfare capitalism. The unwillingness of human beings to work at degrading, routine jobs should be welcomed, both as an advance in the level of men's aspirations and as an opportunity for channeling their talents into socially useful areas. Many dead-end jobs can be mechanized out of existence; as long ago as 1966, the President's Automation Commission demonstrated that there were then 5.3 million public-service jobs in education, health services, beautification, and the like, that could provide decent employment for people displaced by such mechanization—and for millions of the underemployed and unemployed—which would vastly improve the quality of the entire society.[61]

Among the most cruelly used people in the affluent society there seems to be arising a new sense of dignity (conservatives mistake it for laziness), which refutes the old motivations now that brutal compulsions are no longer in force. And this change in psychology could be utilized to help America solve its problems, or it could serve as an excuse—which Heilbroner fears as a possibility and Nixon embraces as a policy—to substitute the coercion of law for the weakened discipline of the market and thereby to drive people to do humiliating work.

Another change in psychology is taking place, not in the slums but in the suburbs of the upper middle class and the rich. A *Fortune* survey taken in October 1968 reports that eight million youths between eighteen and twenty-four are or have been in college. Forty percent of these young people said that they were no longer primarily interested in preparing for commercial careers in the profit sector.[62] This trend will be dealt with in more detail shortly, for it has enormous

61. National Commission on Technology, Automation and Economic Progress, *Technology and the American Economy: Report, 1966* (Washington, D.C.: GPO), p. 36.

62. The Editors of *Fortune, Youth in Turmoil* (New York: Time-Life Books, 1969), p. 43.

political consequences; it is cited here to show that socially conscious motivations are becoming more and more important.

The *Fortune* data describes liberal-arts students for the most part. There is a similar trend in industry, among technicians and engineers. Capitalism went through two successive industrial revolutions—coal, steam, and textiles were the basis of the first, steel and electricity of the second—and both of these resulted in a hierarchical structure with a detailed division of labor. But the third revolution—in electronics, data processing, and petrochemicals—is not so prone to bureaucracy and subordination. Cooperation and informal, transitory team relationships become the norm, replacing fixed and formal lines of authority; groups coalesce around problems and reforms when new issues arise.[63] In May 1968, in France, adult militancy in the general strike was concentrated in precisely these advanced areas of the economy, and the key demands concerned the organization of work rather than simple wage increases.

One of the most important American theorists of the corporation, A. A. Berle, has some fascinating speculations on this development. He argues that profit-oriented decision is not particularly innovative, and that the more secure and wealthy a company becomes the fewer are its incentives to change.[64] The greatest feats of invention, Berle continues, have been accomplished by defense corporations under conditions of war and with survival and patriotism as central motives. The Manhattan Project, which created the atom bomb, is an obvious example.

Berle considers it at least possible that such attitudes can be given a social rather than a military thrust: "A day may come when national glory and prestige, perhaps even national safety, are best established by a country's being the most beautiful, the best socially organized, or culturally the most advanced in the world."[65] If such a profound psychological mutation does not lie in the immediate future, the attitudes of the educated and affluent young suggest that it is not impossibly distant either. Were this to happen, some of the dreams of the anarchists and guild socialists would become a realistic by-product

63. Warren G. Bennis, "Post-Bureaucratic Leadership," *Trans-action,* July–August 1969.
64. Berle, *Power,* p. 211.
65. *Ibid.,* p. 213.

of technical and social change. One could then think of human and communal relationships within the socialized enterprise, and the classic socialist vision—that production will be carried out by the "associated producers"—would become newly relevant.

Taxation as Social Policy

But, before taking a longer perspective on economic development, another quite specific question must come under our scrutiny: that of taxation as social policy. In the past, socialists have tended to ignore the enormous potential of tax policy as a way of getting to a decent society. If there is a tendency under capitalism for reforms, and even in structural changes a tendency to benefit the wealthy more than the poor, a rigorously progressive income tax could provide a major corrective. Not only must the wealth generated by the intervention of the state serve society on a democratic basis; the very organization of inequality itself must be undermined.

In the United States there has been no significant change in the distribution of income since 1944. Moreover, the effective rate of taxation on the rich and the upper middle class (the top 15 percent of the society as measured by incomes) declined in the years 1952–67.[66] Many of the taxes in this country—for social security and unemployment insurance, state and local sales taxes—are regressive. And all of these figures are based on reported rather than actual income: they do not take into account the command over resources in expense accounts, pensions, and other prerequisites that are confined to the upper reaches of the economy.

The American tax system—the same is true for most advanced capitalist countries—is a labyrinth favoring the wealthy who can afford lawyers and accountants. "Income," as defined by the Internal Revenue Service, excludes more than $7 billion a year in capital gains; it does not tax the rent middle-class families save by owning their own houses, worth $8 billion a year; it exempts various state and local bonds; etc. The simple act of making "income" on the tax form equal actual income of the taxpayer would be a major contribution to social justice.

66. Joseph Pechman, "The Rich, the Poor, and the Taxes They Pay," *Public Interest,* Fall 1969.

Even such a modest reform is intolerable on the basis of capitalist ideology. Two items in the *Wall Street Journal,* separated by less than a year's time, illustrate my point. In the summer of 1969 when Congress considered—and then promptly forgot—the idea of limiting some of the privileges of stock speculators by changing somewhat the favored status of capital gains, the *Journal* replied in an indignant editorial. The reform would "punish the nation's most productive citizens," and this disincentive to the stockholder would lead to a decrease in economic activity and lower federal revenues. "Obviously enough," the *Journal* said, "the tax reformers' chief aim is not more money for Uncle Sam but more 'justice' as among individual taxpayers." This plea obviously assumes that the stock market performs important and creative economic functions and that it is peopled by "the nation's most productive citizens."

But in February 1970 there was another report in the *Wall Street Journal.* Inflation had made money so tight that giant blue-chip corporations were doing something out of the ordinary: they were actually trying to raise money in Wall Street. The "nation's most productive citizens," the *Journal* reported, were dismayed at this turn of events. Sidney Homer, a partner in Solomon Brothers & Hutzler, told the paper, "Every time you add $1 billion to the volume through new stock offerings you *take out $1 billion that could be used to push up stocks already on the market*" (emphasis added). This constitutes a marvelous refutation of the *Journal*'s editorial, for it shows that the main form of activity on the market is legalized gambling of a sort that provided no new venture capital whatever. As Joan Robinson summed it up, "the shareholders and rentiers indeed make a great negative contribution to industry, for much of the best talent in every generation is engaged, one way or another, in the lucrative business of swapping securities around amongst them and so is kept from constructive activities."[67]

Effective inheritance taxes would provide another important source of social funds and an opportunity to work toward greater equality. In the United States these taxes are quite low—or quite avoidable, which amounts to the same thing. In classic capitalist theory, a man

67. Joan Robinson, "Socialist Affluence," in *Socialism, Capitalism, and Economic Growth,* G. H. Feinstein, ed. (Cambridge [England]: Cambridge University Press, 1967), p. 177.

must be able to leave his fortune to his children if he is to have an incentive to work hard all his life. That motive could easily be protected by providing for relatively low death duties on the *first* transfer of wealth, from father to son. This would encourage the father, while very high rates on the second transfer, from son to grandson, would give both of them a reason to strive hard. This proposal follows the ingenious Saint-Simonian scheme of abolishing inheritance over three generations and counting on the greed of the first generation to make it indifferent to what happens to its grandchildren.

In all these reforms, the point would be not to penalize hard work or actual risk taking but to limit severely, and eventually to eliminate, the tribute society pays to passive wealth and stock gamblers. For as the process of accumulation becomes much more social, with industry generating its own investment funds or getting them from institutions, it is absurd to pay generations of functionless coupon clippers on the grounds that their distant ancestors made a contribution to the economy. It is property income that should become the target of taxation, a kind of income easy enough to distinguish from the reward for present accomplishment. We should also seek to get at the enormous increase in land value—worth $25 billion a year in the United States between 1956 and 1966—which takes place without any effort on the part of the owner.[68]

Of all the reforms proposed in this essay, the use of taxes to increase justice and equality should be the most politically promising. For it would be a policy attacking the wealth of a parasitic minority, and once all the outmoded rationales for favoring the rich were shattered, a majority of the people might be educated to see the value of a radical system of taxation.

Here, then, are three kinds of programs that move in the direction of a socialist democratization of economic power.

- *the socialization of investment;*
- *the progressive socialization of the functions of corporate property itself, with an attendant increase in the social motivation of the people;*
- *the employment of tax policy as an instrument of social justice.*

68. Pechman, "The Rich, the Poor, and the Taxes They Pay," pp. 30, 35.

Who Will Do the Job?

It may be asked: Who will do the job? Granted that basic new departures in economic and political policy are desperately needed, where can we find the political support for these measures? If the European social democrats have not been able to go beyond the welfare state, isn't it preposterous to suggest that they—and an America that doesn't even have a mass social democratic movement —should now prepare to go much farther? In the nineteenth century, the immediate experience of capitalist society was one of poverty, insecurity, periodic crisis, and the degradation of a mechanized division of labor. As a result there was a revolutionary class consciousness. But as the barbarities of the system were moderated, precisely through the impact of that class consciousness, the consequent new conditions—the new social beings, if you will—gave rise to a new consciousness. The worker in the welfare state has a certain stake in the established order as well as powerful grievances against it. If he still considers himself a socialist, that is either in deference to tradition or as an expression of his essential reformism. We may ask: has utopia, at least for a time, been partially conservatized?

Pursuing this theme, a group of intellectuals in the late fifties and early sixties—Daniel Bell and Raymond Aron prominent among them —declared that we were witnessing an "end of ideology." In effect they argued that the old, militant antagonisms of capital and labor were ended, or largely muted, and that social change had become a question of how experts would divide an ever-increasing Gross National Product. In *The Accidental Century,* I challenged this thesis and contended that revolutionary changes taking place in technology and economic structure could well radicalize masses of people again.

I believe that the second half of the sixties bore out my analysis more than that of the "end of ideology" people. In every advanced nation there was unprecedented student and youth unrest; in the United States there were explosions of black anger; in France, Italy, Germany, and Spain the working class engaged in the most determined struggle since the thirties. And now, looking toward a conscious movement that could make the objective need for socialism into an effective political force, let me suggest a possibility (not an inevitability): that the traditional protest of the workers, the grandchildren of the prisoners of starvation, and the unprecedented rebellion of the youth, the children of affluence, may converge into a force capable of transforming modern society.

To understand the creative potential of the workers, take the United States of America, the advanced nation where labor seems most integrated into the prevailing order and utterly lacking in any kind of revolutionary consciousness.

Now, it is quite true that the *industrial* working class in America is a declining percentage of the population. But, to cite a fact some of the interpreters of this trend forget, the number of the workers is also on the increase; it is their percentage, not their total, that is going down. In 1965 in America, 37 percent of the jobholders, or more than 26 million individuals, were craftsmen, foremen, operatives, and laborers.[69] And a majority of those in the service industries—9 million people and 12.6 percent of the whole work force—were blue-collar. As the Department of Labor projected the evolution of these categories, the number of industrial workers would increase by 1975 to 30 million, even though their percentage would drop to 33.3 percent. Adding in the blue-collar service workers, that would mean over 40 million citizens in working-class occupations in the mid-seventies.

The working class is by no means "disappearing." And, even as various academics were explaining how the proletariat had ceased to be a historical actor, there were tens of millions of workers who continued to face many of the old problems of working-class life. For, as the Bureau of Labor Statistics computed the figures, in late 1966 it took about $9,200 to support an urban family of four in the United States at a "moderate standard of living" (the definition allowed, for example, the purchase of a new suit and a two-year-old used car every four years).[70] With our rampant inflation, it is clear that this figure will have to be revised to somewhat more than $11,000 for 1971.

To achieve that 1966 level required a weekly pay check of $177; the average for industrial workers was actually $114. Indeed, a majority of the American people lacked the resources of this "moderate" budget. In addition to the poor, there were tens of millions of working Americans who, if not hungry, had to struggle and scrape to make

69. *Manpower Report of the President, 1969* (Washington, D.C.: GPO), p. 235, Table E-8.
70. Oswald, "The City Worker's Budget," *Federationist*, February 1969.

ends meet. And many of these citizens were concentrated in factory jobs that were physically grueling. So the "old" issues of wages and working conditions were still very much a factor in the experience of the majority of the people. And in Europe, where per capita wealth is inferior to that in the United States, they were an even greater factor.

Expression of working-class discontent did not take the turbulent, near-revolutionary forms that it did in France and Italy in 1968 and 1969, but it was still a powerful political force. In the elections of 1968 the supposedly decrepit trade unions were clearly the single most important element in the coalition which, despite the most difficult odds, almost elected Humphrey President in 1968. The labor organizations registered 4.6 million voters, printed more than 100 million leaflets and pamphlets, and supplied 72,225 canvassers and 94,457 volunteers on election day.[71]

For—and this point is extremely important—the political potential of social classes cannot be determined by a simple head count. There are nations in which the overwhelming majority is peasant and yet the society is run in the cities. Peasants are dispersed, parochial, and premodern. They can flare into a jacquerie or even provide the troops for a Mao or a Ho Chi Minh. But the decisive technology of the contemporary economy is industrial, and the center of power is therefore urban. Workers, in the cities, are concentrated in very large numbers, subjected to a common discipline in the work process, and forced—in the defense of their most immediate interests—to build collective institutions. They therefore have a cohesion, a social weight, in excess of their numbers.

I stress this aspect of working-class life which is so often ignored by the affluent, college-educated, and issue-oriented people who must form coalitions with the unionists. The new constituency that is emerging as a result of mass higher education is important; but it does not have a solidarity imposed upon it by the very conditions of life and work, as the workers do. Therefore, even if the percentage of blue-collar workers is declining and that of "professional, technical, and kindred workers" is on the increase, it is the working people with

71. Theodore H. White, *The Making of the President, 1968* (New York: Atheneum, 1969), p. 365.

their own stable institutions who must be the decisive component in a socialist majority.

Paradoxically, affluence may yet provoke the workers to political struggle as much as poverty did. As far back as 1849, Marx had recognized the possibility that capitalist success would make labor rebel.

The rapid growth of production capital [Marx wrote] brings about an equally rapid growth of wealth, luxury, social wants, social employments. Thus, although the enjoyments of the worker have risen, the social satisfactions which they give him fall in comparison with the increased enjoyments of the capitalists which are inaccessible to the worker, and in comparison with the state of development of society in general. Our desires and pleasures spring from society; we measure them, therefore, by society.[72]

If one updates Marx's insight into the radicalizing effort of good times, another aspect of recent working-class militancy can be brought into focus. For affluence does not simply narcotize and make men passive, as Herbert Marcuse seems to think. It also makes people angry when they compare what they have with the bountiful pretensions of the society. They contrast their standard of living, not with that of their parents or grandparents, but with that of the enchanted creatures of television. Affluence seems to subvert itself.

Moreover—and here we move toward the line separating the traditional blue-collar working class from the new professionals—there are changes in class structure in the affluent economy which occasion new kinds of discontent. Planned, rationalized capitalism demands higher and higher skills from its labor force, and this opens up the possibility of a very educated opposition among the technicians employed in the most advanced industries. So it was, for example, that in the French general strike of May 1968 the greatest militancy was not found among the coal miners, the classic source of proletarian intransigence, but among men and women working in electronics, the chemical and auto industries, among teachers and the employees of the state-run radio and television network.[73] And the demands of

72. *Communist Manifesto*, 6:412.
73. Alain Touraine, *Le Mouvement de Mai ou le Communisme Utopique* (Paris: Seuil, 1968), pp. 162–68.

these sophisticated workers in advanced industries did not concern wages as much as the democratization of working conditions.

Is There a "New Class"?

There is still a politically potent dissatisfaction, based on the old working-class deprivations and also on the new needs of affluence. Moreover, if the proletariat failed to develop as Marx believed it would, there may now be a totally unexpected agency of social change emerging in the West.

This new class—I use the term loosely—has been glimpsed by many observers. Yet there has been a great deal of confusion, partly, I suspect, because this prodigious age is producing not one but two new social groups, related yet distinct. In addition, this change in class structure has been mistakenly identified so that both the mass media and the pop sociologists see it primarily as a matter of age. What is happening, I would suggest, is not the mere expression of a transitory mood among young people who will forget their egalitarian fantasies once they have to submit to the rigors of the labor market and "grow up." What may well be happening—youth apart—is a change in economic and social structure that could have large political consequences.

As capitalism developed, it needed more and more people who were not engaged in actual production. Long ago Max Adler, the Austrian socialist theorist, had recognized "a new black-coated proletariat altogether unlike the petite bourgeoisie of Marx's day."[74] After World War II this tendency became more and more pronounced. With the third technological revolution within capitalism, electronics, chemicals, computers, and the "knowledge" industry were in the vanguard. And all these fields require a great number of highly skilled people.

Moreover, as John Kenneth Galbraith noted in *The New Industrial State,* because the corporation has become huge and makes multimillion-dollar investments projected over long periods of time, a whole new stratum of industrial planners is needed. This marks, Galbraith suggests, a major new source of power, since society always

74. Quoted in C. D. H. Cole, *History of Socialist Thought,* 5 vols. (New York: St. Martin's Press, 1953–60) 3, Part 3:558.

pays a particular deference to its most scarce resource. Once it was land, then capital; now it is organized intelligence.[75] Daniel Bell has said that the "new men" in this emergent order are

the scientists, the mathematicians, the economists and the engineers of the new complex technology. The leadership of the new society will rest, not with the businessmen or corporations as we have known them . . . but with the research corporation, the industrial laboratories, the experimental stations and the universities.[76]

From this thesis about the new men of "postindustrial" society, Bell drew fairly conservative conclusions. Using almost the same theory, the French sociologist Alain Touraine has said that these changes would result in a "utopian communist" movement and that the French revolt of May 1968 was one of the first expressions of this new revolutionary trend.[77]

In short, responses to this new social stratum come from every point on the political compass. How to interpret the facts about this new group is still a highly controversial matter, but the facts themselves are pretty clear. In 1969 a Department of Labor study predicted that by 1975 this country would have a 45 percent increase in the number of professionals as compared to 1965, a 23 percent rise in the number of managers, and a 32.5 percent growth of the clerical work force.[78] If these projections turn out to be accurate, these three groups could account for over 40 percent of the employment in the United States. There are, of course, enormous differences among and within these categories: a typist is by no means part of the same social stratum as a corporation vice-president or a nuclear physicist. Nevertheless, it is urgent to realize that there is occurring a vast expansion of jobs both distant from actual production and often demanding high levels of education and skill.

Is there evidence to indicate that these statistics point to a group with a consciousness of its own, let alone a special receptivity to radical or socialist ideas? Galbraith is optimistic on this count; he

75. John Kenneth Galbraith, *The New Industrial State* (Boston: Houghton Mifflin, 1967), pp. 46 ff.

76. Daniel Bell, "Notes on Postindustrial Society," *The Public Interest*, Winter 1967, p. 27.

77. Touraine, *Le Mouvement de Mai*, passim.

78. *Manpower Report, 1969*, p. 235, Table E-8.

writes that the industrial system "brings into existence, to serve its intellectual and scientific needs, the group that, hopefully, will reject its monopoly of social purpose."[79] As early as the turn of the century, the American Marxist Louis Boudin applied Kautsky's theory of "state socialism" to the United States and identified the very beginning of the phenomenon Galbraith described. The new middle class or group of propertyless managers, Boudin said, was in favor of regulating the conflicts and crises within capitalism and therefore was disposed to state intervention, but it would never accept a radical transformation of the society itself.[80]

Boudin may be right and Galbraith wrong. The growing stratum of professionals and technicians may simply want to ameliorate, not really change, the existing order. It would then end up with politics similar to those of the American Medical Association, a group organized to exploit the community it is supposed to serve. But there is at least the possibility that the new professionals will be drawn to support more radical transformations. Involved each day with cooperative endeavors in which they debate and discuss and plan, they are open to an appeal to build a more rational, planned order.

Professionals and Technicians as Workers

One could identify this stratum in terms of the traditional Marxist analysis, as some on the Left have done. It would then be seen as a new section of the working class, rather than as a new class. For the great mass of professionals and technicians indeed work for large corporations and universities and often have developed a "trade-union" consciousness of the need to band together and fight for their group interests. It seems quite legitimate to take this view of the phenomenon so long as one recognizes the unique characteristics of the new group: a high level of formal education and an issue orientation. On such issues as foreign policy, civil liberties, and civil rights, this emergent stratum is likely to differ considerably from traditional working-class attitudes.

If, then, the crisis of advanced society will become more pressing

79. Galbraith, *New Industrial State*, p. 399.
80. Louis Boudin, *The Theoretical System of Karl Marx* (Chicago: Charles H. Kerr & Co., 1915), pp. 209 ff.

in the years ahead, and if it can be resolved only through radical innovation, there is a growing group that could become conscious of this fact and decide to act upon it politically. It has, I believe, already provided part of the mass basis for the McCarthy and Robert Kennedy campaigns of 1968 and for the movement to end the war in Vietnam. But if this group decides, out of naïveté or arrogance, to "go it alone" and refuses to work with trade unionists because of the latter's dominant concern with bread-and-butter questions, it will not be able to transform the society. Only if it understands that labor is the best-organized and most powerful force for domestic social change, and if it works with the unions, can it be part of a new, and perhaps radical, majority.

These professionals and technicians, then, are not an age group or a youth phenomenon, but the expression of changes in the American class structure. And they are to be distinguished from yet another stratum, similar to them in certain respects, but with important characteristics of its own. I refer to the young people who are educated— but not for technological functions.

In the *Fortune* survey which showed 40 percent of the college youth to be fundamentally dissatisfied with the values of the society, the majority of this group—*Fortune* dubbed them the "forerunners" —were students in the arts and humanities. The vocational choice that attracted the largest single group among them (39 percent) was teaching. That would, of course, make them part of the "professional" category as defined by the statisticians in Washington, but it would certainly not qualify them as part of the technostructure (since most of them are oriented toward primary or secondary teaching and wish not to participate in either the research institutions or the corporations).

These nontechnicians are the most visible representatives of the "generation gap" that has been so widely discussed in Europe and America. They incarnate not merely a new definition of the meaning of age, but the consequences of changes in class structure as well.

Adolescence, as Kenneth Keniston points out, was an invention of industrial society.[81] Before the rise of urban industrialism, children entered adult society as soon as they were physically able (and, in

81. Kenneth Keniston, *Young Radicals: Notes on Contemporary Youth* (New York: Harcourt, Brace & World, Harvest edition, 1967), p. 264.

the early days of capitalism, even before then). But, with the growth of wealth and the middle class, the children of the well-off were granted (to use Erik Erikson's idea) a "moratorium" in their teens during which they were neither quite children nor adults. Now, as society has grown more affluent, it has created still another period of human life, one that "intervenes between adolescence and adulthood."[82]

The Affluent, Radical Young as a New Force

This new phase, Keniston argues, has been the basis for New Left currents in the advanced nations during the sixties. For the radicals, Keniston discovered, are overwhelmingly the children of the middle, and even upper middle, class; they come from liberal homes; and their bitterness with the existing order is partly the result of having been given the leisure and educational opportunity to take a "disinterested" and critical view. But their antiestablishmentarianism may also reflect a certain self-interest, as Bruno Bettelheim has suggested. For many of these young people understand that, despite or because of their liberal education, they are becoming obsolete in a technological economy. Trained as "gentlemen" in an age that needs technicians, they become, in Walter Lippmann's phrase, "derelicts from progress."[83]

If these theories are correct—and I think there is substance to them—they describe one of the unexpected consequences of our technological revolution. Some writers, myself included, responded in the early sixties to the phenomenon of automation with an excessive literal-mindedness. We assumed it would have the obvious effect of producing chronic, and even mass, unemployment; but we did not realize the various disguises this trend could adopt. One of these was the war in Vietnam, which "carried out" a policy many of us had proposed—the direct governmental creation of 1.7 million jobs —but did so in a murderous fashion. Another was the protracted postponement of entry into the labor market on the part of the liberally educated children of the affluent.

82. *Ibid.*, p. 263.
83. Bruno Bettelheim, "Obsolete Youth," *Encounter*, September 1969, p. 31. See also "A Talk with Walter Lippmann," *New York Times Magazine*, September 14, 1969.

For those among the young who were preparing for careers in the "knowledge economy," this delay was functional. But for others, who sought enlightenment or simply the "credential" of a college degree, the experience was bewildering. True, they were saved from unemployment. But they also found themselves in new mass institutions of higher learning that could give them no convincing reason as to why they should be there. So they rebelled in a thousand ways against the irrationality of their life.

In France, after May 1968, the authorities adopted a version of the foregoing analysis and acted upon it. As *Le Monde* reported in 1969,

> The students in the various faculties are also upset for another reason: the uncertainty of the job market. Almost half the liberal arts graduates no longer find posts in teaching and are not prepared for any other activity. The situation is rapidly going to be just as upsetting for graduates in economics, natural science and even physics, for they cannot all find a place in teaching or research.[84]

As another paradoxical result of the May 1968 student uprising, the technocrats are opening new schools teaching management techniques and introducing the study of technology in the science faculties so that the students will be prepared to work in industry.

Dropouts from Work-Oriented Society

Some of the young drop out of the work-oriented society altogether. This is, of course, an option taken by a tiny minority, yet there is a remarkable response to the hippie style among those who have not disaffiliated completely but share the dissatisfactions of those who have. Theodore Roszak argues that this phenomenon is so serious it marks the appearance of a "counterculture," that is, a radical departure from the mainstream assumptions of the West since the Scientific Revolution of the seventeenth century.[85] It integrates oriental mysticism, psychedelic drugs, and communitarian impulses; and it is profoundly hostile to technological rationality.

84. Girod de L'Ain, in *Le Monde Hebdomadaire* [weekly], October 30–November 5, 1969.
85. Theodore Roszak, *The Making of a Counter Culture* (New York: Doubleday Anchor, 1969), p. xii.

The extreme form of this attitude leads to a dangerous utopianism, in the worst sense of that word. Roszak asks,

. . . how ready are the workers to disband whole sectors of the industrial apparatus where this proves necessary in order to achieve ends other than efficient productivity and high consumption? How willing are they to set aside technocratic priorities in favor of a new simplicity of life?[86]

[And this vision culminates in the proclamation of] . . . . a new heaven and a new earth so vast, so marvelous that the inordinate claims of technical expertise must of necessity withdraw in the presence of such splendor to a subordinate and marginal status in the lives of men.[87]

I take this view seriously, even though it expresses the attitude of only a small number of disaffiliated young people. Portions of this ideology—as, for that matter, hippie styles in clothing—are to be found among a very large number of the growing college-educated constituency. And what Roszak is articulating is, in part at least, a self-righteous call for such people to withdraw into their tight little universe and, in the name of ultraradicalism, reduce the opportunities for basic change.

Politically, it is impossible to persuade the majority of the people of the advanced countries to become voluntary ascetics. Unlike the inhabitants of the counterculture, who usually come from affluent homes and live off the wealth of the society, most people still have unsatisfied material needs. Even more important, dealing with the agony of the poor in the advanced countries—with the hundreds of millions in the Third World who are much more desperate—requires that contemporary technology be used for the creation of food, housing, and clothing. It was, for instance, technological rationality—in this case, applied scientific research—that resulted in the "green revolution" of new strains of wheat and rice, making it possible to generate huge increases in the agricultural production of India. To carry out the program of the "counterculture" would literally threaten millions with starvation. The poetic demand to do away with machines, so compelling to young people who have never run them or realized their own dependence upon them, comes to seem extremely reactionary.

Marx rightly held that the "kingdom of freedom" was one in which

86. *Ibid.*, p. 68.
87. *Ibid.*, p. 240.

there was no compulsory work; and he understood that, if one dispensed with the discipline of the labor market, it would mean a mutation in the psychic character of man—there would be "new" men. But Roszak and those for whom he speaks want to pass immediately into the kingdom of freedom, even though the vast majority of mankind is still forced to live in the kingdom of necessity. Yet the very conditions that make some of the young susceptible to such an appeal might make them open to a socialist program for the humanization of technology. A bit later they might even respond to a realistic strategy for reaching the kingdom of freedom, not through disaffiliation of a sensitive if irresponsible minority, but through the conscious activity of the majority.

In this and other areas of advanced capitalist society, its injustices and perverse values afflict a diverse group of classes and strata, which may possibly join together to transform the society. The workers are confronted by the old and basic problem of not having enough, they are also made discontented when they contrast their own material gains with the affluence enjoyed by a relatively small minority. By virtue of their cohesion and organization, it is this working-class component that must be the spine, the decisive element, of any new socialist movement.

But if the workers have not become the overwhelming majority of society, as the Marxists predicted, the very development of the capitalist economy may be creating new allies for them in the struggle to democratize economic power. The growing stratum of professionals and technicians—whether they are called new class, new working class, technostructure, or what have you—has already had a political impact in the antiwar and civil rights movements. The conditions of their working lives make them susceptible to the appeal for democratic planning and a politics of participation. And then there is a group within the new mass constituency of the college-educated which, because it asserts the traditional values of liberal culture in the midst of a technological revolution, is particularly aware of the insanity of production for production's sake and the dehumanization that accompanies it.

There are reasons to fear that these different groups, all with a practical interest in the transformation of society, will war with one another rather than coalesce in a new radical majority and eventually into a socialist movement. They have profound differences among themselves in style, tradition, and even in politics. But they do share common interests, which, we may hope, will finally render their differences superficial. For if the problems outlined at the beginning of this essay are to be recognized, if the solutions described in the middle of it are to be practical politics, then this new majority that I have just suggested must come into being. It might.

The Vision of Socialism

Although the changes I have been talking about go far beyond any proposals by major political movements in neocapitalist society, they are still only transitional measures. They would profoundly improve and humanize the old order but would not yet constitute a new and revolutionary one. So it is now necessary to look beyond scarcity to the ultimate vision of socialism itself.

Within capitalism, development threatens the very existence of the system: success is suicidal. Capitalism "uses all the power of science and nature, of social cooperation and social exchange, to make the creation of wealth [relatively] independent of the amount of labor time expended."[88] But capitalism also proposes to measure, and consume, this output in terms of labor time, which sets a limit upon what can be sold; the worker, who through technology produces as if he were a thousand men, is paid as an individual. So the increase in productivity within a class society—where the benefits of productivity are necessarily maldistributed—has a tendency to decrease effective demand. An unprecedented accomplishment, Marx concluded, would contain the seeds of crisis.[89]

The basic technological trend Marx predicted has indeed come to pass. Yet the crisis it was supposed to occasion has not. Why?

Marx, it turned out, was wrong in thinking that capitalism was necessarily helpless to deal with its own abundance. There has been widespread state intervention to correct the "natural" tendency of the system to catastrophe (though, more often than not, these measures were introduced at the behest of the labor and socialist

88. Karl Marx, *Grundrisse der Kritik der Politischen Oeconomie* (Berlin: Dietz Verlag, 1953), p. 593.
89. *Ibid.*, p. 594.

movements and against the determined opposition of a significant section of business). But this does not mean that the neo-Keynesian complacency of the National Commission on Technology, Automation and Economic Progress is justified. Federal fiscal policy, the Commission said in summarizing the prevailing reform attitude, could supply the deficiencies in aggregate demand for any rate of technological innovation.[90] If productivity increase eliminated particular jobs, then government action would create an economic environment in which new work would be forthcoming. In other words, Marx's insight was partially validated and partially annulled. The society would indeed have to spend socially in order to buy back its own incredible output; and by doing so it could contain even a revolutionary technology within the established framework.

But this optimism ignores the evidence presented in this essay: that government spending, precisely because it follows a commercial calculus, has "solved" one crisis by worsening other crises. For, if capitalism was more flexible than Marx thought, it still had to design, or stumble into, ameliorative programs that would preserve the structural injustices of the society. It created 1.7 million "jobs" to prosecute the tragedy in Vietnam without hesitation, but it would only fund a handful of social employments; it provided billions in disguised welfare for the housing of the rich and a pittance for the poor; and so on. These perverse appropriations were not miscalculations or the result of ill will, but expressions of the most basic values of the system itself.

This is the key to that paradox presented by the National Commission on the Causes and Prevention of Violence under Dr. Milton Eisenhower: that after the most prosperous decade in the nation's history, it is in imminent danger of building a hate-ridden, strifetorn anti-utopia.

Socialism would be free of precisely those constraints that make it structurally impossible for capitalism to make a truly social use of its productivity. In the immediate future, a democratically socialized society could use this enormous economic power to meet the needs of America and to aid in the industrialization of the world. There is

90. National Commission on Technology, Automation and Economic Progress, *Technology and the American Economy: Report, 1966* (Washington, D.C.: GPO), 1:9 ff.

so much work that needs to be done within this country and internationally that the next several generations, at least, must put the "socialized individual" to work meeting basic needs. Yet in the more distant future it is not only possible, but perhaps necessary, for society to enter that Kingdom of Freedom which Marx described. Once the basic needs of all of mankind are provided for, and productivity still grows, men may be forced to live without compulsory work. The sentence decreed in the Garden of Eden will have been served.

I would not suggest that a psychic transition of this character will be easy. It is a familiar phenomenon that some people are crushed by retirement, bewildered when the compulsion of work is removed from their lives. At a conference sponsored by *Dissent* in 1969, Meyer Schapiro, a brilliant art critic and socialist, placed this kind of crisis in a thoughtful context. The ideal of the artist, of freely chosen and loving work, Schapiro said, is problematic even for the artists themselves and would be infinitely more difficult to apply in the lives of the masses of people. For every successful painter or sculptor there are many others whose hopes are disappointed. And even those who do succeed often require tremendous sacrifice from their family and friends in order to develop their genius.

I suspect that Schapiro has touched upon one of the fundamental social-psychological issues of the twenty-first century: whether, in an economy of abundance, men can find within themselves and their relations with one another, rather than in external necessity, a reason for living. The problem with this aspect of the ultimate socialist projection arises because Marx's cultural vision was so thoroughly aristocratic. He hoped for nothing less than that every citizen become a Renaissance man. "In a Communist society," he and Engels wrote, "there will be no painters, but only highly developed men who, among other things, paint."[91]

But it was Trotsky, among the Marxists, whose optimism was the most audacious:

Man will become immeasurably stronger, wiser and subtler; his movements more rhythmic, his voice more musical. The forms of life will

91. *Communist Manifesto,* 3:378.

become dynamically dramatic. The average human type will rise to the heights of an Aristotle, a Goethe, a Marx. And above this ridge, new peaks will arise.[92]

In part at least, this soaring vision is an expression of that dangerous messianism I described earlier. Yet, if one understands it as the statement of a limit toward which mankind strives but which perhaps it will never reach, it serves to free the mind from the narrowness of the present. The human body has been changing under capitalism: in the United States, Selective Service exams show that height is on the increase in the twentieth century; and of course, athletic records, and presumably biological prowess, have been dramatically extended. A higher living standard, with good diet and medical care, certainly can make people more beautiful, as the rich discovered long ago. In the realm of intelligence there are no comparative statistics but the qualitative growth in the number of scientists, and educated people generally, must mean that some of man's genetic potential has been saved from the savage fate scarcity and starvation used to visit upon it.

We may well be on the eve of psychic mutations. Our unprecedented, man-made environments produce new kinds of people. The question is not whether this will happen but how it will take place: under commercial priorities (Marcuse's pessimistic vision); under totalitarian control (Orwell's fear); or consciously chosen and shaped by a free political and social movement.

In desert societies, including the American Southwest, water is so precious that it is money. People fight and die and connive over it; governments covet it; marriages are made and broken because of it. If one had talked to a person who had known only that desert and told him that in the city there are public water fountains and that children are even sometimes allowed to turn on the fire hydrants in the summer and to frolic in the water, he would be sure that you were crazy. For he knows, with an existential certitude, that it is human nature to fight over water.

Mankind has lived now for several millennia in the desert. Our minds and emotions are conditioned by that bitter experience; we do

92. Leon Trotsky, *Literature and Revolution* (New York: Russell & Russell, 1957), p. 256.

not dare to think that things could be otherwise. Yet there are signs that we are, without really having planned it that way, marching out of the desert. There are some who are loath to leave behind the consolation of familiar brutalities; there are others who, in one way or another, would like to impose the law of the desert upon the Promised Land. It may even be possible that mankind cannot bear too much happiness.

It is also possible that we will seize this opportunity and make of the earth a homeland rather than an exile. That is the socialist project. It does not promise or even seek to abolish the human condition. That is impossible. It does propose to end that invidious competition and venality which, because scarcity allowed no other alternatives, we have come to think are inseparable from our humanity.

Irving Howe

What's the Trouble?

SOCIAL CRISIS, CRISIS
OF CIVILIZATION, OR BOTH?

We must get it out of our heads that
this is a doomed time, that we are
waiting for the end, and the rest of
it, mere junk from fashionable magazines.

—SAUL BELLOW

The rhetoric of apocalypse haunts the air, and naturally fools rush in to use it. Some of it is indeed "mere junk from fashionable magazines," and even those of us who know that we have lived through a terrible century can become impatient with the newest modes in *fin du mondisme.* Yet people who are anything but fools seem also to yield themselves to visions of gloom, as if through a surrender of rationality and will they might find a kind of peace. And there is a feeling abroad, which I partly share, that even if the Vietnam war were to end, our cities to be rebuilt, and our racial conflicts to be eased, we would still be left with a heavy burden of trouble, a trouble not merely personal or social but having to do with some deep if ill-located regions of experience. To be sure, if we could solve social problems of the magnitude I have just mentioned, the remaining troubles would come to seem less ominous. But they would still be there. They would be symptoms of a crisis of civilization through which Western society has been moving for at least a century and a half.

I

A social crisis signifies a breakdown in the functioning of a society: it fails to feed the poor, it cannot settle disputes among constituent groups, it drags the country into an endless war. If local, a social crisis calls for reform; if extensive, for deep changes in the relationship of power. Yet both those defending and those attacking the society may well be speaking with complete sincerity in behalf of a common heritage of values. Even a major social change doesn't necessarily lead to a radical disruption of the civilization in which it occurs. The American Revolution did not. By contrast, the Russian Revolution not only overturned social arrangements, it also signified a deep rent within the fabric of civilization—or so it seemed only a few decades ago, though today, with the increasing "bourgeoisification" of Russia, we can no longer be certain. Romantic writers like Pilnyak and Pasternak looked upon the Revolution less as a step to proletarian power than as an upheaval within the depths of their country that would force it toward a destiny sharply different from that of the West. Trotsky attacked these writers for this heresy, but in retrospect it does not seem that they were quite as foolish as he made out. They were talking about a crisis of civilization.

Though it may coincide with a social crisis and thereby exacerbate its effects, a crisis of civilization has to do not so much with the workings of the economy or the rightness of social arrangements as it does with the transmission of values, those tacit but deeply lodged assumptions by means of which men try to regulate their conduct. At least in principle, a social crisis is open to solutions by legislation and reform—that is, public policy. But a crisis of civilization, though it can be muted or its effects postponed by the relief of social problems, cannot as a rule be dissolved through acts of public policy. It has more to do with the experience of communities and generations than with the resolution of social conflict. It works itself out in ways we don't readily understand and sometimes, far from working itself out, it continues to fester. A social crisis raises difficulties, a crisis of civilization dilemmas. A social crisis is expressed mainly through public struggle, a crisis of civilization mainly through incoherence of behavior.

To speak of a crisis of civilization is not, of course, to suggest that our civilization is coming to an end: it may be, but we have no way of knowing. Nor is it to suggest that every change taking place at the deeper and more obscure levels of our experience should immediately be submitted to a harsh moral judgment. There are many things about which we simply cannot know. We can only say that developments occur which occupy a longer time span and are more deeply lodged in the intangibles of conduct than is true for the issues of a given moment.

II

Let us now turn abruptly away from our present concerns and move backward to a point some seventy-five or eighty-years ago, in order to see how an English Left-Labourite or German social democrat might have felt about the experience of his time.[1]

The main historical fact about the nineteenth century—and for socialists, one of the greatest facts in all history—is that the masses, dumb through the centuries, began to enter public life. A Berlin worker had heard August Bebel speak; he was struck by the thought that, for all his limitations of status, he might help shape public policy; and indeed he might even form or join his "own" party. He would, in the jargon of our day, become a subject of history rather than its object. What the worker came dimly to realize was not merely that history could be made, the lesson of the French Revolution, but that he himself might make it, the message of socialism.

The whole tragic experience of our century, I would submit, demonstrates this to be one of the few unalterable commandments of socialism: the participation of the workers, the masses of human beings, as self-conscious men preparing to enter the arena of history. Without that, or some qualified version of it, socialism is nothing but a mockery, a swindle of bureaucrats and intellectuals reaching out for power. With it, socialism could still be the greatest of human visions. This belief in the autonomous potential of the masses lay at the heart of early Marxism, in what we may now be inclined to regard as its most attractive period: the years in which European social democracy gradually emerged as a popular movement.

Meanwhile there was flowering in England the theory and practice of classical liberalism. By classical liberalism I have in mind not a particular economic doctrine, as the term has come to be understood in Europe, but rather a commitment to political openness, the values

1. The central idea for this section was suggested to me by Max Shachtman, though I cannot say whether he would approve of the way in which I have developed it.

of tolerance, liberties such as were embodied in the American Bill of Rights, and that most revolutionary of innovations, the multiparty system. Among Marxists the significance of this liberal outlook was far from appreciated, and in the Marxist tradition there has undoubtedly been a line of opinion systematically hostile to liberal values. In time that would be one source of the Marxist disaster. So, unless he were the kind of Labourite or social democrat who had become a bit skeptical of his received orthodoxies, our observer of 1895 wasn't likely to grasp the revolutionary implications of the liberal premise, or to see it as part of a large, encompassing democratic transformation that ideally would link the bourgeois and socialist revolutions.

Our socialist observer might also have noted, in the somewhat reductive terms prevalent on the Left, that science was triumphant and religion in decay. He would surely not have suspected that the weakening of religious belief, a development to which he had contributed, might bring unexpected difficulties to the lives of skeptics. Nor would he have paid attention to the views of, say, Dostoevsky on this matter, for as a rule he felt comfortable in the self-contained world that, together with an ideology proclaiming competence in almost all branches of knowledge, socialism had created for itself.

Finally, he might have become aware of certain trends in Western culture, such as the fierce hostility toward bourgeois life shown by almost all writers and artists, including the reactionary ones, and the rapidity of change, indeed the absolute triumph of the principle of change, within European culture. A new sense of time, as Daniel Bell has remarked, came to dominate the arts, and the result would be that thrust toward restlessness and hunger for novelty, that obsession with progress as an end in itself, which has since characterized so much of modern culture.

Let us now propose a brutal exaggeration, yet one that has its analytic uses: *by the time the nineteenth century came to an end, at a point usually agreed to be 1914, the basic direction of world politics starts to be reversed.* The First World War— as it reveals not only the hypocrisies of the European states, including the liberal bourgeois states, but the inability of the social democrats to prevent a global bloodbath—proves to be a terrible blow to the inherited attitudes of the earlier age of progress. If the nineteenth century promised, roughly speaking, an ever-increasing movement toward democracy and liberality, then the twentieth, even while exploiting the catchwords and passions of the nineteenth, would be marked by an overwhelming drift toward various kinds of authoritarianism. This would not of course be the only direction of political change in the twentieth century; vast popular movements, some burned out in defeat and others twisted into betrayals, would also appear in Europe and Asia. But if we remember that ours has been the century of Hitler and Stalin, then my "brutal exaggeration" about the main political drift may not seem . . . well, quite so brutal. The self-activity of the working class, that essential fulcrum of socialist power, would now be replaced in all too many instances by an authoritarian manipulation of plebeian energies (Communism in all its forms) or by an accommodation to the limited goals of the existing society (social democracy in most of its forms). Liberalism as both idea and value came under fierce attack. The expected benefits of Reason were scorned, as being either deceptive or unneeded. Modern culture was recruited as an authority in the assault upon liberal styles of feeling. What I propose to assert is that we have been living not only in the Age of Revolution about which Trotsky spoke but in an Age of Counterrevolution that has assailed mankind from Right and Left.

The central expectation of Marxism—that by its own efforts the working class could transform history—was called into question. Every political tendency on the Left had to face the question: If the working class turns out not to be the revolutionary force that Marxists had supposed, what then? The spectrum of nominated substitutes, from union bureaucracies to insurgent kindergartens, from technocratic experts to soulful dropouts, has not been reassuring.

It is still too soon to speak with certainty. Has the vision of the self-activization of the masses, a vision democratic in its essence, proved to be false? Premature? Or merely delayed by historical interruptions and accidents?[2] I shall not try to answer this question,

2. In 1948, writing on the occasion of the hundreth anniversary of *The Communist Manifesto,* one of Trotsky's close associates remarked about the working class:

It has shown itself capable of outbursts of heroism, during which it sacrifices itself without a thought, and develops a power so strong as to shake society to its very foundations. It can rid itself in an instant of the most inveterate prejudices, while there seems to be no limit to its audacity. But by

in part because I am not certain how to answer it, except to note the cogency of a remark attributed to Cournot: "The fact that we repeatedly fail in some venture merely because of chance is perhaps the best proof that chance is not the cause of our failure." In any case, for us this failure is the central problem of modern political experience, and it helps explain—even while being far from the sole explanation for—the fact that every mode of politics in our century succumbs in varying degrees to authoritarianism.

People employing another set of categories will no doubt see the politics of this century in other terms; but other terms can often veil similar perceptions. What seems likely is that all who share the view that democratic norms are essential to a tolerable life would be ready to grant some credit to the sketch that has been drawn here.

III

How are we now to relate the two lines of speculation I have thus far advanced—first, that we are experiencing the repercussions of a crisis of civilization (a few signs of which will shortly be noted), and second, that we are living through the consequences of the failure of socialism? Perhaps by a third line of speculation: that it is precisely the recurrent political-social difficulties of Western capitalism, significantly eased but not removed by the welfare state, which create a fertile ground for the emerging symptoms of a long-festering crisis of civilization. The social-political problems of the moment and the

---

and by, whatever the consequences of its action, whether victory or defeat, it is finally caught up in the sluggish, quotidian flow of things.

The fetid backwaters of the past seep back; the proletariat sinks into indolence and cynicism. And even in its triumphant moments, it exhibits a want of consciousness in its choice of leaders. The "instinctive sense of reality" attributed to it by Auguste Comte, which it so readily reflects in many a circumstance, abandons it at such moments. Its courage and self-sacrifice are not enough to give it what, precisely, is needed in order to act out the role assigned to it by Marx: political capacity.

Jean Vannier, "A Century's Balance Sheet,"
Partisan Review, March 1948

The question Vannier is raising here is not merely whether the working class can take power—that is an old and well-rehearsed question. He is asking something more troublesome: can a triumphant working class, once in power, display the political "capacity" to rule over a modern society or will it, in effect, cede power to an alliance of bureaucrats, intellectuals, and technocrats?

deeper crisis of civilization have, so to say, a habit of collaboration;
they even maliciously assume the guise of each other. There follows
a terrible confusion in which problems open to public solution become encumbered with metaphysical and quasi-religious issues, while
efforts are vainly made to bring into the political arena metaphysical
and quasi-religious issues beyond the capacity of politics to cope
with.

Why we should be experiencing this confusion of realms is a
question to which the answers are either too easy or too hard. Let us
not rehearse them at length. The atom bomb has made us aware that
the very future of the race hangs on political decision. The Nazi and
Stalinist concentration camps have raised questions as to the nature
of our nature: is there an inherent bestiality in mankind beyond
the correction of collective activity? The Vietnam war, in a more
recent moment, has been felt by portions of the young as an international trauma, serving to break ties of loyalty with both society
and earlier generations. In the West a generation has arisen accustomed to affluence and therefore able to devote itself to problems of
life, sometimes merely life style, as against the problems of making
a living. Higher education on a mass scale is becoming a reality in
Western society, yet no one quite knows what its purpose, content,
or outcome is or should be. A counter society, half real and half myth,
has appeared as the Third World, imbued by its admirers with a
mixture of utopianism and authoritarianism, revolution and primitive
nobility: all arising from a revulsion against advanced society. Such
are the reasons that might be given for a situation in which the crisis
of modern civilization, recurrent for at least a century and a half, is
again felt as immediate and pressing; but what we do not really know
is the relative weights to assign to these reasons, and that means
we do not know very much.

The difficulty—let us say, one difficulty—of living at this moment
in history is that we experience both as *simultaneity and contradiction* the problems of three stages of modern society. Or, to be more
modest, we experience problems that in our thought we have assigned to three stages of society: precapitalist (race, illiteracy, back-
wardness); capitalist (class conflict, economic crisis, distribution of
wealth); and postcapitalist (quandaries concerning work, leisure,
morality, and style, such as are sometimes described as "existential").

But it is crucial to note that we experience these three orders of difficulty within the context of an advanced or "late" capitalism. Problems therefore suddenly appear in this late capitalist society that we had supposed would emerge only under socialism—problems not to be described merely or mainly in terms of social class but rather as pertaining to all human beings. (It ought to be said that the more intelligent socialists had foreseen the possibility that by liberating men from material want socialism might impose upon them a severe crisis of civilization, though impose it under circumstances more favorable to the human imagination than had been possible in the past.)

In the industrialized countries capitalism has entered a phase of unprecedented affluence, not justly distributed yet still reaching almost every class in society. Many people, especially those drawn from the upper and middle classes, have thereby come to experience a certain freedom to see their lives in generalized or abstract "human" terms. In the long run this is surely what one hopes for all humanity—that men should free themselves, to the extent that they can, from the tyranny of circumstances and confront their essential being. In the short run, however, this occurs, to the extent that it does occur, within a social context that distorts and frustrates the newly acquired sense of the human. For it occurs within a context of class domination and social snobbism, as well as at a historical moment forcing upon the young ghastly dilemmas. At one and the same time, a young person of middle-class origin can feel free to experiment with his life, yet must also live under the shadow of a war perceived to be unjust and even criminal. He can feel himself free to abandon the norms of bourgeois society, yet in doing so he will often unwittingly reinstate them as self-alienating masks and phantasms.

I am aware here of a possible criticism: that, in speaking of these three stages of recent history as they had been thought of by socialists, I am referring not to objective realities but to conceptions nurtured, perhaps mistakenly, by people on the Left, and that there is nothing inherent in modern history which requires that certain problems be correlated with early capitalism or others with socialism. I accept this criticism in advance, but would only add that all of us see, as we must see, historical developments through the lens of our assumptions, and that those who reject socialist categories may come to similar conclusions, through their own terms, about the mixture of problems I have been discussing. We might, for example, choose to say that during the past decade we have become aware that the religious disputes of the nineteenth and the social anxieties of the twentieth century are related—with the issues that obsessed the nineteenth century, issues that had to do with the desanctification of the cosmos, surviving into our own moment in surprisingly powerful ways. For what should interest us here is not the "rightness" of a particular intellectual vocabulary or tradition, but a cluster of insights that might be reached through different vocabularies and traditions.

In any case, the jumble of interests and needs I have been associating with various stages of modern history could also be regarded as distinctive elements—elements of conflict and tension—within the welfare state. It is in the very nature of the welfare state that through its formal, ideological claims it should arouse steadily increasing expectations which as an economic system still geared mainly to a maximization of profit it does not always or sufficiently satisfy. The welfare state systematically creates appetites beyond its capacity to appease—that, so to say, is the principle of dynamism which keeps it both in motion and off balance. The welfare state cannot count upon those fierce sentiments of national loyalty, which, precisely insofar as it has come to dominate the industrialized portion of the world, it replaces with an array of group and sectional interests—that much-vaunted pluralism of interests often concealing an imbalance of opportunity. The welfare state has small attraction as an end or ideal in its own right, and little gift for inspiring the loyalties of the young. It is a social arrangement sufficiently stable, thus far, to all but eliminate the prospect of revolution in the advanced countries; but it is also a social arrangement unstable enough to encourage the militant arousal of previously silent groups, the intensification of political discontents, and the reappearance, if in new and strange forms, of those tormenting "ultimate questions" with which modern man has beset himself for a century and a half. That these "ultimate questions," as to man's place in the universe, the meaning of his existence, the nature of his destiny, now come to us in rather modish or foolish ways is cause for impatience and polemic. But we would be dooming ourselves to a philistine narrowness if we denied that such questions do beset human beings, that they are significant questions, and that in our moment there are peculiarly urgent reasons for coming back to them.

IV

How does one know that we, like our fathers, grandfathers, and great-grandfathers, are living through a crisis of civilization? What could possibly constitute evidence for such a claim? Even to ask such questions may strike one as both comic and impudent: comic because it seems a little late to return to a theme that has been pursued to the point of exhaustion, impudent because it can hardly be approached in a few pages. One is tempted simply to say what Louis Armstrong is supposed to have said when he was asked to define jazz, "If you don't know, I can't tell you." For, if felt at all, a crisis of civilization must be felt as pervasive: as atmospheric and behavioral, encompassing and insidious.

How shall we live?—this question has obsessed thoughtful people throughout the modern era, which is to say, since at least the French Revolution, and it has obsessed them with increasing anxiety and intensity. I don't suppose there has ever been a time when the question hasn't been asked, but in those centuries when religious systems were commonly accepted as revealed truth the problems of existence necessarily took on a different shape and eventuated in a different emotional discipline from anything we know in our time. Some of the more spectacular symptoms of disaffection we are now witnessing ought to be taken not as historical novelties revealing the special virtue on wickedness of a new generation, but as tokens of that continuity of restlessness and trouble which compromises the history of Western consciousness since the late eighteenth century.

One major sign is the decay or at least partial breakdown of the transmission agencies—received patterns of culture, family structure, and education—through which values, norms, and ideals are handed down from generation to generation. It would be self-deceiving, if for some comforting, to suppose that we are going through just another "normal" struggle between generations which "in time" will work itself out through familiar mechanisms of social adjustment. The present conflict between generations or, if you prefer, between segments of the generations, is "normal" only insofar as it seizes upon, intensifies, and distorts those philosophical, moral, and religious themes which we have inherited from the nineteenth century.

The decay or partial breakdown in the transmission of values occurs most dramatically among middle-class and upper-middle-class youth secure enough in the comforts of affluence to feel that in the future our primary concern will be existence rather than survival. Some declare an acceptance of received values but cry out against their betrayal by the system or the men who run it; others reject the received values (sustained work, restraint as a social discipline, postponement of gratifications in behalf of ultimate ends, goals of success, and so on). In practice, it is hard to keep the two kinds of response completely separate. Young protesters often believe they are motivated by a fundamental denial of Western civilization when in reality they are unhappy with their private lot; but more important by far is the fact, as I take it to be, that those who believe they are motivated merely by a revulsion against the betrayal of accepted values are in reality being moved, at least in part and at least with partial consciousness, by the more extreme visions of life style that we associate with postindustrial society. One result is that in the name of rejecting their elders' betrayal of liberal values they slide into contempt for those values.

The immediate social form through which such young people try to organize their responses is a cluster of distinctively generational groups lying somewhere between family and occupation. Torn between the problems of too much freedom and the problems of too little, between the fear of an endless chaos and the claustrophobia of rigid social definition, they create, in the words of Richard Flacks, "institutions which can combine some of the features of family life with those of the occupational structure. Youth groups, cultures, movements serve this function, combining relations of diffuse solidarity with universalistic values." One immediate cause for establishing these institutions is frustration with the external society: there is less and less socially useful or meaningful labor for young people to do and the consequence is that while the process of socialization is sped up the prospect of maturation is delayed. These fragile institutions of the youth culture also reveal themselves as testing grounds for experiment with, or acting-out for, the crisis of values which long antedates their appearance. Miniature settings serve as laboratories, sometimes mere sickrooms, for dealing with the largest problems of modern life.

Now, it has been argued by writers who are skeptical of the above description that signs of disaffection, whether trivial or profound, are mostly confined to segments of affluent youth and that the blue-collar young, still facing a struggle for economic survival, cannot indulge themselves in such existential luxuries. Perhaps so. But, even if true, this hardly minimizes the importance of what has happened within large and significant segments of middle-class youth—especially in the United States where the middle class sprawls across the social map and strongly influences the ways in which adjacent classes live.

If your main concern is to plot out lines of voting behavior, then it is indeed crucial to notice the class limitations of the new youth styles; but if you are concerned with long-range social trends, then you must recognize that by their very nature these are likely first to appear among minorities. (It does not follow that everything to be found among minorities will become a long-range social trend.) What needs, then, to be estimated, or simply guessed, is the extent to which such minorities—in our case, a rather substantial one—may shape the conduct of tomorrow. Clearly, it is too soon to say whether we are witnessing a transient outbreak of malaise reflecting the privileges and disadvantages of middle-class youth or a fundamental revision in the patterns of life reflecting the emergence of postindustrial society, the loss of faith in traditional puritan and bourgeois values, and the persistence of moral and metaphysical problems thrown up by the crisis of civilization. To insist merely upon the former might be parochial; merely upon the latter, grandiose. But, even if we lean toward skepticism, we ought to recognize the possibility that a series of intermittent generational traumas, and the current one is hardly the first, might constitute a long-range historical trend of major importance.[3]

3. A few points in rebuttal of those who, in the name of plebeian solidity, minimize the significance of the new youth styles:
• It is hard to suppose that the feelings of disaffection or dismay one encounters among young people are confined to those who come from a single class, though it may well be that such feelings are most strongly articulated by them. Yet even among plebeian segments of our population there are visible strong feelings of rage and resentment, sometimes turned against "the students," but in origin and character often sharing with "the students" sentiments of powerlessness and dismay.

About the gravity of a second major symptom that points to a crisis of civilization there is likely to be less dispute. The whole enterprise of education is in grave trouble. It is marked by anxieties bordering on demoralization and often a retreat from serious purpose that becomes sheer panic. In part this seems due to immediate causes that might let up in a few years; in part it signifies a thread of confusion that has kept recurring throughout the history of modern education. There seems barely any consensus among educators as to what they are supposed to profess, barely any agreement among educators as to what they believe education to be or do. There is little concurrence in our universities, and not much more in our high schools, as to the skills, disciplines, kinds of knowledge, and attitudes of mind we wish to develop. The more education is exalted in our social mythology, the less do we seem to know what it means.

Curricula discussions at faculty meetings are notoriously tiresome, yet they finally do reflect disputes and mirror disorientation concerning the very idea of education and thereby, perhaps, the very nature of our civilization. What, beyond the rudiments of literacy, do people need to know? What, beyond such needs, should they wish to learn? What do we hope to pass on from one generation to the next in regard to moral and cultural values? What is our image of an educated man? Around such questions disputes rage, and rage so harshly that connections can barely be made between the antagonists. For these are disputes that come down to the question of how or whether we shall maintain a vital continuity with traditional Western culture.

• Today's middle-class style can become tomorrow's working-class style. In this country, the lines of social and cultural demarcation between the classes are not nearly so firm as in other capitalist societies. Youth mobility is high; working-class children go to college in increasing, if not sufficient, numbers; they are likely to share at least some of the responses of other students; and they do not bring with them a strong sense of class allegiance or definition to which they feel obliged to cling and which might create psychic barriers between them and their middle-class peers.

• Mass culture quickly provides lower-class equivalents to middle-class styles, and often succeeds in spilling across class barriers. There are overwhelming cultural or pseudo-cultural experiences shared by the young of all classes, certainly more so than in any previous society. Movies, rock music, drugs—these may not figure with equal force in the lives of both working- and middle-class youth, but increasingly they do create a generational consciousness and solidarity that, to an undetermined extent, disintegrates class lines.

When a society does not know what it wishes its young to know, it is suffering from moral and spiritual incoherence. It has no clear sense of the connections it would maintain—or whether it even wishes to maintain them—with the civilization of which presumably it is a part. And when to this incoherence is added the persuasion that young people should be kept in schools for increasing lengths of time (often with the parallel notion that schools should be made to resemble the external society, which is to say, to be unlike schools), then immediate and long-range troubles are thrust into a dangerous friction.

The United States and to a lesser extent other advanced countries of the West have embarked on a project which, we socialists would like to think, might better have coincided with the growth of a democratic socialist order. It is a project that declares every citizen to be entitled to a higher education and soon may enable every citizen to obtain one. Who can fault this premise? But who would deny that there are extremely troubling results from undertaking so revolutionary a task under social circumstances often inhospitable to it? Those of us who spoke for a universalization of culture and education were not, I think, wrong; but we were naïve in our sense of how it might be brought about, or what the cost of bringing it about might be. We failed to see that some problems are not open to quick public solution, and we refused to see that the solution of other problems might lead to new and unforeseen ones. In the short run—and who knows, perhaps even the long run—a conflict develops between the values of high culture and the values of universal education, to both of which we are committed but between which we would hardly know how to choose, if choose we had to. Millions of young people are thrust into universities and no one quite knows why or toward what end. The immediate result is social bitterness and clash. One of the few things these millions of young people may discover in the universities, however, is that learning and culture, since they are but faintly credited by many of the teachers they encounter, need hardly be credited by them. That expresses and intensifies a crisis of civilization.

Ultimately, one suspects, this crisis has to do with residual sentiments of religion and vague but powerful yearnings toward transcendence. For, to the extent that the transmission of values is blocked and a lack of faith in the power of education spreads among the educated classes, there must follow a more pervasive uncertainty as to the meanings and ends of existence. Let me turn to a vocabulary not spontaneously my own and suggest that we are beginning to witness a new religious experience—or, perhaps, an experience of religious feelings. Partly because of the sterility of traditional religious institutions, this experience cannot easily be embodied in religious terms and it must therefore assume the (often misshapen) masks of politics, culture, and life style.[4] Our socialist of seventy-five or eighty years ago, smug in his rationalism and convinced that all would be well once "we" took power, could hardly understand such a development; his first inclination would have been to regard it as a sign of reaction. For that matter, it is by no means clear that a socialist of the present moment can understand it, either. Yet, no matter how alien we remain to the religious outlook, we must ask ourselves whether the malaise of this time isn't partly a consequence of that despairing emptiness which followed the breakup in the nineteenth century of traditional religious systems; whether the nihilism every sensitive person feels encompassing his life like a spiritual smog isn't itself a kind of inverted religious aspiration (so Dostoevsky kept saying); and whether the sense of disorientation that afflicts us isn't due to the difficulties of keeping alive a high civilization without a sustaining belief. All questions of the nineteenth century; all returning to plague us at the end of the twentieth.

Richard Lowenthal has remarked on this score:

We have not yet had a civilization that was not based on a transcendent belief. And what we are trying to do is to maintain our values and move upon the momentum of these values originally created by religion—but after the transcendent belief is gone. The question is: will we succeed?

To such questions a simple answer is neither possible nor desirable. Even if we conclude that the breakdown of religious systems, enormously liberating as in part it was, also yielded unforeseen difficulties for those who might never have stepped into a church or a synagogue,

---

4. This kind of remark, I know, is too easily used as a way of dismissing the radical young; I dissociate myself from such an intent. Many, though not all, of their manifest complaints are valid and deserve to be taken at face value, and my point applies only to the structures of feeling and expression through which these are made known.

this is not to be taken, of course, as a token of support for those who wish to re-create through will the dogmas that were once supported by faith. Perhaps we have no choice but to live with the uncomfortable aftereffects of the disintegration, aftereffects that range from moving efforts at private spiritual communion to flashy chemical improvisations for pseudo-religious sects. I am convinced, in any case, that the coming era will witness a proliferation of such sects, some betraying the corrupting effects of the very technology they will repudiate, others mixing antinomian ecstasies with utopian visions, and still others seeking to discover through simplicities of custom the lost paradise of love.

Again experience proves far more recalcitrant and complicated than any of our theories has enabled us to suppose. It may indeed be that the religious impulse is deeply grounded in human existence and that men need objects of veneration beyond their egos. "The Golden Age," wrote Dostoevsky, "is the most unlikely of all the dreams that have been, but for it men have given up their life. . . . For the sake of it prophets have died and been slain, without it the peoples will not live and cannot die." If the impulse Dostoevsky invokes here cannot be expressed through religious channels, then it must turn to secular equivalents. It turns to the fanaticism of ideology (which may explain the continued hold Marxism has on the imaginations of the young, for is not Marxism the true religion of our century?). It turns to heretical sects seeking an unsullied pantheism. It turns to communities of the faithful who repudiate technology and civilization itself, a repudiation as old as religion itself.

Who can say? Remembering the certainties of our socialist of seventy-five or eighty years ago, good decent and even heroic fellow that he was, we might be a little cautious in dismissing the needs and aspirations of our fellow men, especially those we find difficult to understand. All we can say with assurance or good will is that the themes of religious desire appear and reappear in the experience of our epoch, tokens of "the missing All," whether as harmony or dissonance. And they will surely be heard again.

> *An anxiety,*
>> *A caution,*
>>> *And a caution against the caution.*

The anxiety: whenever there occurs that meeting of social crisis and crisis of civilization I have sketched here, democratic norms and institutions are likely to be in danger. If we look at the collapse of democratic societies in our century, we must conclude that the usually cited causes—economic depression, unemployment, and so forth— are necessary but not sufficient elements; there must also occur some loss of conviction in the animating ethos of the nation or culture, some coming-apart of that moral binder which holds men in the discipline of custom. Anyone observing the intellectual life of the West during the past decade may be struck by the thought that some such loss of conviction, or some such coming-apart of moral binder, seems to be happening, if not among the masses, then certainly among growing segments of the educated classes. The bourgeois myth has been losing its hold on the bourgeois mind, though nothing has come along to replace it. Nothing, that is, except that vulgarized quasi-Marxism which has been improvised by a small though significant minority of the intellectual young. Nor should this, by the way, come as a surprise, for no other twentieth-century ideology has been so powerfully able to stir or corrupt the nascent religious impulses of sensitive and uprooted people.

By an irony too painful to underscore, it is only in Eastern Europe that intellectuals have come to appreciate the value of liberal institutions. In the West, a mere three decades after the ravages of totalitarianism, there is again visible a strident contempt for the ethic of liberal discourse and the style of rationality. In part this arises from the mixed failings and successes of the welfare state, but in part from an upswell of unacknowledged and ill-understood religious sentiments that, unable to find a proper religious outlet, become twisted into moral and political absolutism, a hunger for total solutions and apocalyptic visions. Impatience with the sluggish masses, burning convictions of righteousness, the suffocation of technological society, the boredom of overcrowded cities, the yearning for transcendent ends beyond the petty limits of group interest, romantic-sinister illusions about the charismatic virtues of dictatorship in underdeveloped countries—all these tempt young people into apolitical politics, at best the commune and at worst the bomb, but both sharing an amorphous revulsion from civilization itself.

Why then should one suppose that such sentiments can pose a

threat to democratic institutions? Because, if carried through to the end, they release yearnings and desires that by their very nature cannot be satisfied through the limited mechanisms of democratic politics. Because, if carried through to the end, they summon moods of desperation and fanaticism which lead to a dismissal of democratic politics.

The caution: Nothing could be more disastrous for our political life in the immediate future than to have the modest, perhaps manageable and (as some intellectuals like to suppose) "boring" problems of the welfare state swept aside in behalf of a grandiose, surely unmanageable and (as some intellectuals would feel) "exciting" *Kulturkampf* between the uptight and the loose, the repressive and the permissive. If, say, in the next decade figures like Spiro Agnew and Jerry Rubin, or to choose less disreputable substitutes, William Buckley and Charles Reich were allowed to dominate public debate, people would vote according to their prejudices concerning drugs, sex, morality, pornography, and "permissiveness." A bleak prospect; for while such a situation might arise out of spontaneous passions on all sides, it might just as well have been arranged as a political maneuver for the far Right, the only political group that could profit from it. And, even if I am wrong in supposing that only the far Right could profit politically from a *Kulturkampf*, how much comfort is that? For the one thing that is entirely clear is that a politics or a social outlook devoted to democratic social change and the style of rationality would lose.

What is required here is a measure of social and intellectual discipline, the capacity for keeping one's various interests distinct and in a hierarchy of importance: thus, legalization of marijuana may be a desirable goal but it is as nothing compared to ending the Vietnam war, and if raising the first issue will impede progress on the second, then we must restrain ourselves. Furthermore, we must recognize that at least in a democratic society politics has built-in—and, in the long run, desirable—limitations. It may be possible through legislation to remove some of the socioeconomic causes of alienation but it is not possible through politics to cope directly with that seething cluster of emotions we call alienation; it may be possible through legislation to improve the conditions under which men work, but it is not impossible through politics to cope with the growing uncertainties men have as to work and leisure.

That in a society so beset as ours with ideological noise and cultural clatter we should expect the necessary discipline—give unto the ballot box its due, and leave for your life style what your taste requires—seems all but utopian. But, if we lack that discipline, we will pay heavily.

The caution against this caution: There are limits to common sense and pragmatism, which those who favor these qualities ought to be the first to recognize. The Fabian course, to which democratic socialists in the United States are, by and large, committed, seems to me the closest we can come to political realism; but precisely for that reason we ought to recognize the points at which it fails to stir the imagination or speak to the troubles and passions of many people. Such a politics offers a possible way of improving and extending the welfare state, which is about as much as one can hope for in the immediate future, but it has little to say about all those problems that the welfare state is barely equipped to cope with. A politics of limitation, of coalition, of step-by-step change is desirable; the alternatives are neither real nor attractive; yet we must not allow strategy to blot out vision.

So let us be ready to acknowledge to others and ourselves that between the politics we see as necessary and the imaginative-expressive needs we have as men living in this time there are likely to be notable gaps. The chaotic but profoundly significant urges and passions that sweep through modern society—at once innocent and nihilistic, aspiring and gloom-ridden, chiliastic and despairing—must touch us as well as those with whom we have political quarrels. How could it be otherwise? Who, looking upon the experience of our century, does not feel repeated surges of nausea, a deep persuasion that the very course of civilization has gone wrong? Who, elbowing his way past the wastes of our cities, does not feel revulsion against the very stones and glass, the brick and towers, all the debris of inhumaneness? Who, thinking of our bombs and our pollution, does not wish, at least on occasion, to join in the jeremiads against all that we are and have?

If we felt no impulses of this kind we could hardly call ourselves socialists, since we would have lost the wish for a qualitative transcendence of the given reality. If we allowed such impulses to dominate our minds and our conduct, we could hardly call ourselves socialists either, since we would have lost that fraternal feeling and patience that require democrats to heed the wishes of the people. What we must do is to recognize the distance, perhaps the necessary distance, between political strategy and existential response. We are saying that many things requiring remedy are open to social-political solution (provided intelligence and will are present). We are also saying that we live at a moment when problems beyond the reach of politics—problems that *should* be beyond the reach of politics—have come to seem especially urgent and disturbing. We have learned that the effort to force men into utopia leads to barbarism, but we also know that to live without the image of utopia is to risk the death of imagination. It there a path for us, a crooked path for men of disciplined hope?

Robert Lekachman

Between Apostles and Technicians

MIND-BLOWING AND PROBLEM-SOLVING

I

In the 1970s two ways of examining society, neither of them very satisfactory, will probably continue to vie for intellectual favor. One is the New Left rebellion against the organizational rationalism of a complex technological polity. The second is the style comfortable to the social scientists and bureaucrats who administer such societies, a style ostentatiously prosaic, empirical, and nonideological, lineal descendant to Benthamite felicific calculation and the Fabianism of the Webbs. In extreme versions it manifests itself in essays like Edward Banfield's *The Unheavenly City,* said to be widely admired in the White House. A home for more moderate expression of the problem-solving nonideology is *The Public Interest,* a journal about which more will be said later.

The younger radicals cherish one-to-one relationships, diffusion of power, and immediacy of sensual gratification. They suspect technology and organizational hierarchies.[1] Until they took to criticizing their acolytes' excesses, Herbert Marcuse and Paul Goodman were popular New Left gurus. Their successor appears to be Charles Reich whose *The Greening of America,* an impassioned celebration of youthful virtue, amounts to a prophecy of revolution through a transformation of consciousness. For good or ill, Reich's Third Consciousness bids fair to match the celebrity of such catchwords as repressive

1. I refer only to the libertarian and anarchist branches of the New Left, not to its much less agreeable authoritarian division. The latter is a familiar offshoot of rationalist Marxism, and its organizational expression on college campuses is Progressive Labor.

tolerance, identity crisis, The Medium is the Message, and David Riesman's tripartite construction—inner-directed, other-directed, and autonomous individuals—to which Reich's three consciousnesses display considerable affinity.

Reich is worth consideration as a brand-new cultural phenomenon, or, as Harry Golden might say, Only in America! Reich's transformation is almost as startling as the greening of America that he preaches. He is a forty-three-year-old law professor at Yale, esteemed until only yesterday at his university as an extraordinarily gifted teacher and beyond New Haven's borders as the author of exceptionally provocative law-review articles.[2] These essays on property, government regulation, and twentieth-century feudalism contain the roots of the assault upon organizational power, which is the most satisfactory portion of *The Greening of America.*

"The New Property," the best of the articles, focuses upon governmental "largesse" as a dynamic of alteration in property relationships. This is the rubric under which Reich enumerates the many benefits government confers upon its constituents, extending over additions to income in the shape of welfare, social security, and veterans' pensions; government jobs; occupational licenses; bus, trucking, airline, and taxicab franchises; subsidies to farmers, shipbuilders, and a long list of other clients; access on indulgent terms to grazing, mining, and lumbering on public lands; subsidized commercial mail delivery, cut-rate savings-bank and home-construction insurance; and free technical information for farmers and corporations.

Public functionaries see this largesse as acts of grace; beneficiaries esteem it as similar to older varieties of property. For his part, Reich emphasizes a distinction between largesse and other kinds of property, which simultaneously identifies a danger. Private property in general originates in economic activity performed in private markets, while largesse both reflects and reinforces the existing distributions of political power. *Time-Life* or the *New York Times* secure radio stations and television channels far more readily than Black Panthers.

2. See, as examples, "Individual Rights and Social Welfare," *Yale Law Journal,* 74:1245 (1965); "Midnight Welfare Searches and the Social Security Act," *Yale Law Journal,* 72:1347 (1963); "The Law of the Planned Society," *Yale Law Journal,* 75:1227 (1967); and, most famous of the group, "The New Property," *Yale Law Journal,* 73:733 (1964).

Public largesse enriches the wealthy and adds power to the powerful. Large commercial farmers get most of the agricultural subsidies. FHA loan guarantees facilitated middle-class flight to the suburbs, and in the deserted cities urban renewal has diminished the inventory of low-cost apartments, which have been traded for convention halls and luxury flats. California's tax and fee structures combine to generate subsidies for middle-class youngsters financed mostly by repressive taxes levied upon their financial inferiors. It is a law of public largesse that great social need accompanies small political power. From the law flows a corollary: the powerful, not the needy, get a disproportionate share of the cash.

Worse is yet to come. It is typical of largesse that it can be capriciously granted and removed at the pleasure of administrators endowed with alarming discretionary power either by congressional intention or by their own statutory interpretations. Communications policy illustrates the point. The courts have ruled that the Communications Act, which created the Federal Communications Commission, awarded no property right. Licenses are mere privileges, initially granted for three-year terms and, thereafter, renewed or revoked by FCC decision. Congress originally may have intended license limitation as a pressure upon broadcasters to meet minimum criteria of public service. But in the Agnew era, this precariousness of tenure impresses timid television executives as sufficient reason to tone down news comment. Reich's point is sharp: the networks retain enormously valuable property on the condition that they barter away at least part of their First Amendment rights to free speech. As in the Middle Ages, property is converted into a grant conditioned upon loyalty to the sovereign.

These coercive powers of government over individual access to largesse are extensive and growing. With few signs of popular dissent, Congress has decreed that,

Any person shown by evidence satisfactory to the Administrator to be guilty of mutiny, treason, sabotage, or rendering assistance to any enemy of the United States or of its allies shall forfeit all accrued or future benefits under law administered by the Veterans' Administration.

As a society, we do not take money away from disloyal millionaires. What warrant justifies shearing a veteran of benefits earned by past service because of poor behavior at some later date? Once more the practice of public largesse involves a threat by sovereign power to personal freedoms.

Although recent judicial interpretations have somewhat improved the situation, welfare recipients are most exposed of all to demands for barter of their rights and reprisals when they resist such demands. The Bill of Rights protects ordinary citizens against unreasonable searches conducted without proper warrants issued upon the demonstration of probable cause. Bill of Rights or not, welfare investigators have specialized in midnight searches of their clients' homes, in the attempt to establish male presence and thus terminate benefits. The Supreme Court has recently determined that welfare beneficiaries must trade for public largesse the citizen's constitutionally guaranteed rights to the undisturbed enjoyment of his home.

Reich summarizes these phenomena as the recrudescence of an exceedingly dangerous version of feudalism. Increasingly, property and benefits are linked to status and status is conferred either by the state or, even more dangerously, by a small number of very large private organizations which act as loosely regulated agents of the state, among them corporations, foundations, and universities.

This analysis is persuasive. Unfortunately Reich's powers falter on the threshold of remedy, and rhetoric is made to substitute for programs. Reich leaves his readers with a fair prospect:

The highly organized, scientifically planned society of the future, governed for the good of its inhabitants, promises the best life that men have ever known.

But there is a roaring lion in the path to utopia:

If the individual is to survive in a collective society, he must have protection against its ruthless pressures. There must be sanctuaries or enclaves where no majority can reach. To shelter the solitary human spirit does not merely make possible the fulfillment of individuals; it also gives society the power to change, to grow, and to regenerate, and hence to endure. These were the objects which property sought to achieve and can no longer achieve. The challenge of the future will be to construct, for the society that is coming, institutions and law to carry on this work. Just as the Homestead Act was a deliberate effort to foster individual values at an earlier time, so we must try to build an economic basis for liberty today—a Homestead Act for rootless twentieth-century man. We must create a new property.

Here, upon a dying fall, the witness curiously ends. The vital sanctions and enclaves are never identified. In a curious way the failure of analysis is repeated in Reich's book.

The Greening of America has turned its author into an immediate celebrity. In carrying forward the themes of his law-review essays, Reich has recorded his own rebirth as a child of the new consciousness.

He begins with a conventional checklist of New Left charges: American society is fatally corrupted by "disorder, corruption, hypocrisy, war"; "poverty, distorted priorities, and law-making by private power"; "decline of democracy and liberty, powerlessness"; "the artificiality of work and culture"; "absence of community"; and "loss of self."

Although such a society is overripe for change, successful revolutions require revolutionists. Enter the young as vessels of new truth and heightened consciousness. Their elders are mired either in Consciousness I, the atavistic remnants of frontier individualism, or Consciousness II, the gray spirit of the organizational mentality, bureaucracy incarnate. In entrancing contrast, Consciousness III's converts dismiss with contempt both the alleged inevitabilities and the rewards of hierarchical organization. For them they substitute joy, love, friendship, openness to experience and sensation, immediate communication, and warm community. As Reich would say, oh, wow!

Rejecting hierarchy, competition, and routine, how will the children of the new age inherit the earth, as Reich is certain that they will? Peaceful persuasion and demography will make this revolution. Externally imposing, the Establishment is really little more than a hollow shell. The generals, executives, and college presidents who pretend to run institutions lack conviction and purpose. They are increasingly easy targets of infiltration. The number of the infiltrators steadily rises. As the fifty-year-olds die, decline into their dotage, or, more unusually, join the revolution, their juniors will succeed them in power. At the moment of liberation, Consciousness III will transform the institutions that now oppress us all and liberate even the bureaucrats. In the world struggling to be born, organization and technology, today's enemies, will be made to enlarge the individual and enhance his experience. The universe of work and the private cosmos of sensation will be rejoined and the ancient pangs of alienation at last be relieved. Astonishingly meek in Reich's idealization of them, the young will truly inherit the earth.

The emotional appeal of this sort of thing needs no explanation. Reich will be a hero on the campuses for some time to come. How well does the argument withstand scrutiny? To begin with, *is* there a new consciousness, even as a powerful metaphor for altered cultural and social outlook? Like other academics, I deal with many young men and women who approximate Consciousness III insofar as it is defined by aversion to routine and sustained intellectual effort, and affection for rock music, drugs (on which Reich is fuzzy), and informal human relationships. Reich, not so incidentally, says little about the dark side of Consciousness III, the minority freaked out on drugs, the few attracted by violence, and the many who, according to the campus psychiatrists, are unhappy and neurotic in spite of (or because of?) the new culture of joy.

A Reichian, I suppose, would dismiss this pathology as cultural growing pains. Reich's argument, however, certainly overgeneralizes. An unknown but substantial percentage of the young harbor secret, subversive sympathies for individualism and organizational efficiency. West and south of New Haven, there are campuses where President Nixon is applauded and hecklers must at some expense be imported. A recent poll reported the alarming news that a fifth of the young admire the Vice-President.

Are we dealing with anything more than another leisure class? Ours is larger because we are richer and we make a practice of collecting large numbers of young adults in compounds called universities where their keepers fail to find sufficient diversions for them. The "straight" students are the offspring of poorer families, usually first-generation college attenders, and quite as determined as older predecessors to acquire the marketable skills which will make them eligible for material benefits. Though less noisy, the straight students are more numerous.

I may be quite wrong. Reich may be quite correct in his identification of one of those creative minorities which set the tone for sluggish contemporaries and ultimately convert them to new truths. But even on this hypothesis, it is hard to believe that when Consciousness II and Consciousness III slug it out in large organizations, victory is foreordained for the latter. Hatred of bureaucratic styles is one thing, successful definition of alternative ways of doing the world's work quite another.

At this juncture, Reich offers nothing but more rhetoric. Could Consciousness III run the world? Without organizational routines and hierarchical administration, can there be survival of such life-supporting mechanisms as transportation, power, heat, light, and food distribution? Reich is as vague as he is cheerful about "humane" technology and unrepressive organization, just as in his earlier work he was similarly unhelpful in the identification of the enclaves required to shelter individuals against the enroachments of public power.

Nothing works better than a good Republican recession to remind Americans that the United States is not a land of free goods. Somehow choices must be made about what is to be produced and who is to get it. New capital depends upon past saving. Alas, if men and women save they defer gratification and backslide into the older worlds of sensation. Modern factories turn out work clothes and jeans, not to mention motorcycles, hi-fi equipment, and jet aircraft. Inevitably factories are financed by somebody's savings. Who disagrees with the proposition that there are ways to improve the human environment of work and otherwise to civilize large organizations? On the evidence, I should have no confidence in Consciousness III's capacity to reform factories and offices.

As an intellectual construction Reich's argument amounts to rather little. As a cultural phenomenon Reich is significant—though one should be clear just how. I should not be astonished if on the campuses Reich, a generous but infirm thinker, will enjoy a vogue like that of Hermann Hesse, a sentimental and second-rate novelist. It cannot really be a good thing that intelligent students prefer Reich to Marx and Hesse to Tolstoy.

II

After rhetoric so warm and spirits so high, it is something of a relief to visit the problem-solvers' workshop, a place of comfort for technocrats, economists, cost-benefit analysts, and assorted corporate technicians. As an anonymous reviewer in the *Times Literary Supplement* said of C. P. Snow's *Last Things,* "Many of the characters in his books are scientific civil servants, administrators of one sort or another. These people run the world and it is right that they do so." The engineers, accountants, lawyers, scientists, and administrators who populate Galbraith's technostructure are the real masters of their organizations because they alone can solve the endless stream of technical conundrums presented by science and technology. In principle one cannot distinguish their labors from those of the RAND alumni who at McNamara's behest refined the tools of cost-effectiveness and applied them to Vietnam. In the heyday of the Great Society, Lyndon Johnson's presidential fiat applied Pentagon program-budgeting to the civilian agencies.

The problem-solvers' favorite forum is *The Public Interest,* the quarterly founded by Irving Kristol and Daniel Bell in the wake of the copious arguments over "the future of ideology" stimulated by Bell's famous essay on "the end of ideology." The new journal, said the editors in their opening statement, aspires "to help all of us, when we discuss issues of public policy to know a little better what we are talking about—and preferably in time to make such knowledge effective." In the pursuit of these objectives, ideology was said to be an obstacle:

It is not, however, merely a matter of knowledge or the lack thereof. "Knowing what one is talking about" is a deceptively simple phrase that is pregnant with larger implications. We do not wish to avoid these implications, or pretend to be blind to them. Thus we must admit—or, if you wish, assert—that such an emphasis is not easily reconcilable with a prior commitment to an ideology, whether it be liberal, conservative, or radical.

Why not?

. . . [it] is the nature of ideology to *preconceive* reality; and it is exactly such preconceptions that are the worst hindrances to knowing-what-one-is-talking about. It goes without saying that human thought and action is impossible without *some kinds* of preconceptions—philosophical, religious, moral, or whatever—since it is these that establish the purposes of all thoughts and action. But it is the essential peculiarity of ideologies that they do not simply prescribe ends, but also insistently propose prefabricated interpretations of existing social realities—interpretations that bitterly resist all sensible revision. *The Public Interest* will be animated by a bias against all such prefabrications.

The Public Interest has kept this faith. Its contributors have ranged from Robert Heilbroner's rational radicalism to Daniel Moynihan's emotionally tinged romantic conservatism. Particularly noticeable has been a large delegation from the Harvard-MIT social-science and urban-planning axis. Here are such familiar names as James Q. Wilson, Nathan Glazer, Robert Solow, James Tobin (transplanted to Yale), Carl Kaysen (ditto to Princeton), and David Riesman.

The magazine has been steadily devoted to the evaluation of alternative public policies. Technical comparisons of negative income taxes and family allowances, discussions of cost-benefit measurement, and inquiries into market mechanisms for the control of pollution exemplify the urge to judge existing social mechanisms and design better ones. The editors have naturally been hospitable to the floating establishment of academics and bureaucrats who move in and out of universities, public agencies, foundations, and governments in exile like the Brookings Institution and the Kennedy Institute of Politics. In short, *The Public Interest* has sympathized with an ethic of rational social management by the people who "run the world" as "it is right that they should do." Bell and Kristol possess a Fabian respect for experts and an equally Fabian hope that experts can educate politicians.

In the United States the practitioners of social management are most comfortable during liberal Democratic administrations when there is money to be spent. They flourished on the New Frontier as planners and flourished as spenders in the Great Society, until Vietnam swallowed up the social programs they had formulated, nudged through Congress, and stayed to administer. However, any sensible establishment finds space for flexible souls like Moynihan who are temperamentally equipped to adjust to various holders of office, as well as genuine conservatives of the Edward Banfield stripe.

No need for one's tone to become acid, for there is much to be said in behalf of the problem-solvers. Wouldn't any rational soul join the economist Robert Levine in his preference for "the problem-solving style" over the "politics of provocation"? (Of course there might be other alternatives.) Militants seek excitement and revolution. They (and the rest of us) get instead police repressions, conservative yearning for law and order, plausible justification for new restrictions on civil liberty, and the menace of nativist fascism.

The problem-solver is a dull fellow and it is easy to ridicule his slide rules, office machines, and computers. Yet how sensible he is! *He* wastes no energy railing self-indulgently against the system. *His* enemies are more tangible: ghetto youngsters' poor reading scores, deficient manpower training techniques, gaps in neighborhood legal services, urban housing shortages, congested roads and subways, dirty air and water, and so on.

As he ponders the treatment of these specific ailments, the problem-solver typically is handicapped by neither institutional nor ideological hangups. Since as a practical man he neither loves nor hates major corporations, he is free to convert corporate strengths into the service of effective, curative social action. If major corporations are more efficiently managed than major (or minor) universities, anyone but an ideologue will select Litton, Philco, or Western Electric as a Jobs Corps contractor rather than a university qualified only by a debatable altruism of motive. It is much harder to document the university's altruism than the corporation's efficiency.

In so saying, the problem-solver intends neither to praise corporate officials nor criticize university presidents. The explanation is structural, not personal. Businessmen can rely upon a well-understood and exceedingly powerful set of incentives and penalties. Net income measures corporate performance. Cash and promotion reward individuals who increase net income. Persistent losses result in bankruptcy and the men responsible are thrust into the cold world. No tenure protection and no AAUP shield incompetent corporate executives from the consequences of their inadequacies. As the Penn Central recently demonstrated, even the mightiest may fall. The moral is plain to see. The thing to do is tie the corporate contractor's fees to his success in generating the skill improvements and the behavioral alterations which social programs are designed to achieve.

Altruism, like ideology, is a poor guide to problem solution. Head Start illustrates why this is so. Liberals endorsed the program, as egalitarians and conservatives approved it, out of fiscal anxieties over rising welfare and police expenditures. Both shared a feeling for children. Such sentiments turned Head Start into the most popular of the poverty program's experiments, approximately as safe from attack as motherhood itself. The problem-solver begins rather than stops here. He asks whether the children actually read better, how long the effects last, and which teaching techniques worked best. Only after such technical queries have received satisfactory answers is it reasonable to expand, transform, or replace Head Start. Only ideologues (and congressmen) pour money into programs which careful evaluation reveals to be failing.[3]

Problem-solvers and ideologues have a particularly good war on overeducation: liberal, integrationist doctrine continues to support public education even though liberal parents often enroll their own youngsters in private schools. The familiar public school myth claims that full citizenship is accelerated by common schooling and other common experiences. Hence the integration of Italians, Irish, and Jews, hence the impending integration of blacks. Moreover, what the public school does not do is very nearly as socially virtuous as what it does. Above all, public schools are constitutionally debarred from messing about with religion like the infamous parochial schools. They also avoid the snobbishness of elite Eastern imitations of English public schools and the militarism of the West Point copies.

The problem-solver is prone to identify the realities which ideology masks. In the North residential segregation by color, income, and religion turn the public schoolmen's integrative ideal into farce. And Supreme Court prayer decisions or not, Southern public schools especially have often been conducted as Protestant parochial academies. In the more affluent suburbs everywhere, public schools flourish that consciously model themselves on elite English institutions.

Since real-life public schools differ enormously in intellectual quality, class stratification, ideology, and racial mixture, sensible men will replace their nostalgia for a sentimentalized past with open-minded experiment. Everything then becomes possible. Perhaps a better way than perpetual litigation to cope with Catholic schools might be to consider them as functioning entities, endowed with assorted virtues and flaws. Some Catholic schools have done better at integration than their public rivals. Others do creditable jobs of college preparation.

3. Robert Levine's history of the poverty program, *The Poor Ye Need Not Have with Ye* (Cambridge, Mass.: MIT Press, 1970) presents the evidence of Head Start's failure to effect lasting improvement in reading skills.

A little public money might remedy many of the parochial system's weaknesses.

Once ideological preconception is dispelled, real experiment becomes easy. Performance contracting and educational vouchers are only two of the possibilities. Performance contractors, usually corporations that make teaching machines or other hardware, promise to improve verbal and mathematical skill as measured by standard achievement tests. If the kids do well, the contractors get full payment or even bonuses. Poor performance costs the contractors financial penalties. If greed stimulates teaching ingenuity and the children learn more rapidly and more thoroughly, then educational contracting deserves to flower.

Presumably it will flower most lushly in the gardens of competition. The freer the market, the better. Voucher schemes are one means of devising a free educational market. Milton Friedman was among the first to advocate turning over to parents an allowance in lieu of presently collected school taxes. But in the ongoing OEO voucher experiment, the notion has attracted such liberal sponsors as Harvard's Christopher Jencks. Vouchers start with the critical social observation that the public education coalition has fragmented. On compelling evidence, black parents believe that public-school teachers dislike, undervalue, and humiliate their children. Blue-collar parents rail at racial mixing, sex education, and excessive permissiveness. Middle-class parents are apprehensive about educational quality. Parents of all varieties seem convinced that the schools have done less than they might have to control drug abuse.

These powerful disaffections readily ally themselves with the community power sentiments that now agitate groups as diverse as White Citizens' Councils, campus radicals, homosexuals, black militants, tax avoiders, and white ethnic minorities. If this is social reality, wise men design programs that come to terms with social possibility. Why shouldn't *all* groups of like-minded parents control their schools, as some groups already do? In cities like New York massive educational establishments notoriously smother experiment and deprive parents of effective influence. Reform is all but hopeless. The free market may be a way out, and there doesn't seem to be much to be lost by trying.

Few schools now exist that match the tastes of their prospective customers. As economists know, effective demand soon evokes supply of appropriate quality and quantity. Presented with the new commercial opportunity, educational entrepreneurs will open the sort of schools their customers seek. Should the clients dislike what their children receive, the market will inform the school proprietors that they should either redesign the product or make way for more alert operators. Such a result is considerably more than most people expect from criticizing public-school officials.

This design gives the educational theorists complete freedom to subsidize their favorite nostrums. Altruists can store up treasure in heaven by charging fees below cost. Among them, entrepreneurs, theorists, and altruists will almost certainly hawk a variety of merchandise considerably more diversified than is now available to the ordinary parent.

But all of this is persuasive only for those prepared to jettison the public schools as unsalvageable. If the public schools are valued ideologically, their disrepair is an impetus to programs of rescue. In short, the siren song of the problem-solver lures only those who have made up their minds that the public schools no longer serve or can be made to serve values that they esteem highly. That of course is an ideological decision, and one of considerably more importance than the selection of problem-solving technique.

There is a second controlling ideological element. The problem-solver implicitly declares that organizations differ primarily in their reward structures and relative efficiencies of operation. This is just as ideological a judgment as that of the self-confessed ideologue who frankly prefers altruistic impulse to profit maximization and locates his preferred motive in universities rather than in major corporations. As usual, the problem-solving approach works splendidly if one allows the problem-solver to define the problem.

One more example of the problem-solving technique should suffice. This is public welfare. In the autumn of 1970 even comparatively liberal political candidates were heavily suggesting that many of the poor were lazy, dissolute, and prone to the breeding of large numbers of children for the sake of more generous welfare allowances. The bastard Calvinism implicit in this vein of prejudice enjoins the smallest possible welfare payment, surrounded by the most humiliating conditions ingenuity can arrange. Liberals and most social scientists perceive welfare differently. For them the overwhelming majority of the poor are too young, too old, too disabled, too little trained, too illiterate, or too engrossed by child care, to support themselves. Most would gladly work and earn if only someone would employ them and care for the youngsters. These are the casualties of personal limitation, heedless nurture, racial and sexual discrimination, and neglectful public policy.

According to his custom, the problem-solver defines the issues technically and empirically. He supports an experiment that OEO Administrator Donald Rumsfeld has characterized as "possibly the most significant social-science experiment ever to take place."[4] This is an income maintenance study involving 575 working poor families in New Jersey, 150 more in Scranton, Pennsylvania, and a further 635 in scattered locations. The study's key question is, will income guarantees damage work incentives? Given the chance, will poor people simply down tools and coast along on their subsidies? As far as they reach, preliminary results have been encouraging. The chosen families were offered income guarantees ranging from 50 to 125 percent of the then poverty line of $3,300 for families of four. Those who chose to supplement the guarantee by their own efforts were asked to surrender as little as 30 and as much as 70 percent of their earnings from paid labor. Although some families could have drifted along on higher than poverty incomes without lifting a finger, most chose to work. In fact, 53 percent of the families earned more from their own efforts *after* guarantees were supplied than before they became available, and only 29 percent earned less. Possibly because they alleviated disabling anxiety, cash gifts appeared to encourage individual initiative.

Caution is advisable. The study excluded unemployed female heads of families. Participation in an experiment of itself often generates untypical conduct. Moreover, the time span is too short to allow safe conclusions about the lasting impact upon behavior of no-strings cash guarantees. There is a feature of the New Jersey experiment particularly encouraging to problem-solvers: when the conditions are propitious, scientific research has political effects. The preliminary research findings just summarized apparently sufficed to persuade the House

4. See *Preliminary Results of the New Jersey Graduate Work Incentive Experiment,* OEO Release, February 18, 1970.

Ways and Means Committee, no haunt of Consciousness III, to report the Nixon extension of income maintenance for the working poor to the full House of Representatives, which unexpectedly passed the measure. Wilbur Mills, cautious and conservative (but Harvard Law–trained), was described as particularly taken by the experiment.

All these years apprehensive welfare administrators and humane politicians have been torn between the wish to alleviate hardship and the fear that generosity would damage the incentives of the poor, infuriate the taxpayers, and result in electoral defeat. Are the social scientists really on the verge of the cheerful discovery that the best way to stimulate individual effort even for the poor is to increase the hope of reward? Is social science "truth" a really effective solvent of ideological prejudice?

The story would end better if the Senate were less determined (after receiving the same social science evidence as the House of Representatives) to slaughter the administration's Family Assistance Plan.

III

Problem-solving has held my attention so long because its prestige remains high and also because even in this constricted form, rationality has more appeal to me every day. Nevertheless, the heavily quantitative techniques of the problem-solvers suffer from glaring defects. Some are technical. Cost-benefit analysis, the heart of the analytical mode, struggles unsuccessfully against a very serious bias in favor of the readily quantifiable. In selecting highway routes, it is much easier to compute construction costs per mile than the relative esthetic and scenic penalties attachable to several possible choices. Consolidated Edison's financial savings at Storm King are easier to quantify than the damage to scenery, marine life, and the Hudson River. Conscientious analysts *mention* what they cannot measure. They advise their political masters to *evaluate* the unmeasured and the unmeasurable. Since they don't tell their masters how to turn the trick, the steady political temptation will be to assign low or zero weights to what the computers aren't programmed to evaluate.

Even when amenity and esthetics are not directly at issue, the problem-solving technique is dangerously subjective, and open to the convert influence of individual ideology. I can do no better than cite the testimony of a friendly witness. William Gorham, in better days an assistant secretary of HEW, has spoken in the following terms of the technique which he himself supervised:[5]

The problems of benefits measurement, however, are not just technical; they are conceptual. It is far from obvious how the benefit of most health, education, and welfare programs should be defined. For example, Title 1 of the Elementary and Secondary Education Act provides special funds to local school districts for the education of deprived children. What is it that we want to measure? Should we test the children to see whether their reading comprehension, or their arithmetic achievement, has improved faster than would have been expected? Should we ask them whether they liked school any better or felt more confident of their abilities? Shall we wait and see whether they drop out of school less frequently, commit fewer crimes as teenagers, or go in greater proportions to college? Or shall we wait a decade or two and see how much they earn as adults, and whether, in fact, the cycle of poverty has been broken?

This formidable array just begins the difficulties:

Even if we could conceptualize and measure the benefits of particular programs, there is the fact that benefits of different programs go to different people. Shall equal benefits to different individuals in the population be weighted equally? Is it equally important to raise the educational attainment of a suburban child and a slum child? Should an additional hundred dollars in welfare payments going to a mother with six children in Mississippi be weighted the same as an additional hundred dollars in Social Security payments going to an old man in Chicago? If the weights should not be equal, what should they be? Finally, even if benefits of different programs can be identified and measured and weighted, they cannot always be measured in the same units. Educational benefits may be measurable in terms of achievement test scores, and health benefits in terms of lives saved or days of sickness averted, and welfare benefits in terms of families rescued from poverty. When these benefits are forced into monetary terms, a great deal of violence is inevitably done to their heterogeneity, and useful information is suppressed.

Good questions all. After harkening to Gorham, it is hard not to conclude that cost-benefit analysis is as inescapably imprecise as the

5. The following quotations are drawn from "Notes of a Practitioner," *The Public Interest,* Summer 1967, pp. 6–7.

openly unscientific program choices made by untutored congressmen and overweening presidents. Though Gorham's own final word is naturally more optimistic about his technique's prospects, he sees a narrowly limited role for this mode of problem-solving:

While the big choices may not be greatly illuminated by cost-benefit analysis, the narrower ones can be. It is possible to group programs and potential programs which have the same objective and to examine the effectiveness (relative to cost) of each in reaching the objective. If the objective is to save lives through control of disease, it is clearly helpful to examine various disease control programs and try to estimate how many lives would be saved per dollar expended on each type of program. If we want to raise the earning power of unemployed or under-employed individuals, it makes sense to examine various kinds of training and employment programs in order to compare the effectiveness of these programs in raising the earnings of people being retrained. If we seek to cut infant mortality, rational decision-making will be facilitated if analysts assess relative efficiency of different health programs.

This modest definition of the expert's writ is difficult to quarrel with or, for that matter, to take very seriously as an innovation either in politics or social science. Of course sensible people will estimate program costs by whatever social accounting techniques are plausible. If cost-benefit analysis "forces people to think about the objectives of government programs and how they can be measured," splendid.

Unfortunately, problem-solving techniques leave the difficult issues of social choice just as they were—intractable. At the risk of inflammatory utterance, one must describe these issues in the language of ideology, as any of Gorham's queries serves to illustrate. Gorham asks, "Shall equal benefits to different individuals in the population be weighted equally?" Evidently Congress thought so when it wrote Title 1 of the Elementary and Secondary Education Act. By channeling funds to low-income school districts, the Act explicitly registers a preference for more rapid improvement in the education of the poor than of the rich. The Act implemented a brief American inclination to redeem long neglected promises of racial equality. Extra funds for the poor were Congress's way of compensating for decades of inadequate funding of ghetto schools and decades of preference for the interests of the middle class.

Once Congress states a principle and appropriates the funds to implement it, the money should be rationally administered and its effects reviewed. What else is new?

Little that occurred during the Kennedy-Johnson regime was any freer from ideological overtones, despite the professed attachment by New Frontiersmen and Great Societarians to "nonideological" problem-solving techniques. Thus from its noisy beginnings to its present glum decline, the Office of Economic Opportunity has been a battlefield contested by hostile social theorists. That inflammatory phrase "maximum feasible participation of the poor" expressed a conception of democracy sharply contrasted to the tacit elitism of most social scientists. Within OEO,[6] maximum feasible participation warred with an ethic of opportunity that stressed mobility through existing channels, and job creation instead of community organization.

In the end, the problem-solving style's disabling limitation is its tacit assumption of general agreement upon basic goals and values. Problem-solving is a formula for periods like the 1950s when the natives are calm, politics are placid, and ordinary people leave government and administration to the professionals. In the reign of Eisenhower the Good, Americans agreed on autos and roads. The result was a massive highway construction program that continues inexorably to pave the country long after the consensus upon which it was based has dissolved.

Sputnik legitimized the moon race. Americans, a few sour dissenters excepted, briefly joined hands in a national refusal to lose the Big Game with the Red Machine. In the mid-1960s a somewhat weaker consensus favored more rapid economic growth and accepted tax reduction as the way to get it. The upshot was the Revenue Act of 1964. Moral: where there is general agreement, problem-solving works, especially if a healthy dose of anti-Communist ideology is available as a stimulant.

The problem-solvers have a contribution to make in the handling of small, technical issues. They lack magic as the solvers of major dilemmas of power, income distribution, and racial equity. National consensus on any topic is nowhere in sight. "Problems" are defined

6. The accounts by OEO veterans, though inevitably biased, are revealing. See Levine, *The Poor Ye Need Not Have with Ye,* and Daniel P. Moynihan's *Maximum Feasible Misunderstanding* (Glencoe: Free Press, 1969).

from the start by contending ideologies and they are "solved" or, more accurately, handled in accordance with the political interests of the strongest contenders. Catchwords like *crime in the streets, permissiveness, law and order, pornography* and *drugs* resonate with Consciousness I. For adherents to Consciousness III, permissiveness is personal freedom, pornography is openness to esthetic revelation, and drugs are the well-marked pathway to the expansion of the consciousness. Such clashes of perception, such opposed structures of reality, are at issue every time Congress writes a crime statute and a state legislature considers a university appropriation bill.

On both sides the definitions are ideological. They recall Bell and Kristol's analysis of ideological error: "It is the nature of ideology to *preconceive* reality." I "know," because my students have told me so, that marijuana is a harmless euphoric drug which I am foolish to deny myself. I "know," because narcotics-enforcement administrators have told me so, that marijuana at best is psychologically addictive and at worst leads its consumers toward much more dangerous drugs. I conclude that no quantity of scientific inquiry will modify opinions deeply tied on the one side to a structure of sentiment deeply hostile to the life style of the young and on the other to deep rebelliousness against existing authority and the idea of America cherished by many older Americans.

Crime legislation emanates from a definition of party and generational interest. It is couched in the tongues of ideology, and perceived on all sides as an engagement between old and young, Establishment and radicals, middle Americans and effete Eastern snobs. Hence the Nixon administration's success or failure in enforcing the laws it has sought from Congress is light years away from mundane social-science computation of the relative cost-effectiveness of punitive and rehabilitative approaches to the treatment of criminals. For the administration the political point of the exercise is preservation of the enemy for ritual annihilation during forthcoming electoral hunting seasons. In his successive campaigns, Ronald Reagan has run against student violence, drugs, and high taxes just as though all three had not increased during his term of office.

There is a related point. The techniques of problem solution are themselves judged by all parties ideologically. Among its partisans, community control is much more than an alternative administrative technique comparable to state, regional, or metropolitan modes of organization. An acceptable political solution must emphasize local control because local control is the shared value that precedes and validates policy choice. Implied are confidence in the wisdom of local residents and distrust of experts, mandarins, and professional politicians. The experts share an ideology of their own, a confidence in technique which equips them to generalize beyond specific localities, deploy tools of analysis and choice inexplicable to the laity, and achieve conclusions that are better for ordinary people, but not fully comprehensible to them. The experts can't help themselves. Their mystery converts them into wire-pullers, manipulators, and secret rulers.

Understandably, expert solutions are frequently experienced as the acts of interested parties and the expressions of hostile ideology. Indeed, experts employed by public agencies do represent clients other than the community to which their findings apply. City planning experts implement the policy preferences of the mayors who appoint them. John Mitchell's civil-rights experts interpret the relevant statutes quite differently from the experts who served Ramsay Clark. Experts protect their own positions, opportunities, and reputations, and often they do so most effectively by serving the ideological interests of their employers.

The problem-solvers can at most resolve tiny problems. For everybody's sake one can hope for a time when community agreement upon values and objectives presents the problem-solvers with the agenda of small issues that they are equipped to cope with.

IV

In their different ways, the Reichians and the problem-solvers have taken flight from real politics. The Third Consciousness may be grappling with a substantial vein of youthful romanticism. As far as the young are concerned, their new way of examining experience is nonpolitical or even antipolitical, although it has already been a cause of political response by others. The problem-solvers assume agreement where there is none and thus have nothing to say about the fissures that widen beneath the surface of American life.

For this libertarian radical, contemporary politics is about equality, which is both a value and an ideology. In the long run, the goal remains the good socialist dream of redistribution of privilege, power, property, and income. There is no way to get there except by the patient construction of alliances of intellectuals with unions, blacks, and the poor. Ours is a society blighted by inequality. Our regressive tax structure sufficiently distorts reality so that many people are convinced that we cannot afford Scandinavian standards of public health and communal amenity. Inflation is a disease of distorted expectations, an attempt upon the part of the many to reach for standards of life thrust upon them by the mass media.

I need scarcely say that the immediate prospects for radical economic reconstruction are bad. Accordingly, in the short run I attach myself to a criterion of judgment and a political tactic. I shall support any proposal which, however slightly, diminishes inequality and strengthens potential radical alliances. As for the political tactic, in the absence of a radical party I plan to give what help I can to the more progressive among conventional politicians. It is a good thing to lighten the weight of the Pentagon, diminish tax inequities, agitate for redistributive negative income taxation and universal health care, preserve the environment, and tighten public controls over large corporations. None of this yet constitutes a sufficient or inclusive radical program, but it is an essential immediate perspective for radicals.

Meanwhile, there are other immediate tasks. Ralph Nader is an example of an honorable type, the muckraker. Yet what he has discovered and the opposition he has aroused are educational to the community and grist to the radicals' mill. Radicals need to play conventional politics with the McGoverns and Hugheses and slightly less conventional politics with the Naders and Banzhafs. During the 1970s, conventional politics are unlikely to be uplifting. The alternative to them is far more likely to be universal repression than the sort of radical renewal of our society that socialist egalitarians yearn for.

There may yet come a time when useful employment will be found for the problem-solvers. Perhaps one day the more rational aspirations of Consciousness III will also be approximated. Until then there is no escape from politics and ideology.

Eugene Keller

Social Priorities, Economic Policy, and the State

Twenty-five years ago Lord Beveridge published his *Full Employment in a Free Society,* perhaps the most lucidly argued economic program of social democracy. In this work he assigned three basic functions to public finance. First, total public outlays must always be large enough to ensure full employment. Second, and "subject to this overriding categorical imperative," outlays should be directed within a well-defined framework of social priorities. Third, "subject both to the first and second rule," taxation rather than borrowing should, if possible, be used to finance outlays. This third rule Lord Beveridge did not regard as of prime importance, since either taxation or borrowing could be used to realize the first and second goals. But he favored taxation because in keeping interest rates low it would promote the "euthanasia of the rentier."

Full employment and social priorities were inseparably linked in Beveridge's work. He conceded that digging holes and filling them up again creates jobs, but the very relation between taxation and expenditure that he outlined would go far to ensure that full employment would serve the realization of social priorities—the conquest of "the giant evils of Want, Disease, Squalor, and Ignorance." That relationship was to be determined "not from the angle of public finance, but from the angle of public policy." Taxation was to be viewed as a means of freeing resources for public purposes; expenditures were to be divided into a planned and an unplanned category, the former including investment in physical equipment, the latter spending on goods and services for immediate consumption.

94

Beveridge's prescriptions were of course tied in part to the problems of obsolescence and deterioration of physical plant stemming from the lack of adequate new investment during the depression and war years. But their basic objective was to destroy want, disease, squalor, and ignorance, and like much else that Beveridge had to say, they have lost little of their relevance.

Beveridge left no doubt that his proposals would, if carried out, affect the distribution of political power. "Full employment cannot be won and held without a great extension of the responsibilities and powers of the State, exercised through the organs of the central government," he wrote. "No power less than the State can ensure adequate total outlays at all times or can control in the general interest the location of industry and the use of land."[1] Many new issues would arise, among which perhaps the most difficult would be the transformation of the labor market from a buyer's to a seller's market. But issues such as these could not be evaded if full employment was to be attained and social evils were to be banished.

II

The Beveridge Report continues to be relevant because unemployment, underemployment and poverty continue to be deep-seated problems in the United States, and because official policies for "high" levels of employment, far from being linked with programs incorporating social priorities, have been conceived in deliberate isolation from such programs. And this follows precisely from resistance to the extension of the powers of government which Beveridge thought necessary if jobs for all were to be provided, if poverty was to be eliminated, adequate housing was to be built, and a network of social and medical services was to be created.

The New Economics of the early sixties refined the techniques for estimating the gap between the economy's actual and potential performance, measured roughly in terms of the supply of idle labor and gains in productivity. It improved upon the concepts which in effect rationalized the size of federal budget deficits needed to close the

1. William H. Beveridge, *Full Employment in a Free Society* (New York: W. W. Norton Co., 1945), p. 36.

gap. But it was unconcerned with resource allocation or income distribution, confining itself to the management of aggregate demand along a projected path of gradually accelerating growth. The attainment of social goals was postulated as an incidental benefit; it was not central to the New Economics.

The New Economics represented in large part a response to the challenges posed by Russia's growing military and technological strength (dramatized by Sputnik in 1957) and by the European Common Market's vigorously expanding economies; these challenges would have to be met by policies promoting rapid economic growth in the United States. The problem, however, was to find a balance between the free-market economy—the indispensable source of social power of the American business community—and the civilian and military government bureaucracies whose growth ineluctably accompanied America's assumption of world leadership after World War II, and whose claims on the national product necessarily also grew.

In 1960 Charles J. Hitch, a RAND Corporation economist and subsequently an Assistant Secretary of Defense, wrote that "we must avoid identifying GNP or even expected growth in GNP with economic strength for the cold war," and called for sacrifices to make the required resources available.[2] But others closer to the formulation of economic policy did not accept this point of view. In an essay titled "U.S. Economic Growth and World Leadership" Richard Cooper, a member of the Council of Economic Advisers in the early sixties, wrote that "Growth is the 'great reconciler' among competing claims on output."[3] Growth would ease the task of supplying resources for defense and foreign aid, and would make the sacrifices proposed by Hitch unnecessary, since required tax revenues would increase with growth, obviating higher tax rates that might reduce incentives to work and invest.

The view represented by Cooper turned out to be badly flawed, partly because it failed to take into account the eventual impact upon the American economy of changes in the international situation,

2. Charles J. Hitch, "Resource Limitations," in *The Economics of the New Frontier*, B. Hughel Wilkins and Charles B. Friday, editors (New York: Random House, 1963), p. 191.
3. In *Perspectives on Economic Growth*, Walter W. Heller, ed. (New York: Random House [Vintage edition], 1968), p. 118.

which the steep rises in defense and foreign aid outlays were bound to generate; and partly because the possible results from intensified technological and social changes incident upon accelerated growth were not appreciated, let alone planned for. Between fiscal 1960 and 1964 the budget for defense and space expenditures rose by nearly 25 percent, to $58 billion, and in 1963 Roswell Gilpatrick, a Deputy Secretary of Defense, stated that "a range of credible, usable, military power designed to enable us to deal with challenges all the way across the spectrum of conflict, from guerrilla warfare to thermonuclear war" had been provided. He was hopeful that a reduction in defense costs would now be possible, but in fact the buildup of conventional warfare capabilities that could deal with "wars of liberation" was unquestionably a factor, probably a major factor, in intensifying the Vietnam war; and the metamorphosis in nuclear delivery vehicles— from bombers to missiles in underground silos or on submarines, together with military research expenditures of $7–$8 billion annually—could not but stimulate Russia's defense effort and thus engender a new strategic arms race. The costs of Vietnam and of this new arms race would pre-empt all or most of the increment in federal revenues from stepped-up economic growth which the New Economics had projected as becoming available for whatever purposes Congress would choose, be they social programs, tax cuts, or public debt retirement; and these pre-emptions would in time intensify problems of resource allocation and income distribution.

Increases in defense and space expenditures were important elements in the economic expansion of the early and mid-sixties, but they did not at any time exceed roughly one-tenth of the national product, not even during the height of the Vietnam war. This, to be sure, is not a true measure of their impact upon the economy, since changes in both the mix and the level of these expenditures have a high multiplier effect; but it seems to have been—and to be—regarded as a gauge of their political acceptability: a higher proportion may be viewed as altering the balance of social forces in the United States. Hence, defense and space expenditures have been (and can be) used as stimulative measures only within limits. This is true for government expenditures in general. The then Secretary of the Treasury Douglas Dillon stated that the change in the business outlook between 1960 and 1964 "did not just happen. It was due to the conscious and successful effort of government to provide a climate in which our free enterprise system could flourish—a conscious decision to place primary emphasis on stimulating the private sector of the economy, rather than on massive government actions."[4] The income tax cut of 1964, primarily instituted to put private productive capacity to work (by raising consumer demand),[5] was a result of this "decision."

Pre-empting resources not less than defense expenditures, the tax cut of 1964 represented a reactionary use of Keynesian policies. It was worth $11.5 billion in federal revenues in 1965 alone, a sum that could have been expended to raise the incomes of a substantial segment of the poor (the tax cut benefited mostly families in higher income brackets). Ida C. Merriam, in the *Social Security Bulletin* of October 1963, wrote that if social security benefits were raised to only 50 percent of average preretirement earnings of retired workers, and to 75 percent of those of retired couples, and if eligibility was broadened to 90 percent of the population aged 65 and over (from 70 percent at the time she wrote), *the increase in aggregate benefits would come to $11.5 billion.* (In the fiscal year 1970, average benefits of retired workers were about 35 percent of their preretirement income, and a large proportion of recipients received less.) The premises of the New Economics, with tax policy its center piece, made the elimination of poverty at best a secondary concern; questions of social priorities fell outside its frame of reference. It was preoccupied with the viability of the economic system through innovating new forms of demand management, and it chose not to relate the evils besetting American society to the system or the privileges it secured.

III

Tax and expenditure policies—that is, those measures which in addition to monetary policy are commonly associated with Keynesianism —represent but the broader managerial functions the government has come to assume over the economy. They do not by any means exhaust its role in setting the priorities of resource allocation. These priorities

4. From an address given before the National Industrial Conference Board, September 17, 1964.
5. See "Measuring the Impact of the 1964 Tax Reduction," by Arthur Okun, in *Perspectives on Economic Growth, op. cit.,* p. 28.

are powerfully affected by the government's strong entrenchment in specific sectors of the economy where a symbiotic relation with private interests has developed.

Now, it might be argued that the pre-emptive use of resources for purposes foreign to social needs inheres in an economy oriented to profit maximization. But so to view the problem oversimplifies it and implies that we are in essence dealing with the dichotomy of an "unplanned" versus a "planned" society. The notion of *social* priorities suggests that actual priorities—mainly those determined by government—have damaging effects upon many people, similar to those formerly linked by socialists and other proponents of planning with the workings of the market alone. Unemployment, poverty, lack of job security—all used to be simply related to the way capitalist enterprise operated. This was true of an earlier phase of capitalist development—a phase that, in the United States, more or less ended during the thirties. Since then a new industrial state has presumably evolved. While the market has not been subordinated to the joint control of government and industry to the extent asserted by Galbraith, linkages between the two do dominate the economy. Fiscal and monetary policies are of course geared to the state of demand; and government funds—whether as subsidies, trust funds, or tax aids—exert leverage in varying degree on the direction of private investment, the location of industry, employment opportunities, and the value of social capital. This leverage sets—or keeps—in motion the social and economic forces whose cumulative effects determine the priorities that actually prevail.

For example, the proximate causes for the degradation of inner-city conditions would in the past have been sought in the way the free market works, but now they can no longer be dissociated from government policies. Thus there are tax features, instituted mostly in the fifties, that tend to encourage quick turnover of apartment house properties, resulting in disrepair and deterioration. "Important tax advantages can in most instances be obtained by sale [of a building] after a rather brief interval of holding—commonly 10 years or less—because the tax-saving depreciation allowances are highest in the first few years. . . . [Some] observers have reported a high correlation between frequent turnover and poor maintenance practices, especially for slum housing," writes the National Commission on Urban Problems.[6] The Report of the Commission quotes an expert in the field: "The old-fashioned motives of careful stewardship, conservation, and rational long-term management of investment are apparently subordinated in the tax shelter operation which often characterizes multiple-unit rental housing development, luxury or slum."[7]

More starkly illustrative of the impact of government on the economy and society is the Defense Highway System, which has been of fundamental importance in the decline of American cities. This system, Daniel Patrick Moynihan has written,

the twenty-first century will almost certainly judge to have had more influence on the shape and development of American cities, the distribution of populations within metropolitan areas and across the Nation as a whole, the location of industry, and various kinds of employment opportunities (and, through all these, immense influence on race relations and the welfare of black Americans) than any initiative of the middle third of the twentieth century.[8]

While the population of the country's major metropolitan areas continued to rise during the sixties, that of its great cities dropped, in some instances spectacularly so. The Chicago area population, for example, increased by 11 percent between 1960 and 1970, while that of Chicago itself declined by 6 percent; in Philadelphia, the respective figures show a 10 percent gain versus a 4 percent loss; in Detroit, an 11 percent increase as against an 11 percent loss; in Cleveland a 7 percent rise and a 15 percent drop. There can be no doubt that these trends will persist and perhaps be reinforced, inasmuch as industries now locate predominantly in the suburban rings of central cities rather than inside them: more than three-fifths of industrial construction permits in the late sixties were issued outside cities.

The decline of central cities entailed a momentous change in the racial composition of their population: the number of whites residing in them fell 5 percent between 1960 and 1969, while that of blacks

6. *Building the American City,* Report of the National Commission on Urban Problems to the Congress and to the President of the United States (Washington: Government Printing Office, 1968), p. 402.

7. *Ibid.,* p. 403.

8. In *The Public Interest,* Summer 1970, p. 94.

and other minorities rose by 32 percent. The meaning of these changes cannot be explored here; suffice it to note that suburban sprawl and industrial dispersion have rendered mass transit systems uneconomical, thus precluding low-cost travel by inner-city residents to places of work in the rings. This has probably been an important factor in keeping unemployment at high levels. Social changes of such vast and ominous proportions do not, to be sure, result from only one factor, but the highway program powerfully reinforced the pace of technological change in transportation by creating a vast infrastructure which generated a momentum of its own in transforming locational patterns of industry and population.

The Defense Highway System is but one of a number of key government programs that intensify the evils once associated exclusively with the operation of the free market. Other programs might also be mentioned. Agricultural subsidies, by taking land out of production and by partially or indirectly underwriting farm mechanization, which in turn displaces labor, probably accelerated the exodus from rural areas to a catastrophic degree. Urban renewal, although originally intended "to facilitate the provision of decent low-income housing" is instead "too often looked upon as a federally financed gimmick to provide relatively cheap land for a miscellany of profitable and prestigious enterprises," according to the National Commission on Urban Problems, and "has . . . failed to help the poor and near-poor who make up most of those who have been displaced [by slum clearance]. They have not been rehoused on urban renewal sites, nor has the total volume of public housing been adequate to meet the needs created by demolitions, deterioration, and population growth."[9]

Considering also that the broader managerial policies of government have at times been deliberately designed to increase unemployment, or to finance defense expenditures by inflationary debt creation, *it seems clear that government has become a social and economic force in its own right; it is no mere partner in the new industrial state, it is often the senior partner; it does not necessarily countervail private interests, but frequently adds its weight to theirs.* The simple dichotomy of a "planned" versus an "unplanned" society cannot be applied in this situation, since it refers historically to conditions when

9. *Building the American City, op. cit.,* pp. 152, 153, 167.

government was generally weak in relation to private enterprise. Strengthening the coordinating functions of government, as Moynihan has proposed, would result in improved management and thus reinforce existing tendencies in the activities of government; but it would contribute little to the broadened social vision he expects.

Nevertheless, it must be recognized that social priorities are first and foremost a problem of government. The Republican administration would, as we shall see, "reorder" priorities by reducing the role of government and enhancing that of the private sector; its predilections thus converge with those of many on the New Left who oppose government bureaucracy in the name of "participatory democracy." But, aside from the question of whether any attempt to reduce the reach of government in social and economic programs can be successful, there is the more important point that the very effort to do so would prove damaging. The alternative to responsibility for such programs would not be something more democratic or humane but an accelerated pace of neglect. This is most evident in the deterioration of housing for the poor. Under the Housing Act of 1949, 810,000 public housing units were to be built by 1955. But as of 1967 only about 460,000 additional units of public housing had been completed. Yet, according to the National Commission on Urban Problems, there are about 4 million substandard and overcrowded units in metropolitan areas. "In some places, there is a steady increase in substandard housing," heavily concentrated in poverty areas.[10] Such conditions require more, not less, action by government for their elimination. In the absence of government action, they are bound to worsen.

It seems unlikely, however, that government in America will substantially revise its scale of priorities in the next several years so as to meet the urgent social needs spelled out in official reports that since the mid-sixties have documented the critical problems of poverty, educational neglect, ill health, and social disorganization. Among the chief reasons why such a revision appears to be unlikely are:

1. the attitudes of the leading men of the Nixon administration;
2. the effects of the economic policies pursued in recent years;
3. the increasing pre-emption of resources by private or public in-

10. *Ibid.,* pp. 10, 111.

vestment, compelled by rapidly changing civilian and military technologies;

4. the very terms of the discourse on social priorities.

IV

The more reflective representatives of the Nixon administration, such as Herbert Stein, a member of the Council of Economic Advisers, have attempted to formulate an intellectual basis for minimizing federal activism. They express skepticism about the ability of government to solve the great social problems facing the United States and emphasize the need to rely more on, let us say, the organic processes of society—this is, after all, the meaning of Patrick Moynihan's phrase about "benign neglect." "The priorities problem," Stein has written, "must be faced and ambitions adapted to the willingness of the people to support them. Second, [functions] must be returned to the people wherever possible. Third, [functions] must be returned to the states and localities. Fourth, [functions] must be retained in or returned to the market."[11]

Before attempting a political interpretation of these statements, let us see how these formulations of the "priorities problem" work out in practice. The "leading" example Stein cites to show how functions are returned "to the people" is the Nixon administration's proposed family assistance plan, "which would liberate welfare recipients from the social workers," that is, the welfare bureaucracy. But this is an unwarranted assumption and contemptuous of the needs of the poor, if one considers that the plan as originally submitted to Congress called for $1,600 annually for a four-person family. In New York State, welfare allowances for such a family amounted to over $3,600 in early 1970, a sum representing little more than half the cost of a "low" budget for a family of this size, as calculated by the Bureau of Labor Statistics. "New York City and State will have little relief from welfare spending under the Administration's plan," stated New York City's director of the budget before the Joint Economic Committee of Congress.[12]

11. *The Conference Board Record,* August 1970, p. 15.
12. *The 1970 Economic Report of the President.* In hearings before the Joint Economic Committee of Congress, Part 2, February 1970, p. 355.

The plan will, in fact, abolish neither poverty nor the welfare system. Considering its eligibility provisions, which call for a test of ability and willingness to accept suitable employment, welfare recipients will be more, not less, entangled in the web of administering bureaucracies. A nationwide plan providing an income floor for all could equal the introduction of the eight-hour day in significance; but unless it meets minimal standards of decent living and is free of all eligibility restrictions, it will be nothing but a more efficient and perhaps more oppressive way of administering welfare payments.

The example given by Mr. Stein for the return of functions to the states and localities is revenue sharing. Revenue sharing was first proposed by Walter Heller in the mid-sixties, on the assumption of an "ever-firmer commitment of the Federal government to maintain a high-employment, high-growth economy" generating federal tax revenue at an accelerating rate which would provide the "fiscal dividend" to finance, *inter alia,* revenue sharing.[13] In other words, incipient federal budget surpluses would be used in part to cover perennial state and local deficits. But fiscal dividends have remained fiction, federal deficits reality. Hence, revenue sharing—which involves sharing with the states and localities a certain percentage of annual federal tax revenues, for example, 5 percent under the Heller plan, and 0.33 percent under President Nixon's initial proposal—would reduce the funds available to the federal government for more urgent tasks such as an adequate income maintenance program, which by nature must be national in scope. Richard Musgrave and A. Mitchell Polinsky, both experts in public finance, have written that if substantial new programs oriented toward disadvantaged groups are accepted as priorities,

the case for revenue sharing . . . depends on what it contributes to meeting them. This is to say, it depends on whether responsibility for these programs can be centered at the state-local level; and if so, whether *generalized* sharing will produce the proper distribution of funds. The answer is no on both counts. Any major expansion of income maintenance must be uniform on a nationwide basis. . . . It is clearly a Federal function and has to be performed at that level. Such a program implemented at an adequate scale will cost at least $10–15 billion. . . . Given our premise

13. Walter W. Heller, *New Dimensions of Political Economy* (New York: 1967), p. 140.

that concern with poverty should receive top priority, these programs should outrank revenue sharing.[14]

The contradictions between the ideology guiding Stein and his associates on the one hand, and the actualities on the other dramatize the critical impasse in which American government finds itself. While admitting that "the exchange system . . . contains inequality of command over the use of resources, because it allocates such command more or less in proportion to the ownership of resources," Stein declares that the system "permits more flexible and precise adaptation of the pattern of production to the different desires of different individuals than could be provided by . . . government regulation. It also provides greater incentive to efficiency and innovation because it makes a finer gradation of rewards to performance than is typically found in government operations."[15] Stein's animus is by and large directed against those government operations which, however inadequately, are designed to aid and protect the vast number of disadvantaged persons—estimated to total at least forty million— who have no access to the "exchange system" except as passive consumers and who are more likely to be damaged than benefited by it. Stein would "summon up the real strength of the decentralized free exchange system to replace the evident evils and inadequacies of the present tangle of programs that have grown in response to modern needs."[16] But again, the government programs to which Stein refers were mostly created to deal with the very problems first generated by the "decentralized free exchange system"; their being inadequate, tangled, and bureaucratic has been largely the result of the pressures and antagonisms of the beneficiaries of that system. A case in point is the unemployment insurance program which, while assuring workers of minimal income for a limited time when they become unemployed—and note that only about half of all workers jobless at any one time may be eligible for benefits—provides in most states for less than half of the average weekly wage lost. According to the *1970 Manpower Report of the President,* "opposition to increasing maximum benefit amounts is often based on the alleged

14. *Financing State and Local Governments,* Proceedings of the Monetary Conference, June 1970 (Boston: The Federal Reserve Bank of Boston), p. 23.
15. *The Conference Board Record,* p. 14.
16. *Ibid.,* p. 15.

threat to work incentives."[17] Stringent eligibility and disqualification provisions are additional ways of keeping low the cost of insurance premiums (paid by employers); the resistance by employer groups and the states (which administer the program) to extending coverage to such groups as farm and domestic workers serves the same end.

An equally critical failure of Stein's analysis is its inability to take into account the vast state-capitalist functions assumed by the government. Like its predecessor, the Nixon administration has fought stubbornly for funds to finance such projects as the supersonic transport plane; it has intervened to prevent the bankruptcy of major aircraft manufacturers by guaranteeing payment of huge, cost-inflated debts; and it has eased credit conditions temporarily in order to prevent the liquidity crisis threatened by the bankruptcy of the country's biggest railroad company.

Yet Stein's programmatic statements cannot be dismissed as simply meaningless, for they rationalize a Social Darwinism destructive to the values of equality and democracy. They justify a reactionary kind of "liberalism," which seeks to minimize the intervention of the state in the interests of the poor and deprived. Such analyses reflect the aversion of America's old-line ruling strata to the centralized power of the state. The historical causes of this aversion are related to the unique freedom from public constraints that characterized the expansion of American capitalism in the nineteenth and early twentieth century. That freedom is gone. The rise of the United States to world leadership inevitably imparted immense power to the state, which thus became a rival to finance and industry, even as it sustained their social and economic positions.

Illustrative of this rivalry was the resistance by business to industrial conversion from peacetime to war production in the early forties. So was the latent conflict between business and its congressional allies on the one hand, and John F. Kennedy and his managerial pretensions on the other. But with the exception of the New Deal, no period in American history revealed so dramatically as the years of the Vietnam war the resistance of business, exercised through its allies in Congress, to accretions in the power of government. Lyndon Johnson launched fateful actions unilaterally, although

17. *Ibid.*, p. 14.

he vainly sought to rally the old New Deal coalition of liberals and trade unions through a program of social legislation and full employment. In the absence of idle industrial capacity and with disappearing skilled labor reserves after the Vietnam escalation in mid-1965, large-scale military intervention abroad could not be sustained without rationing of manpower and resources, and this was unobtainable. At the least, substantially increased income taxation was required, as a near-equivalent to consumer-goods rationing. But Johnson's efforts to conduct the war were, finally, thwarted by his inability to get taxes raised sufficiently. He financed the war through huge budget deficits, but these were limited by the gold-dollar crisis resulting from the loss of confidence they created abroad. The unilateral initiative of the executive branch in conducting and expanding the war ran afoul of fiscal limitations, imposed by larger political forces. The slow and ambivalent deescalation of the Vietnam war by President Nixon and the cutbacks in defense outlays over the 1969–71 fiscal years must be regarded as basically conservative measures, designed (even though failing) to restore fiscal balance and thus curb the infringements by the state on the economy. "The dominant persistent budgetary problem of our time will be to hold expenditures in line with what the people are willing to pay for. We cannot afford to be diverted from that task," stated Paul McCracken, the chairman of the Council of Economic Advisers, in the 1970 midyear review of the economy.[18] That federal expenditures should be adapted to willingness rather than ability to pay represents a novel principle of fiscal equity: few taxpayers are "willing" to pay, and the richer they are the more they are unwilling. Yet McCracken's words go beyond the intent of easing the tax load of the rich; they signify a hope that fiscal balance will hold the power of the state at bay.

v

We must now briefly examine some of the key economic policies the Nixon administration has pursued, for these policies, in raising unemployment, sustaining huge losses in output, and failing to slow inflation, have tended to shift the focus of social priorities. First of all,

18. *The 1970 Midyear Review of the State of the Economy.* Hearings before the Joint Economic Committee of Congress, Part 3, July 1970, p. 385.

the Nixon administration deliberately abstained from instituting compensating measures for the job losses incident upon defense cutbacks, and it did not take steps to ensure jobs for discharged soldiers. In an interview with *U.S. News & World Report* (August 3, 1970), Deputy Secretary of Defense David Packard stated that during the fiscal year 1971 at least 1.3 million persons employed by the Defense Department, by prime contractors, and in the Armed Forces would be put "on the job market." The number of civilian defense workers alone would amount to well over 700,000 people. And these figures did not include the number of workers indirectly dependent on defense outlays and adversely affected by cutbacks.

Although it must have been fully aware of the extent of unemployment that would result from lower defense expenditures, the Nixon administration formulated a "game plan" *designed to slow inflation deliberately and almost entirely at the expense of working people.* "At the start of the year [1970] we expected that the gap between the economy's actual and potential output would bring about conditions making for a slower price rise," McCracken stated at the Midyear Review hearings. "With jobs harder to find, labor would find it more difficult to make the kind of wage bargains it had during periods of low unemployment."[19] By the end of 1970, the number of unemployed persons had nearly doubled over the year, to 4.6 million. The unemployment rate for whites had risen to 5.5 percent from 3.2 percent 12 months earlier, and that for Negroes to 9.3 percent from 6.2 percent. According to estimates by Walter Heller, the loss in potential output would amount to $40 billion in 1970, estimates with which the Council of Economic Advisers concurred.

As of early 1971, neither reduced demand nor increased unemployment had seriously retarded inflationary tendencies. To attribute the continuation of these tendencies to "inflationary" wage demands is at best to take effect for cause. Workers can hardly be expected not to resist deterioration in the purchasing power of their income. Inflationary pressures, moreover, have threatened normal standards of living, leisure, and the division of labor in households: in 1965–70, the participation rate in the labor force of married women with children three to five years old rose twice as fast as between 1960

19. *Ibid.,* p. 390.

and 1965 (from 29 percent to 37 percent in the later period, and from 25 percent to 29 percent in the earlier one).[20] This fact cannot be separated from—although admittedly it cannot be shown to be wholly caused by—the decline in real spendable earnings of the average worker since 1965. Sometimes this decline is contrasted with the gain (of 10 percent) in output per manhour in 1965–69, but much of that gain is spurious, since it must largely be attributed to expanded defense production, where productivity improvements mean little in terms of broad economic benefits.

Also pressing on family budgets was the fact that, as money wages rose, there was a faster increase of withheld income taxes; for example, while the earnings of a year-round, full-time factory worker increased 16 percent between 1965 and 1969 (to $6,500), the federal income tax he paid rose by 36 percent, not including either the surtax imposed in 1968 or nonfederal taxes. The proportion the tax took of his gross income rose from 6.9 percent to 8.1 percent.[21] Thus, in an inflationary context, the progressivity of the income tax can become a depressant of real wages. With the onset of the recession, furthermore, losses in weekly work hours contributed to the squeeze on earnings. Considering, finally, the rapid growth during the late sixties in the number of younger workers, who are more concerned with immediate cash income than benefits that tend to postpone it, one could hardly expect that fear of unemployment, potent as it is, would significantly weaken the will—or reduce the necessity—to defend living standards.

Recent inflation has been fueled by the increase in public and private indebtedness. The incurrence of debt in 1965–69 capitalized on expectations of rapidly rising tax revenues or earnings, neither of which materialized. The result has been huge deficits or losses in potential earnings, now being partly made up by increased prices. In earlier days, private debt would have been wiped out through bankruptcies; these today are permitted only on a limited scale and the state bails out the Penn Centrals and the Lockheeds. These debts

20. Release of the Bureau of Labor Statistics, U.S. Department of Labor, January 26, 1971.
21. Statement by Leonard Woodcock, President of the United Auto Workers, in "Impact of the War in Southeast Asia on the U.S. Economy," in *Hearings* before the Committee on Foreign Relations, U.S. Senate, Part 2, April, May, June and August 1970, p. 419.

mortgage the public's savings largely through higher prices. The Nixon administration is unprepared to deal with this phenomenon; imposition of stringent administrative credit controls would be required to deal with it effectively (and they were in fact authorized by Congress in late 1969). Such controls have been anathema to an administration devoted to the "autonomy" of the free market, yet without them talk of reordering priorities remains empty, unless it refers to the priorities of the financial establishment. And these have in fact supervened. One example: financing the enormous federal deficits of the late sixties (and early seventies) raised interest rates to very high levels; funds for socially vital sectors such as housing therefore remained scarce, and periodically nearly unavailable. Here is a striking illustration of the rechanneling of funds into federal finance or private investments, where returns were quicker and higher than in housing: while the Department of Housing and Urban Development had projected a 1969 cash inflow of $23 billion into deposit institutions (such as savings banks), which are the primary underwriters of home financing, an actual outflow of $4 billion occurred.[22] One consequence of the resultant shortage of mortgage funds was a sharp drop in new housing starts in 1969, estimated at about 30 percent below the levels required to attain the ten-year goal of 26 million units set by the 1968 Housing Act.

Now let us reflect on what the deviation of actuality from projection means in terms of social priorities (of which housing is at present perhaps the most urgent one, bearing as it does on the gamut of problems of urban decay, racial integration, employment in suburban areas, and living standards). It means, first of all, that while the need for a steady rise in housing units was clearly recognized, a firm commitment to realizing interim goals was lacking. It means also that the existing priorities in financing were not to be disturbed significantly. Bearing on the first point, Congress allocated funds needed for subsidized housing more than a year after they were originally requested, and then at reduced levels. As regards the second point, the *Second Annual Report on National Housing Goals* blames "inflation" for drawing investments away from traditional types of mortgages, "with their fixed, long-term rate of return, into

22. *Second Annual Report on National Housing Goals,* April 2, 1970, p. 77.

more attractive alternatives—equities and business loans demanded by firms that have little concern about their cost of borrowing."[23]

True, the Nixon administration, recognizing the disastrous effects of the persistent slump in housing, stepped up federal mortgage lending and related financing activity so that in 1970 three-fifths of all home-financing funds were directly or indirectly supplied by the government.[24] In the absence of general credit controls, however, the government can engage in large-scale mortgage financing only at the cost of continued high interest rates. The scale of its activities, furthermore, is likely to encounter budgetary limits, and it is of some significance that the number of housing units built in 1970 remained at least one-fourth below earlier housing-goal projections (an estimated 1.4 million constructed, as compared with 2 million originally projected). Government finance prevented the housing deficit from being worse than it actually was, but certainly did not eliminate it.

VI

There is a fundamental problem in the lack of a reasonable relation between *projections* of the "fiscal dividend" and the probabilities. In early 1970, Charles Schultze of the Brookings Institution projected a fiscal dividend of $13 billion for 1975 (after deduction of a projected $10 billion budget surplus to help finance housing).

His assumption was that there would be (1) no change in present tax rates; (2) a decline in spending on Vietnam to insignificant levels associated with termination of the war but offset by a rise in other military expenditures; (3) continuation of present federal civilian programs plus adoption of proposed programs such as the family assistance plan and revenue sharing; (4) an economic growth rate of 4 percent a year. This is an astonishingly small amount when one remembers the high hopes and projections that were linked with what appeared to be the successful demand management of the economy during the sixties. In 1968, the Cabinet Coordinating Committee on Economic Planning for the End of Vietnam Hostilities pro-

23. *Ibid.*, p. 3.
24. *The Wall Street Journal*, January 6, 1971.

jected a fiscal dividend for fiscal 1972 of $22 billion.[25] This, however, was largely absorbed by the 1969 tax cut, by the continued expenditures for the Vietnam war, and by the expansion of existing civilian programs. Renewed growth of the dividend was foreclosed by the recession that began late in 1969.

Great expectations had been pinned on the growth of the fiscal dividend. Walter Heller as much as predicted that the arena of future social conflict would be confined to struggles over who gets what share of this dividend. The National Advisory Commission on Civil Disorders wrote that its proposals for training, employment, education, housing, and welfare, costed at $30 billion, could without difficulty be financed from the "truly astounding automatic increases in Federal budget receipts" generated by a federal revenue system that was highly responsive to growth—"provided only that the national economy is kept functioning at capacity so that actual national income expands in line with potential. These automatic increases—the 'fiscal dividend' —from the Federal revenue system range from $11 billion to $14 billion under conditions of steady economic growth."[26]

The significance of the very concept of fiscal dividend might also be examined in light of estimates of the funds actually required to finance social priority programs. Here it is well to quote some eloquent statements from the testimony of Joseph Califano, former special aide to President Johnson, before the Joint Economic Committee in mid-1969:

It is easy to point to the recent increases in Federal, State and local spending in these areas [i.e., housing, cities, antipoverty, and crime control] as evidence that many of our domestic commitments are being met. I have often used as examples of Federal increases:

The education budget that grew from $4 billion to over $13 billion in five years.

The health budget that rose from $4 billion to over $16 billion in five years.

25. "Report to the President from the Cabinet Coordinating Committee on Economic Planning for the End of Vietnam Hostilities," in *Economic Report of the President, January 1969* (Washington, D.C.: Government Printing Office), p. 187.

26. *Report of the National Advisory Commission on Civil Disorders* (Kerner Report) (Washington: Government Printing Office, March 1, 1968), p. 229–230.

The cities budget that grew from $900 million in the late fifties to a level of $5 billion last year.

But these large rises are insufficient to meet the urgent national priorities at home. . . . The Federal Government's estimate of the cost of implementing the Kerner Commission's programmatic recommendations was at least $30 billion over and above what we are now spending. The President's Rural Poverty Commission said it would cost $40 billion more than we are now spending to wipe out rural poverty.

Merely to provide for the full development of existing programs and a few modest new programs, the cost in fiscal 1972 would be an additional $37.7 billion. This is not the projection of dreamers. It is a careful calculation contained in a December 1968 report to the President, signed by the Secretaries of the Treasury, Defense, Commerce, and Labor, the Director of the Budget and the Chairman of the Council of Economic Advisers.[27]

These "illustrative new programs or major expansion of existing Federal programs" called for $7 billion more for education, $3.8 billion for health, $9.5 billion for social security and income support alone. Moreover, the list did not include outlays for a comprehensive income maintenance program (whose cost, as indicated, would come to about $15 billion a year were it adequately financed), nor a guaranteed employment opportunities program, which would also require up to $10 billion a year.

VII

We cannot analyze the reasons here for the magnitude of these proposed expenditures or judge their adequacy. It is likely that the need for the programs they were intended to finance will rapidly intensify. There has been much talk of "postindustrialism," but for large numbers of workers and their families, as well as older men and women who do not work, the industrial revolution has not ended. They remain highly vulnerable to the disruptions it continues to generate. Workers are displaced from high-technology agriculture, mechanized factories, automated materials handling activities, and left stranded by changed modes of transport. Older persons are exposed

27. *The Military Budget and National Economic Priorities.* Hearings before the Subcommittee on Economy in Government of the Joint Economic Committee, Part 1, June 1969, p. 269 ff.

to the disintegration of urban communities, and to rapid loss in the buying power of their retirement incomes.[28] It is certain that the social service needs of these workers and their families and of older people will expand.

The federal programs designed to resolve the social and economic problems sketched deal with the effects rather than with the causes of social disruption and economic change; they represent ways to offset some of the social consequences of private market decisions and government programs supporting private or autonomous state-capitalist interests. They do not encumber those decisions or interests. A case in point is agricultural subsidies, which unquestionably have been a major means to provide capital to farmers, enabling many of them to install labor-displacing technologies. These subsidies amounted to $5 billion in 1969, most of it going to the 400,000 or 16 percent of all farmers with $20,000 or more in annual income. By comparison, public-assistance payments by the federal government totaled $4.3 billion in 1969, contributing to the support of 11.5 million needy persons, many of whom had been the victims of the agricultural revolution spurred by farm subsidies.

Admittedly, the causal factors of change can not always be readily identified. Let us cite another example. In January 1971, the Treasury liberalized industry depreciation schedules, at a cost in tax revenue estimated at $2.6 billion merely in the first year during which the liberalization was to be in effect. The loss in tax revenues, however, is unlikely to account for the total social cost of this measure. To what extent will it spur technological change and worker displacement? Will it result in a greater number of factories being built away from central cities, and hasten the obsolescence of plants still located there? Unquestionably it will, yet this particular cause cannot be isolated from others having similar effects.

The dimensions of these effects are suggested by the program cost estimates referred to earlier. How these costs will be met is bound to be a key political question in the seventies, but deeper, more disquieting questions must also arise concerning why they are *not* being met. The debate over "social priorities," hitherto conducted by a

28. "The retirement income problem has become a retirement income crisis," according to a report of the Senate Special Committee on Aging, quoted in *The New York Times*, January 18, 1971, p. 11.

handful of senators and economists in the conventional terms of resource allocation, has yet to develop a concern with the very nature
of the state whose immense taxing and spending power sustains rather
than controls a high-technology capitalism, giving rise to the social
conditions that require large-scale alleviation, while simultaneously
pre-empting the necessary resources for it by accelerating shifts
in the profitability of investments which make great masses of social
capital obsolescent.

VIII

Among the virtually unquestioned assumptions of economic policy
since World War II has been the need to ensure economic growth—
an assumption that also underlies the many discussions of social
priorities. This is implicit in all projections of both the national
product and the federal budget on which estimates of the availability
of funds for carrying out social programs have been based. Charles
Schultze, for example, projected a "resumption" of economic growth
following the 1970 recession at an annual rate of 4–4½ percent.[29]
The Council of Economic Advisers assumed the rate to be 4.3 percent
a year between 1969 and 1975, allowing for annual increases in
output per man hour of 3 percent, rapid increases in the labor force,
and unemployment of 3.8 percent.[30] These projections were based on
the *potential* of the economy. How the actual performance of the
economy would be aligned with its potential the Council did not say.
Yet, in 1970, the actual economic growth rate was less than zero.
But just as the high economic growth rates recorded in the early
and middle sixties were linked to rapid expansion in defense and
capital outlays, so the 1970 recession must be understood in the
context of military spending cutbacks, even if these were not its
only causes.

Here arises a critical question for those who have viewed social
priorities in terms of a "trade-off" between military and civilian expenditures: if economic growth requires large-scale defense spending,

29. *Changing National Priorities*. Hearings before the Subcommittee on
Economy in Government of the Joint Economic Committee, Part 1, June 1970,
p. 4.

30. *Changing National Priorities, op. cit.*, Part 2, p. 298.

the resources needed for new social investment will not be sufficient. But neither will they be sufficient if defense spending is cut back, since this spells recession and a drop in federal revenue required for social investment.

One way to deal with this problem is to deny that it exists. According to the Cabinet Coordinating Committee on Economic Planning for the End of Vietnam Hostilities, prior to the summer of 1965 (when the war was intensified), "the economy was remarkably well-balanced and was in the midst of its longest peacetime expansion in history." This statement is offered as evidence that "prosperity has not depended on the defense buildup and will not need high military spending in peacetime. On the contrary, peace will provide the Nation with welcome opportunities to channel into civilian use manpower and material resources now being devoted to war."[31] What the Committee meant by "well-balanced" or "peacetime" in 1965 is hard to know, considering that the unemployment rate in the first half of 1965 was nearly 5 percent, and that defense and space expenditures had been rising throughout the early sixties.

The linkage between economic growth in the United States and defense spending would seem hard to deny. In a lengthy paper on this question, Professors George Hildebrand and Norman Breckner wrote in 1957 that there is "a persuasive argument for the contention that during 1939–57, security spending promoted a higher realized rate of growth than would otherwise have occurred"—as shown by the increasing injections of military demand beginning in 1940, which ended the depression, and as shown also by the mildness of postwar recessions when contrasted with the boom-and-bust cycles that were typical of the economy prior to 1940. "If, as seems reasonable, we assume a multiplier of 2.5, then even a $10 billion cut in security spending would imply a decline of $25 billion in gross national product, barring offsetting increases in private investment, consumption, or other components of Government demand."[32]

Yet, to maintain full or high employment with a growing labor

31. *Economic Report of The President, January 1969* (Washington: Government Printing Office), p. 187.

32. "Impacts of National Security Expenditures upon the Stability and Growth of the American Economy," by George H. Hildebrand and Norman V. Breckner, in *Federal Expenditure Policy for Economic Growth and Stability*, Joint Economic Committee of Congress, November 5, 1957, pp. 533, 538.

force, large defense cuts would "require extensive Government actions to support aggregate demand." How extensive these actions would have to be is implied by the multiplier mentioned by Professors Hildebrand and Breckner. As already noted, the Nixon administration did not compensate for the defense spending cutbacks it made over the 1969–71 fiscal years. It did significantly raise expenditures on technologically advanced military hardware in its 1972 budget, perpetuating the structural interdependence between the economy and its defense industry components. This interdependence (evidenced also in the 1970–71 recession) would seem to preclude significant reductions in defense spending, such as the 40 percent from 1969 levels recommended by Carl Kaysen.[33] The link between military expenditures and economic growth is thus unlikely to be severed in the foreseeable future.

IX

Does this mean that, given present policy, resources for social priorities must remain inadequate? It does. First, because defense expenditures draw heavily on federal revenues, more so than is commonly recognized, and these revenues of course represent the major portion of that part of the social surplus which is subject to political control. Second, because of powerful resistance to expansion of the tax base on the part of conservatives (they believe it would impinge on the liberties of the private sector) as well as of liberals (they fear it would facilitate higher defense spending).

To deal with the first point: We call attention to a table that appears on page 20 of the federal budget document for fiscal 1971 titled "Changing Priorities," which shows that the share of defense expenditures in total federal outlays was to decline to an estimated 37 percent in 1971, while that of funds for "human resources" was to rise to 41 percent. The actual percent shares will be somewhat different when final figures become available for the fiscal year, but this will not affect the import of the table.

The claim made explicit by the table that "priorities" have been changing under the benign aegis of the Nixon administration is not

33. In *Agenda for the Nation*, Kermit Gordon, ed. (Washington: The Brookings Institution, 1968), p. 582.

of interest here; rather, it serves as a point of departure for a different analysis of the impact of defense expenditures upon the federal budget. As of January 1971, fiscal year 1971 federal outlays directly or indirectly related to the security (which includes more than defense) of the United States tallied as follows (in billions):

National security	$ 76.4
Space technology	3.4
International	3.6
Interest*	19.4
Veterans' affairs	10.0
Total	$112.8

* Interest on the public debt, incurred mostly to finance past and present wars.

These expenditures represented 53 percent of total federal outlays. Funds for "human resources," on the other hand, summed up as follows (in billions):

Manpower and education	$ 8.3
Health	14.9
Income maintenance	55.5
Total	$78.7

These funds made up 37 percent of total federal outlays. It is clear that the actual relation between security and "human resources" expenditures is less favorable than was claimed in the federal budget for 1971.

Moreover, the designation "human resources" for such expenditures as social security, public assistance, or unemployment insurance is misleading, inasmuch as the term is generally used in reference to investment-type outlays, such as education and training. Furthermore, the table in the budget document included veterans' benefits as part of the computation of funds for "human resources," but it is specious to imply that these benefits (or increases in them) are evidence of "changing priorities," since in fact they result from failure to have done so. But these and other possible criticisms are secondary to an examination of the *sources of revenue* from which the two kinds of federal outlays are financed, since it bears upon the constraints that limit genuine and lasting changes in national priorities.

Federal budget receipts essentially consist of general revenue, including proceeds from personal and corporate income taxes; and of trust funds, from which social insurance and Medicare, as well as much of highway construction, are financed. Trust funds draw upon earmarked payroll taxes (or, in the case of the Highway Trust Fund, on special excise taxes) and cannot be diverted to purposes other than those for which they have been designated. General revenues, however, can be and to some extent are used as a vehicle of redistributing income (although tax aids go far to vitiate the redistributional effect).

Significantly, trust fund receipts have grown much faster than general revenue receipts: in 1969, they constituted about one-fourth of total federal budget receipts, compared with one-fifth in 1961. While personal income tax rates have on balance been reduced over the past decade, payroll tax rates, which burden smaller wage and salary earners and businessmen much more than larger ones, have been raised time and again.

Health and income maintenance have been largely financed from trust funds. In the fiscal years 1970–72, trust funds will have financed about 75 percent of all federal health and income maintenance outlays, roughly the same share as in 1961–63. In contrast, expenditures for the security of the United States, as defined in the above table, have been financed of necessity out of general revenue. In fiscal 1971, these expenditures were equivalent to about 80 percent of general revenue. (In no year of the past decade was this equivalent lower than 79 percent.) This is not to say that these or other federal expenditures depend solely on general revenue for their funding, which can be supplemented by deficit borrowing. Deficits, however, have highly regressive redistributional effects of their own since the interest payments on the swelling volume of public debt flow largely to the banks and rich individuals. The revenue equivalent of security expenditures thus would seem to indicate roughly the constraint within which the redistributive function of the federal budget operates, and the extent to which these expenditures pre-empt federal funds for domestic civilian purposes—not all of which of course are linked to social-policy objectives. In sum, to represent shifts (minor in any case) in the composition of federal outlays as changes in priorities benefiting low-income people and the poor is not valid unless these shifts are financed from general revenue and thus stem from a genuine redistribution of the fruits of social labor. That, however, is to a great extent precluded by the huge claims of defense expenditures upon the federal budget.

These claims can be substantially reduced only if the federal government stops investing in the advancement of armaments technology, and adopts a policy of "enough is enough." According to Charles Schultze, $17 billion could be added to the fiscal dividend in 1975 if (1) defense preparedness were reduced, in line with announced intentions, from capabilities of fighting "2½ wars"—one in Europe, one in Asia, and a "minor" one in the Western Hemisphere —to "1½ wars," and (2) strategic nuclear forces were limited to assuring the destruction of an enemy visiting nuclear attack upon the United States.[34] But if the reduction in the number of wars planned for represents a change in strategic policies, it does not necessarily impinge upon armaments expenditures; it may merely mean—and actually seems to mean—that the technological content of military capabilities (particularly those of the Navy and Air Force) is intensified while conventional forces, involving massed manpower, are held down. In his 1969 testimony, Mr. Schultze noted as factors making for increases in the non-Vietnam part of the military budget, (1) prospective raises in civilian and military pay; (2) weapons systems approved by the Defense Department but for which most of the spending had not yet occurred (including the Minuteman III program, Poseidon missile conversion, the antiballistic and multiple nuclear warheads programs, a new strategic bomber, a new Navy fighter plane); (3) cost escalation; (4) new weapons system advocated by the Joint Chiefs of Staff but not yet approved; and (5) mutual escalation of the arms race resulting, for example, from the Defense Department's 1969 request for $12 billion to improve the Poseidon missile, which no doubt compels the Soviet Union to step up its missile development and in turn requires further refinements on the American side. "Continually advancing technology and the risk aversion of military planners . . . combine to produce ever more complex and expensive weapons systems and ever more contingencies to guard against," Schultze said.[35] Certainly the 1972 budget tends to

34. *Changing National Priorities*, Part 1, *op. cit.*, p. 7.
35. *The Military Budget and National Economic Priorities*, *op. cit.*, pp. 47, 50 ff.

bear out Mr. Schultze's pessimism. The "savings" once expected to be realized from "de-escalating" or ending the Vietnam war tend to be absorbed by newly developing generations of weapons, involving steeply rising costs. The new systems funded in the 1972 budget include the Underwater Long-Range Missile System (ULMS); a new missile-firing submarine (still in the design stage); the B1 advanced bomber; an Airborne Warning and Control System to detect low-flying attack planes and to control tactical warplanes in battle zones. This list by no means exhausts the new military technologies currently being funded for research and development, as well as for production.

In view of the seemingly irreducible claims of defense and the seemingly irresistible advance in weapons technology, it has appeared futile to some economists to limit the financing of social priorities to tax rates as they are currently structured. Arthur Okun, a former chairman of the Council of Economic Advisers, has written of the "absurd battle between defense and the cities," which has arisen "because we insist on rather stable tax rates. . . . Defense spending— with its 9 percent of GNP—is pitted against nondefense Federal, state and local expenditures—with their 14 percent of GNP—while the big 77 percent of our GNP that goes into private spending is a bystander." The "trade-off" that would produce the means for broadened social programs and urban rehabilitation has been defined chiefly within the constraints of the federal budget, financed by revenues from stable tax rates, writes Okun. But taxes should be raised when increases in defense outlays are needed, and they should be lowered only insofar as reduced defense outlays permit it.[36]

First of all, Mr. Okun's tax history is wrong. Tax rates, as he himself implies, have *not* been stable. "If the Nation were willing to return to the average income tax rates of 1963, we could have another $10 billion a year to spend on the war against poverty," he writes. That is a surprising statement to come from a prominent representative of the New Frontier, for among its first priorities was the stimulation of capital and consumer spending through reductions in tax rates. Moreover, as has been indicated, payroll taxes to finance social insurance (and levied equally on covered employees and em-

36. *Ibid.*, p. 282.

ployers) were raised throughout the sixties (from 3 percent in 1961 to 5.2 percent in 1971, with maximum taxable earnings rising from $4,800 to $7,800). State and local property, income and sales tax rates have steadily risen or have been introduced in perhaps all major jurisdictions. Lack of "flexibility" in tax rates thus is not the reason why cities obtain relatively less in public money than defense. More to the point, the House Ways and Means Committee's resistance to raising taxes in 1967–68, until a commitment to a ceiling on federal expenditures was made, surely was the single most effective barrier to continued escalation. True, the objective of the Committee was to hobble the Johnson administration's burgeoning civilian programs, and this indeed confronted liberals in the Democratic party with the choice that Okun finds so disagreeable. But the more basic purpose of the Committee was to limit the spending power of the executive branch, precisely in order to maintain a strong private sector—for presumably private-sector spending is the avatar of the system of free enterprise and individual liberties the Committee seeks to defend.

In sum, the claims of what goes under the name of national security limit funds for social priorities to only a minor share of general revenue, and much of this share finances government activities unrelated to social programs. At the same time, the resistance of conservative political forces prevents restructuring of the tax system, except in the direction of easing its exaction of income and wealth. Thus it is improbable that the issue of social priorities will be resolved within the terms posed here. Rather, it is bound to involve a wider arena of social and political contest, which will not limit itself to the fiscal dividend or other such elusive "economic-growth shares" but is bound in time to address the question of distributive justice.

X

The terms in which social priorities have been discussed fixate the political and economic conditions of the early seventies. Yet these conditions by no means permit the indefinite extension of the status quo. In 1960, Seymour Martin Lipset, speaking for many fellow liberals, proclaimed that "the fundamental problems of the industrial revolution have been solved: the workers have achieved industrial and political citizenship." The civil rights struggles and urban rebellions that occurred but a few years later revealed the hollowness of his words no less than the limits of the welfare state. These limits in fact tended to contract, and in 1970, an Assistant Secretary of Labor could address a warning to American industry concerning "millions of full-time workers [who] find themselves in an almost intolerable three-way bind: the basic needs of their families have grown beyond the capacity of their take-home pay; they are unhappy with their jobs but see no way of breaking out; and their total life patterns are less than satisfactory." These workers are "not at the fringes of our economic system. They are at the center, with family income of between $5,000 and $10,000. . . . We are talking about some 20 million families—about 80 million individuals in an income range that makes them ineligible for benefits from anti-poverty programs but does not provide enough money to maintain a moderate family budget. . . . [Given] current conditions, many are permanently trapped . . . in this kind of vise." While these workers are not representative of all American workers, many of whom live quite well, "they represent 40 percent of the American workforce."[37]

How Mr. Rosow proposes to ease the conditions of these workers cannot concern us here; suffice it to say that his proposals largely entail such voluntary actions by industry as are rarely undertaken except under pressure of events or of legislative compulsion. Both depend upon political organization. How such organization will crystallize cannot be forecast; but that the vise of which Mr. Rosow speaks will tighten seems plainly indicated by some of the broad demographic and occupational trends that are likely to emerge in the seventies. According to the Department of Labor, the number of workers in the most active age brackets—the years twenty-five to thirty-four, when family size increases most rapidly and expectations of wage increases are most urgent—will rise four times faster during the seventies than it did in the sixties (49 percent versus 16 percent). These men and women, moreover, will be better educated than their counterparts in the sixties or earlier decades, and 79 percent will have a high school or some college education by 1975 compared with 69

37. "The Blue-Collar Blues (Economic and Social Challenge of the 1970's)," address by Assistant Secretary of Labor Jerome M. Rosow before the fall 1970 meeting of the American Compensation Association, Denver, October 29, 1970.

percent in 1965. Therefore, a much larger number of young workers will have a greater sense of their own potential, bringing higher aspirations to what will be largely constricting jobs. Most of these (60 percent) will open up in clerical, sales, semiskilled blue-collar and service occupations.[38] The restlessness and frustrations, but more important, the evolving consciousness and struggle of these workers will have a powerful impact upon the order of social priorities. Although the eventual shape of that order is scarcely predictable, it is most unlikely to resemble the status quo which President Nixon's Council of Economic Advisers has targeted for the years ahead.

The Vietnam war and the urban rebellions, occurring simultaneously, gave rise to critical, inescapable questions; a nation attempting to change the course of history abroad stood helpless before the bitter fruits of its own history. This antithesis also informed the debate over national priorities—it foreshadowed, as a representative of the Johnson administration put it, a struggle between "diplomacy and domesticity."[39] This formulation represented more than a recognition of political polarization—it was an admission that defense was placing a more and more intolerable burden upon the American economy and society. Both conservative and liberal economists—Arthur Burns and Kenneth Boulding among them—had long maintained or implied in their writings that the American economy could not indefinitely sustain this burden without endangering its very foundations—the freedom, however qualified, of its capital and labor markets. Democratic party spokesmen rarely if ever conceded that there were not sufficient resources to both conduct a vast military effort and promote social progress. The assumption that, given appropriate policies, there was plenty to go round was after all the basis for the coalition of forces that had held the party together since the late thirties. Yet the availability of ample resources was more a political than an economic datum, depending largely on the power to allocate rather than the ability to generate. The Vietnam war, however, devoid of the ideological and moral significance of the struggle against fascism that had

38. *U.S. Manpower in the 1970's—Opportunity and Challenge* (Washington, D.C.: U.S. Department of Labor).
39. "The Battle for Resources—Diplomacy vs. Domesticity," remarks of Undersecretary of the Treasury Joseph W. Barr before the Town Hall of California, Los Angeles, June 25, 1968.

cemented the party three decades earlier, now broke it apart. The power of the executive branch, whose enlargement was once eagerly sought by liberals as a means to give leadership to social advancement, now began to be viewed as a threat embodied by an evil bureaucracy of militarists and technocrats. Significantly, none of those who participated in the debate over social priorities advocated the creation of instruments of national planning to overcome the antithesis of "diplomacy versus domesticity." The political and ideological bases for such planning, weak to begin with, had disintegrated. Had planning been instituted under the changed political conditions of the middle and late sixties, it would have entrenched a warfare-welfare apparatus that would have facilitated the conduct of the war and other, similar "counterinsurgency" actions as well; it would have aggravated the dangers to American democracy which the unilateral exercise of the warmaking power by the executive had already heightened.

Planning would have involved, at the least, the rationing of capital by means of credit controls; the imposition of additional taxes to reduce the need to expand the public debt and control consumer spending; and restraints on prices and wages. Such planning is probably necessary if full employment is to be maintained, since otherwise inflation results, as in fact it did. A cause as well as a consequence of inflation is that economic decision-making power is in part shifted to monopolists and speculators; or better put: much of investment activity turns speculative. Recession ensues when the market no longer absorbs overpriced assets, and debts begin to be called. Thus, planning would avert inflation; recession, if deep enough, aborts it. The Nixon administration was of course committed to avoid any expansion in the power of the executive such as planning implies. But it went further; it fought inflation by fostering unemployment and idling of productive capacity. For the Nixon administration, however, no less than for its predecessor, planning, had it been forced to adopt it, could not have been separated from the context of war and rising defense expenditures; its effects would of course have been just as reactionary. In sum, given the present relationship of forces in the United States, both planning and nonplanning imperil civilized values—the one would largely subserve military purposes, the other generates and intensifies social cleavages and depresses social conditions.

It is hard to see how in the present political and institutional context the issue of planning—and it is an issue—can be resolved. Certainly the debate over social priorities did not begin to broach it. The protagonists of planning confined it to the terms of the federal budget, made assumptions about economic growth and, by extension, the maintenance of high employment which turned out to be fragile, and ignored the state's role in generating the very problems the social programs they advocated were designed to solve.

We have argued that the state frequently acts as the partner or senior partner of powerful private interests, promoting high-technology and other capital-intensive and military investments, about the human and social consequences of which it is as unconcerned as industrialists of an earlier era were about the consequences of *their* decisions. State capitalism pre-empts, possibly on an increasing scale, the resources needed for social reconstruction—the building of highways that strangle cities, the subsidization and management of agriculture that displaces rural people; the support of vast research projects that result in costly but largely useless technology, often threatening to life itself. The claim on resources of activities such as these has been but marginally challenged; their effect on the economy is little understood; and the debate on social priorities has ignored all but their military aspect.

Nor did the debate touch upon the private sector. Yet the investment activities of this sector are more than twice as large as those of the federal government. Although their greater size is not necessarily indicative of greater importance in shaping the basic tendencies of the economy, it is nevertheless probable that they pre-empt resources needed for social priorities no less than do military outlays, and that they continue to function in ways that intensify social problems—although they cannot sharply be separated from the infrastructures which the state provides and which to a large extent ensure their profitability.

Essentially, the debate on social priorities moved within or was premised upon the prevailing system of priorities, whose workings it did not fundamentally question. The terms within which it moved were strongly conservative; like the neo-Keynesian policies of the early sixties, which were designed to manage the economy without interfering with any of its component institutions, the protagonists of the debate abstained from relating social goals to economic growth. They limited it to the allocational potential of the federal budget, but even here they ignored or skirted fundamental questions, such as the impacts of taxation or of subsidies on social conditions which the redirection of federal expenditures was supposed to alleviate. And, insofar as the broader conceptual framework of the national income and product accounts was introduced, it was done to suggest the near futility of any attempt to change actual priorities, except for the presumably overriding needs of defense.

The seventies are likely to witness a deepening conflict between state capitalist interests and human needs. That likelihood is foreshadowed by the debate over social priorities, whose limited, conservative terms and technical jargon should not obscure its bitter origins. It is also indicated by the pattern of economic policy under which inflation is fought by causing workers to lose their jobs, even while costly and unproductive state investment activities and a destructive and futile military effort, themselves causes of inflation, are sustained. How under these circumstances social priorities will be realized depends on the outcome of future political struggles. In these struggles, freedom from poverty and insecurity is at stake. Thus understood, social priorities can be realized only if they become part of the very structure of the social division of labor, if they become inseparable from an undeviating policy of full employment, and if they are uncompromisingly pursued "to conquer the giant evils of Want, Disease, Squalor, and Ignorance." And that should define our tasks in the seventies.

Jesse Pitts

The Counterculture

TRANQUILIZER OR REVOLUTIONARY IDEOLOGY?

In an essay I wrote a while back, "The Hippies as Contrameritoc-racy," (*Dissent,* July-August 1969), I argued that the movement was essentially a response to meritocratic pressures bearing down not only upon youth but upon the society as a whole, and that it represented a first-line structural response that probably would not endure in its initial form. That argument seems to me still decidedly to the point, but I would now like to go a little further. As of the early 1970s the hippie movement has divided itself into four major cultural streams and organizational patterns: the commune, the drug culture, the music culture, and the political youth movement. While all of these could be found in some form prior to the rise of the hippies, it is the hippies who provided them with momentum, style, and legitimation, so that the hippie look came to serve as their badge of allegiance. Various writers have described this phenomenon under the generic term of "counterculture"; I have described it, with an eye toward its structural origins, as a contrameritocracy.

In some form or other, communes have always existed in the United States. There are some in Europe as well, and a number have lasted for several generations, like the Communauté Boismondeau, which, with an 1848 ideology, makes watch cases as a producers' cooperative. Such groups have flourished in the United States, in part because of our abundance of land and space, so that people have been able to "do their thing" without too much popular opposition. Popular historiography presents the Pilgrims as a band of men and women whose religious principles led them to come to the New

World and found a commune of their own. *Newsweek* guesses that there may now be five hundred communes functioning at any one time, with a total membership of ten thousand. But the significance of this movement goes beyond these small figures. On any campus there are a number of students who experiment with "communal living," which means sharing the money and the housework. During the summer and after graduation there are many who try with more or less conviction to live in a communal way in the country and share in the farm labor. The rural commune is where the hippies have retreated in order to escape being swamped by the young "premoral" types and exploited by individuals ready to use any kind of violence that will ensure them bed, board, drugs, and sex. Communes can select their members and impose some sort of vows upon them. And if the mortality rate of communes and the turnover of members seem rather high, only in the communes do the nonviolent themes of hippie culture retain some vigor.

They feature a persistent attempt to organize group life without overt leadership and with a minimum of sex-role differentiation. Yet rural life, because of the premium it places upon physical strength, tends to sharpen the division of labor by sex, especially if there are children around who require close watching. The women find themselves working in the kitchen, doing the sewing, and caring for the babies, while the men work in the fields, fix the fences, repair the barn, and make expeditions to the square world for canned goods, pot, and spare parts for cars. The urban communes, by contrast, find it easier to reduce, if not abolish, the sexual division of labor.

Leadership is repressed as sex was repressed by the Victorians, and just about as successfully. Commune dwellers avoid words like "directed," "requested," "ordered," as Victorians avoided "thigh" and "belly." Efforts are made to resist the crystallization of leadership, and when they are successful during the season when much hard and monotonous work is necessary, the result is often disastrous for the capacity of the commune to survive on its own. Tools are lost or broken through careless use. Weeding is not done. People disappear at harvest time. Luckily enough, there are checks from home or dividend checks, and people can go away to work for wages and return when they have accumulated enough to buy brown rice and beans for several months.

"Group marriage" also creates problems. Some girls are better looking than others, and prejudices against homeliness die hard among liberated men and even liberated women. There seems to be an irresistible tendency for the leading "nonleaders" to exercise a powerful attraction upon the more beautiful girls, a tendency that has also been observed in encounter and sensitivity training groups. Most communes have more men than women and hence some men are always left out. Luckily, commune life does not seem to raise the level of sexual desire among men. Communes frown on "playboy" types, and we know that the threshold of sexual frustration is determined more by the norms of the group than by any sort of biological urge. What seems to work best is some form of monogamy plus some ten to twenty percent adultery. In the commune one would speak less of "adultery" than of "experiences" or "switching." Some switching takes place without too much overt pain. In other cases the best way to describe what happens is to say that a top male is replaced in the affections of one of the best-looking females by another male, with the displaced male leaving for another commune or deciding it is time to go to work outside in the flatland for the wages that will replenish the cash pool. Another common way that resolves the shortage of women is for one or two girls to be on a "promiscuous kick." As long as they don't try to seduce the top males away from their women, their constant state of availability will receive gratitude and amused condescension.[1]

Successful farming or even gardening requires a good deal of repetitive and careful work. Urban types tend, after a while, to miss the excitement and variety, or even more the *privacy,* of city life. Indeed, the commune is different from the urban hippie community in that people in the commune are forced to interact and reach some form of harmony. In standard rural life a sharp division of labor, clear-cut lines of authority, and a stress on getting the work done reduce the areas of "problematic intimacy." But in the commune problematic intimacy is the rule rather than the exception. Some are helped by this atmosphere, some put off.

A common social form in the communes is the incestuous ex-

1. Commune dwellers would fiercely deny that they show amused condescension. New value conflicts lead to new areas of repression. Freudianism is not "in" within the commune.

tended family: an older man, with one or two women attached to him, will form the nucleus of the commune, paying the bills and dealing with the locals. Others who join the commune are content to act as his children, paying for nurturance by a subordination well camouflaged in the rhetoric of equality and liberty. Once in a while, during the "father's" absence, one of the "children" will be able to sleep with the "mother" and take the role of the "preferred son," sometimes even casting out the "father" from his dominant role. The girls can have similar Electra experiences. These are the crises that give psychological zest and opportunities for acting out fantasies not tolerated in the outside world.

Communes may allow for greater role shifts in their members than do most other forms of small group organization. A personality in search of its identity and strong enough to face the demands of others may find in the commune greater support for the changes he is going through than he can find in his own parents. Communes that are successful in limiting the contacts of their members with the outside world can develop private cultures that are very demanding and also sometimes rather deviant. These, however, are rare. Lack of discipline is so much more frequent that it reduces the capacity of the commune to test systematically new forms of social relations. The mystery, the rich fantasies that surround communes, from the Satanic with Manson, to the humorous like the Hog Farm, will ensure a steady supply of mass-media interest. *Time-Life* waxes sentimental over communes.

The urban-based Hare Krishna, which has an involved set of rules and real discipline, is limited in its impact by its conservatism in regard to sex roles and its Hinduist spiritual and vestimentary transvestism. Since communes have the same appeal for people with sexual hangups as nudist camps used to have—and with the same sedative effects—the Hare Krishna also suffer the public-relations consequence of their apparent sexual frugality.

Many communes, even those made up of dropouts from Ivy League and New York universities, attempt a pathetic imitation of Indian life: a search of roots for the rootless; an identification with those too powerless to be guilty; a putdown of the WASP majority for having chased the Red Man from his God-given territory.

Still, the communes represent the *hubris* of the Puritan tradition, the attempt of men and women who feel moved by the spirit to create a perfect community, where the person can meet God face to face and be as unique, as true, as giving as God must be: Promethean arrogance that is the dignity and the curse of our Judeo-Puritan civilization, and that will always deserve our respect and our hope that one day we can make it work. The communes remind us that no man is free not to search for God and that in this search resides his honor even if in the end he meets but his fallible self.

I I

The second major cultural stream picked up and amplified by the hippie movement is the drug culture. Before the late fifties, marijuana smoking was limited to blacks, Puerto Ricans, and Mexicans, and among whites to jazz musicians who had picked it up from black colleagues. In the Eastern colleges, only the few students who were real jazz aficionados might have had some casual contact with marijuana. The radical movement, in its Communist, Trotskyite, or other varieties, was dead set against all drugs.

In the mid-fifties a new phenomenon began: the widespread use of drugs in the treatment of mental disorders. For those not so sick, Miltown became a fashionable remedy against anxiety and tension. In many executive families, where anxiety, hypochondria, and nonconformity describe the social climate, taking tranquilizers became a fashionable exhibit of how many of the world's troubles one had to carry.

The children of these families went to college and there met with at least two currents that would help their conversion to drugs. The first was the poetry-reading fad, often against a background of jazz music, with its heroes the beat poets, Allen Ginsberg, Gregory Corso, Lawrence Ferlinghetti, Gary Snyder, Kenneth Rexroth, and Father Antoninus, who gave recitals in colleges followed by late-hour gatherings where the "in" crowd would "turn on."

The second current was the civil rights movement, whose undeniable greatness was marred by the transformation of the Negroes into angels with black faces: a form of *ouvrièrisme,* probably inevitable, which led some to imitate the objects of compassion in their speech, their ghetto separation, their music, and even their "vices." Since blacks smoked marijuana it had to be a good thing. Heroin addiction, instead of being horrible, became a sort of secret cult—dangerous, of course, but also a curse of greatness that revealed to the initiates how many jazz musicians were addicted to it.

At the same time, one of the barriers to the diffusion of drugs, the frat culture of football games and beer busts, began to disintegrate. A new elite appeared on Eastern and California campuses; instead of claiming upper-class and old-settler connection, it claimed legitimacy on the basis of political awareness and intellectual activism. Its name-dropping related more to the *New York Review of Books* than to the Social Register. The smoking of marijuana became one of its rituals of solidarity, just as the heavy drinking of alcoholic beverages had been the ritual of the frats. Many professors who looked with disdain on the frats looked with approval, if not fondness, on the new student leaders. Whatever their antics, political or recreational, these students supported values in tune with high culture even if the search for the "golden screw" did not allow them to turn in papers on time. Although they might come from prestigious private schools and have rich parents, they did not snub their professors. Many even wanted to join the profession. The period 1957–66 saw the height of the post-Sputnik meritocratic campus, where professors attempted to impose upon adolescents from all social classes the ideals of the intellectual jock.

By 1963–64, however, the ideals of the contrameritocracy—affirming the right, nay, the superiority, of dropping out, and the claim that drugs gave access to a knowledge superior to rational knowledge —became part of the hippie "backlash," which gave the diffusion of marijuana, soon followed by other drugs, a new impulse and legitimacy. By 1964 the whole college scene (that is, the two hundred most selective establishments) was permeated with marijuana, and by 1965 LSD became widely available. In 1967 drugs had begun to infiltrate the high schools. In 1970 a questionnaire, distributed in two middle-class high schools located in the suburbs of a large Midwestern metropolis, showed that only one-third of the students had never taken any drugs, one-third had had only an occasional experience with them, and one-third took drugs (overwhelmingly marijuana or hashish) once a week or more. A tenth of the student body could be called "serious" users. Heroin users (not necessarily addicts) were rare, but 1 percent in a student body of fifteen hundred still makes fifteen users.

The drug culture gets its organization from "dealers," who in turn secure their supplies from wholesalers. The dealer is a semibenevolent merchant who barely makes expenses *over the long run,* wholesalers being the real money-makers. The small-time dealers turn on frequently with their customers. Although sales promotion is not unknown, the dealer prefers to think of himself as servicing a need rather than creating it. Gifts to customers are not uncommon. The small-time dealer becomes a "taste leader" to his clients and this leadership is not necessarily limited to drugs. Clients and dealers meet in an "underground" atmosphere that seems exciting. For many personalities at loose ends the drugs provide a motivational center, a substitute identity, and an occasion to relate meaningfully to others, even if in the process they may kill a certain percentage of those who use them.

Drugs are used, of course, by members of other cultures, such as the communes, the music culture, and the political culture. And with time drugs have lost much of the mystical aura with which the hippie movement had surrounded them. But, especially among some teenagers, drugs have become an end in themselves, a subject of interminable conversations, part tranquilizer, part escape, part dare, a form of Russian roulette with which the middle-class adolescent can demonstrate to himself that he has "heart" without having to engage in the gang bangs dear to the "grease." It is a juvenile delinquency with low risks, where prosecution does not alienate you from your peers; a means of self-assertion and rebellion, yet a way of imitating older adolescents in the search for maturity. As such, it is already spreading to the junior high schools. The drug culture has its own scale of prestige, where the bottom rung belongs to the marijuana experimenter and the top rung to the users of the needle, who inject methedrine, seconal, or heroin.

Drugs were publicized heavily by the underground press until 1968. Youth movies such as *Easy Rider* and *Getting Straight* (there is a lame attempt in *Getting Straight* to oppose the heavy use of drugs by showing the "head" to be unreliable), and the rock songs have glamorized marijuana and LSD.[2] At the present time the irony of drug education programs (they are one way of employing excess language teachers) is that they finish the publicity job that the rock songs and the movies have begun.

Drugs serve an anti-establishment function through the promise of unconditional pleasure (pleasure without having to "earn" the right to it), and through their relation to an antirationality where good or bad astrological "vibes" replace the belief that hard work, learning, and persistence will get you where you want to go. They promote dropping out of structures that require postponement of gratification (college). Through instant nirvana they lure some of the young away from the Puritan establishment culture. Drugs also have an anti-establishment function through the dissonance of illegality. During Prohibition alcohol rarely had this effect, if only because it was part of a traditional male culture resonant with the aggressive toughness of the Puritan ethos and therefore lacking, even in illegality, the tone of subversion. And it had no access to the mass media except as a monster crushed by an establishment that displayed the confidence and self-righteousness of a Saint George.

To evaluate the future of drug consumption in the United States one might look at the problems of the legalization of marijuana. The proponents of legalization find themselves caught in several cross-pressures. It is difficult to press for restrictions on tobacco and pollution while advocating the legalization of a hallucinogen about whose long-range effects little is known. One cannot press for limits to fertilizers, pesticides, and cyclamates, and wish to generalize the unsupervised use of a drug that has a powerful and little-understood impact upon the brain.

Another cross-pressure is that the use of marijuana *does* lead very frequently to further experimentation with other drugs. (A colleague of mine doing research on marijuana effects and using medical students as his subject population noted that it was hard to find cases where marijuana smoking had not been followed by more or less

2. The retort by record companies that most listeners cannot tell the meaning of the words and care only about the music neglects the fact that those who understand the words operate as translators. This is certainly one case where the medium is the message.

broad experimentation with other drugs, so that it became difficult to distinguish between the effects of marijuana smoking and those of other drugs.) Although the great bulk of drug experimenters settle down eventually to a "martini-type" consumption of marijuana or hashish, a certain percentage are sucked into a process of hard-drug addiction, which may last for years before death or remission occurs. Thirty years ago, seventeen-year-old alcoholics were practically unknown. Today middle-class drug addicts on pills or heroin or plain "potheads" are not uncommon, and the group most affected are the children who participate in the antiestablishment culture centering around swingy teachers. Many a potential candidate for an Ivy League college has turned on as a high school junior and found in his senior year his grades slipping to the point where even graduation is in danger.

One frequently hears in liberal circles that dabble in depth psychology that "if it had not been marijuana or barbiturates it would have been something else." This sort of fatalism, based on no data whatsoever, is not very convincing. It comes from the same ideological outlook that sees in the concept of "bad company" an authoritarian or segregationist prejudice, and ignores the insight it contains. The fact is, there are times when in the necessary process of emotional disengagement from parents adolescents do become very vulnerable to outside influences, even if their upbringing has given them "good" principles. In most cases there will be a return to these principles, but the experiences that the adolescent may in the process go through can sear his mind and body for life.[3]

Those whose interest in the legalization of marijuana comes mainly from an antagonism to the Puritan ethos must accept the fact that the illegality of drugs reinforces their antiestablishment significance.

3. In many suburbs, therapeutic youth centers have sprung up with batteries of phones available to give help to anxious youths whose problems range from boredom to "bad trips" to a need for an abortion. Such centers, heavily steeped in the counterculture, are often directed by a swingy psychologist or psychiatrist aided by mother types out of *Alice's Restaurant*. The bulk of the aid they give is precisely the chance to find a congenial group with a new form of self-righteousness which abates the adolescent's guilt. Here it is not a question of learning to dream in a Freudian manner so as to please the "shrink," but becoming innocent through a putdown of the establishment. It probably does help the youth in getting himself "together."

The legalization of marijuana would destroy the social influence of the benevolent dealer, as well as the dissonance of illegality which tends to promote allegiance to the counterculture. Legalization might also accentuate the pacifier aspect of drug intake and facilitate the co-opting of the drug users into the system. This seems to have been one of the major functions of drugs in relation to the lower strata of India, China, the Arab countries, and the South American Indians.

Yet the legalization of marijuana, like the legalization of pornography (already accomplished *sub rosa* by the courts), could have a strong impact as a symbol of the weakening of the Puritan ethos. But if the Puritan ethos were not mortally wounded in the process, the violent attacks upon it could lead to a fundamentalist reassertion that might crush liberalizing movements and lead to drastic changes in the personnel that man the gates of the mass media.

Under these conditions the pros and cons of the legalization of marijuana are complex and there is not likely to be a major push in that direction, certainly not while Mr. Nixon is in the White House. Heavy drug use will probably lose its fad as it reaches the junior high schools, where it can be controlled more effectively by parents. One frequently meets college freshmen who have already been "heavy" into the drug scene and are ready to leave it, now that drug use is becoming identified with the "freak" part of high school culture, rather than with college sophistication.

Marijuana and hashish will probably remain illegal as prostitution is illegal. Drug use of a heavy and prolonged nature will be the tranquilizer of the stagnant and the defeated, the Novocaine of downward mobility. For some middle-class adults who follow the *New York Times Magazine* section in asserting the chicness of marijuana smoking,[4] it will become the equivalent of bathtub gin in the 1920s. For others it may become a middle-class equivalent of what the gin shop in Zola's *L'Assommoir* was to the working class.

III

Now to the third and most creative cultural form in the hippie movement—the music culture. Reaching its apex in the Woodstock festival,

4. Cf. Sam Blum, "Marijuana Clouds the Generation Gap," *New York Times Magazine,* August 23, 1970.

it derives its organization from the musicians, the promoters, the disk jockeys, and the record industry.

This movement finds its roots in several strands of American popular music. There is the folk-singing strand which had remained an antiquarian interest until it began its slow climb to popularity under the aegis of the Popular Front. Folk singing expressed the wisdom of the American folk and as such deserved the support of the progressive. This was the period when the movement took to square dancing and Pete Seeger was a major troubadour. It continued during the war in Café Society Downtown and Uptown and eventually developed its own momentum in the 1950s to culminate in the TV *Hootenanny* (with a little assist from Tennessee Ernie Ford's "Sixteen Tons"). Joan Baez with her voice, Bob Dylan with his poetical talent, were to give a new dimension to folk singing in the first half of the 1960s.

Other strands of the music culture were the rock 'n' roll of black popular music and the blues, the latter being one of the great contributions made by the blacks to American and world culture. A synthesis between the two at the end of the 1950s and the beginning of the sixties gave us the particular Detroit sound known as "Motown." Meanwhile Elvis Presley had made a national fad out of his particular fusion of "mountain" music and rock, getting white audiences to accept a much more orgiastic and openly sexual message within the medium.

It is the Beatles who created the new music by synthesizing the rock of Elvis Presley with Motown sound. They brought to the States their "rocker" or young British working-class style, and it caught fire immediately. One might have expected the hippies to look down their noses at the Beatles and return to the records of Ornette Coleman and Leadbelly; but they did not. On the contrary, the Beatles and the Rolling Stones became new culture heroes. Hippie musicians, combining rock, blues, and English sound (the Yard Birds, the Cream) and using Dylan-type lyrics, gave young America a music all its own, relegating jazz to the paternal generation. It was partially on the wings of the music created and played by John Mayall, Paul Butterfield, Mike Bloomfield, the Fugs, the Jefferson Airplane, the Grateful Dead, Jimi Hendrix, Canned Heat, and many others that the hippie movement became a mass movement, only to explode under the strains of its success, leaving the music culture to develop on its own. The musicians are also close to the drug culture, which they have popularized by their songs and example. Rock musicians (AM rock in working-class districts, FM rock in middle-class districts) have become in the high schools an alternative to the athlete as nonacademic and even anti-academic models.

There is little doubt that the youth who become either players, band followers, or aficionados of the rock culture have a strong antimeritocratic bias. Yet even for them the requirements of professionalization conflict with the cult of spontaneity. Long practice is necessary if one is to obtain proficiency. There is much competition in the music field and the rewards for excellence are enormous, both in prestige and money. The discipline of playing, the organization of the show that accompanies the playing stimulate self-control and self-distance. Drugs on the other hand are a constant temptation for an ego that is put on the block at each performance. But the instability of rock musicians, whether due to their personality types, drugs, life on the road, or the temporary allegiance to music as a career, makes such groups transitory and the quality of their music hard to sustain. Because of their talent, their unusual stability as a group, and the widespread belief that financial success had not spoiled them, the Beatles were the role models. But, now that they have disbanded there seems to be a certain exhaustion of inspiration throughout the rock movement.

Rock music has become a transmission belt for antiestablishment views, through both the lyrics and the orgiastic color of the music. It has contributed to the isolation of youth culture from adult culture by creating a much sharper break between big-band music and rock than there was between ragtime and big-band songs—a process symbolized by the end of the *Hit Parade* program in the late 1950s.

The music culture does not lead per se to political commitment. Musicians tend to be "situationists," prompt to underline and act out the absurd. They find political rhetoric boring, and at the rock festivals the mood seems hardly conducive to radicalization. How much lasting alienation from the Puritan ethos the music creates is a moot point. It may promote a commitment to the "counter culture" through the prestige it gives to deviant life. It also has an impact in promoting the counterculture among a segment of working-class white youth who enjoy the *commercium* and occasional sexual opportunities that rock will give them with college youth.

Drugs and music have made a much bigger impact on youth society than has the "dropout" message of the hippie movement. Yet dropping-out can take place, even while a youth is serving time in high school or college, simply by the withdrawal of motivation from occupational and family roles. For most, the moratorium is temporary; for some, even beneficial.

IV

Perhaps both the drug and music cultures would have developed without the hippie phenomenon. The connection with the latter's love-and-freedom ethos gave the "practitioners" a feeling of group membership and self-righteousness, which greatly increased their proselytizing capacity. The same can be said about the political culture, which was born separately from the hippie movement and eventually merged into it without losing its identity—just as the communal movement, the drug and music cultures have done.

It was probably the collapse of the Communist party as a political force after the 1956 Hungarian uprising that provided an opportunity for the development of a more tenderhearted and expressive oppositional movement, free of the bureaucratic discipline and "rule or ruin" tactics characteristic of Bolshevik politics. This was the New Left. It received considerable momentum from the Free Speech Movement at Berkeley (1964), where it first discovered the vulnerability of the university to political protest.

Three social forces were to give unexpected impetus to the New Left. The first was the development of the "technico-professional complex" as a political tendency led by left-wing academics. The civil rights battles were their first experience with mass politics, after which came the peace movement as it found its real start on the campus in the 1965 teach-in organized at the University of Michigan.

The second force was the cooperation of the mass media, especially the TV networks and the national news magazines (*Time, Life, Look, Newsweek*), which saw in these movements not only a source of dramatic news happenings but also of an ideology commonly shared by cameramen, reporters, news commentators, and even the vice-presidents in charge of editing the six-thirty news show. The mass media and especially TV will give favorable exposure to the New Left, but with this proviso: it must fit the interests of the technico-professional complex of which they are a part. Their coverage of the Vietnam war in 1967–68 was an extraordinary boost to the peace movement and yet remained "invisible" in its political intent.[5] "The Breaking of the President 1968" was also a major success, although of course they had a major assist from their victim.

The third force was the hippyization of the New Left. From the hippies the New Left took its life style, clothing, hair, language, sex life; and from 1967 onward many hippies renounced nonviolence and political indifference. This hippyization of the New Left enabled it to attract the drug and music fans, giving them a political identity of sorts as well as feelings of solidarity. For nonpolitical but disaffected youth, the musicians legitimated the hippie garb. Though it would create difficulties with the world of square adults, the fact that the mass media customarily saw the hippified youth as the exemplars of the new style and the new rebellion also helped bring together the hippies and the New Left. For, when the mass media speak of "youth" or "the students," they certainly don't mean the average youth with short hair, a vocational orientation toward college, good relations with his parents, coolness toward drugs and promiscuous sex, and a political outlook slightly to the left of Hubert Humphrey. No Stalinist front has ever been so successful in endowing the young with its distinctive aura as has the coalition of New Left, hippies, and the mass media, operating without any formal committees, secret accomplices, or central apparatus.

V

From this coalition two major currents have emerged as the standard-bearers of the counterculture. The first is the literary-sociological assault on the Puritan ethos and the WASP establishment; the second, the Che Guevara type of political activism, where the effectiveness of the action is subordinated to the exaltation of the participants.

5. Richard W. Jencks, head of the CBS broadcast group, declared in a recent conference on the problems of broadcasting, where he was being attacked from the Left ("T.V. Neglects Social Needs"): "History will assign television a major role in the black revolution and in the anti-Vietnam war revolution."

The literary-sociological assault has been carried out by a group essentially marginal to the academy, but which desires to keep the aura of the academic commitment to scientific truth. Yet it cannot accept the uncertainty of scientific truth, its perpetual renewal, its rejection of the temptation of power. This group, which might be called the "intellectuoids," searches for a theology in science, a fighting faith which will help to destroy the Country Club set, the Yacht Club set, the Deanery, the professorial establishment, West Palm Beach, the military-industrial complex, and install in their place a brotherhood of freedom. Inevitably many of these "intellectuoids" are young instructors and assistant professors who in their professional fields are ready to accept the burdens of uncertainty but revert to self-serving ideologies when it comes to social issues. It is probably too much to ask that they should approach social science in an intellectual fashion when many of their own peers in sociology, psychology, and political science seem to have transformed their disciplines into a sort of muckraking journalism where the basic "theoretical" orientation is a new version of *delenda est Carthago* or Voltaire's *Écrasons l'infâme*. Too often when opening *Trans-action* and even *Psychology Today* one can predict the argument of the article from a mere knowledge of the title, at least if one follows the principle that the WASP establishment and the Silent Majority are oppressive, dehumanizing, pig-dominated, exploitative, polluting, inefficient, sexist, afraid of sex, racist, authoritarian, rigid, frigid, fearful, paranoid, white-collar criminals, desperate, sick, sadistic, infantile, and ignorant.

Besides *Trans-action* and the *New York Review of Books,* the intellectual ammunition of the counterculture on campus is provided by the radical paperbacks dealing with street violence, racism, and the Third World. Marcuse, Fanon, Kenneth Keniston[6] (who sees in the student radicals a breed of moral supermen as, more realistically, Richard Flacks sees in them the new Social Register), Jerry Rubin's and Abbie Hoffman's nonbooks, Roszak's *Counter-Culture,* and Charles Reich's *Greening of America* are typical resources of the radical faculty. They have organized courses titled "Where It's At"

6. Keniston seems to be having some second thoughts as he discovers the self-serving aspects of moral righteousness in the student radical. Some of the writers used by the counterculture, like Paul Goodman, can become quite distressed by their fans.

and "The Revolution of the Sixties," the prototype of which was Harvard's full-year course Social Relations 148–149, taught to some six hundred students rewarded by easy A's. Part of this counterculture is seeping down to the high schools and private schools, where, in conjunction with the drug and music culture, it contributes to the development of the "freak" grouping, somewhere between the "frats" and the "grease."

The literary-sociological assault has "radicalized" the culture of proper bohemia, the latter being constituted of the young college instructors, the civil liberties lawyers, the Unitarian militants, the Quaker work camps, the mass media specialists (especially those below the $40,000 level), the publishing-house readers and editors, movie directors, actors and actresses between jobs, and other professionals and paraprofessionals who gravitate around the university. A few rich businessmen contribute heavily to the financing of the local underground press and often own the FM stations that provide them with tax write-offs and their younger friends with job opportunities.

The counterculture takes from the upper class its casualness about rules, as also its willingness to use four-letter words that show it to be above middle-class constraints. Most exponents of the counterculture are of petit bourgeois origin, and most petit bourgeois, not having been raised in bourgeois manners, try to bypass them. They imitate the aristocracy's disregard for proper form, believing that they thereby partake in its elegance. They assume the permissiveness of the upper class but not its *noblesse oblige*.

The hippies have provided a pattern of dress which, interpreted by the jet-set boutiques, becomes a badge of being "with it" and a challenge to the status of the traditional Puritan elites. The doctrine of "crystallized establishment violence" has facilitated the transition from the pacifism of the civil rights movement to the legitimation of the violence perpetrated (way downtown) against the establishment and its Irish cops. The worship of the Black Panthers whereby proper bohemia atones its guilt—sometimes intellectual guilt, sometimes a disguise for ethical vanity, sometimes guilt as to the sources of the parental fortunes—has become another badge of membership and a gambit for claiming moral superiority over the conservative old rich.

In the 1930s "proper bohemia," besides being much smaller was influenced by the Stalinist version of Marxism and held real power in some publishing houses.[7] At the present time the ideological tenets are more of the hippie variety. Not that hippies invented them (the sophisticates will refer to young Marx and Wilhelm Reich), but they provided the symbolic rejuvenation for some of the old utopian standbys: arts-and-crafts communism, elegant pastoralism, the poor as noble savages (more specifically the black and Indian poor, certainly not the Polish poor). The hippie cultivation of mood has become the emotionalism of sensitivity training; hippie work avoidance, the put down of manual labor; and hippie stress on the equality of the sexes, the promotion of career aggressiveness in women and of sensualism in men. While the Puritan ethos implied a commitment to abstract values and a suspicion of ascriptive group ties and unearned pleasure, the counterculture promotes a sort of organic groupism in battle against the enemy camp and an existential concern with body pleasures from which active sports are usually excluded. It was used as a weapon of class struggle against the conservative WASP elite.

VI

The meaning of the counterculture is not exhausted by referring to its obvious protection against the pains of possible failure and especially to the way it provides an apparent connection to the fountainhead of wisdom without having to go through the hard work, the patience, the ambiguities and failures of scientific research. This is the contrameritocratic aspect, but not the only one. For there are other aspects which might turn out to be effective solutions to major problems of the postindustrial world: the development of an international community of the young; a blurring of the lines between work and play; a considerable decline in status formalism; a greater equality for women.

All over the world, even in Soviet Russia, there seems to be an erosion of classical patriotism. By contributing to this erosion the counterculture orients the search for the sacred toward an international community of students. On the other hand, the critique of nationalism

7. For a good description of this milieu, see Mary McCarthy's *The Company She Keeps* (New York: Harcourt, Brace, 1942).

too often takes on a shrill quality that denies any obligation of the citizen to the nation. Instead of replacing nationalism by a thoughtful dedication to an entity beyond the nation that requires even more self-sacrifice, there is a tendency toward a premoral affirmation of the primacy of self-interest. The counterculture hatred for the nation is parochial, often too bitter to be the result of a greater love.

Similarly, the counterculture seems to be trying to create the elements whereby the traditional division between work and play can be overcome by a new synthesis. What seems to be wanted is an end to the guilt that attends some of the processes necessary to creative work: the careless as well as the careful experimentation, the trials and errors, the sloth of discovery and the failure to discover anything, the painful fact that most innovations are useless. If we are to solve the problem of work meaninglessness (and I am aware that there is a lot of romantic drivel being peddled under that expression), it is likely that a definition of work less associated with the routine deprivations of discipline must become more generally accepted. Professors know this problem well who feel guilty when they have an enjoyable conversation with their colleagues, a conversation that often leaves a sediment of new ideas, while their superego associates work with the careful reading of Talcott Parsons or the preparation of a lecture which leaves little room for response to the audience. It is possible the current revival of Rousseau's ideas on education may have a positive impact on teaching, although so far the impact of the counterculture upon teaching has been mainly to demoralize professors and to promote camouflaged ways of goofing off.

A greater rate of discovery and change, even if limited to the expressive spheres of life, will demand a greater solidarity, a willingness to put up with the higher rate of obsolescence and disorder that creativity implies. Thus the counterculture's stress upon the legitimacy of ephemeral art, the poetry of mood, the immediate sensitivity and positive response to others, may just possibly create conditions for a solution to the problem of work, play, and rank in the postindustrial world.

Meanwhile, its search for intimacy often seems like a Hollywood version of the shoe salesman's pseudo-*Gemeinschaft,* a ploy for Portnoy on the make. It mocks work discipline and suspects the poor of "Uncle Tomism" if they take "blind-alley jobs." Since most of its adherents work in bureaucratic organizations where they do not own the means of teaching or administration, contempt for private property may seem to have a revolutionary meaning: the property is that of the pig landlord, the pig stockholders, the pig establishmentarian government. It seeps down to the youth society as indulgence for "ripping off." Solid bases for comparison are lacking, hence we cannot be sure that there is really more stealing in the stores than forty or fifty years ago, or much more cheating in school. On a short-run basis, we all know that cheating and thievery on campuses have reached epidemic proportions. Some of it may be due to the changing composition of the student body; some to a redefinition of stealing by middle-class students as a matter of taste.

The decline in status formalism may facilitate social mobility and reduce the costs of marginality. Yet the intolerance that the straight upper middle class reserves for bad manners is more than matched by the intolerance the counterculture shows to those who disagree with its views. In many localities it has created a level of political contentiousness that did not exist before it gained a substantial following.

One might hope that the positive advantages of destruction and reconstruction created by the counterculture will be gained without disorder and reaction. But this hope seems unrealistic. New solutions for tomorrow may come from a few of the communes, but so far the intellectual caliber of the blueprints for tomorrow proposed by the literary-sociological assault has been disappointingly low. Again the medium has been the message.

The weakness of the counterculture analysis, once it tries to go beyond the exaltation of mood and personal freedom, is partly reflected by the weakness of the political movement it sustains, and which I here describe as the Che Guevara movement. This movement contains the political spectrum that made up the non-Bolshevik section of SDS of 1968–69, and groups like the Rainbow People's party, whose leader John Sinclair was one of the original Midwest hippies and a good jazz critic. The core of the Guevara movement is made up of the more romantic and antibureaucratic revolutionaries, who remind one of the Russian Narodniks (Populists) of the 1860–70s, except that our Narodniks have little desire to convert the white working class and peasantry, and are not often welcomed by the blacks. They meet their best response in the swinging and proper bohemians of the middle class, and of course among the college students and/or middle-class dropouts from either high school or college. The Weathermen might well take for their hero Nechaev, who wrote with Bakunin the famous *Revolutionary Catechism* (1869). They have seized the imagination of the revolutionary students by their undeniable courage and flamboyant actions, as well as their luck in avoiding arrest. It will be a while before the police effectively penetrate the organization and corrupt it—which seems to be the fate of all underground movements unable to come quickly above ground and relate directly to the political public.

While the original hippie movement had many aspects of radical Puritanism, this tendency is now found mostly in the rural commune; the Che Guevara tendency is much more overtly anti-Puritan. In contrast with the ascetic patterns of the Bolsheviks, the strength of the American Narodniks resides in their capacity to combine the delights of moral righteousness with the underwriting of sensual release through drugs, sex, music, vandalism, "ripping off," and violence. They have developed a style of leadership that permits their roving bands or campus-based groups to have the benefit of direction without the penalty of felt subordination. To middle-class youth this seems to have more appeal than the authoritarian "delegate from the Central Committee" typical of the Bolshevik tradition.

The Guevara movement has had some success (though more apparent than real) because it was carried along for a time by the peace movement created by professors of the elite colleges and universities. Within that movement—which, for instance, in the mainstream campuses of the University of Michigan, Oakland University, Michigan State University, and Wayne State University receives the support of 70 percent of the liberal arts students[8]—the Che Guevarists were like fish in water. As a result, until 1969–70 the revolutionary activists benefited not only from the support of proper bohemia, but from the indulgence of some antiwar professors and the favorable publicity of the mass media, which played down their provocations but gave maximum publicity to police excesses in

8. These are the results of a poll of 1,200 students in the above-mentioned universities in May–June 1970.

repression. The Guevarists (and the Bolsheviks) thus used the peace movement as a cover and a resonance box, and in return provided an energy and drama that academics could not supply. They also benefited from the inexperience of college administrators and police in coping with the type of disorder created by a group which amounts at most to 1.5 percent of the student body in the Michigan universities, and probably to no more than 3–4 percent of the Ivy League undergraduates.[9]

On the basis of this diagnosis, two scenarios can be constructed. The first rests on the hypothesis that the academic community, no longer influenced by the counterculture, will not attempt to increase its own political power. In that case the liberal-Left faculty would let the peace movement die on the vine and not allow the Guevarists to use the university as a sanctuary. Thus the faculty would take toward the student movement the stance it had toward the jock and fraternity cultures which provided much of the contrameritocratic ideology before 1960. Through an interval in the student movement, an irresistible momentum of social assimilation would be imparted to the ethnic and racial minorities that provide its more determined militants. The 1970s would then see a period of university and social adjustments to the strains of the meritocracy, from which a new creative surge could take place at the end of the decade. The counterculture would be pre-empted of its useful elements and the rest would be encapsulated, so as to provide a permanent justification for those rewards in capitalist-bureaucratic society that do not seem commensurate with their ambitions. And this, paradoxically, would contribute to the long-range stability and productivity of the meritocracy.

Another scenario requires at least two postulates: First, that the faculty—partly because of the threat of downward mobility implicit in the "high-schoolization" of college, partly because of the charisma of science of which it is the depositor, partly because it is the most articulate segment of the technico-professional class—would try to develop the peace movement into a political battering ram, using masses of students and new voters as its army. Second, that the freak

9. Figures derived from the Michigan survey mentioned above. There is a higher percentage of revolutionaries at the University of Michigan than at the three other universities.

culture would take over the grease, that is, the counterculture would reach the white working-class youth.[10]

The politicization of the colleges and universities would lead to the growth of influence of proper bohemia over the "straight" faculty. The disaffection of the intelligentsia and the near-monopoly of the mass media held by groups hostile to the WASP establishment would result in widespread alienation of a youth for whom meritocracy would cease to have much meaning. Both the debunking by faculty and the inability of the system to provide every college graduate with an executive-type job would play a part here. The result would be that economic and military institutions could not be staffed with adequate talent. The WASP establishment, bereft of the symbols of legitimacy, as well as of intellectual advice and support, would lose its nerve and its capacity for social control. The United States would then enter a phase of disorganization, with lesser growth in industrial productivity leading to relative deprivation among the working class. From there one can choose his climax: Berlin 1930 with a fundamentalist reaction, or St. Petersburg October 1917 with the assumption of power by a theocracy of politicized intellectuoids, which would bring back order and the comforts of a sacred orthodoxy. Of course, it is also possible that such a disequilibrium of the capitalist order in America might lead to atomic war.

Somehow, the pessimistic scenario does not seem convincing. The effectiveness of the literary-sociological assault upon traditional American values is hard to evaluate and perhaps easy to overestimate. The mass media have a way of banalizing and sterilizing new cultural forms by giving them instant success. A movement in the United States soon becomes a fad, overwhelmed by the problems of success before it has had time to deepen its insights. Were this Czarist Russia, the disaffection of the gatekeepers to the mass media (if not of the intellectuals) might herald revolution. But this is multicentered America, and the success of the literary-sociological assault in the mass media might testify to its eventual innocuousness.

10. This is the aim of the coffeeshops that have sprung up around Army bases. The penetration of the drug culture into the Army is also a wedge, but Vietnam veterans seem to have sources of supply that do not interact with the student dealer organizations. So far, the assumption of freak styles has not correlated with politicization to the Left.

Most of history is dull rather than dramatic, and the 1970s seem more likely to result in the stabilization of a contrameritocratic movement, which would blunt the cutting edges of meritocratic competition. Furthermore, the professional intellectuals have begun a criticism of the counterculture, which should soon result in a decline of its prestige with the mass media.

The professional intellectual has a crucial role to play in the solution of the problems created by the meritocracy, if he can find a way to show society that the goal of man is the understanding of Nature, and that one can "find God in the anatomy of the louse." In this contemplation the search for the sacred finds a solution in which the problems of ranking, so emphasized by the meritocracy, are shriveled by the *cosmic* perspective of learning. The passion to know can then replace the passion to conquer.

Erazim V. Kohák

Being Young in a Postindustrial Society

Whatever is happening on campus, it is not a revolution in any recognizable sense. A revolution must have an independent socioeconomic base, and the "youth revolution" conspicuously lacks that. Its proponents do not constitute a class, definable in terms of a specific mode of production and capable of offering an alternative mode of meeting men's physical and social needs. Nor do the young have a set of structural proposals that they could put into effect if they were to seize power—or, for that matter, an organization capable of seizing it. The campus upheavals have created a violent, destructive fringe, but the campus mood as a whole is not that. It is a mood of concern and acute alienation, and the upheaval in which it results, while capable of affecting national policy and causing temporary disruption of academic processes, can be represented as a "revolution" only rhetorically, either to justify or provoke repressive measures. For purposes of social analysis it might be more accurate to describe it as a sort of *mutiny*—a bewildered, explosive refusal to continue functioning within a system that has become increasingly alien and alienating.

For this reason, social conditions that shaped the campus upheavals might well prove more significant than the immediate causes sparking this or that explosion. Those causes are real, urgent—and familiar enough. American foreign and domestic policies are passing through a fundamental crisis. It is not simply a matter of specific setbacks like the Bay of Pigs fiasco or the bloody stalemate in Vietnam, or the discovery of poverty and discrimination at home. Rather, basic conceptions which have guided American public policy since the thirties have proved inadequate in the complex world of the sixties. As at the time of the analogous failure of isolationism and *laissez faire* in the early thirties, America is re-examining its basic commitment, foreign and domestic, and the young serve as the leading edge of frustration.

But, while there are clear parallels between the failure of isolationism and *laissez faire* in the thirties and the present failure of anti-Communism and Keynesianism, there are basic differences as well, and these need to be explained in terms of changing conditions rather than recurrent causes. Perhaps the most significant difference is that while in the thirties the revolting young were very much part of a wide upsurge in the whole society, today they are strangely isolated in a world of their own. In the thirties, the "people" of campus rhetoric had a definite empirical counterpart—union workers, dust-bowl farmers, depressed urban middle class. Today, "the people" is largely a mystified concept. The empirical people are to a large extent middle America—as a revolutionary mass they exist primarily in campus imagination.

The impact of campus mutiny on national policy has been significant, but largely indirect. With a few exceptions like the "front-lash" project, the overt content of the youth revolt has tended to create an isolated subculture of youthful imagination rather than significant alternatives for the public world. Not the fact but the form of the youth revolt raises a question about conditions rather than causes—the place of the young in a postindustrial society.

II

What precisely is the youth "revolution"? A great part of the confusion may be due to the fact that it isn't anything precisely. It is an amorphous, discontinuous series of outbursts, which attach themselves to anything from fads in dress and music to radical activism. Their common denominator is distress rather than demand, loneliness rather than confidence.

The positive traits of campus upheaval are common to youth movements of all ages. Any youth movement must stress the special problems and assets of the young—their lack of a firm place in society, their spontaneity, enthusiasm, and idealism. It must degrade those qualities the young do not ordinarily possess, such as skill, persistence, competence; and avoid problems the young normally do not face, such as assuring daily sustenance, public safety, or long-range planning. Youth movements invariably tinge their idealism with a sense of bitter disillusion: brought up on the ideals of their society, the young tend to be shocked by its realities, whether capitalist, Communist, or socialist. The young share a common sense of being in the society but not of it, thereby reflecting quite accurately their relation to the economy. And, for entirely understandable reasons, the young have often shared a sense of mission to redeem their society with their spontaneity and dedication, coupled with a conviction that this cannot be done by humdrum means. Work is vain, dedication and drama alone avail.

In addition to the common traits of adolescence, present-day youth movements share a common perspective of posttechnological affluence. This is a bit more surprising. Even in America, the affluent society is at best twenty years old and remains a class phenomenon. The "affluent young" on state college campuses are, objectively, anything but affluent.

Yet affluence is a state of mind as much as a level of consumption. It reflects relative freedom from ordinary economic cares and preoccupations: in terms of the most elementary immediate experience, it is the mentality of the man who can ask himself, what shall I do today?—and does not receive an immediate, unequivocal answer in terms of daily need. In this sense, affluence can reflect, as in America and Western Europe, the condition of a society whose total productive capacity exceeds its total needs. But it can also reflect the added productive capacity represented by a team of horses in a village where the family cow pulls the plow by day and gives milk at night. In the "socialist" countries of Eastern Europe, comprehensive medical and social care, embracing everything from job security to free vacation tours, creates symptoms of affluence in spite of rather low standards of consumption. Finally, the isolation of the academic community from daily demands, required for academic work, may help to create a very distinctly affluent perspective.

The place of the young in a society that accepts the affluent model as normative is significantly different from that in a society of scarcity.

An affluent society provides for its young a far greater degree of autonomy from many pressing daily occupations, not only objectively but also because it expects far less from the young in terms of cooperation in securing food, shelter, and even an atmosphere of cooperation within the family unit. Unlike his counterpart in the 1820s, a romantic rebel today can "drop out" almost completely for extended periods of time while still enjoying much of the affluence, security, and mobility of an advanced society.

To be sure, there have always been young men who enjoyed this privilege, but in the past they have been relatively few. Being a revolutionary, if we are to trust Cohn-Bendit, is a great way to live; but it requires the time and leisure of a student, and in the past students have constituted a minuscule proportion of the young. Today, some 50 percent of young Americans go on to some form of higher training, only entering the labor force between eighteen and twenty-six. For some years after ceasing to be children they are effectively excluded from assuming adult social roles. The youth "revolution" today can be a mass phenomenon because there is a mass of the young that has the objective prerequisities for engaging in it.

The affluent society makes a youth "revolution" not only possible but virtually necessary. The reason is not simply the inevitable discrepancy between expectations of affluence and objective reality. Even when affluence is quite objective—or perhaps especially when that is the case—the place of the young in society becomes precarious. Given the high degree of skill demanded by modern production, the young have little opportunity for significant participation in the work of the society. They may be enthusiastic—but in economic terms they constitute seasonal unskilled labor. At the same time technological sophistication eliminates many of the marginal tasks that had traditionally provided a bridge between play and work, and where it does not, it makes them appear onerous and insignificant. At a time in life when a young person most acutely experiences the need for a socially significant role to establish his personal identity, a society patterned on the affluent model consigns him to the role of an object of indulgence. It is not surprising that the young seek to establish their distinct identity either by dropping out or by adopting the mock-heroic role of the rebel.

There would be something radically wrong if, for some ten years after ceasing to be children, the young continued to accept without protest the role of pampered children. But there is also something radically wrong with a social model which offers them this role.

III

These observations leave the question of fact unanswered but they do suggest an answer to the question of method. First of all, they establish the lesson of Karl Marx: there is a definite connection between technology and ideology, between the modes and means of production and the modes and means of social existence.

Economic dependence, however, is a necessary but not a sufficient explanatory principle. Analogous economic development is compatible with more than one form of social organization and behavior. A catalytic principle is needed to explain why particular forms emerge at a particular time and place. In part, to be sure, the reasons are historical—the economic prerequisites for a campus revolt existed in the fifties, but America's confidence in the ability of its leadership to cope with the problems of the time did much to prevent an explosion. Only with the loss of confidence—brought about by the failure of basic policies and signalized by the death of a President—did the inherent tensions actually erupt. But an ad hoc explanation deals with causes rather than conditions—for understanding conditions, a generic catalytic principle is needed.

Campus revolutionaries tend to find such a catalyst in the Sombartian principle of power struggle which Lenin singled out as the key to his interpretation of Marxism. Its appeal is understandable enough: struggle, especially the rather indefinite "revolutionary" struggle, is a form of activity that places a premium on the assets of youth. As an analytic tool, however, the Leninist emphasis, more familiar in the West as the "cold-war perspective," is viciously counterproductive. Seeing everything, in R. Roland's words, "from the viewpoint of an army commander" obscures both the complexity of social problems and possibilities of solution. The social strategy of such "Leninism" is to transform problems to be solved into struggles to be won and enemies to be destroyed. Effective in mobilizing energies for battle, it is unable to use them except to do battle: Leninist regimes, having won power, are notoriously incapable of building free, just societies—instead, they are borne into the fratricidal process Stalin described as "intensification of class struggle *following* the Revolution."

For purposes of social analysis and construction, a different historical conception is more helpful. Engels suggests it in his letter to Bloch in 1894 when he writes that his and Marx's preoccupation with economics and revolution was an understandable but unfortunate oversimplification. The structure of society is not a passive reflection of productive relations, but rather a product of the dialectical interaction of economic and ideological factors. Technology alone does not guarantee smooth social functioning or cause social crises. Neither does ideology alone. The crucial factor is their interrelation: a society can function smoothly if its productive processes can meet its physical needs—and if its images of man and society are capable of rationalizing those processes. Ideological appropriation of physical reality is the catalyst—struggle is incidental to it. Social crises reflect a discrepancy between technology and ideology, while social progress is a process of mutual adjustment rather than of forcible imposition of one factor on the other.

This reading of Marxism provides us with the methodological tool for understanding phenomena like the youth "revolution." The Leninist linear reading cannot explain it: neither internal nor international issues fit the pattern of worldwide struggle ranking the "good guys" against "bad guys." There are problems to be solved rather than unequivocal "struggles" between good and evil. In particular, the mutiny of the young is not an extension of a struggle between Soviet and/or Chinese "socialist" power and American "capitalist" power. Rather, it reflects a dialectic of ideology and technology. The place and image of being young in a postindustrial society is far more relevant for understanding the youth "revolution" than the opposition of "revolution" and "reaction."

We need to suspend the fierce imagery of campus rhetoricians and their construction-site opponents. We need rather to ask about the relation of ideology and technology in concrete human experience. First, what is the impact of technological change on the experience of being young? Second, what are the ideological tools in terms of which the young seek to appropriate that change? And, finally, how would our image of man and society have to change to be capable of rationalizing new productive relations, and how would those relations have to be ordered to safeguard the values represented by that image?

To describe the impact of the scientific-technological revolution as "alienation" is accurate but not very helpful. Certainly the young—and for that matter humans *qua* humans—find the postindustrial society alien: bewildering, incomprehensible, threatening. Men appropriate their world through the double process of conceptualization and manipulation. The world becomes familiar as men handle it, work in it and with it, and as they incorporate it in an overall world view. These processes have in fact broken down—but the question is precisely where and how.

The technological-scientific revolution has changed the role of the young by creating a need for extended training periods while at the same time obscuring the relation between training and practice, effort and effect. This is a generic feature of technological complexity. Putting it quite crudely, a subsistence farmer literally eats what he grows: his toil and aching muscles have an immediate personal significance in the feel of a full stomach. His production is not pointless activity, his product not soulless commodity.

The factory worker's experience is different. There is little visible link between the effort he exerts and its effect on his immediate social world. His is alienated labor: effort dissociated from effect. A basic problem for any society beyond subsistence level is one of providing compensatory mechanisms for technological alienation. The industrial age dealt with it in part through the wage system. If the wage functioned objectively, as an instrument for control of labor and distribution, its subjective significance was no less important: the wage packet functioned as a link between effort and effect, translating labor into needed goods. Theoretically, an adequate wage could compensate for technological alienation. The concern of the unions with wages—or of the individual worker with what Karl Marx, living on an unearned income, perceived as "soulless commodity," was not an expression of the greed and materialism of the unenlightened proletariat. It was an expression of concern. The cash nexus may have been a symbol of alienation, but it was also one of its compensating factors.

In the postindustrial age the dissociation of effort and effect increases sharply while the compensating mechanisms become obscured and obsolete. As goods become widely available and payment effectively invisible in a tangle of delayed payment and paper accounting, the significance of effort diminishes. Effort appears pointless, goods become soulless commodity. The split between effort and effect, the two poles of personal identity, becomes endemic.

In the age of scarcity, liberals assumed that once the goods of daily life become available with minimum effort, human life would be freed from drudgery, and human energy would flow into "creative" tasks. They did not anticipate the secondary effect: that human life would be deprived of the token tasks through which man builds a sense of self-confident identity, relates effort and effect, and gains the habits of work demanded by creative effort: in short, that man, no longer forced to manipulate his world, would lose the ability to conceptualize it.

In the postindustrial age, a quasi-magical relation of push-button and instant product replaces effort as the basic, experienced link between man and his world. It not only expresses but also reinforces human alienation in a machine world.

The academic intelligentsia—especially the students—experiences the effect of technological alienation most acutely. Young intellectuals are the segment of the population most completely deprived of—or liberated from—the need and opportunity of handling the world, of linking matter and meaning through effort. Academic effort is real enough and its effects far-reaching, but its connection with need is seldom acted out.

Alienation is finally the result of a sense of the ineffectiveness of effort and anonymity of effect: the gnawing suspicion that what a man does has no relation to what he hopes for or enjoys, and, conversely, that the things he enjoys and hopes for are a fortuitous product of anonymous forces. Students are not alone in experiencing it: it is the problem of the least as well as the most privileged. It has always been the problem of the children of the aristocracy; today it is a problem for national and racial minorities whose traditional forms of effort are not sufficiently sophisticated to produce an effect in a postindustrial society. It is also the problem of women, displaced by technology from traditional roles but barred by old habits of thought and work from assuming new ones. It is the problem of humans in a society in which significant roles appear to be reserved for machines.

IV

Though creating an explosive situation, alienation itself does not bring about the explosion. In the America of Eisenhower and Kennedy it was effectively compensated by the faith that though the forces may be anonymous they are effective and benign. The explosion came when the basic concepts of the Eisenhower era, anti-Communism and Keynesianism, the struggle against totalitarianism abroad and scarcity at home proved inapplicable to new problems. For in the sixties the problem was no longer simply one of "stopping Communism" but rather of creating a viable democratic alternative, no longer one of raising the GNP but rather of distributing affluence.

The quixotic nature of the campus mutiny, however, may well be due to the fact that the ideological alternatives available to the campus are still geared to the realities of the age of scarcity in which total need vastly exceeded total productive capacity. Within such a matrix, any effort is in principle significant as contributing to total capacity—the secret of Adam Smith's invisible hand. Within such a matrix, society is inevitably polarized between drones and drudges—those whose needs are met and those whose needs, because of inadequate total capacity, must remain unmet.

Campus ideologies today reflect this matrix far more than the realities of a postindustrial society. One alternative articulates the situation of the drudges for whom work is drudgery but inevitable. Its strategy is to make virtue out of necessity by stressing the inherent nobility of work and desirability of the compensations it offers. Freedom from drudgery, impossible in any case, is presented as decadent, and experienced as unnecessary: the drones make the decisions and bear the responsibility.

The second alternative articulates the experience of the drones, making a virtue out of privilege. In the experience of the drone, work is unnecessary, for his physical and social needs are met by drudges. From this perspective the proper pursuit of man is not work but pure, spontaneous self-expression. Any concern with needs is degrading, and as the ideal of the drudges is a society in which all men labor and none is exempt, the ideal of the drones is a society in which all are aristocrats and no man labors.

The first alternative is represented by puritan and proletarian ideologies, by Ayn Rand's objectivism of but a few years ago and the present cult of Third World revolutionism. Both are profoundly conservative: both see affluence as the villain and the solution as a reversion to a simpler age. In the objectivist utopia, complexity of technological relations is resolved through strict accounting. Nothing is allowed to appear "free"; everything must be paid for individually. Effort is never anonymous or social; it is always individual, tied to individual needs. In the Third World version, effort becomes radically social and heroic, either by substituting guerrilla warfare for productive activity or by making productive activity heroic. Thus the harvest becomes the "battle for the grain," manufacture becomes a "struggle to fulfill the plan." There is much talk of duty, little of freedom.

The appeal of the proletarian-puritan approach lies largely in its recognition of the need to make effort significant—and of the uses of adversity in achieving this. But for good or bad, neither its puritan nor proletarian version is viable in an affluent society. The heroic model failed disastrously even in much less developed Eastern Europe. It invokes a "struggle" that is theoretic and abstract, though the work it demands is all too immediate and concrete. "Moral incentives," paradoxically dear to materialist theoreticians, proved at best partly effective, and only in situations in which the theoretical struggle had a practical counterpart. On campus, this heroic approach has produced mock heroics. The puritan version did not even have an opportunity to fail. Technological complexity makes Ayn Rand's simplification impossible in principle.

In a sense, the utopian-aristocratic approach is much more congenial to the experience of the young in postindustrial society. On campus, obligations appear and often are conventional, and the effort required to meet them appears arbitrary. A strategy that seeks not to make effort significant but to eliminate it is much more appealing, especially if linked to a vision of spontaneous activity as the genuinely human pursuit.

In a very crude version, this is the alternative offered by Madison Avenue. Its logic is simple: since in an affluent society production is justified by replacement of effort rather than meeting of needs, Madison Avenue holds out the vision of effortlessness as the way to fulfillment. Have, not do.

This approach has had a remarkable impact on America. Not only do a great many of the young consider having to exert effort the chief source of their alienation, but a great many adults, including educators, see the solution to youth protest in making things easier, in doing for the young more and more of what they can do for themselves. Perhaps the most striking testimony to the effectiveness of Madison Avenue is that parents who have "liberated" their children from virtually every opportunity to assume responsibility and whose children are "still" restless, frequently share the conviction that their children need even more freedom from responsibility, more done for them.

In this crude version, this self-destructive aristocratic utopia is persuasive because it reflects rather than challenges the position of man as consumer in an industrially mature society. It is self-destructive because the consumer is also the producer, and the habits of effortlessness and dependence may be virtues in the consumer but are vices in the producer. A modern utopia need not be a utopia for drudges, but it does have to be a utopia of producers rather than of conspicuous consumers.

The problem of man as producer, absent in the Madison Avenue utopia, is very much present in the rather more sophisticated version presented by neo-Marxists like Herbert Marcuse. As interpreted on campus, Marcuse shares the Madison Avenue conviction that the effortless utopia is possible and desirable, and that our failure is the failure to realize it. Thus the mutiny of the young against purposive effort is legitimate, not only because effort has been misdirected but because it is gratuitous.

Marcuse in effect radicalizes Marx in a rather interesting way. In the famous passage in *Kapital* Marx distinguishes the realm of necessity and the realm of freedom, and his reference to a short work day suggests that what he had in mind was economically necessary activity and free-time activity respectively. In Marx, the realm of freedom makes the realm of necessity meaningful: man works in order to enjoy freedom from need. In turn, the realm of necessity makes the realm of freedom possible: the achievements of work win man leisure. According to Marcuse, the realm of necessity has become superfluous: technology is at least in principle capable of replacing all necessary activity. Human life is in principle capable of becoming entirely a realm of spontaneous, unnecessary activity. Only old habits, psychological and institutional, stand in the way.

Marcuse's estimate of the possibilities of technology may or may not be accurate. The odds are against it: the construction, servicing, and control of an economic system so sophisticated that it could meet all productive and distributive needs is likely to demand more rather than less skill, discipline, and dependability on the part of labor. Reliance on spontaneity is notoriously more compatible with beach-combing than with sophisticated technology.

But, even were it technologically feasible, Marcuse's vision would remain problematic. Marcuse is right in seeing work performed under alien, arbitrary constraint as senseless drudgery. But it is not at all clear that its aristocratic opposite, the spontaneous activity "liberated" from all external motives, is the alternative. Traditionally, those sectors of the population which have most closely approximated such "liberation"—the children of the aristocracy, the children of the superrich, and now the children of the affluent—have constituted the most frustrated, decadent, and alienated sector of society. Effort becomes meaningful not by becoming unnecessary but by becoming purposeful and effective. The dichotomy of drudgery and leisure leaves out the uniquely human alternative, necessary work, freely undertaken for good and sufficient reason.

This is the democratic alternative. Even if Marx's scheme of necessity and freedom were economically invalid—which is far from evident —it would still retain its social and psychological validity. Freedom is not empty when it is won through ability to meet necessity through effort—when it is based on democratic work. As long as it is based on dependence on others, whether slaves or robots, it is alienation. Necessity can become meaningful rather than oppressive when man appropriates it as a means of freedom: when it is simply met by the efforts of others, it remains degrading. Marx's hopes for the redeeming role of the proletariat were based on the fact that the proletariat wins its freedom by meeting its own needs through its own labor, not by dependence on others, and so need not itself become an exploiting class.

Marcuse himself may well be trying to say something very similar —that work becomes meaningful when it serves a purpose rather than an external demand. His emphasis on an aesthetic perspective of man and world, his insistence on speaking of *surplus* repression, all hint in this direction. But that has not been his impact on campus. There the lesson of Marcuse has become virtually indistinguishable from the lesson of Madison Avenue: effort is degrading and objectively unnecessary, demanded only by old-fashioned administrators and equally old-fashioned superegos. Hence the response is the "Great Refusal"—chemical or political—to destroy the system which makes demands without, presumably, disrupting the flow of benefits from a self-operating technology, and the "new sensibility" which will replace inner need for effort with instant self-realization. From this perspective, work is polarized between the abstractions of drudgery and play, and the young—some of them—see play as their birthright.

Marcuse's recent loss of popularity on campus may well be due to his misgivings about this bowdlerized version of his ideas. But the misgivings come too late: utopian ideology has inseparably associated all effort with the problems it seeks to resolve. Any effort to resolve them perpetuates them because it perpetuates the age of effort rather than ushering in the age of spontaneity. The only truly "radical" approach is to reject the problems and solutions alike, to withdraw from the world of effort into the world of sensibility.

This version of the utopian ideology fits rather neatly with the campus version of the ideology of heroic effort. Revolution is the praxis of utopia: since problems have to be surpassed rather than solved, "revolutionary" symbolic acts are appropriate. Closing down the university might not improve the quality of education just as "offing the pigs" might not contribute to a more humane and equitable assurance of public safety, but it will render social problems insoluble —and so force the society to transcend them.

v

The success of the new revolutionary-utopian synthesis on campus is due not to any ability to solve the problems of the young but rather to its ability to rationalize them. But while the revolutionary utopianism does accurately reflect the experience of the young, it does nothing to change it. Read in revolutionary-utopian terms, social issues and personal problems may become at once comprehensible and insoluble. The shift in campus strategy makes the point clearly. Social issues have become accessible to campus concern through a translation from the terms of the external world into the terms of emotions, attitudes, and feelings. The issues are real, but the campus "radicalizes" them—makes them subjective, highly general, and charged with the emotions of personal problems. Thus the very real problem of minorities in an increasingly homogeneous society has become the problem of "racism" rather than civil rights, the solution an equivalent of dropping out and turning on—black separatism and black consciousness. Similarly, the complex issues of the place of women in society became the question of "sexism," and even urgent questions of public safety at home and abroad have turned into emotional issues of being "for peace," "for love," "against oppression," or hating "racist, sexist, imperialist pig America." The translation is not always this extreme, and there are still a great many students struggling to retain their hold on reality, but the direction of the revolutionary-utopian ideology is unmistakable and powerful because it makes problems appear amenable to the strategy available to the young —dropping out and turning on.

Yet the demand for "immediate abolition of racism, sexism, imperialism, and pollution" will necessarily be frustrated. It can lead only to greater and greater frustration, sharper and sharper confrontation—and ultimately to repression, whether by reaction or revolution, since even "the revolution" could not meet its own demands. (This is but one sense in which revolution and counterrevolution become equivalents.) The revolutionary-utopian ideology has given the young a superficial sense of instant significance, but the cost is damnably high. The basic problem of rationalizing postindustrial production has disappeared behind a revolutionary-utopian smoke screen. An ideology simply reflecting the conditions of production is not enough. Nor is an ideology that simply reaffirms a perennial ideal. What is needed is an ideology that could play the role of a catalyst between ideals and the realities of the postindustrial age.

Prerequisites for a catalytic ideology do exist today. In spite of the appeal of the revolutionary-utopian strategy, the great escape was not and is not what the great majority of students seek to achieve. The problem, after all, is not that the young refuse to accept the role of pampered, useless children: that was always the positive moment in their mutiny. *The problem is that the society has no real role for its young.* The policy emerging from recent confrontations—roughly, to push off the young into even more luxurious academic sandlots while stationing armed guards around them—is counterproductive. The young have a right to a significant role in society, not only for their own sake but for the sake of society as well. A catalytic ideology would have to be capable of providing social roles both objectively significant and experienced as such.

The objective problem can be solved because it is not simply a matter of technology but of its ideological appropriation as well. Effort loses objective significance not simply because postindustrial society can produce more than it needs, but because it is unable to use its productive capacity to improve the quality of life. A capitalist economy is inevitably bound to reinvest for profit, creating an inflation of unneeded goods, but it lacks the mechanisms to channel its surplus capacity to meet the need for a distribution of affluence—public health, education, housing. When Adam Smith's invisible hand ceases to function with the overcoming of social scarcity, a capitalist society has no way of replacing it. The result is the paradoxical situation of effort invested so that one part of the society will not have to roll up car windows by hand while another part remains deprived of essential services.

Nothing in the nature of postindustrial production demands such a society. Continued reinvestment in surplus production is economically as well as socially undesirable. It has an inflationary effect on the economy as well as on skill levels demanded of the labor force. It creates social and environmental problems not only morally bad but also economically damaging. Modern production requires a social structure capable of coordinating national productive effort, channeling investment into areas of need, and preventing major dislocation of the economy by irresponsible decisions. A postindustrial society requires a socialist social structure to make effort objectively meaningful.

The inherent danger of socialism, however, is that in establishing a social machinery for economic direction it creates a concentration of power—the coercive power of the state and the power of focused economy—far beyond anything capitalism dreamed of and makes men far more dependent than free. Campus rebels, while aware of the limitations of capitalist economy, have been blissfully ignorant of this tendency of socialism. A catalytic ideology would need to take it into account, and counter it with a consistent, radical demand for democracy. The first priority of socialism must be to safeguard rights of free critique, free press, vigorous dissent, individual responsibility and initiative. It has to be democratic both in outline and detail, striving to achieve maximum participation—giving each man an opportunity to function as a member of a community rather than as its beneficiary or victim.

Student slogans about participation grope in this direction. It might be more efficient to have a state agency build low-cost housing than to organize a tenants' cooperative through which to channel funds, but the rebelling young are beginning to recognize that the efficiency is self-defeating. The same is true of community clinics and college dormitories. While social action is necessary to make individual action effective, it is not sufficient—it is the individual action, what Marx called "socially useful labor," which gives men confidence in their identity and a sense of social participation, and can transform campus mutineers into a positive social force.

Postindustrial productive relations create conditions for democracy as a life style not only a political system. To a great extent, the complexity of postindustrial production eliminates economic justification both for the class of drudges and the class of idlers. Income differences tend to be quantitative, differences of earned income. Within a socialist structure, a technologically advanced society can be a classless society of wage earners rather than a society polarized between owners and the owned.

But the anarchist-authoritarian temper of the campus mutiny suggests that posttechnological production does not create the psychological conditions for democracy. Rather, it tends to create habits of dependence, irresponsibility, and anonymity, directly contrary to habits required for a democratic life style. Here a conscious attack is needed. Neither indulgence nor repression is relevant. What is needed is the democratic opportunity *to do,* to accept responsibility and participate in the work of the society, from shared family responsibilities to opportunities for dealing with political and social problems.

In terms of the campus, this justifies the entire range of student participation in academic administration and services, as well as off-campus involvement. But the basic need is to make the students' professional work significant. A student's personal identity is first of all that of a student—and if this is experienced as trivial or insignificant, no amount of marginal activity can replace the self-esteem lost through deprecation of the primary role. Making study significant does not mean making it "relevant" in a fashionable sense of the word by restricting it to the narrow horizons of students' immediate experience. Such strategy may keep students amused, but it gives them little sense of the importance of their work—or of themselves as engaged in it. Rather, making study significant means taking students seriously, showing them the same respect scholars show their colleagues. The scholarship presented in courses deserves to be thorough, and the standards demanded high. Expecting a faculty to teach and paying it for teaching, and expecting students to study and rewarding them for it, are prime requisites. Utilizing the skills of graduates in social service rather than surplus production is their counterpart.

None of this, to be sure, speaks directly to the problems raised by student rebels. Those problems are cosmic ones, stated in intensely personal terms. Any concrete social action will necessarily disappoint them. A person stripped of all the accouterments of personal identity —of skills, interests, obligations—may well be permanently alienated simply because he has lost the ability to function in any social context.

There are signs that Americans are becoming aware of the continuity between responsibility and self-respect. Even on campus, there is increasing evidence of a sorting-out process which separates the desperate from the concerned. It is by no means an automatic development, but it is a possible and a promising one. Given a consistent commitment on the part of all who deal with the young to provide opportunities for participation and assumption of responsibility and an equally consistent resistance to the clamor of the frightened for fewer demands and greater "freedom," it is a development that can effectively compensate for the technological displacement of the young.

Nothing in the nature of postindustrial production guarantees this: quite the contrary, it is entirely possible for most parents and the society as a whole to deprive the young of all participation. But there is everything to make a meaningful participation possible. The mutiny of the young need not end in irrelevance and repression. The displacement of the young that produces it is not simply the result of a technology that makes effort unnecessary, but also of an obsolete ideology that regards it as heroic—and onerous. Socialist recognition of social rights and democratic recognition of individual responsibility make another conception possible: democratic work as the self-expression of a free man in a just society. The growing disillusion of the majority of students with the heroics of their over-thirty ideological mentors, their growing involvement in social, political, and academic processes, and their evident concern with the realities rather than the psychodrama of social change hold out hope for a democratic alternative to violence and repression. They deserve our support. If they can win the freedom to accept responsibility and show a willingness to accept being young not as a privilege or an onus, but as a valid, responsible way of participating in social existence, the youth revolution will become unnecessary. It will also succeed.

Gus Tyler

Generation Gap or Gap Within a Generation?

"Can the American system, which does fairly well at accommodating political or economic conflicts, handle a *cultural* battle, which begins to shape up more and more like the pointlessly violent strife of hostile religious sects?" So asked the *Wall Street Journal* in May 1970. The *Kulturkampf* to which it referred was an "argument over the way people think of themselves and how they should live . . . a cultural conflict [that] is potentially every bit as volatile as conflict over more substantial issues."

To those who think in terms of issues, such a cultural conflict may appear implausible. A confrontation between guardsmen and students at Kent State or hard hats and demonstrators in New York they see as a clash of hawks and doves, or old and young: as ideological or generational struggles. What does culture have to do with it?

Mao Tse-tung's experience with his explosive students may suggest an answer. When the Chinese campuses began to heat up in the mid-sixties, Chairman Mao—in good Leninist tradition—tried to harness the energy. By unleashing the Red Guards on Liu Shao-chi, his favorite scapegoat, Mao took the generational drive and turned it into ideological channels. And he dignified the bloodletting by naming it a "cultural revolution." Once the student crusade began to get out of hand, the Chairman ordered the kids back to their classrooms. No more free bed, board, and travel: return to the parietals. This didn't work, either: the Red Guards continued to tear things up, this time on the campus. There was something about the life style of these zealots that did not yield to Maoist manipulation.

169

It was now that Mao's Marxism came forward—as an inevitable search for the class origins of collective human behavior. The Chairman's conclusion was that the universities were overloaded with children of the privileged, who for too long had been exposed to the temptations and trauma of purposeless leisure and were caught up in unrealistic discourse over abstractions rather than in a serious involvement with matters that mattered. So he simply changed the college curriculum and its constituency. Crap courses were eliminated. Some perennial students were "volunteered" to distant farms, to pitch hay, and replaced in the classrooms by cadres from the unions and armed forces, whose term on the campus was limited to two years lest they also be corrupted by too much comfort. In short, Mao moved to change the life style on campus by changing its class content.

Mao was aware of the generational impulse: he harnessed its energies for his purge against Liu. But Mao also recognized class styles within the young: which he used to purge the purgers.

What Mao knew by heart—life styles derive from class (as well as generational) differences—CBS has recently discovered through the research of a 1969 report prepared by Dr. Daniel Yankelovich. Although the study is entitled "Generations Apart" and described as "a study of the generation gap," it might better have been called "Classes Apart—a study, etc." For the report reveals that, while there is a generation gap, it is not as great as the class gap within generations.

Consider the very first and perhaps most important proposition stated in the Yankelovich questionnaire: "Hard Work Will Always Pay Off." Of college youth (here seen as a class), only 56 percent agreed, of noncollege youth 79 percent agreed. Their parents agreed, respectively, 76 percent and 85 percent. Here the difference among the young is far greater than between noncollege youth and all adults.

The percentage of "revolutionary" youth who say "yes" to this proposition is a low of 12 percent, but the parents of these same "revolutionaries" answer "yes" by a high of 91 percent. Which suggests that for the latter "hard work" did "pay off." It turns out that 44 percent of the "revolutionary" youth have parents making more than $15,000 a year, whereas only 22 percent of the young as a whole have parents in this upper bracket. If black revolutionaries were excluded from the count, the percentage of white "revolutionary" youth from affluent families would even be higher than 44 percent.

One may therefore assume that if a youth is both white and "revolutionary," the chances are better than even that he comes from a well-to-do family and doesn't believe in "hard work."

Among conservative youth, 83 percent believe "hard work" pays—as do 86 percent of their parents. These young conservatives come from families with a disproportionately heavy percentage from the middle-income bracket ($10,000–$15,000 a year). While 29 percent of all youth come from this sector, 43 percent of conservative youth do. Relatively few conservative youth (only 11 percent) come from homes making more than $15,000, whereas 22 percent of all youth come from such homes. The percentage of conservatives in the *lower* bracket (up to $10,000) is 48 percent—almost exactly what it is for all youth. In sum, the conservative youth comes mainly from America's bulge in the middle.

Consider a second proposition posed by the survey: "Belonging to some Organized Religion is Important in a Person's Life." Among the college young 42 percent said "yes"; among noncollege youth, 71 percent. The adults, respectively: 81 percent and 91 percent. These figures clearly show the young are less religious than their parents. But they show even more clearly that noncollege youth are far more like adults than their contemporaries in college.

Among "revolutionary" youth, only 8 percent are religious, while 73 percent of their parents are—a very big generational gap. Among "conservative" youth, 84 percent are religious, while 91 percent of their parents are—nearly no difference.

In their attitudes toward money, sex, law-and-order, and authority, college and noncollege kids differ widely. The latter are far more traditional. Noncollege youths find it easier to accept restraints, whether it be police, "boss," or conventional clothing and grooming. Half the noncollege kids, for instance, assume that for the first couple of years on a job they will have little decision-making power. College youth, by two to one, reject this waiting period. In short, college youth are more reluctant to take orders and more impatient to give them—a not uncommon upper-class trait.

Young people disagree about the nature of the generation gap. While 54 percent of "revolutionary" youth note "very great" differences with their parents, only 11 percent of "middle-roaders" and 12 percent of "conservatives" feel that way. By two to one, the "revolutionaries" believe there is a "large generational gap," while middle-roaders and conservatives believe (72 percent and 70 percent) that the gap "exists" but is "exaggerated."

Above all, the "revolutionaries" think of their parents as immoral. Only 34 percent believe their parents "have strong moral principles and live by them" while 71 percent of "middle-roaders" believe this about their parents. Thirty-six percent of the "revolutionaries" believe their parents "act out of expediency rather than out of any moral principles" while only 10 percent of the "middle-roaders" and only 7 percent of the "conservatives" have this tacky view of their parents. The "revolutionary" youth often sees his parent as a money grubber. Thirty-nine percent believe that what their parents' "way of life brought them" was "material comfort," while only 8 percent of the "middle-road" and 7 percent of the "conservative" youth have this image of their parents.

Parents also differ about the character of youth. The parents of "revolutionaries" have less faith in kids than do conservative folk. Thus, 36 percent of the revolutionaries' parents believe that parents are "more interested in other people" than youths are, while only 14 percent of the conservatives' parents think so. As a corollary, only 9 percent of the revolutionaries' parents think the young "more interested in other people" while 33 percent of the conservatives' parents think so.

These cultural differences appear to have an economic origin. The parents of 41 percent of the college youth earn more than $15,000 and only 24 percent of them under $10,000; fifty percent of the parents of noncollege youth make under $10,000 and only 18 percent make more than $15,000.

From these scattered data a pattern begins to emerge. There are differences of significance within the youth generation as between college and noncollege, upper-middle and lower-middle income, white-collar and blue-collar, "revolutionary" and "conservative." The non-college, lower-income, blue-collar, middle-of-the-road or "conservative" youth is far more like his parent than like his rich intellectual counterpart on the campus. The *Kulturkampf* is less one of age against age than class against class.

Nor is the difference solely ideological—although that dimension is certainly there. The conflict is truly *cultural:* over life styles, authority, bosses, cops, drugs, education, fags, flags, family, girls, hard hats, intellectuals, jobs, kids, love, muscles, neighbors, and so on. The contrast is most apparent as between rich "revolutionary" students and hard-working "conservative" workers. And in between are most of the youth—about 70 percent—with a spectrum of in-between activity. At the center is a big chunk of kids—college and noncollege, affluent and not, Left and Right and Center—whose cultural attitudes are pretty much the same as, or at least not vastly different from, those of the adult generation. The highly dramatized clash of cultures is a conflict among contemporaries fired by atypical extremes who, in a period of high tension, come to appear as spokesmen for the typical.

What are these types? Oversimplified and overdrawn, they are those who come from the polis of work and those who come from the cosmopolis of leisure. Though of the same age and same nation, they are ages apart, locked in combat like warring "nations" arising out of hostile subcultures.

In the work polis, discipline is part of the job. The worker assumes this whether he is "on the belt" or on high steel. In mass production he must move with the ruthless rhythm of the machine; in construction he must swing with the crew—as much as if he were on a PT boat or a bomber crew. Manual labor, except when artsy-craftsy, is a collective effort with built-in congregational compulsions.

This discipline is not as irksome to the worker as it appears (or would be) to the child of leisure, because the blue-collar boy is accustomed to authority before he gets to the job. He is reared with it in his family, where parents traditionally teach their children to "honor your father and mother." This continues into maturity. For blue-collar folk, notes the sociologist Mirra Komarovsky, "the parental family . . . remains their major reference group after marriage." The traditional family structure is further perpetuated among blue-collar workers by the disproportionate presence of Catholics, rural elements (about one-fifth of the blue-collar force is off the farm), and immigrants.

When work discipline comes to seem too oppressive, the worker changes the rules through the structured rebellion of his union. More leisure, greater voice, less pressure. But the rebellion is careful to preserve the work place physically, to seek a settlement, and to run its course in a disciplined way.

In the blue-collar world, two gods preside: Ananke and Eros. The former—the god of necessity, before whom all others must bow—drives the man to work, to hard work, even when it doesn't pay very well. The latter—the god of love—is the maker of his family. No matter how irksome the sacrifices to both these deities, the blue-collar worker continues to pay homage at their shrines. Although probably unaware that Dr. Freud looked upon Ananke ("the compulsion to work") and Eros ("the power of love" with its resultant family) as "the parents of human culture," the plebeians of all ages—including the present—sense the importance of these institutions in the making of a viable society. In the blue-collar family, notes Arthur B. Shostak in *Blue-Collar Life,*

child-rearing is a total activity, possibly the most important in the maintenance of the entire marriage relationship. Together the couple struggles to combine the concern of the wife with the child's self-actualization and the husband's more traditional interest in making men out of boys. . . . In the entire system of rationalizations that blue-collar men derive for life as it is lived (or better yet, tolerated), the working-class family remains the key factor, the beginning and end of all things.

To the worker, the family—like the job—is accepted for better or worse. If he likes his family, so much the better; if he likes his job, he is doubly blessed. But, like it or not, family and job are his cross to be carried to his own calvary for personal salvation and social survival. As a result, the worker is not generally anti-institutional. He may be critical, even cynical, about his institutions—company, family, church, union, political party, or country—but he remains loyal.

This sense of loyalty that starts with family and fellow workers and extends to neighborhood and nation results in such a complex mixture of behavior patterns as class solidarity, family devotion, gang unity, patriotism, parochialism, and prejudice. This set of traditional loyalties is constantly reinforced by the fact that the worker is turf-bound —both at home and on the job. He lives in a fairly homogeneous neighborhood where he mingles with his own kind most of the time. His household is part of an ethnic and economic unity. He worries about safety and stability in his urban village and is prepared to protect its borders. He and his kids may spend all their lives in that enclave, traveling only short distances and at rare intervals. If the family moves, it is likely to do so as part of a tribal migration.

These neighborhoods, points out Shostak, are "social class enclaves relatively untouched by time and emphatically personal in character." Here, adds Scott Greer in *The Emerging City,* we see "not the 'faceless world of megalopolis,' but men in shirt sleeves playing softball, groups of women gossiping on the porches, children swarming in the streets." However slumlike this urban village may look or smell to the visitor, the natives feel at home on this piece of turf that has "an old-shoe comfort and reliability." They are also proud of what Edward Ryan calls their *commonness,* "the strong theme that the good man is the plain man . . . that there is virtue in being of the common clay."

The job, like the neighborhood, is another piece of turf to which workers are attached: by choice, necessity, and habit. Many will not leave a job even for better pay because the work place is a *social center*—a locale of a subculture—with strong emotional ties and loyalties.

One of the propositions in the CBS report that separated college and noncollege youth related to this matter of loyalty. The proposition: "No sane, normal, decent person could even think of hurting a close friend or relative." Of the noncollege youth 43 percent strongly agreed, as against a mere 18 percent of the college youth. This faith in group loyalty on the part of the blue-collar boy was not mere naïveté: they believed in greater numbers than the college youth that "anyone who completely trusts anyone else is asking for trouble." But in the herdish blue-collar world it is natural to believe that a "sane, normal, decent" man will stand *by his own*—will remain loyal.

Traditionalism is reinforced by the fact that the polis of work, shunning change qua change, is basically neophobic. Blue-collar processes tend to be imitative rather than inventive; repetitive rather than innovative. In the case of a man in mass production, this is obvious. In the case of the craftsman—like the electrician—the locale may change but not the chore: installing a switch is, with few variations, installing a switch.

Change may, indeed, be downright threatening. An old dog must learn new tricks. Sometime he may be rendered obsolete by a new process. In any event, comfortable habits and rhythms are disrupted.

Since the worker is expected to turn out as much as possible in as short a time as possible, he is not encouraged to experiment. He is paid to produce—not to probe. He is put on an incentive system rewarding a mastery of routine that speeds output.

At home and at work, he seeks stability—regular employment and regular meals, discipline and authority, predictable production, safety on the job and the street. In this ordered universe, he believes that there are traditional roles to be played by boss and union, by priest and congregation, by friends and neighbors, by "them" and "us," parents and children, men and women.

Men are expected to be men: masculine and muscular. Homosexuals are "queer." In the eyes of the blue-collar beholder, they can't lift big weights or raise big families. When asked about "relations between consenting homosexuals," 72 percent of the noncollege youth thought it was "morally wrong." Less than half the college youth thought so. (Here again the noncollege youth were far closer to the adult generation as a whole than they were to the college kids.) When the same question was put to the "revolutionaries," only 7 percent found it "wrong" as against 83 percent of the "conservatives."

Immersed in a masculine mystique, the blue-collar man accepts combat—at the bar, on the picket line, in the convention hall, at home, overseas—as an inevitable aspect of life. In part, this is a prolongation of boyhood with its street brawls—a commonplace of blue-collar life. In part, it is the result of constant living with physical danger: in the last half-dozen years more lives were lost in industrial accidents than in Vietnam. But basically it is an unstated acceptance that a man cannot go through life without being physically bruised or bruising.

This acceptance of bellicosity, plus a sense of loyalty and patriotism, makes it easier for the blue-collar man to go along with a national war. For instance, in questioning college and noncollege youth on "fighting a war," twice as many noncollege as college respondents felt it worth fighting to "keep a commitment," or to maintain "our position of power in the world," or to protect "our honor." (Again, the noncollege youth are more like adults in general than like their college contemporaries.)

Above all else, the blue-collar worker is reality-bound. No doubt, he has his fantasies; but he quickly separates out the real from the unreal in the crucible of daily demands and deeds. At work and at home he is put to the hard test of personal and familial survival.

In the cosmopolis of leisure, however, a contrary culture is aborning—with play substituted for work, innovation for imitation, style for content, universalism for tribalism, conscience for loyalty, individuality for collectivism, neophilia for neophobia, theater for reality. The carriers of this counterculture are a cadre of youths raised in an elysium whose propagation as a universal life style they envision as a social utopia.

In his *Work and Its Discontents* Daniel Bell concludes with a thought that might well have served as the introduction to a sequel on "Leisure and Its Discontents." In Western civilization, notes Bell, work has stood at the center of moral consciousness and moral unconsciousness: consciously, work was the compelling virtue of Genesis, the Protestant ethic, the Carlylean *homo faber;* unconsciously, work was man's answer to death in an era when the traditional hope of immortality—religion—was in decline. "The significance of work was that it could still mobilize emotional energies into creative challenges. . . . One could eliminate death from consciousness by minimizing it through work." Then comes a closing query: if work (as Freud believed) was "the chief means of binding an individual to reality, what will happen then, when not only the worker but work itself is displaced by the machine?"

This closing query in a section entitled "Ananke and Thanatos" poses the problem of man's ability to relate to reality in a workless world. Whether or not the worker "on the belt" is part of this nonwork unreality because his toil is unvaried and unchallenging is open to debate. But there is little doubt that a sizable body of affluent youths in America, because of the death of that old-fashioned god Ananke, have been liberated from humdrum toil by the very technocracy that many of them yearn to destroy. In *The Making of a Counter-Culture,* Theodore Roszak writes:

A high consumption, leisure-wealthy society simply doesn't need contingents of rigidly trained "responsible" young workers. It cannot employ more than a fraction of untrained youngsters fresh out of high school. The middle class can therefore afford to prolong the ease and drift of childhood, and so it does. . . . The result has been to make of adolescence, not the beginning of adulthood, but a status in its own right: a limbo that is nothing so much as the prolongation of an already permissive infancy.

The notions about the American economy just noted are open to serious doubt; but as prevalent myths they suffice to motivate or justify the extension of infancy through college and beyond.

The prolongation of infancy sustains the notion of life as play rather than work. From the cosmopolis of leisure arises a life style where play's the thing: an attitude nurtured from cradle to college.

As babies [records Roszak], the middle-class young got picked up when they bawled. As children, they got their kindergarten finger paintings thumbtacked on the living room walls by mothers who knew better than to discourage incipient activity. As adolescents, they perhaps even got a car of their own with all of the sexual privileges attending. . . . [The commercial world joined the schools] to elaborate a total culture of adolescence based on nothing but fun and games.

In this life curriculum, discipline appears as an unnecessary evil. Tough problems are resolved through theater. The way to handle the problem of tasteless Pablum, for instance, is to serve it in a variety of containers of varying colors and shapes decorated with characters out of the comics. If that doesn't work, sing a song, play a tape, dance a jig, do anything, even beat a drum—but not the kid. If that doesn't work, offer another food and another and another—change the world, not the child. The well-to-do parent, especially the mother, has time to indulge the whims of the infant. There is also a moral justification, for, as Roszak insists, the young are thus "influenced to believe that being human has something to do with pleasure and freedom."

As in theater, novelty is an essential part of the action. The child is exposed to new décor, dwellings, visitors, places—even new fathers and mothers. Life flickers by like a movie montage with new faces and scenes to excite the senses. The child grows up a neophiliac—yearning for change *per se*. New means good, old means bad, just as youth is virtue and age vice.

Life, like theater, is expected to be instantaneous: to transport the onlooker, to resolve problems, and to render pleasure or catharsis—in a matter of minutes. From high chair to higher education, these youths are reared in a hurrying hothouse. They get instant attention and authority, money and credit. They are surrounded by instant coffee, tea, heat, and refrigeration. They are encouraged to buy instant teeth, nose, hair, and beauty. They sample instant bosoms and a novel bustle touted as "instant fanny." The media make instant heroes, idols, ideas, ideals, and widely imitated idiosyncrasies. A turn of the TV dial turns off one fantasy and turns on another. A pill, a sniff, or a needle makes fantasy instantaneously real. Sex is instant: mate now, meet later.

The yearning for Newness and Nowness is, of course, stimulated by a highly technical society with its magical inventions. Yet, ironically, it is precisely against this technical tyranny with its rigid disciplines that "technocracy's children" are in rebellion. And doubly ironical is the use of modern mechanisms (physical and psychological) by the "revolutionaries" against the technocratic order: cameras, electronic devices, media manipulation, chemistry, image-making, miniaturized high-speed explosives.

Out of this counterculture arises a sophisticated dramaturgy whose real-life enactment is intended to be an instrument of profound social change. Life is expected to imitate art—including the theater of the absurd. Daily dress is costuming, intended far less for comfort or aesthetics than for role playing. Today I'm Sitting Bull or Pocahontas, Fidel or Che, Bill Haywood or Joe Hill, Gandhi or Lumumba: clothes make the man or woman. The revolution itself is theater, inspiring drama critic Robert Brustein to insist that it was within his professional jurisdiction to review the current crop of "revolutionaries" as he would any other batch of plays.

A high percentage of the rich "revolutionary" youth are the children of men who made their wealth recently in the manufacture and sale of images: teachers, preachers, PR men, ad men, artists, writers, foundation executives, psychologists, psychiatrists, lawyers. From such parents, the children learn the power of the word, the repeated cliché, the dramatic act, the surprise move, the subliminal suggestion, the amorphous abstraction with its catch-penny appeal. They learn the superiority of package over content, style over substance. They learn the artifacts of imagery projected in colorful conflict or sweeping symbolism. They become master dramatists, directors, actors, and publicists at an early age, certain—as are their parents—that they know how to merchant dreams.

In some major respects, however, they are unlike their parents. The old man learned his craft to earn a living while the son, taking economic security for granted, feels free—as Roszak puts it—to "build a new uncompromised personality, flawed perhaps by irresponsible ease, but also touched with some outspoken spirit." While the old man must "kowtow to the organization," the son "can talk back at home with little fear of being tossed out into the cold." While the old man made a living out of peddling detergents, cigarettes, or a political candidate, the son makes a religion out of denouncing the parental products as poison.

In such families, the generation gap is great. Fathers appear as hypocrites who, preaching high ideals to their children, practice the mean trade of peddling mischievous myths. The old man, under the lash of Ananke, serves Mammon while the son, believing Ananke is dead, enshrines Thespis. In the fantasy of the son, the father appears as a deceitful, money-mad dictator. When asked whether the adults "considered" their "opinion" or granted them "a full vote in family matters," only 27 percent of the "revolutionaries" said "yes" while 43 percent of the "conservatives" said "yes"—although the latter come from more authoritarian homes.

The rich young "revolutionary" feels no strong tie to work or family. Without such attachment to institutions that are the twin pillars of blue-collar life, the child of leisure lacks a personal model for accepting almost any institution. Loyalty to company, union, family, or nation consequently becomes difficult if not downright craven. The ultimate symbol of loyalty—the flag—is an abomination. The only real loyalty is to the countercultural sect with its own flag, shibboleths, and heroes.

Without strong ties to immediate family, the cosmopolitan child feels no strong attachments to the expanded family—the "tribe"—whether ethnic, geographic, or political. Many of these young have traveled widely during their teens, soaking up the cultures of many peoples. The resulting cosmopolitanism, conditioned by a nonfamilial and antiparental bias, slips easily into a practicing xenophilia and autophobia.

Nor does college change this cultural fix. For the counterculturist, higher education is not intended to have practical consequences. Only 6 percent of the "revolutionaries" thought of college as preparation to "earn more money, have a more interesting career, and enjoy a better position in society." (Seventy-three percent of the "conservatives" saw school in just these practical terms.) Ninety-two percent of the "revolutionaries" found college to be "something more intangible; perhaps the opportunity to change things rather than make out well within the existing system."

For the "revolutionary," college is where you learn how to change the system—not fit into it. The university is not a place to discover reality through work, to accept discipline, to develop institutional loyalty. Quite the opposite. College years are intended to shake institutions, challenge authority, create a workless world. The campus —at this crucial moment of self-assertion—becomes a stage where the "revolution" as theater conducts its rehearsals for the real "revolution" to come.[1]

The children of the work polis and those of the leisure cosmopolis have contrary images of self and of the other. Each thinks he is the true fount of creation: the blue-collar man sees himself as builder of cities, maker of things, defender of the nation; the revolutionary intellectual sees himself as planner of societies, setter of style, maker of eternal peace. The blue-collar man thinks of the rich "revolutionary" as a self-inflated, useless snob; the latter views the "hard hat" as an ignorant, useless slob. Both think of the other as dirty, though in different ways: the blue-collar man works in dirt; the "hippie" lives in it. The blue-collar man looks upon disloyalty as treason; the "revolutionary" sees disloyalty as loyalty to a higher reason. The blue-collar man thinks of this society as his and sees the "hippie" as an alien to be tolerated up to a point and, beyond that, to be chained. The "revolutionary" feels he is alienated from this society and—to find a home—it is not he but the social order and its

---

1. The rich white revolutionary is not the only group conditioned by the unreality of the workless world. There is a "lower class" that is also liberated from the compulsions of labor. Its life style is strikingly like that of affluent counterparts. Here, for instance, is Edward Banfield's description: "The *lower* (as opposed to *working*) class person never sacrifices any present satisfaction for the sake of a larger future one. He lives from moment to moment. This is to say, he does not discipline himself to acquire an occupational or other skill, to hold down a regular job, to maintain stable family ties, or to stay out of trouble with the law. His bodily needs (especially for sex) and his taste for 'action' take precedence over everything else. . . . He likes the feeling that something violent is about to happen." The similarity of life style with this traditional "lower class" has not gone unnoticed by a sector of the counterculturists who have tried to copy habits and make activist alliances with their impoverished twins.

hordes that must be changed. The worker favors social change that is tangible and measurable—job, wage, pension, home, health care, house, vacation—and uses proven methods of collective action, like bargaining and balloting, to make progress through cumulative reform. The rich "revolutionary" favors social changes that are conceptual and abstract—freedom, justice, equality, participation—and turns to novel methods of *individual* action, like booing, burlesquing, or bombing, to make progress through sudden revolution. The worker looks on these "revolutionary" methods as a threat to his existence and to his social order: the "revolutionary" sees the worker as an obstacle to his personal liberation and the freedom of man.

My contrast between the children of "labor" and those of "leisure" is exaggerated. My descriptions are less characterizations than caricatures. Very few individuals totally fit any of these stereotypes, and even within the defined categories there are variations. Moreover, the labels of "revolutionary," "conservative," and so on are—like most modern packaging—somewhat misleading. Revolutionary style does not necessarily signify revolutionary content. And there are the Puritan rebels, the Jacobin squares. A perfect example of a recurrent incongruity between style and substance is the class that the CBS Report calls the "radical reformer."

In discussing the "revolutionaries," Yankelovich notes that "this group is so small (only 1 percent of the youth) that it should be looked at in combination with the radical reformers," making up 10 percent of the youth. On closer examination, it appears that these "radical reformers," no matter how dissident, are traditionalists in life style: 68 percent of them want more emphasis on law and order; 58 percent believe religion is important; 70 percent believe private property is sacred; 82 percent believe society needs some legally based authority to prevent chaos; 82 percent believe compromise is essential for progress; 70 percent favor more respect for authority; 84 percent think education is very important. "While holding radical views on most ideological questions," comments Yankelovich, "these radicals appear more like middle-of-the-roaders on traditional values like patriotism, sex, and religion."

Why? Because a large percentage of them come from working-class families (55 percent from families making less than $10,000 a year), and because nonwhites are disproportionately represented (26 percent). These "black militants," notes Yankelovich, "are radical on domestic issues but highly disciplined in terms of upholding certain standards of personal morality."

If one adds this "radical" group to the "revolutionaries," then the total at the left end of the spectrum is 11 percent. At the right end are the conservatives with 19 percent. In between is 70 percent of the generation. This in-between group covers a wide spectrum, including the "New Left," the "Old Left," people who like to join civil rights protests or favor a "fundamental reform" of the military, big business, and political parties. Some share opinions with the far Left; others share opinions with the conservatives; still others hold a mixed set of views. In life style, this sector is also in-betweenish: a bit obedient and a bit rebellious, liking old shoes but trying new boots, respecting the folks but battling the old man, tied to home and job but on a long elastic tether, remembering that all work and no play makes Jack a jerk. And, like any middle child, it is least likely to be put on public display.

Although composing the bulk of youth in America, the influence (and eventually the size) of this sector could dwindle rapidly. It has little internal cohesion, and is united neither by an easy outlook nor by a recognizable style. (The right wing is swiftly developing a style for public confrontation, a kind of war paint, like the flag decal on the hard hat.) It is underexposed by the media, which prefers the pyrotechnics of confrontation. In a period of polarization its ranks are thinned to Left and Right.

Yet this is a sector of youth that can moderate the cultural clash within its generation and turn politics from theater to reality. Its mood is left-of-center. Its composition is cross-sectional in terms of blue- and white-collar mix, family income, percentage in and out of college, religion. It has natural ties to the nation across economics, education, and ethnicity. It could be the core of a progressive coalition that reaches into both the leftist (especially the radical-reform) and the conservative (especially the trade-union) wings of the nation.

How and whether this can come to pass is an item for another discussion. But the starting point must be a realization that the struggle between generations is far less significant for the politics of our times than the struggle within the generation of the young.

Sanford Gottlieb

State Within a State

WHAT IS THE MILITARY-INDUSTRIAL COMPLEX?

For where your treasure is,
there will your heart be also.

—MATTHEW 6:21

The military-industrial complex today commands power far beyond the measure it knew when President Eisenhower warned in his Farewell Address of 1961 against its "unwarranted influence."

Its clout at the end of the sixties could be measured by a few figures.[1] Americans were spending an annual average of $400 each on "defense." The military was receiving half of each federal tax dollar (excluding the costs of past wars) and more than half the funds spent in the nation on research. Five million men and women were serving in the armed forces and as civilian employees of the Pentagon; four million were working in defense industries, with millions more economically dependent upon them. The Defense Department deployed 339 lobbyists on Capitol Hill and more than 6,000 public relations men in the United States and abroad. Between the end of World War II and 1969, a total of one trillion dollars was spent on the military— a major part during the Kennedy and Johnson administrations.

1. From Senator Edward Kennedy, "National Priorities and the Defense Budget: The Need for New Realities," *Congressional Record,* February 26, 1970; Richard F. Kaufman, "As Eisenhower Was Saying . . . 'We Must Guard Against Unwarranted Influence by the Military-Industrial Complex,'" the *New York Times Magazine,* June 22, 1969; Seymour Melman, *Pentagon Capitalism* (New York: McGraw-Hill, 1970).

This massive investment not only purchased the most destructive military machine in history; it also animated an institution new to American life, the military-industrial complex. The complex is a web of political and economic relationships among defense industries and associations, the military and civilian leadership in the Pentagon, the Atomic Energy Commission, that part of Congress which deals with the interests of the military, some labor unions, universities,[2] and "think tanks" which are heavily dependent upon military expenditures, and the organizations of veterans, reservists, and superpatriots which define their role as promoting "peace through [armed] strength."

The leaders of this complex are not hard to find. On August 12, 1970, the ballroom of the Washington Hilton Hotel was filled with them, at a three-hour luncheon of 1,150 generals, congressmen, and defense contractors to honor the late Congressman Mendel Rivers, then chairman of the House Armed Services Committee. The affair was sponsored by the Washington Chapter of the Air Force Association. Among the treats were music by several Air Force bands; a demonstration by the Army's Old Guard Fife and Drum Corps; a fifteen-page printed program in red, white, and blue, listing seventy-five defense-oriented firms whose "cooperation" or "participation" made the gathering possible, and a speech by Vice-President Spiro Agnew. The latter praised Rivers for his "willingness to go to bat for the so-called and often discredited military-industrial complex." Agnew said he wanted "to lay to rest the ugly, vicious, dastardly rumors" that Rivers "is trying to move the Pentagon piecemeal to South Carolina." South Carolina has indeed been the seat of many military installations, but Chairman Rivers also permitted some important pieces of the complex to move to Massachusetts, Connecticut, Texas, California, Washington, and Alaska. Abundance fosters generosity.

Although he did not spin this web, the President is, in effect, the spider who sits astride it. That the President sometimes finds this posture uncomfortable in no way diminishes his power to rearrange the strands. If he tries to abandon the web, however, he can expect massive resistance, for too many careers are wound up in it.

2. The Massachusetts Institute of Technology has been among the 100 top contractors for years, ranking 67th in the fiscal year 1969 as the result of Pentagon contracts totaling $100.5 million, according to the Defense Department.

The military-industrial complex is a mid-twentieth-century institution. In the past there obviously have been American military establishments, defense industries, war-hawk congressmen, and super-patriotic organizations. But until the 1950s and 1960s there was never such an interlocking directorate as today presides over a key juncture of the public and private sectors of the economy, disburses vast sums for production and research, extends its influence to "every city, every statehouse, every office of the Federal Government" (as described by President Eisenhower), dominates American foreign policy, and even assumes for itself the right to spy on the political activities of private citizens and public officials.

The military-industrial complex has become something like a state within the state.

Part bureaucratic, part industrial, the complex is a network in which even the closest observers fail to detect where government ends and the corporation begins. Indeed, the complex has led to a wholly new form of corporation: a government-created, government-subsidized hybrid earning private profits from the tax coffers and unprepared to compete for commercial markets.

Defense industry is fed by the state, and the state by defense industry. In the process, the military-industrial complex assumes a self-perpetuating momentum of its own, resisting control from any quarter, public or private. This explains in part why strong public opposition to the war in Indochina, to high levels of military spending, and to worldwide military commitments has not been translated into basic changes of governmental policy.

The complex first grew up in response to America's emergence as a major power after World War II and the cold war which followed. Its institutional foundations were laid by a memorandum on "Scientific and Technological Resources as Military Assets" from Army Chief of Staff Dwight Eisenhower in April 1946,[3] and by the National Security Act of 1947, which unified the armed services, coordinated military research and industrial production, and established the National Security Council and the Central Intelligence Agency.[4]

The National Security Council, which brought together the Secretary

---

3. Published in full in Melman, *Pentagon Capitalism*, pp. 231–34.
4. See *The Pentagon Watchers*, Leonard S. Rodberg and Derek Shearer, eds. (New York: Anchor Books, 1970), pp. 10–13.

of State and the civilian and military chiefs of the Pentagon to advise the President, represented the institutionalized fusion of military and foreign-policy interests. It reflected the twin premises of the cold war: military power is the primary component of national security; the United States must defend the "free world" against aggressive Communism.

These premises, in turn, had their source in a confluence of conditions dating from 1942–47: the successful wartime collaboration between American industry and the military; a heady sense of power in Washington after defeat of the Axis and the start of the atomic era; and the mix of business bias with messianic idealism in the American political leadership. The military-mindedness of civilians was then, and still remains, a far greater force than the military itself.

In pursuit of the cold-war version of national security, American decision-makers pressed single-mindedly for ever greater armed might. Members of Congress became conditioned to the automatic "aye" vote whenever the executive branch and the chairmen of the powerful Armed Services Committee discovered another "foreign threat" and recommended another military alliance or another weapons system. Military conscription, approved by the narrowest of margins in 1940, was considered a permanent institution by most Americans only a generation later. In the course of this process, Congress abdicated many of its powers, and the executive branch emerged as the primary force in American government. Since congressmen so willingly granted the Pentagon whatever it wished, canny legislators successfully financed civilian programs in scientific research and education with Defense Department funds.

The economy, too, was altered by the addition of an ingredient that accelerated the militarization of American society and foreign policy. Whole new industries, such as aerospace, and new corporate giants, such as General Dynamics, were nurtured on huge defense contracts, most of them negotiated directly rather than subjected to the risks of competitive bidding, with their way smoothed by the free use of government land and equipment and by tax write-offs for glossy advertisements touting their new, sophisticated products. Some of the products of this industrial hybrid were designed to reach the moon, most to reach the Soviet Union and China.

In 1960, less than a year before he became President Kennedy's science adviser, Jerome Wiesner wrote in *Daedalus* that U.S. Army and Navy studies concluded that two hundred relatively secure sea-borne missiles on each side would constitute an adequate nuclear deterrent. By the end of the decade, the United States could launch forty-two hundred long-range nuclear warheads; the U.S.S.R., two thousand. According to former Defense Secretary Robert McNamara, four hundred of these weapons could annihilate a third of the Soviet population. *Overkill* entered our vocabulary.

Since defense is today defined in terms of deterrence, it is impossible to judge whether the protection of the United States during this period did indeed require such an awesome force. One can always claim that the Minuteman and Titan missiles and the B-52s (which, until the Kennedy administration, tested Soviet defenses by flying directly toward the U.S.S.R. and veering away within a few miles of the border) deterred a Soviet attack. One *cannot* claim, however, that these weapons of mass destruction, buttressed by tens of thousands of tactical nuclear weapons, a two-ocean Navy, conventional forces, chemical and biological warfare agents, three thousand military bases, and more than forty military alliances, prevented a long guerrilla war in Southeast Asia or conflicts in the Middle East, or that they stopped the Russians from repressing the Hungarian revolt or the Czechoslovak liberalization, or that they halted the establishment of a Communist regime in the Western Hemisphere. Clearly, the American people were paying high prices for uncertain service.

One by-product of the pursuit of security through military means has been increased secrecy in foreign policy. It was not until October 1970, for example, that the American public learned that the United States had entered into an unpublicized agreement in 1960 to support a forty-thousand-man Ethiopian army and to oppose any threats to the territorial integrity of Ethiopia. The decade of aid was worth $147 million to the Ethiopian government, in return for permission to construct a large electronics eavesdropping base at Kagnew Station, at Asmara. This agreement and other secret commitments by the executive branch came to light only through the careful work of a Senate Foreign Relations Subcommittee chaired by Stuart Symington.

Similarly, the public was unaware that the Johnson administration had followed a "2½-wars-at-once strategy" until former Budget

Director Charles Schultze returned to private life and spoke out. This strategy was based on the novel notion that the United States should have the capability of simultaneously fighting conventional land wars in Europe and Asia and a guerrilla war somewhere in the "Third World," while holding its nuclear power in reserve. Less ambitious, the Nixon administration cut back to 1½ wars.

Whatever its effects on the international scene, the trillion-dollar investment in the military fueled a huge industrial pyramid at home. The number of prime defense contractors soared to 22,000, served by 100,000 subcontractors. Yet the top 100 contractors received about 65 percent of the contracts awarded in 1967. Between 1960 and 1967, 38 companies received more than $1 billion each in prime military contracts. Lockheed led the parade with a seven-year total of $10.6 billion. While defense contracts spread throughout American industry, the giant contractors took the biggest slice of the pie.[5]

The system of procurement in defense industry has provided high profits at low risk to the corporations, while passing along tremendous cost overruns to the taxpayers. Lavish government subsidies, a tendency to deal directly with a single contractor rather than engage in competitive bidding, and permissiveness toward shoddy performance led to a total of almost $24 billion in cost overruns on 38 weapons systems as of March 31, 1970. According to Gordon Rule, a civilian procurement official for the Pentagon in 1968, "No matter how poor the quality, how late the product and how high the cost, [defense contractors] know nothing will happen to them."[6] The government has a consistent record of extricating them from difficulties.

An incestuous relationship between military procurement officers and their civilian counterparts in defense firms also contributes to high prices and high profits. Upon retirement, many military regulars go to work for the big contractors, and many top officials in the defense firms advance their careers by shuttling to civilian jobs in the Pentagon before returning to government-subsidized corporate life. President Nixon named one top defense-firm official, David Packard, to the second-highest post in the Defense Department.

In response to a request from Senator William Proxmire, chairman

5. The figures in this paragraph are from Kaufman, "As Eisenhower Was Saying . . . ," and Melman, *Pentagon Capitalism*.
6. Quoted by Kaufman, "As Eisenhower Was Saying . . ."

of the Subcommittee on Economy in Government of the Joint Economic Committee, the Pentagon released in February 1969 a list of 2,072 retired regular military officers who were employed by the 95 biggest defense contractors. The ten firms employing the largest number had 1,065 on their payrolls, an average of 106 each and triple the average number they had employed a decade earlier.

Former military officers thus enter positions in which they may negotiate defense contracts with friends and old associates. In addition, according to Senator Proxmire, "there is the subtle or unconscious temptation to the officer still on active duty. After all, he can see that over two thousand of his fellow officers work for the big companies. How hard a bargain does he drive with them when he is one or two years away from retirement?"

The sixteen research centers supported by Pentagon funds also provide opportunities for career advancement. In 1968, seven presidents and five vice-presidents of these "think tanks" had previously held high positions in the Defense Department. The best paid was the $90,000-a-year president of Aerospace Corporation, an offshoot of the Air Force.[7]

The public has no means of knowing the true size of defense profits. No comprehensive study has been done, especially of the giant firms that receive most of the contract awards. The big corporation that sells an entire weapons system to the Pentagon makes much higher profits than the smaller firm that sells soldiers' shirts, but no one knows how much higher. Furthermore, the corporations that sell to both the Pentagon and civilian markets add to the problem by refusing to reveal financial records for the two different kinds of work.

Even if the defense firms' financial records were opened to public scrutiny, the hidden benefits would not necessarily show. For, while the free use of government land and equipment surely contribute to corporate profits, it does not appear on the books. The government makes "progress payments" for expenses incurred rather than work performed, so the defense companies often do not have to borrow working capital. The sheer volume of sales to the Pentagon helps the contractors establish credit and maintain their work force. Moreover, when a contractor is paid for a cost overrun, he may use the money

7. *Ibid.*

for a variety of purposes (including more luxurious offices or bigger expense accounts), although these payments are not called profits.

Occasionally, the informed observer glimpses part of the reality. Such a glimpse proves that a truer picture is revealed when defense profits are calculated as a percentage of return on the contractor's often minimal investment rather than as a percentage of the government-paid cost. Richard Kaufman, a highly competent staff economist on Senator Proxmire's subcommittee, has explained the difference:

An example of the difference was demonstrated in a 1962 tax court case, North American Aviation *vs.* Renegotiation Board. The contracts provided for 8 percent profits as a percentage of costs; the tax court found that the company had realized profits of 612 percent and 802 percent on its investment in two succeeding years. The reason for the huge return on investment was the Defense Department policy of supplying both fixed and working capital to many of the larger contractors. In some cases the amount of government-owned property exceeds the contractors' investment.[8]

Military research and production have spread far beyond the hybrid firms that sell most of their products to Washington. Long-established companies in the private sector, literally household names, operate largely invisible military sidelines. General Electric makes re-entry vehicles for MIRV, the hydra-headed missile which will generate chronic fear of surprise attack in an adversary's military establishment. GE also happens to be the third-largest defense contractor. The Bulova Watch Company manufactures parts for projectiles. Whirlpool and General Motors are engaged in the projectile business. Motorola makes components for 40mm. grenade launchers and classified military electronic equipment. Honeywell's thermostats are for friendly civilian customers; its anti-personnel weapons, torpedoes, and Poseidon missile parts are for the enemy. Dow Chemical has abandoned napalm; now it produces herbicides and nose assemblies for bombs.

But even the wealthiest nation in the world has finite resources. It required the cumulative effect of the Vietnam war on top of cold-war expenditures to teach the lesson that finally this country cannot have both guns and butter—at least, not without wage and price controls and still higher taxes. But that lesson has just begun to come home to the American public.

8. *Ibid.*

The trillion-dollar investment in the military has deprived the public of both material and human resources. The steel used for missiles was not available for housing. The scientists who developed the nuclear-powered missile-launching submarine were not available to develop antipollution devices. Together, the lack of funds and skills depleted the public sector at the very time the country's social and racial problems were growing more volatile. And the diversion of these resources to the military did nothing to enhance the nation's will to meet its internal problems.

The results are seen most starkly in the field of health. While the United States ranks first in the world in gross national product and military spending, it is twenty-third from the top in infant mortality and eleventh in the number of physicians per inhabitant. Nor is it coincidental that the country with the highest productivity rate per employee—Japan—has spent the smallest share of its gross national product on the military, while the United States, which has spent more than eight times as much as Japan on the military in percentage of GNP, has a rate of productivity only one-third as great.

The shortage of available brainpower is probably more devastating to American society than even the lack of material resources. Steel can be shifted easily to civilian use, but scientists, engineers, and managers who have spent years working under the conditions that prevail in defense industry may require considerable retraining before they can perform tasks relevant to the satisfaction of human needs.

When the Kerner Commission issued its report following the explosions in the ghettos in 1967, it attached no cost estimates to its recommendations for programs to provide more housing, education, health care, jobs, and transportation for black Americans. Later, Hyman Bookbinder, a former official of the Office of Employment Opportunity, estimated that it would require $50 billion a year for twenty years to implement the Commission's recommendations. This estimate happens to equal the sum invested in the military during the postwar generation.

The first organized citizens' attack on military spending was launched in 1969. The attack was spurred by growing public disenchantment with the Vietnam war, high taxes, inflation, cost overruns, and such military blunders as the accidental killing of 6,400 sheep in Utah by nerve gas and the designation of the Seattle, Chicago, and

Boston suburbs as sites for the administration's proposed antiballistic missile program.

In the Senate, the campaign, led by Senators John Sherman Cooper and Philip Hart, focused for months on halting ABM. When the vote was cast in August, the opposition failed by only one vote to stop a major new weapons system. For the first time since the nuclear test-ban debate, the relationship between weaponry and national security re-entered the public dialogue. Yet, once the Senate vote on ABM was past, opposition to other military measures largely dissipated. The challengers had not yet developed the staying power of the complex.

In the House, the opposition was spearheaded by a dissident group of five members of the Armed Services Committee. Meeting for the first time on June 10, 1969, Democrats Robert Leggett, Lucien Nedzi, and Otis Pike, and Republicans Charles Whalen and Robert Stafford sought a unified approach to such problems as military redundancy and marginal programs. After discussions among themselves and with specialists, they sent Chairman Rivers a letter outlining their goals. Rivers's answer to the "Fearless Five," as they became known, was to have his staff draw up the military authorization bill and refuse to show it to the dissidents until the evening before it appeared in committee. The five then prepared nine amendments. Each amendment was granted thirty to sixty seconds of discussion in committee. One amendment was ultimately adopted on the House floor.

While the legislative victories by the dissidents in both houses were exceedingly slim, the pressure did succeed in convincing the House Appropriations Committee to cut $1 billion from the bill and in moving the administration to trim its chemical-bacteriological warfare program.

During the debate in the House, some of the "Fearless Five" worked with Members of Congress for Peace Through Law (MCPL), a bipartisan, bicameral group founded by former Senator Joseph Clark (D.-Pa.). For the first time, MCPL hired a professional staff to service its members for the military debate. The beginnings of coordination among the opposition in both houses was thus established.

Four months before the first meeting of the "Fearless Five," the Coalition on National Priorities and Military Policy was born in Washington. Built on earlier efforts at coordination by voluntary organizations, the Coalition mobilized religious, peace, labor, scientific, and social-action groups in the fight against ABM and mindless military spending. Under the leadership of Joseph Clark and the Washington staff members of its affiliates, the Coalition became an important counterweight to the military-industrial complex.

Faced with a new antimilitarist mood in Congress and the country, as well as severe budgetary pressures caused by anticipated deficits, the Nixon administration cut further into the military budget, adopted the rhetoric of "new priorities," and elaborated a new military strategy.

In presenting to Congress the budget for fiscal year 1971, including somewhat reduced military expenditures of $73.6 billion, the Nixon administration claimed that it was in the process of reordering national priorities. Not only were the savings from a diminishing conflict in Vietnam being channeled into programs of human need, it said, but more of the budget dollar (41 percent) would be spent on "human resources" than on national defense (36 percent). Thanks to a detailed analysis by Senator Mark Hatfield, the administration's deceitful use of budget figures was revealed in an address by the Oregon Republican to a town meeting in Corvallis on February 10, 1970. The executive branch achieved its figures of 41 percent for human resources, Hatfield explained, by including under this category the expenditures for such trust funds as social security and railroad retirement (which Congress, as a caretaker, is in no position to touch), all payments for veterans' benefits, and even the costs of operating the Selective Service System.

After Hatfield excluded the trust funds from current governmental expenditures, placed veterans' payments as well as the interest on the national debt under the category of the costs of past wars, moved the expenditures for the draft system into the military column, and made other adjustments, his figures looked far different from the administration's. The true picture of the budget for fiscal 1971, according to Hatfield, was: 48.4 percent for current military expenditures; 16.4 percent for the costs of past wars; 17 percent for human resources, and 18.2 percent for all other expenditures including agriculture and commerce. Very little had changed except the rhetoric.

The Nixon Pentagon prepared for a long-term shift in strategy that would cut costs in manpower while bolstering its firepower. Since general-purpose forces (infantry divisions and the nonnuclear navy and aircraft) consume two-thirds of the military dollar, the Nixon administration intends to cut back troops and bases overseas.[9] The administration will explain this shift primarily in terms of a defense-policy review that has resulted in a modified assessment of the Communist threat on land. It will ask allies to share more of the defense burden and is prepared to grant them increased military assistance. This will result in a new reduction in expenditures for conventional forces.

At the same time, however, the Nixon Pentagon plans to increase conventional firepower and to expand strategic nuclear forces to include MIRVs on land and sea-based missiles, a supersonic bomber (B-1) to replace the B-52, the antiballistic missile system (unless limited by an accord with the Soviet Union), an underwater missile system (ULMS), and a new airborne continental defense system (AWACS). If all of these sophisticated strategic weapons are developed and deployed, the cost will far overshadow the savings expected to result from a reduction in manpower. The mere cost of the weapons systems approved by the end of 1970 (not including the B-1, ULMS and AWACS) would amount to a minimum of $22 billion—plus $25 billion to buy and operate the F-14 Navy fighter intercepter for a ten-year period!

The bigger, more modern defense contractors who make up the vital center of the military-industrial complex have thus laid claim to any "peace dividend" in the 1970s, while the smaller components of the complex struggle to hold what they have.

We can anticipate that this claim will not go unchallenged. There will be a three-way competition during the 1970s for the resources of the public sector. The complex and its ideological supporters, the pressure groups for peace and new priorities, and those who would solve all public problems by reducing taxes to stimulate private consumption will vie for the tax dollar. The outcome of this competition will determine whether the military-industrial complex can be controlled and, ultimately, overcome.

The case for the military-minded was argued by Deputy Director

9. See "The Armed Forces' Reluctant Retrenchment," Juan Cameron, *Fortune,* November 1970.

of Defense David Packard at the annual convention of the Instrument Society of America on October 26, 1970:

Clearly, the world is no less hostile than it has been. In fact, the threat of conflict and violence is, if anything, increasing. The Soviet Union has been building up its development and production of military weapons. At the present time the Soviet build-up of strategic nuclear forces and naval forces is more rapid than it has ever been. One can hardly deny that forces of subversion and revolution inside the boundaries of many free world countries are expanding at an alarming rate, not only in traditionally troubled areas like the Middle East, but even right here at home in the United States, in Canada and in South America.

Then, after estimating that the United States is "from two to four years ahead of the Soviet Union in every important area of weapons technology," Packard defined his fears for the future:

If we ever lose the lead we now have in all major areas of military technology, we will inevitably face the prospect of having to accept a Sputnik not just in one or two unimportant areas now and then, but the prospect of a Sputnik in every important area of military weapons, in strategic nuclear forces, in naval forces, and in conventional ground forces. No responsible administration official nor any member of Congress can afford, in my opinion, to take that gamble with the future security of our nation and the future safety of our people.

An unspoken thought in this presentation was the political calculation of the effects of unemployment. In the previous year, two million workers had been added to the ranks of the jobless. Many had been employees of defense industries and the Pentagon, as well as members of the armed services. The Nixon administration failed to plan adequately to cushion the effects of defense cutbacks on these individuals and their communities. Simultaneously, it sought their votes at election time. One way to reduce the political gamble would be to limit defense-industry cutbacks.

Another constituency, however, had a different view of the security of our nation and the safety of our people. Concerned with peace and a new set of priorities, it included many of the well-educated, affluent professionals, academics, housewives, and students who had supported Eugene McCarthy and Robert Kennedy in 1968, reinforced more recently by a circle of the ecology-minded. Some were active in pressure groups working for peace, quality education, mass transportation, adequate housing, and a clean environment. Others were businessmen aroused over the increasingly depleted central cities. In the late 1960s, they watched the ghettos burn although no enemy missiles had penetrated our defenses. They breathed noxious fumes in the urban areas although no chemical warfare attack had been launched. They found heroin and Molotov cocktails more immediate threats than the Soviet SS-9. They were ready to seek the funds for their favorite domestic programs in the swollen military budget.

Potential allies for this new constituency could be found within two groups that had been growing increasingly hostile to each other: poor blacks and white workers. The needs of the poor blacks were so great that, whatever else was required to meet them, a massive investment of federal funds was clearly a basic ingredient. Yet apathy among the masses of blacks and disunity among the handful of the organized had so far rendered them largely impotent as a pressure group for change. If blacks began to pull together more effectively for their own interests, however, they might meet more resistance from working-class whites. Disadvantaged by the tax structure, harried by unemployment, convinced that their taxes were spent on welfare recipients rather than on services for hard-working, obedient citizens, white workers constituted one of the most insecure and fearful groups in American society. Nevertheless, a number of unions began to take increasingly outspoken positions against military expenditures and for a large budget to meet human needs.

Whether these unions can carry their memberships with them toward this new stance remains one of the questions of the next decade. White workers form an important part of a tax revolt, which was directed largely against expenditures for education in the late 1960s. In the 1970 elections, a *New York Times* survey of the fifty states found that voters generally rejected state proposals to increase taxes or issue new bonds for education. State officials attributed this resistance to "opposition to new taxes of any kind during an economic slump, disgust with student disorders in both colleges and high schools, opposition to busing and integration, and misgivings about the effectiveness of educational institutions."[10]

10. John Herbers, "Survey Finds Voters Across the Nation Opposed Bonds or Taxes for Education," *New York Times,* November 8, 1970.

Yet the mix of socioeconomic resentments directed against educational outlays did not seem to extend to other governmental activities. The same survey reported greater generosity toward state proposals to build highways and antipollution and recreational facilities. When added to the fact that 49 percent of those polled by Gallup in 1970 favored cuts in military spending,[11] it would appear that the impulse to cut taxes can move in a variety of directions in the future. Indeed, sufficiently large cuts in military spending could lead *both* to tax reductions and increased spending on civilian programs.

How realistic is it to assume that the outcome of this political-economic competition is not yet determined by the weight of the military-industrial complex?

While the complex has developed a life of its own, it has not completely escaped the influence of the democratic process. Elected and appointed officials—not some secret, faceless cabal—continue to make decisions about public policies and resources. These officials must choose between new weapons systems and new educational programs, between restrictions on presidential authority to send troops abroad and open-ended commitments, between bailing out Lockheed and writing off a bad investment. Just as men in the executive branch and Congress made decisions in the 1940s and '50s which, in part unwittingly, laid the foundations for the military-industrial complex, so may men in the executive branch and Congress make decisions more consciously in the 1970s which would help to dismantle it.

Because of the institutionalized momentum of the complex, the task is obviously difficult. Yet, at least during the 1970s, it will not be impossible. The power of the complex explains much, but not all, of the federal government's policies. Citizens, too, share some of the blame for their failure to *sustain* an organized effort to pressure and/or replace the decision-makers in Washington. There have been many valiant ad hoc skirmishes, but there has not yet been a protracted political war. Many of the potential troops for such a struggle seem too discouraged, cynical, or tired to wage it. This weakness of will augments the image of an omnipotent enemy—ironically, at a moment when it is on the defensive for the first time.

11. *New York Times,* September 24, 1970.

A political struggle requires a strategy; any strategy which seeks to reduce the power of the military-industrial complex must be based on the urgency of transferring much of its substance to the civilian sector. The major effort—to be undertaken at a time when many Americans feel an undefined malaise and are ready to examine their collective problems—must be directed at persuading the voters, and through them the executive branch and Congress, that most of the federal budget should be spent on people rather than on armed force.

Some structural changes would help, but they are minor. For example, the establishment of a single congressional committee to review all requests for funds would reduce the influence of the all-powerful Armed Services Committees and the Defense Subcommittees of the Appropriations Committees. Yet the national will to shift priorities is infinitely more important than altering this parliamentary procedure. The will to cut the Pentagon's funds means fewer defense contracts, fewer bases, fewer lobbyists, fewer congressional allies. The will to shift funds to domestic programs means that the nation can at least begin to discover whether its problems are susceptible to solution.

Persuasion of the voters should deal with three areas:

1. the concept of national security;
2. the quality of life within the United States;
3. conversion of military production and facilities to civilian uses.

The first requires that a whole series of questions, postponed for a generation, now must enter the public dialogue. What are the vital interests of the United States? How should they be defended? Do more weapons make us more secure? Is the arms race itself a threat to the peace? How much is it worth to society to purchase a specific weapons system, as against expenditures for anti-pollution facilities, quality education, or national health insurance? These questions will have to be continually posed, and answered, through all available public forums.

The second area requires a more organizational, less intellectual effort. A myriad of voluntary organizations exists in the domains of environment, education, health, housing, and social welfare. They all seek federal funds. Almost invariably, they work separately, with a minimum of allies, in each community. Their success will depend on the forging of an urban-suburban coalition of common interests and an awareness that the tax dollars they seek now go to the military.

Here the peace groups can play a crucial role as catalysts. Without broadening their mandate to include purely domestic questions, they can "lobby the lobbies" in the domestic field in order to explain where the tax dollars have really gone and to urge creation of human-needs coalitions at the grass roots and in Washington. In short, the peace groups can help persuade the domestic lobbies that they are the joint underdogs in a very tough competition.

Local leadership of an exceptional quality will be needed before the conservationists agree to support higher pay for teachers in return for the education association's support for a sewage-treatment plant, and before the ghetto leadership agrees to support higher municipal salaries in return for support by the municipal employees of low-cost housing measures. Yet such exchanges are the stuff of which coalitions are forged.

The third area of mass persuasion, conversion of military production and facilities to civilian uses, requires a sophisticated campaign on behalf of planning by defense contractors and by government at all levels. On the one hand, the defense firms possess skills, equipment, and land which would be invaluable to life-serving programs. On the other hand, the managements that have been nurtured on federal largesse are reluctant to endure the vagaries of the commercial market, while the federal government has been both permissive and overprotective toward its industrial offspring. Under the best of conditions, it may take a firm two years to switch to a different line of work. The big defense managements, however, would rather fight than switch.

As voters and taxpayers demand that the federal government press these firms to prepare themselves for civilian life, a chink is opened in the armor of the military-industrial complex. If the managements move to convert, they wean themselves away from dependence on military contracts. If they do not, the federal government will be obliged during this decade to choose between permanent subsidies for the costly monster it has created or making it shift for itself in the cruel world of free enterprise.

The employees of these firms, however, cannot simply be abandoned as military spending shifts or declines. Federal and state governments will have to finance retraining programs, relocation costs, and extended unemployment benefits for the production workers, engineers, and scientists laid off by the defense companies. In supporting measures to cushion the impact of layoffs on these employees, the unions that represent them find another area of overlapping interest with the peace and new-priorities groups which have promoted conversion planning.

In seeking to generate the kind of sustained pressures on the decision-makers in Washington which can reverse the trend toward militarization, the peace and new-priorities forces must work against a deadline. They do not have forever, nor do they face inevitable defeat. But a combination of an increasingly deadly arms race, the mounting pollution and decay in the megalopolis, and the frustration and despair among many Americans mean that the turn must be made during the 1970s. Unless the nation is demilitarized in the coming decade, its problems may well be insoluble.

Ben B. Seligman

Corporate Takeover and Popular Challenge

The post-World War II period in American business has been a success story of seemingly endless prosperity. When the nation entered the war, the depression had been buried in its bones like a never-ending fever. The vast outlays occasioned by the war effort had engendered a repressed demand and unused purchasing power that exploded after 1945 with such force that all the dour predictions of the economists proved groundless. In the early 1940s the population had grown to 137 million; twenty years later, there were 180 million heads to count. In the same period, the gross national product went from $230 billion in real dollars to $500 billion. The result was a marked increase in per capita real income. Steel production jumped in the two decades by more than a third, aluminum output was up ninefold, oil production doubled, almost twice as many automobiles were now on the road, and expenditures for housing had increased by 60 percent. The United States had become a wonder in the world: a perpetually prosperous nation.

Yet two persistent problems gnawed at its vitals: income distribution remained lopsided, so that not everyone shared in the newly attained paradise, and stability kept teetering on the knife edge of recession. While the sort of poverty that had been so pervasive in the thirties had clearly diminished, America seemed unable to grapple with the hard core: the rural poor, the Negro and other ethnic minorities, the aged, and the low-paid workers. The income line that marked off the lowest fifth in the income scale was $2,400 in 1950; but, said the Department of Labor, it required $3,700 to support a family of four on a "modest but adequate budget." In 1935 the lowest fifth got 4.1 percent of total income; in 1950 the lowest fifth got 4.8 percent; in 1967, the figure was virtually the same. In the same years the richest fifth's share hovered between 44 and 45 percent. There had not been much substantial change in relative patterns of distribution. Whatever improvement there had been stemmed from an upward shift in the entire scale. Meanwhile, poverty was threatening to become a chronic ailment.

Meanwhile, business itself was acquiring attributes of elephantiasis. A company that had had assets of $250 million in 1949 would have needed $375 million to hold on to its ranking a decade later. In the 1960s, annual sales of $1 billion were not unusual. In 1968 there were more than one hundred industrial firms with sales in excess of $1 billion; almost fifty banks had deposits exceeding $1 billion; there were almost thirty insurance companies with assets of over $1 billion; sales of twenty merchandising firms went above that figure; and more than thirty utilities showed assets that allowed them to join the circle. Indeed, the sales of one corporation, General Motors, were equivalent to almost 3 percent of the gross national product.

Large corporations so dominated the economy that the welfare of the nation was now largely dependent on their success. Some argued from numbers—after all, there were still at least five million enterprises in the United States—the big fellows did not account for everything. But such arguments ignored the patent fact that most of these enterprises were far too small to exert any weight in the balance. Some 2 million firms could be found in retailing, the last refuge of the individual entrepreneur, who in any case was being displaced by the giant department store and large supermarket operator. Indeed, the five hundred largest industrial firms had sales in 1969 equivalent to almost half the gross national product, a gain of some 8 percent over 1962. Of all the active enterprises in the United States only about twenty-five hundred could be counted as economically significant, and these were controlled by no more than 0.1 percent recorded stockholders. More and more, the major economic activity of the nation was being sustained by the large corporations.

Moreover, new faces began to appear among the billionaires. Paul Getty, one of the newer oil-rich magnates, was reputed in 1969 to be the world's wealthiest man. He had made his first million dollars in 1916 at the age of twenty-three as an oil wildcatter, but an inheritance of $15 million that grew over the years to $700 million constituted the foundation of his fortune. In the 1930s, when prices were low, he began to buy into the Pacific Western Oil Company and Tidewater Associated Oil. Within a few years, an involved sequence of stock purchases brought him control of Tidewater, despite opposition from the Standard Oil people, whom he succeeded in outwitting —no small feat. In 1937, he secured control of another sizable firm, Mission Development Company. Getty now holds almost 80 percent of Getty Oil, which in turn controls Mission; the latter holds majority shares in Tidewater and Skelly Oil. The combined value of Getty, Skelly, and Tidewater is well over $3.5 billion. Though his companies are not as fully integrated as other large oil firms, Getty manages to hold his own, ruling his empire quietly from a mansion near London. In the manner of an old-fashioned entrepreneur, he has avoided publicity and politics.

Other oil magnates have been less retiring about political affairs. H. L. Hunt, whose wealth has been estimated at around $500 million, has sponsored numerous right-wing political ventures, some of them close to the lunatic fringe. Hunt approaches the Henry Ford paradigm, subsidizing radio programs that broadcast sentiments redolent of the red-necked, spittoon-filling, fundamentalist, cracker-barrel philosophy of the Ku Klux Klan. His subsidiaries are funneled through a number of foundations whose purposes have not yet been questioned by the Internal Revenue Service. Hunt has been rather tight-fisted with outright political gifts, even to the Republican party, which for him may not be far enough to the Right. Yet, when oil-depletion allowances are even mildly threatened, as in the early days of the Kennedy administration, Hunt's largesse to the opposition seemed ample enough. The Hunt philosophy appears to be a variant of nineteenth-century Know Nothingism, in the modern version of which all Presidents after Coolidge have been wild-eyed radicals.

But by the 1960s, the personal touch was no longer the dominant motif in American business. It was the impersonal corporate entity that was to set the tone of the economic environment. And the corporation was to grow by acquisition, swallowing other corporations like an anaconda. The merger became the classic American way of building an industrial empire. In Europe, where the cartel had usually been employed, some concession was made to individual corporate identity. But here businessmen preferred to buy out their rivals, taking over plants and assets *in toto* and fusing disparate enterprises into new and wonderfully complex organizations. Bringing together plants, financial structures, and selling apparatuses, the merger, which became something of an imperative in American business, was largely made possible by the ineffectiveness of the antitrust laws. These laws, sufficient for controlling loose arrangements, such as trade associations, were unable until 1950 to place any restraint at all on merger activity. A Clayton Act amendment in that year made mergers tending "substantially to lessen competition" legally dubious. Of course, the question of when competition was *not* reduced in an industrial combination was difficult for a jurist to decide, as is illustrated by the ruling of Federal Judge W. J. LaBuy, who dismissed antitrust charges against Du Pont, General Motors, and United States Rubber. This distinguished jurist held, among other things, that there was no proof that Du Pont controlled General Motors, even though at times it was voting 51 percent of the stock at stockholders' meetings.

The first great merger movement took place in about 1898–1904. The underlying factors in this wave included a rapidly growing market for mass-produced goods, thus irrevocably destroying the century-old grip of local parochial monopolies and markets. When these became national in scope, a smaller merchant or manufacturer might no longer expect to retain leadership at home simply because he held a locational advantage. For this he had to thank the fantastic growth of cheap transportation facilities. In addition, technological advances inexorably increased the ratio of fixed to variable costs. The businessman suddenly faced the problem of idle capacity and overhead. The first solution was a price war, calculated to destroy his rivals; but such a war only created a dilemma, for the ensuing cutthroat competition threatened to wipe out everyone. And so there came a realization that "live and let live" should be the ideal rule. Even better, some thought, would be "living together as one," for then anxieties concerning mavericks who might willy-nilly cut prices could be entirely eliminated.

The kind of forces that were joined during the first wave of mergers was epitomized by the spectacular case of the United States Steel

Corporation. After 1904, the American public, giving vent to its traditional hostility toward corporate bigness, began to clamor for a breakup of the trusts. Businessmen were calling for a temporary halt in empire building, not merely to digest what they had already absorbed, but also to gather strength for the expected economic storms: these broke out in 1907. Then came World War I.

A favorable climate for a second wave of mergers was created by postwar optimism. Professional promoters, discovering that capital was readily available, prepared to turn an easy profit. From 1919 to 1921 mergers were initiated, either through holding companies or outright consolidations, expressly for the purpose of taking advantage of a bull market in securities. New companies meant new stocks, and in a rising market a handsome gain could be easily recognized. So far as industry itself was concerned, the major motivations for mergers stemmed either from a desire to establish vertical combines, thereby ensuring a regular supply of raw materials, or from a need to rationalize sales and marketing operations.

By 1926, the third-wave period, a number of new industries— motion pictures, public utilities, radios, automobiles—had reached a state of economic maturity. But the business community did not hesitate to subject them to reorganization, combination, and merger. Nor did they cease with the onset of the depression. From 1932 to 1938, according to a Federal Trade Commission report, there were numerous consolidations in which the outstanding feature was the absorption of small firms by large ones. In the steel industry, during this time, firms with $3 billion in assets swallowed firms worth $217 million; in auto accessories, $377 million in assets took over $28 million; in oil $832 million absorbed $42 million.

The greatest merger movement of all occurred in the 1960s, yet curiously enough an affluent society paid it little mind. In the post– World War II period, the FTC found that there had been about 700 to 800 mergers a year. Between 1940 and. 1947 more than 2,500 firms with total assets of over $5 billion disappeared: this was equal to 5.5 percent of the total assets in manufacturing industry in 1943. Yet all this was merely a prelude to the wave of mergers that has reached its peak in recent years. Large corporations have been literally hunting for new industrial conquests. In 1967 there were almost 3,000 mergers, an increase of 25 percent over the previous year. It was estimated that more than $14 billion was spent on mergers in that year. Such firms as Litton Industries and ITT have with notable success fed on all sorts of companies. It seemed that the desire to be big could not be suppressed.

The mergers were made easier by offers of convertible securities, rather than cash, on which capital-gains taxes would have had to be paid. Moreover, attractive dividend rates inhibited conversion and protected the remaining common stock from dilution. And so the McDonnell Company, a military aircraft firm, took over Douglas Aircraft, and Ling-Temco-Vought acquired Wilson and Company, a meat packer. A further harvest could be garnered by splitting up the acquired properties and offering to the public portions of the stock on each part. Ling-Temco-Vought not only dismembered Wilson in this way but toyed with its own properties as well. The procedure was called "redeployment of assets."

There was little doubt that businessmen welcomed mergers, particularly the inside managers who kept expressing a concern with growth. Managerial interest appeared to focus on maximizing size rather than profit, thereby insuring control of the market. Pious expressions of faith in the Smithian "unseen hand" notwithstanding, rigorous price competition remained the bane of their existence. The urge to monopolize has not been the sole motivation for mergers. Frequently a profitable firm would buy up unprofitable ones for the purpose of acquiring tax losses to balance against accumulated gains. Tax benefits have been the major consideration in at least 10 percent of the mergers of small firms and in at least 25 percent of the large firms. Some older firms bought younger ones to take over new inventions and ideas; sometimes the motive for a merger was euphemistically described as "diversification," or as the need to produce a fuller line of items. Whatever the immediate reason, the basic acquisitive urge was to achieve a dominant position in their field. The merger movement basically was a struggle for greater market strength, with personal ambition playing a not insignificant part. The natural consequence was to create monopolistic industrial structures.

That concentration in industry is increased by such mergers would seem to be self-evident. George Stigler, a fairly conservative economist, said in 1950 that not one steel company had been able to add as much as 4 percent of ingot capacity through attracting new customers, implying thereby that the greatest part of growth was to be explained by merger, consolidation, and asset purchase.

Yet the government in the 1960s seemed reluctant to hinder the merger movement, despite the fact that some of the mergers were of a wildly improbable sort. Thus, RCA, a leading manufacturer of communications equipment and operator of the National Broadcasting Company, bought control of the Hertz car-rental agency, creating a most curious combination. Aware of the torpidity of the Antitrust Division of the Justice Department, businessmen in the late 1960s decided to merge while the merging was good. The Justice Department, for its part, concluded that prosecution was not necessary, since a mere legal scowl had called off a number of undesirable merger plans. A case in point was the delay in the proposed merger of ITT with the American Broadcasting Company, a stall that impelled ITT to back out of the arrangement. Nevertheless, it appeared that the purpose of antitrust was not to insure "free competition" but to enhance the growth of corporations by directing attacks on them into ceremonial channels. An occasional government foray simply made bigness respectable. Thus antitrust entered into the mythology of American business.

As a matter of fact, antitrust never did halt the march toward bigness. There is little proof that governmental action ever reduced concentration in any sensible way; on the contrary, monopoly in the widest sense increased despite the "concern" of government. All that could be said is that legal action, or the threat of legal action, influenced the shape that mergers have assumed (that is, asset versus stock purchase, or outright amalgamation versus integration). Little effect has been exerted on prices, output, or employment policy. Whatever the form, there has been an undeniable tendency toward control from the center. In many ways, this was the result of the legal philosophy that underpinned antitrust; all too often, real collusion, or behavior close to conspiracy, had to be demonstrated to justify intervention. Yet price maintenance and restricted production can be achieved without actual collusion. Price leadership, "moral suasion," and mutual understanding among giant rivals were all acknowledged social forms for establishing monopolistic control, yet in other instances it was virtually impossible to discover conspiracy within the meaning of the law.

The simple fact was that antitrust had been a failure. The Sherman Act had been emasculated by judicial interpretation, and by 1920 it was useless. The Clayton Act fared no better. The only thing that could be said for antitrust was that it inhibited outright monopoly; business potentates thought it the better part of valor to let a few small rivals stay put. Some critics have suggested that changes in corporation law, taxes, and the patent system could create incentives for industrial giants to disgorge their subsidiaries. Whatever the merit of these notions, the merger movement has continued unabated.

During the 1960s the most dramatic merger development was the growth of conglomerates, combinations of firms operating in disparate fields. The term was derived from geology, where it refers to a mass of heterogeneous material. To some critics it implied that "those who run this new-fangled kind of corporation don't know what they're doing." As the trend accelerated, operators began to talk of "emerging" conglomerates, as if the slow process of geologic time had been speeded up. In reality, the form was nothing new; Andrew Mellon had done it all long before Wall Street started to talk about Litton Industries and Ling-Temco-Vought.

But the conglomerates grew bigger and the mergers more numerous. Steel companies bought TV stations, credit companies absorbed computer manufacturers, railroads acquired apparel makers, petrochemical firms purchased airlines, and hotel chains took over helicopter factories. Increasingly, mergers came to involve companies that had no economic or other logical connection. The FTC estimated that four-fifths of the mergers in 1967 were conglomerate. The agency was concerned that the movement might in fact increase concentration: at any rate, it appeared that conglomerates enhanced economic power. It was dubious that the growth of such companies reflected improvements in products: they reflected, rather, the attraction of empire building. The hunger for acquisitions was assuaged by plunging into debt or issuing new securities to buy up other corporations. Of course, such flotations made the conglomerates the darlings of Wall Street.

One of the more spectacular conglomerates was the one engineered by James J. Ling, a high school dropout, who began with a modest electrical business to build an empire, Ling-Temco-Vought, worth more than $2 billion. His Ling Electronics, which went public with the aid of a Dallas banker, acquired Temco Electronics and Missiles, Altec, and several other firms in 1960. Borrowing $10 million one year later, Ling added Chance Vought, an aircraft and missile manufacturing company with assets of $195 million. In 1967, another conglomerate, Greatamerica, which controlled insurance firms, an airline, and a bank, was brought into the combine. In all, Ling carried through more than thirty mergers after the acquisition of Chance Vought. The technique was always the same: a purchase of majority control with borrowed cash, followed by a transfer of the victim firm's outstanding shares in exchange for Ling-Temco-Vought securities. Most of the debt was then transferred to the new subsidiary. Ling lives as well as any Texas oilman, with a home constructed like a roadside motel, estimated to be worth $1.5 million.

The technique for taking over another firm often resembled an old-fashioned proxy fight or corporate raid. The conglomerate would tender an attractive offer for a block of the victim's stock. Brokers would then move in to purchase as much as they could on the open market and resell to the hungry conglomerate; the prospective takeover might be fought off with counterbids, complaints to the government, press releases, and letters to stockholders urging them to hold the line. Of course, the result was frequently to drive up the price of the stock sufficiently to discourage the conglomerate. Likely prospects for a takeover kept their ears tuned for rumors and unusual activity in their stock. Or they watched the columns of the *Wall Street Journal* and the financial pages of the *New York Times* for takeover bids to be announced, as required by the Securities and Exchange Commission in the interest of full disclosure. Yet most companies that have attracted the lustful glance of others were unable to resist being raped; their only defense was to merge with a friendly suitor, on the theory that seduction was more acceptable. Thus, Sinclair Oil resisted the blandishments of Gulf and Western Industries only to lie down with Atlantic Richfield. Power seemed to be in the hands of the attackers.

Much of the growth has been based on the expansion of paper. There was some doubt that earnings had been really enhanced by the mergers. The operators were arguing that conglomeration had a synergistic effect on earnings, that the whole was greater than the sum of the parts. But as the underlying units in most of these combinations were left to their own devices, just as they had been before they were absorbed, ordinary arithmetic still held—two plus two still equaled four, not five. It was clear that the new corporate setup was simply a matter of enhancing the price of the parent stock on the market. Manipulation of price-earnings ratios by generating "growth" and "distributing" risk over a larger number of subsidiaries drew in the new lambs of the 1960s. The Wall Street wolf was now more sophisticated, but his teeth were still shiny and sharp.

Some were saying that the new conglomerates were frauds, as ever more acquisitions had to be carried through to bolster the "income" of the parent company. Complex financial operations accompanied the mergers with pyramids of paper involving new convertible securities. The "pooling of interests" was sufficient to send the price of stocks skyward like a space missile, without any change in management, production, or marketing. So long as the ratio of stock prices to earnings was low, the parent could create the illusion of having grown rapidly. Reorganizations and new securities added to the merger craze. Fancy terms were applied to new acquisitions: the purchase of a wire firm provided a "synergistic steel fabricating resource base"; a motel chain became a "leisure-time division," with the parent company announcing that it intended "to be a leader in the coming travel revolution." Gobbledygook was by no means limited to government bureaucrats.

Accountants and analysts were not the only ones who were puzzled. Economists were uncertain how these combinations would affect the economy, nor could they say what the effect on competition might be. Some were arguing that bringing together disparate firms would not restrict competition; others said that sheer economic power could submerge the functioning of the market. For one thing, a conglomerate could keep the number of companies competing in a market from increasing. It could "outspend and outdare" a one-product rival; it could survive the failure of one of its items more easily; it could use its enormous buying power to compel suppliers to purchase from one of its subsidiaries. Some economists were not disturbed: to them market power and bigness were like obesity and pregnancy; the conditions were different and required different treatment. Yet it could not be denied that a conglomerate was much less subject to the influences of the market than a company producing a single commodity. Nor were antitrust guidelines very clear. The Supreme Court had specified in 1964 that it would not approve mergers that extended market power. Where acquisition was substituted for direct entry into competition, the court withheld its blessing. The FTC promised a detailed study of the situation. Yet the mergers continued unimpeded, *sans* logic. There was a growing suspicion that it all paralleled the paper expansion of the 1920s.

Interestingly, the Nixon administration appears willing to joust with the conglomerates. In March 1969, the Justice Department decided to move against Ling-Temco-Vought in an effort to divorce from it the Jones and Laughlin Steel corporation, the nation's sixth-largest steel company, which had been ensnared by the Ling-Temco-Vought octopus. Ling-Temco-Vought had acquired no less than 63 percent of the steel firm's shares by an exchange of bonds, stocks, and warrants, as well as by outright purchase. But as of late 1969 the case had not yet come to court, and the Justice Department had agreed to let Ling-Temco-Vought acquire additional Jones and Laughlin shares, so long as it held no more than 81 percent. This ratio, however, represented a victory for Ling-Temco-Vought, since 80 percent control was needed in order to consolidate tax statements, an accounting device that would save the parent company about $25 million a year in taxes. Moreover, it would allow Ling-Temco-Vought to shift debt obligations to Jones and Laughlin, a tactic that the conglomerate described as "redeployment."

It appeared that the Justice Department's sudden antitrust vigor was tempered by a sympathetic concern for Ling-Temco-Vought's financial well-being. Yet the conglomerates were hinting darkly that the Justice Department was attempting to protect old-line Republican leadership in the major industries from a takeover by newcomers. The fact was that antitrust action against conglomerates did not develop until Jones and Laughlin, B. F. Goodrich, New York's Chemical Bank, Great American Insurance, and Pan American World Airways were threatened. Basically, the parties in the battles were the old establishment and the nouveaux riches.

In any case, the conglomerates did not seem to be overly disturbed by renewed antitrust action. Moreover, they had their defenders who argued that much good had come of the search for "investment values," a search that was shaking up otherwise complacent managements. One conglomerate protagonist hoped that the federal government would not overreact "to give undue protection" to the corporate status quo.

Corporations also became transnational in character. American firms developed manufacturing facilities overseas, coming to play a significant role in the economic life of the countries concerned. Not only was it necessary to establish relationships with foreign governments, but it also became more difficult for government policy in the United States to have any effect on such corporations. These included IBM, which produced three-fourths of the world's computers; Standard Oil of New Jersey; General Motors; Ford; and Alcoa. One authority has estimated that by the end of the century the world economy will be dominated by some two hundred large corporations responsible for the greater part of world-industrial production. For all transnationals, domestic and foreign-based, investments had risen from $15 billion in 1940 to about $100 billion a quarter of a century later.

For some companies, foreign investments were even more important than domestic operations. In 1962 the Singer Sewing Machine Company, for example, drew 52 percent of its sales from overseas, and 65 percent of its assets were in foreign nations. Colgate-Palmolive's foreign subsidiaries supplied 54 percent of total sales, and Europe was a more important market for Standard Oil than the United States. There was concern that such development would upset the balance of payments, despite the inflow of dividends, and that the huge flow of transactions internal to the transnationals would escape whatever controls the government might wish to exercise through monetary or fiscal policies. When General Motors decided to halt shipments of cars from Australia to Japan, leaving the latter to its California plants, Australia was confronted by Japanese imports without any car exports to counterbalance the inflow. When Ford and General Motors decide in Detroit to curtail either German or English car shipments to the United States, they can easily generate resentment. Moreover, foreign nations discover that their economic plans may be frustrated by the sheer power and flexibility of the transnational corporation. In self-defense, foreign nations may have to control (through an instrumentality such as the Common Market) the investment plans and capital movements of international corporations. Some of the American-based firms believe that employing nationals in their foreign subsidiaries will minimize hostility. But this does nothing to modulate their impact on foreign economies.

Here corporate power was often expressed through control of prices. Most major industries had long since become oligopolistic, that is, dominated by a few. The rigidities in price structure that oligopolies introduced were bound to have harmful effects on the consumer. A case in point was the drug industry, which was subjected to close scrutiny by the late Senator Estes Kefauver. The industry's advertising had been directed to nonprice features, with emphasis on brand names, though it had been long known that advertised drugs were substantially cheaper when sold under their generic or chemical names. The Senate investigation disclosed, for example, that cortisone derivatives used in the treatment of arthritis were ten times more expensive when sold under brand names rather than generic names. A pill that cost 1.5 cents to make was sold to patients for 30 cents, a twentyfold jump. Drug manufacturers excused themselves by observing that the price was still less than the cost of a milkshake. Further, promotion and advertising costs, they explained, were quite heavy: in one company, these averaged 32.5 cents out of every sales dollar. And, when a drug was controlled by a patent, the price to the consumer really mounted. Drug companies encouraged doctors to prescribe only brand items distributed through "detail" men, a trade euphemism for salesmen. Though the price of a drug might be no more than the cost of a candy bar, for older persons on meager pensions three pills a day amounted to an expensive sweet tooth. The manufacturing cost of one antidiabetic tablet was $13.11 per 1,000: the druggist paid $83.40; it went to the patient for $139. The pyramiding of markups was more than tenfold. As it was a patented item, there was nothing for the patient to do but pay the bill. Senator Kefauver disclosed that foreign drugs had markedly lower price tags. With such a price structure profit rates were astronomical. *Fortune's* list of the five hundred leading industrials showed that some drug companies enjoyed a 38 percent rate of return on invested capital: the average for the entire list was 9.5 percent.

At the same time other industries were insisting on government subsidies, demonstrating that businessmen were still not in the least shy about seeking government aid. An outstanding example was the merchant marine, the industry that builds, sails, and mans ships flying the American flag. Annual government subsidies to the industry averaged $400 million a year in the postwar period. Since 1936, when the present subsidy law was passed, total aid to the merchant marine had come to $4 billion. Yet, as one writer remarked, it was only a leaky ship that the nation had purchased, for the simple fact was American vessels could not compete with those of other nations. The share of foreign trade carried in American bottoms had plummeted from a high of 68 percent in 1945 to 7 percent in 1963. As far back as the 1930s, congressional investigators had demonstrated that the subsidy system merely supported inefficiency and corporate corruption. For all its outlay, when it came to meeting the logistical requirements of the war in Vietnam, the government had to call back old ships long since retired to mothballs. Why was such a situation tolerated? The reasons could be traced to the great political weight and the strenuous lobbying of the industry, often in tandem with the unions.

The conviction has grown that the corporation has become a system of private government, structured along hierarchical lines very much like a totalitarian state. Lacking constitutional guidelines, many threatened to become lawless. Their economic power and strength, and the strength of the nation, rested in the hands of a few thousand men in control of the corporate bureaucracy. In ranking the major United States corporations and state governments by size of income or revenue, there were about eight private corporations that followed the federal government before any of the fifty states were reached.

In recent years a relatively small oligarchy from the same milieu, whose members deal almost exclusively with each other and possess no ownership relation of any sort, have come to represent *the* power center of the corporation. Hence the hope expressed by some corporate defenders that the corporation could be "constitutionalized" to make it responsive to the wishes of its "members," the stockholders, was a rather vain one. In fact, it became technically difficult to impose a proper exercise of the corporate franchise. The First National City Bank once listed fifty-six corporations with more than 50,000 stockholders each, and twenty-seven with more than 100,000. Democracy in the ordinary meaning of the word would simply become chaos. The very diffusion of stockholdings make government in the usual sense impossible. Even the 5 or 6 percent of stock owners who held the bulk of outstanding shares were too numerous to manage the corporations effectively, for they still numbered over 1 million persons. Thus, despite some concentration in stockholdings, dispersion was sufficient to create a passive attitude. Further, most stock owners were much too concerned with prices on the exchange to be genuinely interested in running a corporation. Besides, political analogies holding stockholders to be the ultimate source of power were false, as stockholders were not the ones who governed in a corporation. Rather, the governed were the direct participants in the economic and industrial activities dominated by the corporation; they were mainly workers and suppliers. It was here that government within the corporation began.

The passive nature of the stockholders allowed control to be held by a managerial corps. Sometimes more direct devices were employed, as in the case of the Sears, Roebuck pension plan. Nor did voting rights given to future pensioners in similar arrangements in Standard Oil, Union Carbide, or the Celanese Corporation affect the continuing control of managerial insiders, for there would have to be some unity of purpose and some sort of bloc voting for a real change to take place. The likelihood of this ever occurring was dim.

Robert A. Gordon, a leading economist, once demonstrated that majority ownership was the *least* common mode of control in the larger nonfinancial enterprises. Minority control was most typical in more than half the cases he studied, while stock dispersion was so widespread in another 34 percent of the cases that management was able to do quite as it pleased.

Have increased common-stock purchases by financial intermediaries —banks, insurance companies, investment trusts, mutuals, and pension funds—led to a new kind of finance capitalism? In fact this was unlikely. True, most of the $30 billion or so of the stockholdings of these institutions were concentrated in a few hundred blue-chip issues. Such investments stemmed mainly from a need for safety and a good yield. In almost all instances, those who ran the financial intermediaries transmitted their proxies to incumbent managements without question. If they disliked what management was doing, the stock was simply sold on the exchange. This often did more to rattle a board of directors than a threatened proxy fight.

Of course, managers do frequently own stock in their own corporations, yet Gordon's data showed that all the members of his boards of directors, plus all corporate officers, held only about 2 percent of the voting shares in their firms. In only 20 percent of the companies studied did management hold more than 10 percent of voting stock. This did not mean that officers had no financial stake in their corporations, for 1 percent of $200 million in outstanding shares is $2 million, and at a 5 percent yield this could bring a neat $100,000 per annum. The executive did indeed have a keen financial interest in his organization, even though he didn't "own" it. He thus had sufficient reason to welcome the control provided by the modern corporation; when other stockholders tried to rebel, he was apt to view their action as a peasants' revolt to be crushed.

This was the reality of the corporation: noncorporeal property, proxies, and the centralization of power. We had now a managed economy in which the central question was: for whom is the managing done? Obviously not for those subject to the power of the archon, the man at the top. His rule led rather to a system of commands and internal sanctions which created a tightly knit operational code. As a result, the oligarchs had successfully disfranchised the mass of stockholders and, unless restrained by the countervailing power of a labor union or a government agency, were able to injure workers, suppliers, and customers. And such countervailance was not always forthcoming: as in the case of the electrical conspiracy, "countervailance" often occurred after the damage had been done.

The malefic power of the corporation was most clearly exposed in its relationships with the consumer and his family. Here countervailing power was utterly absent. Here producer and consumer proved to be unequal antagonists. One possessed unbounded economic horizons; the other was severely limited as to what he could do, dependent on the sale of labor services, and subject to ailment and accident. One produced commodities of dubious quality; the other had to buy what was available. One was a paragon of efficiency; the other a backward practitioner of the art of spending money. One had vast financial resources at its command; the other, despite the availability of installment credit, suffered from serious economic disability. One invested in the latest physical equipment; the other was frequently unable to make proper provision for human capital. One could build new plants in the suburbs; the other had to accept such services as the city offered, and these were usually inadequate. Yet it was the consumer who was supposed to be the beneficiary of whatever the corporation did. In reality, the consumer had long since lost his sovereignty and his supposed capacity to influence the social and economic order. Estranged from the sphere of production by technology, he had long since forgotten what property meant, which itself had been attenuated to the point where it no longer had substance.

Large corporations had come to control a significant part of the economy and of society. Indeed as society became increasingly dependent on the corporation, the latter's independence was correspondingly increased. Corporate directives and decisions acquired the force of law, as accommodation to that law became the quintessence of adaptability. Self-appointed corporate guardians emerged, responsible only to themselves. Whatever motion they generated in their capacity as corporate managers became the way of validating their own exercise of power.

P.S. (by the editors):

It is in the light of the situation described by Ben Seligman that the new and still amorphous "movement for corporate responsibility" began to take on, during the early 1970s, an important role. For here, as the possible beginnings of a popular movement, was an effort to bring the corporation, perhaps the single most powerful economic institution in our society, to public check and review. Much of the credit for raising this crucial issue goes to Ralph Nader, who first challenged General Motors and then, through his Center for the Study of Responsive Law, helped initiate similar actions in regard to other corporations. And, while in no instance could such challenges seriously threaten the power of the oligarchs, it served the enormously important purpose of bringing into public discussion the very nature of property in modern American society. Even so moderate a politician as Senator Edmund Muskie was thus impelled to ask: "Are matters of the public health to be left to the decisions of the board of directors of these great motor companies?" And both in universities and labor unions which own blocs of corporate shares, the question had now to be discussed: how should their shares be voted? for or against the small band of critics?

Still very far from a significant challenge to the security of capitalism, the "movement for corporate responsibility"—by insisting that corporations must consider factors other than maximization of profit in making their decisions, by raising the urgent problem of environment and pollution, by proposing that such previously unrepresented constituencies as workers, consumers, and minorities be given seats on boards of directors—might become a wedge for a public campaign against the unchecked powers of the corporations and thereby a first, halting step toward the goal of extending democracy into industrial life.

1970

Alan Dershowitz

Could It Happen Here?

CIVIL LIBERTIES IN A NATIONAL EMERGENCY

At four o'clock on the morning of October 16, 1970, Prime Minister Pierre Trudeau proclaimed the existence of a "state of apprehended insurrection" throughout Canada. Pointing to the kidnaping of a Canadian cabinet minister and a British consul by members of Le Front de Libération du Québec (FLQ), he invoked the "War Measures Act," thereby authorizing extraordinary powers of arrest, search, and detention. Before dawn, the police—who had been strategically deployed in anticipation of the announcement—began their roundup of French Canadians suspected of association with the FLQ. Though most of the 450 arrested were never charged with any crime, many were detained incommunicado for considerable periods of time. The Canadian Bill of Rights—which prohibits such detention— was rendered inapplicable by the emergency decree.

In the middle of the night of December 4, 1970, Irish Prime Minister John Lynch announced that a grave emergency existed in his country. Citing information that Saore Eire (a splinter group of the Irish Republican Army) was conspiring to kidnap "prominent" ministers, he declared that "unless this threat is removed," he would, without further notice, empower the police to "intern any citizen without trial." The government issued instructions "that places of detention be prepared immediately" and that the Council of Europe be notified that "these proposals will involve derogations from certain provisions of the European Convention on Human Rights."

Ten days later—in the wake of kidnaping and demonstrations in support of six Basques on trial for murder—Generalissimo Francisco

220

Franco granted emergency powers to the Spanish police, authorizing them to detain persons for up to six months without a hearing. Franco's proclamation of emergency powers automatically suspended that nation's Bill of Rights.

Within the past months, therefore, we have seen three Western countries suspend, or threaten to suspend, fundamental constitutional protections in response to political kidnapings and other disruptions of a kind not unknown to our own shores. This raises the obvious question: can it happen here? could President Nixon take to the airwaves some night and announce that this nation is confronted with an emergency situation requiring suspension of the American Bill of Rights?

"It could not happen here under any circumstances" was the categorical answer given to me in an interview with then Deputy Attorney General Richard Kleindienst, the man to whom President Nixon has delegated the task of planning for a domestic emergency.

We wouldn't suspend the Bill of Rights even if the whole Cabinet, the Chief Justice, and the Speaker of the House were kidnapped. In the first place, we wouldn't have to, because our existing laws—together with our surveillance and intelligence apparatus, which is the best in the world—are sufficient to cope with any situation. And in the second place, we wouldn't be allowed to; as I understand the law, the courts would have to be closed—unable to operate—before we could invoke martial law.

I pressed him on his last point: What if there were a concerted attack on the courts—judicial kidnapings of the kind attempted in San Rafael, California; bombing of courtrooms, harassment of jurors? Would that constitute an effective closing of the courts and justify a presidential declaration of martial law? Mr. Kleindienst had obviously given some thought to this possibility, because his answer was quite specific:

We would deploy all our resources to get the courts open and to keep them open. We might have to use troops, but we wouldn't use them in place of the courts or the law; we would use them in support of the courts. We have careful plans ready to be put into effect in the event of any emergency requiring federal troops. A team of civilians headed by an Assistant Attorney General is to be dispatched to any crisis city. He would direct the activities of the troops, so there would be no danger of undue military influence. We have a book on every city in which an emergency might occur. We have had numerous rehearsals, but fortunately we have had to act only once: we sent a civilian team under Bill Ruckelshaus up to New Haven last year when it looked like the Panther trial demonstration might get out of hand.

Had he sent that team, I asked, in response to a request from the governor? "No," replied Mr. Kleindienst, "we acted on our own initiative but with full cooperation from the local authorities. Let me assure you once again, however, that our object is to support the local civil authorities, not to supplant them."

I asked whether he thought Canada had overreacted to the two kidnapings. He responded with a twinkle:

We conservatives would not have reacted that way. Cool-headed Wall Street types—like Nixon, Mitchell and me—would never respond emotionally. We would be conservative in invoking extraordinary powers. You liberals, on the other hand, you wait too long before you act; you don't anticipate crises; you worry about upsetting your constituencies. When you finally do act, things have gotten so far out of hand that you have to overreact. That's why liberals are more likely to invoke emergency powers than conservatives. But in fairness to Canada, you have to remember that they don't have the law enforcement machinery that we have. If we had a crisis, we would divert all our existing resources away from non-essential duties and turn them onto the problem at hand. And we would be able to solve it without the need for any emergency powers.

But what if we faced a situation similar to the one that confronted the Canadian government, where those fomenting violence were well known to the authorities, but the absence of admissible evidence made conviction impossible? Wouldn't you be tempted, I asked Mr. Kleindienst, to invoke extraordinary powers of temporary detention in order to break the back of the movement? "We wouldn't have to," he assured me.

There is enough play at the joints of our existing criminal law—enough flexibility—so that if we really felt that we had to pick up the leaders of a violent uprising, we could. We would find something to charge them with and we would be able to hold them that way for awhile.

Mr. Kleindienst's last remark reminded me of something the Canadian Attorney General, John Turner, had told me during a conference he recently convened to evaluate his country's experience under the War Measures Act:

In a certain sense, it is a credit to the civil liberties of a country that it has to invoke extraordinary powers to cope with a real emergency. Some countries have these powers at their disposal all the time.

But whether a country has to invoke extraordinary powers or whether it already has sufficient powers at its disposal tells us little about the actual condition of liberty within its borders. Every legal system has its "stretch points," its flexible areas capable of expansion and contraction depending on the exigencies of the situation. The "stretch points" in our own system include broad police and prosecutorial discretion; vaguely defined offenses (such as disorderly conduct); inchoate crimes (which may also be vaguely defined, like conspiracy); and denial of pretrial release (which can sometimes result in confinement exceeding a year). Some systems employ such devices as "common law (judge-made) crimes," ex post facto (after the fact) legislation, and emergency powers, to achieve similar results. As Attorney General Turner put it: "When placed against the wall, most governments act more alike than differently; they do what they have to do to survive." There are, nevertheless, important differences in the manner by which governments respond to perceived emergencies. Some will take considerable risks to their security in order to preserve a maximum of liberty; while others will become harshly repressive at the slightest threat—real or imagined—to their security. The true condition of a country's freedom can best be seen by stripping away the legal jargon and focusing on the actual balance it has struck between liberty and security.

The fact that Canada invoked emergency powers, while we seem to be relying on "play at the joints of our existing criminal law," does tell us something important about the different status of constitutional rights and their judicial enforcement in our two countries. The Canadian Bill of Rights is subject to suspension by legislative act; accordingly, extraordinary powers can be invoked quite easily in that country without the fear of judicial disapproval. The American Constitution, on the other hand, has been described by our Supreme Court as "irrepealable law . . . for rulers and people, equally in war and peace, [which] covers with the shield of its protection all classes of men, at all times under all circumstances."

But are the safeguards of our Constitution as irrepealable as the judicial rhetoric proclaims? Is Mr. Kleindienst correct when he says that under our law a president would not be "allowed" to suspend the Bill of Rights? Would the courts step in and protect a citizen against the unauthorized actions of a high-handed chief executive during a period of national emergency? Neither American history nor current constitutional doctrine answers these questions unambiguously, as a brief recounting of some episodes from past periods of upheaval will demonstrate.

The great President who proclaimed emancipation also issued another, less well-known proclamation that had the effect of virtually suspending the Bill of Rights. A week after the fall of Fort Sumter, in a communiqué authorizing General Winfield Scott to commence the "bombardment" of certain cities in Maryland "if necessary," Abraham Lincoln also empowered the general to suspend the writ of habeas corpus in designated areas but only "in the extremest necessity." (Habeas corpus, though not a part of the Bill of Rights, is the critical safeguard without which all other constitutional protections would remain largely unenforceable, since its suspension would deny the courts the power to release persons held in violation of other protections.) Shortly after Lincoln issued his "incarceration proclamation," an obscure Marylander named John Merryman, whose loyalties were apparently with the South, was roused from his bed at two in the morning, taken to Fort McHenry, and imprisoned there under military guard. A writ of habeas corpus was sought from the Chief Justice of the United States, Roger B. Taney—a Lincoln protagonist and author of the infamous Dred Scott decision. Taney's opinion gave President Lincoln a failing grade in constitutional law: "I had supposed it to be one of those points in constitutional law upon which there was no difference of opinion," he commented sarcastically, "that the privilege of the writ could not be suspended, except by act of Congress." But, despite the chief justice's order to release Merryman, Merryman remained confined: the general in charge of the fort simply denied the marshal permission to serve the necessary papers, and Lincoln took no official notice of the opinion (which was personally transmitted to him by order of the Court).

Following this confrontation between the executive and the judiciary, Congress enacted a statute giving President Lincoln even more authority to suspend constitutional safeguards than he had requested. And so, when Lambdin Milligan was arrested in Indiana on October

5, 1864, there was little doubt that the privilege of the writ of habeas corpus had been properly suspended.[1] Not content to detain him, the military authorities decided to try Milligan—a civilian—before a military commission, which promptly sentenced him to hang. By the time the case worked its way up to the Supreme Court, the war was over and—in the words of Justice Davis—"now that the public safety is assured, this question . . . can be discussed and decided without passion or the admixture of any element not required to form a legal judgment." The Supreme Court held that since the civil courts of Indiana—a loyal state—had been open and "needed no bayonets" to protect them, it was unconstitutional to try Milligan before a military commission. Recognizing that Milligan was arrested in wartime when passions run high and "considerations of safety" are deemed all important, the Court concluded that the framers of our Constitution

. . . foresaw that troublous times would arise, when rulers and people would become restive under restraint, and seek by sharp and decisive measures to accomplish ends deemed just and proper; and that the principles of constitutional liberty would be in peril, unless established by irrepealable law. . . .

This nation . . . has no right to expect that it will always have wise and humane rulers, sincerely attached to the principles of the Constitution. Wicked men, ambitious of power, with hatred of liberty and contempt of law, may fill the place once occupied by Washington and Lincoln, and if this right [to suspend provisions of the Constitution during the great exigencies of government] is conceded, and the calamities of war again befall us, the dangers to human liberty are frightful to contemplate.

Having delivered itself of its rhetoric about "irrepealable law," the Court then proceeded to suggest that the right to bail could be suspended during emergencies:

If it was dangerous, in the distracted condition of affairs, to leave Milligan unrestrained of his liberty . . . the *law* said to arrest him, confine him closely, render him powerless to do further mischief; and then . . . try him according to the course of the common law.[2]

1. The Constitution specifically authorizes suspension "when in cases of Rebellion or Invasion the public safety may require it," and the civil war was, of course, a rebellion within the intended meaning of that term.
2. Implicit in the Court's reasoning in *Milligan* is a compelling argument against the constitutionality of pretrial preventive detention during normal times. The Court suggested that it required the suspension of habeas corpus to

This view was reaffirmed—and strengthened—by Justice Oliver Wendell Holmes in a case growing out of a private war between Colorado coal miners and owners, which led to a declaration of local martial law. In addition to suppressing newspapers, deposing civil magistrates, and closing all saloons, the governor suspended habeas corpus and ordered the arrest of certain "objectionable characters." One of these "characters," a leader of the miners, was detained without bail for two and a half months and sued the governor after his release. Though Holmes need never have reached the legality of the detention, the Civil War veteran went out of his way to justify the governor's action. Employing "logic" for which he surely would have chastised his first-year Harvard Law students, Holmes argued that since a governor can order soldiers to "kill persons who resist" efforts to put down a rebellion, it certainly follows that "he may use the milder measure of seizing the bodies of those whom he considers to stand in the way of restoring peace." (This non sequitur would, if taken seriously, justify detention of all persons suspected of felonies, since—under the laws of most states—deadly force can be used against anyone resisting a felony arrest.)

Although Justice Holmes intimated that the Court might not sustain a detention of undue duration, his uncritical legitimation of the governor's exercise of extraordinary power was a clear invitation to abuse. And abuse was not long in coming. Numerous governors invoked the magic phrase "martial law" as a kind of "household remedy" to accomplish such diverse and illegitimate ends as closing a racetrack, manipulating a primary election, keeping a neighborhood segregated and—most often—settling labor strikes to the advantage of management. It was inevitable that the Supreme Court could not long tolerate such bogus declarations of martial law. The case that finally wore the Court's patience arose in the east Texas oil fields during the early days of the Depression. The governor declared martial law and ordered restrictions on the production of oil in an effort to raise its price. There were no riots or violence; nor were any troops employed. Martial law was invoked simply to accomplish economic ends. The Supreme Court enjoined the governor's action, reasoning that unless it did so "the fiat of a state Governor, and not the Constitution of the

---

confine a defendant until trial. The obverse of this would seem to be that, in the absence of such suspension, denial of bail is unconstitutional.

United States, would be the Supreme law of the land."

That is where the law stood on December 7, 1941, when the Japanese Air Force bombed Pearl Harbor, throwing Hawaii into turmoil and generating fear of attack in our West Coast cities. Within hours, the governor of Hawaii—at the insistence of the Army—declared martial law, suspended habeas corpus, ordered the civil courts closed, and empowered tribunals to try all criminal cases. The civilian governor handed the reins of government over to the military only after receiving assurances that civilian control would be restored as soon as the immediate emergency was over, within days or, at most, weeks. Relative calm returned quickly to the islands as the threat of renewed attack dissipated; places of amusement and saloons were permitted to open in February of 1942; and life returned to near normalcy after our victory at Midway removed any realistic threat of invasion. But the military still insisted that the civil courts remain closed and the writ of habeas corpus remain suspended. A considerable battle ensued over the next years between the ousted civilian officials and the governing generals. This battle culminated in a contempt citation issued by a federal judge against the commanding general, followed by an order issued by the general threatening to court-martial the judge if he persisted in issuing writs of habeas corpus. It wasn't until after the war (and the restoration of habeas corpus by President Roosevelt) that the Supreme Court decided that Congress, in authorizing martial law in Hawaii, had not intended to permit the "supplanting of courts by military tribunals." By that time, thousands of man days of illegal imprisonment had already been served.[3]

Martial law in Hawaii, with all its abuses, did not include mass detention on racial grounds of the kind employed on our West Coast between 1942 and 1944. The removal and confinement of 110,000 Japanese-Americans, though carried out by the Army, resulted from intense pressure brought by civilian officials (such as the then

3. The main reason this issue did not reach the Supreme Court earlier was that the Justice Department "mooted" prior cases by releasing the defendants as soon as they filed petitions in the Supreme Court.

An extreme—and pathetic—example of the inclination of judges to defer decision until after the emergency has passed was provided by a case growing out of the Hawaiian martial rule. In 1944, a circuit court of appeals had approved the military trial of civilians. Two years later Circuit Judge Stephens filed a belated dissenting opinion, saying he had been reluctant to file it while the war was still going on.

attorney general of California, Earl Warren). The story of this shameful episode has been frequently recounted. Today it is publicly defended by almost no one (including even the House Internal Security Committee, which recently called the episode—"at least in hindsight" —"a dark day in our history").

It is important to recall that the Supreme Court, although it did approve the forced removal of Japanese Americans from the West Coast, did not sustain their long-term detention in the camps. The only detention case decided by the Court involved a woman who the government conceded was loyal. That case reached the Court near the end of the war, when plans were already in progress to return the detainees to their homes, since the threat of Japanese invasion had disappeared. It was easy for the Court, therefore, to order the woman's release on the ground that Congress had never explicitly authorized detention of a "citizen who is concededly loyal [and who] presents no problem of espionage or sabotage." "Loyalty is a matter of the mind," said Justice Douglas, "not of race, creed, or color." The import of that opinion is extremely limited, since it is doubtful that we would ever be so foolish as again to detain a group simply on the basis of their race or color. But we might attempt to detain individuals on the basis of their assumed loyalty or propensity to commit acts of sabotage or espionage. Indeed, not long after the last of the Japanese detention camps were dismantled, Congress enacted just such a law.

On the heels of the Communist invasion of South Korea, the Emergency Detention Act of 1950 was introduced by a group of liberal senators (perhaps in a misguided effort to defeat other provisions of the McCarren Act).[4] After devoting fifteen paragraphs to a recitation of the evils of the "world Communist movement," the statute proceeded to empower the Attorney General to arrest and detain anyone "as to whom there is a reasonable ground to believe that such person probably will engage in, or probably will conspire with others to engage in, acts of espionage or sabotage." The suspect could be kept in a "place of detention" for an indefinite time, but he was denied such basic constitutional safeguards as trial by jury, bail, confrontation of his accuser, and proof beyond reasonable doubt. This extraordinary measure could be invoked in the event of a presidential declaration of

4. The senators included Kilgore, Douglas, Humphrey, Lehman, Graham, Kefauver, and Benton.

"internal security emergency." But such an emergency may not be declared unless our territory is invaded, Congress declares war, or there is an insurrection in aid of a foreign enemy. Had Congress declared war against North Korea or North Vietnam, as many—including some liberals—urged it to do, then the President could have invoked the Detention Act. He also could have invoked it had he agreed with some congressmen who perceived the urban riots as "insurrections in aid of a foreign enemy."[5] But since there has, in fact, been no presidential declaration of internal security emergency since the enactment of the law, the detention provisions have never been employed.[6]

There was a time, however, when serious thought was given to mass detention of potential saboteurs. It was no less a liberal than former Senator Paul Douglas who, in the course of the debate over the Detention Act, made the following statement:

Mr. Hoover says there are 12,000 ["hard core . . . potential saboteurs and spies"]. In my judgment, if we had a period of national emergency —and I think it is pretty close to being a period of national emergency now—the best thing the country could do would be to "put them on ice," so to speak, treating them nicely, but to take them out of circulation so that they could not commit acts of treason.[7]

Following the passage of the Act, the Justice Department established six detention "camps" throughout the country. These camps remained

5. A proposed amendment to the Detention Act would require a "concurrent resolution of the Congress declaring the existence of an insurrection within the United States in support of a foreign enemy."

6. We are now in a state of "national emergency" as a result of President Truman's proclamation of December 16, 1950. The existence of this state has been reaffirmed by subsequent presidents. But we are not in a state of "internal security emergency," which carries very different powers. Other possible states include "extreme emergency," "sufficient emergency," "war or similar emergency," and "public peril."

7. Not all liberal senators supported the detention bill. The late Senator William Langer had this to say: "So now it is proposed to have concentration camps in America! We can be absolutely certain that the concentration camps are for only one purpose: namely, to put in them the kind of people those in authority do not like! So we have come to this! Concentration camps!"

But Senate Majority Leader Scott Lucas observed: "I favor a strong measure. . . . One may call it a police-state measure or whatever else he may desire. . . . One may talk about concentration camps, one may talk about . . . creating a police state if he desires; but when we are dealing with Communists such as we know exist in this country . . . *there is nothing too drastic to meet that situation.*"

unused and generated little concern until a few years ago when a writer named Charles R. Allen achieved some prominence by publishing a pamphlet entitled *Concentration Camps, U.S.A.*, which alleged that the Justice Department had a plan—code-named "Operation Dragnet"—under which it could round up hundreds of thousands of dissidents "overnight." That hysterical document was given considerable credence by the publication of another hysterical document, this one a report by the House Committee on Un-American Activities, entitled *Guerrilla Warfare in the United States.* Among the actions that the report said "could be taken" in the event of a ghetto riot was the invocation of the Emergency Detention Law:

Acts of overt violence by the guerrillas would mean that they had declared a "state of war" within the country and, therefore, would forfeit their rights as in wartime. The [Detention] Act provides for various detention centers to be operated throughout the country and these might well be utilized for the temporary imprisonment of warring guerrillas.

The report also stated that during a "guerrilla uprising most civil liberties would have to be suspended." It is not surprising therefore that mimeographed copies of this report were widely circulated in black areas (at a cost of up to five dollars a copy) and that a Washington *Post* survey found a "deep and abiding" belief in the black community that massive riots would lead the government to "make a vast indiscriminate sweep down the streets of black ghettos and hustle every man, woman and child off into a concentration camp."

Another incident which lent some credence to the concentration camp charge was an interview with then Deputy Attorney General Kleindienst in which he was quoted as saying that demonstrators who "interfered with others . . . should be rounded up and put in a detention camp." On the very day that this charge was categorically denied, Kleindienst wrote a letter to Senator Eastland stating the administration's recommendation that the Detention Law be repealed, because such action would "allay the fears and suspicions—unfounded as they may be—of many of our citizens"; and this benefit "outweighs any potential advantage which the Act may provide in a time of internal security emergency."[8]

8. My own discussions with Mr. Kleindienst convinced me that he did not—and does not—advocate the use of the Detention Law attributed to him.

In 1970 the Senate voted by voice and without debate to repeal the Detention Law, but the House sent the recommendation to the newly named but familiar Committee on Internal Security. Its chairman, Representative Ichord, tried to persuade the House that retention of the Detention Act would be in the interests of civil liberties, since the Act would not permit a roundup on racial grounds such as that directed against the Japanese.[9] The Act was, however, repealed and is no longer on the books. But many other statutes presently on the books that authorize the President to employ extraordinary powers during periods of crisis—powers which include the closing or taking over of radio and television stations; the censorship of newspapers; the imposition of travel restrictions on citizens and aliens; the summoning of the "posse comitatus" (the old "posse" of the cowboy movies); the calling out of federal troops; and the expropriation of private property (subject to subsequent reimbursement). Moreover, the President has considerable inherent powers which are said to derive from the nature of his office without regard to congressional authorization.[10]

The power to declare martial law, for example, is not even mentioned in the Constitution. Nor is the scope of that power anywhere defined, as an opinion of the Attorney General pointed out in 1857: "The common law authorities and commentators afford no clue to what martial law, as understood in England, really is. . . . In this country, it is still worse." "And what was true [of martial law] in 1857 remains true today," observed Justice Black in a 1946 opinion. Some commentators have been content to cite Wellington's cynical

9. Ichord's Alice in Wonderland logic assumes that the President would have more power to detain without a congressional act than he would with such an act. What he neglects to mention is that the Supreme Court specifically relied on congressional ratification in sustaining certain aspects, and in disallowing other aspects, of the Japanese relocation. Moreover, the disingenuousness of Ichord's claim for civil liberties is established by the fact that when repeal was considered in committee, he introduced an amendment explicitly saying that repeal should not be construed to limit the President's inherent powers to order detention.

10. In *Youngstown Co. v. Sawyer,* the Supreme Court held that the President could not, in the absence of congressional authorization, seize the steel mills during the Korean war, but it did say that Congress could authorize the President to take such action. No presidential declaration of emergency should ever, in my view, be permitted to remain in effect for any substantial time unless Congress ratifies that action (probably by more than a mere majority vote).

apothegm that martial law is simply the will of the general; or the equally simple-minded aphorism that "necessity knows no law."[11] The Supreme Court has recognized that "Civil Liberty and this kind of martial law cannot endure together; the antagonism is irreconcilable." (Or, as Groucho Marx might have put it, "Martial law, like military intelligence, is a contradiction in terms.")

While the courts have delivered opinions full of promise and prose about their majestic role during crises and the "irrepealable" nature of our fundamental safeguards, they have acted far more cautiously. And experience teaches us that what courts have in fact done in the past is a far better guide to what we may expect from them in the future than is the rhetoric they have invoked.

What then could we reasonably expect from our courts if an American President during a period of dire emergency were once again to suspend important constitutional safeguards? Our past experiences suggest the following outline: the courts—especially the Supreme Court—will generally not interfere with the executive's handling of a genuine emergency while it still exists. They will employ every technique of judicial avoidance at their disposal to postpone decision until the crisis has passed. (Indeed, though thousands of persons have been unlawfully confined during our various periods of declared emergency, I am aware of no case where the Supreme Court has ever actually ordered anyone's release while the emergency was still in existence.[12]) The likely exceptions to this rule of judicial postponement will be cases of clear abuse where no real emergency can be said to exist, and cases in which delay would result in irrevocable loss of rights, such as those involving the death penalty.[13] Once the emergency has passed, the courts will generally not approve further

11. This aphorism led some New York lawyers to nickname one local judge "Necessity" because he too knew no law.

12. The Japanese detention case was decided while we were still at war with Japan, but well after the danger of a Japanese invasion had ended. Some lower federal courts did order the release of individuals of German and Italian origin who were detained on the East Coast.

13. In ex parte Quirin, the Supreme Court held that German spies captured in the United States could be tried and sentenced to death by a military commission. The Court expedited the hearing in that case "because in our opinion the public interest required that we consider and decide these questions without any avoidable delay." The true dimensions of that scandalous episode in our judicial history are now beginning to emerge in the public record.

punishment; they will order the release of all those sentenced to imprisonment or death in violation of ordinary constitutional safeguards. But they will not entertain damage suits for illegal confinement ordered during the course of the emergency.

When these strands are woven together, there emerges an approach to the limits of martial law that was encapsulated by Justice Holmes: martial law is not "for punishment," but rather "by way or precaution, to prevent the exercise of hostile power." This distinction between "punitive" and "preventive" law runs through the cases and has been echoed by many commentators.[14] But no sharp line exists between punishment and prevention, as Blackstone recognized many years ago: "If we consider all human punishment in a large and extended view, we shall find them all rather calculated to prevent future crimes than to expiate the past." Practically speaking, the distinction means simply that the courts will tolerate preventive detention during an emergency but they will not approve the carrying-out of any part of a sentence after the emergency has ended.

This prediction of "what courts will do in fact"[15] may not, of course, prove entirely accurate. Important changes have occurred since the end of the Second World War. The Warren Court entered "political thickets" into which previous Courts had been reluctant to tread; and its bold record of recognizing and enforcing fundamental rights will not be undone by the Burger Court. Civil rights organizations have proliferated and are better—though probably not well enough—prepared for their roles in the event of an emergency suspension of civil rights. And, most important, the Vietnam war and other recent events may have divided the country beyond any possibility of full repair; short of a nuclear holocaust, we will probably never again see an emergency that will bring the country together in a unanimous display of solidarity and patriotism such as that which accompanied our entry into the Second World War.

But our historical experience—even when tempered by these recent developments—ought to teach us that we cannot place our entire

14. "[M]artial law properly administered is preventive and not punitive." Wiener, *A Practical Manual of Martial Law* (1940), cites numerous authorities to the same effect.

15. Holmes defined law as "the prophecies of what the courts will do in fact, and nothing more pretentious."

reliance upon judges to vindicate our liberties in the midst of great national crises. Learned Hand recognized this when he said: "Liberty lies in the hearts of men and women; when it dies there, no constitution, no law, no court can save it; no constitution, no law, no court can even do much to help it." But just how deeply is liberty engrained in the hearts of American men and women? Can we rely on their "eternal vigilance" to resist suspension of fundamental safeguards during periods of crisis (especially those safeguards designed to protect a small minority)? Our historical experience in this respect is disappointing. When the military took over the governance of Hawaii, few protests were heard from the average citizen.[16] Part of the reason, of course, is that it is in the nature of military rule to discourage dissent: in Hawaii, newspapers were forced to print only what the generals wanted the people to read; and public criticism was punished by court-martial. But there is a subtle, and dangerous, sense in which people—even people whose traditions proclaim liberty—become comfortable with regimentation and authority; they do not necessarily welcome it, but neither are they willing to take risks in order to secure greater freedom. Many Hawaiian businessmen and store owners, for example, resisted the return of civilian authority and even wired the President urging caution in the restoration of habeas corpus. As one businessman commented: "[We] were a darned sight safer as American citizens under that kind of military control, when the fear of immediate punishment was facing the violation of military law, as against cases dragged along in the courts."

It has been indeed fortunate for the survival of our liberties that there have always been some Americans—often only a small group and sometimes not those directly affected—who have been willing to challenge government high-handedness, even during periods of crisis. Under our constitutional system it takes only a single person challenging the government to create a case or controversy suitable for judicial resolution. Even though the Supreme Court has been reluctant to decide these cases and controversies in the midst of the crisis, it has performed an important historical cleansing function by condemning illegal action after normalcy has been restored. But the courts should do more than issue retrospective *pronunciamentos*. This is not to

16. See Anthony, *Hawaii Under Army Rule* (Stanford, 1955), pp. 105–108.

suggest that Justice should remain blind to the existence of a real emergency endangering the survival of the nation. As Justice Arthur Goldberg once wrote: "While the Constitution protects against the invasion of individual rights, it is not a suicide pact." But it is precisely during times of crisis—when the balance between momentary expediency and enduring safeguards often goes askew—that courts can perform their most critical function: to restore and preserve a sense of perspective.

Nor is there any sound reason why the courts should refuse to entertain declaratory actions challenging emergency powers *before* they are invoked in the midst of a crisis. Legal issues can be "discussed and decided without passion" before a crisis as well as after it, and with considerably greater impact. But such anticipatory litigation has been uniformly rejected on the ground that there will be ample opportunity for challenge when the emergency power is invoked. (A constitutional attack on the Emergency Detention Act, for example, has been dismissed on this basis.) In light of the course of avoidance consistently followed by courts during periods of emergency, this "wait for the crunch" argument is indefensible.

Learned Hand is surely correct when he warns us that courts alone cannot save our liberty during times of crisis. But he is wrong when he suggests that "no court can even do much to help it." In the eternal struggle between liberty and security, we have come to expect the executive and legislative branches to champion the latter. The judiciary—with its lifetime tenure, its tradition of independence, and its unique stewardship over our irrepealable Rights—is the institution most able to resist the passing fears and passions of a dangerous moment.

But liberty, like life itself, needs many sources of nutriment to sustain it. It is not a commodity that can be obtained once and for all and then passively held on to. The difficult struggle for liberty must be endured by every new generation and in each new crisis. What Thomas Paine taught us on the eve of our own Revolution remains true today: "Those who expect to reap the blessings of freedom must, like men, undergo the fatigue of supporting it."

Michael Walzer

Violence: The Police, the Militants, and the Rest of Us

Politics is first of all the art of minimizing and controlling violence. It is a taxing and morally dangerous art because violence itself and the threat of violence are two of its instruments. These can be put to use with almost equal ease by the public authorities and by private men and women, but almost always more massively and more effectively by the authorities. So it is best to begin by worrying about them.

War, riot control, law enforcement, "maintenance of order," punishment: all these can involve violence. The word itself calls to mind (to my mind, at least) a charging phalanx of helmeted police, an image fixed, I suppose, as much by the media as by recent events. It is by no means an accurate picture of what it is sometimes said to represent: the state stripped naked. But it does make it impossible to pretend that "the use of physical force to inflict injury" (the dictionary definition of violent behavior) is something other than violent whenever the users are uniformed officials, and it is equally impossible to argue that official violence is somehow presumatively legitimate. Even the justification of punishment, the most ordinary form of official violence, is uncertain and much disputed among philosophers. The intermittent violence of everyday law enforcement is more commonly questioned, especially since historians began to compile the record of police and militia brutality against labor organizers, radical agitators, ethnic and racial minorities. And just as the state's use of violence is often cruel, needless, and illegitimate, so the state possesses no monopoly on legitimate use. We deny its monopoly

236

every time we assert the right of self-defense or of collective resistance to tyranny.

What the state does have and should have is control—in this country it has exclusive control—of the means of massive violence, both human and material: the army and police, planes, tanks, artillery, and so on. Only the ownership of guns is legally the right of individuals in the U.S., and this is a right increasingly questioned—for very good reasons. The case for state control of the means of massive violence is so widely accepted that I need not review it here. I have to stress instead that the existence of such control, however justified, also establishes the state as a threat to us all. The threat is simply that violence will be used, as it has been so often in the past, not to protect everyone's rights or to enforce policies democratically agreed upon, but to defend the privileges of some few of us or to interfere with or repress democratic liberties. Obviously, no guarantees are possible here. Official violence is like unofficial violence, at least in this regard: it too inflicts injury, and it needs (in every case) to be justified. From the time of Thomas Hobbes on, the most successful efforts to justify the use of violence have undoubtedly been undertaken on behalf of the state. But these efforts do not free us from the burden of asking ourselves, over and over again, what are the prospects for the use of military and police power? Insofar as we defend state control, we have an obligation to watch over it.

Recently, however, many of us have focused, except when talking about the Vietnam war, on unofficial violence. Urban riots, street confrontations, terrorism: these claimed our attention, even if only our critical attention. Confrontation and terror suggested a *politics* of un-official violence toward which every leftist and liberal had to adopt a position. That was not hard to do, and no one deserves any special credit for setting himself against it, though there is some discredit to be distributed among those who patronized unofficial violence or apolo-gized for it. "Nothing has ever been accomplished without violence"—this was the peculiarly debased slogan of the apologists, suggesting that it was not *only* in order to make omelets that one had to break eggs. It was necessary also in order to show contempt for the art of cooking, to leave the kitchen as messy as possible, to revenge oneself against bourgeois omelet lovers, and so on. The only trouble is that all this can be accomplished and no one satisfied. And that is true as well of confrontation and terror: they represent a dead end of meaningless militancy. Nor has it taken very long to explore their farthest reaches.

But something happened in the last years of the 1960s that the militants and the rest of us ought to be concerned about. Police power was significantly strengthened and government surveillance over political activity widely extended. That is the usual outcome of un-official violence, but just what it means for our immediate future is not easy to figure out.

It doesn't mean what we are sometimes told by both radical ideo-logists and their critics: that the country has been dangerously polar-ized or that we are in the midst of or on the verge of fascist repression. Instead of polarizing the country, the militants and terrorists have succeeded only in isolating themselves; they are cut off from any hope of a political base or of large-scale (even small-scale) popular support. The country as a whole seems less divided than it was in 1968—I'm not sure how one ought to feel about that. And the repression of the far Left since that time has been less organized and thorough (and the repression of terrorists considerably less efficient) than most of us expected, given the character of the national administration and all the opportunities it has had. There is, nevertheless, a great deal to worry about: above all, the apparent readiness of the police them-selves to engage in confrontation politics; also the nighttime police raids; the shooting down of student demonstrators; the large number of men and women under indictment, often for offenses whose precise character is very unclear; the general and apparently not unrealistic sense of being watched and spied upon. Yet all this does not add up to a countrywide war against the Left. Most of the incidents that outrage us seem rather to be examples of local zealotry, reflecting the con-tinuing and not the new weakness of liberal (and, needless to say, of far Left) politics in many parts of the country.

Nationally, however, things are not the same. Despite the Left's flirtation with localist ideologies, it is protected largely by national forces and would be better protected were this country's politics still more "nationalized." It seems certain that no one would have died at either Kent State or Jackson State had the Ohio National Guard or the Mississippi State Police been under effective federal control. It is significant also that the least bloody of our ghetto riots occurred in Washington, D.C., and, again, that federal courts often overturn the convictions won by local prosecutors. At the present time, and for the foreseeable future, massive repression simply does not have the support of national elites, nor can it be worked through national institutions. The reports of one presidential commission after another—they must reflect *someone's* opinion—point as clearly as one could wish to the absence of any ideology of repression at the national level. Nor does the political campaign for law and order seem likely to change any of this. The 1970 elections suggest instead that far Left violence has not been exploited so as to enlarge the base of conservative support. Given all this, talk of an American fascism seems only a particularly gruesome (and for some people, I suppose, entertaining) escape from the need to face honestly the extent of far Left failure—and the real, if more limited, dangers that failure always brings.

But there is escapism also on what might be called the "near Left" —a term I take to include not only democratic socialists like the editors and readers of *Dissent,* but also many liberals, even those who apologize for far Left violence, since they are apologists at such a distance.

We have been terribly reluctant to face the unpleasant but critically important question: *just what sort of law enforcement do we want?* For example:

• Are we in favor of a national police force or have we opted definitely for local control? A national force would surely be more liberal (and better disciplined) than many local forces; at least it would be more liberal right now; but it would also give to the central government a kind of power that liberals and conservatives alike have always warned against.

• Do we want the National Guard abolished, or its members more widely recruited and better trained? Many of the most disgraceful incidents in the long history of official violence are the work of the National Guard; yet at the same time it is the closest thing we have to a citizen's militia. (But, after reading the polls on the work of the Guard at Kent State, we may be soured on citizens.)

• How do we feel about the many local budgetary decisions that are providing more and more money for the police? Like other municipal employees, they have been badly underpaid, but have they also been underequipped? The Kerner Commission said so, but warned at the same time against supplying policemen with automatic rifles and machine guns. And what about mace and helicopters and other devices tested in Vietnam?

- What do we think of the infiltration of police spies into far Left organizations? into terrorist groups? Is there some line to be drawn between people who can be spied upon and people (like us) who cannot be?

- At what point do we want police called onto a university campus or sent into battle against political demonstrators or rioters? And then do we want them to enforce the law (and collect people for punishment) or simply to keep the peace as best they can?

- Do any of us really think that policemen are "pigs"? And if anyone does believe that, will he refrain from calling on them when faced with a riot or a bombing?

I don't want to suggest by any of these questions that we should be prepared to accept the erosion of civil liberties. The libertarian struggles of the past decade, however, have been largely concerned with the establishment of judicial restraints on police action. These will certainly need to be defended; they are already under attack. I mean to call attention now to the problem of political control. For it is clear that important political decisions have been and will continue to be made by police officials in areas where the courts cannot or will not interfere. They exercise discretion as to what laws they will enforce, with what degree of violence, in what parts of the city, and so on. In some cities, the extent of political control over such decisions is as unclear as is the extent of federal control over national defense. The reasons for the confusion are the same too: larger budgets, advanced weaponry, the freedom that necessarily exists under crisis conditions, and the emergence under these same conditions of the police and the military as political forces in their own right. All this leaves us ignorant of the responsibility (or lack of it) of elected officials. Thus, the war against the Black Panthers looks sometimes like a political campaign (national or, more likely, local) and sometimes like a police crusade. The second would be more understandable, but also more frightening.

The standard Left response is to attack police brutality while insisting that the proper focus of political energy is on those social problems which force public officials to rely on the police. The same response is standard in international affairs, where Leftists generally see in this or that instance of military sadism only the necessary result of a failure to solve the problem of imperialism, capitalism, or war itself. But the police, like the army, are likely to be with us for a long time. It is simply not the case that police powers will cease to be necessary and dangerous once a beginning is made toward solving whatever social problems lie at the roots of our present discontents; nor is it certain that all our discontent has roots that governmental problem-solving can reach. The near Left must face up to the implications of its attack on police brutality: we want the police to act differently, but not to go away. I suppose what we need is a domestic version of the theory of just war—a theory of "civil law enforcement," the appropriate parallel for civil disobedience; but necessary even when disobedience is uncivil.

What kind of a police force do we (of the near Left) want? Surely a force that is, first, carefully selected, well trained, and highly disciplined; these features alone would considerably reduce the quantity of official violence. They would reduce it, that is, to the precise quantity intended by whoever commanded the police and thereby make their responsibility a great deal clearer. Second, a police force that is well paid: for the increasingly narrow social base from which police are recruited plays havoc with law enforcement. Part of what happens when police come onto a campus is simply class war—to be sure of a curious sort, with radical students pretending to represent and the police more nearly representing the working class. It is not a formula for minimal violence. Third, we want or should want a force committed to a fairly rigid professional and legal code (a code, obviously, that requires police to minimize violence). And fourth, a force answerable, within the limits set by that code, to elected officials. These last two requirements are not necessarily consistent or easily maintained together: there is a tension (in the public school system too) between professional commitment and political control. But that is a tension best left unresolved. It's one of the more peculiar notions of the far Left and of many of their liberal apologists that a community police would be better than what we have now. In fact, we have our greatest difficulties precisely with policemen who are little more than ordinary folks with guns. Since it is utopian to hope for an American police force without guns, we must insist that armed men be carefully trained. And the idea of training implies the existence of standards.

I am inclined to think, perhaps naïvely, that a police force better trained and controlled would be less available as an instrument of political repression. Clearly, it would be a purer instrument, its use less violent and more efficient at whatever task it was set, and so its effects more strictly limited to its legally appointed task. The worst effects of police power as we have recently known it (historically too, so far as I can discover) are those that stem from what might be called its "incidental" uses. The police are most repressive not when they are used to prevent or control illegal political activities, but when allowed or encouraged to *punish* those activities—most often by beating up (or killing) the activists. That is not what they are officially told to do, nor is it what they need to do to accomplish their legal purpose. Police violence obviously serves other purposes, but it also expresses ethnic, social, and political feelings—private feelings that ought to be repressed by professionals doing a job. That's a good kind of repression, and it would make the police less repressive.

At the same time, "incidental" violence is exactly the sort of police behavior that activists sometimes seek to provoke, knowing that, insofar as it comes into view, it will be publicly condemned. A great deal of it never does come into view: that, at least, is what we suspect, and it is what makes the police so fearsome. Mere law enforcement is not fearsome, and though revolutionaries may well object to it, they are unlikely to win much sympathy. The far Left lives symbiotically with the "pigs," counting on each outburst of their brutality and then of our indignation.

But if official violence often generates spasms of national anger and self-reproach and "radicalizes" (a word that grossly exaggerates what actually happens) hundreds or even thousands of people, there is no doubt that over time it has a deterrent effect. Unless the political base of the Left (near or far) is very strong, police brutality will erode it, for ordinary men and women, part-time activists and camp followers, will withdraw and seek shelter. The aftermath of Chicago in 1968 was not mass movement, but silence, disillusion, collapse. And it would be foolishly optimistic to imagine that large-scale student demonstrations are going to be easy to organize in Ohio after Kent State 1970. The story may be different in colonial situations, where the mass of the population is already alienated from the authorities and where a particularly brutal incident may trigger a desperate resistance. There, people are not shocked but mobilized. By contrast, the failure of mobilization in this country suggests how far we are (even in the ghettos) from a colonial situation. Confrontation politics, *especially when the police join in,* makes every sort of Left politics more difficult. That is a very important reason for demanding a police force that won't join in.

II

It is also a reason for condemning leftist provocations—like the recent mad campaign to "bring the war home." That effort seems already to have collapsed, though it may continue to have an aftermath of casualties. The career of domestic warfare has been brief and its various moments were so very quick that they can hardly be said to constitute strategic choices in need of careful criticism. Yet it's worth setting out the record of those moments, even as it appears to an outside observer. I don't doubt that there is an inside story, too, more interesting than any I can tell. But it is important here to establish a certain category of militant acts: *those that one wants the police to deal with.* They must deal with them, as I have already argued, without "incidental" violence, without punishing the militants before they are brought to trial, without using far Left madness as a way of attacking other sorts of dissident politics, but deal they must, and, I am afraid, with our support.

The first moment was that of street confrontations, direct attacks (though not with lethal weapons) on massed police. These were intended, if that's not too strong a word, to open the way to full-scale white rioting, comparable to that of the blacks in the ghetto. Working-class youths were supposed to join in, drawn by the *machismo* of the militants and their manifest readiness to break away from the fears and inhibitions of their own past. None did join, so far as I know, during the first dramatic incidents. Indeed, nothing at all happened, except that the police, probably quite happily and certainly rightfully, fought back, and considerable numbers of young militants from the middle and upper classes were injured and arrested.

The second moment was that of collegiate "trashing." Now the ghetto imagery was acted out, not in any of our major cities, but in university towns like Cambridge and Madison. And now young people from the local high schools, some of whom must have been working class, joined the militants, without any discernible political (there may have been social) motives, in breaking the windows and looting the stores of petty-bourgeois merchants. Another example of class war, and again unrelated to any political struggle.

The third moment brought urban terrorism, a surrender of any hope of mass participation, a search for efficacy in the Act rather than the Movement. Or perhaps it is not a search for efficacy at all, but only an expression of hysteria, fury, and failure. Thus far, the attacks have been aimed at buildings rather than at people. I'm not sure if that reflects some murky residue of moral principle or a peculiar sociological sophistication. American society, it may be thought, is built of steel and concrete rather than of men and women. That's wrong, but it's not an error we should seek to correct.

Now, toward activities of these sorts, it's obviously not possible to engage in comradely criticism. Terrorists end without comrades. But, before that, confrontation and trashing already revealed the collapse of any sort of collective discipline on the Left. I don't mean only (though this is important enough) that there is no mass party from which we can expel idiots, adventurers, and plain criminals. There is also no common forum within which strategic options can be debated, no "public opinion" that can exercise any restraint over individual enthusiasts, no stable body of leaders who can be held responsible for whatever happens. In the last years of the sixties, *laissez faire* triumphed on the Left. And, just as in the economy, so in the political arena, and even among radical entrepreneurs, the triumph of *laissez faire* rapidly creates conditions which require state intervention. It also creates conditions in which the state, in this case the police, can be sure of widespread popular support when they do intervene and may have such support even if they intervene inefficiently and brutally.

And what happens to the militants then? With the beginning of terrorist activities, they went underground, and there, wherever it is, they lead a life that I can only speculate about. I find it hard to credit reports that there is an underground *movement*. There clearly are a surprising number of young Americans *hiding,* and there is undoubtedly a network of hiding places and a communications system of some rough sort for sharing information about how to do it. But the existence of a movement implies what is not at all apparent today, a planned and coordinated pattern of activities. Probably no such pattern can be developed without considerable aboveground support, and that the terrorists don't have.

They have, however, found a certain amount of sympathy within that curious American phenomenon, the aboveground underground, the highly publicized perfectly visible subterranean world of the cultural revolution. Despite all the talk about repression, this largely legal "underground" life, typified by the "underground" press sold freely on Cambridge street corners and, I expect, in other cities, has been expanding rapidly. In a more accurate metaphor: the margins of American society are wider than ever before; it has never been easier (though a prolonged recession would change this quickly) to pursue a marginal career. A certain sort of occasional politics is one such career, and terrorism in its turn is marginal to that and might readily be assimilated or reassimilated to it were the terrorists ever to decide that bombing is not the true and only way. Some of them seem already to have made that decision. It is hard to see any other future for them: the cultural revolution is the only revolution they can hope to join.

III

The far Left has split so often, the tale of its internal wars is so tangled and so sad, that the rest of us can be forgiven if we allow ourselves to lose track of its various tendencies and their various ideological excuses. But one division seems to me important. Over and over again the line has been drawn (not always with the same people on the same sides) between those who are willing and those who are not willing to tolerate or encourage cultural marginality. The confrontationists, trashers, and terrorists have been among the tolerant, as well they might be. On the other side are all those groups that have tended toward one or another sort of Marxist (Trotskyist, Maoist) sectarianism, a tendency never free from puritanical impulses, but committed also to relate somehow to the "masses"—even to middle Americans. The sectaries have their own view of violence, which involves theoretical approval of it at some revolutionary moment sure to come but relatively far off and, at the same time, a refusal (mostly) to act violently here and now. The refusal, at least, brings them nearer to the near Left, and it calls to mind a political position on violence that I will try to restate briefly below. The position is worth restating not, I think, because of the Weathermen or the Panthers, whose future is dim, but because of the cultural radicalism with which we are likely to live for some time.

The new culture may indeed turn out to be as nonviolent as some of its friends and publicists suggest. But it is not now and never has been even remotely supportive of a nonviolent politics, or indeed of any politics that requires organization and long-term planning. The radicalism of "Do it!" has no room for prohibitions on trashing or terrorism or anything else. It is, instead, the mirror image of political (and why not of economic?) *laissez-faire.* Against the background of extravagance and fantasy that it provides, there is something attractive about the young sectaries, unlovely as they may be in other respects, who recognize that there are some things that ought not to be done —today, anyway.

Judging from the rhetoric (and the tone, style, voice level) of their spokesmen, their press and movies, the fantasies of many of the cultural radicals are rich in violence. Though they themselves most often appear as victims, part of the fascination is with the possibility of striking back. Not, I think, with the possibility of winning some specific struggle against oppression—the radicals may or may not be victims, but they are not oppressed—nor with the possibility of joining the ranks of the oppressors, temporarily, as has been done so often, for a "good cause." There was a kind of stolid commitment to brutality among Stalinists in the 1930s, but nothing like that exists in the varied ranks of the cultural revolution. Theirs is not the politics of "the necessary murder . . . the flat ephemeral pamphlet, the boring meeting" so much as it is the cult of experience, with violence, for some of them, as the penultimate experience. *Penultimate,* because attacks on the police, for example, are often said to have the happy effect of liberating the attackers, and there must be some further reason for doing that.

But perhaps freedom from moral inhibition is an end in itself: one acts violently in order to free oneself to act violently. It may even be thought that revolutionaries are created through such a process, but I know of no evidence for that claim. The end state is some special sort of grace (or spiritual pride) rather than political effectiveness.

Religious zealots have often in the past set themselves such a goal, and I expect it is even possible to reach it, though there appears to have been some escalation in the necessary means. In the seventeenth century, it was enough, according to certain antinomian sects, to fornicate, or at most to fornicate repeatedly, and so liberation was conceivably available to the millions. Freedom through violence is not so egalitarian a doctrine. It is, however, easily cheapened: violence is an experience that can be enjoyed and is most often enjoyed by its advocates at a distance and vicariously. Nor do I know many people ready to pay the price of a more serious commitment. The greatest violence of the cultural radicals is expressive, not practical. And with *that* the rest of us can live. The problem with the revived and already corrupted cult of experience is not that it is likely by itself to produce more violence than we can endure or the police can handle, but rather that it provides no support for everyday politics. Instead, it sets the stage for once-a-month or once-a-year explosions, bursts of excitement shared through the media, with effects that no one even pretends to think about.

As putative victims, the cultural radicals are more appealing but no more helpful. They have produced a counterimage to the violence of our time, not pacifist but pastoral: the picture of a "green America," themselves the rightful inhabitants, beset by technologically advanced barbarians. As an art form the pastoral has hitherto been a specifically upper-class diversion, and it remains to be seen whether they can make it into anything else. Here I want only to note how innocent their picture of the future is—vaguely anarchist, sternly ecological, sexually bountiful, depopulated—and how incredibly far those who hold it have to go before they can even think of acting it out. Every practical decision lies ahead of them; every political temptation is yet to be encountered; every risk yet to be taken. Now the cultural radicals simply turn away from the violence of the American state and its enemies. If they have to, will they be able to criticize, organize, resist, and still maintain their peculiarly peaceful vision?

IV

Politics, once again, is the art of minimizing violence; a man begins to be a politician as soon as he tries to get what he wants without hitting somebody. But social change, we are told, requires that some-body be hit; nothing has ever been achieved . . . and so on. There is some truth here, but questions need to be asked in each case—just as questions need to be asked of the police. At what point, in what (precise) circumstances was violence used? who used it first? how many people were injured? with what (concrete) results?

A disciplined mass movement is much like a strong and legitimate state: it uses violence artfully and economically; often the mere threat is enough; "incidental" brutality is barred or punished. The classic vision of the near Left is of such a movement, growing steadily over time, winning massive support by means almost entirely peaceful, but then *because of its strength* being challenged by the authorities and forced into strikes, demonstrations, perhaps even street fighting, and so on. It was never thought that this challenge could be success-fully met, however, unless substantial sympathy had already been won among the police and within the ranks of the army. Even "radi-calized" citizens do not conquer policemen and soldiers; they win them over (or they don't). Hence violence is but one instrument of politics, and by no means so ready a choice for the Left as for the authorities.

But the movement grows slowly, and so the shortcut is the first and the perennial political temptation. Violence always looks like the easiest shortcut. Sometimes this or that group of militants hope to seize power all by themselves without waiting for anyone else, or to terrorize the country and win major concessions on behalf of the others; or they hope to provoke police repression and so goad their potential but passive followers into revolutionary action. The last of these is the strategy most often attributed to contemporary militants. They intend to expose the "true character" of American society, it is said, to drive the authorities into an openly fascist posture, and so force the rest of us to resist. What is there to say? I doubt, again, that this is a serious intention, though it is a strategy that might conceivably work if (1) the true character of the U.S. government were fascist, and (2) the mass of the American people were already profoundly alienated from it. Neither of these conditions holds. Nor do strong and legitimate conservative regimes turn fascist in response to leftist provocation; I know of no historical cases. And, if they did, that would surely be a disaster and not a success for the Left. No fascist regime has yet been overthrown by rapid revolutionary mobilization; nor is there time for long-term political organizing; in the short run the militants would be dead. It is, all in all, a policy of insanity compounded.

I have already described the actual results of this "strategy" in the U.S. today. But there is more to say about it, a classic leftist position to reiterate against it. However easy it may be to throw a brick, use a gun, plant a bomb, and however much the cultural atmosphere encourages—and publicists, editors, screenwriters, and so on applaud or "understand"—such activities, they are not likely to be engaged in by large numbers of people. They don't build a movement, because they don't commit men and women to daily work for the cause. Terrorism is not and cannot be a collective effort. It enhances the self-regard of a militant elite, and then the members of this elite celebrate their psychic or moral liberation. But the rest of us have no reason to expect that if they were ever to seize power, they would be any different from the people they call "pigs." The one group is as unlikely as the other to liberate *us*. That we can only do for ourselves, through organizations in which we are actively involved and whose policies we share in making. "The liberation of the workers can come only through the workers themselves."

The liberation of the militants is a waste of violence, just as the beating up of the militants by the police is a waste of violence—and neither is a victory for the rest of us. The only difference between the two is that in the second case there are review boards and presidential commissions to condemn the waste, and in the first there are none. The "movement"—for the moment—offers us no recourse. The democratic state does. So *laissez faire* on the Left makes statists of us all, and our most immediate duty is to be honest about where we are. Inevitably, the police will impose the discipline we have failed to build: the problem of law enforcement—not a problem we are at home with—has been moved onto the political agenda of the seventies. Significant social and political change may well await its working out —may well await, that is, the restoration of a framework of civility within which the police, the militants, and the rest of us can live, more or less, together.

Alice S. Rossi

Women—Terms of Liberation

At least for the moment, Women's Liberation is "in." Its advocates get wide publicity in the mass media, and there is talk, mostly not very serious, about what "those women" want. On campuses, as in professional organizations, there has been mounting pressure to hire and promote more women, to provide child-care facilities for married women students and employees, and to offer courses on the history and the status of women. The voicing of these demands will increase significantly at professional conventions. I predict comparable increases in the political and economic realms, as women organize and demonstrate to change laws and employer practices that discriminate on the grounds of sex. Among activist women there is clearly a new note of optimism.

This optimistic sense does not, however, seem to be shared by many men. The majority of American men appear to be convinced that if they wait out the storm, activism will die down, and they can then continue to run government agencies, businesses, and universities. I do not share the view that the women's rights movement is a passing thing. Indeed, I think the movement has not yet reached its crest, though I also believe it faces hard times. What follows is an attempt to sketch both the encouraging and discouraging developments that may mark the women's movement in the next decade.

At the outset I shall draw upon my personal experiences in academic and private life, upon participation in several reform move-

250

ments in recent years, and upon a commitment to fundamental change in American society.

Personal-Political Background

As an undergraduate and graduate student, I had no particular interest in the status of women, sex roles, or occupational choice. I entered college as an English major, pragmatism dictating an occupational choice of high school English teacher, but romanticism prompting a hope I might become a famous writer. I was one of those thousands of bright, eager New York students attending the city colleges—in my case, Brooklyn College. My first sociology instructor was Louis Schneider, and he began his course by reading a Whitman poem and raising the questions: Who was this man? What does the poem tell about his time, his place on this globe? I found the sociological dimension of literature so fascinating that I fell in love with the field, and began a lifelong affair of the heart and mind that is second only to my own marriage and the three children of that marriage. As a graduate student at Columbia, I was interested in the macroscopic analysis of social institutions; in family and kinship systems rather than the roles of women within family systems; in reference groups, through work with Robert Merton, and in studies of the professions. The occupational role I chose to study in Kingsley Davis's seminar was that of the politician, though not once did I think to look into the sex-linked nature of occupational choice.

No woman in 1970, I hope, could be the total innocent I was in 1950 concerning sex discrimination. I dreamed of being one day the president of the American Sociological Society, and of writing a major opus that would be built on the strengths of my two mentors in theory and research. I discounted as peevish envy the claim of my male peers that I would not get a fellowship "because I was a woman," and then, when I was awarded one, the counterclaim that "someone on the faculty must be trying to make you."

It would have been congenial for me to move from graduate training to an academic position as a teacher and secondarily a researcher. But this is a path difficult for a married woman in academia, particularly if, like myself, she is married to a sociologist. So I spent ten years as a research associate, following not my own interests so much as the availability of funds and openings: intergroup relations at Cornell, generational differences in the Soviet Union at Harvard, kinship in the middle class at the University of Chicago.

Through these research undertakings, I developed a fascination with a problem seldom adequately stated within sociological theory itself: what are the connections, the strains and accommodations, between involvement in the family on the one hand and the occupational system on the other? I was taking a first step away from the predominant theory that the family and occupational systems require "mechanisms of segregation" with only one member of the family participating significantly in the occupational system—a theory I now view as an intellectual putdown providing a rationale for men as the prime movers in work and politics.

The source of this growing interest was not only research and scholarship; it was also my own personal experience as a faculty wife and mother of young children. As a faculty wife, I had ample opportunity to observe that some sociological theorists did a good job of preventing two members of a family from holding significant positions in the occupational system. At Harvard and again at Chicago, I saw numerous instances of women being kept off the academic turf their husbands claimed as their own. I had offended one such theorist by negotiating an appointment at Harvard without first clearing such a horrendous step with him, then my husband's department chairman. I watched women friends leave the university when they became pregnant and being kept out when they tried to return after their children entered school. And during the two years I had my first two children I learned from personal experience the truth of the existential thesis that "one becomes what ones does," for I realized with horror that I was resenting my husband's freedom to continue his full-time academic work despite the addition of parental responsibilities, and even more that I was actually trying to prevent his playing an intimate role in the lives of the children, so that I might at least have ascendancy in parenthood to complement his ascendancy in our profession.

But it took a return to academia, involving a traumatic encounter with the discrimination academic women so often suffer, to jar me out of my innocence. I began a long process of re-establishing connections with my earlier life: intellectual exposure to the ideas of Robert Lynd and C. Wright Mills, personal experiences in a variety of working-class and white-collar clerical jobs, and involvement in radical politics (as an undergraduate in the 1930s and early 1940s). I began to draw together these older layers of the self and to focus the ideas, the personal experience, and the political commitment I now have.

My own trial by fire involved a not untypical story of a bright woman Ph.D. accepting a research associateship to do a study the male principal investigator was not competent to do on his own, and in which he had very little interest. At least initially his interest was low, until I had designed the study, fielded it, and partially analyzed the results. At that point he realized he had a good thing going, and simply announced, despite verbal agreements about co-authorship, that my services were no longer needed. I was a salaried research associate, he a full professor, and as the dean put it bluntly to me, "He is valuable university property; you, unfortunately, are expendable."

My own concern for the status of women, the analysis of sex roles, the study of and active participation in abortion law and divorce law reform, I date to the "slow burn" that began in that first major encounter with sex discrimination in academia. It immediately precipitated the scholarship and writing that led me down the path of immodesty to my first essay on sex equality.

The varied response to that *Daedalus* essay was itself a revealing commentary on American academia. Several male colleagues accused me of troubling their marriages. Young women wrote to say they decided to return to graduate school instead of having another baby. My husband received a sympathetic bereavement card from a West Coast sociologist for having such an upstart wife. A more recent example of this kind was the reaction of male sociologists to the roles my husband and I played at the sociology convention in the fall of 1969. As secretary of the association, my husband was on the platform while I delivered a speech and submitted resolutions for the women's caucus. In the months since then, I have had offers for academic appointments based on the premise that my husband and I are about to be divorced. My husband has been asked how he felt when I delivered that speech, with his male colleagues not knowing how to take his response that he felt pride! During earlier years, my university colleagues criticized me for "not sticking to my last" as research sociologist instead of writing analytic social criticism. Others said it was inappropriate and would "ruin your career" to get involved in the "woman thing," or to be publicly visible as an organizer for abortion law reform, or to write in a woman's magazine that "motherhood was not enough." Nowhere did one hear anything about responsibility for reaching the larger public, nor did one have any sense that there was an obligation for a family sociologist to "do something" about contraception, abortion, or women's rights.

As you may know from reading Eli Ginsberg on life styles of educated women, a supportive husband is an absolute requirement for professional women. Unfortunately, Ginsberg does not understand how a woman gets a supportive husband. It is not a "condition" she is fortunate to have as a base for being something more than homemaker, mother, and husband-relaxer. He is something she looks for, and when she finds him, she marries him. It didn't just happen that my husband is supportive; I chose him in part because he *was*.

From 1964 to the fall of 1969 I enjoyed an unusual status under a research award from the National Institute of Mental Health. This award gave me an academic umbrella to legitimize my status in the university and the independence to undertake my own research. The best education I ever had I acquired on my own during the first year or so of that award: the luxury of getting lost in libraries again, free to acquire that delicious "itch to know," to tackle new fields, turn down any lecture, paper, or course offering that did not interest me. Midway into that five-year award, I undertook a major research study of family and career roles of women college graduates. What time I had beyond this research and family responsibilities was invested in active attempts at social, legal, and political change to benefit women. By early 1969, however, I felt increasingly out of rapport with most of my colleagues in empirical sociology and restless for direct contact with the college-age generation. I had studied these young people; now I wanted to teach them. In the fall of 1969, I therefore shifted from research sociology at Johns Hopkins to undergraduate teaching at Goucher College.

Background of Current Women's Movement

It has become fashionable to link the emergence of the women's liberation movement to the participation of younger women in the

civil rights movement. These young women, one reads, drew the conclusion their ancestors did from involvement in the abolitionist cause
of the nineteenth century: that the arguments developed and the
battles waged to free the black American could apply to American
women, even though women in the abolitionist as in the civil rights
movement all too often found themselves treated as second-class
creatures good for cooking, typing, and comforting their male leaders.
Without detracting from this point at all, I would only remark that
the women's liberation movement is a bit more than two years old,
and there were important, though less visible, changes among American women earlier in the 1960s.

In fact, I would argue that it was the changed composition of the
female labor force during the period beginning with 1940 but rapidly
peaking in the 1950s that provided the momentum leading to the
establishment of the Kennedy Commission on the Status of Women
and the formation of new women's rights organization in the mid-
1960s. So long as women worked mostly before marriage or after
marriage only until a first pregnancy, or lived within city limits where
there was a diversity of cultural activities to engage them, there were
but feeble grounds for a significant movement among women, since
their motivation for working was short-lived. Only among women who
are relatively permanent members of the work force could daily experience force an awareness of economic inequities based on sex and
a determination to do something about them. It was the women who
served on the numerous committees of the Kennedy Commission,
followed by the thousands who worked with the state commissions
established during the Kennedy and Johnson administrations, who
experienced and then stimulated a mood of rising expectations among
American women.

These were committed, knowledgeable, largely middle-aged women
who had high hopes, as they filed their reports, that American society would finally do something to improve the status of women.
Their hopes were dashed by the treatment they experienced at the
spring 1966 conference of representatives from the state commissions
brought together by the Department of Labor in Washington. From
that frustrating experience, a number of women concluded that little
significant change could be expected until a strong organization was
built that would be completely independent of the political establish-

ment. This was how the National Organization for Women was formed in the fall of 1966. The range of women's problems that NOW is concerned with has broadened greatly since 1966, but the core continues to be equal treatment in hiring and promotion.

NOW includes lively, dedicated women who are pressing hard against the barriers that restrict women in American society. Except for its action in behalf of airline stewardesses, however, it has had relatively little public or media attention outside of New York, at least if compared to the extraordinary press coverage given to the women's liberation groups this past year. Why so? The answer, I think, lies in differences of stress and outlook between these two tendencies within the women's movement.

A fundamental assumption of American society is that men's primary social roles are in work and women's primary social roles in the family. It is conventionally supposed that all men will want to work at a challenging job. Nothing is so threatening to conventional values as a man who does not want to work or does not want to work at a challenging job, and most people are disturbed if a man in a well-paying job indicates ambivalence or dislike toward it. The counterpart for women is any suggestion that they feel ambivalent toward maternity, marriage, or homemaking, probably in that order. In more sociological terms, we might put this as follows: social roles vary in the extent to which it is culturally permissible to express ambivalence or negative feelings toward them. Ambivalence can be admitted most readily toward those roles that are optional, least where they are considered primary. Thus men repress negative feelings toward work and feel freer to express negative feelings toward leisure, sex, and marriage, while women are free to express negative feelings toward work but tend to repress them toward family roles.

Applying these hypotheses to the issues that triggered public attention to the women's movement helps explain why reactions are more intense to the women's liberation groups than to women's rights organizations like NOW. There was widespread concern in manpower, government, and university circles when many bright middle-class young men began to depart from an unthinking acceptance of occupational aspirations like those of their fathers, either by shifting away from business, engineering, and science toward teaching, social science, and the humanities, or by indicating that their desire was for a life style with more time spent away from the job. The movie *The Graduate* symbolized this generational contrast in dramatic form. Universities were concerned when men students expressed resentment to advanced training as a preparation for the adult rat race. But I doubt that anyone would have worried if only women had expressed such resentment. They would simply have been told that if they could not take the academic pressure, they should go home.

Public airing of ambivalence or a shift of values toward the place of work in the lives of men touches a vital nerve in American society. For women, the counterpart is any airing of ambivalence toward what the culture has defined as *their* primary roles, in marriage and maternity. However, once even a minority of women begin to reject their role as sex object, postpone or reject marriage, stop smiling over a shiny waxed floor or, heaven forbid, question the desirability of having children or rearing them themselves as a full-time job, then they touch an equivalent nerve in American society.

Hence, it is when men question work and women question family commitment that we find public responses ranging from a shiver of distaste to a convulsion of hate. It has been the questioning of family roles among women's liberation groups that has triggered the current widespread attention to the "woman issue." NOW's focus on employment issues, dealing with an "optional" role for women, cannot compete for media attention with antimarriage and antisexism campaigns by women's liberation spokeswomen.

Employment

What, now, are the immediate problems and possibilities? Let me start with the bread-and-butter issue of women's employment. We must first look at a critical determinant of the changed profile of women's participation in the labor force. A lot of nonsense has been written in the past decade to account for the flow of older married women into the labor force. The emphasis has been on the impact of homemaking simplification via frozen foods and complex gadgetry on the one hand, and the search for self-fulfillment and a solution to the "problem without a name" on the other. This is to look for explanations on the supply side of the economic equation. But in an economy as hard-nosed as ours, such a stress is naïve, for there must be powerful factors on the demand side that prompted employers to open their doors to older women.

A significant factor underlying this willingness lies in the peculiarities of the demographic structure of the American population between 1940 and 1970. Young women were staying in school longer and marrying at an earlier age, thus shrinking the size of the traditional labor pool of young unmarried women. Even more important, the young women of the 1950s were born in the 1930s, when the birth rate was very low, while at the same time there was a vast increase in the number of young children born during the baby boom of those postwar years. As a result of the rippling effect of this low-fertility cohort, employers *had* to seek women workers from other sources than the young unmarried. Consequently, the trigger was in the first place far more a matter of employer demand than of assertive women pressing to enter into the labor force.

These were also years of vast expansion in precisely those segments of the occupational system in which women have traditionally been prominent. Because schools were flooded with the baby-boom children, women college graduates were assured a welcome as teachers despite age and marital and family status. Colleges and universities were expanding at a rapid rate, and married women were taken on as part-time instructors and full-time researchers. Clerical, sales, and service occupations were expanding, and women with high school degrees were able to choose among the available jobs.

This fortunate circumstance is now changing. In the 1970s there will be a reversal in the demographic pattern. The birth rate has declined, in general, between 1957 and the present, although the arrival of the postwar "baby-boom" children at their child-producing years could soon send it back up again. The marriage age has been creeping upward, and the time interval between marriage and childbearing widening. If these trends continue in the 1970s, there may be more young unmarried and childless married women seeking jobs. At the same time, graduate schools will be producing large numbers of young people with advanced degrees, who will face a very different job market from the one that young Ph.D.'s faced during the past twenty years. Up to 1970 the supply of Ph.D.'s was far below the demand in institutions of higher education, but the reverse will hold from 1970 onward: the supply will exceed the demand in universities. This will be especially true for the natural sciences, less so for the social sciences until late in the 1970s. Which is not to say that the society cannot absorb or does not need highly trained people. From one point of view, the excess supply means an opportunity for reducing class size, providing students with better learning experiences, changing graduate curricula to prepare students for non-academic jobs, and so forth. On the other hand, higher education is facing a financial crisis due to the cutbacks in government funding, corporations are pruning staffs of "frills," and government agencies are on an internal economy drive.

It is therefore of critical importance that women press hard during the next few years to secure equal protection of the law and to assure adequate representation in all segments of the economy. There is already a first sign that women are withdrawing from the labor force: in the last quarter of 1969 the Bureau of Labor Statistics showed a drop in the unemployment rate, though the drop occurred not because people found jobs, but because unemployed young people and women were ceasing to look for jobs.

What women must do in the next several years does not require new legislation, though passage of an equal rights amendment to the Constitution would cover a wide range of sex inequities in law and practice. Short of such passage, however, it is true that there has been a legal revolution during the 1960s in regard to protection of women's economic rights. Title VII of the Civil Rights Act of 1964 prohibits discrimination based on sex by all employers of twenty-five or more employees, employment agencies, and unions with twenty-five or more members, with the exception of educational institutions. The Equal Pay Act of 1963 requires equal wages and salaries for men and women doing equal work. Amended Executive Order 11375 prohibits discrimination based on sex by federal government contractors and subcontractors. The Age Discrimination in Employment Act of 1967 prohibits discrimination based on age between forty and sixty-five. While this act does not prohibit sex discrimination, it could play a significant role in enlarging employment opportunities for women over forty who wish to return to the labor market or change jobs. Municipal and state Fair Employment Practices commissions and agencies administering state equal pay legislation can also be used to protect employment rights. Women in colleges and universities are not covered by the Civil Rights Act, but women lawyers in activist groups are now working through the channels provided by Executive Order 11375 rather than pressing for congressional change in the educational institutions exemption in the 1964 act. WEAL, the Women's Equity Action League, has mounted an important campaign designed to apply pressure on colleges and universities to comply with this executive order or face cancellation and future loss of government contracts—something no institution of higher education would care to risk. Labor Department guidelines were announced in June 1970 to assure equal job opportunities for women on work paid for under federal contract.

The mere existence of such laws does not solve anything unless women press for their implementation, first by concerted efforts to educate their sex, and second by developing test cases that will bring real changes in women's employment status. Though unglamorous and hard work, and rarely making a flashy news story, this is of greater long-range significance than any amount of antimen speech-making.

Right now it is not clear how national policies in the coming decade will affect the lives of women. In the post-Sputnik decade, there was a widespread campaign to persuade women to enter the labor force, with the government serving as spokesman for short-handed employers trying to meet personnel needs. The laws serving to strengthen women's economic rights were passed during the sixties. It is only in the past few years that woman power has emerged, with younger women questioning conventional women's roles. Even while expectations are rising, a reversal of national policy may lie ahead, as a brake is put on military expenditure, and as conservative political elements come into ascendancy with the new-old cry that women belong in the home instead of taking jobs away from men or making "outrageous" demands for maternity benefits and child-care facilities.

At the same time there will be mounting pressure for a national population policy. We are witnessing the advance wave of this policy with the unprecedented shift in opinion regarding abortion in the United States. Those of us who worked on this issue early in the 1960s are now gratified and disturbed by the ease with which total repeal of abortion laws looms as a reality: gratified because this represents the fruition of long, hard effort, disturbed by the quite mixed motivations behind the passage of such legislation.

Public dialogue on population is increasing significantly, and we begin to hear large families discussed as undesirable for individual couples and for society at large. But the problem is that women are being told to hold back on their fertility in the same era in which there may be a shift away from encouraging them to seek significant work in the economy, and when much volunteer work is being transformed into paid employment for the poor. Two such conflicting policies—low fertility and minimal participation in the labor force—can have serious consequences in undercutting the confidence of young women. It would be like putting them in a revolving door and spinning it: not permitting them easy entry or significant work *outside* the home, yet not permitting them fulfillment in a bountiful maternity *inside* the home. The social price of such a conflict could well be a rise in alienation, escape into drugs, alcoholism, or joyless sex and an even greater tendency to live vicariously through the few children they have.

I would like to think that women would take the lead in calling attention to the human dimensions of national policies that have particular impact on the lives of women. For the organizations directly involved in action concerning women's rights, such a thorough analysis is difficult. It takes time and some distancing from the heat of battle, and hence becomes a special responsibility of women in academia. But their voice will not be heard nor will their analyses be pertinent unless they keep in close contact with the women's rights movement and national policy formation. A good example can be seen in the congressional hearings on the birth control pill this past spring, at which women's liberation spokesmen engaged in widely publicized protest. Their clamor was, in my judgment, ill-advised. We do not halt smallpox vaccinations because a dozen children die from them each year, or stop using antibiotics because five hundred users die a year; by the same token, an element of risk in contraceptive pills is, in and of itself, no basis for calling a halt to their use. In no way is this to say that women should not have completely safe contraceptives, or that more emphasis should not be put on male contraceptives, sterilization, and abortion as acceptable procedures to control unwanted births. What I am urging is that women be more thorough and thoughtful in their analysis of a problem before rushing to the streets and into print with arguments that may appear sound superficially but are actually political posturing.

Sexuality

Research and education in human sexuality, and the implications of such research for the social roles of the sexes is another matter that merits increased attention in the 1970s. Fifty years of accepting Freudian concepts of female sexuality will not be quickly undone by current research on the human sexual response. Psychoanalytic theories have penetrated deep into the modern consciousness, and are reinforced a dozen times a day through commercials that attempt to sell everything from dresses to detergents. What concerns me equally is to be spared another fifty years of anti-Freudian polemics from the women's movement.

Very often such anti-Freudian analyses are couched in Marxist terms. It may serve unstated political ends, but it is historically false and analytically simplistic to claim that women's sexual role reflects the bourgeois notion of man's desire to possess and amass private property, or to charge that the second-class citizenship of women merely reflects capitalist society's need to coerce them into domestic slavery and conspicuous consumption. Marxist analyses of women and capitalism have an element of truth only if you substitute industrialization for capitalism. As the Communist nations have industrialized, the same hard pinch of double jobs is detectable in the lives of their employed married women, and the same loss of humane values in the work place. Nor is there much evidence that the relations between the sexes are particularly different in Communist nations from those in Western Europe or the United States. The major difference is merely one of intensity: no country can match the United States for media saturated with exploitative and male-dominant sex, typified so well by the infantile or cruel acts of physical rape that fill so many pages of Norman Mailer's books.

A number of radical-feminist analyses begin with a good critique of the Freudian fallacies concerning female sexuality. Let us now assume it to be established that there is no differentiation between a clitoral and vaginal orgasm; that the myth of women's relative asexuality has been shown to be a biological absurdity; and that women's sexuality has been suppressed through a socialization of gender roles that urges passivity and submission to men. Liberation group discussions of these points can be enormously helpful for the psychological release of the submerged sexual selves of many women. But one must also reckon with the fact that the Masters-Johnson research only illuminates the *physiological* dimension of human sexuality. It tells us nothing about the nongenital components of human sexual behavior. Critiques of Freud's notions of female sexuality are now commonplace, but I have seen little as yet that suggests an alternative developmental theory, with the exception of recent work by John Gagnon and William Simon. I would suggest that more critical attention should be paid to two factors bearing upon sexual behavior in American society. One is the view that sex is an intense high-pressure drive that constrains the individual to seek sexual gratification either directly or indirectly. This view is apparent not only in psychoanalytic but in sociological literature as well. Kingsley Davis, for example, considers sex a high-intensity, social constant that must be channeled lest it find expression in behavior that threatens the maintenance of collective life. Part of the Freudian legacy, however, is that we have become extremely adept at weeding out the sexual ingredient in many forms of non-sexual behavior and symbolism while rarely engaging in what may be an equally fruitful analysis: an examination of sexual behavior as an agency for expressing nonsexual motives.

For in truth, sexual behavior in American society serves not merely sexual needs, but also power and status needs compensating for a lack of gratification in other areas of life. A further complication is the pressure on American adults to remain pegged at an adolescent stage of development and behavior. A man or woman of forty-five is not the same person as a twenty-year-old, and to perform sexually as if they were is to require that the man overperform sexually and that the woman persist in a girlish style that is equally inappropriate to her stage of sexual and social maturity. In the case of men, overper-formance can be stoked by extramarital adventures or self-stimulation via pornographic literature or dramatic productions. Men are good at such detached self-stimulation since they learn sexuality in part through masturbation, which itself paves the way for a greater detach-ment in the sexual act than women tend to have. It may also be the case that marital satisfaction and happiness decline with duration of marriage in American society largely because adults are expected to perform at forty or fifty as they did at twenty or twenty-five. This is a reflection of what Henry Murray has described as the retarded adolescent stage of development of American society. If, as a culture, we could move in the direction of mature interdependence between individuals, across social classes, religious, racial, and sexual lines, to say nothing of national boundaries, we might come to develop what Kenneth Boulding has described as "reconciling styles" in which we take primary pleasure in life from identifying with the process of change itself: watching and taking pleasure from our own individual growth and change, and the growth and change of our friends, spouses, and children.

What has this to do with the women's movement in the 1970s? I think we should be prepared for intense male backlash to the demands women make that are rooted not merely in the specific area of work or home management or parental responsibility, but in displacements from a deeper level. Demands for equality for women are threats to men's self-esteem and sense of sexual turf. Some feminists will say, fine and good: men have been our oppressors long enough, now they must give ground. But most women do not wish to live embattled and manless lives, and my impression is there are far more men in the younger generation than there were in my own who are eager to acquire a new life style, a gentler and more meaningful relationship with women. There is much need for research and sober analysis on the social correlates of varying styles of sexual behavior; following that, a great need for a rather different conception of sex education than anything we have seen to date in school curricula or gymnastic sex manuals.

Some women who have recently been active in women's caucuses in professional associations have begun to compare notes on the responses their demands are eliciting from male colleagues. One of the more interesting hypotheses emerging from these comparisons is that the men most resistant to and in some cases almost hysterical about women's pressure for equal treatment are men known to be sexually exploitative in their relations to women students. One such professor whose feathers were decidedly ruffled when the sociology women's caucus displaced a luncheon meeting he was to speak at, complained prettily, with an expectation that it would flatter rather than anger me: "But Alice, what is all the fuss about? There is always room in graduate departments for an extraordinary woman!" It was beyond his ability or willingness to understand that sex equality in academia would not be achieved until there was room for as many "average" women as for "average" men. Some of my caucus colleagues believe that, beneath the surface, men such as this are not able to relate to a woman colleague at the same or higher status rank and feel comfortable only in superordinate positions from which they can dispense professorial and sexual favors.

The male backlash is bound to come, and there are signs of it already. A male friend of mine recently sent me a xeroxed copy of a letter of recommendation to the chairman of his department. The applicant is an unmarried woman who had taught in the writer's department and taken graduate courses with him. He wrote:

When Miss X arrived she was somewhat lacking in self-confidence, uncertain whether there was a place for her in sociology. Now she recognizes that she can, as a female, contribute to the field without becoming a spinster or a swinger. I say this to emphasize that she is a mature person not swayed by the superficial values so evident on campuses today. In short, she is not a participant in the women's liberation movement but a competent sociologist. . . . She is neither seductive nor emasculating and will be a useful colleague.

I cite such examples to point out that we must have thick skins—at least as thick as those of our grandmothers in the suffrage, union, and socialist movements of an earlier day. We shall need every bit of sex solidarity we can get.

Women's Rights Organizations

Everyone knows there has already been a good deal of factionalism within the larger women's movement. We have WITCH, WEAL, Radical Feminists, FEW, NOW, WRAP, and there are undoubtedly more to come. Listening to men, one senses a gleeful pleasure at seeing such sectarianism; many wishfully view this as a dissipation of effort in a noisy fizzle. But this need not be true so long as those who form a new group do not concentrate on fruitless attacks upon the group they left or on styles of protest directed mainly at getting attention from the press. Diversity within a movement can be a strength, for there is no one problem or one solution. Certain women's liberation groups may be trying to recruit for a political revolutionary movement yet find some of their members graduating from informal consciousness-raising group sessions to affiliation with a NOW chapter. In turn, many NOW chapters have lost members to the liberation groups. Women lawyers have on occasion separated from the more diffuse organizations, the better to focus on campaigns making greater use of their skills. Other groups may concentrate on demonstrations protesting sex imagery in the media or beauty pageants. There is far more risk in frantically dissipating one's efforts by doing a great variety of things than in organizational splitting.

Let me end with a comment concerning the relationship between the women's rights movement and the movements of black Americans. There is a serious danger that the essentially middle-class and white women's groups will be as guilty of misunderstanding the problems confronting black men and women today as an earlier counterpart in the middle-class suffrage movement of the nineteenth century misunderstood the political efforts of working-class people.

In recent years, many women in the women's rights movement have taken up with great moral righteousness the task of informing black women that they should avoid the trap of moving through the same series of mistakes that middle-class women were subjected to in the past. A conference on women last February at Cornell culminated in a dramatic session on the black woman in America, in which the largely middle-class white audience hissed black women and men on a panel who spoke of the need for black women to give attention to the black man and his position in the community, to be supportive of their men's struggle for greater self-esteem and dignity. Renee Neblett of the Boston Black Panthers defined the black woman as a strong person who can act independently and make decisions but, most important of all, a woman with an ability to relate to men, one who would do anything to help her man retain or regain his manhood and ensure the survival of her people.

In reading the transcript of this session, I felt anger and shame that the middle-class women in the audience had not appreciated the difference in the positions of the sexes among whites and blacks. John Dollard's description of caste in a Southern town is as relevant today as three decades ago, when he pointed out that within the white caste the man is in the superior position, and within the black caste the woman is more often in the superior position. If black women, largely poor but still more advantageously placed than black men, have the humanity and dignity to help raise the self-esteem of their men—to realize, as one of my black students put it, that the black female is no better than her man despite a history of educational and economic superiority—then this is a great tribute to black women in America that unfortunately is not matched by a comparable dedication on the part of white men toward their women.

Nor do we sufficiently realize the continuing relevance of class differences in the ways a problem is perceived and experienced. Abraham Maslow's need hierarchy thesis is helpful, for it suggests that middle-class women, whose physical needs for food, clothing, shelter, and sheer security of person are relatively assured, are free to concentrate on a higher level of need. A working-class person or group cannot indulge in such luxury until needs for survival and security are met. I think, therefore, that right now the middle-class women's rights movement can find a collaborative arrangement with black women only on such bread-and-butter issues as protecting and expanding economic and political rights. Beyond this, the white women's movement should try to deepen its understanding of the differences between their relations to men and those of black women. Before giving advice, one must understand. Listen, for example, to a black poet's phrasing of the issue:

> blackwoman
> is an
> in and out
> rightsideup
> action-image
> of her man . . .
> in other
> (blacker) words;
> She's together,
> if
> he
> bes.
> —*Don Lee*

What white poet has yet said of a man, "he's together if she is"?

Despite the optimists in our midst, or the pessimists who anticipate revolution in the streets—after which, of course, a magical transformation would follow—I think we are in for a long and hard battle —cultural, legal, and political—before we reach any goal of sex equality for black or white in this nation. It will be won not by quickie-action skirmishes but by the persistent beat of the hearts and work of the minds of at least another generation.

Brendan and Patricia Cayo Sexton

Labor's Decade—Maybe

If we read our stars right, the seventies ought to see, not the dawning of the age of Aquarius, but a new era for the workingman. Of course, some catastrophe or technological breakthrough may make the seventies nobody's decade. But, if history moves on its present course, the worker and his union will again have a place in the sun. They had it in the thirties, during a period of struggle and unrest, when the unions as we today know them were pretty much shaped.

Labor can be expected to achieve renewed strength in the seventies because many Americans do want change in our society, and labor is driven to use its power to win social change. Most of us are sick of violence and guerrilla war, sick of war abroad and at home. Most Americans want to get out of the trenches. Labor will come to the forefront in the seventies because the economic issues, again urgent, will probably remain with us, especially if conservatives persist in fiddling away our resources when not pouring them into war machines. Jobs, income, opportunity, distribution of wealth and power, standard of living—these are basic, and these are the issues of greatest concern to labor.

What will labor *do* with the seventies? A more difficult question. We expect a turn in a progressive direction. Unions in the seventies, for example, will more nearly resemble the Congress of Industrial Organizations of the thirties than the AFL of the sixties. Changing membership and leadership, as well as a thrust into new unorganized areas, will give the unions a strong new momentum. Many will have

269

a membership that will be much blacker, younger, better educated, and probably more militant, and these members will vote in leaders who more nearly resemble them.

Union membership will pick up in the South, among women, among public employees, among the working poor and paraprofessionals, and perhaps also among white-collar and professional workers. As for technology, the major consequence for labor will be to make the work force and union membership somewhat more skilled. Automation, the nightmare of the fifties, will probably have no more profound an impact on the work force in the seventies than it had in the sixties. It will continue to eliminate some unskilled jobs and increase the need for skilled workers—but not dramatically.

Until very recently it has been fashionable to write off the working class as having, at best, small significance in either the nation's present or future. Blue-collar workers, we were told, had grown fat, dispirited, conservative, maybe "neofascist." Social scientists discovered and rediscovered the working class as authoritarian, anti–civil libertarian, white racist, prowar, or in other ways generally repugnant. The workers' unions, naturally, were even worse, led by fat cats, bureaucrats, crooks and sellouts.

In any event, so we were told, blue-collar workers were no longer of much significance because of the "changing nature of the work force" and the disappearance of their jobs. Well, this demise of blue-collar labor has now been impending for at least twenty years, the obituaries have proliferated, and the patient remains pretty healthy.

Neither the work force nor the unions have declined. There are now more blue-collar workers than at any time in history, and more Americans belong to unions than ever before. The 28.2 million blue-collar workers employed at the close of 1969 is the largest number ever so classified.[1] In addition, 9.5 million service workers can probably also be counted as blue-collar—a substantial increase over past years. In all, 37.7 million workers in 1969, compared to 29.8 million in 1950. To be sure, white-collar workers have multiplied even faster, but it is the agricultural workers who are disappearing

1. All statistical citations dealing with the work force are taken from the *Handbook of Basic Economic Statistics,* Bureau of the Census, U.S. Department of Commerce, 1970. In all appropriate cases, we have cited the latest months or years given in that publication.

(and being soaked up into a variety of jobs), not the blue-collar workers. Even as a percentage of the work force, the number of blue-collar workers has remained amazingly constant, fluctuating from year to year only within a few percentage points. In the sixties the percentage actually increased somewhat. More specifically, the male blue-collar work force has increased as a percentage of the total male work force while the corresponding percentage of females has decreased (the proportion of female "service workers" is growing). Almost half of all employed males are employed in blue-collar jobs (craftsmen, operatives, service workers)—47.3 percent in 1968, to be precise.

During the sixties union membership also grew—from 17 to 19 million and held nearly constant as a proportion of the work force.[2] In 1968 union members were 23 percent of the labor force, including part-time as well as full-time workers. In the mid-fifties the percentage had been slightly higher. The big job of unions, in this respect, is keeping up with the phenomenal growth in the work force over the past several decades, from about 59 million in 1950 to about 82 million in 1968. Moreover, the growth has been most rapid in populations and places unfamiliar to unions: clerical, professional, service, women, the South. As unions learn how to organize these new types —and there is evidence that they *are* learning—they may be able to go beyond the one-quarter mark which for the last two decades seems to have been, more or less, their assigned share of the labor force.[3]

Most unions are growing steadily. During the period between 1964 and 1966, for example, 96 unions gained members and 55 lost. Losses were concentrated in sick or dying industries and where employment

2. Materials dealing with numbers of union members are quoted or abstracted from various editions of the *Directory of National and International Labor Unions in the United States*. The most recent edition of this biennial publication of the U.S. Department of Labor, Bureau of Labor Statistics, appeared in late 1970 and reported union membership for 1968–69.

3. For reasons not known to us, union membership is almost always reported as a percentage of the "nonagricultural work force," whereas we choose to measure membership against the total labor force. It makes a difference. From 1960 through 1968 union membership as a percentage of the nonagricultural work force sank from 31.4 to 27.9—but measured against the total labor force the percentages were 23.6 against 23.0. The "nonagricultural work force" measurement reflects a shift away from agrarian jobs rather than a decline of unionism and is therefore less useful for these purposes.

generally declined sharply—such as mining, railroads, textiles, shoe manufacturing, furniture, marine, transportation.

In the fifties and sixties, some long-term assumptions about union growth were drawn from short-term trends. The late fifties were an uncertain and difficult period for unions, especially industrial unions. Losses in some unions were assumed to follow from inroads made by automation and the genetic inability of unions to organize white-collar workers. In fact, many unions were then immobilized by the Eisenhower policy of combating inflation by raising unemployment, a neat trick which Nixon has tried to repeat. Union members were especially vulnerable to this kind of economic manipulation. High interest rates, unemployment, and the periodic recessions of that era reduced the demand for homes, autos, appliances, and all the materials going into them—steel, aluminum, rubber, copper, electrical components.

The Taft-Hartley Law, the various state "right-to-work" laws, and, a little later, Landrum-Griffin, all created new problems for unions, especially in organizing. The more or less liberal interpretation and enforcement of the Labor Relations Act that had marked the Roosevelt and Truman eras began to be reversed as Eisenhower appointees to the NLRB and the federal courts imposed greater restrictions on union organizing efforts.

During the fifties, the McCarthy years, unions again came under assault. The McClellan hearings created general public antagonism to unions. It became fashionable for conservative congressional candidates to "run against" Walter Reuther (who never entered a political race). Noncandidate Reuther was challenged to and participated in national radio and TV debates with both Goldwater and Senator Robert Taft.

Unions were on the defensive, and this made organizing more difficult. At precisely the time when declining membership was reducing dues and income, the new legal complexities drained their finances and energy. Less money was available to pay organizers and the much higher legal expenses incurred in every new organizing campaign. Historically, union organizing efforts tend to be least successful in periods of rising unemployment. During the recession-pocked Eisenhower years, it is a wonder that unions managed to get on as well as they did.

All these factors were often overlooked or minimized by the numerous writers who kept predicting that unionism would wither away. Clichés about the decline of unions were by then so widely accepted that new trends becoming apparent in the middle sixties were almost ignored. President Kennedy opted for high employment levels, and made collective-bargaining procedures a matter of accepted policy for government employees. He thereby stimulated the trend already begun at state, city, and county levels—in areas where organized labor's political muscle could be effectively applied—to guarantee public employees the right to organize and bargain collectively.

Moreover, children born during the baby boom of the forties and fifties became adults and consumers of cars, appliances, homes, and other products made by union members. Increased demand began to compensate for the decline in jobs resulting from automation in industry and partial prefabrication in construction. The growing need for schools, homes, hospitals, autos, appliances, and services caused the work force to grow to an unprecedented size. At the same time, highly publicized and often successful strikes of professionals— teachers, airline pilots, TV commentators—gave the idea of unionization unprecedented public sanction.

The Steelworkers Union, whose membership declined from 1.2 million in 1957 to 878,000 in 1963, climbed back to 1.1 million in 1968. The Auto Workers' 1957 membership of 1.3 million sank to a low of 1.0 million just two years later, but bounced back to 1.4 million in 1968. The rubber workers dropped from 178,000 to 158,000 in the two years 1957–59, but climbed back to 203,000 by 1968. (The membership figures are all rounded.) Among the larger unions, the only ones to suffer permanent damage were those in declining industries.

Barring a dragged-out recession, unions will continue to grow during the seventies. They have finally caught on in some of the fastest-growing sectors of the society and are likely to catch on in others. In those geographic and economic areas where jobs have risen fastest, so has union membership. Between 1957 and 1968, for example, the American Federation of Government Employees grew from 64,000 to 294,000; the State, County and Municipal Employees from 150,000 to 364,000; the Teachers' Federation from 50,000 to 165,000; the Postal Clerks from 97,000 to 166,000; Letter Carriers from 108,000 to 210,000; Retail Clerks from 300,000 to 550,000; Retail, Wholesale from 107,000 to 175,000; Building Service from 230,000 to 389,000; Communications Workers from 259,000 to 357,000; the Teamsters from 1.4 million to 1.7 million.

Meanwhile, major changes were occurring in the racial, social, and cultural composition of the working class. Mainly these changes are making the working class both blacker and younger.

During the fifties and sixties, the average age of the population declined. At the same time that masses of young people were entering the labor force and unions, the older workers were coming out the other end. Pensions have risen and the age of retirement has declined, permitting older workers to make way for the young. During the seventies, there will be increased pressure—from young and old alike —to reduce the number of years spent at routine jobs and to bring the age of retirement down. In 1972, auto workers with thirty years of service will be eligible for retirement at the age fifty-six. By the end of the decade it is likely that many auto workers will be retiring at or before age fifty. These standards will surely spread to other industries also.

II

While the census gives little information about ages of workers in specific occupations, we do know from pension information in the auto industry that hordes of young people are employed there. The same seems true for other industries. In Ford, for example, 32 percent of all workers are age thirty or under, in GM, 39 percent are, and in Chrysler, 41 percent. In all three, the average is very close to four out of ten workers at or under the magical age of thirty.[4] These young workers are beginning to be represented in something close to their numbers in the secondary leadership of the UAW, although nobody on the chief policy-making body—the International Executive Board—is under forty-five. But this, too, inevitably will change, and the union will pay far more attention to its young members. (The young people in the labor force, of course, far outnumber those in schools and colleges.)

As with age, information about the racial composition of the work

4. The percentages were computed from employment reports submitted by Ford, General Motors, and Chrysler to UAW pension committees.

force is sparse. But some reasonable inferences may be made. We know, for example, that black people have been moving North, that the black population of Southern states has declined. Blacks are becoming urban industrial workers—and union members—in the North (and to a lesser extent in the South) at a phenomenal rate. Many whites still come North from the rural South and border states, but they are more likely than blacks to stop off at Memphis, Atlanta, Dallas, Houston, and other Southern cities. Furthermore, the black population is younger than the white, less schooled and, therefore, more likely to enter the blue-collar work force.

Unions in the North, and to a lesser extent in the South, will be a natural center—a new, more realistic and powerful kind—of black power in the seventies. Though their representation is still inadequate, blacks have thus far won more influence in unions than in any other American social institution. A study of black powerlessness, conducted for the Urban League of Chicago and Cook County, Illinois, found that unions had a larger percentage (13 percent) of black "policy-makers" than any other private institution.

In welfare and religious organizations, whose constituents were often largely black, 8 percent of policymaking posts were held by blacks. The universities had a negligible one percent representation. Most of the universities had a few black students, faculty, or administrators. The University of Illinois had one policy maker. Roosevelt University was the sole institution that had a number of blacks at the top. Only *five* out of 380 policy making posts in these universities were held by blacks.

The elected political offices and the elected trade union offices [the study found] account for only 11 percent of all policy making positions in Cook County. Yet, almost half of all the Negro policy makers were found in these areas—137 out of 283.[5]

In three-fourths of the former CIO local unions, blacks were represented in leadership. In two-fifths of the former AFL locals, no blacks were represented, *but one-third had leadership that was 15 percent, or more, black*. Even the much-criticized AFL, in this study, looks better than Chicago's universities, churches, welfare and many other organizations.

More blacks belong to unions than to any other nonreligious organi-

5. Harold M. Baron, with Harriet Stulman, Richard Rothstein, and Renard Davis, "Black Powerlessness in Chicago," *Trans-action,* November 1968.

zation. Black membership of the UAW and Teamsters (the Alliance for Labor Action) is perhaps 750,000, and as many as 2.5 million blacks are members of AFL-CIO unions. Blacks and Latins combined may now be a majority in the ILGWU, the Amalgamated Clothing Workers, and other established unions. Yet they are still underrepresented in the leadership. In the seventies, these unions may be the first really significant organizations to come under black control.[6]

Industrial unions are very likely the most racially integrated organizations in the country—not necessarily out of inherent virtue, but because the CIO saw from the start that it had to include black workers if it was to organize along industrial rather than craft lines.

In the years of the official War Against Poverty, union victories at hospitals and in other service trades probably had as much economic impact on the ghetto as all OEO programs combined. In the South, blacks have begun to see in unions a promise of real social and political advance. Public employees and hospital workers have waged historic strikes in Memphis, Charlotte, Atlanta, Jackson; Martin Luther King went to his death in one of these struggles; and Ralph Abernathy to jail in another.

In the integrated union especially, the activist learns the politics of coalition, a basic part of the art of negotiation. If a candidate wants to win an election for local office, he must advocate a program broad enough to appeal to a majority of voters, which is likely to include a range of racial minorities.

As time goes by, the "minority" in local unions will increasingly be white. Current political roles will then be reversed, with contending groups of blacks seeking white support, just as contending whites now solicit black votes. Where blacks become a majority, the thrust of black separatism is likely to be blunted, just as open white racism be-

6. According to unofficial estimates, almost half the members of the 550,000-member Laborers' Union and the 50,000-member Longshoremen's Union are black. In all, 45 AFL-CIO unions have black membership, which is proportionally larger than that of blacks in the total population (about 11 percent). A number of large unions have more than 20 percent black membership. These include: State, County and Municipal employees (450,000 total members), Meatcutters-Packinghouse (500,000), Letter Carriers (210,000), Postal Clerks (166,000), International Ladies Garment Workers (455,000), Building Service (398,000), Laundry Workers (25,000), the American Federation of Teachers (200,000), and possibly Steel (1.1 million) and Auto (1.4 million).

came politically untenable in locals where blacks form a significant minority.

Though union apologists sometimes stoutly deny it, the history of all unions is scarred by racial discrimination. The AFL, after all, was a leading sponsor of the law excluding Oriental immigrants. Until just a few years ago, many of its affiliates still organized and sanctioned Jim Crow locals in the South. Some craft unions have flatly excluded blacks. Separate seniority lists, negotiated by unions, sometimes guaranteed that blacks would be laid off first and recalled last in periods of recession. Until recently, blacks were restricted in their efforts to enter most of the industrial skilled trades. To this day, they are underrepresented in such occupations as tool-and-die-maker, machinist, patternmaker, machine repairman, and steel mill roller.

Even the best unions have sinned, and the worst have been persistently and callously exclusionist. But unions have been no worse than most other American institutions in this regard, and have been better than many. Their critics—often themselves associated with racially exclusive institutions—have often treated unionists as though they alone were sinners.

What the union apologists might say with justice is "Let him who is without sin cast the first stone." Instead, they often flatly deny any guilt at all. When we measure discrimination we deal not only with blacks and whites, but with all shades of gray as well, and the apologists are wrong in attempting to whitewash union flaws that might better be exposed to the light.

Overlooked by labor's critics, however, is the *present* state of union affairs, obscured as it is by the constant repetition of old charges no longer accurate or valid. So much attention, for example, has been given to conservatism and "racism" in *some* building trades unions that, in the public mind, they have come to symbolize unionism generally. Among the forty-six unions whose membership exceeds 100,000, only eight, as it happens, are building trades unions. One of these, the Laborers, has a membership that may be more than half black, and blacks are prominent in its top leadership. A few of the others, such as the IBEW (Brotherhood of Electrical Workers), have organized industrial workers as well as building tradesmen and include thousands of black workers in their ranks. Even many of the building trades—especially those in the so-called trowel trades—have never been cited for racial exclusion. A good many have joined in programs such as those sponsored by the A. Philip Randolph Institute, which has successfully prepared large numbers of young black workers for admission to apprenticeships in various trades. Others have sponsored their own training programs for both journeymen and apprentices. At least one, the Operating Engineers, administered a Job Corps center in a successful effort to increase the number of blacks employed in driving earth-moving equipment.

In the South, where industry is growing more rapidly than elsewhere, union growth has been dramatic, if rather obscured by the recurrent failures in past decades to "Organize Dixie."

Successful strikes of Southern public and hospital workers have made some local unions the strongest organizations blacks have in Southern communities. These locals are eligible to affiliate with state and county labor groups, in which their representatives find a forum to communicate grievances and political demands to the white community. In almost all cases, unionized whites in these communities have given at least tacit support to the strikes of black workers.

In many industries where Southern unions are growing, blacks form a significant part of the work force. Their impact in those places will be felt, we believe, just as it has been in Northern towns where industrial unions have united workers of all trades and races under one banner. In Alabama, until recently, the only organized opposition to George Wallace came from the State Federation of Labor. In Mississippi, facing terror and intimidation, the state labor organization has nonetheless opposed the Klan and White Citizens Councils. In Texas even now the organized labor movement is at the heart of the liberal political coalition that wins an occasional statewide victory (Yarboro to the U.S. Senate) and sends a good handful of liberal candidates to Congress and to the state legislature.

Union growth in the South has been a rather well-guarded secret. Since 1964, as illustrated in the table, unions have, with some fluctuations, grown in almost every Southern state in both absolute and relative terms.

In these twelve states, unions added 1 million members between 1960 and 1968 and rose to a total estimated membership of about 2.7 million in 1970. By 1980 it will probably come to 4 million. Such growth will have great social and political significance not only in

Union Membership in Southern States

The gross number of members is expressed in thousands and the percentage of nonagricultural work force is enclosed in parentheses.

State	1964	1966	1968
Alabama	158 (18.7)	178 (19.2)	193 (20.1)
Arkansas	73 (17)	83 (17)	97 (19.1)
Florida	214 (14)	234 (13.6)	279 (14.4)
Georgia	166 (14)	188 (14.2)	239 (16.6)
Kentucky	195 (27)	217 (27.1)	235 (27.5)
Louisiana	160 (18.7)	176 (18.3)	187 (18.0)
Mississippi	62 (13.5)	64 (12.3)	76 (13.8)
North Carolina	100 (7.4)	104 (6.9)	124 (7.5)
South Carolina	48 (7.4)	49 (6.7)	66 (8.6)
Tennessee	201 (19.2)	225 (18.9)	246 (19.4)
Virginia	184 (15.8)	199 (15.5)	230 (16.6)
Texas	394 (14.1)	423 (13.7)	474 (13.9)

* The table shows total membership in each state for the years 1964, 1966, and 1968—the only years for which such material is available. In this case the Department of Labor reports show only percentages of the "nonagricultural work force." If the reports showed percentages of the *total* work force, all the percentages almost certainly would have risen.

the South, but in the entire nation. The deaths of Jim Crow locals, for example, will throw blacks and whites together in the same unions where they will find themselves working toward the same goals. An organized base for the Southern populist currents that have never quite died will be created in many communities. Southern unions, playing a healing and ameliorative role in race relations, should begin to push the Democratic party to the left, and diminish the strength of the Northern conservative and Southern coalition that has paralyzed liberal reform for so long.

In the South and elsewhere, much union growth occurred in strategic areas of the economy—especially in government employment. The fastest-growing unions have been the American Federation of Government Employees; State, County and Municipal Workers; and the American Federation of Teachers. Such successes create new agendas for state, local, and federal governments, and a new dynamic in our political life. As they seek support for their goals, the government workers politicize other unions. They create new—and often influential—lobbies for the expansion of public operations. They are generally much more successful than other unions in shaping the policies of the organizations for which they work. Many of them are certain to have a real fling at worker control. The Federation of Teachers, for example, will certainly intervene increasingly in education policy—probably with mixed results.[7]

On the other hand, rising labor costs resulting from unionization will create pressure for technological innovation and improvement in public employment. Teaching machines and TV will become commonplace. Data controls and systems analysis will lead to the replacement of many professional and technical workers. The effect will be to create greater insecurity among publicly employed professionals and accelerate union growth at the upper levels of civil service—which will make unionization of such workers socially more acceptable than it now is.

The effect of the organization of large numbers of public workers is to increase the pressure on unions to campaign for a redistribution of wealth and income. Local and state governments are being pushed to bankruptcy by the need to expand old and provide new services, and by demands of public workers for a greater share of the nation's wealth.

The continuing inflation will add to the pressures. Efforts to control wages, as a pretext for limiting price increases, are sure to be made. Then the Pandora's box of "reasonable profits" will open and out will pop questions of income and wealth distribution.

The expansion of public employment and unionization will probably also have the effect of making public ownership more acceptable to larger numbers of Americans, and certainly will increase public interest and participation in the society. To be sure, racism will not disappear in the South simply because workers are unionized. By the

7. The National Education Association, whose membership is probably five or six times that of the AFT, has a long tradition of participation in policy-making. The NEA is rapidly transforming itself into a real trade union. Many of its state and local affiliates call strikes, and most now bargain collectively for their members. NEA members are not included in our count of union members—though certainly it would not be unreasonable to add their numbers to total union membership. Influential people in both NEA and AFT favor merger of the two organizations. If it occurs the result will be a union about the size of the Teamsters.

logic of their position, however, unionized workers are driven to cooperate, at least for limited goals, across racial lines. Prejudice and discrimination survive—even sometimes flourish—in Detroit, Cleveland, Pittsburgh, Chicago, Los Angeles, and other industrial centers, but unions there nonetheless manage to help elect candidates—including many blacks—who appeal to both black and white workers.

Even the more conservative and lethargic unions transmit information and education for their members about the conduct of public officials. A unionized worker is much more likely than a nonunionized one to be informed about the record of his congressman. He is more likely to register and vote, simply because his union persistently urges him to do so. A majority of Alabama's organized workers, it is true, did support George Wallace, but studies have shown the support they gave was smaller in percentage than among the unorganized.

III

Radicals have a long history of disappointment with American unions, especially the CIO unions, from which they expected far more radicalism than they got. Yet the truth is that the CIO, and those AFL unions that grew along with it, transformed industrial America. Organized workers won some measure of control over their conditions of work and a solid hope that they can win much more. They are protected against arbitrary discipline and discharge. They have access to grievance procedures. They have some insurance against sickness, death, unemployment. They are covered by pension agreements, and enjoy lengthening vacations and holidays with pay. All this may seem trivial to those concerned only with revolutionary abstractions—but it is a great deal to the millions of workers directly affected.

Moreover, the solid strength of unions has underwritten a kind of political and social freedom not previously enjoyed by workers. That freedom is reflected in the kinds of candidates elected to public office in places where unions are strong. In the American political spectrum, unions have been well over to the Left. If there is a prominent liberal officeholder in the country who got there without union support, we can't think of his name. Even John Lindsay had the support of a significant minority of New York's unions, and Gene McCarthy—idol of the New Democrats—was first elected to the House of Representatives and later to the Senate as a candidate of the Minnesota Democratic Farmer-Labor party.

Forced to play coalition politics in order to maximize their political influence, unions have given some impetus to the drive by blacks for political recognition. In a post-1970 election comment on the number of blacks holding public office in the United States, the *New Republic* said that there were sixteen hundred prior to the 1970 election and an increased number thereafter. The largest contingent, the report added, is from Michigan, where the "farsighted policies of the United Auto Workers have contributed measurably to black successes." Those "farsighted policies" are in no small measure attributable to the continuing agitation of courageous and aggressive blacks who found in the UAW a forum where they could struggle for their cause. Increasingly, blacks are taking the struggle to other unions.

Will it all make a difference? We think it will—but our hopes and goals (in contrast to our desires) are limited. We hope not for the millennium, but only for a kind of enlightened social and political equilibrium in which democratic discourse about necessary social change can continue, while the worst burdens are lifted from the backs of the socially and politically outcast.

Actually, if we were to reach the kind of equilibrium that would be achieved if all the candidates supported by labor in 1970 had been elected to the Congress, we would see significant social change. Such a Congress might:

• Pass tax reform that would bring about some redistribution of wealth—especially through the imposition of higher rates on the top income brackets and the elimination of such tax dodges as the depletion allowance.

• Support full employment.

• Adopt an advanced form of national health insurance.

• Adopt a relatively generous form of guaranteed income, and support programs designating the government as employer of last resort to provide work for the unemployed.

• Adopt advanced standards for water and air pollution.

• Raise the minimum wage to $2 an hour.

• Extend the protection of the National Labor Relations Act and

Fair Labor Standards Act (minimum wages) to agricultural workers and others not now covered.

• Reduce the qualifying age and raise the amount of social security payments.

• Increase the amounts of money being spent for education at all levels.

• Increase the number of housing units being constructed.

• Make direct grants to the states and local communities for the support of urban improvements.

• Increase assistance to Appalachia and other areas where poverty is endemic.

• Improve consumer protection, and the enforcement powers of government regulatory agencies.

We are not brash enough to include in this list "a more rapid end to the Vietnam war"—but almost every candidate who won for the U.S. Senate with labor support is classified as a dove. More open and flexible than many of his Left-leaning critics, George Meany personally gave his support to liberals with whom he disagreed violently on Vietnam. While many liberals and radicals in New York, for example, chose the conservative Goodell only because of his position on the war, George Meany made a strong pitch for Ottinger the dove against Buckley the hawk. Meany and his staff also supported Gore, Hart, Hartke, Kennedy, Metzenbaum, Stevenson, Williams, and other doves, though their opponents' position on foreign policy often must have been more to the AFL–CIO's liking.

IV

In summary, we think the obituaries for workers and their unions have been premature, based principally on superficial reading of available materials, and distorted inferences drawn from short-term trends.

We cannot, however, wholly discount the influence of simple anti-labor and anti-working-class bias. Harvard Professor Daniel Bell speaks for many when he says (as quoted in the *New York Times*):

The degree of corruption in labor has become incredible. . . . The pomposity of labor leaders unbearable. . . . A lot of union leaders are corrupted by power. . . . The labor movement has stagnated. . . . Membership has reached the saturation point except in some white-collar unions. Union leadership has grown old. Labor is no longer pushing up the kind of extraordinary leaders that it did in the thirties and who are emerging from the blacks today.

We think, by contrast, that scholars and others increasingly are rejecting Professor Bell's notions. Albert Camus never bought them, and his thinking about workers seems now to have some chance for acceptance.

The confusion of European intellectuals [Camus said] springs from the double hoax, bourgeois and pseudo-revolutionary, and separating them from their sole source of authenticity, the work and suffering of all, cutting them off from sole natural allies, the workers. I know that if they are separated [workers and intellectuals] they will allow themselves to be overwhelmed gradually by the forces of tyranny and barbarousness, but that united, on the other hand, they will govern the world.[8]

Irving Louis Horowitz, a more moderate critic than Professor Bell, says he

does not believe a resurgence of the militant-moralistic unionism of the left is likely in the foreseeable future. . . . American labor, at least after 1880, was not *in the main* of the left in any classically socialist sense of the term. A left orientation has always been modest, if not peripheral, and thus has not suffered such a dramatic decline as is often made out.[9]

We too see no Leftward movement in any "classical socialist sense," but we do see a labor movement supplied with fresh momentum by the newly organized, the blacks, the young, the public workers, and Southerners.

Some years ago Frank Tannenbaum came close to expressing our assessment of unions when he wrote in *A Philosophy of Labor*:

This profound challenge to our time has gone largely unnoticed because the trade-union's preoccupation with the detailed frictions that flow from the worker's relation to his job seemed to involve no broad program. In tinkering with the little things—hours, wages, shop conditions, and security in the job—the trade-union is, however, rebuilding our industrial

8. Albert Camus, *Resistance, Rebellion, and Death,* (New York: Knopf, 1961).

9. Irving L. Horowitz, "Condition of the Working Class in the U.S." (1970), *New Politics,* VIII:3.

society upon a different basis from that envisioned by the philosophers, economists, and social revolutionaries of the 18th and 19th centuries.

A sparsity of general ideas and a lack of any "ideology" kept the trade-union movement from being obtrusively vocal and permitted mesmeric political groups to look upon it as something of no great importance. But its very lack of ideas make it strong and enable it to concentrate upon immediate ends without wasting its energies in a futile pursuit of Utopia.

In terms of the individual, the union returns to the worker his "society." It gives him a fellowship, a part in the drama that he can understand, and life takes on meaning once again because he shares a value system common to others.

That is why the trade-union is a repudiation of the individualism of the French Revolution and of the liberalism of English utilitarian philosophers. It rests upon the group, upon the organized "society" forged by the mine, mill, and factory. Trade-unionism is . . . a social and ethical system, not merely an economic one. It is concerned with the whole man. Its ends are the "good life."[10]

10. Frank Tannenbaum, *A Philosophy of Labor* (New York: Knopf, 1951).

Jervis Anderson

The Agonies of Black Militancy

Although black militancy has been one of the veins of American radicalism at least since the abolitionists, it was only during the early sixties that most people started paying much attention to it or even calling it by that name. More people seem to have been militant in the early sixties than ever before. If that is so, however, it suggests something quite important about that stage of the sixties: that it encouraged more hopes of a breakthrough into freedom, and thus stirred more black activism, than any previous period in the century.

When people started speaking of black militancy, they were not naming the tradition of black militant activity itself, but a mode of activism that seemed to be distinctly part of the style and personality of the sixties. And they were referring to black militancy not in the sense of black nationalism but in the sense of a movement whose controlling impulse was to break down barriers that stood in the way of a full and equal participation in American society, barriers that began to seem quite vulnerable at the turn of the decade. However, the style and personality of the sixties turned out to be more perishable than most of us could have foreseen. And part of what perished as well was that spirit we had come to identify as black militancy. The term is still used, to be sure—however quaint a throwback it may sound, however it may have the forced and somewhat square ring of language no longer quite in fashion. People who still use the term are mostly those who think that nothing much has changed, or those who find it the most convenient catchall for whatever goes on in the precincts of black radicalism.

Whatever happened to the black militancy of the sixties, or the mood that sustained it, is precisely what became of the sixties themselves. Though not everybody sees it that way, the sixties do not seem now to have been the best time to inaugurate new things—except, as it turned out, buildings and highways in memory of dead men and murdered hopes. To a large number of people, and mainly the young, the decade seems now to be littered with the ruins of great expectations: many of its more decent commitments dismantled; its moral language largely discarded; its political sensibility held in contempt; its outlook upon the world withdrawn; its racial promises revoked or betrayed; its moral sense driven up against the wall. Some who do not regard it that way, but mourn it nonetheless, see it as a half-finished house on a deserted road: not a nail has been driven in since the bank canceled its notes; shrubbery has grown up all around it; and vines are climbing over the raw masonry and unpainted woodwork. Some of those who had hoped to find a home in the house have lost faith in banks. Some of them, black militants of the sixties, seem to recall that this sort of thing happened to their forebears several times before. What sense therefore in continuing to believe in promises or in retaining their ties to American idealism?

Anyone who has been raised to respond hysterically to anything with the word black in it—or to find no consoling distinctions between one form of black radicalism and another—may be astonished to hear black militancy associated with the public idealism of the sixties. But such a person should try to remember who the militants were then, what forms their activism took, and what spirit sustained them. They were mostly young people and mostly students. They belonged predominantly to SNCC and CORE, almost the only groups that offered black and white American youth an opportunity to participate constructively in the passions of their time and help set right a society that had long been out of joint. And the tactics they used were sit-ins, freedom rides, disruption of facilities, and a generality of activity described as nonviolent direct action. However irritating most of this may have been to the country, it was somewhat within the American grain. It was certainly what the country seemed to ask of young people then: that they work for change and express their militant energies within the framework of American values. Much of what the young people did then seems rather tame today. But at the time it caused many of their elders in the freedom movement to tear their hair: it was "too provocative" and it could possibly be "counter-productive."

As to the mood that sustained the activism, it was one of optimism —belief that the country was ready and able to respond favorably to demands pressed upon it within the spirit of its own professed ethics. Then came the years between 1963 and 1968 when that belief was shattered by a series of bullets, and the country has not been quite the same since.

Considering whom the bullets struck, they appear to have been aimed directly at the aspirations of the young, the black, and the poor. In any event, most blacks had only one way of seeing it: once again white racism had cast its veto over social and racial progress in America. It does not seem now to be any accident that it was between those years, '63 and '68, that American cities started going up in flames; that young middle-class whites started embracing what have been called un-American heroes and un-American ideologies; that blacks began entertaining—at least expressing—an interest in guns and black power; that the Vietnam war was escalated into a metaphor of contemporary brutality; that this war drove at least half of America out of its skull; that the escape from reality found its most comforting haven in drugs; that almost an entire generation of young people turned to the politics of self-indulgence, self-righteousness, irrationality, violence, and despair.

Today, if there are young blacks who still consider themselves militants, a look at whatever they are "into" will reveal that they are considerably less militant than people who consider themselves something else—people who say that what they are "into" now are things like revolution, liberation, self-determination.

Out of this, where alienated blacks are concerned, two predominant tendencies have taken shape. The first is marked by a set of attitudes which, shared by a variety of individuals and groups, is defined roughly as "nation-building" or cultural nationalism. And the second, a set of political attitudes—roughly described as revolutionary nationalism—is represented most spectacularly by the Panthers.

While it is not the first time that frustration has forced a large number of blacks to withdraw into themselves—and while the black nationalist movement of the twenties was larger than anything that exists today—this is the first time that the withdrawal has appeared so calculated and considered. One cannot recall a time when so many among the educated black young and the lumpen intelligentsia of the streets appeared so utterly at odds with the idea of America, when there appeared to be such a deep and conscious spirit of disaffiliation with the things and processes of the general culture.

Whether it be the movement to salvage and revaluate black history, build up black studies, or talk up the black experience; whether it be the search by young writers and literary intellectuals for a "black aesthetic," different in method, sensibility, spirit, and values from the "white Western aesthetic"; whether it be the claim that black culture is a distinct, independent, and viable element within American society—whether it be any of these, there now seems more intellectual energy and seriousness than ever in the bid to reconsider the blacks' relationship to the society, to define the grounds for dissociating from the culture, and to create "new black men."

Stated simply, perhaps too simply, the black cultural tendency holds a greater feeling for its connection to African cultural forms and roots than for its development within the community of white history and values. Whether such a feeling might have developed in any case—even if blacks had long been accorded what they conceived to be their rightful status in the society—it is hard to say, though it may be worth speculating upon. What seems clear is that the feeling has come about in direct response to a long history of denial in American society.

Much or all of this, however, is in conflict with the ideology of cultural integration held by a more traditional school of black literary and cultural intellectuals. These intellectuals do not so much advocate cultural integration—though the advocacy is clearly implied—as they assert it to be a fact: that there is neither a black nor white American culture but that the one has been irrevocably shaped and influenced by the other. There are no more articulate and formidable proponents of this point of view than Ralph Ellison and Albert Murray, both of whom operate out of a deep sense of the inescapable interconnections of black and white American life. To them the term black American or Negro American is not merely a convenient political combination, but a fine fusion of culture and consciousness and historical experience.

Ellison's ideas, stated and restated in much of his writings, were recently quoted in part by James Alan McPherson in an article, signed by both men, in the *Atlantic Monthly* (December 1970):

I think that too many of our assertions continue to be in response to whites. I think that we're polarized by the very fact that we keep talking about "black awareness" when we really should be talking about black American awareness, an awareness of where we fit into the total American scheme, where our influence is. I tell white kids that instead of talking about black men in white society, they should ask themselves how black *they* are because black men have been influencing the values of the society and the art forms of the society. How many of their parents fell in love listening to Nat King Cole? We did not develop as a people in isolation. We developed within a context of white people. Yes, we have a special awareness because our experience has, in certain ways, been uniquely different from that of white people; but it was not absolutely different. . . . I think . . . that we've looked at our relationship to American literature in a negative way. That is, we've looked at it in terms of our trying to break into it. Well, damn it, *that literature is built off our folklore* to a large extent! I ain't conceding that to *nobody!*

In his book *The Omni-Americans* Albert Murray writes:

White Anglo-Saxon Protestants do in fact dominate the power mechanisms of the United States. Nevertheless no American whose involvement with the question of identity goes beyond the sterile category of race can afford to overlook another fact that is no less essential to his fundamental sense of nationality no matter how much white folklore is concocted to obscure it: Identity is best defined in terms of culture, and the culture of the nation over which the white Anglo-Saxon power elite exercises such exclusive political, economic, and social control is not all white by any measurement ever devised. American culture, even in its most rigidly segregated precincts, is incontestably mulatto. Indeed for all their traditional antagonisms and obvious differences the so-called black and so-called white people in the United States resemble nobody else in the world so much as they resemble each other. And what is more, even their most extreme and violent polarities represent nothing so much as the natural history of pluralism in an open society.

In pointing out these interconnections within black and white culture Ellison and Murray are absolutely right, of course. That certainly seems to be the cultural reality of the United States. But it is not so much the reality itself which troubles those young people who now want to consider themselves cultural nationalists as it is their experience at the hands of the reality. It may be one thing for them to see that American culture is indeed a composite to which blacks have contributed some of the most vital elements. It is quite another thing for them to realize that those who dominate the cultural composite take no more serious and consequential a view of the blacks' part in it than a white household takes of the traditional black help, or a white audience of black entertainment. What most marks the response of whites in such situations is an enjoyment that rests upon a certain fundamental contempt for those who provide it. The general view of such help or such entertainment is that it is after all what blacks do best, almost the only thing they do well, and of considerably less consequence than the role of whites in the life of the culture. As John Corry put it in a recent article in *Harper's,* "One way or another, white America will try to turn blacks into song and dance men."

Not all blacks will oblige. Were they to oblige, it would be almost like saying that one way or another blacks will acquiesce in America's efforts to keep them second-class citizens. That, of course, is not true. And the same smoldering resentment most blacks feel against the effort to keep them second-class citizens marks their refusal to be considered no more than the song-and-dance men of American culture. Not everybody will want to go in the direction of the cultural nationalists; but the effort they make to cut themselves off from the general culture, withdraw into a cultural community of their own, and cultivate the African strains in their historical background, all of this may represent *their* refusal to be seen merely as the song-and-dance men of the culture.

This feeling of tension with the majority elements in the culture is connected not only with periods in the past but also with a tradition of skepticism quite as respectable as the intellectual tradition that supports the idea of cultural integration. As early as the turn of the century, W. E. B. Du Bois was expressing the painful contradictions of the black American cultural situation in these words:

He [the American Negro] would not Africanize America for America has too much to teach the world and Africa. He would not bleach his Negro soul in a flood of Americanism, for he knows that Negro blood has a message for the world. He simply wishes to make it possible for a man to be both Negro and American, without being cursed and spit upon by his fellows, without having the doors of Opportunity closed in his face.

And almost two decades later, during the Harlem Renaissance, Alain Locke noticed a cultural reaction similar if not identical to that of today:

This deep feeling of race is at present the mainspring of Negro life. It seems to be the outcome of the reaction to proscription and prejudice; an attempt, fairly successful on the whole, to convert a defensive into an offensive position, a handicap into an incentive.

While neither of these reactions implies or advocates cultural separation, they have a good deal in common with the reaction of those who today are in effect crying out as Du Bois did against the agony of being an integral part of a culture that nevertheless spits in one's face and declares one not yet worthy of being taken seriously.

Why, anyway, is it blacks who are constantly being reminded that American culture is a composite? Are there not others who appear to be in greater need of the reminder? Why is it that most whites are able to get away with forgetting it? Why is it that remembering it does not seem to make much difference in blacks' experience? Why—since American culture is so "patently and irrevocably composite"—have the experiences and contributions of blacks been ignored, distorted, or otherwise treated so shabbily in American history books? Why has it been left to blacks to salvage much of their past and their pride from the cutting-room floors of white historians? The answer may well have something to do with power, particularly with those who have it: the power of the majority culture to see as it pleases; to define and impose standards; to promote values and pass judgment; to determine what is of consequence and what is not. Whites "do in fact dominate the power mechanisms of the United States," Murray says. They certainly do. And those mechanisms include culture, which in turn includes the power to dominate and influence the shape of a minority's sense of itself.

The point of all this is not that cultural nationalists are justified in their attempt to withdraw into a cultural enclave of their own or that this is even possible in America. One cannot by sheer fiat or a simple act of will undo the complexities and continuities which have been in process since blacks were transported into the Western experience. The point is, though, that there has been a good deal of anguish felt and a good deal of contempt suffered by blacks while trapped in the cultural crucible of these centuries. The point too is that they are entitled to bawl, and deserve to have some attention paid to the cause and nature of their pain.

"There is also," Ellison writes, "an American tradition which teaches one to deflect racial provocation and to master and contain pain." That may be true—though God knows it is hardly a tradition one would choose if he had anything to say about it. But what one knows as well is that experience also teaches us that pain cannot or should not be contained forever, and that a continual deflection of racial provocation may well be achieved at the cost of some awareness of and regard for who and what one is. One can well understand how deep-seated in the white American imagination is the image of silent and noble black endurance—in fact we know this because it is one of the perceptions forced upon us by the power of the majority culture. But it is simply another fantasy built upon wishfulness and contempt. And, even more important, it is a fantasy that has done its part, a very large part, in helping to maintain the status of race relations in this country and the contradictions in the social and political experience of blacks and whites.

It's time we all stopped believing it. It's time we all realized that humanity may consist more in giving utterance to one's suffering than in containing it, resisting racial provocation than in deflecting it, raging against an unjust status than in accepting it.

If it turns out—and as it appears—that no viable rearrangements are possible within the present reality of American culture, the function of intellectual leadership may well be to speak compassionately to that condition, to provide the rationales by which blacks may confront the stubborn irony of it and make some tragic peace with it.

There is hardly anything to be said about the Panthers that hasn't already been said or that everybody doesn't already know. Whatever insufficiencies the Panthers have been victimized by, they do not include an insufficiency of publicity. Almost everyone has heard about their founding in Oakland; of their claims to be the vanguard of an armed black revolution; their breakfast programs and shoot-outs with the police; their alleged connections with international Communist conspiracies; their trials in and out of court; the fascination they hold for rich ladies in pants suits; and their celebration by the intellectuals of chic, machismo, and cultural fashion. Much of what describes the reaction of the cultural nationalists may be applied politically to the Panthers. Only one aspect of this resemblance will be considered here.

As the latest stage in the continuum of black radicalism, the Panthers are as much in reaction against the society's continued frustration of black hopes as against the failure of the civil rights protest movement to fulfill these hopes. This is of course a hard position to take against the protest movement, since the power of that movement is simply to persuade and not to act. It is also a position that ignores the solid accomplishments of the protest movement in the early sixties, accomplishments that dramatically widened the frontiers of black freedom. To be a part of the radical spirit of today, however, is to share in the ideology of instant gratification and to hold a contempt for strategies and tactics that may achieve gratification a twinkling later.

Thus—although almost every bit of racial progress in this century has been achieved by the civil rights movement—it is now held to have temporized and compromised too much, to have wasted its time fighting for integration, to have bitten its tongue in the presence of the white establishment, to have asked for what it could get rather than demanded what it was entitled to, to have sold out on black manhood. Thus too it has come to appear that one of the principal issues around which the Panthers are in motion is the issue of black manhood. An inordinate amount of their rhetoric seems aimed at expressing the essential quality of black manhood which has been denied—a certain mixture of bravery and arrogance. Bravery and arrogance express themselves in a kind of existential revolutionary theater: living dangerously, threatening destruction, cultivating extreme experiences, risking themselves in extreme situations. Since the slave rebels, only a handful of black men have felt the call to live this way—politically. Cleaver: "We shall have our manhood or the earth shall be leveled in our attempts to gain it." Or, as someone less prominent said more recently, the only thing young blacks are prepared for in this country is to destroy it.

The last time that black radicalism was so strident in tone—though more intelligent, more thoughtful, and less sanguinary—was in the years between World War I and the middle twenties when the black economic radicals led by A. Philip Randolph attacked American society and the traditional black leadership with a racial militancy and an ideological vehemence that probably still has not been surpassed. And perhaps it was way back there that the possibilities for rational radical action among blacks began to be exhausted, because the black radical movement of the twenties turned out to be pretty much a spectacular failure. If this is so, then, perhaps the country only has itself to blame that the only possibility for the continuation of black radicalism today lies in the areas of irrationality and violence, or—as Joseph Conrad said in a book that has some relevance to our present political experience—madness and despair. Victories in these areas are measured in martyrdom, in suicide, and in how much of the society a rebel takes with him at the moment of his destruction.

As the seventies grow older, this could even get worse. Who's to say what attractions young and embittered black soldiers returning from Vietnam may find in the Panther movement? How many young ex-convicts may be inspired and emboldened by the revolutionary examples of Cleaver and George Jackson? Urban guerrilla warfare led by Panthers, the young black lumpen proletariat, embittered ex-soldiers and ex-convicts may be a nightmare from which it could take a long time to recover—and which many of us may not survive.

Finally, as periods of black politics have followed periods of intense radical or protest activity, so may the Panther period, as it has been christened by admirers, give way to renewed political activity among many young blacks. Not immediately, of course, for the memory of the more recent frustrations are still too fresh in our minds. The majority of the black population itself represents no more encouragement to the prospect of a revolutionary radical future than America itself does. "The Negro mind," wrote Alain Locke in 1925, "reaches out as yet to nothing but American wants, American ideas."

Ironically, the opportunities for political involvement to which a large number of young blacks may yet turn in the seventies were created by the efforts of the much-maligned civil rights movement. The increase in numbers of registered voters, the training of young people as political organizers, the striking down of many of the legal obstacles blocking the way to an open society, the continued if incomplete integration and democratization of the trade-union movement, the election of black candidates to political offices across the nation—all of these have been made possible by the limited but genuine accomplishments of the civil rights movement. They have also created more space in which blacks can maneuver themselves to the levers of American power. One only has to look at LeRoi Jones's political activities in Newark and his new proximity to the levers of power in that city to realize the uses that may increasingly be made of conventional political avenues to power.

One last word, though, about the Panthers. Even those who believe that blacks can at best share equally and democratically in American power, rather than seizing it, are in no position to carp too cheaply at the Panthers. They are paying an enormous human cost in madness and despair. But madness and despair were not embraced voluntarily; they are precisely where the American experience has driven youthful idealism and activism for the foreseeable future. People like the Panthers are witnessing to the madness that all blacks have felt at one time or another—and to the despair that many of us have avoided only by dint of some tragic and incredibly hopeful conception of the world and of our experience.

Martin Kilson

Black Politics: A New Power

Political Sociology of Racism

For the first half century after slavery was abolished in the United States, the Negro lived mainly in the rural South and, save for a brief ten to fifteen years of Reconstruction, he had no rights of political participation. During this same period, the major white non-Protestant ethnic groups were crowding into the cities of the East, North, and Midwest, and by the end of the nineteenth century they had laid the basis for mastering the politics of the emerging urban society.[1] But the Negro did not enter urban society in significant numbers until World War I, and so for nearly forty years, roughly from the early 1880s to 1915, the typical black had neither political rights (stripped from him by the white racist rule in the post-Reconstruction South) nor access to the social system of urban America.

The cities were becoming the center of sociopolitical influence, and the Negro's belated migration from the South to the cities of the East, North, and Midwest meant that his institutional capability for handling modern urban life was much weaker than that of the white ethnic urban groups which had preceded him by forty years. In fact, their lead in settling in the cities amounted to more than forty years; for although black migration from the South began in earnest around 1910–15, in the succeeding fifty years more than half of the Negro population remained in the South. (See Table 1, page 314.)

1. See Charles Merriam, *The American Party System* (New York, 1924).

In the first sixty years of this century only a minority of the black population, though an increasing minority (for example, 10 percent in 1910, 23 percent in 1930, 32 percent in 1950, 40 percent in 1960), had any opportunity at all to experience modern political life.[2] However, the political experience of this urbanized black minority obviously was part of the kind of political life that was to dominate twentieth-century America. Therefore this black urban sector has been and remains crucial in shaping both current and future Negro politics. What, then, was the experience of this critical urban minority of the Negro population that resided outside the South from 1910 to the post–World War II era?

Of primary importance was that the migration from the South brought hundreds of thousands of Negroes at least some of the political rights they had so long been denied. Without this migration, they doubtless would not have obtained these primary political rights until far beyond the 1960s, when they were secured, at least in the written law. Certainly ruling elites in the South were both willing and able to sustain Negro political subservience to the end of this century; and the connivance of the North, Midwest, and West cannot be discounted.[3] Fortunately, the measure of political freedom available to blacks in other parts of the country was sufficient to allow an attack upon white authoritarianism in the South.

Urbanization provided blacks with the social organization and institutional differentiation that is necessary for effective political power.[4] Essentially, political modernization is a matter of highly differentiated strata and institutions that will sustain political articulation beyond parochial settings (ethnic, religious, regional, economic, etc.) in order to provide public and civil service.

But black urbanization was a *particular* form of city dwelling. Negro city dwelling in this century was stifled by that cluster of norms

2. Negroes did not acquire effective voting rights in the South until the Federal Voting Act of 1965.

3. See Rayford W. Logan, *The Negro in American Life and Thought: The Nadir 1877–1901* (New York, 1954).

4. W. E. B. Du Bois, *The Philadelphia Negro: A Social Study* (Philadelphia, 1899), pp. 233–34, *passim*. Du Bois, one of the first systematic observers of the urban Negro, recognized over seventy years ago that there is a strong correlation between the institutional differentiation available to city-dwelling blacks and their political modernization.

or customs characterized by the term *white racism*. W. Lloyd Warner, the sociologist of mainstream America, discovered this in Yankee City: "The caste barrier or color line, rigid and unrelenting, has cut off this small group [of blacks—0.48 percent of the population] from the general life of the community."[5] As Warner knew well, whatever the general life of a modern community is, surely politics is a salient feature: for politics is, after all, the process through which services and benefits are allocated among competing sectors of society. The restrictions imposed by whites upon blacks necessarily jeopardize the latter's capacity for political adaptation to life in the cities: blacks were victims of the whims and caprice of white politicians, bureaucrats, and party machines, few of which were notable for exemplary political manners even in dealings with whites.[6]

From World War I onward, the coercive regulatory agencies of the cities combined with party and machine organizations to exclude the Negro from an effective political role. Not that the black city dwellers were ignored by white-controlled city politics; their numbers alone argued against indifference. (See Table 2, p. 315.) Rather, white city machines, with the notable exception of Chicago's,[7] simply dealt half-heartedly with the problem of the political inclusion of black ethnic groups on terms comparable to that of white ethnic groups. Even more, special acts of city machines from World War I onward sought to truncate top Negro political development: "The immigrants and their descendants who controlled the [political] machines were anti-Negro," remarked Herbert Gans, "and gerrymandered ghetto neighborhoods so that they would not have to share their power with Negroes."[8] The coercive power of city machines related to the urban

5. W. Lloyd Warner and Paul S. Lunt, *The Social Life of a Modern Community* (New Haven, 1941), p. 217, *passim*. The Lynds discovered a similar situation in their study of a typical American community, the small-sized city of Muncie, Indiana (35,000 population), in the 1920s. So did Frank Quillin, who surveyed Negro status in several cities of Ohio before World War I. See Robert S. Lynd and Helen M. Lynd, *Middletown* (New York, 1929); Frank U. Quillin, *The Color Line in Ohio* (Ann Arbor, 1913).

6. See, e.g., Dayton David McKean, *The Boss: The Hague Machine in Action* (Boston: Russell, 1940).

7. Cf. Harold F. Gosnell, *Negro Politicians: The Rise of Negro Politics in Chicago* (Chicago: University of Chicago Press, 1935).

8. Herbert J. Gans, "The Ghetto Rebellions and Urban Class Conflict," in Robert Connery, ed., *Urban Riots* (New York, 1969), pp. 52–53.

black in ways that demoralized him. As Gunnar Myrdal observed some thirty years ago:

In most Northern communities, Negroes are more likely than whites to be arrested under any suspicious circumstances. They are more likely to be accorded discourteous or brutal treatment at the hands of the police than are whites. The rate of killing of Negroes by the police is high in many Northern cities. . . . The attitudes of the police will sometimes be found among the most important items considered in local Negro politics in the North.[9]

In summary, the rigid and inhuman restrictions placed upon the Negro's access to the modern social system of American cities distorted and truncated his political development in the past sixty years. No other American immigrant group faced comparable barriers to political modernization.[10] It was precisely the white immigrants' reasonably, though not fully, caste-free interaction with the city power structures that enabled them to shape their social institutions.[11]

Ethnicity and the Negro Political Subsystem

Surely an interplay of politics and social structure similar to that of white ethnic groups was required for effective and modern politicization of Negroes. As it happened, however, much less than this occurred. The violence and militancy typical of contemporary urban Negro politics stem directly from this situation. So do the current endeavors of two kinds of black leadership to utilize black ethnicity as an instrument for political efficacy in the black ghetto. One kind of leadership is highly ideological, articulating militancy and black ethnicity as a matter of willed belief; the other is pragmatic, though not without a world view, articulating militancy and black ethnicity as a matter of political necessity. In the latter, militancy and ethnicity

9. Gunnar Myrdal, *An American Dilemma* (New York: Harper & Brothers, 1944), p. 527, *passim*.
10. Cf., Oscar Handlin, *The Uprooted* (Boston: Atlantic Monthly Press, 1951), chapters 7–8; also Lawrence H. Fuchs, ed., *American Ethnic Politics* (New York: Torchbook, Harper & Row, 1968).
11. Cf. Robert K. Merton, *Social Theory and Social Structure* (Glencoe: Free Press, 1956).

are wedded to established city politics, much in the manner of white ethnic late-nineteenth-century and early-twentieth-century politicians. The goal is to facilitate the Negro community's vertical political structure, and to surmount the horizontal class cleavages. This was never realized through other forms of politics available to urban Negroes in this century—not through the second-class version of machine politics available to urban blacks (which I have characterized elsewhere as neo-clientage machine politics[12]) and not through civil rights or protest politics.

The limited relationship between the urban Negro and the white-controlled city machine, from World War I through World War II, deprived the blacks of a primary mode of political development that had been available to white immigrant groups—*the politicization of ethnicity*. This means simply to use ethnic patterns and prejudices as the primary basis for interest-group and political formations, and to build upon these to integrate a given ethnic community into the wider politics of the city and the nation.[13] To the extent that a given ethnic community was successful in so organizing itself, it could claim a share of city-based rewards and, through congressional and presidential politics, of federal government rewards.[14] To fall outside or be only partially integrated into this process, since World War I, was necessarily to be without a basis for sociopolitical power.

As the urban Negro was either outside or only partially linked to this politicization of ethnicity through city machines, his political actions have borne the mark of this experience ever since. First, the Negro lower or popular strata (that is, the working class, the marginal working class, and the chronically unemployed class) have been, until the past decade, deprived of participatory incentives, an experience that had motivated the white ethnic lower strata's political

12. Martin Kilson, "Political Change in the Negro Ghetto, 1900–1940" in Nathan Huggins, Martin Kilson, Daniel Fox, eds., *Key Issues in the Afro-American Experience* (New York, 1971), pp. 167–92.

13. See, e.g., Harold Gosnell, *Machine Politics: Chicago Model* (Chicago: University of Chicago Press, 1937).

14. For a study of city-based rewards stemming from the politicization of ethnicity, see Theodore Lowi, *At the Pleasure of the Mayor: Patronage and Power in New York City 1898–1958* (Glencoe: Free Press, 1964). Since the 1930s the federal government has become the major source of the politically inspired benefits called patronage for ethnic groups that contribute to congressional and presidential victories.

development.[15] This, in turn, has produced Negro urban lower strata that by the 1960s ranked low in all salient indices of modern political life: low political skill and knowledge, a high sense of powerlessness and estrangement from institutionalized processes, and low participation. Second, the city machines' relative neglect of the black ghetto in the years 1915–60 deprived the Negro elites (the black middle and upper classes) of the opportunity and incentives to give political leadership. Whereas the city machines' full-fledged inclusion of white ethnic communities provided a powerful stimulus to the Irish, Italian, Jewish, Polish, and other ethnic bourgeoisies to participate in the political organization (and thus control) of their ethnic lower strata,[16] the black bourgeoisie, for the most part, was indeed not induced to use its institutions to politicize the black lower strata in order to bring their votes to the service of party machines. Only in Chicago did this pattern of political relationship between the black bourgeoisie and the black lower strata evolve between the two World Wars. In Chicago, contrary to the pattern of other cities, the white politicians— especially Republicans—accepted the full-fledged inclusion of the black ethnic turf on terms comparable to those applied to the white ethnic turfs.[17] In other cities, however, the Negro elites, denied full-fledged inclusion in machine politics, turned to civil rights or protest politics.

Civil rights politics was largely a middle-class affair: from 1915 to the 1950s the leadership and membership were mainly middle-class,

15. It is often forgotten how crucial city (and county) party machines were in providing the white ethnic lower strata with viable political organization. Neither interest nor pressure groups such as trade unions or lesser political forms of voluntary associations equaled city machines in this regard. Indeed, interest groups like trade unions and veterans' organizations realized their more effective politicization through city machines. Moreover, the majority of white ethnics in the working class and marginal working class, not to mention those who were lower class, never gained trade union membership anyway, which meant that they could rely only on party machines or paramachine organizations for their politicization. On the central role of city (and county) machines in politicizing white ethnic lower strata, see Gosnell, *Machine Politics,* chaps. I-IV. On the role of party machines in politicizing interest groups that serve the lower strata, see Martin Meyerson and Edward Banfield, *Politics, Planning and the Public Interest* (Glencoe: Free Press, 1955). See also J. David Greenstone, *Labor in American Politics* (New York: Alfred A. Knopf, 1969).

16. Harold Zink, *City Bosses in the United States: A Study of Twenty Municipal Bosses* (Durham, 1930).

17. See Gosnell, *Negro Politicians.*

and the large Negro lower strata had little political relationship to civil rights politics. This meant that the politics pursued by Negro elites in most cities never produced a vertical integration of the elites with the Negro lower strata. In short, the civil rights politics, which the neglect of city machines caused Negro elites in most cities to adopt, had a class and status bias that prevented the black ghetto from taking on the attributes of an ethnic political subsystem—that is, an articulate and politically cohesive group within the structure of the city machine.

Only with the rise of a politically cultivated black ethnicity in the past decade has the Negro ghetto acquired the features of a politically institutionalized ethnic community. But this belated politicization of black ethnicity exhibits features that were uncommon in the development of white ethnic communities at an earlier period. One such feature is sharp conflict with the American political system as such, at all levels—city, state, and federal. This conflict takes the form either of popular-based urban riots, which commenced in 1964 and were initiated largely by lower-strata blacks, or the intensive cultivation of antiwhite perspectives among blacks. Both of these conflict-laden tendencies are directed toward the wider political mobilization of the ghetto and for the growth of Negro political capability. Of course, none of this can be realized without leadership, and two leadership strata now vie for the main role in the politicization of black ethnicity: one is of lower-strata background and so has a special claim to having spearheaded the militant style now common to much of Negro leadership; the other is middle-class, though a good portion of this second leadership group is first-generation middle-class, and this segment is currently leading the bid of the black bourgeoisie to seize a dominant role in the emerging politics of black ethnicity.

Leadership and Black Ethnicity: Lower-Strata Militants

Although the riots initiated by lower-strata Negroes in the mid-1960s stimulated the rise of militant political leaders, it was the federal government's War on Poverty that enabled these leaders to institutionalize their politics. In 1965–70 the federal government allocated nearly $5 billion under the 1964 Economic Opportunity Act to a community action program, which led to the formation of more than two thousand so-called community action organizations. These organizations were quickly politicized by lower-strata black militants throughout the 1960s and became their primary political structure.

The federal government did not intend, of course, to transform the community action organizations into militant political instruments. The government's purpose was rather to provide the Negro lower strata with an opportunity to develop basic administrative and executive skills, a goal some observers claim was realized, though I doubt it.[18] However, federal agencies administering the War on Poverty could not adequately control either what was done at the city level with the resources of community action organizations or the composition of these bodies. In this way the lower-strata militant leaders converted the War on Poverty's action organizations from social service agencies into instruments for politicizing (and radicalizing) such heretofore inarticulate Negro lower-strata groups as welfare mothers, gangs, school dropouts, and semiskilled workers.

Yet little of this politicization of the lower strata represented a long-run political gain. It is, after all, one thing to use community action organizations to attract adherents to ideas of black nationalist militancy and to incite a demonstration by welfare mothers; it is another matter altogether to use community action agencies to encourage welfare mothers to register to vote, to participate in precinct and ward committee elections and activities, to evaluate candidates and issues. Clearly this latter form of politicization in cities would be of more lasting political value than the rather ad hoc politicization used by lower-strata black militants.

The lower-strata militant leaders pursue a policy of short-run rather than long-run politicization of the ghetto because they are accustomed in general to short-run behavior. The turn of many of these militant leaders to politics, after the riots of the mid-1960s, was less a matter of wanting to provide leadership than of utilizing their new status in order to derive benefits on a scale unavailable to them in their previous "hustling" roles, such as pimp, narcotics pusher, small holdup man, numbers writer, and others. A previous experience with hustling,

18. See Sar A. Levitan, "The Community Action Program," *The Annals of the American Academy of Political and Social Science,* September 1969, p. 67.

which is common to some lower-strata militant leaders, has also influenced their political style. For just as their hustling roles afforded them a certain celebrity status—virtually that of "culture heroes"[19]— their concern with such ad hoc political action as confrontations with officials provides them both publicity and celebration. The Black Panther leaders have taken this style to its extreme; but they have contributed little to the durable politicization of the Negro lower strata, since they prefer short-run tactics linked to violent rhetoric and symbolism, and sometimes to violence itself.[20]

It appears, then, that the lower-strata militant leaders lack the habits, values, and skills required for a durable politicization of the Negro population. Though they have become an important force in the new politics of urban black ethnicity, *they have proved incapable of institutionalizing this politics.* Their main contribution is rather different: they stamp the politics of black ethnicity with a lower-class style, which means that the experiences and problems of the Negro lower strata (marginal working class and lower class) rather than the black bourgeoisie have a determining role in the politics of black ethnicity.

One cannot overstate the significance of this. For one thing, it signifies the profoundly important difference between the earlier civil rights politics and the new politics of black ethnicity. And, to the extent that middle-class and upper-strata Negroes participate in the politics of black ethnicity, they must do so at least partly in terms of the lower-class criteria that legitimate this politics. Thus middle-class politicians participating in the politics of black ethnicity now articulate needs, demands, and policies that touch more on problems of lower-strata than of middle- and upper-strata blacks. In making this shift in the style of political articulation, middle-class leaders allow the lower strata a leverage which never before existed. In short, by stamping the politics of black ethnicity with a lower-class style, the lower-strata militants have, largely unwittingly, effected a veritable revolution in the structure of Negro politics. For the first time, in this century, black politics possesses a style and an ideological struc-

19. See Malcolm X (with Alex Haley), *Autobiography of Malcolm X* (New York: Grove Press, 1966).

20. See Martin Kilson, "The 'Put-On' of Black Panther Rhetoric: On the Function of Polemical Excess," *Encounter,* April 1971, pp. 57–58.

ture that facilitate vertical political linkages among the various strata in the black ethnic turf.

Now there is need for a leadership with the skill and political sophistication necessary to institutionalize these vertical political linkages, and thereby to maximize the political power of the Negro ethnic sector on a scale comparable to that realized earlier by other ethnic groups.

Leadership and Black Ethnicity: New Middle-Class Politicians

The leadership necessary for this difficult task is in fact available. This leadership draws upon the Negro working class, a stratum in the urban black ghetto which since World War I has made numerous attempts to facilitate a ghetto-wide leadership but with little success,[21] partly because of the working class's inability to provide enough of its sons with higher education.

In the past twenty years, however, this weakness of the Negro working class has been significantly overcome, and this, along with the marked growth of the Negro middle class, constitutes the most striking sociological change in contemporary Negro society.[22] This new leadership comes out of the post–World War II college-educated generation of the Negro working class. It represents the black working-class segment that reject lower-class life styles and cultivate instead upwardly mobile or middle-class aspirations, occasionally marry up-

21. See Sterling D. Spero and Abram L. Harris, *The Black Worker: The Negro and the Labor Movement* (Port Washington, N. Y.: Kernikat, 1931), chaps. 6 and 20, which deal with the role of independent Negro unions, especially among Pullman workers, from World War I to 1930. See also James W. Ford, *The Negro and the Democratic Front* (New York, 1938). This study, written by the leading Negro Communist in the 1930s, covers the efforts of the Communist party to manipulate the Negro working class into a ghetto-wide leadership role.

22. For example, in 1955 only 9 percent of Negro families had income of $7,000 or more, compared to 31 percent of white families; but in 1967 nearly 39 percent of Negro families fell into this income category, compared to 55 percent of white families. Educationally, 50 percent of Negro males over 25 years of age completed high school by 1967 (compared to 73 percent of white males), while in 1960 only 36 percent of Negro males at 25 years of age had completed high school (compared to 63 percent of white males at 25 years of age). See Bureau of Census, *Social and Economic Conditions of Negroes in the United States* (Washington, D.C., 1967).

ward when opportunity allows, purchase homes, have some savings, and above all inspire sons and daughters to pursue higher education.[23]

This new leadership is exemplified at its best by recently successful politicians like Richard Hatcher, son of a steelworker and first Negro mayor of Gary, Indiana; Thomas Atkins, son of a working-class clergyman, and the first Negro city councilman in Boston in over thirty years; Shirley Chisholm, daughter of an artisan and the first Negro woman to be elected to Congress, representing a new district in Bedford-Stuyvesant. Others in this category include Carl Stokes, first Negro mayor in Cleveland; Louis Stokes, first Negro congressman from Cleveland; Kenneth Gibson, first Negro mayor in Newark. The political resources marshaled by this new group of Negro politicians—the first generation in their families to gain a college education—equip it to begin the task of institutionalizing the politics of black ethnicity. What are these resources?

First, personal attributes. Primary among these is higher education, which affords the new leaders not only skills (for example, Gibson is an engineer; Atkins, Hatcher, and Stokes are lawyers), but a grasp of institutional dynamics in American society—a grasp unavailable to the lower-strata militant leaders.

Second, their background within the lower strata of the black community. This gives them a certain perception of and empathy with the special material and psychological needs of the black lower strata and thus, perhaps, a capacity to articulate these needs in a manner reasonably satisfactory to wide segments of the lower strata. Though these new politicians may not perform this role as convincingly as the lower-strata militants, they will certainly be more acceptable than the established middle-class Negro leaders. The fact that new middle-class politicians like Richard Hatcher are only recently removed from the Negro lower strata strengthens their position in this regard. Some have fathers, mothers, siblings, and kin still residing in

23. An area of major neglect in the sociology of the urban Negro is the study of the life style and social structure of the working-class Negro. For example, a classic description of a ghetto like Drake and Cayton's *Black Metropolis* has virtually nothing to say about the working class, compared to the marginal lower class, and the term "working class" is not even in the book's index. An earlier study does have some data on homeowning tendency among the Negro working class; see Thomas Woofter, ed., *Negro Problems in Cities* (New York: Negro Universities Press, 1928) pp. 106–11, *passim*.

working-class quarters and can readily point to this as evidence of their ties to the black masses.

Third, the rapid growth in the past decade of Negro population in the inner city, together with the emigration of whites to city fringes, must also be counted as a resource. (The rates of Negro concentration in the inner city since the 1950s and of white emigration to the city fringe and suburbs are shown in Table 3; Table 4 shows the percentage growth of Negroes in the thirty largest cities in the 1950s to 1960s.) It is projected that within the next fifteen years the population of some eleven major cities will become nearly 50 percent Negro. Included among these cities are Baltimore (1972), Gary (1973), Cleveland (1975), St. Louis (1978), Detroit (1979), Philadelphia (1981), Oakland (1973), and Chicago (1984).

Fourth and last, the federal government's recognition, since the riots of the 1960s, of the city's problems as a national priority is another and in a way the most crucial political resource available to the emergent middle-class Negro politicians. This recognition, though already acted on by both Democratic and Republican administrations through the War on Poverty, the Model Cities project, and new welfare legislation, still awaits substantial action.

Institutionalizing a Politics of Black Ethnicity

Negro politicians, the main agents of the political institutionalization of black ethnicity, are more numerous today than they were at any other period in this century. There are now about 1,500 elected Negro politicians or officials, 62 percent of them outside the South, representing overwhelmingly city constituencies. They are located in forty-one of the fifty states, and include, among others, 12 congressmen, 168 state legislators, 48 mayors, 575 other city officials, 362 school board members, and 114 judges and magistrates. It is noteworthy that Negro communities in the populous industrial states claim a major share of the congressmen and state legislators, and several of the black mayors head industrial cities. Thus two congressmen (Shirley Chisholm and Charles Rangel) represent Negroes in New York City, two (Charles Diggs and John Conyers) Negroes in Detroit, one (Louis Stokes) Negroes in Cleveland, one (Robert Nix) Negroes in Philadelphia, two (Ralph Metcalfe and George Collins)

Negroes in Chicago, and one (Parren Mitchell) Negroes in Baltimore. Illinois, New York, and Ohio have 14, 12, and 13 Negro state legislators respectively, and the proportion of Negro legislators in Ohio is larger than the Negro share of population. Only in Detroit and Gary do Negroes have a majority of city councilmen, and in Pittsburgh the percentage of Negro councilmen is larger than the Negro percentage in Pittsburgh's population.

As Negroes are more concentrated in cities than any other ethnic group, the city is now more than ever the main arena for institutionalizing the politics of black ethnicity. The political infrastructure necessary to realize the long-run goals of this politics begins in cities and evolves outward, either directly through congressmen to the federal government, or indirectly through county, city, and state offices.

Increasingly, mayors and city councilmen spend more and more of their time seeking federal revenues. This is particularly true for Negro mayors and city councilmen because their primary constituency, the black population, has more poor, unskilled, and semiskilled persons than any other community. This means that resources required to alter these people's lives can no longer be found in the cities but must be acquired from the federal government. In fact, the resources that ultimately enabled the Irish, Italians, Polish, Jewish, and other whites to consolidate their power and improve their conditions also came not from the cities but from the federal government. Without this intervention it is doubtful that the large lower strata of poor, unskilled, and semiskilled persons in the white ethnic groups of fifty years ago would have largely been transformed into skilled workers and homeowners.

Federal government intervention in city politics is required if this politics is to serve Negroes as a means of social change. But, before this can happen, the black city population, like its white ethnic counterparts, must make its contribution to the political forces that make possible such federal government intervention. For it was the ability of political leaders of white ethnic groups to mobilize the votes in their communities that enabled the Democratic party to dominate the presidency in the era 1932–60. The same is now required of the new Negro politicians.

The Negro mayors and city councilmen are in the front line

of this development. For a variety of reasons, mayors and city councilmen, more than congressmen, have in the popular mind been symbolic of the political growth and success of ethnic groups. In cities where the chances to elect Negro mayors and councilmen are good, the problems facing the effective mobilization of Negro votes and some white support are for the most part still unsolved.

This was apparent in rather stark fashion in the mayoralty election in the city of East St. Louis in 1967—a city in which some 84,000 Negroes comprise 60 percent of the total population and somewhat over 50 percent of the voters. Although a Negro had stood for the city office of commissioner (four commissioners and a mayor constitute executive government in East St. Louis) and won as a machine candidate, no black had contested the mayoralty before 1967. But a Negro stood as mayor in 1967, and at the head of an all-black ticket contesting all executive posts; he was confronted by an incumbent ticket, all but one white. Moreover, East St. Louis like other cities experienced some black militancy in the 1960s, including a small riot, and the head of the Negro ticket, Elmo Bush, an educational administrator, conducted the campaign in militant style, which included a visit to the city by Stokely Carmichael, whose address at a mass rally included the remark: "Let me tell you, baby, when we got 52 percent of the voters in a city, we own that city—lock, stock, and barrel."[24]

The election results were the opposite of Carmichael's projection. The incumbent mayor polled 71 percent of the votes and none of the four incumbent commissioners less than 60 percent; Elmo Bush, the Negro mayoral candidate, got 29 percent and his running mates from 20 to 26 percent. What is more, the incumbent mayor won 88 percent of the votes in white precincts, compared to 12 percent for the Negro candidate; and in the black precincts, where some 59 percent of all votes were cast, the incumbent white gained 60 percent against the Negro candidate's 40 percent. The incumbent commissioners received no less than 52 percent of votes in the black precincts, while none of the commissioners on the all-black ticket received more than 35 percent. Of special interest was the fact that the incumbent Negro commissioner on the incumbent mayor's ticket, E. Saverson,

24. *Metro-East Journal,* April 3, 1967.

polled the largest vote of all candidates in the black precincts; and though he received only 46 percent of the votes in white precincts, a return much below his white running mates', no candidate on the all-black ticket received more than 12 percent of the votes in white precincts.

It is clear from the foregoing that the all-black ticket in the 1967 East St. Louis mayorality race was defeated by the weight of the city machine. The racial edge claimed by the all-black ticket was of little moment in face of a well-organized and disciplined party machine. The machine's only Negro candidate, E. Saverson, longtime leader of the city's Negro Democratic organization, brilliantly exhibited the machine's strength. Moreover, the black militant rhetoric of the candidates on the all-black ticket was far from persuasive to the voters in the East St. Louis ghetto. Though they had no illusions about the white city machine, they understood that from it concrete gains in the form of jobs did or could derive. Reasons for the hold of this kind of machine patronage over the Negro vote in East St. Louis, as in many other cities, are suggested by the fact that in 1964 some 33 percent of the city's Negro males were unemployed, and 52 percent of those Negroes holding jobs earned less than $3,000. Clearly anything the city machine did to aid employment and income in East St. Louis would have an important political effect on the Negro vote.

Other Negro candidates for city offices who were unable to see the political limitations of black militant rhetoric have failed in the past five years and will continue to fail until they learn that the rhetoric of blackness, though of some value in the political *mobilization* of the ghetto, is no substitute for viable political *organization*. Candidacies which in the past five years have recognized the limitations of this rhetoric, and have based their campaigns upon sound organization, have registered major victories. This situation characterized the victory of Richard Hatcher in the 1967 mayorality election in Gary, Indiana. As in East St. Louis, Negroes were by 1967 slightly over 50 percent of the population. Also as in East St. Louis, the Democratic city machine was well organized in the ghetto. However, unlike the all-black ticket in East St. Louis, Hatcher did not rely simply upon militant rhetoric; instead, he organized a grassroots campaign—a united front of Negro organizations—which endeavored to overcome the Democratic machine's foothold in the ghetto. He also recognized the need for allies in the white precincts; but since the corrupt Democratic machine opposed him even after he won the primary, his main instrument turned out to be the local press, which though not supporting Hatcher still did not oppose him, thereby allowing some whites to appraise him on the basis of his merit and the issues of his campaign.[25] As a result, Hatcher won by a narrow margin, and though 91 percent of Hatcher's votes came from black precincts, 17 percent came from white ones. It is clear that the 6,762 white votes Hatcher gained were indispensable to his victory.

Another successful Negro candidacy for mayor of a major city occurred in Cleveland, where in 1965 Negroes were 34 percent of the city's 800,000 population. Carl Stokes, typical of the black middle-class politicians, made his first bid for mayor in 1965, unsuccessfully, but stood again in 1967, winning the Democratic primary in a three-sided race with 52 percent of the votes. Like Hatcher in Gary, he recognized the need to confront the Democratic machine, again basically racist in its response to a Negro's candidacy, with a competitive organization in the ghetto. This Stokes's campaign achieved, getting 96 percent of the votes in black precincts, with 74 percent of the Negro electorate participating. Equally significant was his showing in white precincts: he polled 17,000 white votes, a figure that represents nearly his margin of victory—18,736. In the November 1967 mayorality election in which Stokes confronted the Republican candidate Seth C. Taft, Stokes's campaign organization repeated its primary victory. Stokes polled 94 percent of the votes in black precincts and one-fifth of the white votes, which amounted to the balance of victory. The key to the white votes was a brilliantly executed alliance with liberal white Protestants and a scattering of white ethnic supporters, reinforced by the endorsement of Cleveland's most powerful newspaper, the Cleveland *Plain Dealer*.

The Future

The pattern of politically cultivating black ethnicity in order to consolidate Negro voting power and to discipline the black vote in favor of one candidate can be expected to persist through the 1970s

25. See Edward Greer, "The 'Liberation' of Gary, Indiana," *Trans-action*, January 1971, pp. 30–39.

and into the succeeding decades. Additional electoral victories employing this method were registered in 1970 in the mayoralty campaign of Negro candidate Kenneth Gibson in Newark, New Jersey, where blacks are one-half of the population, and in the congressional campaign of Parren Mitchell in Baltimore. In both cases a disciplined use of the black militant style forged vertical linkages among groups within the Negro ghetto, allowing these campaigns to surmount the divisions of the Negro community. But both candidacies combined, as they must, the politics of black ethnicity with alliances with liberal sectors of the white population, and in both instances the white voters provided the margin of victory. These alliances will persist and gain in sophistication as the politics of black ethnicity matures, though some vigilance will be necessary to combat the simplistic and erroneous notion of black-white coalitions as tantamount to a zero-sum game, which was first enunciated by Stokely Carmichael and Charles Hamilton in their book *Black Power: The Politics of Liberation in America* (New York, 1967).[26]

Gaining white voters was central to Mitchell's campaign, for his congressional district was composed of only 40 percent blacks and 60 percent whites (40 percent Jews and 20 percent WASP). Mitchell's forces made a black-white alliance that was based on two (largely Protestant) new politics groups and two Jewish-Negro integrated organizations, backed by liberal labor leaders. These alliances were successful and Parren Mitchell's election as the first Negro congressman from Maryland was assured, as was the election of the first Negro city district attorney, Milton Allen, and the election to the state legislature of sixteen Negroes among the fifty-five legislators representing Baltimore. Furthermore, white liberals gained over twenty of the additional city seats in the state legislature, which enables the Negro and white liberal legislators to be a decisive force if they nurture their alliance.[27]

It would seem, curiously, that a long-run problem for the new middle-class black politicians is less their capacity to forge and main-

---

26. For an excellent antidote to the Carmichael-Hamilton view of coalition politics, see Bayard Rustin, " 'Black Power' and Coalition Politics," *Commentary*, September 1966, pp. 35–40.

27. See Patrick J. McCaffrey, "Black and White in Baltimore," *The Nation*, December 21, 1970, pp. 652–53.

tain alliances with enough whites to ensure victory than the maintenance of discipline within the politics of black ethnicity. Now in its formative period, this politics has yet to encounter major internal conflicts. Two developments will help keep such conflicts at bay: one, the co-optation of lower-class militants by the new black middle-class politicians; two, adequate aid to cities by the federal government.

As for the lower-strata militants' place in the politics of black ethnicity, they will be of little positive value if they persist in a political style emphasizing short-run and merely symbolic political gains. If, however, the lower-strata militants grasp the long-run needs of Negro political development, they will redefine their role in a manner conducive to a division of political tasks between themselves and the middle-class politicians. This division of political roles in the leadership of the ghetto will entail the lower-strata militants' acquiring political roles as local (ward, district, precinct) organizers, while the middle-class politicians would hold the executive political roles. The lower-strata militant leaders would apply their skills to the task of linking the middle-class politicians with the Negro lower classes, rather as do the ward and precinct organizers in the traditional city machine.[28]

TABLE 1

Percent Distribution of the Population
by Region—1950, 1960, and 1966

Region	Negro Population		
	1950	1960	1966
United States	100	100	100
South	68	60	55
North	28	34	37
Northeast	13	16	17
North Central	15	18	20
West	4	6	8

Source: Report of the National Advisory Commission on Civil Disorders (Washington, D.C., 1968).

28. See, e.g., J. T. Salter, Boss Rule: Portraits in City Politics (New York, 1935).

TABLE 2

Number and Percentage of Negroes in Selected Northern Cities
1910–1940

	Number of Negroes				Percent Negroes in Population			
	1910	*1920*	*1930*	*1940*	*1910*	*1920*	*1930*	*1940*
New York	91,709	152,467	327,706	458,444	1.9	2.7	4.7	6.1
Chicago	44,103	109,458	233,903	277,731	2.0	4.1	6.9	8.2
Philadelphia	84,459	134,229	219,599	250,880	5.5	7.4	11.3	13.0
Detroit	5,741	40,838	120,066	149,119	1.2	4.1	7.7	9.2
St. Louis	43,960	69,854	93,580	108,765	6.4	9.0	11.4	13.3
Cleveland	8,448	34,451	71,899	84,504	1.5	4.3	8.0	9.6
Pittsburgh	25,623	37,725	54,983	62,216	4.8	6.4	8.2	9.9
Cincinnati	19,639	30,079	47,818	55,593	5.4	7.5	10.6	12.2
Indianapolis	21,816	34,678	43,967	51,142	9.3	11.0	12.1	13.2
Los Angeles	7,599	15,579	38,894	63,774	2.4	2.7	3.1	4.2
Newark	9,475	16,977	38,880	45,760	2.7	4.1	8.8	10.6
Gary	383	5,299	17,922	20,394	2.3	9.6	17.8	18.3
Dayton	4,842	9,025	17,077	20,273	4.2	5.9	8.5	9.6
Youngstown	1,936	6,662	14,552	14,615	2.4	5.0	8.6	8.7

Source: United States Census Reports.

TABLE 3

Population Change by Location, Inside and Outside
Metropolitan Areas, 1950–1966 (numbers in millions)

	Population					
	Negro			White		
	1950	*1960*	*1966*	*1950*	*1960*	*1966*
United States	15.0	18.8	21.5	135.2	158.8	170.8
Metropolitan areas	8.4	12.2	14.8	80.3	99.7	109.0
Central cities	6.5	9.7	12.1	45.5	47.7	46.4
Urban fringe	1.9	2.5	2.7	34.8	52.0	62.5
Small cities, town and rural	6.7	6.7	6.7	54.8	59.2	61.8

Source: Report of the National Advisory Commission on Civil Disorders (Washington, D.C., 1968).

TABLE 4

Percentage of Negroes in Each of the Thirty Largest Cities

	1950	1960	1965*
New York, N.Y.	10	14	18
Chicago, Ill.	14	23	28
Los Angeles, Calif.	9	14	17
Philadelphia, Pa.	18	26	31
Detroit, Michigan	16	29	34
Baltimore, Md.	21	35	38
Houston, Texas	24	23	23
Cleveland, Ohio	16	29	34
Washington, D.C.	35	54	66
St. Louis, Mo.	18	29	36
Milwaukee, Wis.	3	8	11
San Francisco, Calif.	6	10	12
Boston, Mass.	5	9	13
Dallas, Texas	13	19	21
New Orleans, La.	32	37	41
Pittsburgh, Pa.	12	17	20
San Antonio, Tex.	7	7	8
San Diego, Calif.	5	6	7
Seattle, Wash.	3	5	7
Buffalo, N.Y.	6	13	17
Cincinnati, Ohio	16	22	24
Memphis, Tenn.	37	37	40
Denver, Colo.	4	6	9
Atlanta, Ga.	37	38	44
Minneapolis, Minn.	1	2	4
Indianapolis, Ind.	15	21	23
Kansas City, Mo.	12	18	22
Columbus, Ohio	12	16	18
Phoenix, Ariz.	5	5	5
Newark, N.J.	17	34	47

Source: Report of the National Advisory Commission on Civil Disorders (Washington, D.C., 1968).
  * Estimated.

Also like the traditional ward, district, and precinct party workers, the lower-strata militants who enter this political relationship with middle-class black politicians will be put on city payrolls as patronage workers, which will guarantee them support during the intervals between elections. And the more talented among these transformed lower-strata militants would surely have opportunity to rise to executive roles. Finally, lower-strata militants such as the Black Panthers could —if they come to reject violence—perform the important task of keeping the middle-class politicians informed of the changing needs and interests among the black lower strata, and could thus be a major factor in ensuring the political accountability of the politicians, something few American ethnic groups ever succeeded in maintaining.

As for possible conflicts over the rewards required by the emergent black ethnic politics, clearly these can be derived in adequate measure only from or through the federal government. No other level of government today has the tax power necessary to secure the revenues required to upgrade the Negro's low skills, health care, home ownership, educational facilities, and so on. But this depends upon what kind of regime controls the federal government, whether Republican or Democratic. Unless the latter can regain power in Washington and hold it for another twenty years, it is unlikely that the rewards needed for the politics of black ethnicity will be forthcoming. But, if rewards *are* forthcoming from the federal government, there is little doubt that the politics of black ethnicity will mature in coming decades; it will acquire a degree of institutionalization comparable to the development of ethnic-centered politics among white ethnic groups at an earlier period.

Dennis H. Wrong

Population Growth and Social Policy

Those of us who for years have been concerned, as students of population, with the increasing number of people on the earth feel some satisfaction, though not always of an unmixed kind, over the recent rise of interest in the problem. It seems to be one of those rare instances in which the anxieties of specialists suddenly become converted into a public issue. Most surprising is the new concern over continuing population growth in the United States itself, which has created some popular demand for a national antinatalist population policy. The Nixon administration, though hardly noted for its innovative tendencies, is the first to appoint a Commission on Population Growth and the American Future, assigned to explore the consequences of future growth and distribution and the relevance of government policies in a variety of areas.[1] Social scientists concerned with the underdeveloped countries have long been aware of the need for a slowing-up and even termination of their population growth as a precondition for economic progress. But, except for a few visionaries and conservation or eugenics "cranks," scarcely anyone has bothered about American population growth until very recently. Sociologist-demographers such as Kingsley Davis, Judith Blake, and William Petersen argued that within a few decades government laws and

1. For my references to the President's Population Commission, as well as to several other matters dealing with the future trend in fertility, I am indebted to a seminar talk given at Princeton University by Professor Charles F. Westoff, executive director of the Commission and professor of sociology at Princeton.

policies aimed at discouraging childbearing would be needed, but before the publication in 1964 of Lincoln and Alice Day's *Too Many Americans* virtually no specialists in demography had advocated such a course to a wide nonprofessional audience.

In 1960 I wrote in *Dissent* that the population crisis was "resistant to the old terms of ideological debate between Left and Right." This was an understatement, for the problem of controlling population growth seemed to pose a challenge to basic, though conflicting, assumptions on both sides. Yet today population control has unmistakably become a cause of the Left. Paul Ehrlich's *The Population Bomb* is a best-seller on the campus. ZPG—Zero Population Growth—clubs have been created on many campuses and in liberal, upper-middle-class communities. Women's Liberation advocates of "equal pay for equal work," day-care nurseries, and liberalized abortion laws, and proponents of the removal of all legal restrictions on homosexuality regularly invoke the need for population control. The connection between population increase and environmental deterioration is stressed by those concerned with the ecology issue. Critics of neocolonialism in the Third World have not only called attention to the population explosion there, but have denounced the greater drain on the resources of underdeveloped countries resulting from continued population growth in America itself. Even enthusiasts for communal living have pointed to the advantages of collective child rearing in encouraging lower fertility by enabling childless adults to maintain close contact with infants and children.

Perhaps because there have been so many other startling reversals of attitude on the Left in recent years, the novelty of this new concern with population control has aroused little comment. In the past, Malthusian and neo-Malthusian arguments were usually identified with the Right. As recently as the 1950s a vague antihumanitarian and reactionary aura still clung to advocacy of population control. This goes back, of course, to Malthus himself, who originally put forward his famous theory in 1798 as a refutation of the belief in progress and human perfectibility, cherished by such ideologues of the Enlightenment as Godwin and Condorcet. In the early stages of the Industrial Revolution in England, capitalists and their spokesmen made crassly self-interested use of Malthus's arguments in order to oppose higher wages and social legislation. Malthus himself has often been unjustly blamed for the use made of his ideas by others. Marx was neither the first nor the last to pour invective on Malthus, calling him a reactionary apologist for the worst excesses of capitalist exploitation, and his anti-Malthusian polemics in *Capital* have to this day inhibited full recognition of population pressure as a source of poverty and suffering in the Communist countries.

The birth-control (or "neo-Malthusian" as it was often called) and the socialist movements developed at about the same time in the latter half of the nineteenth century. A few individuals were pioneers in both movements. Annie Besant, for example, whose famous trial with Charles Bradlaugh in 1876 did so much to popularize knowledge of contraception in England, was also one of the first Fabians and a contributor with Shaw and the Webbs to *Fabian Essays*. But, while some of the utopian socialists in the early part of the century had advocated birth control as a solution to the Malthusian dilemma, the parties of the Second International followed Marx's line on Malthus and were generally hostile to birth-control propagandists, seeing them as diverting indignation away from capitalism, the real cause of mass poverty. Nor were the Victorian feminists very sympathetic to the birth-control cause. Most of them, as J. A. and Olive Banks have recently shown,[2] objected to birth control as depriving women of a valid excuse for refusing to submit to the brutish lusts of the male. One is startled to find the identical argument turning up in discussions of "the pill" by some of the more militant contemporary supporters of Women's Liberation.

From the closing decades of the nineteenth century through the 1920s, concern over population growth was often linked to racist and Social Darwinist doctrines and to support for imperialist expansion. Some writers worried about the higher birth rates of the lower classes on the grounds that they were outbreeding the "genetically superior" middle and upper classes. In the era of imperialism, this argument was extended to whole peoples, and concern over the "Asiatic hordes" became widespread in the early part of the century. Scott Fitzgerald's Tom Buchanan in *The Great Gatsby,* depicted as a representative irresponsible rich man of the period, asks, "Have you read *The Rise of the Colored Empires* by this man Goddard?" (no doubt Fitzgerald

2. *Feminism and Family Planning in Victorian England* (Liverpool: Liverpool University Press, 1964).

had in mind *The Rising Tide of Color* by Lothrop Stoddard), and goes on to assert: "The idea is if we don't look out the white race will be—will be utterly submerged. . . . It's up to us, who are the dominant race, to watch out or these other races will have control of things." Indians used to complain as recently as a decade or two ago that the main concern of Westerners seemed to be that there were so many of them, and one finds echoes of this attitude in the fears of "genocide" expressed today by some black militants and in their occasional condemnation of birth control as a white man's plot to eliminate American Negroes. In the debate over the immigration laws fifty years ago, leading American social scientists, even several of liberal persuasion, used racist and eugenic as well as neo-Malthusian arguments to urge the ending of unrestricted immigration.

All this contributed to the bad name of population control on the Left. But there were countercurrents: the Swedish socialists in the thirties, influenced by the Myrdals, encouraged the working class to limit the size of families by birth control. The idea of *la grève des ventres,* a "strike of bellies," to deny fresh cannon fodder to the warmakers, was advanced by socialists before 1914. And the corollary of racist fears of the expanding colored peoples was to encourage higher fertility at home, which the Nazis and Italian Fascists adopted as official policy in the twenties and thirties, thus aligning birth control and abortion advocates with the left-wing opposition to their regimes.

Even in the period since World War II, when alarm over the population explosion in at least the underdeveloped countries became conventional wisdom among demographers, the traditional hostility of the Left to population control was expressed in several books written for a popular audience,[3] quite independently of official Communist attacks on the "reactionary Malthusianism" of American demographers. A far larger number of popular books were published, however, in the late forties and fifties voicing alarm over world population growth. Yet many of these retained the old eugenic concern over the "quality" of population that has always been unpalatable

3. For example: Kirtley Mather, *Enough and to Spare* (New York: Harper & Brothers, 1944); Josué de Castro, *The Geography of Hunger* (Boston: Little, Brown, 1952); Jacob Oser, *Must Men Starve?* (New York: Abelard-Schumann, 1957).

to the Left; or attacked the "illusion" that technological progress and social reform could make much difference; or, though not racist in tone, at least seemed to disparage the cultures of the underdeveloped world, as in conservationist William Vogt's remark that sex was the "Indian national sport."

Ignorance of the facts of population, or their distortion and misuse for partisan purposes, is an obvious danger. Even the well-informed often favor population policies that are in line with their own sentiments and reject or ignore the case for more far-reaching and controversial policies. When professional demographers in the past decade finally became active in antinatalist programs in the underdeveloped countries, they largely confined themselves to encouraging the spread of "family planning" by contraceptive means. It has been, of course, the spread of this practice that has sucessfully lowered fertility in the Western world since the late nineteenth century. The major effort of family-planning programs has, therefore, gone into the mass distribution of such new, simple, and effective contraceptive devices as intrauterine loops and coils on the assumption that, since surveys show family size to exceed the expressed desires of women in the underdeveloped countries, providing them with the means to control fertility will lead to its reduction and therefore to lower overall rates of population growth. Kingsley Davis, however, pointed out in an influential 1967 article in *Science* that the same surveys suggest that even if all women in the underdeveloped areas had no more children than the number they desire they would still produce families large enough to sustain a fairly high rate of population growth in view of continuing declines in mortality.[4] Zero population growth, he argued, must be the ultimate goal of population policy and it has not yet been attained even in the most developed countries, such as the United States, where family planning has been widely practiced for several generations. The elimination of *unwanted* births made possible by the dissemination of contraceptive knowledge is no more than a first step toward population control. People must be induced to *want* fewer children, and to achieve this may require the imposition of new and painful social controls interfering with sentiments and personal

4. "Population Policy: Will Current Programs Succeed?" *Science,* 158, November 10, 1967, pp. 730–39.

freedoms long cherished and taken for granted. Demographers concerned with family-planning programs have, Davis charged, been politically timid in failing to face up to this necessity.

In the last few years concern over pollution and environmental deterioration resulting from high and rising industrial production has focused attention on the population issue in the United States and the developed countries. Many of the alarmist books on population growth of the past quarter century were written by biological scientists with an ecological point of view, but only recently have their arguments been persuasive to a new and larger audience. The proclaimed quest of young people for a more simple and "natural," less materialistic way of life and the allied antitechnological animus of the young and of older ideologues of the New Left have suddenly created a politics of protest over the "ecology issue" in which old-line conservationists have found new allies, and previously conservative or indifferent citizens have been moved to challenge the conventional goals and routines of our economic life. The very title of Charles Reich's overadvertised book eulogizing the new youth culture is a metaphor based on a conservationist slogan: "the greening of America." Presumably, the much-praised new "tribal consciousness" of the young, combined with their alleged freedom from sexual repression and their repudiation of our "plastic" civilization, does not extend to rejection of contraceptive devices, even those made of plastic, nor does it involve, one supposes, acceptance of the high levels of infant mortality that kept population growth rates low in the tribal societies of the past.

This new climate of opinion has rather suddenly placed an anti-natalist population policy on the political agenda of the Left. Population growth obviously increases total demand and thus accelerates the despoliation of the environment. The issue is even adaptable to the ideological identification with the Third World so common nowadays on the Left, for the poverty of the underdeveloped countries can be attributed to the rising levels of demand in the United States, which is allegedly driven to step up its exploitation of their resources as its own population grows. When, at a symposium last year on "The Environment," I argued that population growth caused different and greater problems in the underdeveloped than in the developed countries, I was accused by a fellow panelist, a former editor of *Ramparts,* of "telling the other fellow that his end of the boat is sinking." The population-ecology issue can thus be adapted to the familiar argument that the problems of the Third World are essentially the fault of the West, particularly the United States.

It would be tragic if attention were to be diverted from the enormous task of economic development in the Third World, for which population control is so critical a necessity, by concentration on the lesser problems arising out of population growth in the United States. These problems, however, deserve consideration on their own, quite apart from ideological polemics on global issues. Apocalyptic prophecies that millions of Americans will face imminent death through poisoning by air pollution if people don't stop reproducing tomorrow do a dangerous disservice. I realize that such prophecies are meant to be self-defeating, part of a political strategy designed to jog people out of optimism or indifference. But, though the risk of complacency is perennial, there is also a risk of overwhelming the public with doomsday forecasts, and we surely must have approached the saturation level in recent years—even of forecasts that the air and water are close to saturation level with noxious substances. Resignation rather than strengthened determination to eliminate the evil is a possible response, and if the predicted disasters fail to materialize, apathy and complacency find renewed warrant. Moreover, the apocalyptic imagination of the times often leads to espousal of extreme and "radical" remedies with the result that less dramatic proposals that promise to be effective are made to appear "wishy-washy."

To give a concrete example: both Kingsley Davis and Paul Ehrlich have suggested that the American government might adopt a policy of eliminating tax deductions for more than two children and limiting free public education to the amount necessary to put no more than two children through high school. Davis has proposed that the government might today consider prohibiting couples from having more than *four* children, presumably by making sterilization compulsory for one or both parents who have already had that many. These are far-reaching proposals in light of the pronatalist bias of existing policies. Yet the rhetoric of crisis so prevalent on the campus has led students to confront visiting politicians—and only liberal ones have shown their faces there in recent years—with the demand that they publicly support laws proscribing more than *two* children per couple. Any proposal falling short of this is then viewed—and booed—as a "cop-out."

If ecological disaster truly looms before the end of the century, the cessation *now* of population growth will hardly help to avert it. Banning automobiles rather than babies would be a more immediately effective response. The much-cited statistic that one American consumes fifty times as much of the world's resources as a single Indian is roughly true, and the American's contribution to pollution is undoubtedly greater in about the same proportion. But this applies to *adult* Americans—infants and children do not "consume" cars, jet plane trips, six-packs of beer, or even the products of the chemical industry in anything like the same amounts as adults, and most of the people who are going to raise levels of consumption in the seventies are already alive. There is, in any case, disagreement among experts as to whether population growth is in fact the major culprit in the deterioration of the environment. Paul Ehrlich thinks it is; others attach greater importance to rising levels of per capita demand; while still others, such as Barry Commoner, blame changes in technology independently of higher levels of consumption. Thus the stress on population control as an immediately effective remedy to an imminent ecological armageddon is misplaced.

Major shifts in population trends rarely take place within a few years unless they result from natural or man-made catastrophes. The rapid drop in mortality since World War II in the underdeveloped countries is an exception which has, of course, precipitated their subsequent population explosions. But no unambiguous evidence exists that *any* governmental population policies aimed at influencing fertility, whether pro- or antinatalist, have ever succeeded in doing more than hastening a trend already under way. The Nazis made large claims for reversing the decline of the German birth rate in the 1930s, but detailed analysis suggests that the achievement of full employment as a result of rearmament accounted for the upturn of the birth rate some years before the same thing happened for the same cause in other Western countries. More recently, claims have been made for the success of family-planning programs in lowering fertility in such countries as Taiwan and South Korea, but Kingsley Davis and William Petersen have convincingly argued that a transition to lower birth rates was already under way in both countries when the new programs were introduced.[5] Admittedly, past efforts by governments to encourage fewer births in both developed and underdeveloped countries have been modest by comparison with many proposals currently under discussion.

If, to invert Keynes, we are unlikely all to be dead in the long run—that is, by the year 2000—and if it is an ideologically motivated exaggeration to blame the problems of the Third World on American population growth, or even on the American economy in general, it remains highly desirable that population growth in the United States should approach a zero rate and that we begin to plan both how to achieve this and how to cope with the new "stationary state" once it has been achieved.

What are the present prospects for future American population growth according to the evidence of the 1970 census and recent demographic research?

The census shows a population increase of somewhat more than 24 million in the sixties, from a total population of about 180 million in 1960 to 204 million in 1970. This is the second-largest intercensal increase in the history of the nation (the largest was in the 1950s), but in percentage terms it is the second-*smallest* increase, amounting to about 13.5 percent as compared with an all-time low of 7.2 percent during the depression of the 1930s. Although the 1 percent average annual rate of increase achieved by 1969—less than half the world rate—is still well above zero growth, there has clearly been a considerable decline in the rate of American population growth since the peak of the baby boom in the fifties.

The decline is entirely the result of a reduction in births, just as the post–World War II increases were largely owing to a rise in births. The decline in births in the late sixties so exceeded expectations that in early 1970 the Bureau of the Census revised downward its population projections for the decades ahead. The much-publicized figure of a population of 300 million by the year 2000 now seems too high and the 300 million figure is not expected to be reached until about 2010. Toward the end of the fifties and through the middle sixties, women born during the years of low fertility in the 1930s

5. Davis, *op. cit.*, William Petersen, "Taiwan's Population Problem," In S. Chandrasekhar, ed., *Asia's Population Problems* (London: Allen and Unwin, 1967), pp. 189–210.

made up a larger proportion than either before or since of the total numbers of women in the childbearing years. This "ripple effect" contributed to the downturn from the high birth-rate levels of the late forties and early fifties. But since roughly 1965 the ripple effect has favored higher fertility, with the first cohorts of the postwar baby-boom years entering the parental ages. This will continue to be the case through the seventies, and has already raised slightly the crude birth rates recorded in the last two years above that of 1968, which at 17.5 (per 1,000) was the lowest ever recorded, even lower than that in the depths of the Depression.

However, the fact that the birth rate continued to move downward at a time when the proportion of women in the reproductive ages had become favorable to higher rates indicates a strong desire among contemporary women to have fewer children. Even though the swollen birth cohorts of the mid-fifties will be becoming parents in the seventies, it is unlikely that their numbers will do more than slightly and temporarily increase the birth rate and the rate of population growth. Undoubtedly, the very rapid dissemination of "the pill" and the widespread publicity attending it greatly increased general awareness of the degree to which family size is subject to personal choice. The greater availability of newer methods of contraception, such as intrauterine devices, and of legal abortions, are likely to counteract possible anxieties about the medical effects of the pill which have already somewhat curtailed its use. Yet the American birth rate began its decline some years before the mass marketing of the pill and even more years before intrauterine devices were available. Not the means but the motivation to have fewer children is the crucial consideration.

Some demographers who have long specialized in the study of American fertility go so far as to foresee at least the possibility of widespread concern twenty years from now over the failure of the American population to produce enough children to replace itself. Perhaps the present decline in fertility indicates the resumption of a deeply rooted trend toward small families and low fertility in industrial societies that was interrupted and temporarily reversed in response to the mass traumas of depression, war, and cold war in a period of uneasy prosperity permitting one last acting-out of traditional family values. While new demands and problems have emerged in the sixties, much of the discontent expressed by radical youth, by the women's movement, and, for that matter, by the blacks reflects a desire to complete several of the "compromised revolutions" to which Paul Goodman called our attention a decade ago in *Growing Up Absurd* (though, surprisingly, he failed to mention feminism).

Yet in the case of childbearing decisions there is a new element present. The United States has undoubtedly become the most mass-media-saturated country in the world. The enormous publicity recently given to environmental damage and to the asserted connection between it and population growth has helped convert childbearing decisions into a moral issue, a matter of conscience, for large numbers of people. Greater exposure to the culture of the campus has undoubtedly had a similar effect. Thus decisions on family size may no longer be determined solely by the desires and adaptations to their particular social and economic situations of individual couples; for perhaps the first time in any large-scale society, they may be becoming responsive to public and official concern over the impact of total population size and growth on the general welfare. The very rapid decline of fertility in the last few years and the sharply reduced family-size preferences expressed in surveys by college-age and slightly older women are consistent with this suggestion.

Official pronouncements on American population growth have not gone beyond the family-planning movement's traditional concern with eliminating unwanted births. If this increasingly noncontroversial goal were to be attained,[6] how far would it take us toward zero population growth? Most authoritative estimates place the proportion of all "unwanted" births in the United States at about one-fifth. The ambiguity inherent in the notion of an unwanted birth strongly suggests that this is an underestimate. Demographers have maintained that the elimination in a decade of all unwanted births would bring the United States two-thirds to three-quarters of the way toward zero population growth. If, however, fertility levels sufficient only for population replacement were reached by the end of the 1970s, the present age composition of the population is such that zero growth could not be

6. Not all aspects of it are noncontroversial. A high proportion of increased illegitimate births occurs with teenagers, suggesting the need for more extensive sex education, including contraceptive information, in the schools.

actually achieved for another sixty-five to seventy years.[7] This is a short time according to the usual timetable of demographic change, but impossibly distant by the standards of the doomsday forecasters.

What public policies, in addition to the extension and improvement of effective family-planning services, might be adopted to accelerate this trend? Compulsory restrictions on childbearing by means of required abortions or sterilizations, let alone such measures—still technically impossible—as placing steroids in public water supplies, are politically as well as administratively unfeasible, though it is a good thing that they are at least being discussed as ultimate possibilities. Tax reforms removing extra benefits to large families and penalties for single and childless persons are probably the most obvious initial measures that would reverse the built in, though by no means deliberately planned, pronatalist bias in present tax, welfare, and military exemption policies. It is to be hoped that *all* future government programs will be directly evaluated for their possible effects on fertility, which should rule out such antipoverty measures as the family allowances advocated by Daniel P. Moynihan. Not that present tax or welfare policies have necessarily had a decisive effect on fertility, for, as we have seen, even deliberate population policies in other countries have had little or no measurable impact. But action by the government to remove real or apparent official encouragement of large families may help sustain the present mood of concern, which has independently contributed to the recent decline in fertility. Such new policies might also set limits to a future resurgence of fertility—another baby boom—even though this seems highly unlikely to occur and, if it did, more stringent measures would certainly be required to control and reverse it.

In addition to the volume of direct publicity on the population-ecology issue, the consequences of rapid urbanization and resulting higher population densities are all too visible. Air and water pollution, traffic jams and transportation problems, housing shortages, the spread of suburbia into the countryside, the overcrowding of recreational facilities, even higher crime rates, are plausibly attributed to population growth and have undoubtedly influenced the downward

7. Larry Bumpass and Charles F. Westoff, "The 'Perfect Contraceptive' Population," *Science,* 169, September 18, 1970, pp. 1177–82.

trend in births and family-size preferences. Yet these problems result primarily from a long-standing trend in the *distribution* of the population: the increasing concentration of people in metropolitan areas, which is only indirectly affected by total population increase. Actually, the United States as a whole is not becoming more crowded: fully half our counties have *lost* population since 1950, most of them in the "heartland" rural belt, extending from the agricultural Middle West southward to Texas and Louisiana and eastward across the South to Georgia and South Carolina. Nor are American cities themselves characterized by very high densities if compared with European, let alone Asian, cities. The urban explosion of the last thirty years has taken place largely in the suburbs, creating the familiar problems of racial polarization between black central cities and white suburbs, the declining tax base of central cities, congested transportation arteries between residential suburbs and downtown business districts, and increasing residential segregation by class, race, and ethnic group within metropolitan areas.

The Population Commission's charter includes the examination of trends in population distribution as well as overall growth. But the Commission has been far more gingerly in considering policies aiming at population redistribution than those dealing with total growth. In spite of the association of population control with traditional sexual, moral, and religious values held with emotional fervor, policies designed to alter present population distribution and to slow up or reverse current trends are likely to be even more politically explosive than those aiming at a reduction in fertility. The competition between regions for federal funds and contracts, the acute fiscal needs of the metropolitan areas, the dependence of so many areas on the military-industrial and aerospace establishments, and decisions as to the location of federally financed model cities and new towns—these merely begin to suggest the dimensions of the problem. More than ten years ago, at the peak of the nuclear arms race, Nathan Glazer stated: "Because California needs missile contracts, American civilization may be destroyed."[8] More recently, a similar—if less millennial—disproportion between cause and effect has been indicated in the

8. "The Peace Movement in America, 1961," *Commentary*, 31, April 1961, p. 295.

case of the needs of the Seattle labor market and the noise and pollution effects of the SST.

One may assert with total confidence that there is not a single problem of American society that will be reduced rather than aggravated by the addition of more people to the population. The questions raised by policies of population redistribution, however, are a good deal more complex and politically knotty and fall outside the scope of the present discussion.

Michael Harrington

The Politics of Pollution

One of the main reasons that the issue of the environment has recently become popular is that people wrongly think it noncontroversial. Nobody, David Brinkley said, is in favor of pollution; everybody is against it.

That is a dangerous half-truth. It is quite right to note that filthy air, noise, congestion, and dirty water afflict the middle and upper classes as well as the poor. And that fact certainly does create a huge constituency, for, quite literally, everyone has an interest in cleaning up the environment. It is also true, but less happy, that the pollution crusade may turn out to be a genteel rest home for affluent idealists exhausted by their failures to end either poverty or the war in Vietnam.

But the consensus theory of environmental politics is also profoundly false (and I shall shortly summon up the memory of that great exponent of "reasoning together," Lyndon B. Johnson, to document the point). For, just as everyone was against poverty, but powerful institutional forces refused to do what its abolition required, there are corporations which have become conscience-stricken about pollution only because they fear punitive legislation. They have enlisted in the crusade to ensure that it does not become militant and effective.

And the corollary of this analysis is that the democratic Left must have its own, quite distinctive program to save the environment. It must educate and organize around the proposition that the issue is political and conflict-laden and demands an assertion of social priorities

332

in air and water which will override an entrenched private interest in their abuse.

One must thus prepare for vigorous contention for a simple reason. Ending pollution raises the most explosive of political questions: who pays?

For we have now recognized that the failure of the market system is basic to our current environmental crisis. Air and water were considered to be "free" resources. Therefore, a corporation that would invest enormous amounts of time and money in figuring out how to economize the costs of labor and capital did not give a second thought to using and destroying rivers, lakes, and the atmosphere. The social costs of this pricing system, with its positive incentives for pollution, have now become intolerable, so we are going to decide, in one way or another, to charge for the environment. As Richard Nixon has said, "We can no longer afford to consider air and water common property, free to be abused by anyone without regard to the consequences."

But whenever society determines that it is going to put a price tag on resources that were, up to yesterday, "free," there is an enormous potential for conflict. Moreover, although Mr. Nixon accurately stated the generality, he ignored some of the outstanding specifics. For the corporations that most notably squandered our "common property" of air and water are the largest in the land: pollution tends to grow along with economies of scale. So the industries that must now be forced to change their conduct, or else pay for it, include auto, oil, airlines, utilities, and other giant types of enterprise.

And the recent past provides ample proof that these corporations will not passively submit to a reduction in their profit margins or restrictions on their operations. In his message on the environment President Nixon had to falsify history to evade this reality.

On January 30, 1967, Lyndon Johnson sent Congress his message on "Protecting Our National Heritage." "It is in private laboratories," the President said, "and in private board rooms that the crucial decisions on new fuels, new control of technology, and new means of developing power and locomotion will be made. We should support private efforts now to expand the range of their alternatives and make wiser choices possible." But on the very day that Mr. Johnson was thus engaging in his consensus rhetoric, the *New York Times* reported that Arjay Miller, the president of the Ford Company, was warning of the "threat of over-regulation by government" with regard to pollution. And the *Wall Street Journal* Washington office commented on the Johnson plan, "Business concerns, which have favored state control of anti-pollution programs, will probably fight hard against the proposal."

When Lyndon Johnson finally did sign the Air Quality Act of 1967, he pretended that he had won a great victory: "new power to stop pollution before it chokes our children and strangles our elderly —before it drives us indoors or into the hospital." The *Wall Street Journal* was, once again, more realistic about the law: "This was a major victory for such industrial groups as the coal producers, who vigorously opposed toughening Federal standards."

In his environment message in 1970, Nixon confirmed that the *Wall Street Journal* was right and Johnson wrong. For, as he documented, the "new powers" granted in 1967 had not even slowed down the crisis. But it would not do for an optimistic, preachy Republican President to admit the cause of this failure—that the very corporations to which he was now appealing had subverted the 1967 legislation. So he rewrote history: "Quite inadvertently, by ignoring environmental cost we have given an economic advantage to the careless polluter over his more conscientious rival." That "inadvertence," in point of fact, had been carefully lobbied through Congress by the big polluters and they had prevailed over the wishes of the President of the United States.

But why, then, are the corporations cooperating now? An analogy to auto safety is helpful in understanding this development. Before Ralph Nader had awakened a national constituency and created enormous political pressure for new safety legislation, the auto giants tried to ridicule his charges and, for that matter, to conduct a private investigation of him in order to smear him, blackmail him, or both. But, once Nader's crusade had succeeded, Detroit tried to head off the reform movement at the pass by proposing its safety program and ultimately by proudly advertising the devices which they had been forced to install at political gunpoint.

Today, I am suggesting, the polluting corporations are making a similar tactical retreat: the 1967 strategy of vetoing effective legislation will no longer work; so the new emphasis is to be on making sure that the public, rather than the guilty companies, will pay the bill for cleaning up the environment.

General Motors has already announced that antipollution features in its cars will raise prices by $100. And in the February 1970 issue of *Fortune,* Max Ways quotes Henry Ford as proposing that the government spend money to generate a private, market demand for innovations in protecting the environment. These attitudes account for an interesting phenomenon on the stock market which the *Wall Street Journal* reported on February 3, 1970: in the midst of a bear market, the "ecological" stocks are bullish. If the speculators are right, there is going to be a new, multi-billion-dollar environment industry and filthy air and water will yield a profit.

This approach solves the question of who pays. The consumer is indirectly taxed by the corporation that passes on to him the cost of any government regulations. But there is an even more audacious proposal for seeing to it that the public supports the polluters. When *Fortune* magazine queried some of the most important executives in the nation on how to deal with the environmental crisis, the strategy favored by most of them (57 percent) was for the government to give industry a tax cut so that it could finance antipollution devices. This would mean that the biggest polluters, with the greatest problems, would get the largest subsidies. It would, in effect, reward those who have befouled the atmosphere. And it would, like all other tax expenditures for the private sector, take money away from social uses.

Ecology, then, is a highly political issue. And that is why we need a distinctive program aimed at charging the polluters, rather than the people, for the cost of cleaning up the environment and at relating the solution of this new problem to our older concerns with social needs. Above all the environmental campaign must not become an escape from the domestic priorities which we have identified, but not observed, in recent years.

First of all, the attempt to reclaim our air and water emphasizes the need for comprehensive planning.

In his message on the environment, President Nixon evoked an imminent apocalypse: "Based on present trends, it is quite possible that by 1980 the increase in the sheer number of cars in densely populated areas will begin outrunning the technological limits of our capacity to reduce pollution from the internal combustion engine." That is a clear warning of impending social doom. But, in the budget, the very same President Nixon, after the usual generalities, assigned mass transit 6 percent of the money he is spending on highways. Yet it is obvious that by reducing the "sheer number" of cars by providing new, pollution-free public transit one could take a major step toward dealing with suffocation in 1980. But Mr. Nixon, for all his talk, is actually putting the power of the federal government behind increasing auto congestion with all its fumes.

Here again, if Mr. Nixon observed the logic of his own priorities, he would have to challenge some of the wealthiest vested interests in the nation—that is, the auto-oil-construction alliance for paving the country. Indeed, the *Wall Street Journal* has already warned the President that an attempt to produce an alternative to the internal combustion engine might lead to the "severe disruption of the nation's largest industries." Here, as in the case of most of the other crucial areas of American life, only a political movement based on a noncorporate and radical majority can put forth the solutions we need.

Second, the cost of fighting pollution must be charged to the polluters. And that means some price and profit controls.

If the funds for cleaning up the environment are not to be reflected in higher prices, steps will have to be taken so that industry cannot simply send the bill to the consumer. But then this is only one more case in which the right of huge corporations to follow a pricing policy without any social considerations has to be challenged. And that is precisely what Richard Nixon, with his ideological commitments to the values of the Old Economics, will not do. Under Kennedy-Johnson there were at least attempts to "jawbone" over prices and wages, and sometimes, as in John Kennedy's famous confrontation with the steel companies, the policy worked.

But Mr. Nixon—as a good Republican—is keeping his hands off. The London *Economist*—hardly a radical periodical—commented at the end of January on one consequence of this policy: "With its usual lack of political sense the American steel industry, presumably managed almost entirely by Republicans, is celebrating a new year with yet another price increase." In the ten (mainly Democratic) years between 1959 and 1969, the *Economist* noted, steel prices were up by 6 percent; in the first twelve months of Richard Nixon they soared by 7 percent. And yet, in February 1970 the United States Steel Corporation explained that it was too poor to afford anti-pollution devices at its Duluth, Minnesota, plant.

This clearly will not do. As part of a general policy which insists that all major pricing decisions of large corporations be subject to public debate and that all the necessary data be made a matter of public record, the democratic Left should demand a policing of the price and profit policies of the major polluters. Only in this way can we see to it that corporate wealth pays for the profitable damage it has already done and be given an expensive reason to behave differently in the future.

Third, the details of the Nixon program must be read carefully by experts with a social conscience. For there is already evidence that the President, for all his bold slogans, announced a resolute march to the rear in his pollution message.

As E. W. Kenworthy pointed out in the *New York Times,* Mr. Nixon suggests a "fair allocation of the total capacity of the waterways to absorb the user's particular kind of waste without becoming polluted." This, Kenworthy continued, is a statement of the doctrine of "assimilative capacity"—that is, one pollutes the water up to a safe limit. It is in contradiction to the present principle of "beneficial use," which states that one actually takes a positive view toward the value of the water. Under the Nixon refinement it may even be possible for industries to pollute waters that are now clean. After all, they have not been fouled up to their "assimilative capacity."

This point has larger implications. The Nixon philosophy is that the government should play an essentially negative, limiting role vis-à-vis the private sector. But, in the case of water and in the area of the other profound social consequences of private investment, that is not enough. A technological innovation—the supersonic transport, for instance—affects many crucial areas of social life; it causes pollution by fumes and by noise, it leads to airport congestion; it requires public moneys for highways to carry traffic to and from the planes, and so on. Therefore the major programs of all corporations should be tested for social consequences by an independent public agency. If we do not allow drug manufacturers to market a new product without first checking on its effect on health, we can no longer allow other industries unilaterally to impose their priorities on the nation. And "beneficial use" should be the criterion, not just for water but for technology in general.

Finally, we cannot allow the environment to become a substitute for the struggle against poverty and urban blight. It must be an aid to it.

Mr. Nixon has been very bold in attacking the unions with the Philadelphia Plan (by following fiscal and governmental policies which cut back on construction at the same time he imposes a racial quota on the building industry, he makes a black-white struggle for scarce jobs inevitable—but then maybe that's precisely what he wants, for it splits the two most effective components of the opposition). And he is willing to pay a premium to car makers who come up with pollution-free autos. But the democratic Left must insist that this entire new effort require that the burgeoning antipollution industry hire the unemployed and underemployed poor with special emphasis on the minorities, and that the location of facilities take social as well as economic considerations into account.

We have already discovered through the "new careers" program that poor people can make effective contributions to the economy without a great deal of expensive training, so long as jobs are designed for them (rather, so to speak, than "designing" them for the jobs). If there is now going to be a vanguard industry which does not have a vested interest in the old ways, it provides a marvelous opportunity to redeem some of our promises to the poor, the blacks, and the Spanish-speaking—and to do so by giving the entire society a better place to live. In other words, we must be concerned about the social effect of fighting pollution and not just about technology.

But to carry out this program will require political conflict. For recent experience and the present attitudes of the corporate sector show that it wants to deal with the environment in a conservative way which will yield a profit to those who created the problem in the first place. It is therefore quite wrong to think that all of us men of good will are going to get together and clean up our common air and water. We are going to have to prepare for vigorous conflict if this new crusade is actually going to achieve its goals and, in the process, benefit the entire society and not just the polluters.

Richard Robbins

Perishable Good: Social Ferment
in the American Religious World

Falling into decades—it is a modest version of the archaic practice in European elementary schools of dividing great epochs into convenient categories: the Middle Ages came to an end and then began the Renaissance. In reality, history moves in uneven waves, not by the clock. Yet it is roughly true that the new engagement of American religion with pressing political, economic, and social issues stems from developments that happened to move to a time frame of every-ten-years. To chart the proximate future of our religious social conscience as the seventies unfold, we need to understand that "the will to enter the social arena in force" as Daniel Callahan calls it, the religious impulse to lean more directly on secular institutions in pursuit of social justice and a decent society, was in retreat during the fifties and came to full, if chaotic, expression during the sixties. Nor will it be muted in the seventies.

The principal themes remain what they have been—peace, racial justice, the reduction of poverty, the break-out from worn-out bureaucratic structures (churches included). But the new exuberant commitment, the flood of proposals, programs, and sometimes simply cries of anguish, the "bearing witness" on religion and social activism requires sober analysis even at the risk of being considered morally insensitive. For the alternative—an uncritical blessing of the present religious ferment as good because it is godly or right because it is activist—can mean a repetition of many of the frustrations that eventually undermined the achievements of the predecessor movement

339

of the thirties and forties, the Social Gospel of the Protestants, the Social Action coalitions among Catholics, the Jewish liberalism of the synagogues and secular councils. We owe a debt, even now, to those Catholic critics of that time—Monsignor John Ryan, Dorothy Day, Bishop Sheil, John LaFarge, Paul Furfey, the editors of *Commonweal*—whose views ranged from New Deal liberalism to communitarian-pacifist socialism. All the same, there were limits then, there are limits now.[1] Moral integrity, passion for justice, bearing witness—these count enormously. Yet these characteristics are, at maximum, preconditions for turning the *secular* society around. Put more positively, ethical engagement and prophetic judgment have nothing taken away from them when they are necessarily worked into complex and flexible strategies to shake loose new public policies. Indeed, moral stance on social issues gains from the association with the "tainted" world; morality is prevented from turning into moralizing, righteousness into self-righteousness. The Christianity represented by those two remarkable secular-religious socialists A. J. Muste and Norman Thomas is eloquent evidence of what I mean.

If the religious commitment is vital to, it can never be a full expression of, the political and social order. Its social end is a powerful strengthening of community, achieved broadly with agnostics and atheists, which *then* may be directed from general-theological to specific-political strategies. To seek to fit human action too tightly to the measure of transcendent values is to court that very moral absolutism against which one protests so vehemently in the secular world. As James Finn remarks, "Those who once were tempted to theologize all life are now, apparently, tempted to politicize all life." True enough. Still, on balance, the reappearance of Social Gospel and Social Action, in new and more radical form, is more than welcome. It *is* new; it is no transient thing; it should flourish in the seventies, insistent but not absolutist.

Insistent but not absolutist because religion is no longer, if it ever was, at war with secular society. It has a central place but not a dominant role in the contemporary world. Early Marxism grossly misunderstood the "opiate of the people" by identifying too closely the religious impulse with the power structure of churches. The same

1. See Edward A. Marciniak, "Catholic Social Action: Where Do We Go From Here?" *America,* December 12, 1970.

mistake is not likely to be made again. On the other hand, contrary to the dream of the Social Gospel reformers, religiously based social movements are not prime movers. The religious groups speak *to* power, seek to constrain power, but do not take power. When the secular institutions falter, religious conscience gets blocked off. Or gets itself co-opted by a political leadership ready to invoke the cant of "moral leadership" and "spiritual values" whenever convenient.

All this becomes apparent in a glance at the past twenty years. In the fifties, the American celebration ignored urgent problems pushed aside by World War II, most notably racial discrimination and the failure to extend equality to millions below the poverty line. This slackness in national purpose was echoed in the religious milieu—a muddled religiosity at the top, an ambiguous "revival of religion" out in the growing suburbs. President Eisenhower said it did not matter what faith you had as long as you had one. But this essentially decent man temporized endlessly on racial desegregation of the schools until finally his hand was forced at Little Rock. His secretary of state, John Foster Dulles, a force in the Episcopal church, applied a general religiosity to foreign affairs, as if "the crusade against Communism," through a chain of military pacts around the world, could shore up the faithful against godless evil overseas.

With a few outstanding exceptions, the churches abdicated on the McCarthy threat to civil liberties; on commitment to the awakening minorities; on moral support for the nuclear disarmament campaigns. The moderately liberal National Council of Churches beat off incessant attacks from the Right; so did the World Council. The religiously oriented pacifist groups, the Fellowship of Reconciliation (FOR) and the Catholic peace associations, were as voices in the wilderness. Yet, flat as the fifties may now seem, there were also signs and portents —falling into decades will not quite work. The most important sign was Martin Luther King's Southern Christian Leadership Conference (SCLC), which forged the strategy of nonviolent direct action against racial oppression in the South. Gandhi, Thoreau, and Christian forbearance were joined to militant tactics of civil disobedience capable of attracting the religious and the secular alike. The civil rights movement, organized by young black ministers and black and white students, brought just that moral "leaning" against the racist legal and political structure which enabled the courts and Congress finally to act. By the end of the sixties the civil rights coalition had come apart; but for a brief time a new Social Gospel changed us all. Religion was not completely walled off.

Not surprisingly, the book for the times was Will Herberg's *Protestant, Catholic, Jew*.[2] As far as he advanced the sociological thesis that "the triple melting pot"—the achievement of a religious pluralism from the assimilation of the "new" and mainly Catholic and Jewish immigrants—would open the way to social mobility and an erosion of religious bigotry, Herberg was on firm ground. But when he fashioned the doctrine that the American Way of Life represented the faith of all the people, he only succeeded in creating a thin theological cover for the American celebration. "This secularism of a religious people, this religiousness in a secularist framework," could scarcely provide a motive force for the social conscience of the churches. Instead, religious critics were more inclined to preoccupy themselves with problems of the middle class—"identity," "anxiety," "mass culture"—which cast a troubling shadow over the successful American Way of Life. Herberg did not have in mind what Robert Bellah would later term "the civil religion," the broadly ethical character of the American historical experience, with all its virtues and dangers.[3] His intent was to pronounce religion fit and prospering under the canopy of the American Way of Life, whatever reservations one might have about the foolishness of "the power of positive thinking" or the amiable nonsense of Dial-a-Prayer.

In the sixties that canopy cracked open. The symbolic point of departure, John Kennedy's election as the first Catholic President, was an appropriate coda to Herberg's theme. Thereafter came the

2. Will Herberg, *Protestant, Catholic, Jew* (New York: Doubleday Anchor, rev. ed., 1960).

3. See Robert Bellah, "Civil Religion in America," *Daedalus*, Winter 1967. Involved here is not the worship of the American way of life but "an understanding of the American experience in the light of ultimate and universal reality." I find its expression, for example, in Gunnar Myrdal's now-classic work on the moral ambivalence of white Americans, committed to the value of equality of opportunity and at the same time tenaciously defending a system of devastating racial discrimination. *An American Dilemma* (New York: Harper & Brothers, 1944).

American Disarray of Life, the successive deepening of conflicts in our secular society. It is enough to say that the piling-up of social troubles, especially the war in Vietnam, brought large numbers of clerics into the social arena to denounce, march, organize. And the social crisis, together with the impetus of Vatican II and Pope John, produced a storm of criticism against the church structures themselves. Everything—from theology, liturgy, professional training within the churches, to the secular institutions—would have to be re-examined. This radical change in American religious life constitutes a far more significant event than the "revival of religion" in the fifties. Moreover, the renewal of socially relevant religion was accompanied by a new interest in the relationship of the American religious community to comparable institutions abroad. For Protestants this meant interpretation of radical theology in Europe; for Catholics study of the repercussions of Vatican II; for Jews solidification of the bond with the state of Israel and holocaust dead.

Whatever the validity of the argument that upheaval is bound to be followed by quietism, I foresee more of the same intense social involvement of religious groups during the seventies. Yet we must remember to acknowledge that from the fifties down to the present time *a very large segment, perhaps a majority of the regular church-goers, have been relatively indifferent to and in some cases (mainly Southern Baptists and fundamentalists) actively hostile to "religious liberals."* Once acknowledged, however, this conservative constant should be viewed as a screen against which the smaller, but much more articulate change groups carry on their work.

If the new activism is indeed durable and fairly deep, there ought to occur a falling-off of interest in the religious fads so intriguing to the mass media: the folk-rock mass, the "new breed" of "swinging" young clerics, the priests who leave the Church to marry and "tell their story," the little communes with their patchwork religions— part borrowed Eastern mysticism, part return-to-the-land, part spirit of Woodstock. (On the last point, Margaret Mead is right to argue that the emptiness of the suburban religious revival of the fifties is no reason automatically to delight in the antistructure religious revival of the children of the fifties. She sees the fringe youth groups of the counterculture creating a "mishmash religion." "Young people want to build a new religious movement but they lack the liturgy, poetry, imagery of the historical church.")

For the coming decade there would appear to be at least six central issues, likely even to be with us by 1980. These are:

the continuation of a heightened interest in "radical theology," not so much as abstract argument but as a challenge to theology to speak more directly to the human condition and to enter into philosophical combat with church authority over received theological wisdom; *the willingness of some religious groups to resist at least their own secular states on the issue of war and peace,* with strategy ranging from limited institutionalized "leaning" to massive nonviolent resistance, civil disobedience, and a religious nonviolent "underground revolution";

a more direct commitment to the struggle against the linked problems of racial injustice and poverty, though again it is inconceivable that the religious impulse can be decisive in this area, however powerful the role of the Catholic bishops in helping to sustain the strike of the grape workers in California;

a much firmer consensus on the need for liberalization of laws and practices where "morality" is entwined with family-social relationships;

more insistent reform of church structure itself, especially in Roman Catholicism;

and finally, a rising "spirituality" (for want of a better word) in the American working class and lower middle class, stemming from a sense of loss, of alienation from traditional secular institutions, which no longer seem to sustain traditional values.

The Theological Firmament

What we see in all three faiths, especially Catholicism, is a generalized theological skepticism. The intellectual roots are largely European—the mystical and social thought among French thinkers as diverse as Teilhard de Chardin, Yves Congar, and François Mauriac; the arresting theological argument of a "German school" of Catholics, perhaps best represented by Hans Kung and Karl Rahner; the new Protestant theology centering on a "secular interpretation" and "demythologizing" of religion, which owes a great deal to Dietrich Bonhoeffer and is in some respects transported to America in the work of Harvey Cox and a number of our "death of God" theologians.[4] Jews have had less reason to be involved since "secularizing" Judaism or redefining the tradition has been going on for a long time.

This "radical turn" in theology matters to our discussion of religious social protest insofar as it comes to bear directly on social structure. There is in fact a correspondence between general theological restlessness and specific social movements. For the theologians find themselves compelled to rework their ideas in order to provide a religious rationale for proposed social changes such as might come about anyway for strictly historical reasons. In Roman Catholicism, to take a clear example, such matters as priestly celibacy, the doctrine of the Pope's infallibility, the justification for birth control or abortion, the

---

4. There is a voluminous new literature, extremely variable in depth and in applicability to social action. See Sydney E. Ahlstrom's synoptic essay "The Radical Turn in Theology and Ethics," in J. Gustafson, ed., "The Sixties: Radical Change in American Religion," *The Annals,* January 1970. On the French development, there is a useful, if uneven book: Jean-Marie Domenach and Robert de Montvalon, *The Catholic Avant Garde: French Catholicism Since World War II* (New York: Holt, Rinehart & Winston, 1967). In the European Protestant context see Dietrich Bonhoeffer, *Letters and Papers from Prison* (New York: Macmillan, 1953), which has had more of a direct bearing on social action than the work of Barth, Bultmann, and others whose theology is radical in the technical sense. See also, Karl Rahner, *Theology for Renewal: Bishops, Priests, Laity* (New York: Sheed & Ward, 1965): Hans Kung, *The Church* (New York: Sheed & Ward, 1967). Kung's effort to challenge papal infallibility in *Infallible: An Inquiry* (New York: Doubleday, 1971) is a classic instance of the new interplay between theology and the demand for structural change in the Church. For the situation in American society see, e.g., Michael Novak, *The Open Church* (New York: Macmillan, 1962). On the Protestants in American society, see Martin Marty, *The Second Chance for American Protestants* (New York: Harper & Row, 1963) and Harvey Cox, *The Secular City* (New York: Macmillan, rev. ed., 1966), especially Chapters 5 and 6. Cox now concedes that he may have overestimated the commitment of urban-age man to secular-religious social change and may have underestimated the much deeper spiritual longing for a joyous celebration of life. He now argues that the political radicals and the neo-mystics are equally valuable, but I think he was right the first time out. In any event, *The Secular City* was of great importance to general readers who were not able to see previously how a new theology and the urban crisis could be got together. It spoke directly to the American social conscience. In contrast, "death of God" theology aroused brief, intense debate yet never really left a social imprint. See Thomas J. Altizer and William Hamilton, *Radical Theology and the Death of God* (Indianapolis: Bobbs-Merrill, 1966), the most thorough of a score of books on this subject.

question of collegiality in the definition of the hierarchical system, the accommodation of Christianity to Marxism—such matters are bound to be resolved as much by social conflict within the Church as by the "correctness" of doctrine. Nevertheless, theological ratification is required, whatever the outcome of the clash between "conservatives" and "liberals" within church structure. Theology is thereby drawn into the day-to-day process of change initiated by Vatican II. Further, the sense in the congregations that "eternal truths" are being reconsidered reinforces a general conviction that *anything* is subject to drastic change. To be sure, it is possible for an Ivan Illich to be a theological conservative and a proponent of radical social change, but now that matters less than one might suppose, since the Church would be concerned more with his challenge to its authority structure than with his precise religious beliefs.[5]

For the first time, theology is part of a social ferment instead of a remote, unchanging guardian of eternal truth. I am oversimplifying an extremely complex issue, but it seems incontestable that the consequences of the new theology in Roman Catholicism are favorable to a more wide-ranging, liberalized Catholic social action. It is no longer necessary, for example, for Catholics to tug and haul at "just war" doctrine to express their witness against the war in Vietnam: the war is immoral and un-Christian, and broad theological warrant exists for saying so. So, too, with other problems.

War, the Peace Movement, and the Churches

As nothing else, the war in Vietnam has brought together the leadership of the liberal denominations in opposition. Only some con-

5. It is not surprising that Latin America should show us the priority of a radical critique of an exploitative society and a rigid church hierarchy over a radical critique of Catholic theology. Ivan Illich in Mexico, Dom Helder Câmara in Brazil, are perhaps the two most prominent Catholic critics holding this view. Illich expresses this when he advocates resistance to Church authoritarianism (he has relinquished priestly duties) and advances a program of many-sided social changes (at his CIDOC center in Mexico) but, at the same time warns against a too-easy invocation of God in man's community— "*N'employez pas son nom.*" See Peter Schrag, "Ivan Illich: The Christian as Rebel," *Saturday Review*, July 19, 1969. The same kind of radical humanism informs the work of the Bishop of Recife; see José de Broucker, *The Violence of a Peacemaker; Dom Helder Camâra* (New York: Orbis, 1970).

servative subgroups among Catholics and the Protestant fundamentalists support the war explicitly. The powerful Southern Baptists remain officially neutral but their silence is significant since ordinarily *any* war calls out from this largest Protestant group a patriotic reflex. No one should suppose antiwar declarations in religious national publications are a precise index of sentiment in the congregations. Yet it is clear that moral revulsion against the war has cut deeply into the traditional religious groups' posture of "going along" with the state . . . the things that are Caesar's and the things that are God's. This change, modest as it may be, is unprecedented in our recent history.

Clergy and Laymen Concerned About Vietnam (CLCAV), formed in 1965, remains the organizational focus of the liberal antiwar effort, constantly prodding both the government and the more cautious groups within its own constituency. Its documentation of systematic and deliberate atrocities long preceded the My Lai revelations. Its achievement is especially impressive in the light of extensive research showing that local Protestant clergymen involved in protest movements are likely to encounter strong resistance in their own congregations.[6] CLCAV, although a comparatively small organization, has made religious antiwar protest normative and respectable.

The radical and pacifist religious minority finds CLCAV inadequate. An expansion of religious conscientious objection, in the tradition of the Quakers, does not strike it as sufficient either. It calls for civil disobedience, in the name of a "higher law" invoked as a last resort. In this tradition a man *must* break an unjust law, the military draft system, because he can do no other. The invasion of draft offices, the destruction of federal property, the public burning of draft files—all this does not equate with violence; it is "symbolic speech," for napalm is used to light the fire; and then one calmly awaits arrest and trial. The plea to the judge is that there may be a narrow "guilt" but that these men and women are in the deepest sense innocent; the true crime is in Vietnam. The jury, even in the face of the admitted fact, could thus find them "not guilty," the judge could

6. Jeffrey K. Hadden, *The Gathering Storm in the Churches* (New York: Doubleday, 1969). The primary gap is between conservative laity and liberal clergy. But Hadden notes another gap, between theology and liberal religious social activism; ministers become active in a cause without trying to work out a consistent, yet flexible, ethical position about society. As a result they may rush, ad hoc, from one social commitment to another.

then set them free, and the President would pardon them as they would pardon him. So conceived, religious conscience is expressed, witness is borne, prison accepted. In this I fail to see any moral arrogance or self-righteousness. God's law prevails symbolically while human law is not denied in the specific event.

It is the Catholic radical pacifists in the antiwar movement, clerical and lay men and women, who have most eloquently stood conscience for the rest of us in this way—the Catonsville Nine, the Milwaukee Fourteen, the Chicago Fifteen. The best-known Catholic leaders in the movement, Fathers Philip and Daniel Berrigan, were sentenced with others to prison in 1970 for their part in the burning of the draft files at Catonsville, Maryland, in 1968. It seems to me inconceivable that they engaged, as charged, in the further step of a "conspiracy" to plot violent destruction.

But, taken in its own terms, apart from the outrage of the government's attempt to use charges of "conspiracy" for political repression, there is a point beyond which religious civil disobedience can become self-defeating. The courage and spiritual grace of Father Daniel Berrigan can only command admiration. That does not mean, however, that politically he is right. For unless the society, whatever its grievous faults, is on the threshold of totalitarianism—and it is not—civil disobedience must function on the premise of the legitimacy of the social order, however unjust the draft law or the war. Father Berrigan, Howard Zinn, and others do not agree. They argue that because of the crimes perpetrated by civil government against the Vietnamese abroad and the poor and blacks at home, legitimacy has been forfeited. Why, then, play into the hands of illegitimate authority by quietly inviting arrest and certain conviction? Why not, instead, work to create a nonviolent "revolutionary" underground capable of a real defiance of civil authority gone mad? It is on these grounds that Father Berrigan delayed his inevitable imprisonment by going underground after his conviction—and passed a point of no return.

It is painful but necessary to assert, in the face of Father Berrigan's courage, that this form of religious protest does not work, does not advance the antiwar movement, and simply shifts public attention from the principle of civil disobedience to the story of the chase: when would Father Berrigan be caught? His willingness to suffer further pain does not change the fact that individual religious witness can be translated into an effective social movement only if the secular political order is so overwhelmingly repressive that an organized "underground society" must be developed. That time is not now, or rather not yet, in American society, and so religious civil disobedience must remain an act of individual witness, a just act still subject to unjust law.[7]

In any case, the involvement of both liberal clergy and radical, principally Catholic, pacifists in the antiwar movement points up two somewhat contradictory consequences for the peace movement. Remarkably, the way has been cleared for religious groups to denounce, and even defy, *their own government's* engagement in war, not just the enemy's. But at best the religious conscience can play only an auxiliary role in the organization of a secular antiwar coalition, a role profoundly important but not decisive. To so conclude in no way diminishes either the liberal religious peace movement or the heroism of the Berrigans.

Race, Class, Poverty: The Religious Commitment

The rigid segregationism of the Southern Baptists apart, the major faiths had declared forcefully in the fifties against racism as a direct contradiction of the Judeo-Christian ethic. The Catholic Interracial Councils and the Jewish human relations organizations in particular had worked to translate ethic into action. Yet much remained lip service, not simply because "eleven o'clock on Sunday was still the most segregated hour in America," but because the institutional churches drew back from directly challenging the secular system on

7. The most eloquent case for the opposite view, that the burning of the children in Vietnam, the *real* crime, makes imperative the creation of an underground community of "spiritual criminals," has been stated by Father Berrigan himself. See Daniel Berrigan, *The Trial of the Catonsville Nine* (Boston: Beacon Press, 1970). Most Catholic liberal and radical social activists fully support the bearing witness at Catonsville but are troubled by overtones of moralism and a refusal to communicate with the community, an imperfect community of imperfect men. Gordon Zahn, whose important work on the failure of the Catholic church to confront the Nazi evil in Germany provided part of the intellectual capital on which the Berrigans drew directly, has expressed these and other reservations in "The Berrigans: Radical Activism Personified," *Catholic World,* December 1970. A generally sympathetic and understanding view, but with some criticisms, is contained in the symposium "The Burden of the Berrigans," *Holy Cross Quarterly,* January 1971.

such matters as discrimination in housing. Through the late sixties, however, the civil rights crisis compelled a stronger social activism. The familiar lines of strategy unfolded; the liberal religious establishment worked with secular interest groups in political strategy, which produced the Civil Rights Acts of 1964 and 1965, while the more militant blacks and whites, especially the young, joined the Freedom Rides and voter-registration campaigns. With the wisdom of hindsight, it is now commonplace to fault nonviolent direct action as outmoded, a sop to Christian conscience rather than a meaningful strategy against institutional racism. Perhaps so. Yet those clergymen, black and white, who fought the battle in the rural South and the urban North, were not simply establishing their credentials ("I was at Selma"). And in spite of the opportunism and intramural conflict in the religious civil rights movement of the sixties, there took place at the least that effort to direct conscience into the social arena which is the test of commitment.

But the seventies will be different. A more militant black community will be less concerned with the idea of civil rights and integration, more with the practice of community power and white commitment to support black organized movements. On the white side, then, support, and where possible coalition; on the black, consolidation of political power, community organization, cultural expression. In the religious sphere a dual effort will continue: black caucuses seeking more than token representation in the major denominations, and the growth of both traditional Negro denominations and new separatist black religious groups. Even a new "black theology" is taking shape. The black religious community will share with the secular a pride and solidarity in black life, a refusal to acquiesce in paternalistic white direction.

And yet . . . in the area of religious social action, as in its secular counterpart, we have been caught in an excessive preoccupation with the immediate and novel. The new black community movement invites illusions on both sides. The gravity of the racial crisis, the despair about the ghettos, and the conviction that the U.S. government will not listen—these have led *some* younger blacks to place too much faith in militant splinter groups that claim to speak for the entire black community. On the white side, young ministers and priests, excluded from an interracial movement by black separatism and burdened with "white guilt," have tended also to lose critical judgment about what is central and what peripheral in secular society. The result is a romanticism about black power among the white religious radicals, a disposition to endorse the Black Panthers, for example, as if the Panthers *were* the black community, instead of one, somewhat unstable element within it. A counterpart illusion in the black radical camp is that the mainstream churches can be compelled to pay hundreds of millions of dollars into black community projects as "reparations" for three hundred years of repression. James Forman, previously a leader in SNCC, introduced this strategy toward the end of the sixties with the celebrated disruption of a Sunday service at Riverside Church in New York City. In the wake of other such confrontations, a number of national denominations established funds to channel to black communities. Here, I think, is an example of religious conscience misdirected.

The real "lean" of the churches on secular economic institutions lies in the relationship of the organized churches to the big corporations, not in the pressure of the protest groups on the religious congregations. In the former, churches can exert pressure on governing policy, on corporate investment in South Africa, for example, through the use of blocks of shares. But, in the latter, the money raised is altogether insufficient to initiate any significant economic change in the black community, and demands for much larger amounts succeed principally in producing bitter conflict between national church headquarters and local denominations. Once the "conscience money" is granted, confusion and uncertainty ensue. Among the Unitarian-Universalists, in fact, two rival groups, one integrated and one all-black, battled to an impasse for control of the appropriated half-million dollars.

It seems likely, as the seventies proceed, that white radical romanticism among the younger religious people will give way to more solidly grounded white-black cooperation within a structure loose enough to assure black solidarity and pride. How the liberal religious groups, left groping after the decline of the civil rights coalition, will be fitted into the new political and economic coalitions necessary to a more insistent attack on racial justice I do not know. Probably, at the minimum, it will come to whites not intervening in the rising self-assertion of the black community but instead intervening much more strongly in public conflicts over employment, housing, corporate, and trade union policy.

Because the antipoverty question applies to more whites than blacks (although nonwhite minorities are disproportionately represented), we shall see an intensified participation of religious activists in local and regional programs. Once again, the resources for an actual war on poverty can be located only in secular society, in the federal government. But in this instance the religious auxiliary role can be maintained more forcefully. I have mentioned the intervention of the Catholic bishops in behalf of chicano grape workers; Cesar Chavez's Catholicism is as integral to the primary secular work of trade union organization as was Martin Luther King's Christian doctrine of nonviolent action to his assault on secular racism. A striking number of younger white ministers and priests have chosen to live in central city neighborhoods, only loosely attached to official church bureaucracies and devoting their principal energies to community action groups in the poverty neighborhoods. In the black community a new tough-minded approach of younger clergy, better adapted to the conditions of Northern urban life, is taking hold. The new leader is Jesse Jackson. But in the last analysis, in the absence of a national program of guaranteed employment and income maintenance, the funding of relatively modest projects in urban neighborhoods is about all that religious groups can do in respect to poverty.

Family-Social Relationships and the "New Morality"

Controversy over family relationships, sexual patterns, the position of women, the life style of the young, comes directly within the province of the churches as moral guardians. Power is not so central here. Further, the development of a "situational ethics" and a "new morality" by the religious intellectuals, though largely unknown to the regular parishioners, has had a liberating effect on a whole range of social and sexual norms.[8] As this continues in the seventies we may also expect a "moral backlash" from millions of conservative Christians.

The transition is readily measured in the religious accommodation

8. See Joseph Fletcher, *Situation Ethics: The New Morality* (Philadelphia: Westminster Press, 1966).

to divorce, family planning, and birth control. (Pope Paul to the contrary, it must simply be a matter of time before Catholic doctrine will find a theologically adequate sanction for artificial contraception. Great numbers of Catholic women defy the ban, and they are supported by younger priests.) Premarital sexuality, sexual deviance, freedom of information in sexual matters, sex education—on these matters the liberal and moderate church groups are saying that it is the relationship which counts ethically, and thus traditional judgments must be set aside.

Abortion is more complex and troubling. While many Protestant clergymen continue to support abortion reform, the religious community is split. "Situational ethics" are not so easy to apply to the question of when the fetus becomes "life." The Catholic Church's official position is implacable opposition to "human barbarism." A striking number of the Catholic liberals and radicals who have pressed for change in other areas draw the line at abortion, or at least argue for a more complex approach than "total freedom of the woman to do whatever she wishes with her own body."[9] The conservative Protestant denominations hold fast to a view of abortion as another index of sexual license. In such cases, where a religious social consensus is not developing rapidly enough, the issue is likely to be resolved pragmatically in the secular society, through liberalization of restrictive laws in state legislatures.

Abortion reform is but one aspect of the general revolt of women, protesting second-class citizenship. And the parallel between racial and sexual discrimination has a special relevance for the churches and synagogues. Racism in the Mormon church is echoed by sexism in the Catholic church, as Mary Daly, Sally Cunneen, Sidney Callahan, and other Catholic women writers have made clear.[10] A first step is full ordainment of women clergy; the Lutherans have already done so, the Episcopalians are on the threshold, the first woman

9. The most thoughtful Catholic analysis, favorable to liberalization of abortion law but with careful attention to the need for ethical safeguards, is Daniel Callahan's *Abortion: Law, Choice, and Morality* (New York: Macmillan, 1970).

10. Mary Daly, *Church and the Second Sex* (New York: Harper & Row, 1968); Sally S. Cunneen, *Sex: Female, Religion: Catholic* (New York: Holt, Rinehart, & Winston, 1968); Sidney Callahan, *Exiled to Eden: The Christian Experience of Sex* (New York: Sheed & Ward, 1969).

rabbi (Reform) will be ordained in 1972. But that is only the tip of the iceberg. The real conflict has to do with women's objection to an overwhelmingly "masculine" dominance in the theology and structure of the Judeo-Christian system, a dominance in no way controverted by emphasis on the special place of Mary in Catholic doctrine or the special role of women in the Jewish family. Important work can be done here by the women's liberation movement once its worst enemies, its own splinter groups, have been left behind.

Modernization and Reform

To prepare for the future, to close on the problems of war, race, family life in spite of the centrality of secular power, the religious denominations in America will have to make striking internal changes. (Not all of them, to be sure. One of the surprises of the sixties was the great gain of people in the more traditional faiths, some of them fundamentalist. This trend is likely to continue quietly, while the call for drastic innovation receives most of the publicity. Perhaps we have to do here with the commonplace about the intensification of the search for security and simplicity, the greater the unsettling problems in the secular world.)

Under the spur of Vatican II and its own restless, often angry younger religious, the Catholic Church in America is making a historic transition. The Church of the immigrant era, of the hidebound bureaucracy, of the conservative establishment and narrow diocesan outlook, is giving way, often to the shock and dismay of large numbers of working-class and lower-middle-class Catholics. The great tugging and hauling is summarized in an avalanche of books, in the pages of the *National Catholic Reporter* (which is to *Our Sunday Visitor* as night to day or vice versa). Andrew Greeley is the most prominent among a number of Catholic sociologists who think we may be overemphasizing the upheaval and underestimating the continuity; but the weight of evidence seems on the other side. Many of the changes are largely symbolic—the informal dress, the new liturgy, the effort to bring the laity more closely into parish and diocesan decision-making. More of the changes cut deep. National priests' associations of varying degrees of militancy are contesting the dogmatic authority of local bishops who preside over archaic archdioceses.

Initial steps have been taken to change the training of seminarians, to make more open the sisters' orders—indeed in Los Angeles an entire order simply broke away from the Cardinal's authoritarian control and reorganized on its own. Economic pressures apart, parochial education from grade school to Jesuit universities has lost a good deal of its "ghetto" character and tries to compete more evenly with the public sector. If optional celibacy remains unlikely for now, it is likely in the future, notwithstanding the opposition of Pope Paul.

Of course, no social structure turns inside out overnight. The bishops must continue to mediate between Rome and the local parish, responding to those in the new movement who are angry over failure to denounce publicly the My Lai atrocity or cope more fully with racism within the Church itself, responding to those in the parish who see in this ferment the very faith undermined. All in all, however, it is not an exaggeration to say that the *aggiornamento,* at home and abroad in the Catholic world, is perhaps the most significant development in Western religious life in the twentieth century.

American Protestantism is so diverse that generalizations about modernization are risky. On the whole, the liberal and mainstream denominations have moved further away from the conservative groups, especially in the field of social activism. They have also inched along toward a series of structural mergers that will make for a more cohesive, if still pluralistic, Protestant system. In any case the principal lines of conflict and accommodation are more likely to occur *within* denominations, an oncoming generation of clergy and laity against a presiding establishment. In the short run, with politics under Nixon, and with Billy Graham conducting services in the White House, some of the mainstream Protestant groups will slip back into the traditional "neutrality" of acquiescence. But that is probably a temporary stage. We may expect a resurgence of the Social Gospel, directed toward domestic issues once the government is compelled to undertake complete withdrawal from Vietnam. Part of the price will be an excess of anger and a paucity of skill among the younger ministers concerned to overturn policy at once and inclined to substitute zealous moralism for political realism. It is a small price to pay, however, for the renewal of social relevance in American Protestantism.

Jewish life and Judaic religion are the least likely to take a dramatic turn. But not for reasons of political or social conservatism. It is rather that the lines for social action have been established for some time. Only traumatic events, in Israel or in the relationship of the Jewish to the black community, could conceivably shake them. Secular "Jewish liberalism" is on the defensive for the time being in the cities; however, it has in no sense vanished. The revolt of the young against their middle-class parents in the suburbs is, as usual, more intense among Jews than gentiles. A small group of Jewish radicals has permitted itself to be foolishly boxed into a polemical denunciation of "Zionist imperialism," but such New Left ideology has no real entry into American Jewish life. More broadly, Jewish religious life can absorb any "new theology" of the kind proposed by Rabbi Richard Rubenstein and other counterparts of the Protestant "God is dead" school.[11] I do not mean to present a picture of Jewish complacency and middle-class fatigue, although these elements are there. I would only argue realistically that no other formal religion in America has yielded up, with good reason, so much of its force as an agent of social activism to secular society. Opportunity, mobility, social activism, commitment to arts and letters, all were and are expressions of secular Jewish life. In the main, young believing Jews (the Orthodox possibly excepted) will prefer a separation of elements: synagogue worship on Friday night, a strong Jewish-oriented social activism in the secular system, and modernization of traditional synagogal structure hold a relatively low priority.

Of Perishable Good and Tenacious Evil

There is a revival of religion in America that is very different from its shallow predecessor in the fifties. The depth of our social crisis, the feeling of loss, of "alienation" if you like, only underlines the need for a new and as yet unspecified spiritual quest. At this point in our history, the organized churches, for all their soul-searching and

11. Richard Rubenstein, *After Auschwitz* (Indianapolis: Bobbs-Merrill, 1966). However, in the work of Abraham Heschel, Eugene Borowitz, Emil Fackenheim, and others there is a much deeper awareness of the need to advance "beyond secularism." And there are signs of a new pride in Jewishness among the urban young.

self-criticism, do not yet appear to be the form through which such an inchoate if deeply felt malaise can find expression. But we know that in some way a kind of spiritual crisis is affecting us and that, at the least, the institutionalized religions *used to be* the appropriate form for its expression. A return to social action, a renewal of the Social Gospel, can be helpful in this dilemma, but only in a limited way. A much broader analysis, beyond my competence, is needed to establish the dimensions of this stage in the transit of American society. Here it need only be noted.

It is not, I hope, presumptuous to stress finally that in the secular society religious social activism is vulnerable: it lacks coherent power, it is often forced to fall back on moral exhortation, it has great difficulty in coming to grips with a human situation where falling-short and second-best decisions are the norm. Thus it has sometimes been a perishable good. For the seventies, however, the prognosis is rather optimistic. Religious liberalism and radicalism have much "learning" to do, and it is likely to be done.

Lewis Coser

What Do the Poor Need?

(MONEY)

Writing these pages in Europe allows me to look at the problem of American poverty in a way I might not have chosen had I written in America. Visiting the slums of Naples and North Africa or traveling through the Sicilian or Greek countryside, one realizes that their misery, their utter deprivation, their stark horrors are qualitatively different from the poverty one encounters in the United States. You can, of course, see in the Mississippi delta cases of deprivation similar to those in Mediterranean slums, yet poverty in America is by and large no longer a problem of sheer physical survival, of utter immiseration and pauperism. Poverty in America concerns, in the main, not absolute but relative deprivation. We suffer from a highly unequal distribution of incomes, with the result that a fairly large proportion of the population is daily reminded of the fact that, compared to the rest, it is severely disadvantaged.

Beyond the primary issue of income distribution, poverty raises the question of full citizenship for the poor. Not only are the poor relatively deprived when it comes to goods and services; they are also politically deprived of the rights and privileges that come with citizenship in a democratic society.

The well-to-do and the poor still live as two different nations. To be poor in contemporary America means not only that one disposes of less income but also that one is aware of having little or no access to the levers of political power; that one feels excluded and alienated from the political process; that one is likely to conceive of oneself as

358

a pawn, an object, of social and political developments rather than a self-conscious political subject.

The Need for Income Redistribution

Whatever the merits of the various elaborate standards by which the number of poor is currently estimated and poverty lines are drawn, most uses of these statistics obscure the major fact that, though the number of people falling below statistical poverty lines has dropped considerably in recent years, there has been no redistribution of national income as between the poor and the rest of the population.

The number of Americans below the U.S. Census Bureau poverty level—$3,743 in annual income for a nonfarm family of four, in 1969—dropped from 39 million in 1959 to 24.3 million in 1969; but the percentage of total money income that flows to the bottom 20 percent of American families has hovered at around 5 percent ever since the end of World War II. There has been a reduction of the flow of income going to the top 5 percent of the American population, but this drop, while profiting the middle ranks, has had no discernible effect on the poor. The much-touted Income Revolution has not meant an increase in the share of income of the poor. In absolute terms they are indeed better off, but in relative terms they are almost exactly where they stood twenty-five years ago. And that is the real scandal! Hence radicals, even while supporting this or that measure which promises to alleviate the ailments from which the poor suffer, need most of all to focus on a redistribution of the flow of national income. For unless that is done, the poor will always be with us.

The elimination of poverty in America will not be attained even when almost all of its citizens have moved above one of the statistical poverty lines. It will occur only when the present distribution of income is changed so that the bottom portion of the income distribution is shifted into the middle category. At present a small proportion of the total population earns a great deal of money (the highest fifth earns around 40 percent of all family income). A very large proportion of all families earns a moderate income (the second, middle, and fourth fifths earn roughly 55 percent of all family income). The lowest fifth, on the other hand, earns very little (around 5 percent).

The current income distribution has the shape of a diamond. The only radical strategy worthy of the name must be designed to change income distribution in such a way that it assumes the shape of a pyramid—through moving the bottom fifth into one of the middle categories. This will not bring income equality, but at least it will insure that the 20 percent or so of our population now effectively denied full citizenship will have a secure basis from which to lay the foundations for social and political participation.

Service Versus Income Strategies

Lee Rainwater, on whose work, as well as that of S. M. Miller, I have largely relied in this paper,[1] argues persuasively that basically there are only two strategies for dealing with poverty: the *service strategy* and the *income strategy*. The first, which has been dominant up till now, means viewing the poor as a group of people in need of special aids and services financed by the rest of the population and provided and administered by a welfare bureaucracy. It would be foolish to deny that, compared to the days of *laissez faire,* this approach has been a tremendous step forward. It institutionalized the idea that the total community as well as the government must carry a responsibility for the well-being of all citizens, a well-being that cannot be left to the vagaries of the market. Yet it is by now evident that the service approach has failed to bring about structural changes in the distribution of income. It has helped many of the poor, it may even have enabled many to escape poverty altogether, but it has perpetuated the *condition* of poverty.

Services, though they may have other beneficial consequences, can do little to reduce the overall extent of poverty. A single example: in 1968 the New York Communities Aid Association published a report entitled "The Multiple Problem Dilemma" in which it gave an account of a two-and-a-half-year special-service program for multiple-problem families. Fifty of these families received special and extensive care by highly trained social workers. An equal number of

1. Cf., among other works of these authors, S. M. Miller and Pamela Roby, *The Future of Inequality* (New York: Basic Books, 1970), and Lee Rainwater, "The Service Strategy vs. the Income Strategy" in Fred R. Harris, ed., *Social Science and National Policy* (Chicago: Aldine, 1970).

families with comparable problems were given only routine service. Yet both groups showed almost identical developments. The study director concluded with rare candor: *"You cannot casework poor people out of poverty."*

A major reason, and perhaps the major reason, why such programs fail or even become counterproductive is that the service approach reinforces and perpetuates the dependent status of the poor. By providing services to the poor, the social worker contributes in effect to putting them into a special category of second-class citizens and thereby helps to stamp upon them a stigmatized status.[2]

To receive assistance means to be removed from the ordinary run of men. Once a person is assigned to the status of the assisted poor his role in life is changed, just as the career of the mental patient is changed by the very fact that he is designated a mental patient. Assisted poverty, no matter how well-intentioned the persons who provide assistance may be, involves a status degradation through which, in Harold Garfinkel's words, "the public identity of an actor is transformed into something looked on as lower in the local scheme of social types." Let me give a few illustrations:

Nearly all groups in society can use a variety of legitimate mechanisms to shield their behavior from observation by others; society recognizes a right to privacy, that is, to conceal parts of one's behavior from public scrutiny. Yet this right is denied to the poor. At least in principle, facets of behavior ordinarily not public are in their case under public control and are open to examination by social workers or other investigators. For even to be socially recognized as "poor," a person is obliged to make his private life available to public inspection. The protective veil that other members of society can put between themselves and the outer world is then explicitly denied him.

Where other recipients of social services may occasionally be visited at home by investigators, most of their contact with the agency is likely to be in its offices. Generally, in modern society, the exercise of authority—except within the family—is separated from the home. With

---

2. In the following I have drawn on two of my previously published papers: "The Sociology of Poverty," *Social Problems,* XIII, 2 (Fall 1965), and "Unanticipated Conservative Consequences of Liberal Theorizing," *Social Problems,* XVI, 3 (Winter 1969).

regard to the poor on relief, however, this is not the case. They are typically being investigated at home and hence have much less chance to conceal their private affairs from welfare observers. Because it prevents the usual stage management for visits by outsiders, such an invasion of home territory is necessarily experienced as humiliating.

When money is allocated to members of any other status groups, they have the freedom to dispose of it in almost any way they see fit. Here again the treatment of the poor differs sharply. They are denied free disposition of the money granted them. They must account to the donors for their expenses, and the donors decide whether the money is spent "wisely" or "foolishly." That is, insofar as they are treated much like children who have to account to parents for the use of pocket money, the poor are infantilized.

In the very process, then, of being helped and assisted, the poor are assigned to a special career that impairs their relations with others. Social workers, welfare investigators, welfare administrators, and local volunteer workers seek out the poor in order to help them, yet, paradoxically, are the very agents of their degradation. Subjective intentions and institutional consequences sharply diverge. Even when the help is given from the most benevolent of motives, the very fact of being helped becomes a token of degradation.

Far from aiming to equalize life chances and citizenship rights between the well-to-do and the poor, the service strategy perpetuates inequality. As the dean of British sociology T. H. Marshall once put it, "The common purpose of statutory and voluntary effort was to abate the nuisance of poverty without disturbing the pattern of inequality of which poverty was the most obvious unpleasant consequence."

Patterns of equality in social affairs are established when men deal with others under conditions of reciprocity, that is, when services supplied can be reciprocated. Autonomy and independence are assured to the extent to which benefits received do not exceed services rendered. But the *service strategy,* by its very nature, fosters not reciprocity but unilateral dependence based on asymmetry of power. The poor must approach as supplicants those who have it in their power to relieve some of their misery. By definition they are receivers of benefits who are in no position to reciprocate. Welfare personnel, on the other hand, by supplying services to the poor, establish power over them. They render needed services that cannot be had elsewhere so that the recipients become obligated to them. Hence relations of unilateral dependence come into existence, which are at fundamental variance with the rights deriving from equal participation and citizenship in the society at large. And not only are the poor seen by others as belonging to a special stigmatized category, they also tend to see themselves as others see them. Hence assistance and the service strategy perpetuate the conditions they are designed to alleviate. In an instrumentally oriented society, those who cannot give but only receive are naturally assigned the lowest status.

The Working Poor

So far I have dealt only with the assisted poor, but these are in fact only a minority of the total poor population. While there are about 8 million assisted poor in contemporary America, between 40 and 50 million fell below the poverty or near-poverty level in the late sixties. Millions of people are poor by any standard, despite the fact that they work full-time throughout the year; 25 percent of all poor families (including 8 million persons) are headed by men gainfully occupied for the full working year. These large numbers of families and individuals are, of course, not reached at all by the *service strategy*. They are assumed to be able to take care of themselves. Yet the fact is that they often lead lives just as helpless as those on public assistance. Possessing limited skills, cooped up in areas where the labor market provides no opportunities, they desperately try to hang on to an aura of respectability while knowing only too well that the jobs they perform seldom allow them to gain status and respect. The sociologist Everett C. Hughes has remarked, "A man's work is as good a clue as any to the course of his life, and to his social being and identity." When a man's job does not insure him a decent income and is looked upon with contempt by his fellows, it can only provide him with a negative identity. In this respect the working poor find themselves in a situation not too dissimilar from that of the assisted poor, even though they try desperately to distinguish themselves from them. That the *service strategy* in effect bypasses these huge numbers of men altogether is a further mark of its inadequacy and irrelevance. In an earlier period when the aim of social policy was simply to assist paupers, the *service strategy* made some sense; but it is not in tune with the requirements of our age. Today large-scale income redistribution is on the agenda.

The underlying assumption of the *service strategy* is that the poor need assistance because, unlike the rest of the population, they are unable to make the relevant choices by themselves. The underlying assumption of the *income strategy* is, on the contrary, that what the poor really want is to make their own choices as they see fit. It is based on the notion that the poor are not so very different from the rest of us: *they only have less money.*

I will leave to economists a detailed discussion of the relative merits of a variety of redistribution schemes that have been brought forward in recent years. Whether a negative income tax or another form of income maintenance and support program is adopted does not concern us here. But the principle should be clear: whatever the scheme, the task is to develop a set of economic programs insuring poor families and individuals a basic floor of income not too far removed from the median income of American families as a whole.

There is no doubt in my mind that a great deal of the social pathology now proliferating among the poor would be resolved through an adequate provision of income. At the risk of being taxed with sociological naïveté by social scientific brethren, I would still maintain that what the poor lack above all is money. We therefore need a provision of adequate income for those unable to work and an income maintenance program for those who, because of conditions in the labor market, cannot gain an adequate income.

I am aware of the very special problems that arise in many lower-class families from the lack of authority or the complete absence of fathers and the ensuing pathological matrifocality. But I am also convinced that a man with an adequate income will be much less likely to abandon his family than one whose sense of self-esteem is continually undermined by casual work or by unilateral dependence on public assistance.

In a culture such as ours, which still basically judges a man according to his occupational status, it stands to reason that simple transfers of income to those among the poor who are able to work is not a permanent answer. Even when a man is no longer stigmatized by his dependence on public assistance, even when he has a right to income maintenance as well established as social security benefits, he will still not escape social blame as well as self-blame if he lacks a rewarding and productive job. That is why, for those among the poor who are able to work, a secure job is as important as an adequate income. The fact is, however, that rewarding jobs are likely to come into reach only after immediate worries about current income are relieved. Job training and the development of technical competence can be pursued only when the economic insecurity and anxiety that now mark the poor have at least in part been removed. A man dependent on casual work of an unskilled sort is not likely to have the inclination, time or energy to train himself for new kinds of employment. When immediate worries about income have been removed, when elementary needs have been gratified, it becomes psychologically much easier to prepare for more skillful and hence more rewarding employment. An income strategy should therefore aim at more than simply redistributing income. Ultimately it should be a means to the wider end of creating valued occupational and social positions for those who were formerly casual unskilled laborers or passive recipients of assistance.

This is not the place to spell out the measures that would seem necessary in order to assure that an adequate number of positions is available so as to provide opportunities for all who need them. What is needed is a structural approach counteracting the tendency for unemployment to be much higher among the unskilled than among the skilled occupations. This would involve large-scale federal programs insuring not only very low unemployment rates (reducing unemployment by 1 percentage point would reduce the number of persons in poverty by 1.25 million), but guarantees of entry into the labor force for the unskilled as well as guarantees of on-the-job-training so as to enable the unskilled gradually to move up into skilled categories. It would involve high minimum wages, and federal incentives to employers to retain or even enlarge their labor force rather than replacing expensive manpower by labor-saving devices before the work force has been trained in higher skills. It would entail the creation of a vast number of paraprofessional jobs in schools and hospitals. It would entail the creation of many new jobs in the general area of public employment to counteract the present tendency of neglecting public expenditures so as to enhance the private consumption of middle-class voters. (Think only, as S. M. Miller suggests, how many jobs could be created in the sanitation departments of major cities if lower-class neighborhoods were given services equal to those of higher-class areas.)

Lest I be misunderstood, let me stress that I am not in favor of make-work programs that provide socially unnecessary jobs for the unskilled in order to take them off the streets. Nothing seems to me as degrading for people as to be employed in work that they know is useless. You only have to watch the demeanor of the many persons in the Eastern bloc countries who are employed in raking leaves or sweeping sidewalks to realize that this way of disguising unemployment is deeply humiliating. More generally, when men know that unskilled work to which they are assigned could as well be performed by machines, they often feel such work to be degrading. Washing dishes by hand in the restaurants of the past was a perfectly normal job; washing dishes by hand when mechanical dishwashers are readily available is something else again. The need is not make-work for the unskilled, or to slow technical progress in order to provide jobs. It is, rather, to allow the unskilled to upgrade their skills so that they can work with machines that produce results about which they can feel some satisfaction.

Emphasis on the unskilled and the necessary upgrading of skills need not make us lose sight of the fact that in contemporary American society there exists a large, and growing, category of people who have been so demoralized and pathologized by their social conditions that they cannot, in fact, avail themselves of job opportunities. What I have in mind here are not so much the physically handicapped—their case is largely unproblematic—but rather those who suffer from overpowering psychic handicaps. In the wilderness of every modern city tens of thousands of persons, perhaps many more, have become a kind of permanent underclass or lumpen proletariat that is likely to remain with us no matter what antipoverty strategies are adopted. These people, often under the influence of drugs of various sorts, have become so apathetic and withdrawn from the public scene that they are not likely to be reached by any of these measures. Income maintenance programs may alleviate some of their immediate plights, but it is unlikely that they will lead them to abandon their way of life. The mark of degradation is too deeply ingrained in their psychic structure.

When it comes to this class of men, the limits of public policy may have been reached. They are likely to remain permanent victims of modern society, a vivid reminder of the high price at which modern urban society has made its ambiguous progress. As such they deserve sympathy, understanding, and, above all, tolerance from the ranks of those who have succeeded in carving a more secure niche for themselves. No measure of repression can eliminate them from the social scene, and no appeals to "law and order" offer any effective way of dealing with them. It is possible, I think, to "save" many of their children so that their condition does not become hereditary. But as to most of them, the best that can probably be done is to see to it that they live their dismal lives as free from harassment and direct need as possible.

The "Culture of Poverty"

Though often advanced by writers whose motivations are impeccable, it still seems to me that the notion of a "culture of poverty," bandied about so much in recent years, is a fundamentally mischievous idea. When such writers claim that, far from participating in a common culture, the poor have developed a culture of their own that sets them fundamentally apart from the majority of the population, then, whether they intend it or not, they create the impression that the members of that culture are somehow alien beings who cannot be assimilated and hence must remain beyond the pale.

The notion of a "culture of poverty" creates the impression that, no matter what strategy is adopted, the poor will continue to live in a world of their own, as unassimilated and unassimilable pariahs. This is dangerous nonsense. It is, of course, true that the poor have been forced to make a number of serious adjustments in their life styles in order to subsist at all. But there is a major difference between such adaptations to conditions not of one's own choosing and a culture that is a way of life. A way of life may be adhered to despite poverty, as in the case of the Jews in the *shtetl;* but poverty as such creates no culture.

The notion of culture implies a desired and valued way of life. It is rooted in the idea that men belonging to a culture are devoted to it because it embodies for them prized qualities and virtues. But how can a culture of poverty be valued and desired? Except among religious ascetics, poverty is not a positive virtue. To be sure, deprived persons may present a variety of characteristics that distinguish them from the more fortunate, but they do not choose these characteristics and are not themselves likely to consider them desirable. They are in fact the mark of their oppression. It is only among certain romantic primitivists that life styles from which the lower classes suffer are transmuted into admirable and admired characteristics.

It is one thing to defend the right to diversity in life styles where such divergent and nonconformist patterns have been freely chosen—as among contemporary youth—but it is quite another to defend a situation where such divergencies have in fact been imposed by those who occupy a superior position in society. I know of no evidence to indicate that women who are the heads of matrifocal families in the lower classes desire such positions of their own free choice. They have been forced into them by desertion, by divorce, or by the persistent pressures of male unemployment, the vagaries of the job market for the unskilled, and the inhuman stipulations of current welfare policies. It is deeply offensive to liken, say, Italian subcultural preferences for pasta to alleged lower-class "preferences" for female-dominated households or serial marriage. These are conditions from which the poor *suffer* precisely because in their essential cultural makeup they do not differ fundamentally from the rest of the American population.

Certain intellectuals seem to have a perennial tendency to hunt for noble savages whose traits can be contrasted to the alleged vices of modern civilization. It would be preferable if they were to limit their search to nonliterate tribes. Romantic admiration for the natives of Upper Dahomey is not likely to have many social repercussions in the lives of those people, but the glorification of an alleged "culture of poverty" in our own midst could act as a self-fulfilling prediction. If the poor have indeed cultural characteristics fundamentally at variance with those of the rest of society, then it is of little avail to attempt to eradicate poverty by an income or any other strategy. If policy-makers listen to such vicious advice and refrain from action to eradicate poverty and redistribute income, then indeed the poor will continue to be with us. In any case, an overemphasis on the alleged adaptive functions of the "culture of poverty" can only deter us from taking the needed radical measures to change the opportunity structure and the income distribution of contemporary America. The *status quo* can only be bolstered by attributing some kind of glamour to a way of life, if poverty can be called that, which requires nothing less than radical abolition.

David K. Cohen

Public Schools: The Next Decade

Two ideas have dominated American thought about education during the last half-century. One is that schooling is the key to mobility and social justice; the other that it might be a major instrument of social and cultural integration. Education has long been seen as both the chief antidote to poverty and the principal means for assimilating ethnic and racial minorities. While there always has been evidence to belie these notions, it went virtually unnoticed until the late 1960s. Since then, however, events have cast serious doubt on these two venerable articles of faith. It no longer seems so clear that education is the high road to equality or social integration.

The most perplexing issue is the relation between schooling and social justice. By 1965 the federal government had launched several major initiatives in education—principally Headstart and Title I of the 1965 ESEA—whose main thrust was to improve the life chances of poor people, especially blacks, by improving the quality of their education. A year later, in the federally sponsored *Equality of Educational Opportunity* report, James Coleman announced that differences in the quality of the nation's schools bore only a trivial relationship to differences in the educational achievement of the nation's students. The issue seems clear: *can education be the key to social justice if schools have no effect on children's achievement?*

Early results from the new education programs offered one answer.

An earlier version of this paper was prepared for the American Jewish Committee's Task Force on Group Life.

By 1968, newspaper accounts of the failure of local Headstart and Title I programs had become commonplace. By 1969 several national studies of these programs had found no discernible impact on children's performance in school. And early in 1970 the White House released a special presidential message on education, which argued that federal education spending should be held down until new research could turn up some answers about the schools' effects on students.

All of this is puzzling. If the schools "make no difference," as Coleman's research seems to show, why spend more on them? Several early critics turned up an impressive list of technical problems with which to undermine the report's credibility, but reanalysis of the data (with many of the difficulties corrected) corroborated the original findings. Still, the results boggle the mind. Do they indicate, as some hold, that government will not effect social change by improving social services? Should it then stick to direct income transfers? Others leaped to different conclusions. Arthur Jensen interpreted the reported failure of compensatory programs as evidence of underlying racial differences in the inheritance of intelligence. Many liberals and radicals think the results prove that liberal social welfare programs cannot work as long as they are controlled by centralized bureaucracies. Spending more money on social programs will be futile, they argue, until the programs are made accountable to those they are supposed to serve.

One result of all this has been a sense of trouble within the democratic Left, which has experienced spectacular political fragmentation during the last few years. This fragmentation has been paralleled by growing evidence of disillusion with liberal programs. Just as the political cement of the liberal coalition seems to be dissolving, the intellectual legitimacy of its program has been seriously weakened.

The challenge has come not only from research or program evaluation. Changes in the politics of race during the past five years have created uncertainty about school reform. Until late in the 1960s there was little confusion on the liberal Left about school segregation. Despite much controversy and some reluctance to press ahead, there was never any doubt that racial desegregation in schools and housing was a structural prerequisite for the full social integration of black Americans. Now all that is changing. The debate is no longer over the pace of desegregation, but whether it should occur at all. Outside the South, the most articulate opponents of school integration are blacks who argue that desegregation amounts to little more than brutal assimilation; that black children need education responsive to their special backgrounds; that the only way to attain this is by setting up black community-controlled schools within the public system.

Though many of the arguments for community control or decentralization are historical—stressing the slowness of Southern school desegregation and its virtual absence in the North—these really distract from the main point: the path to social integration for American minority groups is now seen to lie in group solidarity—cultural unity, community economic development, and political control of community institutions. In this view, the public schools should help develop managerial and political competence in the adult community, serve to create and transmit an authentic black culture, and instill a sense of group identity and pride in black students.

Now, whatever one may think about the merit of these ideas, several facts are accepted by all. First, almost no one thinks that this is the way the public schools worked in the past for immigrant children, when blatant assimilation was the rule. Second, the demand for community control violates a cardinal rule of ethnic politics in America: it overtly proclaims ethnicity as the basis for organizing public institutions, rather than leaving the principle undeclared. Third, one of our most fondly held ideas is now bluntly challenged—that in the public schools children of all creeds, colors, and nationalities come together helter-skelter to learn from one another about life in America.

No surprise, then, that the movement for community control has profoundly shaken liberal thought about education and social reform. For it carries the unmistakable suggestion that racial and ethnic integration may not be a good thing; and whatever the *facts* of group life in America may be, the structure of our politics and folklore rests on the notion that this is a nation of individuals, not groups. While we may be able to tolerate the fact of group distinctiveness, it is less easy to tolerate its recognition as the explicit organizing principle of cultural and political life. To say that the schools should create and transmit a distinct ethnic or racial culture, rather than transmit the common culture, is simply heresy when viewed in the light of received doctrine.

The shock these ideas convey has been magnified by the research revelations I discussed above. One obvious rejoinder to pleas for community control has been that political and administrative separation will disadvantage the black community in the competition for scarce educational resources. Yet how can one maintain this argument in the face of evidence that variations in the quality of schools—whether measured in dollars or staff qualifications—relate not at all to student achievement? As Christopher Jencks has argued, if schools have little or no effect on students' achievement, it would seem perverse to resist community control. The only remaining argument against organizing schools along ethnic and racial lines is that it would contribute to divisiveness; but that, after all, is just what the proponents of community control proclaim to be the underlying principle of intergroup relations in America. No wonder they find the objection unconvincing.

If these developments have undermined the legitimacy of accepted ideas about schooling and social reform, they also have encouraged such proposals for diversifying public education as tuition vouchers, performance contracts, subcontracting curricula, and direct public subsidies to private schools. Of course, support for these ideas does not arise solely from the recent crisis of confidence in schooling. It derives in part from a long-standing desire more fully to reflect religious and ethnic differences in public supported education, and in part from a more recent upsurge of interest in free schools, alternative forms of schooling, and so on. Let us pause at these two phenomena for a moment, since they promise to be of increasing political importance in the 1970s.

Several religious groups, especially Catholics, have a strong interest in supporting parochial education, and their legislative activity toward this end has increased markedly during the past few years. Several states have passed parochial aid statutes, and others seem almost sure to do so in the near future. There is, of course, nothing new here, save the greater pressure for public aid. But tuition vouchers, aid to alternative or free schools, and diversification of existing curricula are more of a novelty. The main support for these notions lies outside the established religious and ethnic groups; it is found in certain segments of the urban middle and upper-middle class. Such demands express not a desire to reflect more fully traditional intergroup differences in the school system, but to allow more freedom for individual expression in the quality, style, and character of schools.

They parallel the growing class conflict that has begun to emerge over the character of university education.

What is the source of these demands?

Perhaps the most important development of the last half-century has been the "massification" of social welfare and culture, two sectors of the economy which have experienced enormous growth. The emergence of education, social welfare, communications, and culture as mass industries has begun to create new lines of class and cultural division in American society. This growth can be viewed as an institutionalization of bohemia involving the expansion of values and styles of life radically different from, if not explicitly hostile to, the ethos of industrial capitalism. Workers in the welfare and culture industries are trained to value humanity, openness, and creativity; as professionals, they often deal with the unhappy consequences of market values.

This group has exhibited more and more political discontent over the past several decades. The roots of its discontent are not essentially material: the problem is not increasing misery, or even growing relative deprivation. Its discontent arises from the creation in the bosom of modern society—in the family, child-rearing, and educational institutions—of an ethos and mode of life that is unusually open and democratic. Children from this class have been raised in an atmosphere where individual differences and self-expression are highly valued; parents, consciously seeking to comport themselves in non-repressive ways, teach their children to make their own rules and develop their own discipline. The most highly valued educational institutions are those that stress spontaneity and creativity. Education is esteemed, but there is ambivalence or outright hostility toward the work-oriented and mechanical constraints of urban public schools. As a result, the most typical artifacts of this group have been their schools, expressing for children the values their parents want most to realize for themselves. The institutional history of these schools begins with the turn-of-the-century kindergartens, and moves from there through the Progressive movement to the present fascination with free schools, the Leicestershire movement, and community schools. Through it all, the main themes are similar: children should learn at their own pace, from things that interest them; learning should occur from the inside out, not the other way round—and the only legitimate discipline arises out of the learning situation; school should not prepare for the mechanical routines of the workaday world but should develop individuals toward the outer reaches of their own capacity. Schooling, in short, is justifiable only when playful, not conditioned by the mechanical rhythm of the work place but by the unpredictable rhythm of individual discovery.

All the tables have been turned: the only acceptable work is that which is play, and the only really desirable play is that which is instructive or otherwise useful. In tone as well as character this is reminiscent of the new world Karl Marx described when he ventured a few ideas about Communist society. More than a little, these schools are efforts to create utopian enclaves in the midst of capitalist society. There is, of course, a problem: these schools are only for children, and thus in the ordinary sense of the word partly playful; but the utopia never has been fully realized, either in the free schools or the family—how could it be, in the midst of the existing order? Both unreality and tension mark this new educational world.

Still, the contrasts are clear when the standard of comparison is what already exists. It does not require a superrefined sensibility to discover that on one side the ordering principle is freedom, and on the other the market; for those reared in an atmosphere of freedom, it is not hard to decide which is preferable. And it is hardly surprising that workers in the social-welfare and culture industries—and especially their children—have come into open conflict with the established educational authorities. Whatever position one takes on the politics and ideology marking this clash, it would be a mistake to write it off as an unhappy accident. It is a manifestation of the strains accompanying the development of advanced industrial societies away from the factory system, unregulated capitalism (or, in the "socialist" countries, emphasis on heavy industry), and elite possession of education and culture—toward technological industrialism, greater regulation of the economy in the interest of social welfare and consumer goods, and more democracy in the possession of education and culture. As these changes continue, the strains are likely to increase.

There is no assurance that the outcome will be progressive. For one thing, bohemia always has had a pronounced tendency toward romanticism, the worship of feudal forms and cultural exotica, and religious or quasireligious withdrawal from the world. This was true for the first tiny coteries of early nineteenth-century European bohemians, and there are signs that it is just as true for the mass bohemians of contemporary America. Indeed, the entire history of bohemian and middle-class left-wing culture, since its inception nearly two centuries ago, can be framed in terms of a tension between political and social engagement on one hand, and the urge toward the pastoral life, religious contemplation, or obscure and elitist art forms on the other.

The new culture I have described evokes hostile reactions in the society. We already have a slight foretaste of this in the response of "middle America" to the university-media-liberal-snob axis. Almost everything presently emanating from this "New Left" threatens the working and lower-middle classes: the proclamation of social and cultural freedom is unsettling to those attached to more traditional notions of authority; the advocacy of radical social change is unsettling to those with a minimal stake in economic security; and arguments for massive compensatory treatment for blacks exacerbate both the cultural antagonism and the economic anxiety. Combine all this with the tendencies toward nativism still present in rural and small-town America, and there is the potential for a powerful rightward shift in American politics.

The chief developments of the late 1960s have, then, a remarkable political coherence. Both the "failure" of major domestic programs and the findings that educational institutions have little effect on students reinforce the idea that the traditional liberal approach to social reform is bankrupt. These developments provide grist for radical and conservative elements who—for a wide variety of reasons—believe that liberal reform must or should fail. And just as the evidence of programmatic and institutional "failure" exacerbates the sensibilities of black activists, so does it make way for ever more radical forms of racial separatism. Finally, changes in the class structure have begun to generate fundamental changes in the demand for education among the urban middle and upper-middle class, all tending toward greater freedom for individual expression, more diversity in the character and quality of educational offerings, and increased individual control over the substance and timing of schooling. In the short run, at least, this tendency is hostile to familiar liberal ideas and institutions; its partisans even welcome evidence of failure.

The legacy of the 1960s can be reframed as questions for the 1970s:

• Should choice in public education continue to be constrained by family budgets and school jurisdiction boundaries?

• Should expenditure on education continue to play a major role in government efforts to combat the effects of poverty and discrimination?

One way or another, the main problems in education will turn around these issues. It is worth speculating about what the answers ought to be.

Spending   This issue is so vexing that there can be no quick answers. The pressure to continue the upward trend of educational expenditures will increase, but will greater spending on schools for poor children improve their chances later in life? The evidence on this point is mixed, and likely to remain so for some time. We know, for example, that highly structured preschool child-and-parent-training programs markedly improve the children's cognitive ability; we also know that when the programs are discontinued the children's test ability slumps. But at the moment we don't know how long such efforts would have to be extended to avoid this slump. We also know that the number of years of schooling people complete is strongly related to their later occupational status. We do not know, however, whether less-educated people of the same initial ability and motivation as those who complete college wind up at the same place on the occupational ladder.

There is some evidence that students with better test scores and grades complete more years of school, but it is easy to imagine that those with the higher scores were socialized at home to the sorts of behavior that make for success in school. Whether it is test scores or primary socialization that cause the relationship is presently unknown. But let us suppose we knew that higher test scores caused more years of school to be completed, and that completing more years of school caused higher occupational status; still, very little is known about raising test scores, except at the preschool level. All the experience with elementary-grade compensatory programs suggests that simply spending large sums of money on such gross changes as reducing pupil-teacher ratios has little or no noticeable effect on students' test scores. Some researchers have speculated that more refined approaches —changing teachers' behavior and attitudes—will help, but there is next to no evidence for this, and there are no clues how it might be done.

Research on these issues will be difficult and time-consuming. It demands large-scale study and experimentation, which is both expensive and politically burdensome. The federal government has shown only limited enthusiasm for this, and has not yet developed the capacity for carrying out even the present limited efforts in a satisfactory fashion. In this situation, several courses of action are available. One is to hold all spending at current levels until research provides the "answers." But to do research well requires a political commitment to improving federal social-action experiments, and as the present administration reveals, those politicians who are enthusiastic about reducing costs are ambivalent about experimenting with social-action programs. Help will not soon be forthcoming from this quarter.

A second option is to shift social expenditures to more direct income transfers, such as income maintenance and job-creation programs. This is a sensible approach, not because research shows it to be better, but simply for common-sense reasons. One purpose of the Kennedy-Johnson education programs, after all, was to eliminate poverty. The notion that education is the best and most efficient way to accomplish this is an old one—our faith in its transforming power has been the basis of compensatory and social-welfare programs since the late nineteenth century. Schooling has traditionally been conceived as a mechanism of reform whereby the rewards of adult life would be distributed on the basis of talent rather than inheritance. It is a notion peculiarly suited to liberalism, for the redistribution of social and economic status promised through education does not threaten to reduce the magnitude or importance of class differences. Far from it, schooling-as-reform promised only that inequalities would be more consistent with qualification than with birth. This approach to social reform rests on a desire to promote fairness in the distribution of privilege, but without attacking the distribution or ownership of property. Its appeal is that all problems of the direct redistribution of wealth are deferred, and translated into a matter of individual ability and effort in schools and the market.

Has this ever been the way the schools have really worked?

All the evidence suggests that the school system has "worked" principally for groups well situated to make the most of the academic meritocracy that has evolved over the last six decades. The main prerequisites seem to be competence in the schools' language (formal English), an ability to maneuver in fairly complex urban social systems, and a cosmopolitan cultural orientation. Children from those immigrant groups which consisted mainly of non-English-speaking peasants, oriented toward village societies (southern Italians, for example, or Poles), fared abysmally in the public schools; peasant immigrants from English-speaking countries (the Irish) fared a good deal better; the Jews, who were on the average a good deal more urbanized and cosmopolitan, performed remarkably. What is more, evidence on the relation between schooling and later adult social status suggests that the role of education in promoting upward mobility varies enormously among ethnic groups, and in just the ways we would expect; those groups whose children did well in school show the strongest effect of schooling on social status.

The schools, then, have been most effective in redistributing privilege for already urbanized groups in other ways well prepared to cope with the academic merit system. It is quite a leap from this, however, to the idea that schools can be primary engines of reform for less urbanized groups. Not only is the notion contradicted by the schools' past performance, it seems unlikely on its face. The elimination of poverty seems much more likely to be accomplished by a direct attack on the structural differences in occupation and income, as well as the other barriers to the possibility of a humane life. This course, however, is much more costly, and inconsistent with established ideas about schools and social reform. In my view, therefore, the "failure" of recent social action programs in education simply manifests the results of misdirected efforts. It does not prove that decentralized government is required to make social programs work, any more than it proves that social programs do not work. *If it proves anything at all, it is that greater equality cannot be purchased cheaply.* The new education programs allocate relatively little money to poor children, and almost all of it is used to pay the salaries of school professionals. Although no one knows what all the effects of income transfers would be, any money spent directly on increasing the income of poor people would be much more effective than money spent on the school programs. In any case, since both have the same purpose —eliminating poverty—it is hard to see how income transfers could be less effective.

The fact is, however, that few government programs are ever reduced, let alone halted. The growing power of the education establishment's national lobby (evident in the 1970 session of Congress) makes it doubly unlikely that federal antipoverty funds will be shifted from education to other categories. Thus the new education programs —which were supposed to benefit poor children—will continue to support the educational professions with little visible benefit for the children. Under these circumstances, it is not enough to argue for future expenditures to provide direct income transfers to families— that may be some time off. Other ways must be found by which these programs can directly benefit the people they are supposed to help. In the present circumstances, this can only be accomplished through increased community influence over the allocation of resources. At a minimum, this would increase the likelihood that the programs would be used to support more direct assistance to the poor, in the form of food, clothing, health care, and so on.

Thus, the answer to my second question is that expenditures on education probably ought not to play a major role in any serious effort to combat the effects of poverty and discrimination. But, as existing programs are not going to disappear, the community that is involved should have a major voice in the allocation of these resources. I do not regard this as a pessimistic reflection on the efficacy of liberal social programs, but rather a reflection on the limitations of the liberal notion that schooling is always a suitable instrument for redistributing wealth and status. *We may be learning that equality cannot be gotten in the bargain basement, by trying to teach the children of the poor to behave differently, while all the other conditions of their lives remain unchanged.*

Diversity Pressures to widen the framework of educational choice come from two sources: those who want to abandon district lines altogether in favor of individual decisions, and those who simply want to redraw jurisdictional boundaries around smaller and more homogeneous school communities. Both notions rest on what appear to be similar assumptions:

1. Smaller units of educational choice would provide greater effi-

ciency—there would be a better match between the schools' taste in pupils and the parents' taste in pedagogy. Because parents would have more leverage on schools, students would perform better.

2. Smaller units of educational choice would provide the material with which those blacks and whites now disaffected from public institutions could regain a legitimate polity, since smaller units of choice would establish a new social contract around the schools.

3. Smaller units of choice would allow more educational variety than is possible within the present overregulated and standardized school system.

Despite such similarities in assumption, the two sorts of proposals are by no means identical. They rest, for example, on fundamentally different ideas about the role of government. The individual-choice schemes suit the taste of those who have an antipathy to government and bureaucracy; by now these sentiments are no less strange on the political Left than on the Right. By way of contrast, proposals for decentralization and community control appeal to those who regard government as an agency for social change. The notion is that government at the community level should have more impact on educational decisions; this assumes that political communities, not individuals, are the proper units for making decisions about the allocation of public goods. Once we strip away the rhetoric about bureaucracy, it becomes clear that *one likely implication of community control is that education would be governed more rather than less.* The other group of proposals, by contrast, rests on the notion that decisions about education should be based on individual choice, and that government should have a much smaller role in making them than it now does. This assumes, of course, that the public interest in education is relatively small compared to private interests, and it implies that school reform is mainly a matter of reducing government control over schools.

Diversification of some sort is desirable. School government in the cities has grown in ways that weaken accountability without improving efficiency: transportation and other support systems require metropolitan or regional government (because they would be either economically more efficient, or administratively and politically less clumsy). There is, however, no evidence that this is needed for schools. In addition, city schools do not reflect as well as they might the large underlying diversity of taste in education: in fact, for most of their history the public schools have sought to avoid or deny these differences, especially if they were related to class or ethnicity.

The question is whether diversification could be arranged without becoming politically retrograde. The two leading schemes are decentralization and tuition vouchers, but both could increase segregation by race and class, and they might produce greater disparities in the distribution of educational resources than exist now.

Decentralization would be a desirable alternative if there was any evidence that smaller school districts would permit a greater range of alternatives for parents. But that is not the case. Decentralization would presumably increase diversity within a given city by giving communities more voice in decisions about staff, curriculum, and style. For parents in any given district, however, the range of choice would be no greater—it might even be less; black parents in black districts, for example, might have more difficulty transferring children to integrated schools than is at present the case. Decentralization would probably not only increase segregation, but by drawing new district boundaries around "neighborhoods," would lock residential patterns into place with new jurisdictions.

Decentralization is a suitable alternative, then, if one believes (1) there are no important variations in the demand for education within communities, and (2) no values in integration. The first is clearly untrue, for while the major variations in the demand for schooling probably do lie among ethnic and class groupings, residential segregation by ethnicity and class is far from complete. As for the second, whatever one's own view, many black and white parents do prefer integration. Other things being equal one would not want to impede the expression of *that* variation in taste for schooling while allowing the expression of others.

Tuition vouchers would not be subject to this difficulty, for they would permit parents to choose whatever school they liked. Blacks in mostly Negro districts who preferred white schools would not be restrained by their community of origin; upper-middle-class families in working-class neighborhoods would not be restrained by a local governing board from enrolling their children in a "free" school. This, of course, is the great appeal of vouchers: by allowing "communities" of very limited liability to come together around schools, vouchers permit the fullest expression of variations in the demand for schooling.

But therein also lies their great difficulty: would not the individual freedom to choose schools also imply freedom to restrict the attendance of others? Negro parents might want to enroll their children in mixed schools, but whites could prefer it otherwise. An unrestricted voucher scheme could harden patterns of segregation even more effectively than decentralization.

There are ways in which these problems might be avoided. If racial discrimination in admission were forbidden, and if fiscal incentives for accepting poor children (and thus promoting economic and racial integration) were offered to schools, many of the problems would probably disappear. If in addition a large proportion of students in all schools were admitted by some device for random choice (a lottery, for example), there would probably be more integration under a system of voucher-financed schools than there is now in most public school systems.[1] The difficulty is not in conceiving ways to avoid segregation, but in imagining how they might be implemented. It is not easy to see how the legislature in states like New York or Michigan would approve legislation of this sort, when they have recently evidenced such distaste for other, more limited, approaches to school integration.

Racial segregation is not the only major problem that would arise under these schemes. If either neighborhoods or individuals were made the basis of educational choice, the existing class disparities in the allocation of school resources might grow. State equalization formulas would retard this somewhat in many states, but the disparities there are still great. Poor districts—those with low assessed valuation and/or a greater burden of municipal services—typically must tax themselves much more severely to raise school funds than districts with less burden and greater wealth. At the individual level tuition vouchers could avoid part of the problem, at least, by making the size of vouchers an inverse function of family income, and prohibiting parents from spending more on the children's schooling than the value of the voucher. While the first would not be a major problem

1. This discussion is a condensed version of suggestions that can be found in *Education Vouchers*, a report on various voucher schemes produced by several staff members of the Center for the Study of Public Policy, in Cambridge.

(schools could be given more money for enrolling poor children), it is hard to see how the second could be effectively enforced without creating the sort of bureaucracy that tuition vouchers are supposed to dissolve.

It would be a mistake to suppose, however, that under either scheme the educational advantages of wealth would be eliminated. At best they would be somewhat reduced, within the narrow limits that are politically acceptable. Thus, the question is whether the inequalities likely under decentralization or vouchers would be greater than those we now have. If we assume the sort of admissions restrictions discussed just above—present levels of state equalization for decentralized districts, and moderately strong fiscal incentives for enrolling poor children—I suspect there would be little change. There would, of course, still be plenty of private schools outside the system (most of the exclusive schools would not accept lottery admissions), just as there are now; but, as is also now the case, they would receive no direct tax subsidy. Within decentralized or voucher-supported schools, inequalities in the ability to support schooling would surely remain; but given the assumptions I have made, it seems unlikely that they would be larger than those we now have.

Even this cursory review of these two alternatives suggests that diversification schemes are worth considering. On balance, I have come to regard the voucher plan as more desirable. It does not restrict individual choice as narrowly as community government would; it would be likely to result in more integration and provide the foundation for greater diversity.

The problems, however, lie not in the scheme, but in the restrictions I have assumed. Their desirability is probably an inverse function of their political feasibility. The voucher scheme most likely to succeed in a state legislature would be one that satisfied the most powerful interests—none of which are poor or black. Such a scheme would be unacceptable to liberals and radicals. Similarly, the most likely decentralization schemes are those that change the balance of power only slightly. It would be no surprise if the decade passed with little progress on either front.

There are, of course, other approaches to diversification, most of which center on the idea of contracting out the school program. James Coleman has suggested that segments of public school curricula (math or reading) be subcontracted to nonschool agencies, such as community corporations, profit-making firms, or nonprofit institutions. Their scale of payment and/or parents' patronage would be contingent on the contractors' performance in teaching the children. This idea has been carried further by the Office of Economic Opportunity recently, in experiments with contracting the entire school program. The "performance contract" experiments involve conditioning contractors' fees on children's performance. Although this approach has some promising elements—unlike the present school system, educators would be rewarded for doing better with the students they have, rather than for teaching in schools where the students already do well—there is a swarm of problems, including fraud, social class differentials in access to information, and antiunion practices. Chief among the difficulties, however, is that the criterion of success in all cases is the children's standardized test performance and, as I pointed out earlier, there is little evidence that this is salient in any way to later success. It would be perverse to further entrench reliance on test scores, and to restructure incentives more firmly around them—unless we knew that they bear some powerful intrinsic relationship to adult achievement.

The outlook for significant progress toward diversification of the school system is not terribly hopeful. The most desirable scheme—an egalitarian version of tuition vouchers—seems not to have nearly the political promise of performance contracting—the least desirable scheme.

One thing seems certain: for the foreseeable future the main issues in education will center on diversity. This is not a trivial matter, but much of the interest in it—indeed, the concern for the school "crisis" —arose from efforts to eliminate race and class disparities in the outcomes of schooling. There is, however, no evidence that changing the framework of choice in education will have much effect. It may be that the schools' "failure" to affect the transmission of status from generation to generation will only serve to focus attention on the political arrangements governing education, rather than on the more important need to attack directly the underlying social and economic inequalities.

Bernard Rosenberg

Crime On and Off the Streets

Neither the clamor for "law and order" nor alarm over "crime on the streets" will soon subside. These are the highly exploitable catch-phrases that cluster around a gut issue on which local, state, and national candidates for important office have increasingly had to take a stand. Cynical manipulation of these phrases has made cryptographers of us all. Decoded, the invocation of "law and order" to oppose "crime on the streets" often mutes what it cannot disguise: the impulse to destroy "them niggers," other poor people, bothersome hippies, and obstreperous students. The sloganeering is so understood by a far-out Right-wing constituency loyal to politicians like George Wallace and Spiro Agnew. At the same time, a certain portion of the more privileged, educated, and liberal public, without a racist taint or inordinate hostility to exotic life styles, is simply scared, a feeling it conveys to leaders who are implored to provide better protection for them, their families, and their property. So-called conservatives advocate repression which, when it does not work, prompts them to ask for more repression. Self-styled liberals reflexively favor elimination of the causes, but nobody really knows the causes. Thus, when meliorative measures fail, these liberals call first for further inquiry, and then for more meliorative measures. Meanwhile, solid white citizens of nearly every political persuasion feel that noxious foreign matter exuded by the other America is too great a threat to their personal safety and security, so that, one way or another, it must be contained. Fright precedes the flight to suburbia.

Urban-suburban or black-white polarization crystallizes demographically and geographically.

This is the grim reality that no amount of good will and compassion can obscure from those who inhabit megalopolis. Rational observers will weigh that reality against a few additional data, which will help them keep their balance even if they remain depressed. We need to remember what the National Crime Commission reported in 1967 and the Eisenhower Commission reaffirmed in 1969: that crime off the streets is much more prevalent than crime on the streets (and crime in rice paddies may have exceeded any other kind, as our chief counsel at Nuremberg, General Telford Taylor, has recently suggested); that only a small fraction of officially recorded and duly adjudicated crime is violent—even when the term "violent" is stretched to include robbery of items valued at as little as fifty dollars; and that, to quote the National Commission on the Causes and Prevention of Violence, ". . . deaths and personal injuries from violent crime cause only a small part of the pain and suffering which we experience: one is five times more likely to die in an auto accident than to be criminally slain, and one hundred times more likely to be injured in a home accident than in a serious assault."

With all that, and much, much more that needs to be repeated and remembered, the most widely and deservedly publicized passages of a document too few people have read are also the most nightmarish and prophetic. They ring, alas, even truer now than they did in 1969. Milton Eisenhower and his associates solemnly warned then that, lacking effective public action, our cities were likely to take on these characteristics:

—Central business districts in the heart of the city, surrounded by mixed areas of accelerating deterioration, will be partially protected by large numbers of people shopping or working in commercial buildings during day-time hours, plus a substantial police presence, and will be largely deserted except for police patrols during night-time hours.

—High-rise apartment buildings and residential compounds protected by private guards and security devices will be fortified cells for upper-middle and high-income populations living at prime locations in the city.

—Suburban neighborhoods, geographically far removed from the central city, will be protected mainly by economic homogeneity and by distance from population groups with the highest propensities to commit crimes.

—Lacking a sharp change in federal and state policies, ownership of guns will be almost universal in the suburbs, homes will be fortified by an array of devices from window grills to electronic surveillance equipment, armed citizen volunteers in cars will supplement inadequate police patrols in neighborhoods closer to the central city, and extreme left-wing and right-wing groups will have tremendous armories of weapons which could be brought into play with or without any provocation.

—High-speed, patrolled expressways will be sanitized corridors connecting safe areas, and private automobiles, taxicabs and commercial vehicles will be routinely equipped with unbreakable glass, light armor and other security features. Inside garages or valet parking will be available at safe buildings in or near the central city. Armed guards will "ride shot gun" on all forms of public transportation. . . .

—Between the unsafe, deteriorating central city on the one hand and the network of safe, prosperous areas and sanitized corridors on the other, there will be, not unnaturally, intensifying hatred and deepening division. Violence will increase further and the defensive response of the affluent will become still more elaborate.

When, since *1984,* has extrapolation of the dismal present come so close to the mark? And so rapidly? It is a painful situation, and anyone who claimed he had quick or easy answers would be a knave or a fool. What I want to do here is to step back from the immediacies of the problem, so entangled with passion and blood as to be almost beyond solution, and to see if there may be some value in reflecting upon the matter of crime and punishment from a dispassionate, yet intensely concerned, perspective.

Winston Churchill once said that the public attitude toward criminals constitutes "a sure test of the level of civilization."[1] If so, then

1. The reference is a famous one and appears in, among many other places, the concluding chapter of a book by John Barron Mays, *Crime and the Social Structure* (London: Faber & Faber, 1967), p. 228.

these essentials of the liberal doctrine as set forth by Leon Radzinowicz should not be forgotten:

Since law, and especially criminal law, placed restrictions upon individual freedom, there should be as little of it as possible. To prohibit an action unnecessarily increases rather than decreases crime. Moreover, it was not the function of the law to enforce moral virtue as such, but simply to serve the needs of a particular society. . . .

As to the administration of justice: It was here above all that the rights of the individual had suffered most in the past and here that it was most necessary to build secure lines of defense against the encroachments of the State. . . . Presumption of innocence should be the guiding principle: the maxim, so fashionable at the beginning of the nineteenth century, that it is better that ten guilty persons escape than that one innocent man should suffer, tersely expressed this deeply felt concern.[2]

Men like Cesare Beccaria and Wilhelm von Humboldt (who believed that the evils occasioned by police regulations outweighed those they prevented) set forth a general position that not even its Western heirs can take for granted. This position declares that insofar as a society attempts to legislate sin out of existence, seeking thereby to govern private morals by criminal law, it reverses the historic trend away from tyranny. If this assertion is construed as a pure value judgment—which some of us view also as a demonstrable fact—no one need feel constrained to accept it. That the criminalization of many common acts helps to account for our crime problem is another matter.

This argument has taken two contemporary American criminologists to a point where they see current police practice as the bearer of a serious totalitarian potential. Jerome H. Skolnick and J. Richard Woodward offer their empirical findings to underscore a real and present danger.[3] They know how easily the delicate legal fabric can be torn apart when law becomes the major device for imposing conventional morality. To a large extent the police, who are our official

2. Leon Radzinowicz, *Ideology and Crime* (London: Heinemann, 1966), p. 2.
3. Jerome H. Skolnick and J. Richard Woodward, "Bureaucracy, Information and Social Control" in *The Police,* David J. Bordua, ed. (New York: John Wiley and Sons, 1967), pp. 99–136.

guardians of that morality, have been prevented from achieving full success, or total competence, by their very human limitations. Even now, it is impossible for them to be everywhere; nor are they argus-eyed agents of the conformist behavior that society theoretically demands.

The police have always needed to persuade, pay, threaten, or coerce informants to help them gather intelligence. Perfected or not, any system of surveillance and enforcement consisting solely of human contacts is necessarily fallible. So long as we rely only on people for the production of incriminating evidence, most "immorality" goes undetected, unprosecuted, and consequently unpunished. But, as police efficiency increases, the crime rate looks more alarming, and totalitarian control draws closer. The puny human factor diminishes before an awesome technology.

Skolnick and Woodward draw our attention not only to new means for observing and recording transgression—hidden microphones, wire-taps, high-powered binoculars—but also to the computerized and centralized information they supply. Data banks, with instant retrieval, which may include police, court, probation, school, welfare, and health records, are already under way.

Skolnick and Woodward address themselves to one small but para-digmatic situation in the state of California. There, statutory rape is an offense that occurs when a man has sexual intercourse with a willing girl under the age of eighteen who is not his wife. At the time of this study, no allowance was made if the male honestly and with reason believed the girl to be over the age of consent. Since a 1964 California Supreme Court decision, *People versus Hernandez,* the defendant may plead that he mistakenly but in good faith took the girl to be eighteen years of age or older. The research is concerned with all statutory rapes reported in two jurisdictions: that of the Westville Police Department between January 1962 and October 1963 (a total of 235 cases) and, for comparative purposes, that of a nearby community, Mountain City, where 87 cases were reported for the year 1961. The population of Mountain City is larger than that of Westville. Nevertheless, for the period studied, more cases of statutory rape were reported in Westville than in Mountain City, where, for instance, 40 cases came to the attention of Westville police in 1961. Skolnick and Woodward explain this difference as the statistical artifact that it is. Available figures grossly distort both the incidence and the distribution of an offense whose actual magnitude we cannot know. Those in the upper and middle reaches of American society are not given to lodging complaints that would reveal the sexual indiscretions of their offspring. Parents from the lowest stratum of that society, though they may appear somewhat less reluctant, are also not overeager to act as complainants. Yet it is this stratum, and not only in a corner of California, that supplies most of the known-because-reported cases. If so, why the difference between Westville and Mountain City in numbers and in racial composition (67 percent Negroes compared to 22 percent)? More Negroes live in Westville, but not nearly enough to account for the disproportionate ratios. In a meticulous examination of the police process, Skolnick and Woodward reveal many pertinent details, and of these one emerges as decisive:

> The Mountain City family support division does not systematically report violations it discovers while taking welfare applications, and it is largely to this difference in policy that the different outcome is attributable. . . . As a result, many of the features of the Westville cases are lacking in Mountain City: fewer reporting persons wait until they are certain the girl is pregnant before reporting the offense . . . offenses are reported more quickly . . . ; and Negroes are involved in far fewer of the cases.[4]

One agency in possession of facts otherwise unavailable to the public passes them on to another agency. If A tells B, and B—using its broadly discretionary powers of enforcement—decides to prosecute, nonvoluntary complainants are found, and statutory rape looks like a serious matter. Actual fluctuation in rates remains unknown and unknowable, but when information about welfare recipients is exchanged with police officials, a larger than ordinary number of these people will be included as offenders. Hence, for the record, poor men have a far greater propensity to commit acts of statutory rape than rich men. Where this reporting system has yet to be adopted, the propensity is officially less pronounced. The system implies an increase in police efficiency, which will be further facilitated by improved technology. It exposes much that would remain unexposed about the "wicked ways" of those in an affluent society who receive public assistance. Skolnick and Woodward conclude that the

4. *Ibid.*, p. 111.

Westville policeman is significantly more successful than his Mountain City counterpart in locating "crime," not because of his superior skill or his more rational administration, but basically because he taps welfare records.

These criminologists believe that, for their kind of data, Philip Selznick has posed the most appropriate question, namely, "Do we need or want agencies of control so efficient and so impartial that every actual offender has an equal chance of being known and processed?"[5] Selznick's question answers itself in the negative. For a condition where every offender has an equal chance of being known and "processed" presupposes the politicization and totalitarianization of everything. We are some distance from that extremity. So far, it is only a criminological nightmare that threatens to materialize as mechanical detection replaces merely human effort in order to maintain "law and order." If instant exposure and swift punishment followed the commission of all acts defined at this moment as violations of existing statutes, then our society would be nothing but an enormous prison.

Therefore, one cannot lightly dismiss either Selznick's disturbing question or his implicit answer. Yet we greatly doubt whether that question is quite the right one. Skolnick and Woodward have shown that consequential public policy can be set when welfare department records are transmitted by a family support division to police officials. Specifically created to uncover fraud and nonsupport, the family division may be instrumental in reporting crimes outside its sphere.

The authors ask us to consider what would happen if public policy of this sort extended into other institutional spheres. They offer public schools as an example: "Many acts routinely dealt with by school officials under the label of school discipline—petty theft, carrying of knives, assaults, sport 'pools'—could conceivably be reported to the police for criminal processing."[6] And so they are—not always, or the public schools would be depopulated, but often enough to help overcrowd nearly every reformatory in the land. These offenses, petty theft and so forth, cover a large part of juvenile delinquency.

5. Philip Selznick, "Foundations of the Theory of Organization," *American Sociological Review,* February 1948, p. 84.
6. Skolnick and Woodward, "Bureaucracy, Information and Social Control," p. 112.

The urban public school year by year comes closer to being synonymous with the slum school, in contrast to the private school, the parochial school, and the suburban white school; it is filled with children who learn soon enough that they belong to persecuted minorities. Today's slum school is one of many conduits through which some of these children are remanded to punitive and "rehabilitative" agencies where detention rather than education is the rule. Social critics like Paul Goodman have characterized the average public school as an institution very much like a penal colony.[7] If still more police discipline is substituted for the fairly rigid school discipline that already prevails, then an even larger number of dark, or not so dark, and impoverished youths will be caught directly in the coils of the law. Far from attaining impartial justice, such that "each actual offender has an equal chance" of being apprehended and punished, we would achieve a marked enlargement of the discriminatory treatment chronically accorded underdogs. That such criminal justice shows no sign of abatement is a major component in the strife besetting America.

One cannot overemphasize this point: discriminatory treatment before the law in a formal framework of equality weighs heavily, oppressively (and, among both victims and offenders, more consciously than ever) on the poor. The poor, moreover, are likely to discover that unhappy truth early in life. Unlawful conduct *which results in arrest and adjudication* is overwhelmingly found among the young. Teenagers (and subteenagers), not deemed to have reached the age of reason, are technically irresponsible. Special courts exist to protect them from being branded as criminals. They and slightly older youths comprise the hard core of our highly publicized crime problem. Given a national population of which nearly half was born after 1945, those in the age bracket of 16–21 are by far the largest criminal category. On this datum all authorities are agreed—as they are agreed on the low socioeconomic status of most youthful offenders. To be pigeonholed as offenders they must first have been convicted. Mere arrest cannot be equated with guilt, especially when "According to a recent estimate based on 1963 F.B.I. crime reports approximately

7. Paul Goodman, *Growing Up Absurd* (New York: Random House, 1960).

two and one-half million persons arrested annually for non-traffic offenses are not convicted."[8] Edward V. Sparer, who cites this estimate, goes on to say, "Despite the court's finding that such persons are not guilty, social punishment for the *fact of arrest* is often quick to follow."[9] He quotes from a New York memorandum, which in his opinion accurately describes one countrywide form of inequity:

The major handicap from an arrest record appears to be in securing and retaining employment, membership in a labor organization, or apprenticeship training. Applications for both public and private employment sometimes ask not only whether an applicant has ever been convicted, but also whether he has ever been arrested on charges, and sometimes even whether he has ever received a summons. . . .

The persons most affected by this practice are almost invariably those who reside in disadvantaged areas, of whom a high proportion are Negro and Puerto Rican. Wholesale arrests of "suspects" on vagrancy charges are often made when a crime or a "rumble" has occurred in a high-delinquency area. Most of these "suspects" are released after questioning, but their job opportunities have been endangered without any proof of guilt.[10]

The disadvantaged boy living in a "high-delinquency area" may seem disrespectful, uppity, mischievous, or idle. The policeman, who enjoys a social status higher than that boy and his family, must decide whether or not to include him in a roundup of "suspects." If he chooses to make the "pinch," it will be a first arrest in about one case out of four. Guarantees of confidentiality and anonymity notwithstanding, this experience can blight the rest of the boy's life. Arrested, booked, interrogated, and discharged as innocent, he now has "a record," ostensibly unavailable to others who represent a society that wishes to protect him even if his conduct *has* been judged wrongful or harmful. The statutory language used in New York is similar to that of other jurisdictions: ". . . no person adjudicated a juvenile delinquent . . . may be denominated a criminal by reason of such adjudication." Further:

8. Edward V. Sparer, "Employability and the Juvenile 'Arrest' Record," *Work, Youth, and Unemployment,* Melvin Herman, Stanley Sadofsky, Bernard Rosenberg, eds. (New York: Thomas Y. Crowell, 1968), p. 470.
9. *Ibid.*
10. *Ibid.*

All police records relating to the arrest and disposition of any person under this article . . . shall be withheld from public inspection. . . . Loopholes *are* specified; such records shall be open to inspection upon good cause shown by the parent, guardian, next friend, or attorney of that person upon the written order of a judge of the family court in the county in which the order was made or, if the person is subsequently convicted of a crime, of a judge of the court in which he was convicted.[11]

These exceptions do not include possibly prejudiced employers, union leaders jealously guarding the ethnic exclusivity of their membership, or personnel in nonjudicial branches of the federal government. All are supposedly barred, as are neighbors, pressmen, and laymen at large, from scrutiny of presumably private and confidential documents. And all have fairly free access to them. Job applicants, as well as would-be apprentices and soldiers, with "records," can lie about their past, which is itself an actionable practice, or they can compromise themselves by admitting the truth. Alternatively, young people sign waivers to their legal right of confidentiality. Privileged information is released, legislative intent is contravened, and anyone who in his minority was justly or unjustly *charged* with an offense can be incriminated.

Sparer emphasizes the abuse, not to say the impropriety and near illegality, which most heavily penalizes young people, who, in any event, are three or four times less employable than their more advantaged peers. Years ago, Austin Porterfield found no statistically significant difference between the waywardness of court children and of college or precollege students. He defined the official delinquent as a friendless youth, moving under maximum exposure to arrest, usually on the street because there was no other place for him to be.[12] Such youths are hauled into station houses, where their names appear on police blotters. Later on, out of school and out of work, countless numbers of them are disqualified from employment, from job training, and from service in the armed forces because they are held to be "poor risks"—with "records" they cannot erase.

The difficulties of slum-bred youths are thus compounded. Private employers, craft unions, and sections of the government disqualify

11. *Ibid.*, p. 472.
12. Austin L. Porterfield, "Delinquency and Its Outcome in Court and College," *American Journal of Sociology*, November 1943, pp. 199–208.

precisely those whose employability is in the first place most restricted. It is usually considered too dangerous to hire these "potential" criminals. Sparer reports a study made by the New York Civil Liberties Union of employment agency practices, in which fully 75 percent of the agencies sampled ask job applicants about *arrest* records, and "as a matter of regular and automatic procedure," would not refer those with arrest records, irrespective of any judicial determination that may have been made. Adjudications of "Delinquency," "Youthful Offender," and "Wayward Youth"—all are supposed to be purely "civil," and never "criminal" proceedings. The perversion of this principle exercises thoughtful judges, legal philosophers, and criminologists.

Every few months, crime is reported to be on the upswing, but it is not accidental that the full force of penal and social sanctions falls only on some offenders. The regular upswing can be partially attributed to greater efficiency in detecting and reporting crime committed not just by any citizen, but by a certain kind of citizen. When two humane criminologists, Richard R. Korn and Lloyd W. McCorkle, ask, "How far may the State go in enforcing social values?" they correctly perceive ethical issues that transcend crime and punishment. We agree with them that "To press for unlimited enforcement efficiency is, in effect, to assert that the ends justify the means. To set limits on the reaches of the law is, in effect, to assert that the individual is himself a social end."[13] The inference is valid and we salute the praiseworthy sentiment that underlies it. But once again, as with Selznick, sight has been lost of a differential, selective, and invidious process. No one presses for truly *unlimited* enforcement efficiency. Those who press wish to achieve greater and greater enforcement efficiency in the *same limited* area of class and race that has never ceased to be their concern.

Korn and McCorkle, in passages immediately preceding their critical question, draw upon a prominent legal authority, William Seagle, who neatly circumscribes the area. Seagle finds most justices of the Supreme Court of the United States expounding the view that efficiency in criminal law enforcement is irreconcilable with decency and

13. Richard R. Korn and Lloyd W. McCorkle, *Criminology and Penology* (New York: Henry Holt, 1959), p. 97.

liberty—which, in the profoundest sense, renders it unconstitutional. He sees the open exposition of this philosophy in Justice Jackson's statement, "The forefathers, after consulting the lessons of history, designed our Constitution to place obstacles in the way of a too permeating police surveillance, which they seemed to think a greater danger to a free people than the escape of some criminals from punishment." To which Seagle appends an aphorism of his own: "The inefficiency of the criminal law is indeed the pride of democracy."[14] Except for an additional appraisal, all this could still relate to unlimited efficiency. The key paragraph follows:

Power can be curbed only by making the law inefficient. Indeed the establishment of every limitation upon political power has been a tacit recognition of the undesirability of legal efficiency. Humanity has constantly drawn back from legal efficiency as from the brink of an abyss. When threatened by efficient law enforcement, it has loudly demanded Twelve Tables, codes, bills of rights, declarations of the rights of man, and full-fledged written constitutions—*all for the purpose of protecting the weak against the strong, and the individual against the state.* In short, it has always demanded inefficiency as an inalienable right of man. Of course no one literally demands "inefficiency," which as an ideal has always been in bad odor. Everyone actually demands "liberty." Liberty, however, is only inefficiency in false face. [Emphasis added.][15]

"Protecting the individual against the state" is without any possible respite a matter of the utmost urgency. Safeguards built into criminal law are a political shield against authoritarian and totalitarian rule. So long, however, as democratic forms persist and we continue to cherish them, protecting the weak against the strong must remain uppermost in our minds. In the first instance, every full-blown twentieth-century dictatorship, whether of the Right or the Left, has taught us anew how heavily civil liberty and the principle of legality depend upon criminal law. That much should have been learned by anyone who has lived through the past fifty years of world history. Once in power, the Bolsheviks, the Nazis, the Maoists, and the Fidelistas, having enjoyed such civil liberty as they found (sometimes a great deal, sometimes very little), destroyed every vestige of the rights on which they had capitalized.

14. *Ibid.*, p. 96.
15. *Ibid.*, pp. 96–97.

Over two decades ago, Jerome Hall summed up several traits common to revolutionary authoritarian movements:

Special police are exempt from legal constraint: they arrest, try, execute, and exile without legal restraint. Appeal is limited or non-existent. Special tribunals for the trial of political offenders may be depended upon to effectuate the will of the government. There is sweeping abrogation of constitutional guarantees. All of this is rationalized and sustained by controlled philosophic thought, as interpreted by the leaders to implement their political aims. . . . Thus, during revolution, law, especially criminal law, is used as a party weapon.[16]

And we may say that this is still so, long after the revolution has run its course!

Hall has referred us to the Russian Penal Code of 1926, which stated:

A crime is any socially dangerous act or omission which threatens the foundations of the Soviet political structure and that system of law which has been established by the Workers' and Peasants' Government for the period of transition to a Communist structure.

In cases where the Criminal Code makes no direct reference to particular forms of crimes, punishments or other measures of social protection are applied in accordance with those Articles of the Criminal Code which deal with crimes most closely approximating, in gravity and in kind, the crimes actually committed.[17]

Similarly in Nazi Germany, the Act of June 28, 1935, provided:

Any person who commits an act which the law declares to be punishable, or which is deserving of penalty according to the fundamental conceptions of penal law and sound popular feeling, shall be punished. If there is no penal law directly covering an act, it shall be punished under the law of which the fundamental conception applies most nearly to the said act.[18]

The arbitrariness which this Act exudes lasted only as long as National Socialism. Its spirit, by which the rule of law was temporarily expunged for Germans, has proved to be more durable in Soviet Russia. Fifty-one years after the October Revolution, James Reston

16. Jerome Hall, *General Principles of Criminal Law* (Indianapolis: Bobbs-Merrill, 1947), p. 57.
17. *Ibid.,* p. 42.
18. *Ibid.*

supplied a pertinent postscript. Reston, writing from Russia for the *New York Times* on November 21, 1968, noted:

Moscow has its own "law and order." If justice is "incidental" to order, as J. Edgar Hoover is reported to have said the other day, he would be happy in Moscow. This is a policeman's paradise, and "crime in the streets" is manageable.

At this writing, the United States has still declined to opt fully for such "law and order" as Moscow confers on a disenfranchised citizenry. No higher priority has as yet totally eclipsed or absolutely subordinated that concept of justice which runs like a golden thread through British and American criminal law. Those who have not collapsed into totalitarianism, like those who have wrenched themselves free from its confinement, are better protected in their struggle for "the individual against the state" than they are in their struggle for "the weak against the strong." Pending a politically calamitous resolution of our many social and economic crises, which would require us to suspend the Constitution and the Bill of Rights, we are markedly more vulnerable on the second score than on the first.

Before suprafamilial control or centralized state authority came into being, when man's existence was still coterminous with the band, the clan and the tribe, reparation and revenge were identical. Attacker and defender, criminal and victim, and their kindred, all governed by an unshakable belief in collective or consanguineous responsibility, and involved one another in endless acts of retaliation. Most important in primitive or preliterate and early Western law was that "Injury was scaled in accordance with the seriousness of the trespass and the social evaluation of the aggrieved party."[19] Whoever attacked also ineluctably provoked defense and counterattack—setting two families in motion, touching off a vendetta or blood feud. (The term "blood feud" suggests kinship, which always mattered most, rather than bloodshed, which was often present.) Punishment was carefully graded to the litigant's social position.

This theme is the subject matter of all sagas, of all epic literature—whether that of nomadic tribesmen or more settled peoples like the

19. Norman C. Cantor, *The English* (New York: Simon and Schuster, 1968), p. 33.

ancient Greeks, Romans, Icelanders, Gauls, and Anglo-Saxons. Gradually, the blood feud gave way to other forms of reparation, "composition," or compensation. Survivals of the very old tradition remain in virtually every society, including our own. How could it be otherwise when "The blood feud in Anglo-Saxon society was as central to social life as employment and taxes are today"?[20] By modern standards, the violence of medieval Europe was prodigious. In the end, it must have been too enervating and too dangerous to be borne. With plague and hunger never far behind, only so much manslaughter, murder, and robbery-by-stealth could remain unchecked. An alternative to the blood feud, a legal process, had to be worked out. Christendom, of which Britain was a part after the seventh century, sorely needed an authority both broader and more powerful than that of angry kinsmen. It was on this social necessity that Anglo-Saxon society founded the folk or community court.

From the late sixth century onward, a folk court or *moot* operated, at least among the leading warrior class in the small kingdoms of Wessex, Kent, Northumbria, and Mercia. It endured until Anglo-Norman times and then, in uneven stages after 1066, to the indigenous Angle and Saxon nations. By the eighth century, moots were differentiated into local courts, called hundreds, and others, encompassing subkingdoms or whole kingdoms, which were designated as shires. Norman F. Cantor, in his history of England, graphically describes how they worked:

Whether it was the hundred or the shire court, the leading men of the community presided and arrived at decisions by a kind of consensus of the meeting. These leaders of the court may be called doomsmen or elders or wisemen but in all cases they were inevitably the men of greater substance and influence whose task was to work out and perpetuate legal processes in accordance with customary law. In the case of the hundred court the elders of the court could be ordinary peasants; in the case of the shire court they would always be the great warlords in the community. The first task of the folk moot was to build upon the old Germanic tradition that the blood feud could be abrogated in return for monetary compensation, the *Wergeld* (literally, man-money), to the dead man's kin. The kin were not required to take the wergeld and waive the right of revenge; it was the first obligation of the court to urge them to accept

20. *Ibid.*, p. 16.

it. It was their second task to prepare lists of wergelds for every possible kind of violence, from the loss of a toenail, to the killing of a slave, to the killing of a nobleman or king (the king's wergeld was placed so high that no man, no matter how many cattle he owned, could afford to pay it).[21]

The folk moot was designed to inhibit, and, if possible, to abolish, the exercise of family vengeance. It sought, without the sophistication of Roman law—which left no perceptible mark on early Britain—to determine who committed murder and robbery by stealth. Neither the rules of evidence nor rational procedure for the interrogation of witnesses had come into being. Moots reached a verdict by invoking divine aid as it was made manifest in the ordeal and by compurgation. A defendant was unlikely to survive either the ordeal of hot iron or the ordeal of cold water. In the former, he touched a piece of red-hot iron, and if after three days his hand showed signs of festering, he was promptly hanged. England, with its many lakes and streams, seems to have favored the ordeal of water, in which the defendant, bound hand and foot, was flung into a body of water. "If he sank he was innocent and if he floated he was guilty, on the premise that water, being a holy element, would not receive a guilty man. The defendant thus had a choice between probable death by drowning and certain death by hanging."[22]

The historical record shows refinements and variations (the use of boiling caldrons from which stones had to be retrieved, or two- and three-fold ordeals), but in essence this was the judicial process. Christian churchmen initially found it repugnant, but while they added oaths and efforts to extract confessions, the ordeal had become so essential a part of Anglo-Saxon life that it could not be extirpated. Cantor argues that the folk court provided an element of rationality: "Only those defendants were put to the ordeal who were either commonly suspected of guilt"—which is an element of rationality—"or were of the lower social strata"—which is something else. Cantor informs us, "It was a process almost exclusively designed for those who were peasants or who were 'ill-famed,' which to the medieval mind with its strong class biases meant almost the same thing." Then

21. *Ibid.*, p. 37.
22. *Ibid.*

the historian cannot refrain from ruminating upon what he has just written: "Those who are horrified by this deep social prejudice might reflect on the kinds of people who have suffered capital punishment in the United States, noting the overwhelming proportion of Negroes and poor people. In this respect we have remained faithful to the traditions of Anglo-Saxon law."[23]

As long as society is divided into the noble and the ignoble (which is to say, always and everywhere, and with or without ideological support), special provision must also be made for those of wealth and prominence. In this too we have remained faithful to the tradition of Anglo-Saxon law. Compurgations against indictments in the folk court were for noblemen what ordeals were for peasants. Again, divine intercession was called for but in a much less exacting and arduous manner than the harsh method reserved for the common populace. In compurgation, the defendant swore to his innocence, and oath helpers, graded by their wergelds, swore that his oath could be taken as "clean," in other words, that he was a man of good repute.

The court could decide only who should have the privilege of compurgation and how weighty the oath helpers needed to be. As Cantor writes,

Beyond this, a rich man who was oblivious to the heavenly perils of perjury and who had powerful relatives and friends of like dispositions could commit murder and robbery with impunity. He might be dealt with by the kin of the victim, but the court could not convict him. Thus Anglo-Saxon process tended to provide one procedure for the rich and the powerful and another for the poor and the unknown.

It is an understatement to conclude that "This class bias in somewhat less flagrant forms was to have a long history in English law and has not entirely ended at the present time."[24] Class bias, complicated by race, never ceased to operate. More opaque, subdued, and genuinely humane in the modern era, its recrudescence is apparent as crime becomes a public obsession.

The idea of individual autonomy was alien to all feudal law. Subjects, not yet citizens, were divested of will: they could only obey. In

23. *Ibid.*
24. *Ibid.*, p. 38.

a strict hierarchical order, thought to be ordained by Almighty God, no inferior could legitimately bring any accusation against a superior. Subjects were not entitled to invoke the help of a law court except against those of equal or subordinate status. In the feudal theocracy, no layman could charge a cleric with any crime. Walter Ullman, the eminent medievalist, has shown that in terms of ecclesiastical and secular law, *people* of every age were defined as minors, requiring the undisputed protection of their overall superiors, who, in turn, had been deputized by God to act *in loco parentis*. And what of the folk court? Ullman's answer is, "One can best understand the meaning of the Munt [moot] if one compares it to the guardianship of a child: it is the kind of protection which a father affords to a child, or a guardian to his ward, or in Anglo-Saxon and Anglo-Norman England, the husband to his wife."[25]

High treason could be committed only against the king, or rather, against his "highness," his *majestas,* a term pointing to the sublime office and function of him who was major. No royal persona could and, where the monarchy survives, none can today commit a crime. By the same token, no mere vassal but only a subject could commit high treason. "Petty treason" was of a lower order: it consisted in murder of the master by his servant, murder of the bishop by a clerk or a layman of his diocese, or murder of the husband by the wife. A remnant of old Roman law, elaborated by medieval jurists, namely, "What pleases the prince has the force of law," is quoted in modern canon law to this day. In a unique blend of Hellenistic, Roman, and Christian elements, the High Middle Ages produced a high legal synthesis. By it, law, already apotheosized in the Invisible Ruler, was literally embodied in the visible ruler. An organic, functional, collectivist metaphor—precluding any such novel idea as individual citizenship—underlay the whole conception. "The body politic" and related imagery, as Michael Walzer has pointed out, served to justify a rigid hierarchy of persons which gradually supplanted the chaos of feudal arrangements:

. . . as the head rules the body, medieval writers argued, so God the world and the king the polity; as the angels stand below God in nine

25. Walter Ullman, *The Individual and Society in the Middle Ages* (London: Methuen & Co., 1967), p. 21.

ranks and orders, so the nobler parts of the body politic below the king and the priests of the body of Christ below the Pope.[26]

Walzer maintains that the inequality thus defended also established persistent patterns of obedience and deference. His conclusion is unexceptionable. And yet the curious system, which comprises so large a part of our cultural heritage, carried with it in embryonic form what we today would call the rule of law. The premodern world (and a whole assortment of metaphysical underpinnings) had to decompose before that rule could become a widely held ideal. For a while, with the spread of equalitarianism from Western Europe, the ideal seemed to have triumphed. Actually, in waxing and waning, its precarious nature is clearly exposed.

At best the rule of law never fully banished gross inequality before the law. A veteran English magistrate, reflecting on his long career, found it most appropriate in 1969 to use as the epigraph to a book of selected memoirs[27] this passage from King Lear (IV:6):

See how yond justice rails upon yond simple thief. Hark in thine ear. Change places; and, handy-dandy, which is the justice, which is the thief?

By and large, and handy-dandy, Shakespeare's mad king knew enough to ask the question without which no criminological answer is worth a moment's notice.

26. Michael Walzer, *The Revolution of the Saints* (New York: Atheneum, 1968), p. 7.
27. John Watson, *Which Is the Justice?* (London: Allen & Unwin, 1969).

Lewis Lipsitz

A Better System of Prisons?

DECENTRALIZATION AND PARTICIPATION

Adieu Prince I have tasks a sewer project
and a decree on prostitutes and beggars
I must also elaborate a better system of prisons
Since as you justly said Denmark is a prison. . . .

ZBIGNIEW HERBERT, *Elegy of Fortinbras*

Imagine, if you will, Hamlet alive at the end of Shakespeare's play. Fortinbras, just returned from battle, stands with him on the stage. The audience must choose: which man will rule Denmark? How shall we go about making such a choice?

We know something about each of them. In contrast to Hamlet's terrible inner conflicts, we sense Fortinbras's blunt decisiveness. He appears capable of assuming power while Hamlet has seemed barely able to maintain control over himself. But then Hamlet has faced a different series of problems: matters of the inner life, of murder, guilt, love, and salvation. Then we hear Fortinbras speak the words quoted above. What is he telling us? Perhaps something about bureaucratic rule. Perhaps something about the inevitability of "prisons," social arrangements which deform and punish our capacities for freedom. Perhaps he is asking us to face the boredom, craft,

A somewhat longer version of this essay was prepared for a conference on New Public Administration and Neighborhood Control held in Boulder, Colorado, in May 1970. The Conference was sponsored by The Center for Governmental Studies, Washington, D.C. That version of the essay will appear in H. George Frederickson, ed., *Politics, Public Administration and Neighborhood Control* (San Francisco: Chandler Publishing Company) scheduled for publication early in 1972.

and tension which are a necessary part of rule. Perhaps he is speaking for the dignity of that reformism which aims to obtain as much as it is possible to obtain. Perhaps he is communicating to us the emptiness of a politics that is without tragedy and inner questioning.

Yet, even if we knew these men better than we do, how should we decide between them? It may be there is a polity for which Hamlet would be suited; and another, quite different, that would prosper under Fortinbras. On the other hand, we might conclude that they both should take extended vacations. In order to make up our minds, we would be wise to inquire about Denmark itself.

Here we must hesitate, for we do not know enough to pass judgment. We do not know if they are tired of war or of peace. We do not know if the bureaucracy is reasonable and sensibly structured, or if it perpetuates it own privileges. We do not know of mass movements and agitations that may be occurring in the hinterlands. Until we can grasp the larger context, we cannot make a decision about who is to rule.

This same issue of "context" plagues current discussions of decentralization and participation. Often the debate between proponents and opponents of decentralization and participation appears as if it were a debate over eternal truths. How much hierarchy is necessary? How much participation does it take to create a healthy personality? How fully should professional norms override popular preferences? Can poor people be rational? Can bureaucrats act like human beings? As with the question about Fortinbras and Hamlet, without some understanding of the political context we cannot know whether decentralization in the U.S. today will be a real improvement or simply create a "better system of prisons."

A few of the questions just mentioned are, perhaps, real,[1] but when they are brought to bear on the issues of participation and decentralization in America today, they often function as a disguise for normative preferences; they mask the real issues rather than unraveling them. They obscure the limits of what is possible by defining the possible without context. Other discussions focus too narrowly on the more immediate political considerations. We hear about troubles caused in

---

1. For a discussion of some of these issues among professionals in public administration see the January-February 1970 issue of *Public Administration Review*.

a particular town, or the pacification produced. We hear about a federal program undermined, or of small successes in making the bureaucracy knuckle under. Again, this is talk that needs to be aired, but it does not in itself constitute a broad enough discussion.

To make judgments about the issues involved in decentralization and participation, we have to know more about the polity we are talking about, and about the nature of the times. If we know that corporate and economic power is abusive and cannot be controlled locally, we might opt for national regulation. If we know that religious cleavage is acute and destructive and being exacerbated by excessive central regulation, we might opt for greater local autonomy. If we know that libertarian principles are widely held, but opposed by elites, we might favor greater local law-making powers. In all such cases, various mixes of central-local initiative might be worked out, depending on the circumstances.

How then do we establish a meaningful context for deciding about decentralization and participation in the United States today?

The first question we need to answer is: how effectively are Americans now participating in political life? I do not propose to attempt a full answer, but only to set out a few main issues for discussion. Ordinarily, in more or less democratic societies, political parties serve as the main forums for political discussion and the main vehicles for participation. In the United States, as Walter Dean Burnham has pointed out, the parties have not performed this function very effectively and, in fact, have deteriorated in these respects since the late nineteenth century. Burnham traces the relatively low levels of political participation in America to two primary factors: first, the growth of one-party systems in many areas of the country after 1896, a situation the New Deal did something, but not enough, to change; second, the failure of a major party of the Left to develop in this country, leaving a "hole" in our political system. This last point is most significant, Burnham argues, because it means that no party is attempting to mobilize the poorest sectors of the population in any sustained way. Burnham's picture of the American party system over time looks like this:

. . . the reality of American politics appears quite different from a simple vision of pluralist democracy. It is shot through with escalating tensions, periodic electoral convulsions and repeated redefinitions of the rules and general outcomes of the political game. It has also been marked repeatedly by redefinitions—by no means always broadening ones—of those who are permitted to play. And one other very basic characteristic of American party politics that emerges from an historical overview is the profound incapacity of established political leadership to adapt itself to the political demands produced by the losers in America's stormy socio-economic life. As is well-known, American political parties are not instruments of collective purpose, but of electoral success. One major implication of this is that, as organizations, parties are interested in control of offices but not of government in any larger sense. It follows that once successful routines are established or reestablished for office-winning, very little motivation exists among party leaders to disturb the routines of the game. These routines are periodically upset, to be sure, but not by adaptive change within the party system. They are upset by overwhelming external force.[2]

True, the Democratic party has, as Burnham himself notes, mobilized *some* of the less privileged groups in America. But it is just this matter of degree that makes for sharp contrast between our political system and that, say, of the Scandinavian countries, where Labor and Social Democratic parties have been able to incorporate a considerably larger percentage of working- and lower-class groups. The same contrast holds in regard to trade unionism. Millions of American blue-collar workers are still not unionized, and the overall percentage of unionization is far lower than in most Western European countries. This means that a significant portion of the American population has not been educated about economic and class-related issues, and that it does not see a clear relationship between its problems and politics.

This is not to denigrate what portions of the Democratic party have achieved. It is to note, however, the larger problem of nonparticipation that America continues to have. The future prospects of the Democratic party as a vehicle for social change will depend, in part, on its ability to reduce this problem to smaller dimensions. Without a party that consciously aims to organize and politicize those with low incomes and little education, participation will remain low in these groups, and such people will be unable to relate their grievances to larger political

2. See Burnham's two articles: "The Changing Shape of the American Political Universe," *American Political Science Review,* March 1965, pp. 7–28; and "The End of American Party Politics," *Trans-action,* December 1969, pp. 12–22. Quotes are from the latter.

questions; and they may also be attracted, when they are aroused, by demagogic or personalist appeals. We have then a long-term fact about the American political system: the failure to mobilize fully that portion of the population most likely to support egalitarian social change.

The second point of reference concerns the rates and meanings of social change. What sort of change is taking place? Do people feel it is under reasonable control? Is the distribution of privileges and deprivations felt to be legitimate? On these scores, much has gone wrong in our society. At every turn, we are confronted with massive "unplanned" social changes with profound consequences: migrations from rural areas; environmental pollution. Here people experience at first hand the impact of social forces beyond their control. Here the economically useless, or the marginally useful, find that their condition is a secondary consideration in a profit-oriented economy. Many of these developments impinge most directly on the poor and the powerless, who must bear the brunt of those changes they cannot halt.

In addition, over the last twenty years in this country, the distribution of wealth has remained relatively unaltered. Again, it is those at the economic bottom of society whose condition has improved least. Despite all of the loose talk about an "affluent society," most Americans are far from economically comfortable. Many, in all classes of society, feel the pinch and are not certain that the future will be better. In any case, it seems reasonable to suppose that the failure to redistribute wealth in recent years, though not consciously perceived, has led to feelings of discontent and a certain lack of hope.

Third and finally, we must ask about the "legitimacy" of authority structures in America. The sixties were a time for questioning the "legitimacy" that social scientists believed was so solid in the late fifties. Schools, local governments, police, national bureaucracies, major corporations, the military, the electoral process, have all had sharp challenges not only to aspects of policy, but to their very styles of functioning.

John Schaar has argued that we are seeing a general crisis of legitimacy in modern societies, a crisis which has multiple roots.[3] Without exploring Schaar's arguments here, let me note that he

3. "Legitimacy in the Modern State," in Green and Levinson, eds., *Power and Community* (New York: Pantheon, 1970), pp. 276–327.

criticizes the Weberian model of the "rational-legal" form of authority and maintains that the bureaucratic style cannot be a genuinely satisfactory form of authority. He emphasizes here the specific sort of "rationality" bureaucracies cultivate. This "rationality" involves depersonalization, detachment of personal feelings, interchangeability of individual bureaucrats. In contrast to this bureaucratic conception of authority, Schaar describes what he calls "natural" or "human" authority." This sort of authority involves a

kind of knowledge which includes intuition, insight, and vision as indispensable elements. . . . One who possesses and values this kind of knowledge bases his claims to its validity on grounds which are quicksand to the objective and rational man. One of the foundations is strength of conviction. . . . The other ground is the resonance set going between leader and followers when communication "makes sense."

In our time, Schaar writes, "the established processes and formal structures of control are at war with the conditions necessary for authority." In the end, however, Schaar, while recognizing a "crisis" of authority, does not try to predict what new forms of authority may develop in the future.

There are many ambiguities here. It is possible, with opinion data, to "prove" that most Americans believe in the "legitimacy" of the national government. But it is equally possible to show that large numbers of Americans show strong mistrust of local and national governments, of courts, and of political parties. All of these attitudes exist side by side, and choosing to represent only one portion of them distorts both reality and the potentialities of the future.

If I have now established at least a portion of the context for a discussion of the issues involved in participation and decentralization, I have not shown how this context might help us come to some conclusions about these issues. I have already argued that participation is lower than it ought to be in America and that many widespread grievances are not mobilized. These positions certainly look friendly to increased participation, but they do not tell us anything about where that participation ought to take place, nor do they tell us anything about the decentralization of bureaucracies and increased citizen involvement at the local level. But how do poor Americans feel about these matters? As one further preliminary to answering these questions, we can turn briefly to some data on the attitudes of the poor in a city I have studied, Durham, North Carolina.

How It Looks in Durham

Let's say we go to Durham and ask some poor whites and Negroes how they feel about the relationships between themselves and the various levels of government. What do we find?[4] First, we find a lot of ignorance, especially among poor whites. Nearly half of both racial groups have heard neither of the antipoverty program nor of Head Start. Approximately 40 percent of the whites and approximately 30 percent of the Negroes do not know about Operation Breakthrough, although this community-action program was extremely controversial and made the papers frequently. Three-quarters of the whites and between 40 and 50 percent of the Negroes do not know whether or not there is a neighborhood council in their neighborhood. Finally, we find that when asked whether the poverty program would help most of the poor, or only a few of the poor, 60 percent of the Negroes and three-quarters of the whites, perhaps wisely, said they didn't know.

Next, we find that most poor people do not feel that the government is helping them with their most important problems, which in their minds are overwhelmingly financial—problems of food, clothing, shelter, and health care. When asked if the governments in Washington, Raleigh, or Durham had ever helped or hurt them, these men responded as indicated in the table below:

Has the Government Ever Helped (Hurt) You?

	Washington		*Raleigh*		*Durham*	
	Helped	Hurt	Helped	Hurt	Helped	Hurt
Negroes	48%	21%	7%	21%	21%	14%
Whites	42	15	23	11	17	4

We can see here, first, a relative absence of the sense of connection with government. In no case do even half of the men say that a partic-

4. The Durham survey, based on three- or four-hour interviews with a sample of poor whites and Negroes, was carried out in 1966 and 1967. For a fuller discussion, see Lipsitz, in *Power and Community*.

ular level of government helped them or hurt them. Second, one sees a predominance of "helping" over "hurting," except in the case of Negro feelings about state government. Much of this predominance, however, results from the fact that these men largely do not see the government as hurting them by what it fails to do, but only by the harm it inflicts, mostly in the form of taxes. Third, we see a sharp drop-off in the sense of receiving help from the government, once we focus on the state and local level. On the whole, most of the help received from the federal government was seen in terms of social security, public housing, unemployment benefits, and jobs. If we look more carefully at the comments these men make about the government, we find a mix of feeling, ranging from deference to cynical detachment to specific criticism to a sense of loyalty. For example, here is a fairly typical, positive response, but an unusually revealing one:

—What are the biggest problems you face?
—I don't have any too big problems to worry about right now. The biggest problem I have is worrying about health and things like that.
—Has the government in Washington ever done anything to help you?
—Yes, my social security and the protection and all they give me in this country.
—Has the government in Washington ever done anything to hurt you?
—Not that I know anything about.
—Has the state government in Raleigh ever done anything to help you?
—Yes, not helped me directly, but they helped when my mother was an invalid. They helped me with that, with her care and upkeep. That was welfare and old-age benefits.
—Has the state government ever done anything to hurt you?
—Not that I know anything about.
—Has the city government here in Durham ever done anything that helped you?
—I don't know anything specific, but they've never done anything to hurt me.
—They haven't hurt you?
—No. In fact, I've never called on them to help me.

A certain self-awareness and sense of the citizen's potential "activity" comes through in this last answer. This is what ranks as unusual. Others have complaints beneath which one senses broader frustration:

—Has the government in Washington ever done anything to help you?
—No, they ain't never done nothing. . . .
—Has the state government in Raleigh ever done anything to help you?
—I don't ever want to talk about them crackers in Raleigh.
—Has the state government ever done anything to hurt you?
—Yeah . . . Too many taxes, raggedy streets.
—Has the city government in Durham ever done anything to help you?
—No.
—Has it ever done anything to hurt you?
—They don't fix the raggedy streets either.

Often people have a sense of governmental inadequacies without being about to pinpoint their own recommendations or complaints. For example:

—Has the state government in Raleigh ever done anything to help you?
—No, I can't say that it has directly. Just like everybody else, I go along with the state, the people in it.
—Has the city government in Durham ever done anything to help you?
—No, that's on the same footing. You can't find any one person that can come right out and say the state has done them any harm, any damage, but still, it looks like everything they do, everyone don't agree with it.

If we look in other ways at their attitudes toward political institutions, we find a heavy dose of mistrust and feelings of alienation. For example, we asked a series of questions about the political parties, the laws, and the relationship between "rich people" and the government. In the table on page 414 we compare the Durham findings with those of a national sample.

In addition to the strong dose of mistrust seen in these responses, we also find that two-thirds of these men believe that half or more of all Americans are poor. Close to 90 percent believe there will always be poor people. And close to half the Negroes and two-thirds of the whites believe there will be the same number of poor people, or more, ten years from now. Their picture of the world then is not an optimistic one. They are resigned to the existence of poverty and largely to

Attitudes Toward Political Institutions

	DURHAM DATA		NATIONAL SAMPLE
	Negroes	Whites	(McClosky, 1956)*
1. Govt. pays more attention to rich?			
Yes	28%	60%	—
No	41	28	—
Don't know	31	6	—
2. Parties controlled by the rich?			
Yes	45	51	32.1%
No	41	40	—
Don't know	14	9	—
3. Laws are rich man's laws?			
Yes	62	53	33.3
No	35	43	—
Don't know	3	4	—
4. Representatives not connected with citizen?			
Yes	53	52	43.7
No	21	24	—
Don't know	26	24	—
5. Parties are too big?			
Yes	65	79	67.5
No	23	17	—
Don't know	12	4	—

* Herbert McClosky, "Consensus and Ideology in American Politics," *American Political Science Review,* June 1964.

their own poverty as well, though this is truer of whites than of Negroes. They have a heavy dose of distrust about government that has surely been thoroughly earned.

If we look at what has happened in Durham in the 1960s, we see a history that has many parallels elsewhere. Negroes have become more organized and self-conscious and have been somewhat successful in pressuring local government and institutions. But organizing among the white poor has had only the most limited success, though these people are in no less need of better chances. Negroes have fought on such issues as desegregation, housing-code enforcement, representation on local boards, welfare regulations, health care, employment, and so on. Only one successful white neighborhood group has been organized. It has fought through a few small neighborhood issues.[5] Though Negroes in the future may demand decentralization and greater control over local bureaucracies, poor whites are more in need of local organization and are more locked into the feelings of political futility.

Decentralization and Participation: Issues and Methods

There are many problems in America, not one. And there will have to be many solutions. Paul Goodman, an early advocate of decentralization and citizen participation, has cautioned that the present movement toward local control and self-determination could well be a dead end, leading to the development of enclaves of neglect, like the Indian reservations.[6] Looking at the problems of the poor, for example, we can see that local control and decentralization will not *in themselves* avail much. The changes needed are clear and many of them cannot be made locally: for example, altering of national priorites in such a way that health care, housing, education, apprenticeship training, and the like have the resources necessary to help poor people, and others as well, restructure their lives.[7]

Local initiative and local conflict can supply, and have already supplied, the beginnings of political organization and self-help, a sense of potency and hope, and the possibility of correcting these priorities close to home. The poor in Durham, the white possibly more than the black, are in need of the effective national movement of the Left that we have lacked for decades. In the meantime, localism can be a considerable virtue if it does not lose sight of the larger issues.

Calls for community control of education, however, will not necessarily mean better schools. Calls for community control of police will not necessarily mean a more effective and intelligent police force, or a more honest one. Arthur Waskow, for example, in a recent discussion

5. See the discussion in Elizabeth Tornquist, "Standing Up to America," *New South,* Fall 1969.

6. Paul Goodman, "The Limits of Local Liberty," *New Generation,* Summer 1969.

7. Bayard Rustin, "The Failure of Black Separatism," *Harper's Magazine,* January 1970.

of police argued that community control is both workable and a reasonable solution to many of the abuses that currently plague minority areas.[8] But in Waskow's argument, as in much of the current literature about local control, it is not made clear how community power will serve other than essentially defensive functions. The "community" perhaps can make certain that local enforcement officers are "of" the community and accept the "mores" of the people they police. But this defensive achievement, preventing abuse, does not reach the fundamental problem: that it is precisely the ghetto areas that need more and better policing. This can probably be accomplished only by better recruiting and more thorough training, and through those changes in the law and the penal system that both minimize and deal reasonably with criminality.

If we look at community control of the welfare system, we see a similar pattern. A community predominantly of chicanos, for example, might reasonably seek a say in the location and weekly schedule of a welfare office in its area. It might ask that the office remain open on weekends when it would be easier for working people to get there. Or the community might seek a say in hiring, hoping to get jobs for their own, or to make sure that the people who process applications have a real "understanding" of local problems—perhaps even down to the first names of clients. Such demands help ensure against a bureaucratic arbitrariness and a coldness that would limit the efficacy of welfare efforts as well as antagonize the local people. But the local people would also recognize that the financing of the welfare system was a matter beyond local control, as would be the definition of eligibility. They could not reasonably hope, locally, to determine the size of the welfare budget or the definition of poverty.

Perhaps, in the context of these examples of combining local and national initiatives, we can turn to the question of whether the usual democratic optimism about decentralization isn't altogether out of place. Theodore Lowi, for example, argues in his recent book, *The End of Liberalism,* that the current press toward decentralization is only a further development of what he terms "interest group liberalism." From Lowi's point of view, such a development, like the rest of interest group liberalism, will only serve to fragment governmental

8. *Trans-action,* December 1969.

authority, to create laws without standards, and to undermine the legitimacy of the political order. In addition, decentralization will lead to increased parochialism and, among blacks, to a focusing-in on the ghetto when it is the very existence of the ghetto that is the problem.

Lowi's case is convincing at several points. Decentralization has already led, and will continue to lead, to a narrowed focus for protest; it will undermine authority by leading to differential applications of law in response to community pressures. It will increase chaos. Lowi proposes instead the re-creation of a government of laws—the imposition of genuine standards in legislation, particularly standards that would thoroughly and effectively provide Negroes with first-class citizenship. Yet, Lowi is missing part of the point. First, many issues are genuinely local and are rightly dealt with at the community level. Second, the national majority willing to create and enforce new standards of social justice does not yet exist. One way to create it may be through local organizing, as long as these local efforts are not antithetical to broader movements for change. Third, interest group liberalism has its reasonable aspects, and is not likely to disappear soon. One way to improve upon the obviously inadequate system we have is to bring into it precisely those groups that have been excluded for so long, rather than to freeze out such groups in the name of impartial bureaucratic standards.

Altering political priorities in America will not be accomplished by getting clearer standards into legislation or, as Lowi suggests in a weaker moment, by encouraging the Supreme Court to return to its sick-chicken ruling in the Schechter case. Here he mistakes the form for the substance of change. It seems extremely quixotic to opt for the form in the *absence* of substance. But this is precisely where Lowi's argument leads. This is why he ignores the realities of power that would compel him to be more sympathetic to locally based movements for a voice in decision-making, even if such movements have their shortcomings.

But Lowi is right to some degree in his emphasis on standards, because community control cannot, in most cases, mean total control. This extends far beyond the immediate political arena itself. Teachers must retain professional standards of their own; so must police and civil servants. Some policies must be immune from local decision-making, such as the notion of equal treatment itself. Community-controlled policy, for example, should have no power to discriminate among citizens. Nor should school boards be capable of resegregating a system. Though these are obvious examples, they make clear a more general point: that decentralized control cannot be complete control, that national and/or professional standards ought to prevail regardless of local sentiments in many situations.

If we look back again at the Durham data, we can see that local control is itself not simple to accomplish. For poor whites particularly, political activity is suspect and political ignorance widespread. The blacks, though less fatalistic and better organized, face formidable barriers to effective access and have the problem of building a sustained movement. The problems then are different for these groups. Blacks are attempting with limited success to get into the pluralistic ballgame from which they have been effectively excluded. What they seek is both control and control over something worth having, and these are not necessarily the same. Here considerable experimentation will have to be the rule, both for blacks and for the local bureaucracies with which they deal. Poor whites, on the other hand, have rarely demanded any local control since they accept their situation fatalistically and, despite deep resentments, are unable to organize themselves. The temptation then is to forget about poor white power. The question here is, wouldn't some local organization among poor whites, on a nonracist basis, help to create the preconditions for a better life for the poor in America generally? The answer is, clearly, yes. How then can this be done? More generally here, the question is what particular forms of local participation and control might prove interesting and effective.

Paul Goodman again is a good critic. He points out that many of the most promising avenues of local initiative have not been developed very effectively. For example:

. . . in both theory and practice, the liberty of occupation and function have been neglected. There has been little mention of workers' management and the kind of education and apprenticeship of the young that are necessary for this. Professional and guild autonomy has been readily sacrificed for narrow economic advantage. Producers' and consumers' cooperatives are in eclipse.

Goodman is emphasizing here that concentration of political forms of power and participation provides too narrow a focus. This criticism has most relevance to poor whites for whom, say, cooperatives might be a way out of passivity. The important point is not only that people must be engaged in the issues that affect them, but that they only have a chance of becoming engaged when they personally experience the connection between themselves and larger social issues. This is one of the reasons that participation at the work place might be fruitful and possible.

Bureaucracy has become a dirty word. This is only because it is associated with bureaucrats. But the bureaucrat is himself, oddly enough, a person, and he often finds himself in a position of great strain. He can respond to this strain constructively or destructively, depending on who he is and what the situation allows.[9] The demands for participation and decentralization have commonly put considerable strains on bureaucrats at many levels who, starting with inadequate resources, have found their routines disrupted, their norms challenged, and their motives attacked. How to deal with this?

The trouble is that teachers, social workers, police, and other civil servants get themselves locked into combat with militant local groups. Sometimes this combat is fruitful, but often not. From the bureaucrat's point of view, there are several things to be done. First, the bureaucrat's self-image, although it incorporates professional standards and norms of due process, also should involve a commitment to equality and dignity. Second, this means that bureaucrats must try to transcend the conflicts and look for a common ground—and often this must involve increased local decision-making. Moreover, bureaucrats need to think carefully about the very programs they administer, whose content they cannot take for granted simply because they have proceeded down the line of command. Some real innovation is called for within bureaucracies, and clearly some of this is coming. Bureaucratic action can, also, take on a nonbureaucratic character where needed—modeling itself on an example like Danilo Dolci's

9. Michael Lipsky, "Street-Level Bureaucracy and the Analysis of Urban Reform," to appear in *Politics, Public Administration, and Neighborhood Control (op. cit.).*

"reverse strike," which put unemployed men to work on socially constructive tasks and then called for payment and appropriate acknowledgment. Mayakovsky, writing around the time of the Russian revolution, talked about "crossroads crucifying policemen"—a line that conveys the implacable, tragic, and socially structured conflicts that set men against each other and themselves. It is only the consciousness of this dilemma that may make it possible to break out of it.

What lies before us then is a politics of slow chaos and possible constructiveness. The growth and humanization of the welfare state, the creation of durable political vehicles for popular control, the righting of the blatant and subtle wrongs of our present domestic life, the establishment of a saner set of national priorities, all of these will probably require an interaction between national and local initiatives. Here, ideology may be the largest stumblingblock if it pits potential allies against each other in struggles for a crumb of the local pie.

Increased participation and decentralization have certain obvious virtues, especially when they provide hope for those who have been hopeless and an arena for action to those previously fatalistic. But participation is never universal, nor is it necessarily always the greatest value, nor is decentralization necessarily the healthiest or most significant method of solving political problems. We must face the fact that without a significant restructuring of national priorities, without alterations in our social system, much local work will be in vain.

Arthur M. Schlesinger, Jr.

Nixon and Neo-Jeffersonianism

For American historians, President Nixon's 1971 State of the Union message had an agreeably nostalgic ring. "The further away government is from people," he said, "the stronger government becomes and the weaker people become. . . . Local government is the government closest to the people and more responsive to the individual person; it is people's government in a far more intimate way than the Government in Washington can ever be."

This is the purest Jeffersonian gospel, and the familiar phrases strike deep and reassuring chords in all our breasts. On the other hand, our national experience has seen a steady movement away from Jeffersonian localism. Does this mean that American history was all a mistake? Or did Jeffersonianism in practice turn out to have fatal flaws? This is not just a question for the Nixon administration. It is also a question for those on the Left who denounce the national government and cry "power to the people."

The reason why Jeffersonianism has receded through our history, it may be suggested, is precisely because local government has *not* been, most of the time, "responsive to the individual person"—because it has *not* been, in fact, "people's government." For local government is characteristically the government of the locally powerful, not of the locally powerless; and the best way the locally powerless have found to sustain their rights and welfare against the locally powerful is through resort to the national government. Jeffersonianism, in short, has ordinarily meant in practice a system by which the strongest local

421

interests, whether planters, landlords, merchants, bankers, or industrialists, have been able to consolidate their control. Local government is generally the last refuge of reaction. This is why liberals have long since abandoned Jeffersonian localism—and why conservatives, from the American Liberty League to President Nixon, like to flourish the neo-Jeffersonian standard.

Seventy years ago Theodore Roosevelt explained that the national government was the only means by which we could correct the injustices in a national economy and a national society. He knew that industrialism had long since destroyed the rural utopia of Jefferson and that Hamiltonian means were now required to achieve Jeffersonian ends. Woodrow Wilson even insisted that Jefferson himself would have changed his mind. "I feel confident," Wilson said, "that if Jefferson were living in our day he would see what we see. . . . Without the watchful interference, the resolute interference of the government, there can be no fair play."

It is the national government, for example, that has vindicated racial justice against local bigotry. It is the national government that has protected the Bill of Rights against local vigilantism. It is the national government that has preserved natural resources against local greed. It is the national government that has civilized our industry, that has secured the rights of labor organization, that has defended the farmer against the vagaries of the free market. The growth of national power, far from producing government less "responsive to the individual person," has given a majority of Americans far more dignity and freedom than they could win in a century of localism.

It is little wonder that those who dislike civil rights and civil liberties, who want to loot our timberlands and break our unions and dismantle our regulation of business, should propagate the fraud of local government as the only true "people's government." It is a little harder, though, to see why the New Left should join in this crusade against the national authority.

Other considerations argue against Nixon's neo-Jeffersonianism. It demands, for example, a really stupefying act of faith to suppose local government more incorruptible, more efficient, or more expert than national government. The national authority is less vulnerable to selfish local pressures, more flexible in the transfer of resources, more economical in the use of trained personnel. To say this is not to say, as

Nixon suggests, that "a bureaucratic elite in Washington knows what is best for people everywhere." Obviously more money should go to cities and states, though under stringent national standards; obviously national agencies, bureaucratized and ossified by time, too often lose contact with local needs and interests; obviously we need a great deal more of what David Lilienthal used to call in New Deal days the "decentralized administration of centralized authority." There is a particular argument for the promotion of local initiative through the creation of specific community institutions outside the formal governmental structure—like Robert Kennedy's Bedford-Stuyvesant project, for example, which local residents control and through which they can express their wishes.

But decentralization on the Nixon model—decentralization that would simply turn money and power over to local government and private business—would only defeat the humane hopes of contemporary America. Nixon's notion that this would be "government that truly is by the people" and would give the people "a bigger voice in deciding for themselves those questions that so greatly affect their lives" is refuted by the whole course of American history. As for Nixon's proposition that inadequate enthusiasm for local government "is really a contention that you cannot trust people to govern themselves," this is sheer demagoguery. The national government is just as "truly . . . by the people," just as legitimate an instrument of self-government, as local government—and an instrument that, through our history, has served individual freedom and social justice a good deal more consistently than the currently fashionable nostrum of all power to the neighborhood oligarchs.

Sidney H. Aronson

The City: Nostalgia, Illusion, and Reality

How different would our view of the city be had the Jewish scribes who wrote the Book of Genesis been urban dwellers rather than members of a nomadic, desert tribe; had they located paradise amid the market place or the theater of a thriving town rather than in a pastoral Garden of Eden; had they not held up to an impressionable posterity the "cities of the valley"—Sodom and Gomorrah—as archetypal images of appalling evil? We can only speculate on the answers to such questions while knowing full well that we are both the spiritual and lineal descendants of people who deeply distrusted the life of cities and who imaged the Golden Age of freedom and happiness as a sylvan oasis. The City of God was a self-evident self-contradiction.

Historical attempts to deal with the city's origins have always been in the nature of guesswork and ingenious speculation based on the most fragmentary of evidence. The archaeological record of city life for the first few thousand years of its existence is a record more of gaps than of facts. Nor has the analysis of the modern city always been on firmer ground, informed as so much of it has been, especially in America, by the antiurban bias that pervades so much of our history

I wish especially to thank my colleague, Richard Greenbaum, for his assistance in the writing of this article. He read the entire manuscript and made innumerable suggestions that greatly improved its organization and clarity. Such felicity of style as it now exhibits is also largely the result of his efforts. I also gained much from exchanges with Israel Gerver.—S.H.A.

424

and our social attitudes, a bias that has effectively obscured the nature of the city and led to an obsession with its worst features to the almost complete neglect of its best. The standard, contemporary sociological view of the city sees it rather as a human theater of horrors than as the matrix of inexhaustible choices and opportunities, the provider of endless stimulation, and the seedbed of all that goes by the name "civilization."

Yet the city's origin and its early history may be worth brief attention if only because such an examination may uncover aspects of the city which have too long been obscured or casually assumed. Then too, a historical perspective should make it easier to avoid that reverse evolutionary thinking which, beginning with Hesiod and the Book of Genesis, has placed man's Golden Age in the past and has gone on to yearn for what Roger Starr has called the "City of the Imagination." This is not to deny the real things that are wrong with the cities of today but to suggest that that is only one facet of the story and not perhaps the most important one.

For most of his time on earth man was a roving hunter and predator, forced to wander and to forage for food because the latter was so limited and the competition for it so fierce that even the most bountifully supplied areas could support no more than a handful of people. The first permanent settlements (not cities, to be sure) probably began as resting places in a nomadic existence and as burial sites. At some point in the development of man's mind, he attributed to the spirits of the dead such powers over the living that the former had to be ceremonially buried, commemorated, and propitiated. What converted these temporary settlements into permanent ones was that series of events, occurring during the Neolithic period, which we are justified in calling the "Agricultural Revolution": the domestication of plants and animals and, ultimately, man himself.

The resulting increase in food production made possible the support of a larger population than ever before. It also made it both necessary and possible to excuse some of the adult population from food-growing and to divert their energies to the processing and storage of food and to the maintenance of the settlement itself. While the greater food supply made such specialization possible, the specialization, in its turn, led to more efficient food production and utilization, thus setting in motion those cycles, vicious or beneficial, that have remained with us to this day. Lewis Mumford's definition of the city as a container of containers reflects implicity the greater complexity and differentiation of village life.

The invention of the plow and, perhaps, of the political institution of kingship made it possible for the village to develop into the town, and ultimately the city, by producing, on the one hand, a food surplus large enough to free whole groups from direct involvement with food production and, on the other, by creating an instrumentality that could effectively organize and utilize surplus resources. In consequence the village artisan, once a part-time peasant, became a full-time craftsman producing for a more or less dependable "market." It was not long thereafter that fairs and regular markets supplanted the system of barter among individuals.

Whether between the village and the true city there is a homology or only an analogy remains a matter of dispute among historians and urbanists, but we know that in the city the natural features of the landscape to which the villages resorted for protection gave way to well-planned fortresses or citadels; temporary markets to permanent, regulated ones (the *sine qua non* of a city for Max Weber); and wooden altars to imposing stone temples. At this point in history, political institutions were not differentiated from religious ones—the king was at the same time the chief priest of the cult and was often himself considered divine—and under the threat of religious sanction the people of the city and the surrounding hinterland that depended on it (the suburbs of an earlier era) could be made to build those imposing monuments that ever since have denoted the beginnings of civilization. Civilization is coeval with the city; the etymological connection between the two words is far from gratuitous.

For Emile Durkheim, on the other hand, the key to urbanism is not in monuments or material artifacts but in the social processes that underlay them and, specifically, in the division of labor that made possible such complex living arrangements. For Durkheim the city was, above all, a place where different people did different things and by so doing developed relationships of mutual interdependence. But this is tantamount to saying that the city by its very nature creates diversity. For the division of labor, by producing different kinds of work, created different personalities since every work situation shapes human character congruent with its own demands.

Thus, the greater the variety of social processes in a society, the more distinctive and varied are the psychological types that it exhibits. What could truly be said of the peasant, that he "looks into his neighbor's face and sees his own image," was no longer true for the city dweller. The city thus became an inexhaustible spectacle.

Concomitant with this increase in size and diversity that in part defines the city went an equal increase in "impersonality" or "anonymity." Where a large population inhabits a confined area (and most premodern cities were quite small in area, primarily because of the needs of defense), it becomes impossible for the individual, in Weber's terms, to have "personal reciprocal acquaintance" with all or any substantial part of his fellow inhabitants. In other words, the individual often finds himself a stranger in his own city, an insight forcefully developed by Weber's contemporary Georg Simmel.

In considering those features of the city that seemed to make urban living so eminently desirable to many of our ancestors, we must be careful to distinguish between the advantages of life in permanent settlements as such and the advantages to be derived from living in true cities. Many of the benefits of settled life were almost as available to the inhabitants of hamlets and villages as to city dwellers. These included a respite from wandering, relative safety, and the comforts of a permanent dwelling. What the city added to these but the village and hamlet could never supply were diversity, an abundance of choices, an incomparable range of opportunities—economic, political, artistic, and religious; and a setting in which one could exploit and exchange the fruits of one's creativity, whatever its form. Furthermore, there was the stimulation that inevitably arose from living among diverse types of people, of being at the center of power, commerce, and the arts, of meeting visitors from the other great cities of the world. To live in a city was thus to be present at the creation and the endless re-creation of all that the word "civilization" connotes.

But the advantages of life in permanent settlements were not all on the side of the city nor did the advantages of cities necessarily increase in lineal fashion as they grew larger. Village life meant more comfortable and secure living at the same time that its smallness permitted the luxury of certain dangerous habits. The sloppy housekeeping customs villagers carried over from their nomadic past were tolerable in the relatively uncrowded conditions of village life. Nor did villages and small towns present the kind of tempting targets to marauders that wealthy and populous cities did. If the city nurtured civilization it also and simultaneously encouraged warfare, often for the same reasons.

Cities were thus beset by hazards within and enemies without. The more people were crowded into urban centers the more hazardous did the traditional habits of housekeeping become. The disposal of refuse was not perceived as a problem by the early urbanite; in fact, in the ancient city, human excreta and other wastes were customarily thrown into the street in front of one's dwelling and were removed only through biological degrading and the medium of rain, or, occasionally, of flooding. The hazards to health posed by this method of waste disposal are obvious and plagues were correspondingly common. The appearance of New York City's streets during the sanitation strike of early 1969 may give one a faint idea of what the streets of ancient metropolises were like year after year, although, in fairness, most of the waste produced in the premodern city was of an organic character and did ultimately decay.

Even the introduction of indoor plumbing—which occurred as early as the Minoan Period (circa 3000 B.C.), did little to improve waste disposal since it was available only to the rich while the poor continued to use the streets as a convenient refuse dump. This was true even in the Athens of Pericles and the Rome of the Empire. Meanwhile, the invention of the high-rise apartment building—the Roman *insula*—so discouraged what little care had been exercised in the process of garbage disposal that new laws had to be passed, forbidding the emptying of chamber pots from the upper-story windows of such buildings onto whatever unfortunates happened to be passing in the streets below. And, as has been a persistent irony of technological innovation, what improved one condition simultaneously worsened another: the water which flushed privies in Roman *insulae* was later used for washing and cooking, drawn as it was from the same conduits and streams. And so the city became the seedbed of disease and pestilence as well as of civilization, able to maintain its population only as a result of high birth rates and of a constant influx of rural inhabitants drawn by its myriad attractions and opportunities.

The greatest threat to early cities was other cities. "In reality," wrote Plato, "every city is in a natural state of war with every other." For urbanization and the political development that accompanied it also produced the capacity to organize larger and more effective armies than ever before. In consequence, cities, the storehouses of wealth and political power, became irresistible targets for those who sought one, the other, or both. The history of civilization is replete with the sacking and plundering of great cities, the slaughter and enslavement of their inhabitants. In premodern time Babylon, Nineveh, Carthage, Rome, Jerusalem, Ch'angan, Baghdad, and Constantinople all suffered such a fate at least once.

One of the more paradoxical aspects of the city's history, considering its seminal role in the rise of civilization, is what a relatively small percentage of the world's total population has actually resided in cities. Most of the people who have ever inhabited this planet have not been urbanites. Until the nineteenth century all but a relative few of the world's cities, by the standards of today, were no larger than fair-sized towns. The earliest cities, those that arose some 5,000 to 8,000 years ago in the Mesopotamian culture area, probably did not contain populations much in excess of 5,000. Even in the first millennium B.C., when city life was at least 2,000 years old, it was only the exceptional urban center that could boast a population larger than some 30,000, although Periclean Athens at the height of its power and influence may have had a population of as much as 300,000 including slaves and metics. The only two premodern cities that seem at all comparable to those of the industrial age are Rome of the second century A.D. (especially in the period of Trajan) and Ch'angan of the first half of the T'ang Dynasty, each of which appears to have had a million or more inhabitants. But even in the heyday of the Roman Empire and the urban development it fostered, most cities were modest in size and most Romans did not live in them. With the invasions from the North, the disintegration of the Roman Empire, and the consequent disruption of commerce, urban life in Western Europe entered on a half-millennium period of decline as many city-dwellers returned to the towns and the countryside and took up once again an agricultural life. Many cities, including Rome itself, were reduced to a fraction of the population they had once supported. It was not until the tenth century, with the reopening of the Mediterranean to

Western traders and the general revival of economic life consequent upon that event, that cities entered upon a renaissance. Most of the later Medieval and Renaissance cities of Europe contained fewer than 50,000 inhabitants. As had always been the case up to that time, the vast majority of the world's population lived physically if not politically, economically, and spiritually apart from the cities.

The Industrial Revolution radically and rapidly changed that state of affairs. Just as the expansion of commerce and trade had spurred urbanization in the preindustrial age so did industrialization lead, everywhere in the world, to the rise and growth of the modern city. Beginning in England in the late eighteenth century the Industrial Revolution spread first to Western Europe and then to America despite Thomas Jefferson's admonition to "let our workshops remain in Europe." It brought in its wake a profound and thorough restructuring of virtually every human activity and social institution—in agriculture, manufacturing, business organization, transportation, communication, government, religion, and family life. The city building which the Industrial Revolution set in motion differed from that of the preindustrial age in that industrialization and its accompanying changes made possible the concentration of millions of people within the metropolis itself and of further millions, economically and socially dependent on the city, in adjacent suburbs. We have at last reached the point at which every region of the world has its megalopolis and it has become customary to speak of the "urbanization of the world," to refer to the spread and growth of cities as "irreversible and inexorable," and to predict that eventually three-fourths of the world's population will live in cities of more than 500,000 inhabitants.

The industrial metropolis that was often superimposed on an existing preindustrial city overwhelmed existing urban institutions that had, at best, been no more than adequate to their tasks. This would have been true even if the source of the rapidly increasing urban population had been primarily or entirely from the natural increase of the existing urban population (that is, from an accelerating increase of the birth rate over the death rate). But, in fact, most of the tens of millions who flooded into the cities in the aftermath of industrialization were drawn from the ranks of peasants, farmers, and landless agricultural laborers for whom the countryside had no further use or who had no further use for the countryside. Throughout the Western world, and especially in the United States, the rustic, the yokel, the country bumpkin—scarcely characterized by "urbanity"—became the typical new city dweller. In the United States the inevitable problems posed by the differing values and life styles of urban-born and rural-born groups were aggravated by the huge foreign immigration that began in earnest after the mid-1840s. Yet, the peasant is always a foreigner in the city, and European cities were not appreciably better off simply because of their greater ethnic homogeneity. In every major city the problem of acculturation of rural immigrants has been a real and pressing one. In American society the movement from rural areas to the cities has gone on virtually to the present day although, since the 1920s, the chief source of this migration has shifted from foreign-born peasants to native-born rural blacks.

The great transformation of the city in the drive toward mature industrialization was experienced so acutely by both European and American sociologists that it became a dominant concern—almost an obsession—of modern sociology (an intellectual activity which is itself a product of the conflict of ideologies that ushered in the industrial age). Many sociologists, writing from an essentially romantic ideological position, deplored the loss of warm, intimate, primary-group relations and that sense of belonging to an organic, solidary community which they believed—or affected to believe—to have characterized earlier small-town and rural life. In its place they depicted a fragmented and impersonal urban society in which isolated, anonymous individuals had only the most temporary and superficial contact with one another.

Following the First World War, Robert Park and his colleagues at the University of Chicago, strongly influenced by the German tradition of Tönnies and Simmel, tried to provide the empirical evidence that would support the more philosophical and impressionistic analyses of the European sociological romantics. In the America of Harding and Coolidge—the redoubt of "normalcy"—they found cities (more particularly, Chicago) characterized by slums and racial ghettos, by bohemias and skid rows, by crime and delinquency, by jack-rollers and hoboes, by prostitutes, taxi dancers, and schizophrenics. Although the members of the Chicago School felt bound by the canons of dispassionate scientific inquiry to maintain a semblance of objectivity in their writings, they could scarcely conceal their dismay. Surely this was not what Durkheim meant when he said that the moral order of modern society was based on the division of social labor. Urban dwellers seemed able to sustain only impersonal, fleeting, and exploitative relations with one another. City dwellers, wrote Park, were like so many guests in a hotel "meeting but not knowing one another."

Thus, the Chicago School brought the prestige of science (in an age enamored of science and "scientism") to the support of an antiurban tradition in America that long antedated the development of sociology and that had numbered among its adherents some of America's most creative and influential thinkers. Surely the city has changed (if not always for the better) since Jefferson in the early nineteenth century warned of its poverty, depravity, and corruption, yet that characterization of American urban life has enjoyed remarkable continuity both in our philosophical and literary traditions. This may suggest that the preindustrial city despite several millennia of history had still not become the truly congenial home for man, or that there may be biological reasons, as some evolutionary biologists have suggested, why even confirmed and satisfied city dwellers yearn for the quiet and beauty of the countryside, even though their only real concession to such a desire may be a tree planted in the back yard of a Manhattan brownstone. The rapid and momentous changes wrought by the Industrial Revolution were, in most instances, forced upon a set of living and working arrangements that had never been able to make its residents feel "urbane."

And so instead of celebrants the American city has had few but critics—often vitriolic ones—from Thomas Jefferson to Frank Lloyd Wright and Lewis Mumford. The case for the city as a twentieth-century version of Dante's Inferno is too well known and too depressing to bear detailed review here. Any hardened urbanite would readily recognize the chief counts of the indictment: poverty, ugliness, filth, violence, substandard housing, foul air, nerve-shattering noise, political corruption, crime, drug addiction, mutual fear, crowds, loneliness, exasperating traffic jams, inadequate health and welfare services, inadequate transportation facilities, mediocre public schools, a criminal justice system so overburdened and ineffectual that all but a handful of crimes go unpunished, and everywhere a pervasive incivility of man to man. As always, these failings are not evenly distributed among all the residents and residential areas of the city but fall most heavily on the poor and especially on the blacks and other ethnic minorities.

Even those problems once thought definitively solved threaten to recur. Enclosed sewer systems, first introduced in mid-nineteenth-century London (such a system had existed in Knossos of the Minoans but that was in another country, and besides the civilization was dead), and the later chemical purification of water effectively put an end to the ages-old threat of cholera and typhus epidemics. But now detergent residues flood the sewers and even seep into the drinking water of cities and the ground water of the countryside itself. Natural epidemics may thus be replaced by man-made epidemics. Solid wastes, most of which used to be organic in character, now are composed largely of glass, metal, and plastic containers that will not decay for hundreds of years, if ever, leading to the creation of unsightly and undisposable mountains of refuse. And the excreta deposited every day by scores of thousands of pet dogs on the streets of every major American city serves to give each resident and visitor a faint idea of what the streets of most ancient cities probably were like.

As though this indictment were not devastating enough there are those who believe that the city's greatest offense is the absence of "community" or, in other terms, the presence of widespread *anomie,* social disorganization or social and psychological isolation. In the eyes of its authors, the City of the Imagination was always characterized by geographically compact, close-knit groups of kinsmen and neighbors who satisfied the ubiquitous and imperious human need for emotional warmth, friendship, and protection. In such an ideal city all the needs of its inhabitants were satisfied by those who knew and cared for the individual personally, without any intervention by formal, impersonal service organizations.

The decline of the old neighborhood community is paradoxically unlike most of the other urban maladies in that the economically better-off residents are said to suffer from it most acutely. Although those who hold this view do not specify by what processes it comes to pass, they appear to believe that poverty, crowding, and the deprivation of human dignity encourage the development of communal sentiments and institutions. Would Katherine Genovese, the most striking symbol of the breakdown of community in the American city, have been saved from death had she resided in a black or Puerto Rican ghetto rather than in a middle-class white neighborhood?

It was the German philosopher-sociologist Georg Simmel who, in his 1918 essay "The Metropolis and Mental Life," provided the first coherent characterization of the city as an arena of impersonality, secondary relationships, and *anomie*. (In fact Simmel did not use the word *anomie,* but his characterization is close enough to the accepted meaning of that word so that we may use it as a convenient shorthand.) Twenty years later his student Louis Wirth repeated and embellished Simmel's analysis in his well-known article "Urbanism as a Way of Life." It was through Wirth and his writings that this ideological position (for that is what it is) passed into the mainstream of American sociology under the guise of factual descriptions. Precisely because this ideology has been so prominent and persistent both in American sociology and popular social criticism, it deserves some close scrutiny.

There is little doubt that the quantitative increase in the population of a city ultimately causes qualitative changes in the life of the city's inhabitants. At some critical point in the growth of a city (it is not necessary for the argument that it be able to identify that point precisely), it becomes impossible for every inhabitant to know everyone else even by reputation. Attention to sheer numbers does not, of course, deny the importance of other sociological variables in understanding the life of a city or the attitudes of its inhabitants. Once past the critical point, cities are composed essentially of strangers, that is, individuals who tend to be suspicious of and even hostile to those they do not know personally. When, in addition, the strangers are of different races, ethnic groups, or social classes competing for scarce resources, the possibilities of misunderstanding and conflict increase sharply.

The effect of increasing numbers on the character of urban life is to increase the probability that certain kinds of events will occur and that certain conditions will prevail while decreasing the probability of certain other kinds of events. For example, increasing the numbers and thus the density of a population of any given area will increase the probability of a high noise level, of large accumulations of refuse, of traffic jams, of overcrowded public transportation facilities at peak travel hours, of crowding in stores on weekends, and of long ticket lines for popular plays, movies, and sporting events. The very same conditions will, on the other hand, decrease the probability that any two randomly selected inhabitants will meet on the street and will similarly decrease the likelihood that one will be intimately acquainted with all of one's co-workers or physically close neighbors. Furthermore, an increase in the number of inhabitants will tend to increase the absolute numerical representation of many types of people whose proportion of the total population may be very small. Thus, every city of substantial size has its set population of psychopaths, drug addicts, hoodlums, lovers, lawyers, prostitutes, homosexuals, hippies, and so on *ad infinitum*. Finally, as with all voluntary migrations, that to the city was selective and thus increased some probabilities while decreasing others. Historically, it has always been the younger, the more energetic, the more ambitious, the more restless, and the more unscrupulous who have been attracted to the city; but also those whose deviance or idiosyncrasies could only be tolerated in the atmosphere of privacy (for which anonymity is but a pejorative name) that the numbers, the diversity, and the psychological distance of the city makes possible.

But these very same factors account for the existence of an entirely different city: the city of the museum and the cathedral, of the playhouse and concert hall, of the bookstore and the research laboratory, in summary, that seedbed and storehouse of the products of man's most creative impulses. Cities provide not only the time but the physical and psychological conditions necessary for the creation of art: large numbers of people from whom the gifted can be selected; teachers and critics; physical facilities and money; literacy; the stimulation of exhibits and performances and of people meeting people. While some of the opportunities offered by the city attract the antisocial, others attract another kind of deviant: the talented provincial. And, in fact, the two are often the same. Essential for the creation of art or of any high culture is the availability of audiences— those willing and able to buy or support the work of artists. Much has been made of the fact that relative to the total population of a city the proportion who support the "art trade" is small; that may well be, but the absolute number is large enough to provide an adequate market for at least some creative artists. The village, the town, even small cities produce only the dilettante and the amateur, not the artist; orchestras and theatrical performances, but not music or drama. First-rate artists may be found in towns and small cities but only after they have been formed in the crucible of the metropolis.

Once the city is seen as composed of an almost infinite number of publics making for an almost infinite number of choices, many of the amenities and delights of urbanity become clear. The diversity of publics is assured by that very migration to the industrial city that has made it into a living ethnographic museum. For example, the glossary in Kate Simon's *New York Places and Pleasures* directs the reader to places that sell attayef, barracuda loaves, bialys, boccie balls, bouillabaisse, brioches, cherimoyas, cholent, chladdegh ring, couscous, découpage, fhidara, ipon, kimchee, kompe, kouraber, and scores of other things that demonstrate that the city remains what it has always been, the great bazaar of infinite choices. Indeed, the audiences for such urban amenities gradually grow larger not only because the cosmopolitanism of the city exposes people to the exotic, but also because the increasing prosperity makes it possible for many to join in who previously could not afford to be part of a particular audience. As Roger Starr has observed, the increase in the number of customers for the products of the city further alienates its critics either because the latter, usually arguing from an aristocratic position, object to the leveling of taste or because they are inconvenienced by the heavy demand. They are totally unaware that the essential diversity of city life depends on the existence of many substantial publics. For example, even with an attendance of 250,000 the New York flower show of 1970 lost money. The greatest threat to urbanity would seem to lie not in the excessive size of publics but in the danger that those publics will not be large and diverse enough to sustain the multiplicity of markets and choices.

This image of the city as a cross-cutting system of publics, markets, and choices clearly runs counter to the prevailing dreary view that social *dis*organization is the defining characteristic of city life, if indeed disorganization can be a defining characteristic of any viable institution. Present evidence suggests that the city still is viable, though ailing. From this point of view the organization of urban life seems a far more prominent characteristic than its disorganization.

Not all urbanites, to be sure, share equally in the remarkable range of choices offered by the city. True, the decades since 1940 have produced a growing middle class that is both able and eager to enjoy the diversity of city life and to make use of the choices it offers. But for the poor, the excluded, and the disadvantaged the city remains a giant tease, offering much enticement but little fulfillment. The future of the city depends heavily on the capacity of its leadership to make those groups into publics, able to participate in the city's diversity and able to make meaningful choices from among alternatives which it offers.

As the city increases the chances that the individual will be able to satisfy his tastes and interests, whatever they may be, it is also able to satisfy the human need for other people. Since its very invention the city has been a gathering place for different kinds of people, and the industrial metropolis especially, as we have seen, attracts and concentrates every conceivable personality type. This means that any individual urbanite, whatever his attitudes and behavior idiosyncrasies, has a reasonable chance to find congenial others to share those attitudes and idiosyncrasies. The other side of that cohesion and face-to-face intimacy so extolled by the champions of the village and the small town was that it forcibly imposed a set of attitudes and values on all its members and inhibited the expression of any views or feelings that were not consonant with the dominant ethos. It is not accidental that the one aspect of the small town that is not idealized by its nostalgic defenders is the difficulty of escaping the watchful eye of the community. Sherwood Anderson's *Winesburg, Ohio* serves as a model of the small town's hostility not only to deviance but to difference.

Despite this, critics of the city continue to "view with alarm" what they call the impersonal, fragmented quality of urban life and compare it unfavorably with the warm, face-to-face relationships they believe to have characterized villages, towns, and even the urban neighborhoods of half a century or more ago. They contend that the extended family, the single most important primary group, has disintegrated and dispersed under the impact of large-scale industrialization as its constituent units, responding to opportunities presented by economic development, have scattered across the landscape. Although more recent studies have demonstrated that the American conjugal family is less isolated than once believed and although new types of primary groups have been discovered by sociologists, the latter have tended to see these as "temporary systems," grounded either in work situations or informal activities rather than in enduring groups such as the nuclear family. Sociologists, bemused by the confusion between physical and psychological closeness, have almost completely overlooked how large-scale urban life makes it possible for the urbanite to take advantage of the multitude of human choices the city offers him.

The urbanite can become an integral part of a network of satisfying human relationships precisely because in the city there exist publics of every conceivable taste and interest and because forms of transportation and communication—especially the telephone—makes it possible for the individual to extend his range of personal associations far beyond the limits of his physical area of residence ("his neighborhood" in its original meaning). Unlike the town dweller, the urbanite can form primary groups based on personal attraction and shared interests rather than solely on the accident of physical propinquity. The very density of urban population makes it impossible to know all one's physical neighbors even if one wished to do so and makes of every street and virtually every building a physical point at which dozens or even hundreds of social networks intersect.

Some sociologists now speak of "dispersed" social networks to denote that many urbanites form primary groups with others who are scattered throughout the metropolitan area, groups which interact as much over the telephone as in face-to-face gatherings. From the point of view of the individual, such groups constitute his "psychological neighborhood" as opposed to his physical neighborhood of residence. Modern transportation, of course, makes it possible for such groups to forgather in person but it seems doubtful that such dispersed groups could long remain cohesive without the communication made possible by the telephone. The city has not lost community, it has rather developed a different *kind* of community more appropriate to its physical setting.

Sociologists have only recently discovered these "telephone communities" (as Suzanne Keller calls them) and their precise character still remains obscure. I myself have discovered one such "neighborhood" that consists of a group of elderly widows living alone who maintain scheduled daily telephone contact as a means of ensuring the safety, health, and emotional security of the group's members. The telephone also plays a key role in maintaining the cohesion of physically dispersed families: private telephone calls seem to be made most frequently among close relatives with mother-daughter calls probably the most frequent of all.

Of course, psychological closeness not dependent on the telephone is also possible in the modern city and probably exists in a few neighborhoods such as the Chinatowns of New York and San Francisco and the Italian North End of Boston. The communes that have recently sprung up in various parts of the country represent a new form of primary group, one that differs both from the extended family of preindustrial society and from the conjugal family of industrial society. What the future of this new form will be and how successful it will be in meeting psychological as well as physical needs of its members remains to be seen.

If we are to believe the ideology which has come to surround it, rural life provided emotional security at the expense of privacy and individuality; the modern city, on the other hand, can provide both physical privacy even amidst high-density living and intimacy within one's psychological neighborhood or neighborhoods. Needless to say, this arrangement does not always work satisfactorily: there are times, as the Genovese case showed us, when a neighbor in the old-fashioned sense of the word is sorely needed. But it is just as easy to blame such incidents on the lack of adequate police protection, a protection needed the more as the meaning of "community" shifts from physical to psychological and as many of the activities that used to be the province of informal neighborhood groupings are assumed by large-scale, bureaucratic governmental organizations. Moreover, in the modern industrial city it is virtually impossible to determine who speaks for "the community" since each psychological neighborhood draws its residents from diverse parts of the metropolitan area.

Those critics engaged in writing the city's obituary speak as though the chief hope of the future lies in alternative living arrangements. Much has been made of the recent census findings (both 1960 and 1970) that show decline in the population of many American central cities and a more than corresponding rise in the suburban population. Yet many of those who flock to the suburbs are the middle- and upper-middle-class supporters of the "art trade" and the "great bazaar." To ask how readily such people would live in small towns not situated near a major metropolis is to answer the question. Those who have chosen suburban life have not created new institutions but have tended to make second-hand imitations of existing urban forms. The suburban shopping center offers convenience and adequate parking space but at the price of a narrower range of choices than those offered by central-city department stores and specialty shops. Suburbs are widely believed to offer superior public education and that belief has itself been a major motive for the exodus from the central city. But, except for towns such as Newton, Massachusetts, and Scarsdale, New York, there is precious little evidence for the superiority of suburban over central city schools. We now know that middle-class suburban schools attract eager, highly motivated, well-socialized white students; but the quality of education in blue-collar suburbs is no better than that of urban schools that cater to similar populations.

It is, of course, possible that increasing dissatisfaction with the quality of urban life may produce a new migration out toward the suburbs and exurbs which, in its magnitude, may be comparable to that which first created the industrial city. Some demographers and sociologists have claimed to see evidence of such a migration in the results of the 1970 census, results which disclosed that America's suburban population (exceeding 71 million) is now its largest single sector. In comparison, the central cities now contain some 59 million people, while another 71 million live in the nation's smaller cities, towns, and genuinely rural areas. Should such a suburban or exurban migration prove, in fact, to be the trend of the future, the ultimate result will be the gradual filling of the sparsely settled countryside, the still further diffusion of standardized housing developments and shopping centers, a still greater dependence on the automobile, and the total uglification of the American landscape. It may be little enough to say in its favor, but at least the concentration of the American population in large metropolitan areas has preserved a real distinction between urban and rural. That in itself may be a positive value.

But perhaps the most remarkable tribute to the city is the ability of its inhabitants to endure and to surmont virtually every catastrophe, every abomination, every one of the many affronts to their senses, to adapt to each successive trial, to survive and, by surviving, to triumph. As always, wars remain the greatest threat to the city, yet war has come to be accepted, much as fire used to be, as the "ultimate municipal germicide." The typical New Yorker, that intrepid veteran of municipal crises, has become a master of survival. At the Museum of Modern Art recently, I observed an elderly woman demonstrating to a companion the best way to keep a robber from making off with a handbag. Millions of subway riders know that any day they may be trapped in their trains and forced to exit through the labyrinth of tracks, tunnels, and underground passageways—as many thousands already have. And all city dwellers know that from time to time, as the result of strikes, job actions, and political disputes they will have to make do for shorter or longer periods without essential services. The dream of permanently leaving New York is but the New Yorker's latest wish-fulfilling fantasy and has replaced the older dream of leaving the employ of another and starting one's own business.

Recently, in the *New York Times* John Canaday wrote something that may sum up both the glory and the horror of the contemporary American city. He wrote of the increase in his rent, the mugging of his mother-in-law, subway delays, and a pickpocket in the elevator, but then he added: "In how many towns outside New York would 15th-century prayer books and Japanese screens attract the large audiences they do here?" Where else but in New York or, more generally, in a true city? Such experiences incarnate the uniqueness of the urban experience: the coexistence at the same time in the same place of the wonders and the terrors of human life, the visionary and his audience side-by-side with the criminal and his victims.

By now everyone knows about the numerous and grave problems our cities face. Everyone can check off the list of disasters that may come to our cities if financial help is not available to them and if social imagination is not applied in their management. It has become an accepted part of our social discussion to speak of the sickness of our cities, and an all-too-familiar part of "advanced" thought to predict their imminent death. I should not like anyone to suppose that what I have written here is meant, in the slightest, to minimize the gravity of our urban problems, or the urgency of the need to cope with them. But what I do want to stress is that the city as both place and idea is central to the survival of civilization, that the city is the locale of our freedom, and that without cities modern life would be unimaginable. It is too late to indulge in romantic-pastoral fantasies. We are men of cities, and we must try to make them more livable because it is in them that we will live.

Speculation over the supposed obsolescence of the city and its ultimate decline seems both premature and unfruitful. Around the world a new wave of the great urban migration is gathering force and the clamor for those products of civilization that only the city can provide rises apace. Robert Park, despite his concern over the city's *anomie,* was one of the first to realize that as a result of living in the city man produced civilization. The end of the city might well signify the end of that civilization. Our task in the seventies and beyond is not to bury or replace the city but to humanize it, to make of it a decent home for all its residents, to make it urbane as well as urban.

Henry M. Pachter

The New Shape of Foreign Policy

Let us assume that at some time during the seventies the United States will have withdrawn the last GI from Vietnam, that other GIs are preparing to leave Germany and Japan, that Taiwan is again Chinese, Okinawa Japanese, and most other overseas bases either have been abandoned or are under heavy political fire; that the NATO command is in the process of being dismantled, SEATO and CENTO have been shelved; that most American assets abroad have been nationalized or repatriated, and the United States has discontinued most of its foreign aid operations. Let us also assume that all countries that have not yet done so will have established diplomatic relations with the Soviet Union, the Chinese People's Republic, and even the German Democratic Republic, recognizing thereby the Communists' conquests of 1939–49.

Some may find this picture shocking; but on reflection it is consistent with expectations most of us thought realistic back in 1945—with the exception that few expected Mao to win all of China. At that time, long before we invested $100 billion abroad and acquired garrison rights in overseas countries, many thought we were entering "an American century." Technologically, politically, and economically, perhaps even morally and artistically, we felt superior to the Russians.

But what appeared as the foundation of a bright future now seems difficult to accept as the result of twenty-five years' contestation. In politics as in personal life, "you can't go home again" is a truism painful to admit. Not only has twenty-five years' experience made us wiser; unforeseen forces have become visible in the meantime, and the old starting point may not actually be what we thought it was. Those who blame all our woes on the mistake of ever having left that position certainly have no sense of history; those who imagine that we need only go back to the illusions of 1945 and everything will be all right have not understood what happened in these twenty-five years.

Nor is it sufficient to criticize specific errors such as a certain formulation of the Truman Doctrine, an excessive reliance on nuclear power, the conclusion of alliances, and other measures of the "cold war." All these were attempts to cope with the main but unforeseen postwar problem: the militancy of revisionism. To be a have-not country is not something that can be defined by statistics; it is a state of mind. For historical reasons a nation may seek its identity in rivaling, surpassing, getting even with certain others. The revolutionary nationalism that developed after the post–World War II liberation may be unhealthy, immature, and easy to belittle as mere "resentment"; but it will not come to rest before it has put the old ruling powers in their place. Not even the benevolent leadership that many conceived as America's role in this world of rising expectations is to be tolerated.

America's plan had been to fulfill and even to raise the economic dynamics, while containing the political expectations, of revolutionary nationalism. To the new nations, however, rising political influence matters more than social and economic gains. In this respect the Soviet Union and the Chinese People's Republic are still new and unsatiated nations and act as the leaders of all other revisionist powers. The combination of Russian imperialism, intent on surpassing the Americans, with revolutionary nationalists who have accounts to settle with all Western powers has unsettled the old power equations. The resulting dynamism continues to negate any new equilibrium in the world.

This is the main reason why the United States cannot simply go back to zero commitment. The security of many countries is based on the assumption that the United States cannot tolerate its impairment without jeopardizing its own security. We may retreat from positions which we never planned to be permanent, which we had occupied precipitately to meet a special emergency, or which proved to be untenable; but that does not imply a renunciation of all involvement. The universe in which we are living is different from the one we imagined in 1945; but we still have to seek influence and mutual relationships in this universe, and the greatest error would be to envisage a new isolationism as a return to America's "natural" attitude after a spree of misconceived "globalism." To isolationism we cannot "return" because we never were isolationist in the sense of being "detached from world affairs." The alternative between isolationism and interventionism is a false one, as will be shown later, and the meaningful choices will be discussed at the end of the paper.

I

For twenty-five years Americans have viewed their foreign policy in the light of a myth. Originally founded to provide a haven from the quarrels of Old Europe, so we were told, this country had little foreign involvement for a hundred years and more. Fairly recently did Woodrow Wilson arouse its sense of global responsibility. But after a brief spurt of internationalism, we relapsed into our natural stance—isolationism; then two unforeseen events precipitated us into "globalism." First, Hitler and Tojo forced us to intervene again. After V-Day, we might once more have retreated from world politics had not Stalin's shadow, hovering ominously over Europe, stirred our conscience: this time for good, we recognized our duty to shoulder our share of the burden to preserve international peace. A textbook widely used only ten years ago, and aptly entitled *The Revolution in American Foreign Policy,* told of our late conversion to "collective security." In this view, George Washington committed the country to abstentionism in foreign policy,[1] but in the hundred and fifty years

---

1. Incidentally, the Farewell Address is consistently misquoted. The first President did not warn against "entangling alliances" but against "permanent alliances," and for that he had good reason: in concluding the alliance with France he had neglected to set a term for renewal, and he was anxious to correct this violation of an elementary rule of diplomacy. Two years later, the United States broke the alliance, and then Jefferson did speak contemptuously of "entangling alliances"—only to exclaim, another two years later, that "we must marry ourselves to the British fleet and nation." The first Presidents started the bad habit of their successors: to justify opportunistic policies by invoking *principles* manufactured for the occasion.

since his Farewell Address the world has shrunk and our conscience has been sharpened; the new state of the world requires our help to keep its joints together. While liberals hailed and conservatives deplored this turn toward the "One World" concept, both sides agreed that our fall from the paradise of innocent isolation had occurred at some time in the forties.

Any discussion of America's future policy must start with a repudiation of this isolationist myth. For the obvious conclusion from the outline of history quoted above is: with Stalin gone, the dangers of the cold war situation have receded; hence we may once again safely relegate power politics to second place, confident that people abroad now know that we would again rush into any breach in case of emergency. America's interventions abroad have indeed given the impression of being ad hoc precipitate actions, often decided in the nick of time to prevent great disaster. We never conceived of our role as that of "the world's policeman,"[2] but perhaps as its fire brigade.

But this picture is not quite correct. While the means and the intensity of our involvement were changing from time to time, the Republic has followed, from its earliest days to the present, a balance-of-power policy, never allowing any one nation to dominate either Europe or Asia. Far from being dedicated to pacifism, the country always defended vigorously what it considered its "neutrality" in European affairs—but with two provisos, the first of which was spelled out fifty years after Washington's Farewell Address by William H. Trescot, a conservative Democrat from South Carolina: "Wherever the changes among European powers are such as to modify the respective weights of their colonial empires, we are directly interested in the resulting balance of powers." The other proviso was that America must secure for herself freedom of action in its own hemisphere. Isolationism was merely the verso of continental imperialism and, right down to the beginning of the First World War, it was consistent with interventions in this hemisphere, in Africa, Asia, and Polynesia, and even with the acquisition of colonies. Perry "opened Nippon," Beveridge and Josiah Strong hailed the Anglo-Saxons'

2. I have not been able to find this claim in any administration source, but only as a charge in the mouth of opponents. The average American probably saw his government's interventions in world affairs in the light of Gary Cooper's role in *High Noon*.

"destiny"—a term beloved by Hitler, too. Again, isolationists who fought America's entry into the European War in 1941 were imperialists for the Pacific area—with a few honorable exceptions, such as Norman Thomas. Senator Taft felt at the time that we were in the wrong war, and later he attacked Truman for "losing China" and for concluding an armistice in Korea. The isolationism of the forties and fifties was actually nothing but anti-Europeanism; more recent writers who were tarnished with the "neoisolationist" epithet have rightly repudiated any connection with the earlier breed. They should more properly be called anti-interventionists.

Even so cursory a survey reveals that we did not pass from a state of introverted innocence to an eruption of exuberant expansionism in this century, and there is little substance to the prediction that, after the shattering experience of Vietnam, we might "return" to the earlier mood of humility. Apart from the fact that innocence, once lost, cannot be recovered, this country has never displayed any particular taste for Hegelian triads, and its foreign policy has been informed by need and opportunity rather than metaphysics. Like any other country, we have had periods of more intensive activism and periods of relative inactivity or retrenchment. Weakness suggested a defensive attitude during the Civil War; but even in periods when the official philosophy was isolationist, as under Herbert Hoover, we did not turn our face away from Europe, but were one of the principals in the quest for disarmament and for a solution of the reparations question.

It is true, however, that new policies always have to be "sold" to the American people by invoking ideologies. As other nations had their crusades, we have fought the uncivilized Indians and the over-civilized English, the absolutist Queen of Spain and the bolshevist Russians, the wild Asiatics and the sophisticated Europeans. Whenever such a crusading ideology lost its usefulness, the people and its policy-makers found it difficult to switch signals at the right moment. The danger of overshooting the mark had to be countered by a counterideology of "isolationism." Thinkers who just wanted us to mark time had to propagate retrenchment. People who saw no point in pressing on Europe our own conception of the millennium had to profess a deep disappointment over our inability to fire others with our own messianism.

Many innocents had indeed experienced this disappointment. Having supported the crusading policy in the honest belief that its aim was a transcendent ideal, they felt utterly let down when they suddenly saw that no such aim was reached or even intended and that their dream could not be realized with the means employed. Having assumed that our foreign policy must be more beautiful than that of any other country, they were shocked to discover that it was just as ugly. But strangely, instead of blaming the realism of the actual policy, they blamed the idealism in which they had believed, and thereupon turned their back on all principles of foreign policy, especially that of collective security. Paradoxically, this disgust with foreign policy, or perhaps with all politics in the established framework, was now called "realism" or even by the German word "Realpolitik."

The ideological swings of the pendulum tend, therefore, to be wider than the swings in our actual foreign policy. A comparatively slight change in the pace of activism, a shift in the geographical direction of our concerns, an overhauling of the means and instruments used—any such alteration will be hailed or condemned as a fundamental change of ideological direction and basic philosophy, engendering enthusiasm or dejection. Whenever we are forced to intervene somewhere, those who say "we have to" find support from others who say "we ought to"; whenever we find our policies checked somewhere, those who admit that "we cannot" make it sound like "we must not." It is not surprising, therefore, that our failure in Vietnam should be accompanied by a resurgence of "isolationism" or "neo-isolationism," whose representative speakers claim to be both more realistic and more idealistic than the proponents of the previous policy.

II

The targets of isolationist—or revisionist[3]—criticism are both the means and the philosophy of America's political behavior in these

3. The word "revisionism" is used here, of course, in a sense different from that on page 444. There it meant countries which feel that the present distribution of power in the world gives them less influence than is their due. Here it means critics of the conventional views on U.S. interventions in World Wars I and II, the Korean war, and the cold war. It is sheer accident that these critics also identify themselves with Third World revisionism.

last thirty years, as well as its two kinds of agents, the liberal internationalists and the military nationalists. On the one hand the protesters charge that our policy was shaped by the Pentagon, on the other hand the realists deplore that it was conceived without due regard to our military capabilities; some see our interventions abroad as dictated by sinister business interests, others as the work of doctrinaire fanatics and the outflow of liberal idealism. We shall divide the charges into two categories: those directed against the ideology of internationalism or collective security, and those directed against the practice of interventions, which often is elevated to an alleged philosophy of "interventionism."

As for the latter, there is no such thing. There have been interventions, sometimes appropriate and often ill-considered, though usually engaged in with great reluctance and after due agonizing. There may be greater disposition to intervene on the part of some policy-makers than of others; but there is no "interventionism" from which flow the individual interventions as milk flows from the cow or as fantasies about secret conclaves flow from the fertile imagination of extremist politicians. Yet there is no denying that in the past thirty years we have intervened directly with American might where it would have been preferable to work through proxies or to allow the dust to settle of its own accord. Where we have adopted the latter course (as in China), we have done so with so little gracefulness that a hidden impatience to intervene seemed to shine through the apparent abstentionism. Having gained the valuable, if costly, experience of interventions that backfired, our future policy-makers probably will go through more prolonged agonizing sessions before they engage in another direct intervention; but they are unlikely to discard and forswear this instrument of foreign policy. They will always try, as they have done before, to prompt international organizations, such as the OAS and the UN, into necessary actions or, like a good judo fighter, if they are clever enough, they will incite two of our enemies to fight each other rather than do it themselves.

But in the last resort a nation's power is not believable, and therefore is ineffective, without a minimum preparedness to use it in an emergency. The Guam Doctrine—so-called, though it really says nothing a student would not learn in his first semester at the Fletcher

School of Diplomacy—does not renounce force and does not abandon intervention as a means of U.S. foreign policy; it merely assures the Asian nations of our continued support and assigns to the U.S. forces a standby role of last resort instead of the front-line role they have played in Korea and Vietnam. (If there was any doubt about the meaning of the Guam Doctrine, Nixon resolved it in Cambodia.) Likewise, when Senator Fulbright untiringly assures us that "the most powerful nation in the world" need not use its power to see it respected, he actually is concerned with appearances and methods rather than with the essence of the problem of power. He is getting undeserved laurels for seeming to say that power need not be wielded. Neither he nor other "neo-isolationists" like Kennan or Lippmann or Morgenthau say that. They merely disagree with the administration (and among themselves) on the place where and the time when to use U.S. power—and as we shall see, there is a good chance that the administration will adopt more of their advice, even though it may not say so either.

The critics would like to extricate U.S. power from undesirable involvements regardless of the consequences for our local protégés. Nixon would like to extricate us with as little damage as possible to these clients. The difference may be significant but it is one of judgment (specifically as to the value of those clients and of promises made to them) rather than of basic attitudes. Even Dean Rusk, the former Secretary of State who is the neo-isolationists' *bête noire,* would agree that one must not make promises one cannot keep; he scored before a hostile Senate Foreign Affairs Committee by boasting that "this Administration has not undertaken a single new commitment." The real question, indeed, is whether the United States should be committed to the defense of other nations or should wait and withhold intervention until it perceives a clear and present danger to its own interests. Here Rusk, with Kennedy, Roosevelt, Acheson, and Stevenson, stands on one side; Nixon with his senatorial and professorial critics on the other side. The latter feel that this nation should stick to its own business; the former hold that other nations' independence is our business. Therefore they have been called, not quite accurately, internationalists or even, derisively, globalists. More appropriately, they might be called collectivists or equilibrists, since in the late forties they committed the United States to the defense of a certain status quo which seemed to them to keep world affairs in a state of perfect balance.[4]

If an association of independent states was to counterbalance Soviet power and its ideological-political dynamism, they had to develop a spirit of group solidarity. Collective security was to be understood, not as a series of individual commitments, but as the readiness of all to prevent any change in the relations of international power anywhere and by whomsoever.[5] This, after all, was the lesson these men had learned in the thirties: failure to repel the first aggression eventually resulted in world war. The antifascist origins of the insight seemed to make it a slogan of the Left, and internationalism part of the liberal ideology. It also is true that, to realize such a policy of solidarity, one had to have that generosity which is characteristic of Left-wing politics: for instance, one had to spend money for development aid and identify with people of other races.

Nevertheless, it is erroneous to treat the idea of collective security as a liberal ideology. Today, when Acheson, Lilienthal, and George Marshall are being denounced by revisionists of the Left, one remembers with a smile that in their own day they were denounced by the Right as Communists or protectors of Communists. In reality, they were internationalists because internationalism was a practical idea.

4. This may imply the obligation to keep promises one did not make. Dean Rusk said on August 25, 1966: "No would-be aggressor should suppose that the absence of a defense treaty . . . grants immunity to aggression." The full speech is the most extreme statement of the philosophical rationale of unilateral intervention: even in the absence of an explicit mandate, this argument runs, the United States must act as though it had received one. For, according to Kant's categorical imperative, each of us must act in accordance with a maxim that could be the maxim for the conduct of all others; and this must apply to foreign ministers as to other mortals.

5. In his popular book *A New Foreign Policy for the United States,* Hans Morgenthau charges that we defend the status quo not only with respect to the international distribution of power, but in the social constitutions of overseas countries, too. This is neither true nor necessary. We have imposed reforms on Japan and Formosa; we urged them on Diem; we even offered to finance Castro's agrarian reform. The Alianza para el Progreso was especially designed to force beneficiary countries to institute reforms. I agree that, had we gone farther in that direction, we would have lost the support of the parasitic classes in Latin America. But I deny that it was logical for us to support Nasser, Papadopoulos, Somoza, Thieu, etc. Of all revisionists, George Kennan alone had the courage to carry isolationism to its logically mad conclusion; he has argued that we must take a business-as-usual attitude to Ian Smith and Vorster.

Their apparent idealism rested on a solid foundation of enlightened interest. Their ideology of global responsibility—though propounded with the righteousness of liberal activism—served as a cover for the policy of containment which, besides saving Europe from Russification, also established an American hegemony in the Atlantic community. Far from being starry-eyed philanthropy, that policy clearly was consistent with the long-range economic interests of the United States.

Moreover, it merely continued a trend that had been apparent in our policies for over fifty years. An increasing involvement in "world politics" had become inevitable; since two powers, allied by ideology and treaty, threatened to dominate both Europe and Asia in the thirties, the United States had to provide the balance. Not only noblesse—bigness, too, obligates, as George Washington had foreseen. But then the policy was conceived as one of alliance. It was not until after the victory over fascism—the most virulent kind of chauvinism—that the idea of a "world order" or of "collective security" took hold.

Such a world order can be conceived in several forms:

1. as "concert of powers": In eighteenth- and nineteenth-century Europe, the "concert" of England, France, Russia, Austria-Hungary, and Prussia-Germany guaranteed to each nation that none of them should gain preponderance; after 1945 the UN Security Council was constructed as such a "concert" where England, France, China, the U.S.S.R., and the U.S.A. were to sustain and contain each other. It is silly to blame "lack of unity" for the failure of a body that was created as a bargaining table, a place not to dispense justice but to distribute power. The system failed, not because the powers were divided but because the three first-named powers were not strong enough to bargain. Hence we were left with—

2. the bipolar system: Two superpowers stood at the head of two alliance systems, again sustaining and containing each other while fighting over influence among the uncommitted. Their rivalry was seen as either "cold war" or as "coexistence." In the next section, I shall briefly indicate how this system broke down. The question is whether it will resolve itself into

3. polycentrism (which is to be discussed later), or

4. multi-isolationism, the utopia that each country can withdraw into its shell and leave the others in peace. The conditions of success for such a multi-isolationist system are manifold: To prevent the big from swallowing the small countries, large units should be broken up and no state should be larger than, say, Massachusetts. At the same time, in order to survive, these smaller units must surrender much of their sovereignty to regional planning boards. There would have to be rapid retreat not only from national policies but from national ideologies. In short, the present big and small states are utterly unsuitable for such an experiment; they cannot help getting involved in other nations' affairs and they are not prepared to give up, nay, they wish to increase, their national sovereignties and identities.

5. Another way of overcoming sovereignty would be the gradual enlargement of certain essential services which the United Nations is now offering on an almost eleemosynary basis—regional planning, investment aid, health care, ecological surveys, energy supply, transportation policies, and, above all, the establishment of a body of international law governing the various encounters between nations, formation of an international civil service, and so on. The rudimentary form of all these services does not allow any hope that during the seventies they will generate authorities to which the nations might bow.

To put it bluntly, there is no system of collective security in sight, and there never was one either in the old League of Nations or in the present United Nations. In both cases the ideology of collective security was debased to provide legal cover for the protection of big-power interests.

This is even more true of regional arrangements such as the Organization of American States, which for most of its life was a screen for U.S. hegemony in this area, or the Warsaw Pact, which permits Soviet intervention in other countries. A new version of such false "security" arrangements is the Soviet proposal to convene a "European Security Conference"—a device to sever Western Europe from the United States. The Europeans are indeed eager to conclude special security treaties with the Soviet Union, provided that security is guaranteed by the United States. The model for this procedure is found in the Locarno Treaty of 1925 by which England guaranteed the Rhine frontier. Likewise, it has now been recognized that peace in the Middle East will require the guarantees of all the big powers concerned.

We have here an interesting reversal of previous U.S. positions. At the time of the Baghdad Pact, Mr. Dulles tried to keep the U.S.S.R. out of the region; now, after the Kremlin has shown that no peace is possible there without its specific consent, we are interested in making the U.S.S.R. shoulder its responsibilities. We are returning to the insight of liberal internationalists, at the end of World War II, that the organization of peace requires the involvement of all the big powers. It was for this reason that FDR was so anxious to secure Stalin's adherence to the United Nations.

III

The ideology of internationalism ruled for twenty-five years, though it was not always matched by practice.[6] It came to grief, not because people changed their minds about the merits of its underlying principles but when the policy associated with it in Vietnam proved unsuccessful. Opportunistic as we are, we did not react to the shock by inquiring into the specific causes of the disaster but by jumping to the conclusion: internationalism has failed, interventionism has failed.[7]

6. It was not liberal, for it required us to support regimes no liberal would touch with a pole; nor was it consistently anti-Communist, as Acheson's treatment of Yugoslavia and Dulles's treatment of the Hungarian revolution showed. Even Dean Rusk, as Secretary of State, was always at pains to point out that "there are many kinds of communism." A speech of 1951, often quoted to the contrary, was not a policy paper but a pure propaganda harangue.

7. This failure is often misunderstood. It is said, for instance, that we were "overextended" and had no "vital interest" in a country "five thousand miles away." Now France was only five hundred miles away from Algeria and certainly had "vital" interests to defend there. On the other hand, our interests are "vital" in Berlin and in Israel, though these places also are thousands of miles away. The limitations of Western powers in the Third World are not logistical but political, inasmuch as guerrillas are always able to resume any fight they appear to have given up: as long as they don't lose totally, they win. Failure in Vietnam discloses not any "limits of U.S. power" in state-to-state relations but the different abilities to take punishment, on the one hand, of a professional army and, on the other hand, of fanatical kamikaze fighters. Perhaps this fanaticism is best mobilized when the war is also racial: the Czechs are no less devoted to freedom than the Vietcong but they do not wish to destroy their own country.

The ensuing debate has had all the earmarks of a conversation in an insane asylum, with each participant answering to a fourth person the question that a second had asked of a third, while addressing a fifth. The liberals used the idealistic language of collective security to defend military policies they might have attacked under different circumstances; the conservatives found themselves in the company of radicals who claimed to be guarding the tabernacle of traditional neutrality in foreign affairs. The opportunistic policy of shoring up friendly governments of whatever description was denounced as the bastard child of an ideological preconception and defended as a service to "democracy." On the other hand, the preconception that the United States must not commit itself to collective arrangements of mutual security was given out as *Realpolitik*. The standoff that in Europe clearly had been accepted by both sides was not greeted with relief but vilified as "cold war," while Soviet invasions and proxy wars came under the heading of "coexistence."

The debate also led to new and strange kinds of polarization. The liberal internationalists, whose original concern had been with organizing world peace, now modified their home-grown faith in legalized collective action to maintain that the United States had an implicit mandate to police the status quo. The critics of such various police operations, by contrast, all too soon came to question America's right or duty to engage in any peace-keeping venture outside its proper defense perimeter. Having rejected NATO, they felt obliged to disapprove of America's entry into World War I and World War II. Historical revisionism—a legitimate reconsideration of past policies in the light of new information—degenerated into a self-lacerating ritual of purging America of its "arrogance of power."

The military debacle of Vietnam and the moral debacle of Santo Domingo have in this country tipped the balance of articulate opinion toward revisionism in its extreme form. Americans who formerly thought that "the most powerful nation" could do *everything* now find that the price of doing *anything* is too high. They can think of hardly any provocation, short of an actual attack on the United States itself, against which the use of U.S. power might be justified.[8] They

8. The issue was joined in May 1967, when the shipping rights of a democratic country and of all other countries, including the United States, were being attacked by a willful dictator who also was waging war in Yemen. But

are not sure that we either should or can protect Israel, and they are anxious to extricate from Berlin the ten thousand American soldiers whom the Germans hold there as hostages for the safety of their former capital. Senator Mansfield thinks that now or soon the six U.S. divisions can be brought home from Europe, so that NATO can be transformed into a purely political alliance. We would then have the choice of not rescuing Europe a third time, or of limiting our guarantee to certain countries. If some Europeans still think that the American troops in Germany serve as a trip wire to unleash instant massive retaliation in case of a Russian attack, very few Americans today are likely to agree that this is a realistic assumption. Just as French opponents of collective security at the end of the thirties did not want to "die for Danzig," it is equally true that Americans do not want to die for Berlin or Jerusalem.

Like most great debates in history, however, the battle between American globalists and isolationists is not being resolved by either party's victory but has been brushed aside by the events. It no longer matters whether Americans do or do not agree to intervene on behalf of their clients in other parts of the globe. The clients no longer wish to be rescued by us if rescue means all the things we are doing in Vietnam. The strongest argument for Americanization of the Vietnamese war—in fact the only argument that seemed realistic in the framework of cold-war thinking—held that the U.S. guarantee for Berlin and other threatened places might lose its credibility unless we made good on our promises to our Vietnamese clients. But since "Vietnamization" of that war has become our official policy, it is doubtful whether in the future we shall find many who wish to be protected by our guarantee. By now they suspect that our suggestions of "flexible response" to possible Soviet aggression amounts to nothing but "Europeanization" of the war. This is at the bottom of our difficulties in NATO: our allies don't wish to fight our wars on their soil; they would prefer a strategy requiring instant exchanges of nuclear rockets between the Soviet Union and the United States. Reviewing his options for the seventies, Willy Brandt understandably concluded that it would be wiser for him to seek an accommodation

---

precisely those who previously had complained that "we always support dictators" now came to Nasser's aid by denouncing any action we might have taken to prevent the outbreak of a war for which he professed to lust.

with the Soviet Union. Even before we have abandoned the role of protector, we are running out of nations that wish to be protected.

The case for retrenchment, therefore, no longer rests on purely ideological grounds and does not even have to rely on the argument that interventions do not serve our best interests; in the near future it will be based on the fact that we have not been invited to intervene and that other nations will place their trust in their own diplomatic agility rather than in our promise to help them. Having failed to obtain a fair peace for Israel, we need not wonder why so few small nations find it necessary to vote our way in the U.N. General Assembly.

This development is consistent with two trends that have become evident over the past ten years: increasing nationalism of the de Gaullist type among our allies, and decreasing efficacy of the big deterrent in the most current types of conflicts. The superpowers seem to have lost stature; they no longer enjoy absolute hegemony in their spheres of influence. Their superweapons are of little use in small wars and they cannot even overcome colonial rebellions. Atomic weapons are just threatening enough to provide an umbrella under which the small powers are able to conduct their own independent policies. De Gaulle saw that he did not need to pay for the umbrella by assuming reciprocal obligations; Germany is on the verge of emulating his example, thereby opening Eastern markets to German industry. It is true that the Soviet Union's satellites have less freedom to stray from the fold; but they are straining at the leash, too. World politics is visibly moving away from the polarized, binomial model of the fifties and sixties, toward a more "polycentric"—an unfortunate coinage which seems to mean multicornered—or even chaotic model.

Peace-keeping will be more difficult in such a universe of nations than under the Soviet-American "condominium," which kept the world divided but also kept its conflicts manageable for twenty-five years. Any circus clown knows that juggling is easier with two balls than with five. When there were only two superpowers, Khrushchev could confidently tell us: You watch your Germans, I'll watch mine. When the restraining hands of the hegemons are no longer steady in their respective orbits, small wars may be impossible to localize; conflicts may multiply as smaller countries find support in defying the presumptions of the big. Even if it wanted, the Soviet Union now could not settle the Near East conflict by offering the United States a reasonable proposal—not with China in the wings to shout betrayal in the halls of the Bandung countries. Even before China joined, the United Nations General Assembly had become quite unruly—to the point of adopting resolutions it knew it could not carry out. The veto is now in the hands of rival powers vying for leadership in the Third World, and no longer are U.N. resolutions respected, at least in those areas where the U.S. has power. Now even NATO resolutions are not necessarily carried out by all partners—except when they have been so carefully watered down as to be acceptable even to the most independent members.*

IV

Seen in this light, America's newly resurgent isolationism seems merely a reflection of the nationalism that is becoming the practical guide for every country's foreign policy. Global responsibilities were costly for the United States taxpayers and therefore at all times difficult to sell to Congress. But now hidebound nationalism is no longer confined to the backwoods constituencies; it finds eloquent advocates among the educated and worldly-wise who can show how little the United States has received in return for worrying over the fate of the world. Other nations' indifference to what the United States considers their best interest is cited as justification for our indifference to what they consider their business. Unrequited love and sour grapes provide the emotional underpinning for the return to a policy of cumulative disengagement: our retrenchment diminishes our partners' zeal, which in turn decreases our feeling of concern, and so on.

The question is, how long can this process of disengagement be continued without creating utter chaos in the international balance of powers? It is very clear that there must be a point beyond which the United States cannot retreat without unsettling the equilibrium and endangering its safety. While theoretically it is not necessary that one side must win what the other side has abandoned, in practice the Soviet Union has pressed hard on the heels of the Western powers wherever their retreat left a vacuum. Smaller powers were not strong

* This paragraph has been updated—Ed.

enough or not united enough to fill such vacuums; or if they thought they did, they have not been able to defend vital interests against Soviet encroachments. Some naïve neutralists may have hoped that American retrenchment would result in everybody's retrenchment, as though good examples were as contagious in foreign affairs as they are supposedly in the nursery. Such expectations have been disappointed; practical isolationists of the Right have therefore concluded that retrenchment must be accompanied by even heavier armament and by constant preparedness to re-enter the contested areas. This was the essence of Herbert Hoover's conception of "Fortress America," and it is no less topical today: paradoxically, the more seriously President Nixon takes his Guam Doctrine, the less conciliatory can he allow his negotiators to be in the SALT negotiations. If America's border is to be the continental shelf, our military can have no strategy except "massive retaliation."[9] The price tag on this return to Eisenhower's strategy is said to be staggering.

Unfortunately, the paradox may even extend into another region. Proponents of retrenchment in foreign policy usually argue that our first business should be to "put our own house in order." But in practice we may find that retrenchment in foreign policy increases difficulties in domestic affairs, and just the opposite of the desired effect may result: more economic and financial controls, more burdensome defense expenditures, restriction of liberties, or even a military dictatorship to meet the more stringent conditions of international political rivalry. Experience shows that the quality of liberty suffers when its area is restricted. Incidentally, this danger might be even

9. American military doctrine states that the strategic equilibrium can be maintained only if the balance of forces is asymmetric: the defender always needs more power than the aggressor, who can concentrate his forces on a point of his selection. At first sight one should think that this need of defensive superiority diminishes as the United States disengages itself from overseas obligations. However, as the U.S. defense perimeter shrinks and limited engagements become less practical.le, the fear of total war becomes once more a strong argument for heavy modern arms. Unless he holds that total unilateral disarmament is realistic, an advocate of retrenchment cannot readily oppose ABM, ULMS, FOB, and MIRV: the deterrent must be strong enough to make war impossible. For without room for "flexible response," a war, once it breaks out, can be neither stalled nor won. *Newsweek* quoted Mr. Laird as saying: "Our policy is based on preventing war, not planning to fight wars." Translated: there is no middle thing between deterrence and annihilation; the only weapons our generals have are those of total destruction.

greater for other nations; for of all countries the United States is least dependent on foreign markets and foreign suppliers.

Under these conditions it is fair to predict that many who now are working hard to dismantle the alliances and to liquidate the cold war will be even less happy under the new system of promiscuously antagonistic multi-isolationism. There are now five atomic powers, and a dozen more nations could become atomic powers at short notice. If once we had one enemy in the Kremlin, we shall now have any number of potential enemies the world over. Shall the unfreezing of the cold war restore the old merry-go-round of diplomatic jealousies and rivalries? Is there really more safety in a fluid state of diplomacy than in a more structured order?

One hesitates to enumerate the problems that may still be unresolved at the end of the seventies or that may result in minor wars. Neither the Chinese nor the Russians are likely to abandon their respective claims to pre-eminence in the Communist world. The Vietnamese, united under the banner of Ho Chi Minh, may try to reassemble the Indochinese empire once owned by the French. India may have fallen apart; part of Pakistan may have joined Afghanistan. Japan will have restored—without military, through commercial conquest—her old Pacific empire. A savage war may be fought in Africa over the question of who should unite the continent. Arabs may fight among each other, or once again with Israel, with other powers backing either side. Soviet power will almost certainly continue its drive toward the Moslem areas south of its borders, into the oil-rich Arab countries and toward the Indian Ocean. Italy never agreed that Nice and Savoy are French departments; Yugoslavia and Austria did not acquiesce in Italy's possession of Trieste and South Tyrol. Nor can Pakistan forget Kashmir, and so on. Germany divided will fill the air with laments over its frustrations, or united will be a danger to its neighbors. These sources of conflict are now visible; but the list of new conflicts that might arise during a decade must be much longer —and at least one of the contestants is likely to seek support from a big power.

Many conflicts will have no other reason than some megalomaniac's desire to assert the sovereignty of his country. Under the old system of bipolarity the big powers had a good chance to call such adventurers to order; but for a time now they have vied with each other in pressing the most sophisticated arms into the hands of wreckers of the peace. The temptation to enlarge such deliveries is great since the big powers are equipping their armies with more and more futuristic hardware and would not know how to dispose of the dated equipment if they could not hand it down to beggars and bandits.[10]

Space does not permit here a discussion of civil wars, which might degenerate into confrontations between national powers. A diplomacy that merely aims at preventing the outbreak of war may find itself busily engaged in the affairs of seven continents, and in the absence of any rational system of collective security the job might be desperately difficult.

V

Yet the picture may not be quite as chaotic as the notion of multi-isolationism suggests. There are countertrends, too. The big will grow more efficient; at least some small ones will merge into larger units. The United States, let us hope, may overcome its present dissensions and once more be a stabilizing factor in world politics. We do not know what regime will govern in the Soviet Union, but we must assume, as it is technologically superior to China, that it will be the world's greatest power. With a larger population than the United States, it is bending all its energies and resources on the attainment of its strategic aims. As a residue from its past, moreover, it still feels strong incentives to take the former colonial powers' place. It will strive for atomic superiority and try to expand its influence on the Third World—possibly even over some countries of Central Europe which today are officially neutral. Finally, there is no reason to doubt that sooner or later its systematic research efforts will lead to technological breakthroughs that will relegate the United States to second place. Though the Soviet Union still may lag in consumer goods for its population, it will be first by all measurements of power. Its saturation then may transform it from a destroyer into a defender of the status quo.

The Common Market will become a major power comparable to the United States and the Soviet Union—at least potentially, though

10. An agreement to have a yearly bonfire of disposable arms should be the first desideratum for the seventies.

it may be less ruthless in exploiting its capacity for political purposes. Through the accession of most countries once belonging to the Outer Seven, there may emerge a United States of Europe—U.S.Eu.— capable of holding its own between the United States of America and the Soviet Union, or of mediating between them. We may assume that this new unit will exercise a stabilizing influence after the lapse of NATO; though for some time the Soviet Union can forbid Austria to join, ultimately the United States of Europe may attract even Yugoslavia and Czechoslovakia, too.

Meanwhile, Japan is likely to emerge as a strong power center in East Asia. Her young leaders' nationalism and energy are ferocious forces that may compensate for her lack of numbers, space, and facilities. Japan may once more become the hegemon of the area she tried to make into her political empire in the thirties. Both the Soviet Union and China must watch this new rival, and as a result we shall have three triangles of power: in the East among Japan, China, and the U.S.S.R.; in the Pacific among the United States, China, and Japan; in the West among the U.S., U.S.Eu., and U.S.S.R.

There may emerge, during the seventies or eighties, a common market for South America and a political confederation of black Africa, perhaps also an Arab-Moslem community encompassing the former Ottoman Empire. None of them will have much political or industrial weight, but put together they may manage independently the resources which foreign masters were once able to monopolize. (I also assume that most U.S. property and assets abroad may be nationalized, after which friendly relations can prevail between the United States and the revolutionary juntas.)

At the end of the seventies, the United States will clearly not be "the most powerful nation in the world" but find itself as one of four more or less equal powers, with the prospect that two to five other such powers might emerge in the eighties. Of its former alliances (NATO, SEATO, CENTO) it may have retained the empty shells and some isolated clients (Israel? Australia?).

Nuclear weapons will continue to be the instruments of an arms race, but strategically they will be almost worthless since no nation can use them without bringing destruction upon itself. The nuclear weapons deter each other but they do not deter an aggressor using conventional or political weapons.

Nevertheless, no one expects that the superpowers will renounce these weapons voluntarily. At best, the SALT talks might result in a stabilization of the present balance of terror—an agreement to add no further weapons of the ABM, MIRV, ULMS, FOB types to the present arsenal, perhaps a tightened test-ban treaty prohibiting more experiments with newer weapons, and a tighter nonproliferation treaty restricting nuclear weapons to the present owners of such weapons. But even should, by good luck, some of the existing A-weapons be destroyed in the process, the remaining overkill would still be the multiple of anything that was thought tolerable in 1941.

We might then return to our previous assumption: if and when the Soviet leadership will be satisfied that they hold a slight superiority in arms and can consider their empire safe, then internal changes inside the Soviet society *might* permit the rise of a new leadership with a new perception of its place in the world. These new leaders might declare themselves saturated and stop the arms race (which, once more, does not mean to reverse it!), perhaps even allow some satellites to escape.

Until that time, ideological vectors and the dynamic forces in the structure of national-revolutionary states are likely to carry the Soviet Union and its allies toward expansionist policies. No matter what importance one may attribute to Communist and national-revolutionary ideologies as policy-inspiring factors, it is clear that a dynamic faith with a promise of world domination is a much stronger cement for any alliance than the merely defensive ideologies of the Western powers, which do not claim to be doing more than preserving an unsatisfactory status quo. Once such ideologies have been used and set in motion, they induce a dynamism in the behavior of their believers. Any have-not alliance includes junior members whose ramshackle governments must show successes in foreign policy, or at least stir up hate campaigns which the major powers may be unable to control. The Brezhnev doctrine gives satellite leaders a hold on Soviet policies: by declaring himself a Leninist, Castro could force Khrushchev to stand by him. In the May 1971 treaty the U.S.S.R. recognized that the U.A.R. is "setting itself the aim of constructing its society along socialist lines."

Even if the Soviet Union and the United States were to enter into a tacit agreement to withdraw from areas of friction and to avoid confrontations, their respective clients would force them to remain watchful in world politics. Both are constantly involved in negotiations that concern the security of smaller nations and, by implication, their own. So are the other partners of this or that diplomatic and strategic triangle.

VI

The system described in the preceding section resembles the old model of the "concert": it sustains itself through the mechanism of a mutual containment, but that same mechanism may destroy it. An unstable equilibrium is exposed to adjustments which may become necessary for any number of reasons—demographic, economic, ideological. But where there is need for change, there also are forces that resist and others that are impatient. Thus our collective security will be neither very secure nor very collective; the five powers which sustain and contain each other do not really act in "concert"; the term suggests some degree of harmony, but conceals their rivalry with each other. Yet they are not completely in the "state of nature" which Hobbes said is the state of nations with respect to each other. They follow certain rules that keep the game of equilibrium going. But the condition of continuing the equilibrium is that the checks be effective, that is, that each of the participating powers plays its role to the hilt, not shirking the risks others might be taking too. For the risk of not playing is usually greater than that of playing.

Previous examples of such an unstable concert are not too encouraging. A Frederick II might not play by the rules; a French Revolution might suspend the rules altogether; a Chamberlain might fumble the ball. While the system is not entirely chaotic, it is not self-adjusting and dependable. Its rules may be realized, as Marx said, like the law of gravitation when the house collapses on us. There is no permanent security within the system.

Radicals, therefore, will have to think of methods to break the vicious circle. The easiest and most common suggestion of a remedy is to abolish foreign policy and to substitute public-relations programs for the use and show of power. Proposals that amount to this are as naïve as the wish that presidents should adopt only policies with which pacifists can live. We have seen that Presidents get themselves elected on a no-war pledge only to find themselves forced to override their own promises and even their political interests. As a remedy to this, the obvious appeal must be to change "the system," which may be defined as either the capitalistic-imperialistic, or the military-industrial complex. But we see that the Soviet Union and China, neither of which is, whatever they may be, capitalistic by any classical definition, also engage in warlike policies against each other, and that in both countries it is not the military but the civilian leadership that fans the flames of their conflict. In his memoirs Khrushchev boasts that he himself ordered the missiles put into Cuba, not his generals. Likewise, the advice of U.S. generals has often been sober; they warned us not to get involved in any land war in Asia; the Korean war was "Truman's war" to its critics and the Indochina war is McNamara's or Bundy's or Johnson's war, but certainly neither General Westmoreland's nor General Abrams's war.[11]

When we specify "the system," we must conclude, therefore, that it is the power game itself, the rivalry of nations or what Lenin called "the system of states." Since there is little hope that states will be abolished within the next decade, the question is how to make this system, immoral as it may be, habitable for human beings—a task perhaps self-contradictory because the system that is built on nationalism in turn creates more nationalism. Created by conflict, it creates more conflict. No arrangements, pacts, organizations, or political conceptions can change these foundations unless the change has first occurred in the minds of people, in their attitudes to their own nations, in their ability to understand our current problems as world problems. They must be overcome by institutions affecting the daily life of every nation—international boards dealing with the distribution of raw materials and the exploitation of energy sources, of traffic by sea and air, of money management, of health services and environmental conservation. As the interstate commerce clause in the U.S. Constitution has given the federal government powers transcending the states, so perhaps the nations can be transcended by regional development authorities and international agencies. The growth of

11. Nor Mr. Helms's war. The CIA consistently warned Johnson against committing American troops in Vietnam, and I for one would not be surprised if one day we were to learn that some of the violent kinds of opposition to the war had secretly been fomented by the CIA.

such functional associations, it seems to me, would be the most meaningful development that can realistically be expected in the seventies.

I am not advocating world government or world economic planning, but the erosion of national governments and the supersession of national economic interests by international boards. Recently, the development of multinational corporations has come under scholarly scrutiny, and it is clear that for international relations even more than in domestic affairs Reinhold Niebuhr's dictum (rephrased after Marx) is true: when private enterprise ceases to be private, it should become public. When national enterprises cease to concern only one nation, they ought to become international, at the same time that they become public, i.e., democratically controlled. I don't expect an early abolition of national authority, but I hope that the course of developments will render it irrelevant.

At the same time, socialists should encourage the growth and strengthening of subnational authorities and centers of power. This idea, made popular by the various youth movements in recent years, represents a decisive departure from previous efforts on the Left. So far, our ideas on foreign policy were addressed to national governments, and most efforts to curb the power of nationalism and militarism were based on the assumption that international agreements or international councils are able to impose transnational law upon reluctant national establishments. But whenever such laws were established, they left the national governments in as strong a position as before and free to break the agreements whenever they saw fit. The new idea is not incompatible with this approach but supplements it: it aims to weaken the national governments' ability to violate international law. It strengthens the people's ability to withhold cooperation or even enjoins them to resist a government that has violated international law. The so-called Nuremberg Law was faulty only because it was imposed by conquering governments, some of which did not have clean hands. The recent My Lai case, however, has returned the fundamental idea of this law to the people; in this instance, an increase in subnational power was simultaneously an increase in transnational law.

The complementary effects of subnational and transnational checks could be further enhanced if governments could be induced to sign an agreement on free international information or, as we might name it, cultural and moral disarmament. The proposal would oblige governments to disseminate each other's releases through the news media on a periodic and reciprocal basis, i.e., to publish, in the periodicals, the press, through radio and TV, maybe in the movies, the other side's point of view especially during negotiations, in litigation, or in case of conflict. Such information will not eliminate the causes of conflict but may prevent the escalation of its hostility. Likewise, disarmament will not eliminate the causes of the arms race, but may help to limit its course and its cost. In negotiating such agreements, governments so far have considered primarily the relationship of their respective forces and capabilities to hurt each other. Therefore, it did not seem very realistic for pacifists to exhort and implore them to disarm. The question is whether the development of national means of destruction and of international organizations can create a situation where governments may have to revise their priorities.

Leon Shull and Stina Santiestevan

What Do We Want Right Now?

LEGISLATIVE PROPOSALS FOR REFORM

Legislation as a way to the Good Society is in bad repute, a passage beset with pitfalls and infested with outlaws. Jefferson once said, "No good measure was ever proposed which if duly pursued failed to prevail in the end." But the legislature has the power to be negative as well as affirmative, and anyone who remembers the long and tortuous history of winning federal aid to education or medical care for the aged can testify to the enormity of congressional roadblocks. Though the legislative process is the chief expression of national purpose in this country, it can require an age for an idea to ripen into a proposal and a proposal to become law.

Why?

One reason is the weakness of the American party system as an instrument of political purpose. The inability of our political parties to exercise any form of discipline prevents them from playing a role in the development of programmatic legislation. The freedom of American candidates from party domination, healthy enough in some respects, means that legislators cannot be pressured by their parties into supporting legislation—in fact, such pressure is often considered bad form in this country.

The congressional seniority system tends to retain in power those least interested in reform. Consequently a disproportionate share of conservatives control major committees, and these committees, unrepresentative of the ideological outlook of Senate and House Democrats, hold immense power.

Furthermore, those who devise good legislation and push for its passage—liberals especially—do not know how to deal with the arthritic bureaucracies which set in. We let the conservatives, the businessmen, and the influence peddlers deal with the administrative bodies which take over after legislation is passed—and then we may cease even to think of it as good legislation.

And we are all infected with Madison Avenue fever. Any new law must be described in superlative terms, yet the results can rarely live up to the language. Each of our programs is oversold, each raises impossible expectations, and so we build into them disappointment and cynicism.

Sometimes we lack knowledge. We adopt Medicare without really understanding what is entailed in providing health services for twenty million aged persons. We push for programs in ecology, some of which are inconsistent with others, because we do not as yet understand the ecology of our planet. We develop civil rights programs without perceiving the true depths of the rage and the desperate needs of our minorities. Each new law that strikes with any degree of success at a fundamental flaw in society raises vast new problems we had not foreseen.

And it cannot be denied that the nation's faults remain monstrous.

We are a long way from achieving even an approximation of equality for all our citizens. Millions of our minority members—to say nothing of U.S. women—are denied equal rights and justice before the law. The rights of young people—especially students—all too often are abrogated; the rights of the poor are annulled daily. Their struggles for self-determination are met with denials, repression, brutality—sometimes death, often prison.

Our environment is polluted, but despite a river of rhetoric, little is being done. Our cities are close to uninhabitable. Our transportation policies appear to have been designed by an idiot. Crime—whimsical, petty, terrorist, organized—is a growing part of the American way. Drugs obsess our children. Many of our public schools—some would say most—have all the flexibility and compassion of a crowded prison. And the terrible war in Vietnam goes on.

Some have prophesied doom, and some have sought revolution— the school of thought which holds that it-has-to-get-worse-before-it-can-get-better. The latter in their anger and impatience want society to pay a terrible price, greater than any supposed benefits they might bring. Those of us who are incapable of accepting doom and reject revolution are challenged to produce alternatives. Our only alternative to totalitarianism is a functioning democracy.

Because our problems are monstrous, it is understandably easy to forget the progress that has been made. During certain periods in American history legislation has flowered profusely—the early New Deal years were such a time. During the first half of the sixties some of the deep concerns of the American people were again expressed in legislative innovations that spoke to the national need: federal aid to elementary and secondary schools, the war on poverty, a fiscal policy designed to create jobs, health care for the aged, the extension and protection of civil rights.

Granted their inadequacies, these laws have had enormous effects on our society. The New Deal brought about basic changes in national attitudes which we now take for granted. As a nation we declared then that unemployment and its miseries are usually the product not of individual failure but of social failure, and that society has an obligation to its victims. We declared that we wanted a strong labor movement and would support it. We devised social security, unemployment insurance, workmen's compensation—all measures designed to soften the impact of disaster, and we accepted deficit financing as a way of controlling the economy.

Even a few years earlier these accomplishments would have been impossible. As late as World War II the Civil Rights Acts of 1964 and 1965 would have been unthinkable. The laws of the New Deal and the Great Society did not accomplish all that we should have liked to achieve. Yet each represented something new and somewhat better in American life. And if we seriously doubt their significance, let us imagine what our lives would today be like without these laws.

There are many steps to be taken that do not involve legislation. Our task now, however, is to set forth the major problems susceptible in some measure to legislative solutions and the laws we ought to pass so as to begin to solve these problems.

The Economy

The stability that characterized the period from 1961 to 1965 was ended by the expansion of the Vietnam war. A period of inflation began. The Nixon administration's efforts to deal with this inflation then produced what was unmistakably a recession.

The Employment Act of 1946—a landmark in social legislation—had provided directions for achieving and sustaining high levels of employment, income, and production. It was, alas, never implemented. Other measures have been enacted to cool overheated and support sagging economies; all suggest ways to deal with the Nixon administration's recession/inflation.

We need a public-service employment program similar to that proposed by Representative James O'Hara (D.-Mich.), enacted by Congress in 1970, and vetoed by President Nixon: a program under which the federal government would provide most of the money to enable public agencies to hire extra workers in health, housing, education, neighborhood improvement, consumer protection, rural development, mass transit, and so on. Eventually, up to one million new jobs could be provided in this way, but the benefits would touch many more than a million workers and their families. Their communities and neighborhoods would find themselves with taxpayers instead of welfare clients; hospitals, schools, neighborhoods would benefit from the services these workers would perform—services desperately needed. A plan to upgrade the skills of unskilled workers would be included, with the government providing perhaps 90 percent of education and training costs to employers who participate.

We must also improve unemployment compensation so that it provides more money for a longer time, and extend its benefits during periods of sharp recession—again, not only to reduce the impact of economic disaster on the individual family but to reduce the impact of personal disaster on the community at large.

To control inflation, we must increase productivity and the supply of goods and services, through manpower training, housing stimulators, sales of government stockpiles, adjusted government purchases, a suspension of tariffs and quotas in areas of rapid price increases, reduced military spending, wage and price guidelines—and selective wage and price controls if they prove to be necessary.

We must also face the growing danger inherent in increased centralization of economic power—the conglomerates. Congress, through a joint committee, before which representatives of both the Justice Department and the public would be heard, should review these huge corporations to determine their social, political, and economic roles. *A new merger law is needed, applying special legal standards to very large mergers and requiring that, before a large merger is permitted, the Federal Trade Commission must find that the proposed corporation would not substantially lessen competition, and that the merger would be generally in the public interest.*

Finally, we must devise and apply economic conversion plans for defense and aerospace industries. The strength of the military-industrial complex is rooted in the nation's economic dependence on defense work. It is fashionable now to talk about setting new national priorities but nothing except talk will come of it unless the power of the military-industrial complex can be reduced, and we shall never reduce it until we can find jobs for all in peacetime industries. We must put to use—not waste—the technology, skills and capital goods which a decline in defense contracts will free.

De-escalation and withdrawal from Vietnam will eliminate hundreds of thousands of jobs—civilian and military—within government and the private sector as well. Congressional scrutiny of military programs will continue to reduce spending in defense industries. The space program, too, is being cut back, and hopefully the arms limitation talks will produce a U.S.–U.S.S.R. agreement to limit nuclear forces, permitting further defense reductions.

Senator George McGovern (D.-S.D.) has estimated a future job loss—stemming from all causes—of over 5 million, on top of the 5–6 percent of the population already out of work. The Senator says some 2.4 million workers will lose their jobs as a direct result of the end of the Vietnam war; additional job losses will come about as a result of the factors discussed above, plus the multiplier effect—the loss of local nondefense business when defense work in a community shuts down. The 5,200 towns and cities where military projects are presently concentrated will feel the impact—in economic depression, declining business opportunity, declining tax bases, and unemployment.

Senator McGovern and others are proposing the creation of a National Economic Conversion Commission, to include representatives from the Cabinet, NASA, AEC, the Arms Control and Disarmament Agency, the Council of Economic Advisers, and business and labor.

The commission would administer the nation's economic conversion program.

The McGovern bill would require that 12.5 percent of each contractor's profits from defense and space work be put into a conversion reserve and held in trust by the commission. The funds would be used (1) to finance the implementation of conversion plans and (2) to pay benefits to workers adversely affected by declining defense production. Supporters of the idea say it would motivate defense contractors to develop conversion plans. After a contractor has converted to civilian production, he would be permitted to reclaim all his remaining funds—with interest and free of taxes. Since the amount of the remaining funds will depend on his ability to employ his former defense workers in civilian production jobs, he will have strong economic reasons for working hard at conversion plans. During the transition period the contractor could borrow back his impounded profits to finance his new ventures. Contractors failing to file conversion plans might have up to 15 percent of any payments owed them withheld by the government.

Income for All—Guaranteed. Despite extraordinary national affluence, U.S. income distribution has not changed significantly since World War II; the poorest 20 percent of the population still receive only 5 percent of the wealth. The poor simply need money, but beyond that is another fact: relative deprivation or economic inequality. We must raise the income of the poor not only absolutely but relative to the income of the average American. Herbert Gans, professor of sociology at MIT, lucidly presented this idea to the Senate Finance Committee during its 1970 hearings on welfare reform.

Gans told the senators that the federal poverty line, now about $3,750, is based on budgets calculated to keep the family and its members alive. But mere physical survival, Gans said, does not reduce "the many pathologies that stem from poverty." During the 1960s, he said, the number of people below the federal poverty line dropped from 22.2 percent to 12.8 percent.

Yet during these same years, there was no equivalent decline in the pathologies associated with poverty, e.g., crime, delinquency, mental illness, alcoholism and drug addiction.

Gans said that although incomes had risen for everyone, including the poor,

the poor were as far behind the average American family as ever. In fact, their position has not really changed in the last generation, even though for many people those years brought about the greatest increase in affluence in American history. In 1947, 19 percent of Americans earned less than half the median income; in 1957, 20 percent; in 1967, 18.7 percent. Thus, one possible explanation for the fact that the pathology associated with poverty has not declined is that the number of people whose income places them so far below everyone else has not declined.

The Nixon administration's family assistance program represents a historic breakthrough in concept, despite inadequacies: acceptance of a guaranteed income, federal standards and federal responsibility, and the incorporation of financial incentives to work. According to Gans, the program should be amended to increase benefits annually so that within three years the minimum payment is equivalent to 60 percent of the median income of all families in the United States. (In 1969 this equivalent figure for a four-member nonfarm family would have been $5,659, for example. OEO's poverty cut-off point in 1970 was $3,300; the administration's proposal calls for less.) Beyond an increase in amounts, the program should provide for an upward adjustment in geographical areas of high prices and for automatic adjustments for cost-of-living increases.

Beyond family assistance, which is aimed at making most families independent, there is need for programs to assist those who truly cannot work and who will therefore always be at the bottom of the income ladder: legal service centers, federally financed; food cooperatives, to return middleman profits to consumers; a national housing-loan bank, to insure housing loans during tight money periods, to provide low-interest loans, and to lend money to help establish cooperatives among the poor.

Workers and Consumers. Serious economic problems are not confined to the long-time unemployed and the unemployable. In 1970 the Democratic Study Group reported that the 48 million nonsupervisory workers in private, nonfarm employment are suffering for the first time since 1960 a significant loss in buying power. From 1960 to 1965 their buying power went up 9 percent. It held steady until 1969, but in the past year that buying power has dropped over 1 percent and is still declining.

In mid-1970 the Labor Department said an urban family of four required $6,900 per year to live on its lower budget (a little over a thousand more than Gans's 60-percent-of-median-income figure for 1969) and $10,000 a year to live at what it calls a modest standard of living. In the same year the average take-home pay for a production or maintenance worker in manufacturing was $6,024. For a non-supervisory clerical worker in finance, insurance, or real estate, it was $5,100. In gas and oil mining it was $7,296. A construction worker who worked 42 weeks took home $6,940, a worker in whole-sale or retail goods $4,940.

These workers and their families live on the edge of poverty, though not counted among the poor. Add to their ranks those temporarily laid off or underemployed, the aged, workers who become seriously injured or ill, most women workers, and most minority workers, and you have a very large and significant segment of the U.S. population that is presently not sharing in the national af-fluence.

The Fair Labor Standards Act is now cruelly inadequate. *The minimum wage is stuck at $1.60 an hour; it should be raised to $2.50 and increased regularly thereafter, in response to both cost-of-living increases and the principle of equitable income, which we discussed above.* Fully thirteen million persons are not covered by the law, including many state and local government employees, workers in small retail trades, domestic workers, and most farm workers. The law should be amended to cover all workers; no one anywhere should work at less than the minimum wage, and disability pay, unemploy-ment compensation, and retirement pay likewise should not fall below the minimum wage.

Workers are consumers, and all consumers—rich and poor—suffer from unsafe products, badly made products, poor repair work, deceptive labeling and packaging, power shortages, and the like. Consumers need an independent consumer protection agency to represent their interests in Washington. The right to bring class action suits in court would be a long step, too, toward justice for consumers.

Fifty-one percent of the population is female; women constitute a large part of the labor force; and of these working women, a large and significant number are heads of families. These are the economic facts that make passage of the Equal Rights Amendment to the U.S. Constitution so important, not only to women themselves, long relegated to second-class citizenship, but to the success of any war on poverty. Working women are paid some 50 percent of what men are paid for comparable work. Simply paying working women equitably would take many families out of the poverty category.

Like consumer problems, housing problems and education problems beset alike the just and the unjust, the rich and the poor, but their impact is always greater for the poor, because their options are curtailed. The poor, in fact, have no options to speak of in the areas of housing and education, yet poor schools and slum housing continue to breed "the many pathologies that stem from poverty."

U.S. housing is a sick industry. The United States has a history of good housing laws, however, beginning with laws to stimulate mortgage credit and provide public housing in the thirties and including the Housing and Urban Development Act of 1968, which provided comprehensive legislation to meet the housing crisis. That law included a goal of twenty-six million new or rehabilitated units in ten years, six million of them for low- and middle-income families. That the goal has been attacked as unrealistic does not detract from the constructive features of the act. A far more serious limitation is the lack of full funding by Congress.

Congress should fund the Housing Act of 1968, liberalizing funding for public housing and moderate-income housing, eligibility, and rent levels.

Both local and national housing goals probably ought to be set and reviewed each year. If the private building industry fails to meet the goals Congress has set, then the federal government should act as the builder of last resort and construct the needed housing.

It is time we considered a further step. *House ownership should be limited to those who live in it or to community institutions (probably excluding small owner-occupied multifamily structures) and Congress should take steps to enable everyone to own or share in the ownership of his dwelling.* Legislation phasing ownership of rental units to tenants and the the community should be introduced, to begin a national dialogue through which the nation can examine housing problems and proposals. Immediate authorization and funding should be provided to enable community institutions, including cooperative and nonprofit or limited-dividend companies, to acquire and operate the large numbers of residential structures presently being abandoned by the owners. We cannot afford to throw away used houses as we throw away old washing machines and auto tires.

Further, Congress should make possible open-land acquisition and land banking in suburban communities so that land will be available for public purposes. It should promote uniform and realistic building codes that permit technological innovations.

Congress should reduce the general level of interest rates on indebtedness for publicly assisted housing. It should provide that no one be displaced unless relocation housing is available at a cost within 20 percent of his income and in a location of his choice. It should guarantee residents of areas slated for urban renewal or development the control of those programs and options to the land. It should provide funds to rebuild and rehabilitate inner cities. Congress especially should discourage suburban barriers to low- and moderate-income housing.

The Nation's Health

Health care as a basic human right is a comparatively new idea, only now becoming widely accepted. As a nation we spend $60 billion a year on health care, using what the Committee for National Health Insurance calls "a fragmented, wasteful, duplicative, inefficient, semi-functional nonsystem" in which costs are skyrocketing; a shortage of hospital beds, physicians, nurses, and other health personnel is exacerbated by our failure to make proper use of the resources we have; too much emphasis is placed on expensive hospital-based treatment and not enough on preventive and ambulatory care; and millions of citizens are excluded from all but emergency services, while millions more receive inadequate treatment.

The United States ranks thirteenth in infant mortality, seventh in maternal mortality, eighteenth in life expectancy for men, eighth in physicians per population, and so on and on. Nevertheless, for this "nonsystem" of health care Americans pay more—an average of $300 each in 1969—than the citizens of any other country. The average daily cost of hospitalization in the U.S. has risen to $75.

Our present providers of health insurance leave 25 million citizens with no health insurance at all. And, according to *Group Health and Welfare News*, in 1968 one-third of the under-sixty-five population had no insurance that paid for in-hospital medical expenses, and one-half had no insurance covering X-ray and laboratory examinations not performed in a hospital. Close to two-thirds had no insurance against the cost of prescribed drugs. Almost no one had insurance against dental expenses.

The U.S. Public Health Service tells us that the nation faces a shortage of health personnel, with 481,000 spots unfilled, including 48,000 doctors, 17,000 dentists, 150,000 nurses, 105,000 environmental health specialists, and 161,000 others. By 1980 the figure will nearly double.

Right now we need 250,000 more hospital beds—and the same number of existing beds are in facilities that require extensive modernization, while 10 percent of our medical schools are at the point of closing owing to lack of funds.

With significant bipartisan support, Congress has extended ten basic health programs enacted during the Kennedy–Johnson years: hospital construction and modernization; aid to medical libraries; community mental health centers; grants to schools of public health; help for migrant workers; training; regional heart, cancer, stroke, and kidney programs; communicable disease control; and so forth. But of the $1.46 billion authorized by the ninety-first Congress to carry out these basic health programs, the Nixon administration has requested only $620 million, or 42 percent, in actual appropriations.

Even if the administration were to request and receive full appropriations for the programs Congress has approved, we would not have solved our basic health care problems. There is widespread agreement that only through a system of national health insurance can we approach a solution. This idea has been growing for nearly thirty years—ever since Representative John Dingell, Sr., introduced the first national health insurance bill in Congress in 1943. Surely its time has come.

National health insurance should be made a part of the national social insurance system, meeting the total health needs of all U.S. residents, financed by contributions from employers, employees, and general tax revenues. Adoption of the Health Security Program, introduced in 1970 by Senator Edward Kennedy, would be a giant step in that direction.

Briefly, the Kennedy proposal would provide comprehensive medical care for all, including preventive and rehabilitative care, hospitalization, some home health care, some nursing home care, some psychiatric care, and, through a series of steps leading to ever-wider coverage, eventually comprehensive dental care. *The bill proposes the establishment of a Health Security Trust Fund, with 40 percent coming from general revenue, 35 percent coming from a 3.5 percent payroll tax, and 25 percent coming from a 2.1 percent tax on income up to $15,000 a year.* Five percent of the total would be put into a Resources Development Fund. The program would seek to supplement existing programs in health manpower, including the provision of incentives for development of group practice. It would compensate individual providers of health services directly, on a fee-for-service or other elective basis.

Backers believe that if Congress approves the bill, it will presently be obliged to go further and take in hand the delivery system itself.

Serious gaps in the present nonsystem should be plugged and the system itself reorganized. It should be structured so as to increase the productivity of highly skilled physicians, dentists, *et al.,* encouraging teamwork, organized patient care, and preventive medicine through regular checkups, mental health resources, child care, and the like. To some extent the existing comprehensive group plans offering prepaid care—CHA in Detroit, GHA in Washington, HIP in New York, Kaiser on the West Coast—provide models, combining relative economy and high-quality care. These groups operate on the premise that it is cheaper to keep people well than to cure them when sick.

Writing in *Scientific American,* Sidney R. Garfield, director of the Kaiser Foundation Health Plan and Hospitals, has proposed that the medical industry take several further steps. Traditionally, he says it is the patient who decides when he needs care. The point of entry is an appointment with a doctor and the patient enters by paying a fee. Garfield says four kinds of patients consult doctors: the well, the worried well, the early sick, and the sick. The fee tends to regulate somewhat the flow of patients, since most people wait until they are sick to seek care. But the fee must be eliminated for it discourages preventive care, and with its elimination Garfield predicts an uncontrolled flood of all kinds of patients at the point of entry—the doctor's office. Kaiser has devised a new point of entry—an intake multiphasic screening or health evaluation process, which combines a detailed computerized medical history with a comprehensive series of physiological tests administered by paramedical personnel. The results are computerized and the computer "advises" further tests, an immediate appointment with a doctor, or a routine appointment. The record is stored permanently by the computer as part of a growing health profile of every individual.

Garfield says this procedure sorts the entry mix into those needing health care, those needing maintenance care for chronic illness, and those needing the care of a doctor for acute illnesses. Using primarily paraprofessional workers in the intake process, in providing health care, and to a considerable extent with those requiring maintenance care, Garfield estimates Kaiser will be able to save 50 percent of the doctor's time and so use his skills more efficiently in the service of many more patients.

While he sees his plan working well with the prepaid groups, he believes it can work with private physicians as well, and suggests that local medical societies sponsor health testing and health care services for patients of the private practitioners.

Whether a combination of national health insurance, group practice, and Garfield's multiphasic screening, or some other organization of medical resources is to provide the answer, the nation and the medical community will have to determine. It is up to Congress to provide the money to make the determination possible.

Environment: The Highest Priority

The doomsayers predict we can't do it, and the optimists say we can if we want to, but both agree that the struggle to save the environment is the struggle to save mankind itself.

The first need is research, supported through adequate appropriations and directed by scientists independent of political considerations. Whether it be a joint effort by the United Nations or purely a U.S.

effort, it is vitally important that the scientists of the world keep in close touch with one another.

By environment we mean here the total environment in which people live, and so we consider housing, streets and neighborhoods, transportation, land use and planning as components of the problem, as well as more familiar concerns: air and water, big and little parks and recreation areas, forests, wildlife, wilderness, wild rivers, shorelines, wetlands. As we learn more, we may find it necessary to change our techniques and perhaps even our goals, but until we do possess more information, there are many things we can do legislatively.

Take air. Our finite quantity of air is daily polluted with gases and solids from cars and trucks, factories, incinerators, power companies, furnaces. Increasingly we suffer lung cancer, heart disease, respiratory ailments. It is understood that already there is no more clean air to be breathed in the United States. But our crisis is more than a matter of pollution. To have clean air we must first stop mixing it with garbage—and then we must be sure that enough green plants remain on the surface of the earth to preserve the balance between red and green life. There is reason to believe that already in some parts of the U.S. we are using oxygen faster than the vegetable kingdom can replenish it.

Take water. It covers most of the earth but we will never have more of it than we have now. Whole lakes and rivers are dead, and the margins of the oceans are dying, in various parts of the world, of industrial wastes, oil spills, pesticides, fertilizers, sewage, detergents. Congress should set effective standards now covering the water-aging properties, biodegradability, toxicity, and health effects of detergents, and the government should guarantee sufficient capital for construction of water treatment plants—not only full funding for currently authorized programs but a significant increase in federal funds, to the tune of an estimated $40 billion over the next six years.

Congress should establish a valid national air and water quality policy and should require cities and industries to use the most advanced and efficient methods to reduce pollution. As fast as improvements are made, more efficient techniques and equipment must be put to use. Government research and development programs must be put to the task of finding ways to neutralize, dispose of, and recycle all wastes.

Like the nation's wildlife, we are being poisoned by pesticides used on trees, lawns, crops, even national parks. Mother's milk contains more DDT than the law permits in cow's milk. Congress must end production and use of the chlorinated hydrocarbon pesticides, which include DDT, Dieldrin, and Lindane, and the inorganic nitrogen- and phosphorus-compound fertilizers.

In the U.S. each year we discard 48 billion cans, 26 billion bottles, 30 million tons of paper, 4 million tons of plastics, and 100 million rubber tires. Congress must require the use of reusable or degradable containers as soon as technically feasible. Industry should be required to pay special charges on all packaging that does not degrade or cannot be reused.

Twenty-seven states now have nuclear energy plants—all emit some radiation. We simply do not know the safe level for such radiation. Congress should establish an agency to regulate all kinds of electric power production—including water, atomic energy, and fossil fuel plants. The agency should be given the task of developing long-range plans to meet the nation's power needs, taking into consideration such factors as air and water pollution, disposal of spent fuels, and location of plants, dams, and transmission lines. Conservationists believe that regulation of atomic energy power production should be taken away from the AEC because of the conflict between advocacy and regulation.

Liberals who favor an economic growth policy to provide full employment and end poverty appear to be on a collision course with at least some of the environmentalists, who blame runaway technology for our ecological problems. We may, indeed, be forced to make some changes in the way we live if we are to survive, but a more cheerful viewpoint holds that technology can get us out of the mess it has gotten us into if we use it properly, and that already we have the technology necessary to eliminate very nearly all of our major pollutants, if we are willing to pay the bill, estimated by *U.S. News & World Report* as over $70 billion for the next five years. Other estimates say $50 billion a year. The same financial and emotional commitments we devoted to the exploration of space, for example, could be turned to saving us from ourselves. The energy, money, and materials still being poured into the Indochina war could be diverted to this vastly more significant challenge.

Planned obsolescence as an economic way of life must end. Corporations produce commodities and generate a large share of pollution as by-products. A system of steep fines for misuse of resources should be enacted. The automobile presently produces up to 92 percent of air pollution in cities. Pollution levels must be set by the federal government, and standards—based on what the cleanest feasible propulsion system is capable of achieving—should be applied. The quality of our air should not be determined by what the inherently polluting internal combustion engine can or cannot do. Pollution control standards must be properly drafted, kept up-to-date, vigorously enforced and supported by sanctions when violated: nonreimbursable fines, suspensions, rechartering of corporations, required disclosure of violations in company promotional materials, and more severe criminal penalties.

Two further arguments can be produced to support a policy of controlled growth instead of no growth. It is doubtful, first of all, that the nation could be turned around; we cannot go back to nineteenth-century ways. And if the industrialized nations were to abandon growth it would be at the expense of the underdeveloped nations, as well as their own poor.

"The very real danger is that this new heady concern with the environment will be the final nail in the aid coffin," writes Stanley Johnson in *Vista,* the magazine of the United Nations Association.

Johnson cites a substantial list of current conflicts between environmentalists and economists: the proposed hydroelectric scheme at Murchison Falls in Uganda, a project that will have far-reaching effects on the wildlife of the area—and possibly on Uganda's tourist industry; the Matto Grosso in Brazil, virgin forest, presently being destroyed to provide grazing; the use of insecticides, an important element in the Green Revolution's success in feeding people; ditto for malaria control; the conversion of game reserves into agricultural settlements.

Stanley Johnson proposes instead of a no-growth policy the adoption of the Arusha principle—enunciated at the 1961 Arusha Conference—which held that, if African wildlife, for example, is a world resource, then the world should help pay for its preservation. Other nations should help Brazil for the preservation of the Matto Grosso. Johnson also asks for basic new research into the Ice Box Effect, the Greenhouse Effect, and other worldwide effects of pollution. Rather than ask underdeveloped nations to forgo development, he suggests that the developed nations must learn to conserve and recycle, to reduce their own pollution while aiding the less-developed countries.

Congress must involve itself with these difficult problems. It should:

1. Establish a national planning and development agency, with authority and funds to articulate development policy and to acquire and develop land in any area where needs are not being met by either private enterprise or local public bodies.

2. Make a deliberate and sustained effort to limit private control over development and use of land and natural resources. A root cause of the ineffectiveness of planning at any level is the influence that private ownership of land and resources exercises over public decision-making.

3. Establish democratically controlled metropolitan or regional land development agencies, with powers of eminent domain, to undertake major land development in accordance with a metropolitan or regional plan.

Conclusion

> *We've tried everything else, now let's try money.*
> —JOHN KENNETH GALBRAITH

The national budget and the government's way of raising and spending money express the real national purpose. The enormous growth of the American economic machine makes social problem-solving possible on a scale heretofore unimagined. It is entirely appropriate for the nation through its Congress to decide how the income of the country will be divided.

About 75 percent of our national income now goes to private consumers and business firms, allowing some 6–7 percent of the government's income to be transferred back to individuals to use as they wish. Under normal full-employment conditions and assuming an annual 2 percent price inflation, Charles Schultze estimates that the money value of the nation's income will grow by 6–7 percent annually, an increase of $55 to $65 billion a year during the next decade. Public expenditures, therefore, can also rise—from $16 to $20 billion a year. This fact in itself, as demonstrated by the last so-called tax reform law, represents a hazard. The first impulse of the Nixon administration was to give the country tax cuts. Schultze estimates that by 1974 the annual fiscal dividend, over and above what we are spending today, can amount to some $40 billion, and if in fact the power of the military-industrial complex is reduced this can be even greater. The most important gain we could make in the seventies would be a willingness among politicians to propose and approve the tax programs necessary to achieve a just society.

There is no economic reason why a larger share of the private sector's 75 percent of national income cannot be made available for social purposes. A much larger share of our wealth could be used for social purposes and the living standards for the affluent could still rise within reasonable limits. The conventional wisdom tells us that it is unwise to increase taxes except in time of war, and it is somehow comforting to say that money alone isn't the answer to our problems anyway. Liberals and conservatives alike buy these conventional wisdoms. Now, it is true that it is easier to reduce than to increase taxes, and certainly money is not the entire answer. But it is equally clear that not a single major problem this nation faces can be solved without money. It is the essential, if not a sufficient, ingredient.

As time goes on new problems will arise. Perhaps we need a Department of Problem Identification, or a Joint Senate-House Committee on the Identification of National Priorities. Certainly a way of stating, relating, and researching the larger problems needs to be found, and a way of translating what is learned into public awareness and then legislation. It may be, as some have said, that those who worship the growth of the gross national product must eventually confront those determined to restore and preserve the natural environment. We may have to learn that to achieve the good life in general we must do without some of the particulars. Perhaps we will have to restrict the uses of the automobile. Perhaps we will determine that we can tolerate some pests better than some pesticides. We may have to learn to reuse materials rather than turn the entire nation into a vast dump.

Certainly, too, we must learn how to decentralize. Would the neighborhood of Blushing Heights prefer its shaggy trees and less-than-ideal dwellings to the disruptive grandeur of urban renewal? Would the little city of Twiddle prefer to do without the superhighway that threatens to impale it? The days when all wisdom seemed centered in Washington are over. We must leave in the hands of people, organized in their own communities, some decision-making about their own lives. This can give the nation a diversity, healthy competition, and satisfactions missing in a society where those who live in it participate so little in making its decisions.

How is our society to find the leadership and provide the money—the bare-bone essentials for social problem-solving?

What we need is a series of simultaneous actions. We can assume that the reason so many Americans fail to vote is an understandable lack of faith in the effectiveness of their votes. And yet, in order to make our government responsive, a larger number of citizens will have to participate. This change in attitude will take much hard work by many people. But it can be accomplished. We can create a participatory democracy by using the only instrument a complex, huge nation can use—the ballot box. At the same time we can make our political system more sensitive and responsive to the needs of the people. We can develop a high degree of sophistication on the part of both the leadership and the led, in a relationship that can enrich our political life.

There also is a need to express the national purpose in institutional reform in Congress itself. We can no longer afford a situation that makes it almost impossible to pass legislation desperately needed. We must bring the leaders of Congress closer to the political movements they pretend today to represent. In the House changes are necessary in the committee's operations, particularly the Rules Committee, to safeguard legislation, to permit the committee to function, and to permit the administration to get its proposals to the floor for consideration, at least. In the Senate only fifty-one members should be required to end a filibuster. Here, too, the administration should be able to get its proposals to the floor. Changes also are needed in the operation of the House Democratic and Republican caucuses, especially in the selection of committee chairmen and members. All important votes should be record votes.

To some, these proposals may not seem very exciting. Our programs will not win to the beat of drums, the whine of bullets, or the whirl of rhetoric. But, if duly pursued, such programs can begin to make the difference between a country that understands and responds to its problems and one that is doomed at best to mediocrity and decay.

Arnold S. Kaufman

A Political Strategy for Radical Liberals

One of Jules Feiffer's cartoons captures the mood of political hope-lessness that pervades the American Left. A long-haired militant asks a short-cropped liberal whether he voted in the last election. "Yes." "Did your man win?" "Yes." "How will you feel about him a year from now?" asks the militant. "Betrayed," the liberal answers. "Then why did you vote?" "To be effective." The liberal then asks the militant whether he voted. "No." "What did you do?" "Blew up a university," answers the militant. "Why did you blow up a university?" "To be effective." "How will you feel about it a year from now?" "Ineffective." To which the liberal responds, "I can get the same results a lot easier."

My aim is to dispel this sense of profound discouragement. I offer a political strategy that is, I think, better than betrayal or ineffectiveness—at least for those who are radical and liberal.

I am liberal in believing that "a good society is one in which each person possesses the resources of materials, mind, and spirit, as well as the opportunities, to carve out a career in conformity to that person's own nature and reasoned choice."[1] This simple expression of basic social faith will have to serve for present purposes.

I am radical because the United States is so far from a good society that institutional arrangements must be thoroughly trans-formed before it can become one. The sense of *radical* I intend is a

1. Arnold S. Kaufman, *The Radical Liberal* (New York: Clarion Books), p. 6.

matter of what political programs one embraces, not of the political tactics favored. So radical liberals favor radical policies for eliminating poverty and racism, guaranteeing full employment, providing decent housing and medical care to everyone, drastically paring military appropriations, purifying and beautifying our common environment, reconstructing our prisons and mental institutions, implementing a universal right to higher education—to mention only a few minimal points. Radicals know that to achieve these goals vast corporate powers must be subordinated to wise and democratic governance: that bureaucracies must be humanized, pursuit of private profit ethically subordinated.

Radical liberals are not and for the foreseeable future will not be a majority of the population or the voting public; but there are many of us. Our numerically significant but distinctly minority status is the foundation on which any sensible political strategy must be built.

The Possibility of a Radical Majority

Radical liberals must regard electoral politics as an essential part of the strategy for political change. But since we comprise a distinct minority both of the voting public and of the Democratic party —the major party with which we most identify—our strategic aims must be to build a radical majority in the long run and to deploy our minority strength effectively in the short run. What are the prospects?

There are two bases for a new majority coalition: self-interest and moral concern. Many think that only self-interest provides a reliable basis for building a coalition. Such a view goes too far in the basically healthy effort to debunk the moralism that has plagued American politics. People *are* capable of acting persistently and energetically out of primarily moral motives. Richard L. Stout provides evidence for this claim in a book that describes the significance of the effort thousands of morally concerned people made during the McCarthy campaign.[2]

If we are to build a radical majority, there is no realistic alternative to relying on what has been called a constituency of conscience. For consider the alternatives:

2. Richard Stout, *People* (New York: Harper & Row, 1970).

First, we might rely on a broadly based movement that has workers, especially trade unionists, the racially oppressed, and the very poor as its primary base. Such a coalition would not have to wait for some distant future to effect radical change. For it is, or is close to being, a voting majority of the population. But this in itself is not a valid alternative, for such a coalition would not be radical. Those who favor this approach cling to a neo-Marxian faith in the radical potentialities of organized workers,[3] even though a plausible basis for their optimism has disappeared. It is a fact of American political life that whatever radicalism is found among workers, and trade unionists in particular, tends to diminish as their precarious hold on a marginally comfortable life grows firmer. Relatively little education, growing security and comfort, constant concern to satisfy desires that press against income, the still frightening realities of an uncertain labor market—in combination these cause the near-poor and the affluent poor to draw back from genuinely radical commitment, *even while remaining a generally progressive force for change.*[4]

This is a crucial point. A distinction must be drawn between progressive and radical majorities. Radical liberals should view organization of progressive voting majorities as a vital part of their strategy for change. Without doing so, it is unlikely that repression can be contained or the basis for a radical future laid. But the ameliorative, reformist programs such majorities are disposed to support are far from radical enough.

I am not saying that the working class is authoritarian or the trade union movement conservative. Many within the trade union movement are deeply committed radical liberals. They form an indispensable part of the new coalition. And the possibilities for progressive coalition between racial minorities and white workers, especially in the South, now is great and growing. Yet a coalition whose core consists of organized workers, though generally progressive, will not be radical.

3. I have in mind especially writings by Bayard Rustin and Gus Tyler. Their position is widely held within liberal and democratic socialist circles— e.g., in the ADA, the League for Industrial Democracy, and the Young Peoples Socialist League.

4. That Rustin regards his approach as conflicting with a new coalition strategy indicates that he does not make the distinction between a radical and a progressive coalition. Cf. "From Protest to Politics," in Irving Howe, ed., *The Radical Papers* (New York: Doubleday, 1965).

A second alternative is to rely mainly on those who are most abused racially and economically—a constituency of the oppressed. This group must be an important part of any new radical coalition. As they become more aware of the causes of their misery the poor increasingly seek radical perspectives. The Poor People's Campaign and the Welfare Rights Organization represent a new kind of radical assertiveness among the very poor. Still, they comprise a small proportion of the total population, and even their absolute strength is likely to diminish over time. For there is a good conservative sense in trying to buy social stability by using a portion of America's prodigious wealth to provide them with modest increments in income. No doubt this is the main political thought behind Nixon's conversion to a minimum income program.

As people who have been long deprived begin to consume more, their expectations rise and they tend to become more overtly frustrated and angry. Their ire tends to focus on whatever frustrates their effort to consume, not on the forces that hold them down. Not for them the counterculture. Barring economic catastrophe, in twenty to thirty years some of those who yesterday joined the Poor People's Campaign may be among the most consumption-oriented segments of our population. Groups afflicted by scarcity cannot generally be made to skip this cultural stage—as the Communist states of Eastern Europe have discovered and China will discover. This is not said critically, but in an effort to assess the prospects for radical liberalism.

A third alternative for building a new radical coalition is to appeal to the more affluent on the basis of their narrow interest. War, ecology, the debasement of our culture affect them, too, vitally. While this must be done, it is delusive to suppose that the affluent can be radicalized on the basis of self-interest alone. For them life usually is too comfortable, and the cost of activism too great. Whatever effort they can make on behalf of radical programs will depend on the depth of their moral commitment.

Each of these alternatives is an important part of any effort to forge a new radical majority; but separately they are doomed to failure. Our ability to create a radical future depends on our ability to fuse a radical constituency of the oppressed with a radical constituency of conscience. And the prospect of organizing a conscience constituency that will in time be sufficiently numerous rests in turn on what is happening to our young people, primarily the more affluent young on the nation's campuses.

The Centrality of the Campus

While higher education is neither essential nor enough to produce liberals, every study reveals a significant correlation between the two. Examining the available evidence, Kenneth Keniston and Michael Lerner declare:

The most decisive refutation of the leftist charge that the universities are centers for reactionary indoctrination is the growing liberalism of college students. Radicals who claim universities castrate their students intellectually find it impossible to explain why American students are taking an increasingly active role in attempting to redress the injustices of American society.[5]

Young people, especially the more affluent ones, are less afflicted by economic fear and careerism than any generation of advantaged youths before them.[6] They feel, with some reason, that they will *make it* economically and professionally. And they know that anxieties of budget-cutting conservatives bear no plausible relationship to what this society can do to end human misery.

So today's young people are uniquely predisposed to use education not only as a stepping stone to personal security but as a means of examining their lives and their society. They bring to these tasks commitment to the ideals of American culture—such as belief in liberty and justice and in the efficacy of reason. And they take these ideals seriously. The basic mission of our universities is to provide what has traditionally been called, not without reason, a liberal education. When this task is competently fulfilled, the ideas and knowledge it opens to students affect them profoundly. Now they quickly, sometimes intolerantly, demand that material be presented in a man-

5. *New York Times Magazine,* November 9, 1970, p. 66.
6. A survey by the American Council on Education shows that the percentage of entering college freshmen who consider themselves "far left" or "liberal" has risen to more than 36 percent while the percentage who consider themselves "far right" or "conservative" has declined to 18.1 percent. In the *New York Times,* December 20, 1970. If my analysis is correct, education will intensify these trends.

ner that breathes life into study. They demand relevance, though they are often too impatient and therefore self-defeating.

As the conventional American ideals are taken seriously and as students are confirmed in their suspicions that the rhetoric is remote from the reality, education comes to promote both the liberal ideal and a commitment to making it real. The potential ranks of the con-science constituency will swell as long as increasing numbers of the young receive an honest liberal education. Barring economic catas-trophe, there is only one way in which the trend can be impeded or reversed—through politicization of the university.

The serious danger of politicization emanates not from the bulk of the students or faculty but from those who accurately perceive the long-range political threat implicit in the very idea of a liberal educa-tion—a danger they try to counter in three ways: (1) by forcing curricular changes that divert educational resources from liberal edu-cation; (2) by repression, crude and subtle; (3) by cutting college budgets enough to insure that standards of educational competence will erode.

To cope with this assault, the universities' internal political resources are inadequate. Those who want to protect the integrity of liberal education need political allies, and there are no more reliable allies than those who have a natural political interest in preventing inter-ference with the campuses' doing well what they are supposed to do. None have a more natural interest in protecting the universities than those forces that are trying to build a new radical coalition.

The views just sketched contrast sharply with the rage for counter-culture. I find that the currently fashionable works of countercultural theorists are naïve and politically muddled.[7] It is dangerous to sup-pose, as Charles Reich does,[8] that successful cultural revolution is inevitable. Unless we maintain continuous effective political awareness and action on every front, minds will ultimately be destroyed, not liberated. Ideologues of the counterculture do not appreciate the extent

7. See Theodore Roszak, *The Making of a Counter Culture* (New York: Doubleday, 1969); Philip Slater, *In Pursuit of Loneliness* (Boston: Beacon, 1970); Charles Reich, *The Greening of America* (New York: Random House, 1970). I am not passing a general judgment on these works; only on those parts that have political relevance. In other respects these authors have im-portant things to say.

8. In Reich's *New Yorker* abridgment, September 26, 1970, p. 111.

to which the young are moved, not by new ideals, but by the traditional values of American culture. At their best and most politically relevant, the changing styles of American consciousness are efforts to redeem the pledge of liberty and justice for all. Although much that the chroniclers of counterculture write is useful background to the serious business of building a decent society, it is dangerous to regard their prescriptions as an alternative to hard, sustained political effort.

Building the New Coalition

To criticize a new coalition strategy on grounds that it would not build winning majorities in the immediate future would miss my central point. The basic aim is *radical* change. But, as present majorities are not radical, the most urgent aim is to transform the center of American political life from moderation to radicalism. To do that we must build a radical coalition now, deploying its substantial but minority strength effectively on behalf of programs that are radical when possible, and at least progressive. As the radical coalition consists primarily of two groups—constituencies of the oppressed and of conscience—it is paramount to increase and fuse their respective strengths.

I have already indicated what is important in shaping a growing constituency of conscience: to protect and adequately fund a system of higher education committed to liberal education for everyone who wants to go to college. Beyond this, the conscience constituency must be organized wherever the potential exists—in unions, churches, businesses, towns, city neighborhoods, suburbs, and so on. For not only the young seek to redeem the promise of their own lives and the promise of American society. There is something in the air that stirs millions of Americans of all ages.

The Black Power movement was first and foremost an effort to transform the consciousness of black Americans; to destroy attitudes of slavishness and deference; to engender self-respect and autonomy. The same urgings are plain in the movement for women's liberation, among radical clergy, within segments of the industrial community. Affluent people in growing numbers are trying to feel free, to live with dignity, without lying. And their needs fuel political interests in ways that erode constraints of self-interest. Criticism that dwells primarily on political defect and rhetorical excess misses the most hopeful thing about these liberation movements. If these urgings are an outgrowth of middle-class attitudes, then all power to that aspect of bourgeois culture. In response to these currents the politics of the new coalition should, in part, be redemptive. But its primary aim must be to radicalize and politicize what is too often merely redemptive.

There is no blueprint for what needs to be done. Each segment of the emerging conscience constituency must be convinced that its special interests are important; that people within the coalition care. Yet each must be brought into the coalition not merely on the basis of interest, but on the basis of moral concern. Political activity must become a means of endowing with significance lives despoiled in other respects.

The central difficulty in building the constituency of the oppressed is their sense of powerlessness resulting from political isolation. And the main barrier to joining it to a constituency of conscience is this sense of powerlessness often expressed in mistrust of those who are moved primarily by moral concern. This is neither surprising nor unjustified. For what is a moral matter to the conscientious may, for the oppressed, be a condition of survival. And it is inevitable that, faced with less catastrophic options, the affluent will not usually be willing to absorb comparable personal costs for the sake of social justice. Those black activists of the South who in the early days of the civil rights movement doubted that their affluent white helpmates could stay the course once the going got rough or, more likely, tiresome, showed good sense. Tension and disharmony can never be completely eliminated from a coalition that is primarily a fusion of these two constituencies.

However, there are many ways in which mistrust can be reasonably allayed. Four general issues are crucial. Each involves dissolution of traditionally liberal hangups about mere forms of equality and lawfulness. Each has symbolic importance that sometimes transcends its direct importance to people's lives.

First, relatively affluent whites should respond affirmatively to claims for reparation. The moral case for doing so is strong; the strategic case, decisive. Suppose an easily identifiable group has, by and large, suffered the effects of original injustices from which another easily identifiable group has generally benefited. The disabilities and advantages have been transmitted to the respective groups by social inheritance, much by deliberate design of unjust social institutions. This is the situation of most black people in relation to most whites in our society. There is a compelling case for a transfer of resources from whites to blacks. It is not a matter of visiting the sins of the fathers on the sons, but of transferring undeserved benefits to those who suffer undeserved disabilities.[9] This perspective is, moreover, compatible with acknowledging that distinct groups—for example, the poor—have claims equal to or greater than black people as such.

Second, the issue of minority representation is crucial. Whether X, who is white, will make a better congressman than Y, who is black, is often less important than the fact that the election of a black representative has political significance for black constituents everywhere. In California, Democratic legislators have gerrymandered chicano candidates out of contention so often that many key Mexican-American leaders are no longer willing to play the Democratic electoral game. They demand representation. To intone that merit alone should be decisive is morally evasive. Minorities must be accorded representation at every level of American power. As a group, minority representatives will tend to make greater personal sacrifices for the sake of important policy goals than comparable alternatives.

Third, economic boycott is an important weapon for poor minorities. Whether organized on behalf of the grape or lettuce workers of California, the black residents of Cairo, Illinois, the white miners of Appalachia, successful boycott is effective power. Members of the new coalition should bring economic muscle to bear in communities that otherwise cannot be influenced by minority economic pressure. The conscience constituency should become the lens through which the power of poor and racial minorities is effectively magnified in communities where the oppressed are politically insignificant.

Fourth, one aspect of the law-and-order issue is pre-eminently important to all oppressed groups, especially ghetto dwellers: the injustice of *official* lawlessness. They view lawless action, not only by police but by every segment of the legal system, as a plague that

9. I have discussed the moral and political case for reparations more fully elsewhere. Cf. Chapter 6 of *The Radical Liberal,* and "Black Reparations: Two Views" (an exchange with Michael Harrington), *Dissent,* July-August, 1969, pp. 317–320.

specially afflicts them. One recent issue of the *New York Times* (November 21, 1970) carried stories about the determination of black policemen in Hartford, Connecticut, to protect members of minority communities who are physically interfered with by "white bigoted police officers"; about a grand jury report that indicated "there was probable cause to believe that State policemen committed a criminal offense in a case in which they shot and killed two unarmed brothers in a stake-out and then planted a gun to cover themselves"; about a New York detective who was tried for conducting illegal checks of police records on behalf of a private business firm. And beneath the surface of reported events is greater abuse of official power that is never publicly aired. The new coalition should fight for that favorite ideal of conservatives, genuine rule of law. Doing so would produce a dramatically favorable response among those who primarily suffer the harm of official lawlessness.[10]

These four issues have great symbolic and policy significance. But, taken together, they are only an aspect of the general political effort to empower the oppressed. A program of progressive change that achieves meaningful *reform* is a precondition of successful *radicalism*. To complete the work of the welfare state is the surest route to a radical future. The sooner everyone has access to a decent share of affluence, the sooner will a subsequent generation know in their gut that achievement of material well-being is only a way station to a truly satisfying existence. Fear that welfarism is co-optative is morally arrogant, and politically senseless from the point of view of genuine radicalism.

The Tokenism of American Democracy

A major obstacle to significantly ameliorative social programs is a political system whose hallmark is tokenism. That is, the maintenance of social stability by means of payoffs to the victims of injustice— payoffs so small as to be mere tokens. The system has worked primarily

10. This observation is, unhappily, partly based on personal experience. I testified in the case of a UCLA professor who was assaulted by policemen, then charged with felonious assault. In this instance the state's case was so flimsy, the number of eyewitnesses so great, that the judge terminated the proceedings before the defense had finished giving all its evidence, summarily declaring the defendant innocent without even retiring to his chambers.

because those who have least have traditionally accepted least in return for their compliance with established forms of law and order. From the Republic's beginning, this system of token payoffs has worked remarkably well. Radical strategy cannot rid us of tokenism until radical majorities can act within a genuinely majoritarian system. But we cannot even navigate the intervening waters unless there is at least mitigation of the evil.

Tokenism has three main causes.[11] (1) The entire social system is institutionally skewed in favor of the tiny minority at the top that has most power, wealth, and status. (2) Since majorities are not presently radical, even the majoritarian aspects of the system tend to promote tokenism, especially in relation to poverty and racism. (3) Manipulation and co-optation are so common that most Americans, especially those at the bottom, are too often inculcated with political attitudes that frustrate basic interests.

1. Social stability is important to anyone who has something he wants to protect against society's boat rockers. In a just society, just men would seek social stability to protect those institutions that promote what they cherish most. In an unjust society, powerful men do the same.

American democracy's historic genius, throughout the era of industrial expansion, has enabled groups highest in the social hierarchy to protect what they have with minimum reliance on repressive force. By contrast to other political systems, primary reliance on a token carrot instead of a big stick has enabled American democracy to promote social peace efficiently and with a minimum of jeopardy to structures of injustice.

The institutional devices by which the interests of the mighty have almost always been protected at the expense of the weak are many, varied, and mutable. At one time, the Supreme Court was a main bulwark; today it is a less reliable tool of the powerful. At one time, limitations on the franchise were effective; with gradual extension of the suffrage, devices like the congressional seniority system and the poll tax were introduced to take up the slack. Our federal system was designed to frustrate the will of urban majorities, something it has done remarkably well as the present madness of our system of agri-

11. I have analyzed *tokenism* more fully in "Democracy and the Paradox of Want-Satisfaction," *The Personalist,* Spring 1970 issue.

cultural subsidies attests. In fact every aspect of American political life—party organization, electoral practices, municipal governance, legislative redistricting, governance of the mass media—betrays an institutional skew that favors the upper classes.

Today the practices by which majorities are frustrated is vulnerable to political attack. For the American electorate increasingly supports efforts to translate theoretical majoritarianism into institutional practice—a development reinforced by the Supreme Court's one-man one-vote decision. The new coalition should ally itself with every effort to erode the unequal political power of the socially mighty; but it should do so with care. For majorities are not more inclined to govern justly than ruling elites. And, paradoxically, in some cases the vestiges of class rule have become important defenses for oppressed minorities.

2. Our short-term coalition aim should not be majoritarian democracy; rather, what we should seek is a democratic order that most effectively promotes social justice. For example, direct primaries often harm the interests of urban minorities who, through strategic concentrations, have acquired a political leverage within nominating conventions that more majoritarian practices might dilute. Radical liberals who are carried away by majoritarian bias will ignore such practicalities at peril of frustrating their primary goal—to build the coalition.[12] Because majorities usually act against the victims of extreme poverty and racial discrimination, the new coalition should deliberately try to modify adherence to the principle of majority rule. I can do no more here than suggest the range of possibilities open to creative political minds.

The following specific measures may prove useful: community control that increases the power of oppressed minorities over municipal decisions affecting their lives; a cabinet post that deals exclusively with minority interests; systematic and sustained effort by the Democratic party organization to bring minorities into positions of influence and power out of proportion to their numbers; gerrymandering electoral districts to guarantee minority representation; a national party

12. For example, a proposal for a direct presidential primary went down to defeat in a special 1969 convention of the Michigan Democratic party partly because so many black Democrats thought a convention system gave them more political leverage.

committee structure that magnifies the representation of minorities; even the use of weighted votes when feasible.

3. The fact is that a free marketplace of ideas as John Stuart Mill proposed it does not exist. Despite the current fashions of counter-culture, in political thought and feeling the great mass of the American people are too often manipulated "right down to their very instincts." Autonomy is a word more honored ceremonially than in practical political ways. Even those who are genuinely autonomous can rarely make themselves heard. That is partly why so many of them are inclined to "speak" disruptively. But these problems are so basic and so deep that any remedies proposed in this brief space would be too superficial to be helpful. Besides more emphasis on liberal education, there is a need for more political education, more participation in decisions that affect one's life, more democratic control over the media of communication, more sympathy for liberation movements despite their rhetorical excess.

Electoral Politics: Keystone in the Arch

The vote is the keystone in a strategic arch that includes many other forms of political action. Nonelectoral tactics will fail unless there is effective use of the ballot. For example, the vast concentrations of corporate power cannot be democratically and wisely mastered without vigorous use of voting power. The task is not more likely to be accomplished by bloody revolution, or the Great Refusal, or "socialism in the ghetto," or the politics of the shaman—to mention only a few of the more frivolous alternatives that have recently been suggested.[13]

Yet the keystone is useless without the other stones in the arch. When Hubert Humphrey proclaimed that "liberalism and violence are deadly enemies,"[14] he betrayed devastating historical ignorance about how almost every radical program of liberal change has been achieved in this society. Foreign domination was lifted, slavery ended, the franchise extended to women, the trade unions were organized, the conditions of racial minorities generally improved by a complex

13. By Tom Hayden, Herbert Marcuse, Christopher Lasch, and Theodore Roszak, respectively.
14. *New York Times Magazine*, October 11, 1969.

set of events and political activities that included much essential disruption, disorder, and violence. But American revolutionaries also used their votes to control colonial legislatures. Abraham Lincoln had to be elected before he emancipated the slaves. Women were enfranchised only when enough elected public officials were willing to endorse a constitutional amendment. New Deal legislation promoted and consolidated trade union organization. And right now legislative willingness is essential if the lives of racial minorities are to be steadily improved. It is morally wrong and politically opportunistic to urge radicals to pledge unconditional nonviolence. But it is more absurd to urge them to forgo electoral activity. Only a complex strategy that promotes flexibility about tactics can get the job done.

Lest I be misinterpreted in a climate of public opinion that is only a little less hysterical about violence than it was about Communism during the McCarthy period, I do not think violence is particularly useful at this time. All forms of disorder tend to be counterproductive. By and large, the sporadic violence that has occurred has been manipulated by the Nixons, Agnews, and Reagans for political advantage. There is even evidence that they have, on occasion, not been loath to encourage violence.[15]

My point is not to defend violence, but to liberate the tactical imagination. I had principally in mind neither violence nor any other form of social disorder when I used the metaphor of the arch. Political education that goes on outside the electoral process as such is far more important and persuasive.

The role of secondary political groups that focus on a narrow range of issues needs to be stressed in this connection. Peace, civil liberties, and ecological groups play an indispensable role whose effectiveness tends to be blunted by their engagement in electoral politics. This is something Ralph Nader, to his credit, understands very well. There must be division of labor within the radical movement. Appropriate linkage of such groups with a radical coalition that is directly involved in electoral activities provides the best assurance that an obsessive desire to win elections will not undermine a politics of issues.

15. I have in mind such statements as Ronald Reagan's when he welcomed a bloodbath on the campuses, as well as hard evidence that President Nixon went out of his way to encourage rock throwing at San Jose, California, for the sake of its effect on the 1970 elections.

With regard to electoral strategy itself, the main problem is how to deploy most effectively a minority of substantial strength. As they have only the support of a minority, candidates who run as radicals and liberals cannot normally hope to win. By the same token, those who place exclusive emphasis on winning erode prospects for radical change. When winning is the measure, the disheartening impact of losing is magnified. And demoralized former activists swell the ranks of the apathetic—not because they don't care, but because they can't hope.

Apathy is not, however, the worst consequence of a mania for victory. Practitioners of the old politics who are disposed to pay any price to win demote even the gravest moral issue. By 1967 Hubert Humphrey was already convinced that the war in Southeast Asia was wrong and had to be ended. Asked why he did not say so at the 1968 Democratic Convention, he explained that President Johnson "was absolutely paranoid about the war" and that, after all, "there I was, supposed to be running for President of the United States. All I had for a party to start with were the Johnson remnants."[16]

Radical liberals who cannot normally win elections are yet sufficiently numerous to veto the election of candidates who desperately want simply to win—especially the ones who have tended to take for granted our willingness to march lock-step in the cadres of the lesser evil. And while we should always support a lesser evil when evils are our only alternatives, the mistake is to suppose that support of marginally better candidates is always, in balance, the lesser evil.

The opposite is often true. By exercising an electoral veto we can, in those instances where the opposite *is* true, exert maximum pressure on the entire political process—educating the center when we defend our use of the veto; educating candidates, or at least forcing them to reassess their inclination to move to the soft side of every tough policy question; giving heart to those who despair by enabling them to count some losses as victories; eventually moving the whole center of gravity of American politics toward an authentic liberalism.

Two broadly conflicting approaches to the problem of applying the veto vie for the favor of radical liberals; formation of a new political party on the one hand, retaining a loose affiliation with the Demo-

16. *New York Times Magazine,* October 11, 1969, p. 26.

cratic party on the other. In present conditions, the latter is more rational.

A new party that really tries to win elections would not be sufficiently better than the Democratic party to justify the enormous effort that would have to be expended in the building. At best, such a new party effort would be slightly more progressive and less corrupt than internal Democratic party politics. Those who think otherwise fantasize. It is the process of seeking power, not the Democratic party, that co-opts. Immunity results, not from new organizational forms, but from rationality and morally authentic commitment—another reason why a new political coalition based solely on self-interest would merely initiate new political horrors. Granting that a new party would make political education easier, the critical test is whether such a shift would make application of a veto strategy more effective. The answer to that question is plainly negative. For a new party would organize a minority of an already distinct minority. In the process it would fragment our strength in those other ways that anyone who has ever been involved in internecine political conflict knows too well. Not only would deployment of the veto be less effective, but a new party effort would make us look far weaker than we are. That is precisely the illusion independent antiwar candidacies have fostered during the last few years.

Many who might be attracted by a new coalition strategy that broadly gears itself to Democratic party activity will not be drawn to a new party. The bulk of the racial minorities, the more radical trade unionists, all in the conscience constituency who have acquired significant leverage within the Democratic party are not about to abandon the organization they continue to view as their main vehicle for electoral effort. The election victories of genuine radicals like Bella Abzug in New York, Ronald Dellums in California, the successful gubernatorial race of Pat Lucey in Wisconsin, Joseph Duffey's near-miss in Connecticut are among the gains I have in mind. Those who have in the face of growing repression made this limited progress are not about to yield it for the sake of party purity. And those who look to liberal Republicans for radical leadership, who try to induce men like John Lindsay and John Gardner to join a new genuinely radical party, pursue a will o' the wisp. Common Cause, for example, is a hopeful development, but hardly radical.

Moreover, any new party would be the fourth, not the third. It is true, as Senator McCarthy has emphasized,[17] that habits of major-party loyalty have been eroding. But, though generally healthy, the main benefits of this development have gone to those who are conservative or reactionary, not to radical liberals. Buckley's success in New York, Byrd's in Virginia, and the general threat George Wallace poses, all indicate that a new party would likely be the weakest of the four. And because a party is a less flexible instrument than the alternative I will propose, a new party effort is likely to play right into the hands of conservative and reactionary forces. For, by splitting the vote that would normally go to progressive candidates, conservatives and reactionaries hope to gain by pluralities what majorities normally deny them.

To some extent people find a new party attractive because they despair of reforming the Democratic party in even its procedural aspects. Reform of the Democratic party, state by state, and at the national level, indeed is urgently needed. And the little that has been done—reports by the McGovern and O'Hara commissions, proposals by a few reform commissions in such states as Michigan—is mostly a matter of blueprints awaiting implementing action. Progress is being made, but the omens are, at best, problematic. Yet well-justified skepticism about party reform efforts is a sandy foundation on which to build fourth-party effort and a very weak basis for a new coalition strategy.

The time for a new party has not yet arrived. The alternative is loose affiliations with the Democratic party, primarily by successfully deploying our power to veto.

In order to do so most effectively, we must understand what makes very good politicians tick. Senator Edmund Muskie, for example, is a man who possesses integrity, intelligence, moral sensibility, and enough *amour propre* to project great dignity. He reminds many of Lincoln. Moreover, like Lincoln, he is very ambitious—a man who seeks and enjoys the exercise of power. Most important within the frame of broadly decent but quite flexible moral commitments, his decision-making mechanisms function so that he comes to perceive the world and to make judgments in ways that accommodate his

17. In his general defense of a new party effort in "A Third Party May Be a Real Force in 1972," *New York Times Magazine,* June 7, 1970.

political ambitions. When he does form judgments that conflict with views held by people who can advance or impair his career, he displays a fine humility. He is, and perceives himself to be, a bridge across troubled waters.[18]

In brief, Muskie's instinctual tendencies move him toward the center of any system of political pressures that is relevant to his electoral success. Clearly such a man will be affected by credible pressure from radical liberals. An intelligently conceived, vigorously applied veto strategy can contribute to the moral education of men like Muskie. But this must be done in a rational, credible fashion. The purpose is to limit the range of acceptable candidates; and to make sure that those who qualify and run conduct their campaigns in ways that most advance radical liberalism's long-term aims.

To see how this approach might work, consider a concrete case. Liberals want the Democrats to nominate a presidential candidate in 1972 who can win without betraying certain critically important, minimal commitments and values. That is to say, we would support a man who, if he wins, will at least be pledged to defend us against repressive force, will generally encourage the demographic trends on which we found our hope for future majorities, will energetically try to advance the welfare state, will enable us to be heard by keeping channels of governmental and party power open, will treat with reasonable sympathy programs we favor, the moral aspirations we voice. He cannot be radical and win. He can be progressive, reasonable, and tolerant. With these thoughts in mind, we should formulate a set of minimal but definite criteria of acceptability. Presenting these to all plausible candidates, we should warn each that unless he subscribes to these reasonable standards, we will work to defeat him in the general election should he be nominated. By gently reminding him of what many of us did in 1968, we can make it plain that this is not an empty threat.

Of course circumstances could arise in which all threats are void. Suppose an Agnew is nominated. Or suppose the danger of another

18. "The American people don't like extremists or extreme positions. If I'm pushed to try to please the left, I lose some Democratic votes and the independent and Republican votes I've always needed and gotten in Maine. I'm one of the few politicians who can still talk to the hard-hats and the blacks." *New York Times Magazine*, November 22, 1970, p. 130.

Vietnam, or of a great depression, is imminent. We might have to swallow our convictions and our threats, support a nominee who does not satisfy even our minimal criteria. But, barring such unfortunate contingencies, we should make the veto threat, and carry it out if it becomes necessary.

The same process, with appropriate variations, should be adopted whenever we are in a minority so definite that candidates of our own cannot win. The veto is applicable at every level of the electoral process. In each case we should assess our strength, assess the alternative to the lesser-evil Democrat, and, where the alternatives are tolerable, apply the veto. The processes by which criteria are hammered out, limits of tolerability fixed, are crucial. No component of the existing or potential coalition of radical forces should be excluded. The very process of participating in setting minimal demands that satisfy all segments of the coalition will be a factor in building it.

It is argued that we cannot organize a veto effectively enough to be credible. But it has been done, notably in 1968, and should be done much more explicitly. We have no alternative to going the veto route—except acquiescing in the kind of pseudo-realism that permits fundamental evils of our society to fester while candidates continue merrily to appeal to majority prejudices at the center. To permit this to happen will result in more than burning ghettos; our hopes for a liberal future will also go up in flames.

To accept the veto as basic to our electoral strategy does not preclude our running candidates who are genuinely committed radicals. In those rare instances where assessment yields a rational prospect of winning, the fight should certainly be made. Nor do radical liberals have to restrict themselves to candidacies that have prospects for victory. At times it is important to make the race for mainly educational reasons—though, unless this is done without illusion, the resulting loss will be demoralizing.

The basic approach should be clear. Electoral effort, precisely because it is so important, should be conducted with all the intelligence and determination needed to exert a maximum influence on the entire political process. The tension between short-term gains and long-term prospects should always be in the forefront. Skill at using our minority strength most effectively in building toward future majorities is, to repeat, the keynote of the arch which has the veto at the center.

A New Political Persona

The new politics sketched in what has gone before needs a new political persona, able to handle baffling tensions without losing either moral élan or political effectiveness.

The tensions are many. For at the heart of this new politics is the effort to build a radical coalition that is cohesive without being monolithic, progressive in ways that do not weaken more basic commitment to radicalism, tactically bold yet mindful of political consequence. The new coalition seeks to exert a steady pressure on the Democratic party. Above all, the coalition neither overestimates its present strength nor underestimates its future potential.

Possessive individualism—the need to appropriate and control all things, people, organizations as one would a toothbrush—is the scourge of our culture. It is, not surprisingly, a special vice of our politics. The radical Left has not been spared. Through the period of Vietnam protest, insurgents frequently suffered leaders who treated the many movements and groups they helped to build as personal fiefdoms. Some wheeled and dealed, manipulated and lied, betrayed trusts. Others displayed more integrity, but not less possessiveness. Unless this atavistic need to control is curbed, unless we become more capable of substituting the satisfactions of common effort for the satisfactions of ego-fulfillment, the new politics will in time become indistinguishable from the old.

The new political man will view all political leaders, especially candidates and officials, as neither devils nor saints, but as fallible creatures too often caught in a web of conflicting pressures to which they respond out of a variety of motives. But such understanding compassion should not prevent us from adding to the officials' predicament. For our basic task is to generate pressures that by influencing judgment and action serve our ultimate aims. We will not succeed if we role-play, if we act *as if* we were at the center of the system of pressures rather than as a part of its source. The tendency to role-playing comes to the fore when successful candidates or officials emerge from our own ranks. It is then that the dangers of harmful identification, of false loyalty and misplaced gratitude are greatest. Part of the price of success is that old intimacies must give way to the imperatives of a politics of impersonal, radical pressure.

My remarks no more than scratch the surface of the topic. Unless those qualities that constitute this new political persona become typical rather than exceptional, our radical minority cannot hope to be effective. But if radicals learn to find their gratifications through communal accomplishment within a strategic frame set by long-range moral perspectives, then the present mood of cynicism and despair may lift.

1971

Emanuel Geltman and Stanley Plastrik

Coalition Politics Revisited

Though the events of recent years have bruised its image, the idea of political coalitionism is still very much with us. Among some of the young and disaffected, coalition politics may not be this season's vegetable but it remains this season's political strategy—provided we recognize that its virtue rests not in repetition but in changing political relationships and styles.

The argument is not all that abstract. It is a plain and demonstrable fact that politics by coalition is a commonplace of political life everywhere, at least in democratic societies. Could Golda Meir rule Israel without a coalition? Or Indira Gandhi steer India along progressive lines without a coalition? Would any alternative but chaos and confrontation exist for Chile's President Allende without a coalition?

Writing on the politics of coalition in what now seems a distant past, when progressive forces in the labor, civil rights, and liberal-radical movements were working together as never before, we said:

"A new style of politics" is certainly the order of the day. But the content of that new style can be given a wide range of meaning, from isolated, if brave, sorties, to turbulent intervention in American political life *as it is lived*. Surely the happiest and easiest solution for the radical condition is to think we can agitate the disaffected into our welcoming organizational arms—if only they would come! It is not quite that easy to rub against the realities of American politics, to educate people, convince them, move them. Easy or not, it is possible to accomplish these ends if we use the resources that are available to us in *coalition* with others of more or less similar purpose and mind. [Emphasis in original.][1]

Admittedly, the politics of coalition has not fared well since these words were written. Yet there have been significant advances. In its own way, the present turmoil in our cities reflects the taste for "more," as stimulated by the achievements of coalition activity during the early and mid-sixties. But it was a politics that could barely withstand the successive shocks of the Martin Luther King and Robert Kennedy assassinations, the sour smell of the 1968 Democratic party convention, the appearance of new movements, the aggravation of old issues.

Yet we feel we are right in asking: what political course *has* met with success, what brave new political worlds have revealed themselves to us over, say, the past ten years? It is our contention that had a more vigorous coalitionist policy been pursued and preserved, a policy designed to unite people behind desirable goals, the tone and level of political life in the United States would not be in its present dismal condition.

Changes in the Making

A recent Labor Department study contains projections of great relevance to our subject.[2] Estimated to reach 100 million workers by 1980, the labor force will show a major increase in the number of young adult workers, particularly in the number of young black workers. In addition to a doubling of the number of women workers as compared with 1950, *there will be, for the first time, as many professional and technical workers by 1980 as blue-collar workers.*

This represents a growth in the country's labor force of 15 million workers within the next decade, of whom 50 percent will be 25–34 years old, a carry-over of the famous post–World War II "baby boom"; in other words, that section of today's youth population which does not succeed in getting into the ranks of the professional classes.

1. "The Politics of Coalition," *The Radical Papers,* Irving Howe, ed. (New York: Doubleday, 1966).
2. *United States Manpower in the Nineteen-Seventies,* U.S. Labor Department pamphlet, 1971.

More significantly, it is estimated that the number of young black workers entering the work force will outnumber—perhaps as much as fivefold—the entering young white workers. These changes are bound to generate social and economic problems that will require the broadest kind of political coalition to supply the mass basis for new and humane solutions.

Or consider the role of women. By 1980 there will be an estimated 37 million working women, as compared with 30 million in 1969 and 18 million in 1950—very near a doubling of the female labor force within two decades. This fact alone will initiate major changes in our society. Among other things, job training for mothers who re-enter the labor force and day-care facilities for the children of working mothers are less likely to be dismissed as luxuries, for they will have become social necessities.

All in all, fundamental shifts in the composition, activity, and personnel of the world's most gigantic labor force are bound to have major political consequences and to act as a stimulus to forming alliances between this mass of human labor and other sectors of our society—alliances that may well assume fresh and unforeseeable forms.

Even the coalitionism of a few years ago differed sharply from the classic coalitionism familiar in the United States since the days of the New Deal. By the 1960s it had acquired a new context: the context of the civil rights movement, of the struggle to right the wrongs of the Vietnam war and to prevent similar national catastrophes. Now, in the 1970s, the task of a progressive coalitionism is still more demanding.

First, there is the burning need for a redistribution of the nation's wealth, at present concentrated in the hands of those whom Gus Tyler calls the "superrich," so as to make possible funding of the tens of billions required to solve the problems of school building, housing, health care, poverty, hunger, and so on.

Second, there is the whole ecological problem, under which must be included such matters as a voluntary population redistribution in order to decongest urban density, the colossal issue of pollution, and the more conventional questions of resource conservation. It is calculated that ecological rebirth in the United States will involve sums running into the trillions of dollars. A vast number of policies must be worked out: population control, land usage, recycling of wastes, readjustment of resource allocations, re-establishment of control over the use of air, water, fuels, and so on. Third, there remain the familiar but urgent social issues which condition the daily responses of almost all Americans, such as crime, drugs, racism, campus life. And, in the early seventies, the traditional union preoccupation with whether a man has a job or not (full employment) has assumed new importance.

The very magnitude of the issues precludes any other solution than that of coalitionism, that is, *the mobilization of the broadest number of people coming from all sorts of "interest groups" in an effort to find common answers.* Given the American political structure, the diversity of this country, and the deep tradition of political and social pluralism, it seems unlikely (to put it mildly) that any single political constituency or social group, no matter how large or powerful, can expect to gain sufficient support or power in order to cope effectively with the issues we face.

The November 1970 elections back up these conclusions, if sometimes only negatively. Because the liberal and radical forces in New York were unable to work together, Conservative James Buckley was elected a senator. Though Buckley ran on an independent ticket (with veiled support from large sections of the Republican party), he benefited from a conservative version of coalition strategy. By welding together the sizable minority of conservative forces, mainly through working with and through the Republican party, they could exercise an effective, and often decisive, voice in national politics.

Independents of the Left and radical-progressive candidates, recognizing that the mass of people still speak through the traditional parties, have similarly had little choice but to use the Democratic party if they wanted to get anywhere. Had they run as independent or so-called peace candidates, people like Julian Bond, Shirley Chisholm, and Allard Lowenstein, as well as the growing number of black mayors across the country, would probably have suffered utter defeat. The skepticism that coexists in the electoral mood together with traditional voting habits is not very receptive to "freakish" or "wasted" political effort. Whether or not one likes this isn't nearly as important as recognizing that for the present, and very likely the immediate future, it is a fact.

Third- or fourth-party activity was so feeble and distant from any reality in the 1970 elections that it barely surfaced, with the one partial exception of the Right-wing Buckley campaign, which, as we have noted, was as much coalitionist as independent. For all their "revolutionary" rhetoric, even the Panthers accept the practical necessity for a coalition with whites—in their own version, of course—but nonetheless a coalition such as had previously been ruled out by Rap Brown and Stokely Carmichael, the first of whom has vanished and the second been reduced to calls from Guinea for a return to "Mother Africa."

A Coalition in New Dress?

Our goal is a broad-based, majority coalition for major social change in America, capable of winning elections and built around a concentration on domestic issues, though not to the exclusion of foreign problems.

Such a coalition can probably not be constructed simply along the lines of the classic New Deal–FDR pattern of the thirties (Democratic party, labor unions, and urban poor), any more than it can simply rehash the slogans of that period. The issues raised in that period are by no means completely resolved; not at all. And the welfare state solutions proposed in that period still remain urgently to the point. But now the problems are much more complex, and even a coalition trying to limit itself to thirties-style issues would have to acknowledge the presence of new forces, such as the organized blacks and the peace movement. Further, the new American middle class (technicians, experts, the vastly expanded academic community, white-collar specialists in electronics, social engineers) will simply not accept a coalition in which they do not have a prominent role. Some of the academic spokesmen for this new class reveal ambitions in excess of their probable power and a snobbism toward the plebeian classes in excess of their democratic convictions; but even after such spokesmen are deflated, the power of the new class of technicians and specialists will be considerable. At best, they will share the leadership of the coalition movement with other forces in the Democratic party, most of all the labor movement, which, in addition to supplying experience, political drive, and organizing capacity, influences large numbers of voters.

If liberalism was the ideology of classic American coalitionism, what may replace it in the coalition of tomorrow?

While American liberalism may not be nearly as exhausted a force as some maintain, its strength as both ideological tendency and practical force is at a low point. Scorned by many of the young New Leftists, whose attitudes toward conventional American liberalism often parallel those of traditional conservatism, the liberal forces are at the moment in disarray. But we do not think that an outlook as deeply ingrained in the American experience as liberalism is likely to go under—though, for revival, it may have to rethink its premises and take on a sharper radical edge. In any case, during the seventies it seems likely that because of the troubles of liberalism there will flourish a sophisticated conservative ideology stressing self-centered individualism (plight and flight of the individual when faced with the machine) and state and local "decentralization."

Is there any reason to suppose that such a Rightist mixture of nostalgia and cynicism is likely to help the country? For our part, we think that the outlook of a new liberal-Left coalition must be that of social cooperation; that its philosophy must be based on the conviction that man can make the machine do his work; that only on a national scale can our social problems be solved; and that the society is the arena in which we act as brothers.

While the terrain for political realignment remains the Democratic party, too much can be made of the questions whether all progressive coalitionist roads lead to the Democratic party, whether one should work "outside" or "inside" the party, and so on. If recent investigations have indicated that a growing number of voters classify themselves (and act) as independents (probably the emerging younger voters, hopefully a substantial percentage of those in the new 18–21-year-old electors category; newly married couples; the new middle class referred to above), there is all the more reason to be flexible about labels and organizations. There will be much shifting of political chairs in the next decade. People come together politically around issues and personalities to a greater extent than before, particularly if the personality involved strongly symbolizes a position on a critical issue. Traditional party labels could melt away before the growing number of "swing" or mixed-ticket voters. Nevertheless, and of much more immediate import, a strong tradition remains according to which the Democratic party is the more liberal, responsive, loose, and free of the two parties. All this is only comparative, which is to say, far from ideal; no one would claim the Democratic party is a beacon of enlightenment; still, it is in comparisons that we have to deal if we want to participate in American politics at all. Just about all parties in American life have been coalitions of one or another sort, brought into existence by leaders of fairly well-defined "interest groups" heading constituencies that make up the coalition. Even without having formally declared themselves, these coalitions have as a rule been easily recognizable and definable. Now, however, this has changed somewhat. It has become more difficult to grasp the interests and aspirations of the multitude of groups making up an infinitely complex society. Hence, forming coalitions is a process at once looser, less clearly definable, and harder to arrive at. No one, not even the heads of powerful organizations that number in the millions, can simply declare by fiat the fixed shape of tomorrow's coalition—and expect sufficient acquiescence for political success. People are these days too uneasy for that, too itchy, too independent. Or, to put it another way, coalitions already formed fall apart much more easily than before. Groups tend to coalesce around *issues* (or personalities associated with issues), but new issues constantly arise which strain and break apart yesterday's coalition. We ought to expect a phase in our history during which coalitions will seem rapidly to come and go, though in practice what may happen will be the shifting of tactical realignments (like European cabinets) of pretty much the same forces. Those, however, who stress one issue above all else—the "peace" candidates— aren't likely to thrive. Americans believe that the war is a major issue, but one in a series of related problems. It is not so much Vietnam that divides us any longer; it is what to do about the United States.

Reforming the Democratic Party

The most-powerful and best-established coalition in America worked traditionally in the Democratic party—a coalition of workers (trade unions), liberal city middle-class, and minority groups. It used to command such cities as New York, Chicago, Boston, and Philadelphia, as well as such old factory towns as Scranton, Duluth, and dozens of others. In addition, it commanded national power for most of the period from the early thirties onward. That day is perhaps over.

Where this old coalition once ruled, we now find decline, loss of influence, or outright disintegration. We think this decline may well continue if only because the 1970 census figures indicate a steady population loss in these towns and cities. The "population explosion" is centered in what may be described as the "neoconservative" places —Tulsa, Shreveport, Orlando, Albuquerque—relatively new towns, with a population quite different in ethnic and social composition from the old industrial and commercial centers of the country.

Who are these "conservatives"? Some lower middle-class workers and service employees (mainly white, of course); prosperous citizens, at least until the Nixon recession, either owning or running some service industry (insurance, auto sales, supermarket); homeowners and taxpayers whose central political concern tends to be the white man's fear of the black man's presence. Any proposal for restructuring the Democratic party in the seventies must take this influential group into account.

Concretely, this means that a liberal coalitionist politics in the seventies—even as it places heavy stress on domestic economic issues, along the lines of greater federal expenditure in behalf of jobs, housing, education, antipollution, and smaller expenditures on the military—must take great pains to speak in a language that would connect with the feelings and troubles of mainstream segments of the population. It must recognize that the popular concern with "law and order" isn't simply or always a code name for racism, though sometimes it is that. Often enough, this concern is an authentic one, the response of people who feel harried and threatened, and who have a perfect right to want to live under conditions of reasonable personal security.

Meanwhile, the question of Democratic-party reorganization is high on the agenda. Minor local and statewide reforms have been begun. Is a major reorganization possible? In the defeatist mood after the 1968 election, the McGovern Commission was appointed. It met and discussed the enormous task of the internal reform of a party heavily larded with bureaucracy and outworn rules designed to frustrate insurgent forces.

Now the Commission's proposals, many of them sensible and

concrete, face opposition from the revived "regular" wing of the party, a group anxious to maintain control over the party, and trying to do so through a clever appeal to "unity." A key issue, as of this writing, will be the matter of qualifying delegates for the 1972 convention, a convention that some would like to see as "safe and sane" as the 1968 convention was stormy and dangerous.

While no single proposed new rule is drastic, the McGovern package as a whole is striking. Party "regulars" have so far responded with hostility or studied indifference. These reforms deal with access to power rather than with distribution of power within the party. The "mandatory" proposals include a welcome to the new eighteen-year-old national voter, urging his full participation at every level of party activity regardless of state law; an end to corrupt proxy voting practices; a banning of secret caucuses; an end to closed, slate-making sessions. There are recommendations for proportional representation of minority groups on all delegations, so as to include young people and women; reiteration of the Chicago decision barring use of the unit rule (state voting as one unit); and a rule that delegate selection should start in the calendar year of the convention.

The McGovern proposals, indicating that the first round of the struggle for major reform of the Democratic party is under way, are now in the hands of the party state machines for compliance and implementation. This, together with the presidential nominating drives already in progress, places the Democratic party at the center of the struggle for political change.

The Democratic Party

Whatever may happen in the eighties, the Democratic party is the party of the politics of the seventies. And, if the party succeeds in appealing to the new breed of independent "swing" voters coming largely from the ranks of youth and the new middle class of professional and white-collar workers, it will quickly regain strength. If a moderate-toned middle-of-the-road-but-leaning-rightward politics works for the Republicans, then a moderate-toned, but progressive left-of-center policy is indicated for the Democrats. Single-issue candidates and reformers will find themselves hopelessly outflanked. If there are now more secretaries and garage and gas station attendants in this country than college students, we ought to drop the notion that radical students can lead or change society or, in its smaller aspects, reform the Democratic party. Social and demographic facts are against such propositions, and showdown challenges usually encourage Rightist victories at the polls. Which is not to say that the radicalized students cannot play a ginger role, as they did in the McCarthy campaign. Their commitment, idealism, energy, and even their freedom to move about make them indispensable allies in a restructured democratic politics.

Professional and technical workers who constitute the new middle class are undergoing their first serious shock in the loss of jobs, under-employment, and a darkening of what had yesterday seemed the endless vistas of prosperity. This middle class has experienced the most rapid growth rate of any sector of the American population in the last decade, and even if this rate falls in the future, its absolute numbers will continue to grow. Parts of the traditional lower middle class, however much against its will, may now be shoved into working-class ranks, a kind of belated quasi-confirmation of the old Marxist view that the lower middle class will be reduced to proletarians. At this point, sections of the white middle class and white working class form the source of Wallace support, even though in 1968 the trade unions did an effective last-minute job of keeping blue-collar workers out of Wallace ranks. Still, he received 10 million votes, 50 percent of them in the South and the other 5 million in the North (in such states as Kansas, Michigan, Ohio, and Indiana it came to 10–12 percent). An overly drastic transformation of the Democratic party, or an enlarged influence of confrontationist elements, or efforts to initiate a radical new party—such developments would probably speed up "Wallace-ization," no matter how heroic the efforts of the unions to oppose it.

Goals

Our goal is a broad-based majority coalition of progressive forces for major social change, fulfilling and expanding the welfare state. As for foreign issues: an end to any remaining illusions about the "American century," or a *Pax Americana,* and the subordination of military (Pentagon) objectives to domestic priorities. Needless to say, we are not proposing an isolationist absurdity this late in the twentieth century. If only on the simplest level of helping the developing nations to survive, the United States cannot avoid a leading role in the world. And a radicalized domestic program could influence foreign policies by encouraging a more tolerant view of radical alternatives in other countries.

We see the politics of coalition taking three possible roads during the seventies:

First, a *traditional coalitionism,* modeling itself after the New Deal coalition of the thirties. This would be built around the professional, machine wing of the Democratic party, dominated by men in their fifties and sixties, together with the cautious trade union leadership of the AFL-CIO executive council. Such a coalition can claim credit for real achievements in the past but is not likely to turn on the important new segments of the population we have already mentioned, including, by the way, the young workers. Its outlook on foreign policy is essentially attached to the administration in power (Johnson, Nixon), and inflexible in its world view.

Second, at the opposite pole, a *radical coalitionism* modeling itself on the tradition in American history that consists of sharp breaks with past politics (the Abolitionists' Liberty party, Teddy Roosevelt's Bull Moose party, Henry Wallace's Progressive party); built upon such issues as Vietnam, imperialism, "quality of life"; particularly emphatic in proposing radical justice for minorities and disturbingly confrontationist to the bulk of the citizenry. Such a coalition has barely the slightest chance for political success in the next decade, though if it acted independently at election time it could virtually assure the success of the Nixon and still more conservative Republicans. Apart from the enormous difficulties that follow whenever former McCarthy supporters, New Politics people, and New Leftists come together in the same room, such a gathering on the Left might well find itself unrelated to the very people—racial minorities as well as others—it proposes to serve.

Finally, the alternative of a *progressive coalitionism,* of those who believe that it is still possible to rally a large majority of the United States electorate for change. We view this as an empirical approach to progress because it preserves, but intensifies, a strong relation to long-standing ideals and the traditional way in which we have lived our political life. Though we have emphasized domestic issues, we take it as given the quickest end to the senseless engagement in Vietnam is a *sine qua non* for innovative reforms and the huge expenditures they will require. If progressive coalitionism works, that is, if numbers and ideas can be brought together, it could propel the country along progressive lines that will lead us into the eighties with cleaner horizons and greater cheer.

72 73 74 75 10 9 8 7 6 5 4 3 2 1